ITALIAN
Regional Cooking

ITALIAN

Translated by
Maria Langdale and Ursula Whyte

Regional Cooking

Ada Boni

Bonanza Books · New York

Library of Congress Catalog Card Number: 74-89975

This material was first published in slightly different form in *Arianna*.

This edition published by Bonanza Books,
a division of Crown Publishers, Inc.,
by arrangement with the owner of Copyright
a   b   c   d   e   f   g   h

Printed and bound in Italy by Arnoldo Mondadori
Filmset in Malta by St. Paul's Press Ltd.

PIEDMONT

In its mysterious and incalculable way, the truffle grows spontaneously in the clay soil of the Langhe in Piedmont. There are no clues to its presence and only the most experienced *trifolau* or truffle-hunter will succeed in finding it. With his vast experience, which in many cases has been transmitted and increased from generation to generation, and aided only by a mongrel dog whose sense of smell has been trained to enable it to recognize the truffle even when it is hidden several inches beneath the ground (pedigree dogs do not have the same skill), the *trifolau* works secretly at night to avoid betraying to others the spot where he knows he will find this elusive treasure.

Truffles serve as an ideal introduction to Piedmontese cooking. They are an exciting ingredient of so many dishes of this region, from *fonduta* to risotto and game. With its penetrating aroma, the truffle enhances a cuisine which is rich in every detail, from the aperitif (vermouth was invented here) to dessert (sweets are a great specialty of the region).

The capital city of Piedmont, Turin, has a long and honorable gastronomic tradition. The city itself is of great interest—regular streets crossing at right angles, built by far-sighted engineers according to a plan whereby the city center retained the grid pattern of the ancient Roman *castrum*, with the via Garibaldi as the *decumana maxima*, and the via Santomaso and via di Porta Palatina as the *cardo maximus*. There is nothing quite like it anywhere else in Italy. And although Turin's fame may now rest on its importance as the center of Italy's automobile industry, it nevertheless remains one

More delicate and prized than black truffles, white truffles are Piedmont's pride and glory. They thrive among the roots of oak and beech trees, and in the clay soils where willows grow, ripening from October to December.

Photographed in the historic Ristorante Cambio in Turin, once frequented by the great Italian statesman Camillo Benso di Cavour, three typical Piedmontese dishes—a *fritto misto* or "mixed fry" which, according to some experts, should include at least thirteen different ingredients, risotto, and the traditional *fonduta* or Piedmontese fondue (see page 17)—accompanied by a bottle of vintage Barolo.

Bagna cauda (see page 19), a hot dip with garlic and anchovies, is one of the gastronomic specialties of Piedmont, thought to date from the beginning of the eighteenth century. Its place of origin is disputed: whether the Monferrato region or Chieri, home of the biggest and best *cardi* (cardoons), which are dipped, along with other raw vegetables, into this delicious sauce.

Perch is one of the most sought-after fish caught in Lake Maggiore. The delicate fillets are dipped in beaten egg and breadcrumbs, then fried in butter flavored with sage (see page 25).

of the few Italian cities where the population still seems to be able to find enough time to sit in cafés during the afternoon, drinking tea and nibbling at cakes and sweets. In spite of industrial progress, the windows of the pastry shops are as elegant and old-fashioned as they were a hundred years ago, so much so that they could easily be mistaken for jewelers' shops.

In culinary matters, too, the Piedmontese are gentlemanly and old-fashioned. Piedmontese cooking is "good" cooking in the old sense of the word, sober but substantial, simple yet counterpointed by rich flavors and pleasing aromas. Only the finest ingredients are tolerated. For instance, garden produce is so essential that all Piedmontese, be they politicians, artists, economists, writers or business tycoons, insist on having their own kitchen gardens. Garlic, an ingredient regarded with some suspicion by the cooks of many other regions, is used frequently, together with every other kind of raw vegetable. We find it in *bagna cauda* or *caôda* (see page 19), cut lovingly into small pieces, together with raw sweet peppers, celery stalks, cardoons and boiled potatoes, and in hundreds of other dishes it is used to balance flavors and counteract heaviness.

On the basis of a law of dietetics, which may be empirical but is scientifically beyond dispute, cheese serves the same purpose. Piedmont produces a wealth of cheeses, from Tome to Robiole and the world-famous Fontina. Cream and other milk products are used generously in many dishes. As for butter, we find it everywhere, reducing the harshness of certain dishes, and increasing the lightness and delicacy of others.

From the Ristorante Belvedere in La Morra in the province of Cuneo: casseroled guinea fowl, *finanziera*, a rich sauce flavored with Madeira (see page 21), mushroom salad and *dolcetti Belvedere* topped with caramelized sugar (see page 28). To go with them, three Piedmontese wines, Barbaresco, Grignolino and Dolcetto delle Langhe.

Photographed on the tranquil bank of the Po, some of the fine dishes of game served at the Ristorante San Giorgio al Valentino. These include pheasant, hare and chamois. Their ideal partner is Barolo, full-bodied and generous.

There is an old saying in Piedmont that even in the condemned cell a man should not be refused a cup of broth, for broth is another of the region's specialties. Unlike the majority of Italians, the Piedmontese are inclined to prefer broth or soup to rice and pasta.

The Alpine slopes by which three sides of the region are bounded, and fertile plains between the Dora Baltea and the Dora Riparia, and between the Po and Tanaro rivers, ensure an abundance of meat and game. Fish, of which the finest is trout, are to be found in the pure, crystal-clear torrents of the mountains, especially in the Val d'Aosta, in the shelter of Mont Blanc.

A meal worthy of the name should end with a dessert of the same quality. Many such specialties were created in the golden environment of the Court of Savoy—*zabaglione*, and countless other custards and sweets. Boiled candies (sweets) were invented in Turin, and cocoa was introduced into Italy by King Emanuele Filiberto of Savoy. *Grissini* or crisp bread sticks, *les petits bâtons de Turin*, as Napoleon called them, are synonymous with Turin, as characteristic as the River Po and the Mole Antonelliana which, built at the same time as the Eiffel Tower in Paris, stands high over the city.

The wines of Piedmont, noble by origin and tradition, are worthy of a book in themselves. Barbera, from the valley of Tignone near Asti, is a strong red wine particularly good with roasts and red meat in general. Barolo, another excellent wine with roasts, is produced in the Langhe, south-west of Alba; it has a powerful *bouquet* which becomes splendid after the fourth or fifth year. Gattinara comes from the province of Vercelli and together with Ghemme,

Cocconato, in the province of Asti, is an agricultural center renowned for its salted meats, and local cheeses known as *robiole*. Gourmets gather at the Ristorante Regina, whose specialties include veal cutlets Regina and chicken *al babi*.

Lessona and Mottalciata, is a product of the Nebbiolo vine—the name comes from the word *nebbia*, meaning "fog", because the grapes are not fully mature until the first mists of autumn. Barbaresco is similar to Barolo, more delicate perhaps and slightly less alcoholic, and it makes excellent drinking after three years. The Dolcetto delle Langhe goes splendidly with any dish containing truffles, while the *bagna cauda* blends perfectly with Freisa, a good, semi-sparkling wine with a low alcoholic content, which is produced in the area between Turin and Casale. This short list of the best red table wines closes with Grignolino, which comes from the hills near Asti and Alessandria and which, unfortunately, is becoming scarce. Of the local white wines, Cortese is by far the best with fish, while the Muscatel of Asti is sweet and delicate. The sparkling wines from Asti would require a chapter on their own, and as we have already noted, the region boasts of having invented vermouth, which is now enjoyed all over the world.

Crostini di Tartufi Bianchi
Piedmontese Rarebit

US		UK
6 slices	bread, crusts removed	6 slices
1 small	white truffle	1 small
4 tablespoons	butter	2 ounces
2½ tablespoons	grated Parmesan cheese	2 tablespoons
	juice of 1 lemon	

Cut the slices of bread in half, toast them and keep hot. Grate the truffle. Melt the butter over a very low heat, add the truffle, and let it heat through for a few minutes without actually cooking; add the Parmesan cheese. Remove from heat, mix well and stir in the lemon juice. If this mixture seems too thick, dilute with a little stock (preferably veal or chicken).

Spread the toast with the truffle and cheese mixture, and serve very hot.
Serves 6.

Fonduta – "Fondua"
Piedmontese Fondue

US		UK
¾ pound	Fontina cheese	¾ pound
	milk	
6	egg yolks, well beaten	6
½ cup	butter	¼ pound
1	white truffle, thinly sliced – optional	1
	white pepper	
	fingers of toasted bread	

This is one of the most famous Piedmontese dishes. To be successful, best-quality, genuine Piedmontese Fontina cheese should be used. It will still be a genuine Piedmontese *fonduta* even if the truffle is omitted, but not if Gruyère or Edam is substituted.

Pare off the rind and cut the cheese into small dice. Put it into a bowl, cover with milk and leave to steep for at least 8 hours or overnight.

Pour the cheese and milk into the top of a double boiler; the water in the bottom should be hot but not boiling. Add the egg yolks and the butter. Cook over a low heat, stirring constantly but gently with a wooden spoon. The moment the cheese is smooth and creamy, pour it into deep, heated plates and sprinkle with truffle and pepper. Serve with fingers of toast.
Serves 6.

Polenta e Fontina in Torta
Savory Polenta and Cheese Pudding

US		UK
7½ cups	water	3 pints
1½ teaspoons	salt	1½ teaspoons
3 cups	cornmeal	1 pound
5–6 tablespoons	butter	2½–3 ounces
½ pound	Fontina cheese, thinly sliced	½ pound
	white pepper	

Bring the water and salt to the boil in a large pan. Add the cornmeal, stirring continuously with a wooden spoon to prevent lumping. Cook over a moderate heat, stirring frequently, for about 45 minutes, or until the mixture comes away cleanly from the sides of the pan and has the consistency of mashed potatoes. Rinse a deep dish with cold water and turn the polenta into it. Leave to cool. When it is cold, cut the polenta into ¼-inch-thick slices.

Generously grease a baking dish with butter. Place a layer of sliced polenta on the bottom and cover with a layer of cheese. Season with pepper. Repeat these layers until the ingredients are used up, finishing with a layer of polenta. Dot with butter and put into a hot oven (450°F. Mark 7) to brown.
Serves 6.

Gnocchetti alla Piemontese
Piedmontese Gnocchetti (Gnocchi)

US		UK
	all-purpose (plain) flour	
3 tablespoons	semolina	1 ounce
3	egg yolks, beaten	3
pinch	freshly grated nutmeg	pinch
pinch	sugar	pinch
	salt and white pepper	
2 cups	milk	¾ pint
⅔ cup	grated Parmesan cheese	2 ounces
¼ cup	diced Emmenthal cheese	2 ounces
1 small	white truffle, finely chopped – optional	1
	olive oil	
1	egg, well beaten	1
	fine dry breadcrumbs	

Beat ½ cup plus 2 tablespoons (U.K. 2½ ounces) flour and the semolina with the egg yolks, grated nutmeg and sugar, and a little salt and pepper to taste. Pour into a pan and gradually add the milk, stirring constantly until smooth. Bring to the boil and cook over a moderate heat, stirring, for about 15 minutes. The mixture must be so thick that a spoon will stand up in it.

Take the pan from the heat and stir in the Parmesan cheese. Let the mixture cool a little, then add the Emmenthal cheese and the truffle, if used. Mix thoroughly and turn out on to a cold surface (marble, or even a large plate) brushed with olive oil. Smooth out with a wet knife blade until the paste is ½ inch thick. Leave until cold, then cut into diamond shapes. Dip these into flour, egg and finally into breadcrumbs, and deep-fry in plenty of hot olive oil. Drain on paper towels and serve very hot, with additional grated Parmesan and a smooth white sauce into which you have stirred a few tablespoons of heavy (double) cream.
Serves 6.

Gnocchi alla Bava
Potato Gnocchi with Cheese

US		UK
4 pounds	potatoes	4 pounds
4 cups	all-purpose (plain) flour	1 pound
	salt	
½ pound	Fontina cheese	½ pound
½ cup	butter, melted	¼ pound

Wash and boil the potatoes until soft. Drain, cool and peel them. Mash the potatoes in a bowl until quite free from lumps and very dry. Add the flour, a little salt and quickly work the mixture into a dough. Break off small pieces and shape them into sausage-like rolls the thickness of a finger, each about 1 inch long. Press each piece with the thumb against the concave surface of a cheese grater (or a fork) – this will give each *gnocchi* the appearance of a shell with a ridged pattern on its back. Place the *gnocchi* on a floured surface to prevent them sticking together.

Bring a large pan of salted water to a gentle boil and drop in the *gnocchi*, removing them with a perforated spoon as soon as they rise to the top, approximately after 3 minutes' cooking. (It is usually better to cook them in batches rather than all at once, as if there are too many they will stick together.) Fill a fireproof dish with alternate layers of *gnocchi* and slices of Fontina, sprinkling each layer with melted butter. Cover and bake in a moderate oven (375°F. Mark 4) for 5 minutes. Serve immediately.
Serves 6.

Agnollotti alla Piemontese
Piedmontese Agnollotti or Ravioli

US		UK
6 tablespoons	butter	3 ounces
2½ tablespoons	olive oil	2 tablespoons
1 small	onion, finely chopped	1 small
1 clove	garlic, finely chopped	1 clove
1 sprig	rosemary, finely chopped	1 sprig
1 pound	lean beef	1 pound
	salt and pepper	
2 tablespoons	flour	1½ tablespoons
⅔ cup	stock	¼ pint
3 canned	Italian peeled tomatoes, puréed	3 canned
¾ cup	cooked spinach, finely chopped	6 ounces
⅔ cup	grated Parmesan cheese	2 ounces
2	eggs, beaten	2

Dough		
4 cups	all-purpose (plain) flour	1 pound
4–5	eggs	4–5
	salt	

Stuffing

Heat half the butter and all the oil together in a pan, and sauté the onion, garlic and rosemary. Add the meat, season to taste with salt and pepper, and brown it well on all sides. Sprinkle with flour and add the stock and tomatoes. Cover and simmer for about 2 hours.

When the meat is tender, take it from the pan, cut it into pieces and put it through the fine blade of a meat grinder (U.K. mincer). Mix this with the spinach, the Parmesan and the beaten eggs. Rub the sauce through a sieve and return it to the pan. Let this simmer.

Dough

Put the flour on a large pastry board. Make a well in the middle and add the eggs and salt. Work the eggs into the flour, then knead to a smooth, elastic dough, about 10 minutes.

Roll the dough out as thinly as possible and divide into 2 sheets. On one sheet arrange teaspoons of the stuffing in little heaps at regular intervals 1½ inches apart. Cover with the second sheet of dough and press with the fingers round the heaps of stuffing. Cut round the *agnollotti* with a pastry wheel or a sharp knife and make quite sure the edges are firmly sealed. Sprinkle lightly with flour and let them rest for 30 minutes, turning them after 15 minutes.

Bring a large pan of salted water to a fast boil, add 15 *agnollotti* and cook for 10 to 12 minutes. Lift out with a perforated spoon and transfer to a heated serving dish. Repeat until all the *agnollotti* are cooked. Add the sauce from the meat and the rest of the butter, toss gently and serve with additional grated Parmesan cheese.
Serves 6.

Risotto con Tartufi
Truffled Risotto

US		UK
6 tablespoons	butter	3 ounces
¼ pound	fat salt pork, diced	¼ pound
2 ounces	Parma ham, shredded	2 ounces
3¾ cups	rice – see page 66	1½ pounds
10 cups	boiling meat stock	4 pints
1 teaspoon	meat extract – optional	1 teaspoon
¾ cup	grated Parmesan cheese	3 ounces
1 small	white truffle, sliced paper-thin	1 small

Heat half the butter in a large, heavy pan, add the fat pork and ham, and sauté gently for a few minutes. And the rice and stir it thoroughly but gently to absorb the fat. Cook for 5 minutes. Add a little

stock, stirring gently, and when it is almost absorbed add more. Continue to cook the rice in this way, adding 2 or 3 cups of boiling stock each time it shows signs of drying out. It should be ready in about 20 minutes.

Dilute the meat extract in a little of the stock. Add this to the rice with the remaining butter and the Parmesan cheese. Stir well. Arrange the rice on a hot platter and cover with slices of truffle.
Serves 6.

Salsa Verde alla Piemontese
Piedmontese Green Sauce

US		UK
2	salted anchovies	2
1	hard-boiled egg yolk	1
5 tablespoons	finely chopped parsley	4 tablespoons
1 clove	garlic, minced or finely chopped	1 clove
1 tablespoon	capers	2–3 teaspoons
4 teaspoons	fresh breadcrumbs	1 tablespoon
	milk	
	olive oil	
	salt and pepper	

There are several versions of this sauce. Some omit the capers and/or the egg yolk; others include finely chopped onions, peppers or pickled gherkins, and dilute the sauce with lemon juice.

Wash the anchovies, fillet them and chop them finely together with the egg yolk. Add the parsley, garlic, capers and the breadcrumbs, soaked in milk and squeezed dry. Pound this mixture to a paste. Very gradually add enough olive oil to make a fairly liquid sauce, beating between each addition. Season to taste with salt and pepper.
Serve with boiled meat or fish.

Salsa Piemontese
Piedmontese Sauce

US		UK
1 cup	water	½ pint
1 teaspoon	meat extract	1 teaspoon
4	salted anchovies, filleted – see method	4
1 small	white truffle, grated	1 small
1 small	shallot, finely chopped	1 small
1 clove	garlic, finely chopped	1 clove
2–3 sprigs	parsley, finely chopped	2–3 sprigs
1	hard-boiled egg yolk	1
1 teaspoon	potato flour	1 teaspoon
	olive oil	
	lemon juice	
pinch	white pepper	pinch

Bring the water to the boil and add the meat extract. (If meat extract is not available, use half a bouillon cube or even better, substitute meat stock for the water and meat extract.) Keep at simmering point.

Pound the anchovies, truffle, shallot, garlic, parsley and egg yolk to a paste in a mortar. Rub this paste through a sieve into the simmering liquid and continue to cook gently.

Mix the potato flour with enough cold water to make a thin paste. Stir this into the pan and continue stirring until the sauce thickens.

Add a few drops of olive oil and lemon juice to taste, stir thoroughly, add the pepper, and stir once more.

This sauce is usually served with steak, roast beef or tournedos.

Some salted anchovies are inclined to be over-salted and should be quickly washed in warm water or vinegar before being added to the sauce. Canned anchovies can be used in this recipe but should first be wiped free of oil.

Bagna Cauda
Piedmontese Garlic and Anchovy Sauce

US		UK
1 cup	butter	½ pound
4 tablespoons	olive oil	3 tablespoons
4 cloves	garlic, finely chopped	4 cloves
6	anchovy fillets, chopped	6
	salt	
1 small	truffle, thinly sliced – optional	1 small

This sauce is one of the specialties of Piedmontese cooking, served whenever the Piedmontese feel hungry, accompanied by coarse red wine. The name literally means "hot bath" because raw vegetables, in particular tender cardoons, celery, peppers, artichokes and chicory, are dipped into it. It is usual to serve *bagna cauda* in the pan in which it has been cooked, kept hot at table over a small spirit stove.

Heat the butter and oil together in a shallow pan, earthenware if possible, and sauté the garlic gently without letting it brown. Take the pan off the heat and add the anchovies. Stir well with a wooden spoon. Return the pan to a low heat and continue cooking, stirring, until the anchovies have dissolved into a paste. Season with a pinch of salt, and add the truffle. Serve hot.

Consommé alla Benso
Consommé with Chicken Royale

US		UK
½	cooked chicken breast	½
1	egg	1
3	egg yolks	3
	salt	
10 cups	chicken consommé or clear stock	4 pints
	butter	
1	white truffle, sliced paper-thin – optional	1
	grated Parmesan cheese	

A *royale* is an egg custard, usually prepared with eggs and a purée or flavoring of some kind. *Royales* are easy to make and transform a simple stock into an elegant soup.

Pound the chicken breast in a mortar and rub through a sieve or purée in a blender. Beat the egg and the 3 yolks together. Add salt to taste and the chicken purée. Blend thoroughly, then stir in 1 cup (U.K. scant ½ pint) of the chicken stock.

Pour the custard into a well-buttered mold (mould). Remove the scum that forms on top and cook, covered, in a pan with water to come halfway up the mold, for 30 minutes, or until the custard is set. Take care never to let the water boil. Take the custard from the pan and leave to cool completely. Turn the custard out, cut it into thin slices and then into rounds or fancy shapes. Divide these between the soup bowls and to each bowl add a slice of white truffle, if used. Bring the chicken stock to the boil and pour it into the bowls.

Serve immediately, accompanied by a bowl of grated Parmesan cheese.

Serves 6.

Minestrone d'Asti
Vegetable Soup Asti Style

US		UK
1 pound	shelled fresh white (haricot) beans	1 pound
4 quarts	water	6 pints
1 small	cabbage, shredded	1 small
4 medium-sized	potatoes, peeled and diced	4 medium-sized
2	carrots, diced	2
2–3 stalks	celery, chopped	2–3 stalks
	salt	
¾ pound	ditalini noodles – see method – or rice	¾ pound
½ pound	fat salt pork, diced	½ pound
2 cloves	garlic	2 cloves
2–3 sprigs	parsley, finely chopped	2–3 sprigs
10–12 leaves	basil, finely chopped	10–12 leaves
1 cup	grated Parmesan cheese	4 ounces
	white pepper	

Ditalini are tiny, thimble-shaped noodles. Failing these, any other Italian noodles may be used, provided they are small and round.

Put the beans into a large pan, cover with the water, bring to the boil, and cook them slowly for 1 hour. Add the cabbage, potatoes, carrots, celery and salt, and continue to cook for 40 minutes. Add the noodles and cook for another 10 to 12 minutes over a high heat (15 to 20 minutes for rice).

Meanwhile, pound the salt pork to a paste with the garlic, parsley and basil (or use an electric blender). Add the grated cheese, and dilute with a few tablespoons of the stock. Pour the mixture into the soup, stir well, season with a little freshly ground white pepper and serve immediately.

Serves 6 to 8.

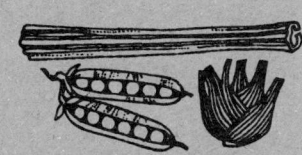

Minestra di Trippa
Tripe Soup

US		UK
2 pounds	dressed calf's tripe – see page 46	2 pounds
2	onions	2
2	cloves	2
1	carrot	1
2 stalks	celery	2 stalks
	salt	
4	black peppercorns	4
¼ pound	fat salt pork	¼ pound
1 small	cabbage, shredded	1 small
4	potatoes, peeled and diced	4
2	leeks, chopped	2
	pepper	

Wash the tripe, scald it and cut into strips. Put into a large pan with 1 onion stuck with the cloves, the carrot, 1 stalk celery, a little salt and the peppercorns. Cover with plenty of water and simmer for 1 hour. Take out the tripe and strain the liquid.

Pound the salt pork to a paste and fry it in a large flameproof casserole (the Italians prefer to use earthenware). Let the fat begin to run, then gently sauté the remaining onion and celery, finely chopped. Add the tripe, cabbage, potatoes and leeks. Add the tripe stock, check seasoning, and cook very gently for another hour. Serve the tripe very hot in the same casserole.

Serves 6.

Zuppa di Fontina
Bread and Cheese Soup

Slice 1 pound Fontina very thinly. Slice 1 or 2 long French loaves, depending on size, into rounds and toast them. Put alternate layers of toast and cheese in a large earthenware bowl or soup tureen. Bring 10 cups (U.K. 4 pints) stock to the boil and immediately pour over the toast and cheese. Leave in a warm oven (250°F. Mark ¼) for 10 minutes before serving.
Serves 6 to 8.

Manzo Stufato al Barolo
Beef in Barolo Wine

US		UK
2–2½ pounds	lean beef	2–2½ pounds
1	bay leaf	1
1 clove	garlic	1 clove
	salt and pepper	
	grated nutmeg	
2 cups	Barolo or good red wine	¾ pint
1 medium-sized	onion	1 medium-sized
4 tablespoons	fresh pork fat	2 ounces
2 tablespoons	butter	1 ounce

Cut the meat into 6 large pieces of equal size. Put into a bowl with the bay leaf, garlic, a little salt, a pinch of pepper and a pinch of grated nutmeg. Add the wine, stir and leave in a cool place, covered, for at least 8 hours, or overnight, turning the meat occasionally.

Dice the onion and the pork fat. Heat the pork fat and butter in a large pan, and when the butter is hot and the pork fat begins to run, sauté the onion gently until soft but not brown.

Take the meat from the marinade, drain thoroughly and pat dry with paper towels. Add the meat to the pan and brown over a moderate heat. Strain the marinade and pour over the meat. Check seasoning, cover the pan and cook slowly for 2 hours, or until the meat is very tender.
Serves 6.

Costata di Manzo al Barolo
Boned Rib of Beef in Barolo Wine

US		UK
a 3-pound	boned rib of beef	a 3-pound
1	onion, quartered	1
1	carrot, sliced	1
1 stalk	celery, roughly chopped	1 stalk
1	bay leaf	1
	salt	
4–5	black peppercorns	4–5
1 bottle	Barolo or good red wine	1 bottle
2 tablespoons	pork fat, chopped	1 ounce
4 tablespoons	butter	2 ounces
1 teaspoon	potato flour or cornstarch (cornflour)	1 teaspoon

Put the meat into a large bowl, add the onion, carrot, celery, bay leaf, a little salt and the peppercorns, and pour over the wine. Leave to marinate for 24 hours, turning the meat from time to time.

Take the meat from the marinade and dry it carefully. Tie it into a neat round. Heat the pork fat in a pan large enough to hold the meat, and as the fat begins to run add the butter. Stir until melted, then add the meat and brown it on all sides.

Strain the marinade into another pan and cook over a fairly high heat until reduced by half.

Season the meat with salt and pour over the reduced wine. Cover and cook over a low heat for about 2 hours, or until very tender. When the meat is really tender (one should be able to eat it with only a fork or even a spoon), transfer it to a heated serving dish and keep hot in a warm oven. Skim the sauce of fat and bring it to the boil

again. Mix the potato flour to a thin paste with water and stir this into the boiling sauce. Cook, stirring constantly, for 5 minutes. Pour a little of the sauce over the meat and serve the rest separately.
Serves 6 to 8.

Costolette alla Valdostana
Veal Chops Stuffed with Cheese

US		UK
6	veal chops	6
¼ pound	Fontina cheese, thinly sliced	¼ pound
	salt and white pepper	
2½ tablespoons	flour	2 tablespoons
1	egg, well beaten	1
¼ cup	fine dry breadcrumbs	3 tablespoons
6 tablespoons	butter	3 ounces

This dish is a specialty of the Val d'Aosta.

Slit each chop horizontally almost to the bone to make a pocket for the filling. Push slices of Fontina cheese into the pockets, lay the slices flat and then press the top and bottom together again and seal the edges by beating hard with the dull end of a heavy kitchen knife. Sprinkle lightly with salt and pepper on both sides. Dip the chops in flour, then in egg, and finally in breadcrumbs. Sauté in hot butter on both sides until golden brown, about 10 to 15 minutes.
Serves 6.

Vitello alla Marengo
Veal Marengo

US		UK
2–2½ pounds	boned breast or loin of veal	2–2½ pounds
½ cup	olive oil	6–8 tablespoons
1	onion, finely chopped	1
	salt and pepper	
4 teaspoons	flour	1 tablespoon
1 cup	dry white wine	scant ½ pint
1 cup	meat stock	scant ½ pint
6 large	ripe tomatoes, peeled and sliced	6 large
1 clove	garlic, crushed	1 clove
½	bay leaf	½
pinch	thyme	pinch
4 tablespoons	butter	2 ounces
12	pearl (button) onions	12
12 small	white mushrooms	12 small
2–3 sprigs	parsley, coarsely chopped	2–3 sprigs
6 slices	bread fried in oil and cut into triangles	6 slices

Cut the veal into large cubes. Heat the oil in a large pan and brown the meat on all sides. Add the chopped onion, a little salt and a pinch of pepper. Sprinkle with flour and continue stirring until smoothly blended with the other ingredients. Add the wine and stock, stirring constantly and scraping all the crusty bits from the bottom and sides of the pan. Bring to the boil and add the tomatoes, garlic, bay leaf and thyme. Cover the pan, lower the heat and simmer for 45 minutes, or until the meat is tender.

Heat the butter in another pan and quickly brown the pearl (button) onions without letting them soften. Discard the stalks from the mushrooms; wash and dry the caps, if necessary. Add the onions and mushrooms to the meat and cook for 15 minutes longer. Let the meat cool slightly so that the fat comes to the surface. Skim this off with a spoon and reheat the meat. Arrange the veal on a hot serving dish with the sauce poured over the top. Sprinkle with parsley and serve garnished with fried bread triangles.
Serves 6.

Tournedos con Finanziera
Tournedos à la Financière

US		UK
½ pound	calf's sweetbreads	½ pound
	salt	
½ cup	veal bone marrow	3 ounces
	pepper	
4 teaspoons	wine vinegar	1 tablespoon
1 small	onion, chopped	1 small
1	carrot, chopped	1
1 stalk	celery, chopped	1 stalk
⅝ cup	butter	5 ounces
	Madeira wine	
¼ pound	pickled mushrooms, diced	4 ounces
2 ounces	pickled gherkins, diced	2 ounces
6 slices	veal, cut from the leg ½ inch thick	6 slices
4 teaspoons	flour	1 tablespoon

Remove all the hard tubes, etc. from the sweetbreads, then wash and soak them in cold water with a pinch of salt for 1 hour to remove the blood. Drain and rinse. Put them into a pan with the marrow, cover with cold water, add a pinch of salt and pepper, the vinegar, onion, carrot and celery, and bring slowly to the boil; simmer for 4 minutes. The sweetbreads are done after the water reaches boiling point. Take them from the pan and drop immediately into cold water. Remove any fat and left-over membrane. Cut the marrow and the sweetbreads into cubes. (The stock with the chopped vegetables can be used later for a soup.)

In another pan, heat 4 tablespoons (2 ounces) butter and sauté the sweetbreads and marrow very gently until golden. Season with salt and pepper, and add ½ cup (U.K. 6 to 8 tablespoons) Madeira. Let the wine reduce, then add the mushrooms and gherkins. Mix well, cover and keep hot. This is Financière Sauce, Piedmont style.

Shape the veal slices into tournedos, tie with thread and flour lightly. The thread keeps the tournedos in shape while cooking and can be omitted if perfection of shape is not demanded. Heat the remaining butter in a frying pan and brown the tournedos on both sides. Add salt, sprinkle with 2 to 3 tablespoons Madeira and let the wine reduce very slowly. When the meat is tender, take it from the pan. Remove the threads, arrange the tournedos on a heated serving dish and top each one with a little of the sauce. Serve immediately.

Serves 6.

Coda di Bue alla Cavour
Oxtail Cavour

US		UK
3½–4 pounds	oxtail	3½–4 pounds
¼ pound	fresh pork rind	¼ pound
	olive oil	
2	onions, finely chopped	2
4	carrots, finely chopped	4
2 stalks	celery, finely chopped	2 stalks
3 sprigs	parsley, finely chopped	3 sprigs
	salt and pepper	
2½ cups	red wine	1 pint
2 ounces	dried mushrooms	2 ounces
2 tablespoons	butter	1 ounce
4 tablespoons	potato flour	1 ounce

Wipe the oxtail with a damp cloth and saw or cut it into neat joints. Cut the pork rind into thin strips. Heat ½ cup (U.K. 6 to 8 tablespoons) olive oil and the pork rind in a large pan, add all the chopped vegetables and the pieces of oxtail, and sauté gently. Season with salt and pepper, and pour in the wine. Cover and cook very slowly until the vegetables begin to soften and the wine has reduced a little. Add enough hot water to cover the meat. Cover the pan tightly and simmer for 2 to 3 hours longer, or until the oxtail is tender.

Soak the mushrooms in hot water for 30 minutes. Drain and pat dry. Heat ¼ cup (U.K. 3 tablespoons) olive oil and sauté the mushrooms for a few minutes.

Remove the scum from the oxtail liquid and bring to the boil. Knead the butter and potato flour together until smooth. Stir this into the oxtail liquid in small pieces, and continue cooking until the sauce has thickened. Skim off any surplus fat, stir in the mushrooms and continue cooking for a few minutes longer. Transfer the pieces of oxtail to a deep, round dish. Pour the sauce over the meat and serve immediately, with plain boiled potatoes.

Serves 6.

Rane Fritte
Fried Frogs' Legs

Skin and trim about 3 dozen frogs, removing the breast and gall bladder, and retaining only the legs. Cut off the feet. Skewer the legs and soak them for 1 hour in iced water with 2 to 3 tablespoons milk. Drain and soak in a fresh portion of iced water for 2 hours. This will draw out all the impurities, and whiten and swell the flesh. Drain the legs, wash carefully and dry.

Make a marinade with ½ bottle dry white wine, 2 or 3 sprigs parsley, a small onion, thinly sliced, a pinch of grated nutmeg and salt and white pepper, to taste. Add the legs and leave to marinate for about 1 hour. Drain and dry them, dust them with flour and deep-fry in hot olive oil until golden brown. Sprinkle with salt and serve immediately, garnished with chopped parsley.

If liked, the legs may be dipped in beaten egg after flouring. The marinade may be strained and used again for either meat or fish.

Serves 12 as an appetizer.

Rane in Guazzetto
Stewed Frogs' Legs

US		UK
3 dozen	prepared frogs — see method	3 dozen
5 tablespoons	olive oil	4 tablespoons
3 tablespoons	butter	1½ ounces
2 large	ripe tomatoes, peeled and chopped	2 large
1 clove	garlic, finely chopped	1 clove
4 teaspoons	finely chopped parsley	1 tablespoon
2–3 leaves	sage, chopped	2–3 leaves
6–7 leaves	basil, chopped	6–7 leaves
2 large	anchovy fillets, chopped	2 large
½ cup	dry white wine	6–8 tablespoons
	salt and pepper	
pinch	grated nutmeg	pinch

Prepare the frogs exactly as directed in the preceding recipe, up to and including dusting them with flour.

Heat the oil and butter together in a large pan, and add the frogs' legs. Cook over a high heat for about 10 minutes, turning them from time to time. When they are lightly browned, lift them out and put them aside. Add the chopped tomatoes, garlic and herbs to the pan, and cook over a moderate heat until the tomatoes are soft. Add the anchovies and the wine, and raise the heat to let the wine reduce a little.

Return the frogs' legs to the pan. Season to taste with salt, pepper and a pinch of nutmeg, cover and cook over a low heat for another 10 minutes.

Serves 12 as an appetizer, 6 as a main dish.

Pollo alla Marengo
Chicken Marengo

US		UK
1	young chicken – about 2½ pounds	1
½ cup	olive oil	6–8 tablespoons
2 cloves	garlic, crushed	2 cloves
4–5 large	ripe tomatoes, peeled and sliced	4–5 large
	salt and pepper	
1 cup	dry white wine	scant ½ pint
4 slices	bread, crusts removed	4 slices
4	eggs	4
4	cooked shrimps (UK prawns) – optional	4
2–3 sprigs	parsley, finely chopped	2–3 sprigs
	juice of 1 lemon	

Cut the chicken into pieces – wings, thighs, drumsticks and breasts. Heat the oil in a shallow pan. Brown the legs first, then add the remaining chicken pieces. When all the pieces of chicken are golden brown, pour off the surplus oil and reserve it. Add the garlic, tomatoes, salt, pepper and wine, and continue cooking until the chicken pieces are tender.

Re-heat the oil poured off from the chicken in a frying pan, and fry the bread on both sides. Put aside but keep hot. In the same pan, fry the eggs, adding more oil if necessary.

Serve the chicken in its sauce, garnished with the fried bread, eggs and shrimps (U.K. prawns), if used. Sprinkle with parsley and lemon juice, and serve.

Serves 4.

Budino di Pollo
Chicken Mousse

US		UK
1	boiled chicken – 3 to 3½ pounds	1
	salt and pepper	
2	eggs, beaten	2
	grated rind of 1 lemon	
1	black truffle, diced – optional	1
½ cup	heavy (double) cream, lightly beaten	6–8 tablespoons
	butter	

A good way to deal with an elderly bird.

Skin and bone the chicken. Put the meat twice through the fine blade of a meat grinder (U.K. mincer). Mix with salt, a pinch of pepper, the eggs, lemon rind, truffle if used, and the cream. Pour into a well-buttered soufflé dish and tap the dish firmly on a hard surface to eliminate any air pockets in the mousse. Cover with wax paper or foil, and set the dish in a pan of hot water. Bake in a moderate oven (375°F. Mark 4) for 1 hour.

Take from the oven, leave to settle for a few minutes and turn out on to a hot, flat, round serving dish.

Serves 6.

Spezzatino di Pollo
Chicken in Tomato and White Wine Sauce

US		UK
1	chicken – 3 to 3½ pounds	1
4 tablespoons	butter	2 ounces
4 tablespoons	olive oil	3 tablespoons
	salt and white pepper	
½ cup	dry white wine	6–8 tablespoons
1 pound	ripe tomatoes, rubbed through a sieve	1 pound
1	white truffle, sliced paper-thin – optional	1

Only a tender chicken can be cooked in this manner. If fresh tomatoes are not available, use a can of Italian peeled tomatoes.

Chop the chicken into 4 pieces. Heat the butter and oil together in a large pan, add the chicken legs first and brown them over a high heat; then brown the breasts. Season with salt and pepper, lower the heat and continue cooking until the chicken pieces are tender. Remove from the pan and keep hot.

Scraping off any bits adhering to the bottom and sides of the pan, and stir in the wine. Let it reduce a little over a high heat. Add the puréed tomatoes, salt and pepper to taste, stir well, and cook over a moderate heat for about 10 minutes. Return the chicken pieces to the pan, spoon over the sauce and cook for a few minutes longer. Serve the chicken in the sauce, sprinkled with truffle, if used.

Serves 4.

Filetti di Tacchino al Marsala
Turkey Breasts with Marsala Sauce

US		UK
6	turkey fillets, cut from the breast	6
	flour	
½ cup	butter	¼ pound
	salt and white pepper	
1 cup	Marsala wine	scant ½ pint
1	white truffle, sliced paper-thin – optional	1

An 8-pound turkey will give 8 to 10 good-sized fillets. Flatten them out lightly with a meat bat and dust them with flour.

Heat 6 tablespoons (3 ounces) butter and brown the turkey fillets gently on both sides; do not have the heat too high or the butter will burn. Cook the fillets for 5 minutes on each side, sprinkle with salt and pepper, and transfer to a heated serving dish. Keep hot in a warm oven.

Stir the butter in the pan, scraping the bottom and sides, and add the Marsala. Stir well, then add the remaining butter. Continue to stir and cook over a high heat until the butter has been incorporated into the Marsala sauce. Pour the sauce over the turkey fillets and serve immediately, sprinkled with truffle slices, if used.

Serves 6.

Lepre alla Piemontese
Hare Piedmontese Style

US		UK
1	hare, dressed	1
	salt	
1½ bottles	Barbera or other full-bodied red wine	1½ bottles
3	cloves	3
2	bay leaves	2
3 stalks	celery, roughly chopped	3 stalks
1 large	onion, sliced	1 large
2–3	carrots, roughly chopped	2–3
pinch	marjoram	pinch
pinch	thyme	pinch
3–4	black peppercorns	3–4
¼ cup	olive oil	3 tablespoons
2 tablespoons	butter	1 ounce
2 tablespoons	bacon fat	1 ounce
1 small	onion, finely chopped	1 small
1 square	bitter chocolate, grated	1 ounce
4 teaspoons	sugar	1 tablespoon
3–4 tablespoons	cognac	3 tablespoons

Cut the hare into joints. Reserve the blood and strain it into a bowl. Add a little salt to the blood and put it into the refrigerator together with the heart and liver.

Wipe the pieces of hare and put them into a bowl, preferably earthenware. Add the wine, cloves, bay leaves, celery, onion, carrots, marjoram, thyme, a little salt and the peppercorns. Stir well, cover the bowl and leave it in a cool place for 2 to 3 days, depending on the age of the hare.

Heat the oil and butter together in a large pan or casserole. Add the chopped bacon fat and sauté the onion gently until it begins to change color. Take the pieces of hare from the marinade, drain and dry them, and add them to the pan. Brown the hare over a high heat, turning the pieces frequently. Add the marinade, including the vegetables, lower the heat, cover the pan tightly and simmer for 2 to 3 hours.

Chop the liver and heart, and mix them with the blood. Pour all this into the pan and continue cooking slowly for another 30 minutes. Lift out the pieces of hare and put them aside. Rub the sauce through a sieve into a bowl. Stir the grated chocolate and sugar into the sauce, and return it to the pan. Add the hare, re-heat slowly and finally stir in the cognac. Serve with a thick, hot polenta.

Serves 6 to 8.

Lepre alla Marengo
Hare Marengo

US		UK
1	hare, dressed	1
½ cup	olive oil	6 tablespoons
1½ ounces	dried mushrooms	1½ ounces
2 tablespoons	butter	1 ounce
2½ tablespoons	tomato paste	2 tablespoons
	salt and pepper	
1 cup	dry white wine	scant ½ pint
2–3 sprigs	parsley, finely chopped	2–3 sprigs
Marinade		
¼ cup	olive oil	3 tablespoons
1	onion, chopped	1
1	carrot, chopped	1
1 stalk	celery, chopped	1 stalk
1	clove	1
3–4 leaves	sage	3–4 leaves
1	bay leaf	1
1 sprig	rosemary	1 sprig
1 clove	garlic, crushed	1 clove
	salt	
3–4	black peppercorns	3–4
2½ cups	Madeira wine	1 pint
¼ cup	wine vinegar	3 tablespoons

Wipe the hare with paper towels. Cut into joints and put into a large earthenware or porcelain bowl.

Marinade
Heat the olive oil in a large pan with the chopped onion, carrot and celery, and cook over a very low heat until the vegetables are soft but not brown. Now add the clove, herbs and garlic, a little salt and the peppercorns, and cook for 2 minutes. Stir in the Madeira and vinegar. Bring to the boil, remove from the heat and leave to cool. Pour this marinade over the hare and leave in a cool place for at least 18 hours, or up to 48 hours if dealing with an elderly hare.

Drain the pieces of hare and dry them well. Reserve the marinade. Heat 3 tablespoons (U.K. 4 tablespoons) olive oil in a casserole or large pan and brown the hare pieces. Add the marinade, pouring it slowly through a strainer over the hare. Cover the pan and cook slowly for 2 to 3 hours, or until tender.

Soak the mushrooms in hot water for 30 minutes. Drain and dry them. Heat the butter with the remaining olive oil in a frying pan and sauté the mushrooms. After 5 minutes, add the tomato paste diluted with a little hot water. Season to taste with salt and pepper, and pour over the hare. Add the white wine and cook for another 15 minutes.

Transfer the hare with all its sauce to a deep, heated serving dish and serve, sprinkled with chopped parsley – or serve the hare in the casserole in which it was cooked.

Serves 6 to 8.

Fagiano con Funghi
Pheasant with Mushrooms

US		UK
1	hen pheasant, dressed	1
5 tablespoons	olive oil	4 tablespoons
3 tablespoons	butter	1½ ounces
	salt and pepper	
¼ cup	brandy	3–4 tablespoons
1 small	onion, finely chopped	1 small
2 stalks	celery, finely chopped	2 stalks
2–3 sprigs	parsley, finely chopped	2–3 sprigs
3–4 leaves	sage, chopped	3–4 leaves
pinch	thyme	pinch
2 cups	stock	¾ pint
½–¾ pound	mushrooms – see method	½–¾ pound
	juice of 1 lemon	
1	white truffle, thinly sliced – optional	1

The mushrooms used should be well-flavored ones – *cèpes* or *boletus edulis* – preferably not cultivated white mushrooms.

Wipe the pheasant and cut it into serving pieces. Heat half the oil with the butter in a pan or heavy casserole and brown the pheasant pieces. Season to taste with salt and pepper. Pour over the brandy and ignite it. When the flames have died down, add the onion, celery and herbs (not the mushrooms), and continue to cook until these are soft. Add the stock, cover the pan and continue cooking over a low heat until the pheasant pieces are tender, about 40 minutes.

Clean the mushrooms, discarding the stems. Slice the caps and drop them into water acidulated with lemon juice for a few minutes. Drain and pat dry. Heat the remaining oil in another pan and sauté the mushrooms for about 10 minutes. Transfer them to the pan with the pheasant. Stir gently and continue cooking for a few minutes longer to impregnate the sauce with the flavor of the mushrooms.

Serve the pheasant with the sauce on a hot platter, sprinkled with truffle, if used.

Serves 3 to 4.

Fagiano Tartufato
Pheasant Stuffed with Truffles

US		UK
1	young pheasant, dressed	1
2–3 small	white truffles	2–3 small
4 tablespoons	pork fat	2 ounces
3 slices	fat bacon	3 slices
	salt	
¼ cup	olive oil	3 tablespoons
	watercress	

This dish should be started the day before it is to be served.

Wipe the pheasant and truss it, pressing the legs tightly against the breast. Clean the truffles and slice them thinly. Pound the pork fat to a paste and stuff the pheasant with the truffles and fat. Put it into a deep, heavy casserole with a tight-fitting lid and leave in a cool place for 24 hours.

Secure the strips of bacon on the breast of the pheasant. Place the bird on a rack in a baking pan, season with salt and sprinkle with olive oil. Roast in a hot oven (425°F. Mark 6) for 30 to 45 minutes, depending on the size and age of the bird.

Take the pheasant from the pan, carve it, re-shape on a heated serving dish and return to a low oven to keep hot. Put the pan with the cooking juices on top of the stove and re-heat, stirring well. Strain over the pheasant. Insert a few feathers in the tail end of the pheasant and garnish with little bunches of watercress.

Serves 3 to 4.

Piccioni alla Cavour
Pigeons Cavour

US		UK
4	pigeons or squabs	4
6 tablespoons	butter	3 ounces
	salt	
4 teaspoons	flour	1 tablespoon
½ cup	Marsala wine	6 tablespoons
¼ pound	chicken livers, chopped	¼ pound
1	white truffle, thinly sliced – optional	1

Wash the pigeons and wipe them dry. Truss them with their feet folded inwards across the rear. Melt the butter in a shallow pan (it must not be too hot or the delicate flavor of the pigeons will be lost), add the pigeons and brown them lightly all over. Sprinkle with salt and flour, then add the Marsala. Cook rapidly for 5 minutes, then stir in ½ cup (U.K. 6 tablespoons) hot water. Check seasoning, lower the heat and continue cooking over a moderate heat for 30 to 45 minutes, or until the pigeons are tender.

Ten minutes before the pigeons are ready, add the chicken livers and the truffle, if used. Take the pigeons from the pan, discard the trussing threads and arrange the birds on a heated serving dish. Stir the sauce in the pan and pour it over the pigeons.

Serves 4.

Faraona alla Campagnola
Guinea Fowl Country Style

US		UK
1	guinea fowl	1
¼ cup	olive oil	3 tablespoons
	salt and pepper	
3 tablespoons	butter	1½ ounces
2	onions, finely chopped	2
2	carrots, finely chopped	2
2 stalks	celery, finely chopped	2 stalks
2–3 sprigs	parsley, finely chopped	2–3 sprigs
1 sprig	rosemary, finely chopped	1 sprig
1 cup	dry white wine	scant ½ pint
1	white truffle, sliced wafer-thin – optional	1

The guinea fowl, a rather dry, delicate-fleshed bird, a little reminiscent of pheasant, is a native of Africa. It was, however, known to the gourmets of ancient Rome, who called it Humidian or Carthagenian hen. It can be cooked in any of the ways in which chicken is cooked.

Singe the guinea fowl, clean it carefully and reserve the liver. Put the guinea fowl in a roasting pan with the olive oil, and season with salt and pepper. Roast in a moderate oven (375°F. Mark 4) for 35 to 45 minutes, or until tender, basting frequently to counteract dryness.

Melt the butter in a pan, add all the vegetables, herbs and the guinea fowl liver, and cook very gently until the vegetables are very soft. Add the wine, season to taste with salt and pepper, and continue cooking until the wine is reduced a little, then add

½ cup (U.K. 6 tablespoons) warm water and reduce this over a high heat. Rub the vegetables, liver and liquid through a sieve to make a sauce; return it to the pan, re-heat and, if necessary, reduce the sauce still further – it should be fairly thick.

When the guinea fowl is tender, carve it into serving pieces and arrange them on a hot serving dish. Pour over the sauce and sprinkle with slices of truffle.

Serves 3 to 4.

Quaglie ai Tartufi
Quails with Truffles

US		UK
6	quails, dressed	6
4 small	white truffles	4 small
	salt and white pepper	
	brandy	
6 slices	fat bacon	6 slices
2 tablespoons	butter	1 ounce
1 small	onion, finely chopped	1 small
1 small	carrot, finely chopped	1 small
1 stalk	celery, finely chopped	1 stalk
½ cup	stock	6 tablespoons

Wipe the quails carefully and dry them. Place half a truffle, a little salt and pepper, and a teaspoon of brandy into the cavity of each bird and wrap the bird in a slice of fat bacon. Tie with thread. Arrange the quails side by side in one tight layer in a shallow pan or heatproof casserole.

Melt the butter in another pan and sauté the vegetables lightly until soft but not brown. Arrange the vegetables round the quails, filling in all the spaces. Pour in the stock, cover the pan tightly and cook for 25 to 30 minutes. Take the pan from the heat, add the last truffle, cut into wafer-thin slices, cover again and leave to stand in a warm place for 5 minutes. Discard the thread and the bacon from the quails. Put the little birds on a hot serving dish. Rub the sauce through a sieve and re-heat quickly.

Serve the quails with polenta or rice, and hand round the sauce separately.

Serve one or two quails per person.

Trota alla Piemontese
Trout Piedmontese Style

US		UK
1 large	trout – about 2½ pounds	1 large
2 tablespoons	seedless white raisins (sultanas)	1½–2 tablespoons
¼ cup	olive oil	3 tablespoons
1 small	onion, finely chopped	1 small
1 clove	garlic, finely chopped	1 clove
1 stalk	celery, finely chopped	1 stalk
1 sprig	sage, finely chopped	1 sprig
1 sprig	rosemary, finely chopped	1 sprig
5 tablespoons	wine vinegar	4 tablespoons
	grated rind of 1 lemon	
1 cup	fish stock	scant ½ pint
	salt	
4 teaspoons	flour	1 tablespoon

There is more variety in trout than many people realize, especially in their coloring. The Italian lakes and northern rivers have some excellent trout.

Clean the trout and wash it under running water to rid it of any muddy flavor. Soak the white raisins (sultanas) in lukewarm water (or white wine). In a large pan, preferably an oval fish frying pan, heat the oil and sauté the chopped vegetables and herbs very gently until soft but not brown. Add the fish, vinegar, lemon rind, stock, a little salt and the white raisins with their liquid. Cover and simmer over a low heat for about 10 minutes.

Remove the trout, bone it and arrange it on a hot, oval serving dish. Keep hot in a warm oven.

Mix the flour with enough cold water to make a thin paste. Bring the fish sauce to the boil, add the flour and water paste, stir thoroughly and cook until the sauce is thick and smooth. Pour over the trout and serve immediately.

Serves 4.

Pesce Persico alla Salvia
Fillets of Perch with Sage

US		UK
12	fillets of perch	12
	flour	
2	eggs, beaten and lightly salted	2
	fine dry breadcrumbs	
½ cup	butter	4 ounces
¼ cup	olive oil	3 tablespoons
12 leaves	sage	12 leaves
Marinade		
½ cup	olive oil	6–8 tablespoons
	juice of 1 lemon	
1	green (spring) onion, finely chopped	1
	salt and pepper	

This hump-backed fish is one of the most delicate of the freshwater fish. If dealing with whole fish, the prickly dorsal fin, which begins almost above the head, must be cut off before attempting to clean the fish, in case of scratches from the sharp spines, which are said to be poisonous.

Stir the marinade ingredients together. Put the fillets of perch in a fairly deep dish and pour the marinade over them. Leave for 1 hour, turning occasionally.

Drain and dry the fish. Dip each fillet in flour, then in egg and finally in breadcrumbs. Heat 6 tablespoons (3 ounces) butter with the oil in a large, shallow pan; add the fillets and brown them well on both sides. Drain and arrange on a heated oval serving dish. Add the rest of the butter and the sage leaves to the cooking fat, re-heat and stir thoroughly. Pour this sauce over the fish and serve immediately.

Serves 6.

Tinche Marinate
Tench in Vinegar

US		UK
12 small	tench	12 small
	flour	
	oil for frying	
Marinade		
½ cup	olive oil	6–8 tablespoons
2 cloves	garlic, finely chopped	2 cloves
1	onion, finely chopped	1
3 tablespoons	white wine vinegar	2–3 tablespoons
3 tablespoons	dry white wine	2–3 tablespoons
	salt	
4–5	black peppercorns	4–5
12 leaves	sage	12 leaves

Clean and thoroughly wash the tench. Dry them, dust with flour, and shake gently in a sieve. Fry in plenty of hot oil. Arrange them in an earthenware dish.

Prepare the marinade. Heat the olive oil in a small pan and sauté the garlic and onion until golden brown. Add the vinegar, wine, salt, peppercorns and sage. Bring this mixture to the boil, and pour at once over the fish. Cover and leave in a cool place for at least 2 days before serving.

Serves 6.

Acciughe Tartufate
Truffled Anchovies

Fillet about ½ pound salted anchovies (not canned ones) and wash them thoroughly. Arrange them in layers in an earthenware dish, covering each layer with a little chopped parsley and a few paper-thin slices of white truffle. Add 1 or 2 cloves crushed garlic and enough olive oil to cover. Cover the dish and leave in a cool place for 3 or 4 days before serving.

Branzino al Vino Bianco
Sea Bass with White Wine

US		UK
a 2½-pound	sea bass	a 2½-pound
	salt	
2 cups	dry white wine	¾ pint
2 tablespoons	butter	1 ounce

Bass are found in temperate and tropical seas. We read that gourmets in ancient Rome would boast that they could distinguish between a bass caught in the sea at the mouth of the Tiber, and one caught between the bridges, a fine distinction.

Clean the fish through its gills or through a small incision in its stomach. Scrape off the scales, taking care not to break the skin, which is delicate, and wash well. Score the fish and sprinkle inside with salt. Place in an oval casserole large enough to take the fish comfortably. Add the wine, butter and a little salt. Cover and bake in a moderate oven (375°F. Mark 4) for about 20 minutes, or until the fish is tender. Transfer the fish to a hot oval serving dish, make 2 or 3 incisions with a knife in its back, and pour the remaining sauce over the top. Serve immediately.

Serves 6.

Insalata con Tartufi
Lettuce and Celery Salad with Truffles

US		UK
1 large	lettuce	1 large
1 large stalk	white celery	1 large stalk
2–3 tablespoons	olive oil	2 tablespoons
	salt and white pepper	
4 teaspoons	lemon juice	1 tablespoon
1	white truffle, thinly sliced	1
6 tablespoons	cream	4–5 tablespoons

Discard the outer leaves of the lettuce. Wash the heart, take the leaves apart, then tear them into small pieces. Wash the celery stalk, pull off any coarse strings and cut it into chunks. Mix the lettuce and celery in a salad bowl. Dress with olive oil, salt, pepper and lemon juice, adding more oil or lemon if preferred. Toss lightly, then sprinkle with the truffle slices and spoon over the cream.

Serves 4 to 6.

Insalata di Sedani
Truffled Celery Salad

Remove the coarse outer stalks from a large bunch of celery. Pull the inner stalks apart, wash and trim them, discarding any strings, and cut them into small, even chunks. Slice a white truffle very thinly, mix with the celery in a salad bowl and dress with well-flavored, home-made mayonnaise. Serve very cold but not chilled.

Serves 4.

Insalata di Fontina
Pepper and Fontina Cheese Salad

US		UK
6	yellow sweet peppers	6
½ pound	Fontina cheese, diced	½ pound
¼ cup	green olives, pitted	2 ounces
	olive oil	
1 teaspoon	French mustard	1 teaspoon
	salt and pepper	
2–3 tablespoons	cream	2–3 tablespoons

Cut the peppers in half, discarding cores and seeds. Bake them in a hot oven (450°F. Mark 7) or broil (grill) under a high heat until the skins blacken and blister. When cool enough to handle, pull off the thin outer skin and cut the flesh into long, even strips.

Put the strips of pepper in a salad bowl with the cheese and olives. Mix lightly and add a dressing made with olive oil, mustard, salt, pepper and cream in quantities to taste.

Stir well and chill for 2 hours before serving.

Serves 4 to 6.

Peperoni alla Bagna Cauda
Sweet Peppers with Bagna Cauda Sauce

US		UK
2 pounds	sweet peppers	2 pounds
4 large	ripe tomatoes, peeled and sliced	4 large
3 large	anchovy fillets	3 large
2 cloves	garlic, sliced	2 cloves
1 recipe	Bagna Cauda – page 19	1 recipe

Wipe the peppers, cut in half lengthwise and discard cores and seeds. Roast them in a hot oven (450°F. Mark 7) or under a broiler (grill) until they blacken and blister. Take from the heat, cool, then strip off the thin outer skin. Cut the flesh into strips.

Arrange the strips of pepper in a deep serving dish. Cover with tomato slices, the anchovy fillets, halved lengthwise, and the garlic. Pour the Bagna Cauda Sauce over the entire dish and serve immediately.

Serves 6.

Cipolline d'Ivrea
Pearl (Button) Onions Ivrea Style

US		UK
1½ pounds	pearl (button) onions	1½ pounds
2–3 tablespoons	olive oil	2 tablespoons
4 tablespoons	butter	2 ounces
1 small	bay leaf	1 small
⅔ cup	stock	¼ pint
	salt	
⅔ cup	dry white wine	¼ pint

If possible, choose onions all of the same size. Peel them carefully and blanch them in boiling water for a few minutes. Drain well.

Heat the olive oil and butter in a frying pan, add the onions, bay leaf, stock and a little salt to taste, and cook very gently until the onions are golden brown and beginning to soften. Add the wine and continue cooking until this has reduced and the onions are soft. Serve hot.

Serves 6.

Asparagi in Salsa Tartare
Asparagus in Tartare Sauce

US		UK
2 pounds	asparagus	2 pounds
	salt	
Tartare sauce		
4	hard-boiled egg yolks	4
1	raw egg yolk	1
1¼ cups	olive oil	½ pint
1 teaspoon	French mustard, or to taste	1 teaspoon
1 teaspoon	chopped capers	1 teaspoon
1 teaspoon	finely chopped pickled onions	1 teaspoon
1 teaspoon	finely chopped gherkins	1 teaspoon
2–3 sprigs	parsley, finely chopped	2–3 sprigs
	salt and pepper	

Clean and scrape the asparagus stalks if necessary, tie them in bundles and stand them upright in a tall, narrow pan. Pour in salted water up to the tips, cover with a lid which has a hole to let out steam (or leave the lid slightly off the pan), bring to the boil and cook for 15 to 20 minutes. In this way the stalks will boil while the tender tips simply cook in steam. Take the bundles from the pan carefully to avoid breaking the tips.

Tartare sauce

Mash the hard-boiled yolks with a wooden spoon. Add the raw egg yolk and the olive oil very gradually, beating between each addition as you would a mayonnaise. Finally, stir in the mustard, pickles and parsley, and season to taste with salt and pepper.

Serve the sauce with the asparagus.

Serves 6.

Spinaci alla Piemontese
Spinach Piedmontese Style

US		UK
2 pounds	fresh spinach	2 pounds
	salt and pepper	
½ cup	butter	4 ounces
3–4 large	anchovy fillets, finely chopped	3–4 large
1 clove	garlic	1 clove
8	croûtons	8

Wash the spinach very carefully in several changes of water. Tear off the leaves from the ribs and put the wet leaves (whole or shredded) into a pan with a little salt. Do not add any more water. Cover the pan and cook the spinach until it is quite tender. Drain in a colander and squeeze as dry as possible.

Heat the butter gently in a frying pan until it begins to brown; add the spinach, pepper, the anchovies and the garlic clove. Turn the spinach over and over to mix the ingredients thoroughly, and cook over a low heat for 5 minutes to bring out flavors. Serve with croûtons.

Serves 4.

Castagne Stufate
Stewed Chestnuts

US		UK
50 large	chestnuts	50 large
1 cup	dry white wine	scant ½ pint
1 stalk	celery, chopped	1 stalk
	salt	
1 teaspoon	meat extract	1 teaspoon

Split the skins of the chestnuts at the pointed end. Put them in a pan with cold water to cover, and bring to the boil. Take the chestnuts from the pan and peel off the thick outer skin.

Put the chestnuts into a perforated pan or strainer and leave them over a low heat for a few minutes to dry. This process makes it easier to peel off the inner skin.

Return the chestnuts to the pan, add the wine, celery and a little salt. Cover with water, stir in the meat extract and cook over a moderate heat until the chestnuts are soft. Take care that they do not disintegrate.

Serves 4 to 6.

Crêpes Piemontese
Piedmontese Pancakes

US		UK
1¼ cups	all-purpose (plain) flour	5 ounces
	salt	
3	eggs	3
1¼ cups	milk	½ pint
2 teaspoons	melted butter	1½ teaspoons
4 teaspoons	brandy	1 tablespoon
6	salted anchovies	6
6 tablespoons	butter	3 ounces
1	white truffle, diced – optional	1

Make a smooth batter with the flour, a pinch of salt, the eggs and milk. Stir in the melted butter and brandy, and leave to rest for 30 minutes.

Bone the anchovies and wash the fillets in cold water to rid them of some of their salt. Let them dissolve to a paste in 4 tablespoons (2 ounces) of the butter over low heat. Stir in the truffle, if used, remove the pan from the heat and leave to cool.

Heat just enough of the remaining butter in a small frying pan to grease the bottom. Pour in 2 to 3 tablespoons of the batter, or enough to cover the bottom of the pan thinly. Turn and twist the pan to spread the batter evenly over the entire surface. Fry over a moderate heat until the pancake is set and golden brown underneath, and can be shaken free in the pan. Turn and as soon as it puffs up in the pan, remove it – this side should not brown at all. Turn the pan upside down and gently drop the pancake on to paper towels. Keep hot in a warm oven. Repeat this process until all the batter is used up.

When all the pancakes are made, spread each one with a little of the anchovy and truffle butter. Quickly roll up the pancakes and arrange them side by side in a well-buttered fireproof dish. Dot with the remaining butter and glaze in a very hot oven (475°F. Mark 8).

Serves 6.

Omelette Piemontese
Piedmontese Truffle Omelette

Clean 1 white truffle carefully and wipe it with a damp cloth. Cut it in half. Dice one half and slice the other. Put the diced truffle in a frying pan in which you have melted 4 tablespoons (2 ounces) butter and heat it through without letting it cook. Scoop out of the pan and keep warm. Heat the truffle slices in the same butter, remove them to another plate, cover and keep warm.

Beat 6 eggs very lightly, season with a pinch of salt and white pepper, and make an omelette with them in the same butter. When the omelette is creamy and set, put the diced truffle in a row down the middle and fold the omelette over it. Slide out on to a heated serving dish, garnish with the sliced truffle and serve immediately.

Serves 2 to 3.

Uova Fritte alla Fontina
Fried Eggs with Fontina Cheese

US		UK
6 slices	bread	6 slices
½ cup	butter	¼ pound
6 slices	Fontina cheese	6 slices
6	anchovy fillets	6
6	eggs	6
	pepper	

Cut the bread slices into rounds about 2½ inches in diameter. Heat half the butter and gently fry the bread slices on one side only until crisp. Arrange the slices in a large, shallow casserole, fried side up.

Place a slice of Fontina cheese on each slice of bread, and on the cheese put half a chopped anchovy fillet. Sprinkle with pepper and transfer the dish to a moderate oven (375°F. Mark 4) long enough for the cheese to melt.

Fry the eggs in the remaining butter. Put 1 fried egg on each slice of cheese. In the same pan quickly fry the remaining anchovies until dissolved to a paste. Sprinkle over the eggs and serve immediately.

Serve one or two eggs per person.

Uova in Cocotte
Eggs en Cocotte

Butter 6 cocotte or ramekin dishes and scatter a little diced Fontina cheese and ham in the bottom of each dish. Bake in a hot oven (450°F. Mark 7) until the cheese has melted. Take the little dishes from the oven and carefully break an egg into each dish. Sprinkle with salt and top with a sliver of butter. Set the dishes in a baking pan, add about ½ inch boiling water and return to the oven for 8 to 10 minutes, or until the eggs are set. Serve immediately.

Serves 6.

Uova alla Torinese
Eggs Turin Style

Hard-boil 6 large eggs, cool them under running water and shell them carefully. Cut each egg in half.

Collect 2 to 3 sprigs parsley and a sprig each of sage, rosemary and thyme. Chop them together finely, mixing them thoroughly. Melt 2 tablespoons (1 ounce) butter in a heavy frying pan and sauté the herbs until limp over a low heat. Leave to cool completely.

Beat 2 eggs thoroughly with a pinch of salt, pepper and grated nutmeg, and stir in 2 or 3 tablespoons grated Parmesan. Pour over the herbs and beat with a fork until thoroughly mixed.

Dust the hard-boiled eggs with flour, dip them into the herb and egg mixture, and deep-fry in hot oil until golden. Serve immediately, allowing one or two eggs per person.

Tartufi alla Piemontese
Truffles Piedmontese Style

This splendid dish is not easily made outside its homeland. Quantities are to taste.

Thoroughly clean some white truffles, brushing them and rubbing them with a damp cloth. Cut into paper-thin slices. Fill a small fireproof dish with alternate layers of truffles and thinly sliced fresh Parmesan cheese, brushing each layer with a little olive oil and seasoning it with a pinch of salt and white pepper. Bake in a hot oven (425°F. Mark 6) for about 10 minutes.

Serve immediately, garnished with lemon wedges.

Ciliege al Barolo
Cherries in Barolo Wine

US		UK
2 pounds	large ripe (US sour) cherries, pitted	2 pounds
1½ cups	sugar	12 ounces
2½ cups	Barolo or any full-bodied red wine	1 pint
1¼ cups	heavy (double) cream, whipped and sweetened	½ pint

Put the pitted cherries into a pan or casserole, preferably an earthenware one. Add the sugar and wine. Bring slowly to the boil, lower the heat to simmering point and cook for 30 minutes, or until soft. Leave to cool, turn into a glass bowl and cover with whipped cream.

Serves 6.

Budino Freddo Gianduia
Cold Gianduia Pudding

US		UK
1	egg	1
1	egg yolk	1
½ cup	sugar	4 ounces
2½ squares	bitter chocolate, grated	2½ ounces
5 tablespoons	butter	2½ ounces
scant ½ cup	hazelnuts, roasted and chopped	2 ounces
¼ pound	plain cookies (UK petit beurre biscuits)	¼ pound
	butter for cake pan	
	whipped cream	

Beat the whole egg, egg yolk and sugar together for 15 minutes, or until very light and fluffy. Add the grated chocolate. Melt the butter in the top of a double boiler, add the egg and chocolate mixture, and cook, beating constantly, until the mixture thickens. Fold in the nuts and finally the cookies (U.K. biscuits), crushed.

Line a rectangular cake pan with wax paper and grease with butter. Add the pudding mixture, which should come level with the top of the pan. Cool, then chill in the refrigerator until firm.

Turn out, cut into slices and serve with whipped cream.

Serves 6.

Dolcetti Belvedere
Belvedere Creams

US		UK
5 cups	heavy (double) cream	2 pints
	vanilla pod – see method	
	granulated (caster) sugar	

This recipe is a specialty of the Belvedere Restaurant in La Morra in the Province of Cuneo.

Pour the cream into a heavy pan, add a piece of vanilla pod and slowly bring to the boil. If a vanilla pod is not available, use vanilla powder or extract to taste. Stir in 1⅛ cups (½ pound) sugar until dissolved, remove from the heat and leave to settle. Pour the cream into individual little soufflé dishes.

In a small pan, dissolve ¼ cup (2 ounces) sugar in 2 to 3 tablespoons water. Boil rapidly until the sugar has caramelized to a clear amber color. Pour over the tops of the creams and chill in the refrigerator. Turn out just before serving.

Serves 6 to 8.

Pesche alla Piemontese
Piedmontese Stuffed Peaches

US		UK
7 large	fresh peaches	7 large
2½ tablespoons	sugar	2 tablespoons
4 tablespoons	butter	2 ounces
1	egg yolk, beaten	1
5	almond macaroons, crumbled	5

Wash 6 of the peaches, dry them and cut them in half; remove the stones. Scoop out a little of the flesh in the middle and put this into a bowl. Add the flesh of remaining peach and mash to a purée.

Add the sugar, 2 tablespoons (1 ounce) butter, the egg yolk and the crumbled macaroons to the puréed peach. Mix well and fill each peach half with some of the mixture, piling it up in the middle. Arrange the peach halves in a fireproof dish and dot with the remaining butter. Bake in a moderate oven (375°F. Mark 4) for about 1 hour. Serve hot or cold.

Serves 6.

Bicciolani di Vercelli
Sweet Spiced Cookies (U.K. Biscuits) Vercelli Style

US		UK
1⅜ cups	butter	11 ounces
⅔ cup	granulated (caster) sugar	5½ ounces
	grated rind of 1 lemon	
pinch each	ground cinnamon, cloves, coriander, grated nutmeg and white pepper	pinch each
2	eggs	2
3	egg yolks	3
3 cups	all-purpose (plain) flour	12 ounces
¾ cup	very fine cornmeal (UK maize flour)	3 ounces
	butter for baking sheet	

Cream the butter and sugar together. Add the rind and spices. Beat in, separately, first the whole eggs and then the yolks.

Sift the two flours together and quickly mix into the creamed butter and eggs, working the dough as little as possible. Butter a baking sheet. Put the dough into a piping bag and pipe it out on to the baking sheet in strips about 4 inches long. Bake in a moderate oven (375°F. Mark 4) for 10 to 15 minutes. Cool before serving.

Store in an airtight container.

Zabaglione

Zabaglione is surely the most famous of all Italian puddings. It is served in glasses, either hot or cold, and eaten with a spoon.

For each egg yolk you will need about 1 tablespoon sugar and 2 tablespoons Marsala or white wine. Put these in the top of a double boiler and beat until well blended. Then continue to beat over boiling water, taking care that the water below does not touch the bottom of the pan, until the *zabaglione* is thick, light and fluffy.

The pudding may be flavored with vanilla, liqueur, or grated orange or lemon rind.

LOMBARDY

Right: Some of the excellent cheeses produced in the countryside around Lodi, displayed with other local dishes: *tortionata lodigiana* (see page 51), a risotto with cream, and trout from the River Adda.
Below: With the Castello Sforzesco in the background, some of the great dishes which have given Milanese cooking its world-wide reputation: *ossobuco* (see page 47), a thick *minestrone, risotto giallo*, or "yellow risotto", so called because of the saffron with which it is tinted, and *costolette alla milanese* (both on page 46).

On February 24, 1525, Francis I, King of France, was losing the battle of Pavia. Pursued by the Spaniards and about to surrender, he stopped at a cottage near the city and asked for a meal. As it happened, a classical vegetable *minestrone* was being prepared in the kitchen, and the cook, with a proper sense of occasion, decided to enrich it. She added a few slices of stale bread, toasted and buttered, broke a couple of eggs over them, threw in a few handfuls of Parmesan cheese, and poured the boiling vegetable broth over the top. Francis ate this strange new dish with great curiosity, and as the Spaniards closed in he thanked the peasants for their hospitality, declaring, "What you have given me was a King's soup!" And that, according to authorities on Lombard cooking, was the origin of Pavia soup, or *zuppa alla pavese* (see page 45).

The cottage where this is said to have happened still stands, and as you travel by train from Milan to Pavia you may catch a glimpse of it between the paddy fields a few minutes before passing the Certosa—the famous Charterhouse of Pavia. But soon little may be left of the sad plain of Lombardy, and within a few years perhaps even the cottage will have fallen victim to the urban sprawl of Milan, where all but the center of the city has changed almost beyond recognition in the last fifty years or so. Business is now the dominating factor and the "working lunch" has replaced the more leisurely, civilized meal of earlier times. True, at midday the Milanese still drink their usual aperitif, *bitter*, with olives and potato chips (crisps), as their fathers did in the past, but the majority of restaurants have been taken over by Tuscans, who have altered

Below, left: La Brianza is a traditional meeting place for Milanese gourmets. Seen against the background of the Villa Taverna are some local specialties: guinea fowl *alla creta* (lit: "in clay"), liver Mortadella with lentils, *cassoeula* (see page 48), and risotto with Luganega pork sausages.
Right: In the cloister of the Certosa (Carthusian monastery) of Pavia, some local delicacies: frogs' legs *in guazzetto* (see page 49), *cotolettine del priore*— little veal cutlets in cheese and tomato sauce, served on rice— *risotto alla certosina* (see page 44) and the famous *zuppa pavese* (see page 45), light and elegant.

The most typical dish of Bergamo,
polenta e uccelletti, or *polenta*
with small birds (see page 43),
photographed with other
local delicacies, including the
famous *casonsei* or ravioli of
Bergamo (see page 41). In the
background, the Romanesque
prothyrum or vestibule
of the Basilica of St. Mary Major
in Upper Bergamo.

In the heart of Mantua's historic center, with the rotunda of San Lorenzo in the background: *tortelli di zucca*—ravioli with pumpkin stuffing (see page 42)— the pride of Mantuan cooking, accompanied by *anolini*, one of the many other versions of ravioli made in this region, *coppa* and local salami sausage, and *risotto alla pilota* (see page 44).

Lombard cooking to suit the needs of the busy executive. Good Milanese cooking is rare in the city itself, but in the old part of the city and in certain *trattorie* in the outer suburbs it may still be found by the enterprising and inquisitive gastronome.

Those familiar with Milanese cooking will know that many of its dishes are colored with saffron. As with the recipe for *zuppa pavese,* there are historical reasons for this. In fourteenth-century Milan, as in other great European cities, food was often gilded before it was brought to the table. This was not mere ostentation, but often because, it was said by the alchemists of those days, gold was a remedy for most of man's ills. In such days of general poverty, however, only the most affluent could afford this luxury. It was then that, according to another Milanese legend, a painter from Brianza decided to gild the risotto to be served at his wedding breakfast with a harmless coloring agent used for strengthening yellow paints. Thus with risotto, gold reached the tables of the poor. This tradition is perpetuated in many dishes besides risotto, especially the golden brown of veal cutlets cooked *alla milanese.*

Contrary to many of the other regions of Italy, butter is the preferred cooking fat in Lombardy. It is said that butter was first invented near Lodi, a few miles from Milan, and, indeed, Julius Caesar is thought to have been the first great man to appreciate its culinary value. Until then, the Romans had used it for greasing their bodies before sporting competitions and battles. Other Milanese dishes also have strange origins; some, for instance, link the *cassoeula* with the ancient custom of eating soup made with

Left: The wines produced in the sun-drenched Valtellina blend admirably with the robust food of the region: *pizzoccheri*, a delicious casserole of pasta and vegetables (see page 42), and *polenta taragna* (see page 43), shown here with local cheeses, rye bread, and *bresaola*, a type of dried salt beef.
Right: Some of the finest freshwater fish in Italy are caught in the waters of Lake Garda.

The *misoltitt* of Lake Como are a species of shad, dried in the sun and then canned with bay leaves. They are a specialty of Lecco, which has been called ''the town of the *misoltitt*''. Here they are accompanied by other local dishes of fresh shad and trout.

Panettone, the pride of Milanese pastry-cooks, was originally simple, rustic fare, hardly more than spiced bread, but over the centuries it has been transformed into a light cake, rich with butter and eggs, candied citron and raisins. With the Villa Comunale in the background, it is seen here surrounded by *amaretti di Saronno* (almond macaroons), two versions of aniseed-flavored buns known as *pan de mei*, little spiced *oss de mord* (lit: "bones to bite"), and *torta paradiso*, a superbly light sponge cake.

pork and Savoy cabbage in the depth of winter on the feast of St. Anthony.

Lombardy offers many specialties. *Busecca*, a dish of tripe, is hardly known outside Milan, whereas *ossobuco* has now become part of international cuisine. Pavia is renowned not only for its soup, but also for its frogs, and Certosa for its *risotto alla certosina*, prepared with locally grown rice. In Bergamo, the specialty consists of birds roasted on a spit and served with *polenta*. Cremona, the birthplace of Stradivarius and other great violin-makers, offers salami, fruits preserved in a mustard-flavored syrup and nougat. Mantua is famous for its inimitable *tortelli di zucca*, small ravioli stuffed with pumpkin, its *risotto alla pilota*, and its fish, which are at their best when eaten in the inns dotted along the banks of the Po. Brescia is also famous for its fish, and at Lake Garda you may enjoy trout, eels, carp and *carpione* (salmon trout).

Salami sausages have an important place in the cooking of Lombardy. There are the salami of Cremona, the incomparable *bresaola* from the Valtellina, made from beef, and that of Varzi, made in the hills overlooking the Po near Pavia.

The Milanese claim the credit for inventing *panettone*, a cake which is to be found on the table of every Italian family at Christmas, and which the great food firms now export all over the world. There are several legends to explain its origin, the most common one related with the recipe on page 52.

Lombardy is also a land of cheeses, the home of perhaps the finest cheese in the world, Gorgonzola. Others, although they may not have achieved the household name of Gorgonzola, are no less delectable: Taleggio, Stracchino (of which Gorgonzola itself is but one variety), Grana Lodigiana, the goat's milk cheeses of Valsassina, Quartirolo and the delicate cream cheese Mascarpone.

Lombardy has some fine wines, too. The best come from the hills that overlook the Po, among them Cortese, Clastidio, Frecciarossa, Barbera, Sangue di Giuda (or if you prefer it, the blood of Judas), Buttafuoco and Montelio. The Valtellina offers Sasella, an excellent wine with roasts and game. Inferno, the grapes for which are grown in Sondrio, Grumello, which has a slight taste of strawberries, and Valgella, are also well known; and from the district around Brescia come Chiaretto del Garda, Retica and Lugana.

Whatever the expansion of industry and the urbanization of Lombardy may do to its towns and its countryside, let us hope that those old-fashioned *trattorie*, where the discerning traveler can still find the traditional cooking of Lombardy and sample the magnificent wines she offers with them, will survive.

Fitascetta
Onion Bread Ring

US		UK
¾ pound	once-risen bread dough, made with 2 cups (8 ounces) flour	¾ pound
3 tablespoons	olive oil	2½ tablespoons
1½ pounds	Italian red onions – see method	1½ pounds
6 tablespoons	butter	3 ounces
	salt	
1 teaspoon	sugar	1 teaspoon
	butter or oil for baking sheet	

Failing the red onions, any large mild onions, e.g. Bermuda or Spanish, may be used.

Punch down the risen bread dough and work in the oil, kneading vigorously until incorporated. Leave to rise in a warm place while you prepare the onions.

Slice the onions thinly and sauté gently in butter until soft and golden but not brown. Season to taste with salt and a sprinkling of sugar.

Take the dough, knead it lightly and roll it into a long sausage. Coil it into a ring, transfer to a buttered or oiled flat baking sheet and leave to rise again in a warm place. When doubled in bulk, spread with the onions and bake in a hot oven (450°F. Mark 7). After 15 minutes, lower the heat to 375°F. (Mark 4) and continue baking until the bread is golden brown, about 15 to 20 minutes longer. Serve hot or cold, sliced and spread with butter.

Serves 6.

Although the onion ring is extremely good as it is, it is even more delicious if the onions are covered with thinly sliced Mozzarella cheese before baking.

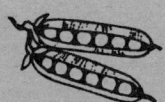

Pizzette al Gorgonzola
Gorgonzola Biscuits

US		UK
6 tablespoons	butter	3 ounces
6 ounces	Gorgonzola cheese	6 ounces
2 cups	all-purpose (plain) flour	8 ounces
2	egg yolks, lightly beaten	2
¼ teaspoon	grated nutmeg	¼ teaspoon
	salt and black pepper	
	butter and flour for baking sheet	
1	egg white, lightly beaten	1

Cream the butter, add the cheese and mix thoroughly. Add the flour, egg yolks, nutmeg and a little salt and pepper. Mix to a dough and pat gently into a square. Wrap in a clean cloth or foil and leave to rest, preferably in the refrigerator, for 30 minutes.

Sprinkle a pastry board lightly with flour and roll out the dough about ¼ inch thick. Cut into circles 3 inches in diameter. Arrange them on a buttered and lightly floured baking sheet. Brush each circle with egg white and decorate the edges with a fork. Bake in a hot oven (450°F. Mark 7) for 15 to 20 minutes. Serve cold – the biscuits have a good flavor of cheese and can be eaten alone or with cheese.

Makes 18 biscuits.

Frittelle della Valtellina
Valtellina Cheese Fritters

US		UK
2 cups	buckwheat flour	½ pound
1 cup	all-purpose (plain) flour	¼ pound
	salt	
¼ pound	Valtellina fat cheese – see method	¼ pound
2 tablespoons	grappa or vodka	1½ tablespoons
	olive oil for deep-frying	

Taleggio would be the right cheese for this recipe, but failing this, use a fat, soft cheese such as Bel Paese, although the taste of the latter is not as strong.

Sift the flours into a bowl together with a good pinch of salt and gradually work in enough cold water to make a smooth, stiff batter. Leave for 1 hour, covered with a damp cloth.

Dice the cheese and stir it into the batter together with the grappa. Deep-fry the batter, a teaspoonful at a time, in hot oil until golden brown. Drain on paper towels and serve immediately.

Serves 6.

"Casonsei" di Bergamo
Ravioli Bergamo Style

US		UK
Dough		
4 cups	all-purpose (plain) flour	1 pound
	salt	
4–5	eggs	4–5
Stuffing		
1 clove	garlic, finely chopped	1 clove
4 teaspoons	finely chopped parsley	1 tablespoon
¼ cup	butter	2 ounces
1 cup	ground (UK minced) beef	½ pound
2½ tablespoons	soft breadcrumbs	2 tablespoons
¼ cup	grated Parmesan cheese	3 tablespoons
	salt and pepper	
	freshly grated nutmeg	
2	eggs, well beaten	2
2½ tablespoons	stock	2 tablespoons
Dressing		
½ cup	butter, melted	¼ pound
¾ cup	grated Parmesan cheese	3 ounces

Dough
Sift the flour with a pinch of salt and make a well in the middle. Break in the eggs and work to a dough, kneading vigorously until elastic. Roll into a ball, cover with a cloth and leave to rest while you prepare the stuffing.

Stuffing
Sauté the garlic and parsley gently in butter for a minute. Add the meat and continue to fry until well browned, crumbling it with a fork. Turn into a bowl, add the breadcrumbs and cheese, and season to taste with salt, pepper and nutmeg. Mix thoroughly, work in the beaten eggs and the stock (or milk or water).

Roll the dough out thinly and cut into 3- by 4-inch rectangles. Add a heaped teaspoonful of the stuffing and fold in half lengthwise. Press the edges tightly to seal them and shape the ravioli into crescents.

Have ready a large pan of salted water at a bubbling boil. Drop in the ravioli, a batch at a time, and cook for 8 to 10 minutes. Take them from the pan with a perforated spoon and serve immediately, dressed with melted butter and grated Parmesan.

Serves 6.

Tortelli di Zucca
Ravioli with Pumpkin Stuffing

US		UK
Dough		
3 cups	all-purpose (plain flour)	¾ pound
3 large	eggs	3 large
	salt	
Stuffing		
2½-pound	pumpkin	2½-pound
¼ pound	Cremona mustard – see method	¼ pound
1 cup	grated Parmesan cheese	¼ pound
1 cup	crushed almond macaroons	¼ pound
2½ tablespoons	breadcrumbs	2 tablespoons
1 teaspoon	sugar	1 teaspoon
2–3 tablespoons	brandy – optional	2 tablespoons
	grated nutmeg	
	salt	
Dressing		
½ cup	butter, melted	¼ pound
¾ cup	grated Parmesan cheese	3 ounces

Cremona mustard is a sweet pickle made with fruit (whole cherries, plums, greengages, halved pears, peaches etc.) preserved in a mustard-flavored clear syrup. It is easily available, not only in Italian shops but in most well-stocked stores.

Dough
Prepare the dough as directed in the preceding recipe. Divide this into 2 pieces and leave until required, covered.

Stuffing
Slice off the top of the pumpkin. Scoop out all the seeds and replace the top. Stand the pumpkin upright in a baking pan, add a little water and bake in a moderate oven (375°F. Mark 4) for 1½ to 2 hours, or until the pumpkin is tender. Take the pumpkin from the oven and leave it until cool enough to handle.

Take off the pumpkin lid and scoop out all the flesh. Mash this with a fork until smooth, then rub it through a sieve, or purée in a blender. Put the pumpkin purée into a bowl, add the Cremona mustard, finely chopped, grated Parmesan, macaroons, breadcrumbs, sugar, brandy if used, nutmeg and salt to taste. Mix thoroughly and put aside until required.

Roll out the pieces of dough into two thin, even-sized sheets. On one sheet of dough place teaspoons of the stuffing in small heaps at 2-inch intervals. Cover with the second sheet and press firmly down with the fingers between the small mounds. Separate the ravioli with a pastry wheel or sharp knife, making sure the edges are tightly sealed. Place the ravioli on a floured board and leave to dry for 30 minutes, turning them after 20 minutes.

Bring a large pan of salted water to the boil, add the ravioli, a batch at a time so that they do not stick together, and cook rapidly for 8 to 10 minutes, or until they are soft and have all risen to the top of the pan. Take the ravioli out with a perforated spoon, drain them quickly, put on a hot platter and sprinkle with melted butter and Parmesan cheese.

If for some reason it is not possible to serve the ravioli immediately they are cooked, take them from the pan when still slightly underdone, turn them into a fireproof dish, pour over the melted butter and Parmesan cheese, and put them into a hot oven (450°F. Mark 7). Turn off the heat at once and leave the ravioli for 10 minutes before serving.

Makes approximately 30 ravioli.

Salsa Verde alla Milanese
Milanese Green Parsley Sauce

US		UK
1 clove	garlic – optional	1 clove
4 teaspoons	breadcrumbs, soaked in vinegar	1 tablespoon
1	hard-boiled egg, finely chopped	1
1–2	anchovy fillets, finely chopped	1–2
1 teaspoon	capers, finely chopped	1 teaspoon
4 tablespoons	finely chopped parsley	3 tablespoons
	olive oil	
	salt	

Rub the inside of a small bowl thoroughly with the cut garlic clove and discard. Add the breadcrumbs, egg, anchovies, capers and parsley. Mix well and stir in olive oil, a little at a time, until the mixture is of a semi-liquid consistency, rather like bread sauce. Check seasoning. Leave for 2 hours before serving. Whisk lightly and transfer to a sauceboat.

This sauce is usually served with boiled meat or fish.
Serves 6.

Pizzoccheri di Teglio
Casserole of Noodles and Vegetables

US		UK
6 cups	buckwheat flour	1½ pounds
2 cups	all-purpose (plain) flour	½ pound
4	eggs	4
	salt	
1½ pounds	potatoes	1½ pounds
1½ pounds	white cabbage	1½ pounds
½ cup	butter	¼ pound
1 large	onion, finely chopped	1 large
1 sprig	sage	1 sprig
¾ cup	grated Parmesan cheese	3 ounces
½ pound	Valtellina fat cheese, e.g. Taleggio, thinly sliced	½ pound

This casserole might at first reading appear to be stodgy. On the contrary, it is both light and moist. Failing Taleggio, which is a fat, soft cheese, use Mozzarella or even Bel Paese.

Those who do not have time to make their own noodles can prepare this dish with commercially made wide ribbon noodles broken neatly into 2½-inch strips. These should be cooked in boiling salted water until *al dente* before being added to the other ingredients in the casserole.

Sift the flours together into a large bowl. Add the eggs and a pinch of salt, and mix well, gradually adding as much warm water as needed to make a firm, elastic dough. Knead until smooth and roll into 2 or 3 sheets, not too thin. Cut these sheets into strips ½ inch wide and 2½ inches long to make *pizzoccheri*. Leave on a floured board or cloth to dry.

In the meantime, prepare the remaining ingredients. Peel the potatoes and cut them into thick slices or cubes. Drop them into a large pan of boiling, salted water. Wash and shred the cabbage, add this to the pan with the potatoes, and continue cooking until the potatoes are almost soft. Add the *pizzoccheri* to the vegetables and cook them until *al dente* – tender but still slightly resistant to bite.

Melt the butter and fry the onion and sage; then add the Parmesan cheese. Stir this to a sauce and discard the sage.

Drain the *pizzoccheri* and vegetables, and arrange them in layers in a fairly deep casserole, alternating each layer with a generous layer of sliced cheese spread with the onion and Parmesan sauce. The top layer should be one of *pizzoccheri* and vegetables. Put the casserole into a hot oven (450°F. Mark 7), turn off the heat and leave it for a few minutes to settle.

Serves 6.

Polenta alla Lodigiana
Polenta Lodi Style

US		UK
2 cups	milk	¾ pint
	salt	
½ cup	fine cornmeal	3 ounces
6 ounces	Gruyère cheese	6 ounces
	flour	
1	egg, well beaten	1
	fine dry breadcrumbs	
6 tablespoons	butter	3 ounces

Bring the milk to the boil and add salt to taste. Sprinkle in the cornmeal and cook for 30 minutes, stirring constantly, until thick. Once this has happened, continue to stir frequently to prevent it sticking. When the polenta is thick and smooth, turn it out on to a wetted flat surface – a pastry board will do – and spread it out to a thickness of ¼ inch. Let it cool.

Cut the polenta into small circles or squares of equal size. Cut the cheese into ¼-inch-thick slices, then into pieces the same size as the polenta but half the number. Sandwich and press firmly a slice of cheese between 2 slices of polenta. Repeat this until all the polenta and cheese are used up.

Dip each "sandwich" in flour, then in lightly salted, beaten egg, and finally in breadcrumbs. Melt the butter and fry the sandwiches, a few at a time, turning them once to brown both sides. Serve hot.

Makes 18 sandwiches.

Polenta Taragna
Polenta Valtellina Style

US		UK
4 cups	buckwheat flour	1 pound
½ cup	fine cornmeal	3 ounces
8 cups	water	3¼ pints
	salt	
1¼ cups	butter, diced	10 ounces
½ pound	fresh Valtellina cheese, cut into thin strips	½ pound

This dish is a specialty of the Valtellina district. When Valtellina cheese (e.g. Taleggio) is not available, either Bel Paese or Mozzarella may be used.

Sift the flour and cornmeal into a bowl. Bring the water to the boil in a large pan, add salt and gradually sprinkle in the flour, stirring constantly with a wooden spoon. Cook for 1 hour, by which time the mixture will be firm. It must be stirred very frequently to avoid sticking. Add the butter, stirring until this has been completely incorporated into the polenta, then the cheese. Mix well and continue cooking for another 10 minutes. Turn out on to a heated platter and serve at once, as hot as possible.

Serves 6.

Polenta e Uccelletti
Small Birds with Polenta

In some Italian provinces many of the choicest dishes are prepared with small birds. This taste for fieldfare has existed since the days of the Romans, and larks and thrushes in particular are considered to have a very delicate flavor. We are apt to be more squeamish about small birds, especially song birds.

The birds are plucked but not drawn and their heads are left on. They are then threaded on to long skewers interspersed with thin slices of pork and bacon and sage leaves, and spit-roasted quickly with frequent basting. The small birds are served very hot, resting on a dish of polenta.

Before preparing any of the rice dishes below, please read the general introduction to cooking risotto on page 66.

Risotto alla Milanese

US		UK
7 tablespoons	butter	3½ ounces
1 small	onion, thinly sliced	1 small
2 tablespoons	bone marrow	1 ounce
½ cup	dry red or white wine	6–8 tablespoons
3 cups	rice	1¼ pounds
about 6½ cups	boiling meat stock	about 2½ pints
generous pinch	saffron, soaked in water	generous pinch
¾ cup	grated Parmesan cheese	3 ounces

Melt half the butter in a large, heavy pan and sauté the onion and bone marrow gently until the onion is transparent and golden. Add the wine and cook until reduced. Stir in the rice and sauté gently until it begins to brown.

Pour in 1 cup of boiling stock (it will sizzle alarmingly, but this is as it should be). Continue cooking until the liquid has been absorbed, then add another cup of boiling stock. Continue to cook the rice in this manner, stirring carefully, until all the liquid has been used up and absorbed.

When the rice is almost ready, after about 20 minutes, add the saffron, stirring this into the rice to color it. If all the rice does not change color this does not matter – a two-color risotto is very effective. Turn off the heat, and gently but thoroughly stir in the remaining butter and the cheese. Cover the pan and let the risotto settle for 2 minutes. Serve at once, accompanied by a bowl of additional grated Parmesan.

Serves 6.

Risotto alla Valtellinese
Risotto Valtellina Style

US		UK
¾ cup	dried red kidney beans – see method	½ pound
	salt	
1 small	cabbage	1 small
2½ cups	rice	1 pound
½ cup	butter	¼ pound
1 sprig	sage	1 sprig
½ cup	grated Parmesan cheese	2 ounces

Red kidney beans are known as *borlotti* in Italy and are sometimes sold under this name abroad.

Soak the beans overnight in plenty of lukewarm water. The following day, boil them until tender in their soaking water with additional salted water to cover.

Wash the cabbage, discard any damaged leaves and blanch the heart for 5 minutes in boiling salted water. Drain and shred. Bring a large pan of salted water to the boil, add the rice and boil hard for 5 minutes. Add the shredded cabbage and continue cooking rapidly for 15 minutes longer. Drain thoroughly and turn out on to a large, heated serving dish. Keep hot in a low oven while preparing the remaining ingredients.

Drain the cooked beans and heap them round the rice and cabbage; return the dish to the oven.

Melt the butter in a small pan and cook the sage gently until the butter is impregnated with its flavor. Discard the sage. Pour the butter over the dish, sprinkle with grated Parmesan and serve immediately.

Serves 6.

Riso alla Pilota
Rice Mantua Style

US		UK
about 4 cups	water	about 1¾ pints
	salt	
2½ cups	rice	1 pound
½ pound	Italian pork sausages	½ pound
3 tablespoons	butter	1½ ounces
pinch	grated nutmeg	pinch
pinch	ground cinnamon	pinch
¾ cup	grated Parmesan cheese	3 ounces

This is a traditional dish of the country around Mantua. It takes its name from the *piloti* – the men who winnow (*pilano*) the rice.

Pour the water into a flameproof, earthenware casserole or a large, heavy pan, add salt and bring to the boil. Pour the rice into the middle of the pan so that it forms a heap. The tip of the rice should just show above the water; if not, ladle out a little of the water. Cook rapidly for 5 minutes, then take the pan from the heat. Shake it a little to settle the rice and cover the top of the pan with a cloth folded in four. Clamp on the lid and wrap the pan in another cloth so that the rice will continue cooking off the heat. Leave for about 25 minutes before uncovering the pan. Rice varies and times for cooking can only be approximate. When cooked, the rice should be almost dry.

While the rice is cooking, skin the sausages and crumble them lightly. Fry gently in the butter, then stir in the nutmeg and cinnamon. Pour this mixture over the rice, add the grated cheese, stir well, cover the pan again and leave to settle for 2 minutes.

Serves 4 to 6.

Risotto ai Funghi
Mushroom Risotto

US		UK
½ cup	butter	¼ pound
1 small	onion, very thinly sliced	1 small
¾ pound	field mushrooms – see method	¾ pound
1 cup	dry white wine	⅓ pint
3 cups	Italian Arborio rice – see method	1¼ pounds
about 7 cups	boiling meat stock	about 2¾ pints
¾ cup	grated Parmesan or Lodigiano cheese	3 ounces

Fresh wild mushrooms should be used for this recipe – *cèpes* or *boletus edulis*. Arborio rice has plump, golden brown grains with a nutty flavor.

Melt half the butter in a large, heavy pan and sauté the onion over a low heat until soft and transparent but not brown. Clean the mushrooms and slice them thinly. Add these to the pan and stir well. Pour in the wine and continue cooking until almost completely evaporated. Add the rice and continue cooking until it begins to change color, then add ½ cup of the stock. Cook until the stock has been absorbed by the rice, then add another ½ cup stock. Continue in reis manner until all the stock has been absorbed. This process will take about 20 minutes, and by the end the rice will be perfectly tender, each grain separate.

Add the rest of the butter and the cheese, stir well, cover the pan and leave the risotto to settle for 2 or 3 minutes before serving. Serve with a bowl of additional grated Parmesan cheese.

Serves 6.

Risotto con la Zucca
Pumpkin Risotto

US		UK
about 2 pounds	pumpkin	about 2 pounds
6 tablespoons	butter	3 ounces
2½ tablespoons	olive oil	2 tablespoons
1 small	onion, finely chopped	1 small
about 7 cups	boiling water	about 2¾ pints
	salt	
2½ cups	Arborio rice – see previous recipe	1 pound
¾ cup	grated Parmesan cheese	3 ounces

Peel the pumpkin and discard the seeds. Cut the flesh into small pieces.

Heat half the butter and all the oil in a large pan, and sauté the onion very gently until soft but not brown. Add the pumpkin, pour over 1 cup boiling water, season to taste with salt and continue cooking for 15 minutes, or until the pumpkin is tender.

Stir the rice in thoroughly but gently, and continue cooking until it has absorbed the liquid. Pour in another cup of boiling water as the rice dries out, and continue adding water in this manner until all the water has been absorbed and the rice is tender. This will take about 20 minutes.

Stir in the remaining butter and the cheese very gently, cover the pan and leave the risotto for 2 minutes to settle. Serve hot, sprinkled generously with additional grated Parmesan cheese.

Serves 6.

Risotto alla Certosina
Crawfish (U.K. Crayfish) Risotto

US		UK
1½ pounds	freshwater crawfish (UK crayfish)	1½ pounds
14-ounce can	Italian peeled tomatoes	14-ounce can
½ cup	olive oil	6–8 tablespoons
1 small	onion, finely chopped	1 small
1	carrot, finely chopped	1
1 stalk	celery, finely chopped	1 stalk
1 clove	garlic, finely chopped	1 clove
3–4 sprigs	parsley, finely chopped	3–4 sprigs
	salt and pepper	
6 tablespoons	butter	3 ounces
1 small	onion, thinly sliced	1 small
½ cup	dry white wine	6–8 tablespoons
3 cups	rice	1¼ pounds

Thoroughly wash the crawfish (U.K. crayfish). Rub the tomatoes through a sieve.

Heat the oil, add the chopped vegetables (not the sliced onion), garlic and parsley, and sauté gently until they turn golden. Add the crawfish, stir well, then add the tomatoes, salt and pepper, and about 8½ cups (U.K. 3½ pints) water. Bring to the boil and cook over a brisk heat for 10 minutes.

Take out the crawfish; strain the liquid and reserve it. Shell the crawfish, put aside the best pieces and pound the rest in a mortar, or purée in a blender. Return the cooking liquid to the pan, add the puréed crawfish and stir well.

In another large, heavy pan, melt half the butter and lightly brown the sliced onion. Add the wine and let it simmer for a few minutes. Stir in the rice, mixing it thoroughly into the onion, then little by little, add the crawfish liquid. After 10 to 15 minutes, when most of the liquid has been absorbed, add the reserved crawfish pieces, cover the pan, and continue cooking slowly until the rice is tender – it will take about 25 minutes in all. Add the rest of the butter, stir gently, re-cover and leave to settle for 2 minutes before serving. It is important not to stir the rice too often, or it may become soggy.

Serves 6.

Risotto al Salto
Fried Risotto

This is an excellent way in which to use up left-over rice.

Melt a large knob of butter in a deep frying pan; add the left-over rice, smoothing it down with a palette knife. Cook over a moderate heat until a thin crust forms underneath the rice, shaking the pan from time to time so that the crust becomes brown and crisp but does not burn. Turn the rice out, upside-down, on to a plate, and then slide it back into the frying pan. Continue cooking until a crust forms on the underside.

Serve the rice cut in portions like a pie, with plenty of grated Parmesan cheese.

Omelette di Riso
Rice Omelette

Mix a good plateful of left-over cooked rice with ¼ pound Gruyère cheese, diced, and 2 ounces salami, skinned and diced. Beat 8 eggs lightly with a pinch of salt and pepper to taste. Heat 2 or 3 tablespoons butter in a heavy frying pan and when it is bubbling pour in the eggs. Cook like an omelette and when the eggs are set but still very moist, spread the rice mixture down the middle. Fold the omelette over with a spatula, turn the heat down to low and cook the omelette very gently for 5 minutes longer, or until the rice mixture is thoroughly heated through.

Serves 4.

Zuppa di Ceci
Chick Pea Soup

US		UK
2 cups	dried chick peas, soaked overnight	12 ounces
2 pounds	pig's head	2 pounds
4 tablespoons	butter	2 ounces
2 small	onions, finely chopped	2 small
3 stalks	celery, finely chopped	3 stalks
1	clove	1
1	bay leaf	1
1 cup	dry white wine	scant ½ pint
	salt	
3 tablespoons	fat salt pork, diced	1½ ounces
2	carrots, finely chopped	2
1 sprig	sage	1 sprig
4 teaspoons	tomato paste	1 tablespoon
2–3 sprigs	parsley, finely chopped	2–3 sprigs

Cover the soaked chick peas with plenty of water, bring to the boil, lower the heat and simmer until tender. This will take up to 4 hours, depending on their age and place of origin. Drain.

Wash the pig's head thoroughly and pat it dry. Melt the butter in a large pan, add the head, half the onion and 1 stalk celery, finely chopped. Fry the head, turning it rapidly until brown all over. Add the clove, bay leaf, wine, salt to taste, and 10 cups (U.K. 4 pints) lukewarm water. Cover the pan and cook gently for 2 hours, skimming the top from time to time.

In another large pan, sauté the salt pork gently until the fat runs, then add the remaining onion and celery, the carrots and sage. When these are golden, add the chick peas. Dilute the tomato paste with a cup of the pig's head broth. Stir this into the chick peas and leave to infuse for 20 minutes. Lift out the head from its broth and let it cool. Pull off the flesh and cut it into thin strips. Add this to the chick peas. Strain the broth and stir it into the pan with the chick peas. Bring once more to the boil, discard the sage and serve the soup sprinkled with chopped parsley.

Serves 6.

Zuppa alla Pavese
Soup Pavese Style

US		UK
12 thick slices	French bread	12 thick slices
½ cup	butter	4 ounces
12	eggs	12
½ cup	grated Parmesan cheese	6 tablespoons
	salt	
8–9 cups	clear stock	3½ pints

Fry the bread quickly in butter until golden brown on both sides but still soft inside. Put 2 slices of bread into each soup bowl or cup.

Break 2 eggs carefully into each bowl; sprinkle with Parmesan cheese and a very little salt. Bring the stock to a bubbling boil and swiftly but as carefully as possible pour a cup of this into each bowl. Let the stock continue boiling as you work. This is important for the stock must be so hot that it cooks the eggs in the bowls. If added carelessly, the eggs will break and spoil the appearance of the soup. Serve immediately.

Some cooks poach the eggs before putting them into the bowls. Although this does ensure that the eggs will not be underdone, contrary to the first method whereby they remain slightly underdone, it does change the flavor of the soup, making it somewhat less subtle. However, if the stock is really boiling hot, the eggs will be cooked enough for most tastes.

Serves 6.

Minestrone alla Milanese
Milanese Vegetable Soup

US		UK
⅔ cup	dried white (haricot) beans, soaked overnight	¼ pound
¼ pound	fat salt pork	¼ pound
1 clove	garlic	1 clove
2–3 sprigs	parsley	2–3 sprigs
1	onion, thinly sliced	1
½ pound	mild bacon, cut into thin strips	½ pound
3 large	potatoes, peeled and cubed	3 large
2–3	carrots, diced	2–3
3 stalks	celery, sliced	3 stalks
2	zucchini (courgettes), thinly sliced	2
2	ripe tomatoes, peeled and chopped	2
	salt and pepper	
1 small	cabbage, shredded	1 small
2 cups	shelled green peas	½ pound
1 cup	rice	6 ounces
4 teaspoons	finely chopped basil – optional	1 tablespoon
	grated Parmesan cheese	

Cook the beans in plenty of water until they are almost tender but still firm. Do not add salt, or the beans will toughen. Drain.

Finely chop the salt pork, garlic and parsley, and sauté in a very large pan over a moderate heat until the fat begins to run; then add the onion and let this cook until soft but not brown. Add the bacon, beans and all the vegetables except the cabbage and peas. (If preferred, the preliminary frying of the onion and salt pork may be omitted and all these ingredients placed together in the pan cold. This means that the soup will be less rich, but it will also lose its characteristic flavor.) Cover with plenty of water – 12 cups (U.K. 5 pints) – add salt to taste and bring to the boil. Lower the heat and let the soup cook gently for 1½ hours. Then add the cabbage and peas and, 15 minutes later, the rice. Continue cooking for another 20 minutes, or until the rice is tender but not overcooked. A little fresh basil may be added at the last moment.

Serve hot with plenty of grated Parmesan cheese to sprinkle over each individual bowl. Italians also eat this kind of minestrone cold.

Serves 6 to 8.

Busecca
Tripe with White (Haricot) Beans

US		UK
3–3½ pounds	dressed calf's tripe – see method	3–3½ pounds
1 large	onion, stuck with 2 cloves	1 large
3 stalks	celery, chopped	3 stalks
	salt	
4 tablespoons	butter	2 ounces
4 tablespoons	pork or bacon fat, diced	2 ounces
6 small	onions, finely chopped	6 small
2	carrots, chopped	2
1 sprig	sage	1 sprig
14-ounce can	Italian peeled tomatoes, drained and chopped	14-ounce can
	pepper	
3–4 cups	cooked white (haricot) beans	1 pound
¾ cup	grated Parmesan cheese	3 ounces

This is a thick, rich soup and very much a local specialty.

Tripe is usually sold "dressed", i.e. cleaned and almost completely cooked. It may have to be blanched simply for extra cleaning but even this is seldom necessary. The butcher selling the tripe should know how much it has been processed.

Wash the tripe and cut it into 3-inch squares. Put it into a pan together with the onion stuck with cloves, 1 stalk celery, chopped, a little salt and enough cold water to cover. Put on the lid and bring to the boil, then lower the heat to moderate and cook for 2 hours, or until the tripe is quite tender. Take it from the pan, cool it and cut into narrow strips.

Melt the butter and pork fat in another pan. Fry the small onions, the remaining celery, carrots and sage, stirring to mix thoroughly. As the vegetables are beginning to brown, add the tomatoes. Cook over a moderate heat for 10 minutes, add the tripe, a little salt and pepper, and ⅔ cup (U.K. ¼ pint) hot water. Bring to the boil and cook gently for a further 30 minutes. Finally add the beans, check seasoning and cook gently for another 15 minutes to bring out flavors. Sprinkle generously with Parmesan before serving.

Serves 6.

Manzo Brasato
Braised Beef

US		UK
3 pounds	rump or top round (topside) of beef, rolled and tied	3 pounds
2 ounces	fat bacon, cut into thin strips	2 ounces
1 clove	garlic	1 clove
¼ cup	butter	2 ounces
¼ cup	olive oil	3 tablespoons
1	clove	1
1	onion, chopped	1
3	carrots, thickly sliced	3
2 stalks	celery, thickly sliced	2 stalks
1 cup	Barbera or Barolo wine – see method	scant ½ pint
	salt and pepper	
4 teaspoons	tomato paste	1 tablespoon
½ cup	stock or water	6–8 tablespoons

This rich, succulent dish is always prepared the day before required. It is almost true to say that it cannot be over-cooked – in fact, the chief characteristic is that the meat should be simmered until it can be "cut with a spoon", certainly so tender that even when thickly sliced the meat crumbles.

If Barbera or Barolo wines, both from Italy, are not available, any other full-bodied red wine may be used.

Lard the meat with the strips of bacon and rub with garlic. Heat the butter and oil together in a large heavy pan, and brown the

meat on all sides. Add the clove, vegetables and wine. Cover the pan and cook gently for 3 hours, turning the meat occasionally. Season to taste with salt and pepper, pour in the tomato paste, diluted with stock or water (or, if preferred, whole peeled fresh tomatoes). Continue cooking for at least another 2 hours.

Turn off the heat and leave the meat with its vegetables and liquid in the pan. The following day, re-heat gently – or the meat can be simmered for another hour if liked. Take it from the pan and cut into thick slices. Arrange on a hot platter and keep hot in a warm oven. Strain the sauce through a sieve, re-heat it and pour it over the meat. The vegetables may be served as a garnish.

Serves 6.

Stufato
Beef in Red Wine

US		UK
3–3½ pounds	stewing beef, in one piece	3–3½ pounds
¼ pound	pickled pork belly	¼ pound
	flour	
6 tablespoons	butter	3 ounces
1 small	onion, finely chopped	1 small
1	bay leaf	1
Marinade		
2	carrots, diced	2
1 small	onion, thinly sliced	1 small
1 stalk	celery, chopped	1 stalk
1 clove	garlic, crushed	1 clove
1	bay leaf	1
2	cloves	2
2½ cups	Barbera or Barolo wine	1 pint
	grated nutmeg	
	salt and pepper	

A *stufato* is a rich beef stew and one of the important Italian dishes. There are, naturally, several recipes for its preparation, just as there are many different recipes for making *ragoûts* in France. The following version is typical of Lombard cooking.

Lard the meat with half the pork belly, cut into long, thin strips. Tie it into a good shape and marinate it for at least 6 hours – or better still overnight – in the marinade ingredients.

Lift the meat out of its marinade, drain it, wipe it dry and coat lightly with flour. Melt the butter in a large pan, add the remaining pork belly, chopped, and the onion. Sauté the onion until it begins to change color, then add the meat and bay leaf, and brown the meat on all sides. Strain the marinade and pour over the meat. Cover the pan tightly and cook over a gentle heat for 3 to 4 hours. The sauce should be fairly thick but it may be necessary to add either some more wine, stock or water.

Leave the meat in the pan in which it has been cooking until the following day. Then re-heat it over a moderate heat. Take the meat from the pan, cut it into thick slices and arrange on a hot serving dish. Any remaining sauce may be used to garnish the meat.

Serves 6 to 8.

Costolette alla Milanese
Milanese Veal Cutlets

US		UK
6	veal cutlets, on the bone	6
2	eggs, beaten	2
	fine dry breadcrumbs	
½–¾ cup	butter	4–6 ounces
	salt	
	lemon wedges	

Trim the cutlets, flatten them lightly with a cutlet bat, and with a sharp knife or kitchen scissors make nicks round the edges so that they will not curl up when cooking. Dip the cutlets into the beaten eggs and then coat them with breadcrumbs, pressing them well into the meat to form an even coating.

Heat the butter in a large frying pan until just beginning to change color; add the cutlets, all at the same time if the pan is large enough. Cook briskly without moving them until a golden crust forms on the underside. Then turn the cutlets carefully with a palette knife and let them form a crust on the other side. Lower the heat and continue to cook gently for another 5 minutes to make sure they are cooked through. Just before serving, sprinkle lightly with salt and arrange the cutlets on a heated serving dish. Garnish with lemon wedges.

Serve one or two cutlets per person.

Vitello Tonnato
Cold Veal with Tuna Fish Sauce

US		UK
2–2½ pounds	boned leg of veal	2–2½ pounds
7 ounces	tuna fish canned in olive oil	½ pound
6	anchovy fillets, finely chopped	6
1 small	onion, finely chopped	1 small
2	carrots, finely chopped	2
1 cup	dry white wine	scant ½ pint
½ cup	wine vinegar	6–8 tablespoons
½ cup	water	6–8 tablespoons
	salt and pepper	
Sauce		
	olive oil	
2	hard-boiled egg yolks	2
1 tablespoon	capers, finely chopped	1 tablespoon

Vitello is meat from a young, milk-fed calf not more than a few weeks old. Its flesh is a delicate pink with a fine texture. If somewhat older veal is used, cook it more slowly and for a longer time.

Put the veal, tuna, anchovies, vegetables, wine, vinegar and water into a large, heavy pan. Season lightly, bring once to the boil, lower the heat, cover and simmer very gently for 1½ hours, or until the meat is tender.

Take the veal from the pan and leave it to cool. Rub the sauce through a fine sieve and then gradually add enough olive oil to make a fairly fluid dressing. Beat in the egg yolks, mashed to a paste, and continue beating until the sauce is smooth, then add the capers.

Cut the veal into thin slices, spread each slice with some of the sauce and arrange them in a deep serving dish. Cover the veal with the rest of the sauce and leave in a cool place for 24 hours. Garnish with lemon wedges and serve with Italian pickles and a fresh green salad. This dish will keep for several days in a refrigerator.

Serves 6.

Ossobuco Milanese
Stewed Shin of Veal

US		UK
6 slices	shin of veal – see method	6 slices
	flour	
6 tablespoons	butter	3 ounces
½ cup	dry white wine	6–8 tablespoons
14-ounce can	Italian peeled tomatoes	14-ounce can
	salt and pepper	
1 clove	garlic, finely chopped or minced	1 clove
	grated rind of ½ lemon	
3–4 sprigs	parsley, finely chopped	3–4 sprigs
1–2	anchovy fillets, finely chopped	1–2

Slices of shin bone of veal sawed crosswise into 2½- or 3-inch pieces should be used.

Roll the bones in flour. In a large pan, fry the bones in butter, turning them once or twice to ensure even browning. Pour the wine over them and cook for 15 minutes, then add the tomatoes and season to taste with salt and pepper. Cover and cook for 2 hours over a low heat, or until the meat is so tender it almost falls off the bones. If necessary, some hot stock or water may be added during cooking.

Prepare a *gremolada*, an essential part of the *ossobuco*. Mix the garlic, lemon rind, parsley and anchovy together. Sprinkle this over the bones a few minutes before serving and turn them once to distribute the flavor of the *gremolada*.

Ossobuco is always served with a large dish of rice, usually a Risotto Milanese. An important part of the dish is the marrow from the bones, and for this a small narrow fork is supplied with which to dig it out. Failing this, the marrow may simply be dug out with the point of a knife and spread on small chunks of bread.

Serve one or two slices per person.

Vitello in Gelatina alla Milanese
Veal in Aspic Milanese Style

US		UK
2½ pounds	veal fillet	2½ pounds
2 small	carrots, diced	2 small
2 stalks	celery, finely chopped	2 stalks
2 large slices	raw ham, medium-thick	2 large slices
	salt and pepper	
3 tablespoons	butter	1½ ounces
2 ounces	fat pork belly, finely chopped	2 ounces
2	bay leaves	2
1	calf's foot, chopped	1
1	clove	1
	Marsala	
2 envelopes	unflavored gelatine	½ ounce
Garnish		
¼ pound	pickled tongue, sliced	¼ pound
¼ pound	pickles	¼ pound

The aspic turns a dark, wine-red color in this recipe. Do not add too much gelatine, otherwise the aspic might become too hard. Remember that the calf's foot alone is almost enough to set the stock in time.

Lightly flatten the fillet – not too much, simply enough to give it length – and then press half of the carrots and celery into it. Fold it over into a neat shape and sandwich it between the slices of ham. Sprinkle with salt and pepper, and tie it securely but neatly with string. (When it is cooked it should have a good shape and the ham should still be firmly attached to it.)

Melt the butter in a pan large enough to take the meat, and sauté the remaining vegetables, pork belly, bay leaves, and finally the roll of veal. Let this brown, turning it round and round so that it colors quickly and evenly on all sides. Add the calf's foot and clove, and cover with water. Cover the pan and bring to a gentle boil, then lower the heat and simmer for 2 hours, or until the meat is tender. Let the veal cool in its own liquid.

Lift the meat from the pan, remove the strings and cut it into medium-thick slices. Arrange these in a deep serving dish.

Strain the liquid twice through muslin and pour 4 cups (U.K. 1½ pints) of it into a clean pan. This is important, otherwise the aspic will be fatty. Flavor with Marsala – how much depends on individual tastes – and bring to the boil. In the meantime, dissolve the gelatine. Stir this into the boiling stock and when it has completely dissolved, strain the hot stock over the meat. Cool and put into a refrigerator to jell. Serve garnished with pickles and tongue.

Serves 6.

Involtini alla Milanese
Milanese Stuffed Meat Rolls

US		UK
1½ pounds	pork or veal, thinly sliced	1½ pounds
2 small	Italian pork sausages, skinned and crumbled	2 small
6	chicken livers, chopped	6
1 clove	garlic, finely chopped	1 clove
2–3 sprigs	parsley, finely chopped	2–3 sprigs
2–3 tablespoons	grated Parmesan cheese	2 tablespoons
2	egg yolks, lightly beaten	2
small pieces	fat bacon	small pieces
	sage leaves	
	flour	
¼ cup	butter	2 ounces
	salt	
½ cup	dry white wine	6–8 tablespoons
½ cup	boiling stock or water	6 tablespoons

Only very tender meat is suitable for this dish. Flatten the slices carefully until very thin, trying to make them all the same size, approximately 3 by 4 inches.

Combine the sausages, chicken livers, garlic, parsley, Parmesan cheese and egg yolks. Mix to a paste and spread some of it on each slice of meat. Roll up the slices tightly and secure with tiny skewers or toothpicks. Thread on to each skewer a piece of bacon and 1 sage leaf. Dust the rolls lightly with flour.

Melt the butter and fry the meat rolls until brown all over, turning them occasionally. Sprinkle lightly with salt, add the wine and continue cooking over a moderate heat until it evaporates. Add the stock, cover the pan and cook gently until the rolls are tender, about 20 minutes. Serve with a risotto or a dish of polenta.

Serves 4 to 6.

"Cassoeula"
Casserole of Pork

US		UK
1	pig's ear	1
1	pig's trotter	1
½ pound	fat pork or bacon ends	½ pound
	salt	
4 teaspoons	olive oil	1 tablespoon
2 tablespoons	butter	1 ounce
1	onion, thinly sliced	1
2 pounds	lean pork, thickly sliced	2 pounds
½ cup	dry white wine	6–8 tablespoons
2 stalks	celery, finely chopped	2 stalks
2	carrots, finely chopped	2
3 pounds	white cabbage	3 pounds
6	Luganega pork sausages – see method	6
	pepper	

Luganega sausages are long, thin pork sausages, but if these are not available other types of sausages can be used instead, e.g. Cotechino, provided they are made of pure pork and are fresh.

Wash the pig's ear and trotter thoroughly – if there are any hairs remaining on the pig's ear, singe these off. Cut the ear in half and chop the trotter roughly with a cleaver. Cut the fat pork into large pieces. Put all these ingredients into a large pan of water, add salt and cook slowly for 1 hour. Lift out the pieces of meat and bones etc., with a perforated spoon. Cut the ear into thin strips.

In another large pan (preferably a heavy casserole) heat the oil and butter, and lightly brown the onion. Add the lean pork slices and brown them on both sides. Add the wine, celery, carrots, the pig's ear and trotter, the fat pork and 2 cups (U.K. ¾ pint) of the broth. Simmer for 30 minutes. Wash the cabbage, cut it into

quarters and cook it for 10 to 15 minutes in boiling, salted water. Drain well and put it on top of the meat. Continue cooking a further 30 minutes, add the sausages (whole, unless using large sausages, in which case cut them into chunks) and cook for another 20 minutes. Skim off surplus fat from time to time and check seasoning.

This is a dish which should not have too much liquid. It is rather rich and extremely good as well as inexpensive. Serve in the casserole in which it has been cooked.

Serves 6.

Fritto Misto alla Milanese
Milanese Mixed Fry

This is one of the classic preparations of which the Milanese cuisine is justly proud. The more varied the ingredients the better. Any or all of the following may be used: liver, heart, sweetbreads, brains, slices of beef, kidneys, veal of any kind, bone marrow, cockscombs, potato croquettes, one or more vegetables such as young artichokes, zucchini (courgettes), cauliflowers etc.

Brains
Soak the brains for 30 minutes in tepid water, then remove the skin and membrane. Simmer for 15 minutes in salted water acidulated with a little mild vinegar or lemon juice. Drain, dry and cut into thick slices. Dip in beaten egg and roll in a mixture of grated Parmesan and breadcrumbs. Deep-fry until golden brown.

Bone Marrow
This is extracted raw from the bones, cut into thick slices, dipped in flour and beaten egg, and fried in hot butter.

Heart
Cut away the walls of the large blood vessels but leave the fleshy flaps intact. Soak the heart for 10 minutes in salted water and rinse it well to remove the blood from inside. Cook gently until tender, then cut into thick slices, roll in flour and fry in hot butter.

Thin Slices of Veal
For this, the slices of veal are cut almost paper-thin and nicked round the edges to prevent curling while cooking. Heat as much butter as required for the number of veal slices being used, add the veal, sprinkle with dry white wine and season to taste with salt and black pepper. Lightly brown on one side, then turn the veal slices and brown them on the other side. Sprinkle with finely chopped parsley.

Calf's Liver
Have the liver cut into very, very thin slices. (Make sure that all the outer skin and blood vessels are removed.) Flour the slices of liver, and fry quickly on both sides in hot butter.

Calf's Kidneys
Remove the skin from the kidneys before washing them, then split them into halves and slice each half lengthwise. Fry in hot butter.

Calf's Sweetbreads
Soak these in cold, salted water for several hours to remove the blood. Drain, cover with fresh salted water, and simmer slowly until tender. Take the sweetbreads from the pan, cool and remove any fat and membrane. Cut the sweetbreads into slices. Dip them into beaten egg and then in fine breadcrumbs. Melt some butter, add the sweetbreads and fry them on both sides for approximately 3 minutes – make sure that the heat is not too fierce.

Potato Croquettes
Mix thoroughly 2 pounds mashed potatoes with 2 beaten eggs, ½ cup (2 ounces) grated Parmesan cheese and finely chopped parsley to taste. Roll into fat, sausage-shaped rissoles, each about 2 inches long. Coat with breadcrumbs and leave for 1 hour in the

refrigerator. Heat enough olive oil for deep-frying, add the croquettes, a few at a time, and fry them until golden brown all over.

Zucchini (Courgettes)
Wash and thinly slice the zucchini lengthwise or, if preferred, into thickish rounds. Fry in oil until tender and brown. The zucchini may be peeled before frying, but if they are really young and tender, this will not be necessary.

Artichokes (very young)
Cut off the stalks and the tips of the artichokes, and remove any tough outer leaves. Cut them into rounds, discarding any choke (very young artichokes have had no time to form a choke). Drop them into a bowl of water acidulated with lemon juice. Leave for a short while, then drain, pat dry and cut into slices. Dip the slices in flour and beaten egg, and fry in hot butter.

Cauliflower Flowerettes
Cut out and remove any bruised portions from a large, firm cauliflower. Place the cauliflower top downwards in a pan of cold, salted water, and leave for 30 minutes. Drain and break into flowerettes, keeping them all the same size if possible. Cook in boiling salted water for 15 minutes. Drain carefully and cool. Dip the flowerettes in flour, then in beaten egg, and fry in plenty of hot butter until brown.

No exact measurements are given for *fritto misto*. One may serve two or three of the above ingredients, or as many as six. When preparing a *fritto misto* it is important that all the ingredients should be of the best quality and all much the same size, i.e. more or less bite-sized. It is equally important to remember that the *fritto misto* must not be kept waiting for, like all fried foods, it is not worth eating if lukewarm. Serve with halved lemons.

Lumache alla Milanese
Snails Milanese Style

US		UK
3 dozen	large live snails	3 dozen
	coarse salt	
	wine vinegar	
½ cup	olive oil	6 tablespoons
¼ cup	butter	2 ounces
1 clove	garlic, crushed	1 clove
4–6	anchovy fillets, finely chopped	4–6
4	fennel seeds	4
2–3 sprigs	parsley, finely chopped	2–3 sprigs
1 small	onion, finely chopped	1 small
1 teaspoon	flour	1 teaspoon
1 cup	dry white wine	scant ½ pint
	salt and pepper	
	grated nutmeg	

Drop the snails into a large bowl or pan of cold water to which you have added some coarse salt and a tablespoon of vinegar. Stir thoroughly with the hands. Repeat this operation, changing the water, salt and vinegar four times, or until the water is clear. Wash in running water until the last trace of scum has disappeared.

Drop the snails into a large pan of cold water and bring to the boil over a high heat. Cook for 10 minutes, skimming foam off the surface as soon as it rises. Drain and cool. Take the snails out of their shells, removing the little black bits from each snail.

Heat the oil and butter together in a deep frying pan, and brown the garlic clove; discard it. Add the anchovies, fennel seeds, parsley and onion, and sauté until the mixture browns. Sprinkle with flour and stir until it is completely incorporated. Add the snails. Again stir so that the snails are mixed into the sauce, then stir in the wine, salt, pepper and a dash of freshly grated nutmeg. Cook over a low heat for 1 hour, stirring occasionally. Replace the snails in their shells, and arrange them in snail plates. Pour the sauce over the snails and serve at once.

Serve 6 or 12 snails per person.

Snail plates are round with small indents just large enough to hold the snails. They are usually made to take 6 to 12 snails. With these are served snail pincers to hold the shells, and a fork to dig out the snails. This is all part of the mystique of eating snails.

It is sometimes possible to buy snails ready for cooking, their shells splendidly polished. If buying such snails, follow the recipe from the point of making the sauce, cooking them for as long as the instructions on the particular brand of snails advocates.

Rane in Guazzetto
Frogs' Legs in Butter and Wine

US		UK
2 pounds	frogs' legs, skinned and cleaned	2 pounds
1¼ cups	dry white wine	½ pint
6 tablespoons	butter	3 ounces
1 teaspoon	flour	1 teaspoon
	salt	
2–3 sprigs	parsley, finely chopped	2–3 sprigs
	juice of 1 small lemon	

Prepare the frogs' legs as directed on page 21, using wine to marinate them.

Melt the butter in a deep frying pan. Take the frogs' legs from their marinade, put them aside and pour the wine into the pan. Mix this thoroughly with the butter, then add the legs. Cook over a moderate heat until the wine is reduced by half.

Mix the flour, a pinch of salt and the parsley with 2 tablespoons water. Stir this into the pan and continue to cook over a moderate heat for another 15 minutes. Sprinkle the frogs' legs with lemon juice just before serving.

Serves 6.

Fagiano alla Milanese
Pheasant Milanese Style

US		UK
1	hen pheasant, well hung	1
	salt	
4 tablespoons	butter	2 ounces
2 ounces	fat pork belly, chopped	2 ounces
2 ounces	calf's liver, chopped	2 ounces
½ cup	ground (UK minced) beef	4 ounces
1 small	onion, finely chopped	1 small
1	clove	1
	pepper	
1 cup	Marsala or sherry	scant ½ pint
⅔ cup	stock	¼ pint

Pluck the pheasant, clean it well and singe it if necessary. Rub with salt inside and out, and truss like a chicken.

Melt the butter and pork in a heavy pan or casserole, and brown the pheasant, turning it from time to time. Add the liver, beef, onion, clove, and salt and pepper to taste, and moisten with Marsala and stock. Cover the pan and cook over a low heat for about 1 hour, or until the pheasant is tender. Test the leg with a skewer to see if it is cooked.

Take the pheasant from the pan, put it on a heated serving dish and keep hot in a warm oven. Rub the sauce through a fine sieve, scraping round the sides of the pan, return to the pan and re-heat. Pour the sauce over the pheasant immediately before serving.

Serves 3 to 4.

Tacchina Ripiena
Turkey Stuffed with Chestnuts

US		UK
1	turkey – 8 to 10 pounds	1
	salt and pepper	
6–8 tablespoons	butter	3–4 ounces
1 sprig	sage	1 sprig
1 sprig	rosemary	1 sprig
Stuffing		
18	fresh chestnuts, skinned, *or*	18
½ pound	dried chestnuts, soaked	½ pound
½ pound	dried prunes, soaked, pitted and chopped	½ pound
½ cup	ground (UK minced) veal	¼ pound
¼ pound	fat pork belly or bacon, finely chopped	¼ pound
3	apples, peeled and cubed	3
3	pears, peeled and cubed	3
12	walnut halves, chopped	12
5 tablespoons	grated Parmesan cheese	4 tablespoons
1 teaspoon	salt	1 teaspoon
¼ teaspoon	black pepper	¼ teaspoon
¼ teaspoon	grated nutmeg	¼ teaspoon
2	eggs, lightly beaten	2
1 cup	dry white wine	scant ½ pint

Rub the turkey inside and out with salt and pepper.

Mix all the stuffing ingredients together in a bowl, adding the turkey liver and heart, both ground (U.K. minced).

Stuff the turkey loosely with this mixture and sew up neatly and firmly to keep the stuffing securely in place. Place the turkey on the rack of a large roasting pan. Spread it thickly with butter, sprinkle lightly with salt and place the sage and rosemary on the top. Roast in a moderate oven (375°F. Mark 4), allowing 20 to 25 minutes per pound of weight. Baste every 30 minutes, the first time with boiling water, then with the juices from the turkey. (Many Lombard cooks also baste with white wine.) If the breast of the turkey begins to brown too quickly, cover it with foil.

When the turkey is quite tender, take it from the oven, place it on a large heated serving dish and return it to the oven to keep hot. Pour off most of the fat in the pan, add a little water (or better still stock) to the pan juices, stirring and scraping the sides of the pan, and cook on top of the stove for 5 minutes. Strain over the turkey.

Serves 8 to 10.

Lepre in Salmì
Jugged Hare

US		UK
1 large	hare, well hung	1 large
	flour	
4 tablespoons	butter	2 ounces
4 tablespoons	olive oil	3 tablespoons
1	onion, finely chopped	1
	salt and pepper	
Marinade		
2	carrots, thinly sliced	2
1	onion, thinly sliced	1
2 stalks	celery, diced	2 stalks
2 cloves	garlic, crushed	2 cloves
1 sprig each	thyme, marjoram and sage	1 sprig each
2	bay leaves	2
3	juniper berries	3
4–5	black peppercorns	4–5
	salt	
5 cups	Barbera or Barolo red wine	2 pints

Clean the hare, wipe it dry and chop it into pieces, carefully catching its blood. Usually hare does not need washing as this is thought to

spoil its flavor. However, if it should be necessary, wash it quickly in cold water and dry thoroughly. Cut up the heart, lungs and liver.

Combine the marinade ingredients in a large bowl. Add the pieces of hare, cover the dish and leave in a cool place for up to 48 hours.

Lift the pieces of hare from the marinade; drain them and wipe dry with paper towels. Coat lightly in flour.

Heat the butter and oil together in a large pan, add the onion and the pieces of hare, and brown them all over. Stir in the blood, heart, lungs and liver. Strain the marinade and measure 2½ cups (U.K. 1 pint). Pour it into the pan together with all the marinade vegetables (the left-over marinade can be used in another dish). Season and cook slowly for 2 hours, or until the hare is tender.

Arrange the pieces of hare on a heated serving dish and keep hot in a warm oven. Rub the sauce through a fine sieve, return it to the pan and re-heat. Strain this over the hare and serve.

As with other game in Italy, hare is usually served with boiled polenta. Jugged hare is all the better for being left overnight in its own sauce.

Serves 6 to 8.

Agoni Seccati in Graticola (Missoltitt)
Dried Shad, Broiled (Grilled)

US		UK
2 pounds	dried shad – see method	2 pounds
1 cup	red wine vinegar	scant ½ pint
	olive oil	
12 slices	cooked polenta, toasted	12 slices

Missoltitt are the shad caught in Lake Como in May and June, dried in the sun and then pressed into cans with bay leaves.

Place the *missoltitt* on a hot griddle and let them swell up over a low heat. (They are at their best when cooked over the dying embers of a fire.) Remove the scales with a sharp knife and arrange the fish, still warm, in a deep serving dish. Sprinkle generously with wine vinegar and leave to marinate for 1 hour.

Serve lightly sprinkled with olive oil on slices of hot, toasted polenta.

Serves 6.

Baccalà alla Milanese
Milanese Salt Cod Fritters

US		UK
2 pounds	dried salt cod	2 pounds
1 small	onion, chopped	1 small
2–3 sprigs	parsley	2–3 sprigs
2	lemons	2
	olive oil for frying	
Batter		
2	eggs	2
5 tablespoons	all-purpose (plain) flour	4 tablespoons
4 teaspoons	olive oil	1 tablespoon

Baccalà or *stoccafisso* is cod, sometimes haddock, that has been dried in the sun and preserved in salt. It requires at least 24 hours' soaking in running water (or several changes of cold water) before it can be used. In Italy, the soaking is often done by the grocers who sell *baccalà*. There it can be purchased dry, i.e. unsoaked, partially soaked and completely soaked, the cost of soaked fish being higher.

In the following recipe it is assumed that the *baccalà* has not been soaked.

Soak the dried fish in water for 24 to 48 hours, changing the water every 8 hours. Drain the fish, skin and bone it, and cut into pieces about 2 to 3 inches square. Make sure no bones or bits of skin are left. Put the squares into a pan of water with the chopped onion, parsley and ½ lemon. Cover the pan and bring to the boil. Let it boil for 1 minute, then remove it from the heat, and leave, covered, for 15 minutes.

Meanwhile, prepare a batter: beat the eggs and gradually add the flour and enough water to make a fairly thick, smooth batter. Stir in the olive oil and leave the batter to rest for 30 minutes.

Heat plenty of olive oil in a deep frying pan until smoking hot. Drain the cod and dip the pieces into the batter. Drop these one by one into the boiling oil and fry on both sides until golden brown. Drain the fritters on paper towels and serve hot, garnished with lemon wedges.

Serves 6.

Carpione al Vino
Carp in Wine

US		UK
3–3½ pounds	carp – one fish	3–3½ pounds
4 tablespoons	olive oil	3 tablespoons
1	onion, finely chopped	1
3 tablespoons	butter	1½ ounces
4 teaspoons	flour	1 tablespoon
2–3 sprigs	parsley, finely chopped	2–3 sprigs
1 cup	dry white wine	scant ½ pint
	salt and pepper	
4 teaspoons	wine vinegar	1 tablespoon
1	lemon	1

Carp is an excellent table fish and when in season has a good flavor. Carp are, however, sometimes muddy and it is advisable after scaling and cleaning to wash them well in running water or to soak them in 2 or 3 changes of salted water. If the scales are difficult to remove, dip the fish into boiling water for 1 minute. Cut off the head and be sure to remove the gall stone which lies at the back of the head, otherwise the fish will acquire a bitter taste when cooked.

When the carp has been cleaned, wipe it dry and cut it into large steaks. Heat the oil in a frying pan and gently fry the onion until soft but not brown. While this is cooking, work the butter to a smooth paste with the flour and stir it into the pan. Add the parsley and finally the wine, and continue stirring until the mixture is smooth and thick. Add the pieces of carp, salt and pepper to taste, the vinegar and about 1 cup (U.K. ½ pint) water. Cover and cook slowly for 30 minutes, stirring the sauce from time to time, and gently turning the pieces of fish.

Serve the carp hot with its sauce, garnished with lemon wedges.
Serves 4 to 6.

Filetti di Pesce Persico alla Milanese
Perch Fillets Milanese Style

US		UK
12	perch fillets	12
2½ tablespoons	flour	2 tablespoons
2	eggs	2
	salt	
	fine dry breadcrumbs	
½ cup	butter	4 ounces
	lemon wedges – optional	

Wash the fillets and gently pat them dry. Roll them in flour, dip into the eggs, beaten with salt, and coat in breadcrumbs. Fry the fillets very slowly in butter until golden brown on both sides. Serve hot, either with lemon wedges or with a risotto.
Serves 4 to 6.

Luccio alla Marinara
Pike Sailor's Style

US		UK
2	pike – about 2 pounds each	2
2½ tablespoons	olive oil	2 tablespoons
4 tablespoons	butter	2 ounces
6 small	onions, finely chopped	6 small
2 stalks	celery, cut into neat rounds	2 stalks
2	carrots, cut into thick rounds	2
4 teaspoons	flour	1 tablespoon
	salt and pepper	
2–3 sprigs	parsley, finely chopped	2–3 sprigs
	croûtons	
Marinade		
4 teaspoons	olive oil	1 tablespoon
	salt and pepper	
1 small	onion, sliced	1 small
1 stalk	celery, chopped	1 stalk
1	carrot, chopped	1
4–5 cups	dry red wine	1½–2 pints

Sometimes pike attain enormous size, but the larger fish are apt to be rather coarse, so choose smaller ones for this dish.

Clean the pike well and wash them thoroughly in salted water. Combine the marinade ingredients in a large shallow dish and marinate the fish for 2 hours. Heat the oil and butter together in a pan. Add the onions, celery and carrots, and sauté gently until they begin to brown. Lift the fish from the marinade, dry them and coat lightly with flour.

Strain the marinade and measure out 2½ cups (U.K. 1 pint). Pour this over the fish and vegetables, and season with salt and pepper. Cover the pan, lower the heat and simmer for 30 minutes. A few minutes before the fish are ready, sprinkle with parsley.

Take the fish from the pan, arrange them on a hot serving dish and strain the sauce over the top. Serve the fish generously garnished with croûtons.
Serves 6.

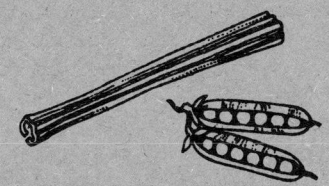

Verzada
Cabbage with Pork Sausages

US		UK
1 large	white cabbage – about 2 pounds	1 large
2 tablespoons	butter	1 ounce
½ cup	pork belly or fat bacon, diced	3 ounces
1	onion, thinly sliced	1
2½ tablespoons	wine vinegar	2 tablespoons
	salt	
6 small	Italian pork sausages	6 small

Discard the outer leaves of the cabbage, shred the cabbage coarsely and wash it thoroughly. Drain. Heat the butter and the pork belly in a large pan, and sauté the onion until soft but not brown. Add the cabbage and stir well so that the leaves are coated with fat. Cook over a moderate heat until the cabbage begins to brown. Sprinkle with vinegar, and add salt to taste. Arrange the sausages, pricked all over with a fork, on top of the cabbage, cover the pan and simmer for 1 hour. Serve the cabbage on a hot platter, garnished with the sausages.
Serves 4.

Laciaditt
Apple Fritters Lombardy Style

US		UK
2 cups	all-purpose (plain) flour	8 ounces
pinch	salt	pinch
1	egg	1
1¼ cups each	milk and water, mixed	½ pint each
2–3 large	green (cooking) apples, peeled and thinly sliced	2–3 large
	grated rind of ½ lemon	
	oil for deep-frying	
	granulated (caster) sugar	

Sift the flour into a bowl with the salt. Make a well in the middle. Drop the egg into the well and stir it into the flour until thoroughly mixed. Gradually add the milk and water, beating all the time until the batter is smooth. Leave for 1 hour.

Add the slices of apple and the lemon rind. Have ready a deep pan of hot olive oil. Deep-fry the apple slices, a few at a time, until a pale amber color, turning them once. Take them from the pan with a perforated spoon, drain them quickly on paper towels and serve very hot, sprinkled with sugar.

Serves 4 to 6.

Crema al Mascarpone
Cream Cheese with Sugar and Rum

US		UK
1 pound	fresh Mascarpone cheese – see method	1 pound
½ cup	granulated (caster) sugar	4 ounces
4	egg yolks	4
½ cup	rum	6–8 tablespoons
4–6	plain cookies (UK biscuits)	4–6

Mascarpone (Mascapone, Mascherpone) is a very soft Italian cheese made in the winter from cow's milk in Lombardy and Tuscany. It is somewhat like Devonshire clotted cream and is sold in little muslin bags, each cheese weighing about ¼ pound. It is eaten with fruit, such as strawberries and raspberries, or sprinkled with cinnamon. Sometimes lemon juice is added, or it is beaten up with rum and eggs and sweetened as in the following recipe. Like Ricotta cheese, Mascarpone is sometimes smoked.

Mix the cheese and sugar together, and add the egg yolks, one at a time, beating constantly. Add the rum (brandy may be used instead if preferred). Fold in the egg whites, scoop the mixture into individual glasses and chill for several hours. Serve with plain cookies (U.K. biscuits).

Serves 4 to 6.

Busecchina
Stewed Chestnuts

US		UK
1 pound	dried chestnuts	1 pound
1¼ cups	white wine	½ pint
pinch	salt	pinch
2½ tablespoons	sugar	2 tablespoons
1¼ cups	light (single) cream	½ pint

Dried chestnuts are usually available from Italian shops and also in large stores and delicatessens. They are apt to be seasonal, so check with the vendor that his stock is fresh. When cooked, especially as in the following recipe, they can be delicious.

Soak the chestnuts overnight in the wine plus enough water to cover. The following day, place them in a pan with their liquid, add salt and sugar, and cook over a low heat for about 20 minutes, or until they are tender and have absorbed most of their liquid. Serve chilled, with cream.

Serves 4 to 6.

Budino di Panettone
Sweet Panettone Pudding

US		UK
¾ pound	stale panettone, sliced – see method	¾ pound
¼ cup	rum	3–4 tablespoons
¼ cup	Marsala	3–4 tablespoons
5 cups	milk	2 pints
	grated rind of ½ lemon	
pinch	ground cinnamon	pinch
5 large	eggs	5 large
½ cup	granulated (caster) sugar	3½ ounces
	butter	

Panettone is a type of sweet brioche bread and a specialty of Milan. It is said to have first been made by a baker called Toni and became so popular that, lacking a name, customers simply asked for Toni's bread or "panettone". But there is also *panettone* of Venice and of Turin; and Genoa claims that the first *panettone*, called *pandolce*, came from that town, and dismisses all other *panettone* recipes as mere imitations. However, whatever its origin, *panettone di Milano* is the most popular in Italy.

When *panettone* is not available, almost any light, sweet white bread can be used instead in this pudding.

Soak the slices in the rum and Marsala. Bring the milk to the boil, stir in the lemon rind and cinnamon, then let it cool. Separate the eggs. Beat the yolks with the sugar until the mixture is smooth, and stir in the warm milk. Add this to the soaked *panettone* slices. Beat the egg whites stiffly and fold them carefully into the bread mixture. (It is essential not to break up the slices too much.) When all this is blended, pour the mixture into a buttered baking dish. Put this into a baking pan and add enough hot water to come halfway up the sides of the dish. Bake in a very slow oven (290°F. Mark 1) until the pudding is firm – about 1½ to 2 hours. Turn off the heat and let the pudding cool in the oven. Turn out and serve cold.

Serves 6.

Tortionata Lodigiana
Lodigiana Cake

US		UK
1 cup	almonds, peeled and toasted	6 ounces
1 cup	butter	½ pound
4 cups	all-purpose (plain) flour	1 pound
1 teaspoon	baking powder	1 teaspoon
1⅛ cups	granulated (caster) sugar	½ pound
2–3	egg yolks	2–3
	grated rind of 1 lemon	
pinch	vanilla powder or vanilla extract to taste	pinch
	butter and flour for cake pan	
	confectioners' (icing) sugar	

This cake is a sort of shortbread.

Blanch the almonds and quickly sauté until golden brown in a very little of the butter. Watch them carefully as they brown, for even a second's over-cooking will produce burnt almonds.

Sift the flour and baking powder together. Put all the ingredients into a bowl and work to a thick paste. Butter and lightly flour a 10-inch cake pan. Pat the paste evenly into the cake pan and bake in a hot oven (425°F. Mark 6) for 30 minutes, or until a skewer inserted in the middle comes out clean. Turn the cake out on to a wire rack and cool. If liked, sprinkle generously with sifted sugar.

Serves 6.

VENETO

When they returned from their long voyages in the Mediterranean, the great vessels of the Venetian Republic sailed into Venice along the Giudecca Canal and dropped anchor within sight of the Campanile of St. Mark. During the sixteenth century a vessel arrived one day loaded with gold, oriental carpets, perfumes and other treasures brought from the far-flung possessions of the Republic. Included in its hold was a sack of maize, the first to be imported into Italy. It had come from America, which had been discovered by Columbus only a few years earlier. As most good things brought to Venice by sea came from Turkey and its Empire, this new cereal was assumed to be Turkish, and to this day maize is known in Italy as *granoturco*, or Turkish corn. In the Rialto market, where the bag of maize was taken to be sold, it caused a sensation, and it was here perhaps, near the Rialto, that the first *polenta* was made.

Today, *polenta* is a staple food of a large area of Northern Italy, but nowhere is it more popular than in the region of Veneto. *Polenta* blends superbly well with innumerable dishes of meat, game and fish. It can be eaten with or without sauce, roasted, toasted, fried, or boiled and served straight from a copper pan.

Next in popularity to *polenta* is fish. Most of it comes from the fishing port of Chioggia at the western extremity of the Lagoon, where small fishing boats, known as *bragozzi*, bring ashore the very finest fish from the teeming banks of the Adriatic. The Venetians are past masters in the art of cooking fish. Nothing is more typically Venetian than the little restaurants and *rosticcerie*, often wrapped

Bacalà alla visentina, or salt cod as cooked in Vicenza, is a fine example of the cooking of the Veneto (see page 74). Steeped in olive oil and milk, and cooked very gently over a low heat, the dried fish becomes tender and succulent. It is best eaten with a stiff *polenta*. In the background is the Villa Cordellina-Lombardi at Montecchio Maggiore.

Risi e bisi, or rice with peas (see page 68), is the Veneto's most famous first course. It is seen here with another well-known local dish, *fegato alla veneziana*, paper-thin slices of liver fried for only a moment or two with thinly sliced onions (see page 70), and served with the traditional *polenta*. In the background, the island of San Giorgio.

Three inviting fish dishes, photographed at Duino, a placid little fishing port on the Gulf of Trieste.
Left: Da Romano (Romano's) on the tiny island of Burano, a typical Venetian *trattoria*, and a meeting place for painters and poets. Here one can feast on the fish and other seafood which abound in the waters of the Lagoon.

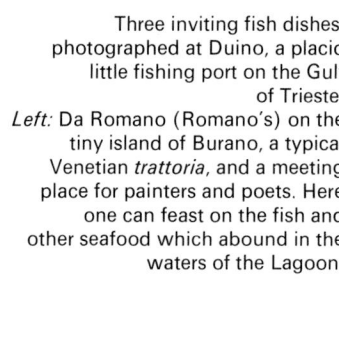

in a billowing cloud of smoke and steam, that line the *calli, rive, campi, rii,* and the principal canals of Venice. The fish are cooked according to strict rules—either deep-fried in oil, or broiled (grilled) on a fierce charcoal fire, or else boiled. Indeed, fish is the most important element of Venetian cooking, whether it be served as an hors d'oeuvre, consisting of shrimps and prawns, cuttlefish and lobsters; as a first course, especially in the form of an exquisite fish soup known as *broeto*; or as an entrée—fried or broiled (grilled) fish, scampi, squid, angler fish, sea bream, mullet, sole, sardines and eels; or boiled fish, from sea bass to red mullet.

And almost as if nature had not provided them with enough, the Venetians have gone in search of more fish in the Lagoon, in lakes, in rivers and in Alpine streams. From northern seas they have brought back stockfish or sun-dried salt cod, and used it to make *bacalà* or *baccalà alla visentina*, one of the finest of all Venetian dishes. It should be remembered, though, if you are thinking of making it in the traditional manner, that it takes three days to prepare. After being beaten with a wooden hammer, the fish is soaked for forty-eight hours in order to soften it and remove some of the salt. It is then simmered in a bath of milk and oil, with onions, garlic, anchovies and parsley. *Bacalà* blends perfectly with *polenta*, and the Venetians like it even better warmed up, a test that only a perfect dish can survive.

Traveling through the hinterland of the Veneto from Vicenza to Treviso, you will find the *radicchio rosso*, a form of chicory (curly endive), which is the most popular salad plant of the region. In

Goose cooked with celery is a specialty of Treviso, home of the famous *radicchio rosso*—see facing page.
Below: A hearth with the traditional *ciavedal* (Friulian firedog) and some specialties of the Friuli region: Montasio cheese, San Daniele ham with Friulian sausages, sauerkraut with Cotechino sausages, and *dolce gubana*, a spiral of pastry stuffed with fruit, nuts and chocolate.
Below, left: Photographed against the impressive backdrop of the Marmolada range, several specialties of the Trentino: sausages, smoked fat pork, polenta, trout from Lake Fedaia and roast veal, accompanied by Terlaner wine.

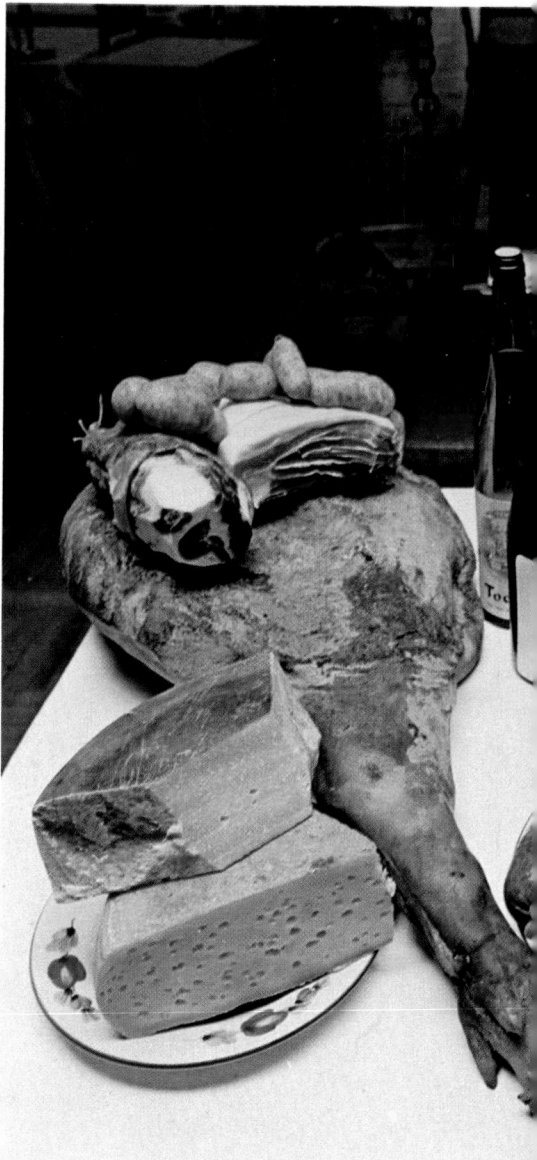

Radicchio di Treviso, wild chicory (curly endive), a crisp salad vegetable with a faintly bitter taste, which grows only around Treviso. *Below:* At Giavera del Montello in the province of Treviso, laden spits are turned slowly before a charcoal fire and the famous local mushrooms are prepared in a variety of ways.

December it looks like a fleshy purple flower, as fresh as if it had been specially created to bring spring to the dinner table in winter. A close relation of the *radicchio rosso*, although substantially different in flavor and appearance, is the chicory of Castelfranco Veneto, which is sweet and has leaves speckled with all the colors of the rainbow. And there are many other vegetables that are used with great effect in Venetian cooking; peas, for instance, known locally as *bisi*, are one of the main ingredients of a classical dish that now belongs to international cookery, *risi e bisi* (rice and peas).

The Venetians make great use of rice, which may seem strange, because apart from the delta of the Po, the largest rice-producing areas are to be found outside the region, in Lombardy. However, the Venetians do not treat rice in the same way as the Lombards. Saffron, for instance, is unknown here, and rice is never eaten by itself but always cooked and served with other ingredients, such as lamb, sausages, chicken livers, tripe, beans and raisins, as well as with fish and shellfish (baby clams, eels, scampi and squid). Next to rice, which dominates the first part of the meal, there are various kinds of pasta, e.g., the famous *pasta e fagioli* and the gnocchi of Verona. Verona has a culinary tradition of its own, and its proximity to Lake Garda ensures a good supply of trout.

Venetian cooking bears witness to a great and proud past. The luxury of the Venice of the Doges, and of the wonderful villas that still line the banks of the Brenta Canal, has not entirely vanished from the tables of the Venetians, the richness of whose cuisine is evidence of the fastidiousness shown by every good Venetian when he sits down at table. (Venetians claim to have invented the table napkin and the fork at a time when most people were still eating with their fingers.) Nowhere is the fastidiousness and elegance more apparent than in certain Venetian dishes: the sweet and fragrant San Daniele ham, the inimitable *torresani*—small, semi-domesticated pigeons which are hung for a couple of days before being spit-roasted, and served with boiled *polenta*—or young turkeys, known locally as *paeta*, cooked with pomegranates—these are served at Montebello in the province of Vicenza. Then there are freshwater shrimps (U.K. prawns) from San Paolo di Piave, the delicious liver *alla veneziana*, asparagus from Bariano, and the traditional *polenta e osei* (*polenta* and small birds). The *pandoro* (golden bread) of Verona, which is appreciated not only in Italy, and a variety of pastries, conclude the classical bill of fare.

The best wines of Verona are Valpolicella, Bardolino, Soave (a perfect white wine for hors d'oeuvre and fish), Amarone, Recioto, which is a sweet, slightly sparkling red wine with a delicate *bouquet*, and Tokai, a very clear, slightly fragrant wine, excellent with roasts and fish. Pinot (of which there are three varieties, white, rosé and red), Merlot, Riesling and Cabernet, are to be found almost everywhere throughout the region. In the Alto Adige, where the cooking has a Germanic flavor, there is Terlano, a dry white wine, Caldaro, Santa Maddalena and Santa Giustina. The Trentino, where they make good local wine, produces among others Tiroldego and Marzemino. And this list could easily be extended, for there are over sixty wines in the Veneto, all of excellent quality.

Frico del Friuli
Fried Cheese Friuli Style

US		UK
½ pound	low fat cheese	½ pound
¼ pound	mature Carnia cheese – see method	¼ pound
3–4 tablespoons	butter	1½–2 ounces
3 tablespoons	fat salt pork	1½ ounces
a few slices	onion	a few slices
2	eggs, beaten	2
	salt and pepper	

This is a simple little recipe which can be prepared with any piquant cheese which will fry. Carnia is a fairly piquant cheese of the Provolone type.

Cut all the cheese into small pieces. Heat the butter and sauté the salt pork and onion until the onion is soft but not brown. Add the cheese and continue to cook slowly until it melts. Turn it over, add the eggs, season to taste with salt and pepper, and cook the eggs until they are firmly set and slightly crisp around the edges.

Serves 4.

Salsa Peverada
Venetian Savory Sauce

US		UK
5 ounces	chicken livers	5 ounces
3	anchovy fillets	3
4 ounces	sausage – see method	4 ounces
	grated rind of ½ lemon	
2–3 sprigs	parsley, finely chopped	2–3 sprigs
⅔ cup	olive oil	¼ pint
1 clove	garlic	1 clove
	salt and pepper	
⅓ cup	wine vinegar or dry white wine	½ gill
	lemon juice	

The sausage traditionally used in this recipe is the *sopressa veneta*, which is made with a mixture of pork and beef.

Finely chop the chicken livers with the anchovy fillets and the sausage meat. Put this mixture in a bowl and add the lemon rind and parsley. Heat the oil, brown the garlic lightly and discard it, then add the chopped meat mixture. Season lightly with salt and pepper, and let it simmer slowly, adding the wine vinegar and a few drops of lemon juice, until the sauce is smooth and fairly thick.

Serve hot with poultry or game.

"Pasta e Fasoi col Pistelo de Parsuto"
Noodles and Beans with Ham Bone

US		UK
2 cups	dried white (haricot) beans	¾ pound
½ pound	fresh pork skin	½ pound
1	ham bone	1
1	onion, finely chopped	1
1	carrot, finely chopped	1
1 stalk	celery, finely chopped	1 stalk
4 tablespoons	olive oil	3 tablespoons
	salt	
½ pound	ribbon noodles or spaghetti	½ pound
	pepper	
	grated Parmesan cheese	

Soak the beans overnight or for several hours. Cut the pork skin into pieces. Put the beans, pork skin, ham bone, onion, carrot, celery and 2½ tablespoons (U.K. 2 tablespoons) oil into a large pan and cover with water. Season with salt and cook slowly for 2½ hours. Discard the ham bone.

Take about half the beans from the pan and rub them through a fine sieve. Return the bean purée to the pan and bring the soup back to the boil. Add the noodles and cook over a good heat until just tender. Sprinkle with salt and pepper, and stir in the remaining oil. Pour into soup bowls, leave to cool (this dish is served warm, not hot) and sprinkle lightly with Parmesan cheese before serving.

Serves 6.

Bigoli coll'Anatra
Noodles with Duck Sauce

US		UK
Dough		
6 cups	all-purpose (plain) flour	1½ pounds
3	eggs	3
	salt	
4 tablespoons	melted butter	2 ounces
	milk	
1 large	duck	1 large
1	onion, quartered	1
2	carrots, sliced	2
1 stalk	celery, chopped	1 stalk
¾ cup	grated Parmesan cheese, to garnish	3 ounces
Sauce		
	duck giblets	
4 tablespoons	butter	2 ounces
1 sprig	sage, chopped	1 sprig
	salt and pepper	

To make these noodles, which are like spaghetti without holes, a special instrument called a *bigolaro* is necessary, and most people outside Italy will probably resort to commercially made noodles.

Dough
Sift the flour on to a pastry board. Make a well in the middle and drop the eggs in, one by one. Add a pinch of salt, the melted butter and about ⅔ cup (U.K. ¼ pint) milk. Work to a firm, smooth dough, adding more milk as required. An exact quantity of milk cannot be given as eggs vary in size and flour in quality. When the dough is pliable, cut it into small stick-shapes and press them through the *bigolaro*.

Clean the duck, reserving its giblets. Put it in a large pan with the onion, carrots, celery, plenty of water and salt to taste. Bring to the boil slowly, lower the heat to moderate and cook, covered, until the duck is tender, about 1½ hours, depending on size and age.

Take the duck from the pan and keep hot in a warm oven. Strain the stock. Return it to the pan, bring to the boil again, add the noodles and boil rapidly until tender but firm. They will take only a minute or two if freshly made.

Sauce
While the noodles are cooking, chop the giblets finely. Melt the butter and add the sage, giblets and a pinch of salt and pepper. Simmer gently until the giblets are cooked.

Drain the noodles and turn them into a deep, heated dish. Cover with the sage and giblet sauce, and stir lightly but carefully.

Serve the noodles as a first course, garnished with Parmesan cheese, followed by the duck as a main course, accompanied by Venetian Savory Sauce (see above).

Serves 4 to 6.

Gnocchi di Patate
Potato Gnocchi or Dumplings

US		UK
2½ pounds	potatoes, boiled and mashed	2½ pounds
2 cups	all-purpose (plain) flour	8 ounces
	salt	
1 teaspoon	baking powder	1 teaspoon
2	eggs, beaten	2
6 tablespoons	melted butter	3 ounces
¾ cup	grated Parmesan cheese	3 ounces

Put the warm mashed potatoes into a bowl. Add the flour, salt to taste, baking powder and eggs, and work lightly to a dough. Form into long, thin cylinders about the thickness of a finger, and cut these into inch-long pieces. Press each small cylinder of potato against the concave side of a small cheese grater and use the pressure of your fingers to make a hollow. (Or more simply, make a dent with the fingers so that the small cylinders become almost crescent-shaped.)

Have ready a large pan of boiling salted water. Drop the gnocchi, one by one, into the water and cook them, a few at a time, until they float to the top – about 3 minutes. Take them from the pan with a perforated spoon and drain them. Put them in a heated fireproof dish and keep hot in a warm oven until they are all cooked. Serve hot with melted butter and grated Parmesan.

Serves 6.

Polenta "Pastizada"
Venetian Polenta Pie

US		UK
1½ ounces	dried mushrooms	1½ ounces
¼ pound	chicken giblets	4 ounces
3 cups	cornmeal	1 pound
	salt	
	butter	
5 ounces	Parmesan, half grated and half very thinly sliced	5 ounces
Sauce		
¼ cup	olive oil	3 tablespoons
	butter	
1	onion, finely chopped	1
2	carrots, finely chopped	2
1 stalk	celery, finely chopped	1 stalk
½ cup	finely chopped bacon	2 ounces
1 cup	finely chopped raw veal	8 ounces
½ cup	dry white wine	6–8 tablespoons
1 pound	ripe or canned tomatoes	1 pound
	salt and pepper	

Sauce

As all Italian sauces require prolonged cooking, it is wise when preparing this dish to make the meat sauce first and, while this is cooking, to deal with the remaining ingredients.

Heat the oil and 2 tablespoons (1 ounce) butter, and gently sauté the onion, carrots, celery and bacon until they change color. Add the veal, let this brown, then pour in the wine. Cook for 5 minutes. Peel, seed and finely chop the tomatoes. Add these to the pan, season with salt and pepper, cover and cook gently for 1½ hours.

Soak the mushrooms in warm water and finely chop the giblets. Put the latter aside until required. When the mushrooms have been soaking for 30 minutes drain them, pat them dry and chop finely.

Bring a large pan of salted water to the boil, at least 8½ cups (U.K. 3½ pints). Pour in the cornmeal, stirring constantly, lower the heat and cook gently for 30 minutes, or until it is a thick,

smooth mass. Stir frequently while the polenta is cooking. Pour it into a square baking pan, let it cool and then cut into ¼-inch-thick slices. Put aside until required.

Melt 3 tablespoons (1½ ounces) butter and sauté the mushrooms and giblets gently for 5 minutes. Sprinkle lightly with salt.

Rub a fairly large pie dish generously with butter. Cover with a layer of polenta and spread with a layer of the meat sauce, another of polenta and one of mushrooms and giblets. Sprinkle with grated Parmesan and add a layer of sliced Parmesan. Dot with butter. Continue in this manner until all the ingredients are used up, finishing with a sprinkling of grated Parmesan cheese and slivers of butter. Bake in a very hot oven (475°F. Mark 8) until heated through, and serve very hot.

Serves 8.

Italian Risotto

As rice dishes are such a feature of the cooking of Veneto, it is worthwhile at this point to set out in detail the correct method of making a risotto.

Generally, the idea is that the rice is *insaporito* – gently fried in a finely chopped mixture of onion and garlic, parsley, anchovies, etc. (*soffritto* or *battuto*) which has been sautéed lightly in oil and butter to develop flavors. Then a hot liquid (stock for preference, but water will do) is added, about a cupful at a time, as the rice cooks, swells, absorbs the liquid and begins to dry out. The rice should always be kept simmering and at no point be allowed to dry out completely. An Italian risotto is far more moist than, for example, a Spanish or Indian rice dish – in fact, it may often be too mushy for American or English tastes.

As Italian rice, Arborio and Vialone for example, is better suited to this method of cooking, it is well worth trying to get it. There will be less danger of this type breaking down into a mush than if ordinary rice is used.

A risotto must be watched carefully all the time that it is cooking. Stop adding liquid when the rice is tender with still a little "bite" to each grain, and there is just enough liquid left to bubble gently. Rice with its liquid still bubbling is called *riso all'onda* or "rippling rice" and many recipes specify that this is how it should be when ready. Do not strain before serving. The risotto is sometimes left for a couple of minutes before serving to "settle", especially if any flavoring has been added at the last moment, to give it time to impregnate the rice.

(Translator's note)

"Risi e Bisati"
Rice with Eel

US		UK
1 pound	eel, cleaned and skinned	1 pound
5 tablespoons	olive oil	4 tablespoons
1 clove	garlic, finely chopped	1 clove
2–3 sprigs	parsley, finely chopped	2–3 sprigs
1	bay leaf	1
	lemon juice	
2½ cups	rice	1 pound
about 10 cups	boiling water	about 4 pints
	salt and pepper	

This pleasant if somewhat substantial dish is traditionally served in Venice on Christmas Eve.

Chop the eel into small pieces. Heat the oil in a large heavy pan and sauté the garlic and parsley gently until golden. Add the pieces of eel, the bay leaf and a few drops of lemon juice. Cook for about 20 minutes, then stir in the rice until it has absorbed some of the fat. Gradually add the boiling water, a cupful at a time, until the rice is tender but still moist. Season with salt and plenty of pepper. Serve very hot, without cheese.

Serves 4 to 6.

Risotto con i "Caparozzoli"
Shellfish Risotto

US		UK
3–3½ pounds	caparozzoli – see method	3–3½ pounds
	salt	
5 tablespoons	olive oil	4 tablespoons
2 cloves	garlic, finely chopped	2 cloves
2–3 sprigs	parsley, finely chopped	2–3 sprigs
1 cup	dry white wine	scant ½ pint
	pepper	
2½ cups	rice	1 pound
6½ cups	boiling fish stock	2½ pints

Caparozzoli are shellfish rather similar to baby clams, which may be used instead. Failing these, use any other small shellfish available, including oysters. Canned or bottled clams may be used, provided they are not preserved in vinegar.

Wash the shellfish thoroughly in plenty of salted water. Put them into a thick, very hot frying pan and shake them over a good heat until they open. Cool and shell them.

Heat the oil in a large pan, add the garlic and parsley, and sauté until the garlic begins to change color. Add the fish, lower the heat and simmer for a few minutes, rather more to absorb the garlic and oil flavor then actually to cook the little fish. Add the wine, cook until it evaporates and season generously with pepper.

Add the rice, stir gently into the ingredients in the pan and fry until the rice begins to change color. Add a cupful of the stock, cook it over a moderate heat until it has been absorbed, and continue in this manner until all the stock is finished and the rice is tender. Check seasoning and serve immediately.

Serves 4 to 6.

Risotto "a la Sbiraglia"
Chicken and Veal Risotto

US		UK
1	plump chicken – about 2½ pounds	1
4 tablespoons	butter	2 ounces
2 tablespoons	olive oil	1½ tablespoons
1 small	onion, sliced	1 small
1	carrot, finely chopped	1
1 stalk	celery, finely chopped	1 stalk
1	chicken liver	1
5 ounces	lean veal, chopped	5 ounces
½ cup	dry white wine	6–8 tablespoons
	salt	
2½ cups	rice	1 pound
	grated Parmesan cheese	
Stock		
1	onion	1
2	carrots	2
1 stalk	celery	1 stalk
	salt	
about 12 cups	water	about 5 pints

Clean the chicken and cut off the wings, legs and head – if still on. Put the wings, etc., into a large pan with the giblets (not the liver), and add the stock ingredients. Cut off as much of the meat from the chicken as possible and drop the carcass into the pan with the stock. Bring slowly to the boil and simmer for 3 hours.

Strain the stock and discard the vegetables. Heat the butter with the oil in a large pan, and gently sauté the onion, carrot, celery, chicken liver, the pieces of chicken meat and the veal until brown. Add the wine, season lightly with salt, cover the pan and cook slowly for 30 minutes.

Add the rice to the pan and sauté until brown, stirring all the time. Add a cupful of the strained stock and cook it over a moderate heat until it has been absorbed into the rice, stirring constantly. Continue adding stock in this way until all of it has been absorbed into the rice. Serve on a heated platter with plenty of grated Parmesan cheese.

Serves 6.

"Risi in Cavroman"
Rice with Mutton

US		UK
1½ pounds	lean mutton – see method	1½ pounds
4 tablespoons	butter	2 ounces
1 small	onion, sliced	1 small
1 pound	ripe or canned tomatoes, peeled and seeded	1 pound
	salt and pepper	
pinch	ground cinnamon	pinch
2½ cups	rice	1 pound
about 10 cups	boiling meat stock	about 4 pints
¾ cup	grated Parmesan cheese	3 ounces

The meat used in this recipe should be mutton or lamb cutlets (best end of neck), cut into small pieces.

Melt the butter in a large pan and sauté the onion over a moderate heat until golden brown. Add the meat and brown it all over. Add the tomatoes and season to taste with salt, pepper and cinnamon. Cover and cook slowly for 1½ hours. Take the pan from the heat, let it cool a little, then take out the meat and bone it. Return the meat to the pan, stir it into the sauce and bring to the boil.

Add the rice, stirring, and cook for 5 minutes, stirring frequently. Add a cup of boiling stock and when this has been absorbed into the rice, add another cup. Continue in this manner until all the stock has been absorbed into the rice and the rice is tender, stirring very frequently. Stir in the Parmesan cheese and serve at once.

Serves 6.

Risi e Luganeghe
Rice with Pork Sausage

US		UK
½ pound	pure pork sausage(s) – see method	½ pound
2 tablespoons	butter	1 ounce
¼ cup	ham fat	2 ounces
1 small	onion, finely chopped	1 small
½ cup	dry white wine	6–8 tablespoons
7–8½ cups	meat or chicken stock	3–3½ pints
1 cup	rice	7 ounces
2–3 sprigs	parsley, finely chopped	2–3 sprigs
¾ cup	grated Parmesan cheese	3 ounces

This dish is traditionally prepared with *luganeghe*, the famous home-made pure pork sausages of Treviso. Best-quality commercially made sausages may be used instead. Skin the sausage(s) and cut into pieces.

Heat the butter in a large pan and gently sauté the ham fat and onion. When the onion begins to change color, add the sausage meat and let it brown. Pour in the wine and cook gently until it has evaporated. Add the hot stock, bring to the boil, sprinkle in the rice and cook slowly until it is tender, stirring frequently – about 20 minutes. When the rice is cooked and the liquid has been absorbed, stir in the parsley and the Parmesan cheese. Serve immediately.

Serves 3 to 4.

Risi e Bisi
Rice with Peas

US		UK
3 tablespoons	butter	1½ ounces
2½ tablespoons	olive oil	2 tablespoons
⅔ cup	diced lean bacon	3 ounces
1	green (spring) onion, sliced	1
3–3½ cups	shelled green peas	1 pound
10 cups	stock	4 pints
1⅔ cups	rice	10 ounces
	salt	
¾ cup	grated Parmesan cheese	3 ounces
2–3 sprigs	parsley, finely chopped	2–3 sprigs

This dish is considered by the Italians as a soup, but it is even thicker than most Italian thick soups. It is a specialty of Venice and said to have been served to the Doges of Venice at banquets to celebrate the Feast of St Mark. As with all traditional dishes, there are several versions. It is eaten with a fork, not a spoon, and basically should be rice with a green motif.

Heat the butter and oil together in a large pan, and gently sauté the bacon and onion. When the bacon is brown, add the peas and moisten with a few tablespoons of the stock. Cook gently for 15 minutes. Add the rest of the stock, which must be hot, and bring it to the boil. Pour in the rice, stir well, lower the heat and cook gently for 20 minutes, or until the rice is tender and still fairly moist. Add salt if necessary, and sprinkle generously with Parmesan cheese and parsley.

Serves 4 to 6.

"Risi col'Ua"
Rice with Raisins

US		UK
⅔ cup	raisins, soaked in water or wine	¼ pound
2 cloves	garlic	2 cloves
5 tablespoons	olive oil	4 tablespoons
2–3 sprigs	parsley, finely chopped	2–3 sprigs
2½ cups	rice	1 pound
about 10 cups	boiling stock	about 4 pints
¾ cup	grated Parmesan cheese	3 ounces

Drain the raisins and pat them dry with a cloth. Leave one clove garlic whole and chop the other finely. Fry both in oil together with the parsley in a large heavy pan. When the whole garlic clove browns, discard it and add the raisins.

Add the rice, stir it thoroughly into the oil and cook for 5 minutes, stirring gently all the time. Add a cup of boiling stock (or water) and when this has been absorbed, add another cup. Continue in this manner until the rice is just tender and still moist. Depending on the type of rice, up to 10 cups (U.K. 4 pints) liquid will be used. Serve garnished with grated Parmesan.

Serves 4 to 6.

Risotto con i Finocchi
Risotto with Florence Fennel

US		UK
1 pound	Florence fennel	1 pound
7 tablespoons	butter	3½ ounces
1	onion, thinly sliced	1
3–3¼ cups	rice	1¼ pounds
10 cups	boiling meat stock	4 pints
	salt	
¾ cup	grated Parmesan cheese	3 ounces

There are several varieties of fennel, some bitter and some sweet. In this recipe it is sweet bulb fennel with a large white heart which is

called for. It is a highly popular vegetable in Italy and not difficult to find abroad. One pound yields 2 to 3 bulbs, depending on their size.

Wash the fennel bulbs thoroughly and slice thinly. Melt 5 tablespoons (2½ ounces) butter, add the onion and fennel, and sauté gently until the fennel begins to soften. Add the rice and fry until it begins to brown. Pour in a cup of boiling stock, cook over a moderate heat until it has been absorbed, and continue in this manner until all the stock has been absorbed and the rice is tender.

Add salt if necessary (the stock may be sufficiently seasoned), stir in the remaining butter and the Parmesan cheese, cover and leave the risotto to settle for 2 minutes over a low heat.

A similar risotto can also be prepared with asparagus.

Serves 6.

Risotto con le "Zuchete"
Risotto with Zucchini (Courgettes)

US		UK
1 pound	small zucchini (courgettes)	1 pound
4 tablespoons	butter	2 ounces
½ cup	finely chopped bacon	2 ounces
1 small	onion, finely chopped	1 small
1 clove	garlic	1 clove
2–3 sprigs	parsley, finely chopped	2–3 sprigs
	salt and pepper	
3–3¼ cups	rice	1¼ pounds
about 8½ cups	boiling meat stock	about 3½ pints
¾ cup	grated Parmesan cheese	3 ounces

Wash the zucchini (courgettes) and slice them thinly.

Melt the butter in a large pan and sauté the bacon, onion and garlic until the onion is golden. Discard the garlic, then add the zucchini and parsley. Cook slowly until the zucchini are brown, season with salt and add the rice. Fry this for 5 minutes, stirring all the time. Add a cupful of the boiling stock, cook it until it is absorbed, then add another cupful and continue in this way until the rice is tender and all the liquid is absorbed.

Check seasoning, stir in the Parmesan and leave the risotto to settle for 2 minutes over a low heat before serving.

An excellent so-called "spring" risotto can be made in the same way, using almost any vegetable in season, including potatoes and mushrooms.

Serves 6.

"Sopa Coada"
"Hatched" Pigeon Soup

US		UK
3	plump pigeons or squabs, dressed	3
5 tablespoons	butter	2½ ounces
1	carrot, finely chopped	1
1 small	onion, sliced	1 small
1 stalk	celery, chopped	1 stalk
1 cup	dry white wine	scant ½ pint
	salt and pepper	
12 slices	bread, crisply fried	12 slices
about 5 cups	meat stock	about 2 pints
1½ cups	grated Parmesan cheese	5 ounces

Wipe the pigeons and singe them if necessary. Melt the butter in a large pan or casserole and gently sauté the carrot, onion and celery for a few minutes. Add the pigeons and brown them all over. Pour in the wine, season to taste with salt and pepper, and continue to cook slowly, covered, until the pigeons are tender.

Take the pigeons from the pan and let them cool, then pull as much meat from the bones as possible. Soak the fried bread in stock. Lay 3 slices of bread on the bottom of a deep baking dish, add a layer of pigeon meat and a sprinkling of Parmesan cheese. Continue in this order until all the ingredients are used up, finishing with a layer of bread. Pour the remaining stock over the top and put the dish into a very low oven (250°F. Mark ¼) to "hatch". Bake for 4 hours, or until the bread is dry but still soft, moistening with a little more hot stock during this time if necessary.

This popular soup is considered even better if left until the day after it has been made, then slowly re-heated in the oven. If by chance it has become a little too dry, extra stock may be added. Serves 6.

Zuppa di Pollo
Venetian Chicken Soup

US		UK
1	chicken – about 3 pounds	1
2½ tablespoons	olive oil	2 tablespoons
4 tablespoons	butter	2 ounces
½ cup	chopped bacon	2 ounces
1 sprig	rosemary	1 sprig
1 small	onion, sliced	1 small
½ cup	dry white wine	6–8 tablespoons
6½ cups	meat or chicken stock	2½ pints
6 slices	toasted bread	6 slices
	grated Parmesan cheese	

Clean and bone the chicken, and cut the meat into strips. Heat the oil and butter together in a large pan, and sauté the bacon, rosemary sprig and onion until golden. Add the chicken meat and brown it lightly. Discard the rosemary. Sprinkle with wine, moisten with a little stock and cook, covered, until the chicken is tender. Pour in the remaining stock, bring to the boil and serve, garnished with crisp slices of toast and plenty of grated Parmesan. Serves 6.

Iota Friulana
Vegetable Soup Friuli Style

US		UK
1⅓ cups	dry white (haricot) beans	½ pound
½ head	Savoy or firm white cabbage	½ head
1 clove	garlic	1 clove
2–3 sprigs	parsley	2–3 sprigs
3 tablespoons	pork fat	1½ ounces
1 small	onion	1 small
2 leaves	sage	2 leaves
1 bunch	celery	1 head
	salt and pepper	
	grated Parmesan cheese	

Soak the beans overnight or for several hours. Wash the cabbage and shred it finely, discarding any damaged leaves. Mix the garlic, parsley, pork fat, onion and sage leaves on a board, and chop finely – this makes what the Italians call a *pestat*. Wash, trim and chop the celery.

Cook the beans in water without salt until tender. Add the cabbage and celery, the *pestat*, salt and pepper, and make the liquid up to 10 cups (U.K. 4 pints) with boiling water. Cover the pan and cook slowly for 1 hour. Serve the soup sprinkled with Parmesan cheese.

Instead of cabbage, many people in the Friuli area use a cup of *brovada*. This consists of turnips macerated with their leaves for several months in the dregs left after the grape pressing. Serves 6.

"Sguazeto" alla Friulana
Lamb Stew Friuli Style

US		UK
2½ pounds	leg of lamb	2½ pounds
3 tablespoons	butter	1½ ounces
4 tablespoons	olive oil	3 tablespoons
1 clove	garlic	1 clove
1	onion, finely chopped	1
6 tablespoons	pork fat	3 ounces
	salt and pepper	
pinch	ground cinnamon	pinch
1 teaspoon	tomato paste	1 teaspoon
⅔ cup	stock	¼ pint

Cut the meat into cubes – if preferred, use stewing lamb for this dish.

Heat the butter and oil, and sauté the garlic, onion and pork fat for 5 minutes, or until the onion is golden brown. Discard the garlic and add the pieces of lamb. Season with salt, pepper and a pinch of cinnamon. Brown the meat well, turning it over to ensure even browning. Dilute the tomato paste with the stock and add this to the pan. Cover and continue to cook slowly until the meat is very, very tender and the sauce thick – 1½ to 2 hours. Serve the stew with boiled polenta. Serves 6.

"Pastizada" alla Veneta
Beef Pot Roast Veneto Style

US		UK
3½ pounds	bottom round or rump (leg) of beef	3½ pounds
6 tablespoons	butter	3 ounces
1 small	onion, finely chopped	1 small
	salt and pepper	
¼ cup	Marsala	3 tablespoons
¼ cup	white wine	3 tablespoons
Marinade		
2 cloves	garlic	2 cloves
2	cloves	2
pinch	ground cinnamon	pinch
2½ cups	wine vinegar	1 pint
2 stalks	celery, coarsely chopped	2 stalks
1 sprig	rosemary	1 sprig
	salt	
5–6	black peppercorns	5–6

Mix the marinade ingredients in a large bowl, add the meat and leave it to marinate for 12 hours. Strain the vegetables from the marinade and put them aside – the marinating vinegar may be used again if wished.

In an earthenware pot if possible – otherwise in a thick-bottomed metal pan – melt the butter and sauté the chopped onion and the vegetables from the marinade. When the vegetables are soft, add the meat and brown it all over. Sprinkle with salt and pepper, and moisten with Marsala and white wine. Cover the pan with buttered wax paper or foil, then with the lid, and cook very gently for 2½ hours, or until the meat is very tender. Cut the meat into medium-thick slices and arrange them on a heated serving dish. Pour over the sauce and serve immediately, accompanied by polenta. Serves 6 to 8.

Arrosto di Maiale al Latte
Pork Pot-roasted in Milk

US		UK
2–2½ pounds	loin of pork	2–2½ pounds
5 tablespoons	olive oil	4 tablespoons
1 sprig	rosemary	1 sprig
½ clove	garlic	½ clove
	salt	
2½ cups	milk	1 pint

Have the pork boned and rolled. Heat the oil in a heavy casserole, one into which the meat will fit snugly. Add the rosemary and garlic, then the meat and salt. Fry the meat, turning it from time to time, until brown all over. Discard the rosemary and garlic. Pour the milk over the meat, cover the casserole and cook for about 1½ hours.

Cut the meat into medium-thick slices, arrange them on a hot platter and keep hot in a warm oven. Bring the sauce in the casserole to a quick boil, pour over the meat and serve immediately.

Serves 6.

Sguazzetto "a la Bechera"
"Butcher's" Stew

US		UK
2 pounds	variety meats (offal) — see method	2 pounds
	salt	
4 tablespoons	butter	2 ounces
4 tablespoons	olive oil	3 tablespoons
1	onion, finely chopped	1
1 clove	garlic	1 clove
1 stalk	celery, finely chopped	1 stalk
2	carrots, finely chopped	2
⅔ cup	dry white wine	¼ pint
	pepper	
1 sprig	thyme	1 sprig
4 teaspoons	tomato paste, diluted with	3 teaspoons
2 cups	stock	¾ pint

Use calf's heart, liver, lung and spleen in this recipe. Blanch them for 5 minutes in boiling salted water, drain and chop into small pieces.

Heat the butter and oil in a large pan, and gently sauté the onion, garlic, celery and carrots until they begin to brown. Discard the garlic and add the meat and wine. Simmer until the wine has evaporated a little, season with salt and pepper, and add the thyme and diluted tomato paste. Cover the pan and continue to cook slowly until the sauce is reduced. Discard the thyme and serve the meat very hot in its sauce.

Serves 4 to 6.

Fegato alla Veneziana
Liver Venetian Style

US		UK
2 pounds	calf's liver	2 pounds
2–3 tablespoons	olive oil	2 tablespoons
4 tablespoons	butter	2 ounces
1½ pounds	onions, thinly sliced	1½ pounds
2–3 sprigs	parsley, finely chopped	2–3 sprigs
	salt and pepper	

Italian liver is sliced much more thinly than is customary in the United States or in Britain. For this and other dishes which call for thinly sliced liver, it should resemble thinly sliced bacon.

Heat the oil and butter in a frying pan. Add the onions and sauté very gently until soft but not brown. Add the liver and cook for about 5 minutes over a brisk heat, browning it on both sides. Sprinkle with parsley, season with salt and plenty of pepper, and serve immediately with thick slices of hot polenta.

Serves 6.

Pâté di Fegato alla Veneziana
Liver Pâté Venetian Style

This recipe originated as a way in which to use up left-over *fegato alla veneziana*.

Chop the liver until reduced to a pulp or put it through a blender. Put the pulped liver in a bowl and blend thoroughly with an equal weight of butter. Flavor with a little brandy.

Butter one large deep dish or several small ones, depending on how much liver there is, and fill with the liver mixture. Put into a refrigerator and leave for at least 2 days before serving.

The pâté can be served either directly from the dish or turned out and cut into thin slices.

Fegato "Garbo e Dolce"
Sweet and Sour Liver

US		UK
2 pounds	calf's liver, very thinly sliced — see above	2 pounds
1–2	eggs	1–2
	salt	
	flour	
	fine dry breadcrumbs	
¾ cup	butter	6 ounces
	juice of 1 large lemon	
1½ teaspoons	sugar	1–1½ teaspoons

Beat the egg(s) with a pinch of salt. Lightly flour the slices of liver and dip them first into the beaten egg and then into breadcrumbs. Heat the butter in a frying pan and quickly fry the liver until brown on both sides. Transfer to a heated serving dish and keep hot in a warm oven.

Slowly heat the lemon juice with the sugar, stirring until the sugar is dissolved. Pour this mixture over the liver and serve hot.

Serves 6.

Trippa alla Trevisana
Tripe Treviso Style

US		UK
2½ pounds	dressed calf's tripe — see page 46	2½ pounds
4 tablespoons	butter	2 ounces
4 teaspoons	pork fat, finely chopped	3 teaspoons
1	onion, sliced	1
1 sprig	rosemary	1 sprig
2½ cups	beef stock	1 pint
12 slices	toasted bread	12 slices
	grated Parmesan cheese	

Wash the tripe, scald it and cut it into thin strips. Heat the butter and the pork fat in a large pan. Simmer for a few minutes, then add the onion, and when it begins to brown add the tripe and rosemary. Simmer for 5 minutes. Stir in the stock, cover the pan and continue cooking over a low heat for 30 to 45 minutes, or until the tripe is tender. Add more stock if necessary.

Put 2 slices of toast into each individual bowl and ladle the tripe over the top. Sprinkle with Parmesan cheese and serve immediately.

Serves 6.

"Polastro in Tecia"
Casseroled Chicken Veneto Style

US		UK
1	tender chicken, dressed – about 3 pounds	1
1½ tablespoons	olive oil	2 tablespoons
4 tablespoons	butter	2 ounces
1	onion, sliced	1
1	carrot, finely chopped	1
1 stalk	celery, finely chopped	1 stalk
½ cup	dry white wine	6–8 tablespoons
10-ounce can	Italian peeled tomatoes	10-ounce can
	salt and pepper	
2	cloves	2
pinch	ground cinnamon	pinch
1 pound	fresh button mushrooms	1 pound

Wipe the chicken and cut it into serving portions.

Heat the oil and butter in a fairly large casserole, and gently sauté the onion, carrot and celery. Add the pieces of chicken and brown them lightly, then add the wine and the tomatoes, season to taste with salt and pepper, and flavor with cloves and cinnamon. Continue cooking over a moderate heat until the chicken is tender. The cooking time depends entirely on the quality of the chicken. A young, tender chicken will be ready in about 1 hour, but an elderly bird will do better if allowed longer and slower cooking.

In the meantime, wash and slice the mushrooms (discarding their stems, which can be used in a soup). Add the mushrooms to the chicken about 20 minutes before serving.

Serves 4 to 6.

Anatra Ripiena
Stuffed Duck

US		UK
1	duck, dressed – about 4 pounds	1
	salt	
¼ pound	bacon, thinly sliced	¼ pound
½ cup	olive oil	6 tablespoons
4 teaspoons	butter	3 teaspoons
2 sprigs	rosemary	2 sprigs
Stuffing		
4 ounces	ground (UK minced) lean veal	4 ounces
3 tablespoons	pork fat, very finely chopped	1½ ounces
2 ounces	mixed pork and beef sausage meat	2 ounces
1	egg	1
2½ tablespoons	grated Parmesan cheese	2 tablespoons
1 clove	garlic, finely chopped	1 clove
2–3 sprigs	parsley, finely chopped	2–3 sprigs
	pith of 1 small bread roll, soaked in milk and squeezed dry	
	salt and pepper	

Put the duck giblets and liver aside; they can be used to make a soup stock. Wipe the bird with a damp cloth and rub inside with salt.

Mix all the stuffing ingredients together, adding salt and pepper to taste. Push this mixture into the duck and sew up the vent. Wrap the bacon slices round its breast and secure them with string or tiny skewers.

Put the oil, butter and rosemary into a casserole into which the duck will fit snugly. Add the duck, breast side uppermost, and roast, uncovered, in a hot oven (425°F. Mark 6) for 30 minutes. Take the duck from the oven and prick it well on the thighs and legs. Return it to the oven, lower the heat and continue roasting until tender, about 1 hour longer.

Take the duck from the pan, place it on a hot platter, and keep warm in the oven. Strain the sauce and serve it separately.

Serves 3 to 4.

Anatra in Salsa Piccante
Duck in Piquant Sauce

US		UK
1	duck, dressed – about 4 pounds	1
4 tablespoons	butter	2 ounces
½ cup	finely chopped bacon	2 ounces
1 sprig	rosemary, finely chopped	1 sprig
2–3 sprigs	sage, finely chopped	2–3 sprigs
1	lemon, halved	1
	salt and pepper	
¾ cup	mixed pork and beef sausage meat	6 ounces
1 clove	garlic, finely chopped	1 clove
2	anchovy fillets, finely chopped	2
½ cup	wine vinegar	6 tablespoons

Take out the giblets and liver from the duck and wipe the bird with a damp cloth. Melt the butter in an ovenproof casserole and add the bacon, rosemary and sage. Fry these ingredients for a few minutes, then add the lemon and the duck. Sprinkle with salt and pepper. Put the casserole in a hot oven (425°F. Mark 6), and roast the duck, uncovered, for 30 minutes. Take the duck from the oven, pour off any excess fat and prick the skin of the bird over the breast and thighs. Return the duck to the casserole and roast for another 30 minutes, basting frequently with the liquid in the casserole.

In another pan, gently fry the sausage meat, garlic and anchovies. When the sausage meat is brown, add the vinegar and continue cooking until reduced.

Take the casserole from the oven. Cut the duck into serving pieces and return them to the casserole. Cover with the sauce and return the casserole to the oven; lower the heat and simmer for another 30 minutes before serving, to allow the flavor of the sauce to penetrate the duck meat.

Serves 4.

"Masoro a la Valesana" – Anatra Selvatica alla Valligiana
Wild Duck as Cooked in the Valleys

US		UK
1	wild duck	1
2½ cups	wine vinegar	1 pint
pinch	thyme	pinch
pinch	marjoram	pinch
	salt	
½ cup	butter	4 ounces
4–5 slices	bacon	4–5 slices
1	onion, finely chopped	1
3	anchovy fillets, finely chopped	3
4 teaspoons	capers, finely chopped	1 tablespoon
1¼ cups	dry white wine	½ pint

Draw the duck and wash it quickly in cold water. Put it into a bowl with the wine vinegar and a good pinch of thyme and marjoram. Leave to marinate for 12 hours.

Drain the duck thoroughly, wipe it dry and sprinkle its cavity with salt. Spread the duck with half the butter. Cover its breast with the bacon slices and secure them with toothpicks, skewers or thread. Place on a rack in a roasting pan with a little hot water in the bottom of the pan. Roast in a hot oven (450°F. Mark 7), basting two or three times with its own juices – it should not cook longer than 20 minutes, less for those who like wild duck really underdone.

While the duck is cooking, heat the remaining butter and sauté the onion, anchovies and capers gently.

Take the duck from the oven and cut it into serving portions. Add these, together with the wine, to the simmering onion mixture, and continue cooking very slowly until the wine is reduced.

Serves 3 to 4.

"Capon a la Canevera"
Capon with Bamboo

US		UK
1	capon, dressed — about 6 pounds	1
1 cup	finely chopped beef	½ pound
1 cup	finely chopped guinea fowl meat	½ pound
1	pig's bladder	1
1 small piece	hollow bamboo cane	1 small piece
	salt and pepper	

This is a most unusual recipe and probably the most difficult part will be finding a suitable piece of hollow bamboo cane, although the pig's bladder may also present a problem. The bladder must be sound, without any holes, and large. If guinea fowl meat is not available, substitute chicken or duck meat.

Put the capon with the beef and guinea fowl meat into the pig's bladder, season with salt and pepper, and sew up the bladder, leaving a hole just large enough in which to insert the bamboo cane. Bring a large pan of salted water to the boil and cook the capon in this for about 3 hours, or until no more steam escapes from the bamboo.

Take the bladder from the pan, open it up and take out the capon. Cut the bird into serving portions and serve immediately, together with the beef and guinea fowl meats.

Serves 8.

Dindo alla Schiavona
Spit-roasted Turkey Slavonic Style

US		UK
1	young turkey, dressed — about 6 pounds	1
	salt	
6 large	raw chestnuts, peeled and skinned	6 large
8	dried prunes, pitted	8
2 hearts	celery, washed and chopped	2 hearts
¼ pound	bacon, thinly sliced	¼ pound

Rub the turkey inside and out with salt. Fill it with the chestnuts, prunes and celery. Pull back the skin over the neck and sew it up. Truss the turkey and tie the bacon slices round it, securing them firmly.

Thread the turkey on to a spit and roast in a gentle heat, basting from time to time with its own fat, collected in a pan under the spit. (It is difficult to give the exact cooking time, but allow at least 2½ hours.) To test whether the turkey is cooked, pull gently at the leg. If the meat behind looks white, then the turkey is ready.

Serve the turkey carved into portions, garnished with its stuffing and accompanied by fried chipped potatoes.

Serves 8.

"Paeta Arosto col Malgaragno"
Spit-roasted Turkey with Pomegranates

US		UK
1	turkey, dressed — about 8 pounds	1
3	pomegranates	3
	salt	
4 tablespoons	butter	2 ounces
4–6 slices	bacon	4–6 slices
2½ tablespoons	olive oil	2 tablespoons
	pepper	

To get the juice from a pomegranate squeeze it again and again (or roll it on a hard surface) until the seeds inside come loose. Make a small opening in the skin and pour the juice out. The pomegranate juice darkens the turkey sauce and gives the flesh a pleasing, somewhat bitter taste.

Rub the turkey inside with salt and butter. Sew up the loose crop neatly. Wrap the bacon slices over its breast and secure them firmly with thread or with skewers. Thread the turkey on to a spit and roast in a fair heat for 2 to 2½ hours, depending on the size of the bird. Baste it frequently with its own juices. After the turkey has been roasting for 1½ hours, baste it generously with the juice of 2 pomegranates and season lightly with salt. Continue roasting until the turkey is quite tender. To test whether it is ready, pull gently at one leg. If the meat behind it looks white, the turkey is ready.

While the turkey is roasting, chop its giblets and brown them in olive oil. Add the juice of the remaining pomegranate and the seeds of 1 pomegranate. Season to taste with salt and pepper, and continue cooking until the giblets are tender.

Carve the turkey into serving pieces, arrange them on a heated platter, and pour the giblets with their sauce over the top.

The turkey can also be oven-roasted in the usual manner.

Serves 8 to 10.

Faraona con "Peverada"
Guinea Fowl with Savory Sauce

US		UK
1	guinea fowl, dressed — see page 24	1
2 ounces	bacon, thinly sliced	2 ounces
	butter	
	salt	
Sauce		
1 cup	olive oil	scant ½ pint
3 slices	lemon	3 slices
2 cloves	garlic, finely chopped	2 cloves
	guinea fowl giblets, finely chopped	
½ cup	wine vinegar	6–8 tablespoons
	salt and pepper	

Wipe the guinea fowl inside and out with a damp cloth. Cover it with the bacon slices, securing them with toothpicks or skewers. Spread the guinea fowl generously with butter to counteract its dryness. Place in a casserole, sprinkle with salt and pot-roast very slowly on top of the stove until tender, about 45 minutes, depending on the heat and the age of the bird. Baste frequently with its own juices.

Sauce

Heat the oil, fry the lemon and garlic, add the giblets and let them brown slowly. Add the vinegar, season with salt and pepper, and cook for a further 15 to 20 minutes. Discard the lemon slices.

When the guinea fowl is tender, cut it into serving portions and arrange them on a heated serving dish. Pour over the sauce, boiling hot, and serve immediately.

Serves 3 to 4.

"Cape Longhe a la Capuzzina"
Razor-shell Soup

The razor-shell, of which there are several kinds, is a variety of clam. Its flesh is considered a delicacy.

Wash 4½ pounds razor-shells thoroughly in plenty of salted water. Heat 1 cup (U.K. scant ½ pint) oil and gently sauté 2 cloves garlic and 2 or 3 sprigs parsley, both finely chopped. Add the razor-shells and cook until the shells open in the heat.

Take the meat from the shells and put into a soup tureen. Pour over the strained cooking oil and serve with bread slices fried in oil.

Serves 6.

"Broeto" — Brodetto
Venetian Fish Soup

US		UK
5 pounds	assorted fish — see method	5 pounds
½	lemon	½
3 large	ripe tomatoes, peeled and chopped	3 large
	salt	
½ cup	olive oil	6–8 tablespoons
2 cloves	garlic, finely chopped	2 cloves
1 small	onion, finely chopped	1 small
2–3 sprigs	parsley, finely chopped	2–3 sprigs
12 slices	bread, crisply fried in oil	12 slices
	grated Parmesan cheese	

The following fish would be used in this version of an Italian fish soup: a grey mullet weighing about 3½ pounds, a ½-pound gudgeon, ½ pound gragnons or snapping shrimps, 6 sea-hens (*trigla lyra*) and 2 heads of *scorpaena porcus*. The mullet will require very careful washing to rid it of its muddy flavor. The gudgeon is a small, rather pretty fish and extremely tasty. Instead of the *scorpaena porcus* heads, a red fish related to the *rascasse* might be tried. Snapping shrimps can be replaced by ordinary shrimps. As for the sea-hen, this is a funny-looking fish with more head than body, and can be replaced by some cod or haddock heads.

Cut off the mullet's head, tail and fins, and put them into a large pan. Cut the mullet itself into rounds and put aside. Add all the remaining fish, lemon, tomatoes and salt to taste to the mullet trimmings, and cover with 10 cups (U.K. 4 pints) water. Cook over a moderate heat for 30 minutes. Strain.

Heat the oil in another large pan, sauté the garlic, onion and parsley until golden, then add the pieces of mullet. When the mullet is cooked, add the fish stock and bring to a slow boil. Put 2 slices of fried bread into each soup bowl, sprinkle generously with Parmesan and ladle the soup over the top. Serve immediately.

Serves 6.

"Sfogi in Saor" — Sogliole in Sapore
Venetian Fried Marinated Sole

US		UK
6	sole, filleted	6
	flour	
	oil	
	salt	
1	onion, sliced	1
1 cup	wine vinegar	scant ½ pint
1 cup	dry white wine	scant ½ pint
2	bay leaves	2
4 tablespoons	seedless white raisins (sultanas)	3 tablespoons
4 tablespoons	pine nuts	3 tablespoons
2	cloves	2
pinch	ground cinnamon	pinch
pinch	pepper	pinch

Traditionally this dish is served on the night of the Feast of the Holy Redeemer, the third Sunday in July. It is a day of great celebration, finishing with fireworks in the evening.

Lightly coat the fillets in flour. Heat plenty of oil and gently fry the fillets until golden brown on both sides. Drain on paper towels and sprinkle lightly with salt. In the same oil, lightly fry the onion until soft but not brown. Add the vinegar and the wine, and bring to the boil. Simmer for 5 minutes.

Arrange the fried fish in a large, flat, earthenware dish and pour over the onion and vinegar mixture. Add the remaining ingredients. Leave to marinate, covered, in a cool place for 2 days. Serve cold.

Serves 6.

"Bisato in Tecia"
Stewed Eel Venetian Style

US		UK
3–3½ pounds	small eels	3–3½ pounds
2½ cups	wine vinegar	1 pint
3	bay leaves	3
	salt	
3–4	black peppercorns	3–4
	fine dry breadcrumbs	
2½ tablespoons	olive oil	2 tablespoons
3 tablespoons	butter	1½ ounces
2 cloves	garlic, crushed	2 cloves
¼ cup	Marsala	3 tablespoons
4 tablespoons	tomato paste	3 tablespoons
	pepper	
2–3 sprigs	parsley, finely chopped	2–3 sprigs

Clean the eels and cut them every 2 or 2½ inches without slicing right through. Marinate them for several hours in all but 2 or 3 tablespoons of the wine vinegar with the bay leaves, a little salt and the peppercorns.

Drain the pieces of eel, dry them thoroughly and roll them in breadcrumbs, taking care that the pieces do not separate.

Heat the oil and butter in a large wide pan, and brown the garlic cloves. Discard them and add the eel. Brown the eel all over, add the remaining wine vinegar and Marsala, and continue cooking until they evaporate. Dilute the tomato paste with a little hot water and pour over the eels; season to taste with salt and pepper, and continue cooking until the pieces of eel separate – this will take about 20 minutes. Garnish with parsley and serve very hot.

Serves 6.

"Bisato sull'Ara"
Baked Eels

The literal translation of this recipe is "eels on the sacrificial altar". It is a favorite dish among the people of Murano, the island renowned for its glass furnaces. The eels are baked in the ovens used for the famous glass.

Clean 2 medium-sized eels and rub their skins with a piece of paper generously sprinkled with wood-ash to remove the fat. Wash them and cut them into largish pieces. In a baking dish, a copper one if possible, arrange a layer of 12 bay leaves and place the pieces of eel on top. Salt generously, moisten with a little water, and cover with another 12 bay leaves. Bake in a moderate oven (375°F. Mark 4) for 1 hour.

Serves 4.

"Bacalà Mantecato"
Cream of Salt Cod

US		UK
2½ pounds	pre-soaked salt cod—see page 50	2½ pounds
	olive oil	
2 cloves	garlic, finely chopped	2 cloves
2–3 sprigs	parsley, finely chopped	2–3 sprigs
	salt and pepper	

If the salt cod has not been pre-soaked, soak it in fresh water for at least 24 hours, changing the water every 8 hours.

Put the soaked cod into a large pan and cover with cold water. Bring to the boil slowly, remove the pan from the heat and leave the cod to soak for about 20 minutes. Drain, skin and bone the fish. Pound the flesh to a paste, gradually adding as much olive oil as it will absorb. Finally add the garlic, parsley, a little salt if necessary and a generous pinch of pepper. Serve cold with polenta.

Serves 6.

"Bacalà a la Visentina"
Salt Cod Vicenza Style

US		UK
2 pounds	pre-soaked salt cod – see page 50	2 pounds
1¼ cups	olive oil	½ pint
3	onions, sliced	3
2 cloves	garlic, finely chopped	2 cloves
2–3 sprigs	parsley, finely chopped	2–3 sprigs
3–4	anchovy fillets, finely chopped	3–4
¼ cup	flour	3 tablespoons
	salt and pepper	
2½ cups	milk	1 pint
2½ tablespoons	grated Parmesan cheese	2 tablespoons

If the cod is not pre-soaked, soak it in fresh water for at least 24 hours, changing the water every 8 hours.

Skin and bone the cod, and cut it into largish pieces. Heat the oil and fry the onion and garlic until they begin to brown. Add the parsley and anchovies. Lightly coat the pieces of cod with flour. Arrange them in a baking dish into which they will fit snugly, and pour over the onion mixture. Season with salt (if necessary– remember the fish is heavily salted) and pepper, cover with milk and sprinkle with cheese. Cover tightly and bake in a very slow oven (250°F. Mark ¼) for 4 to 5 hours, gently stirring from time to time. Serve with a stiff polenta, cut into slices.

Serves 6.

Aringhe in Insalata
Salt Herring Salad

US		UK
½ pound	salted herrings	½ pound
2 cups	cooked or canned white (haricot) beans	½ pound
1	onion, thinly sliced	1
¾ cup	black olives, pitted and halved	3–4 ounces
	salt and pepper	
¼ cup	olive oil	3 tablespoons
4 teaspoons	wine vinegar	1 tablespoon
2–3 sprigs	parsley, finely chopped	2–3 sprigs
2	hard-boiled eggs, quartered	2

Soak the herrings in cold water for at least 2 days, changing the water frequently to remove the salt and to soften them. Carefully remove heads, tails and skin. Split the herrings in two lengthwise, and remove the dorsal fin. Cut the flesh into small pieces.

Place the pieces of herring in a shallow salad dish, add the beans, onion and olives, mix lightly and dress with a very little salt, plenty of pepper, olive oil and wine vinegar. Garnish with parsley and hard-boiled eggs.

Serves 4.

"Moleche a la Muranese"
Soft-shelled Crabs Murano Style

Soft-shelled crabs are found in shoals in the Venetian lagoons in the spring and autumn, the two seasons when the crabs are changing their shells. They are then so light that they float to the surface of the lagoons and can be easily caught. At this time they are a slaty-greenish color. The little crabs are cooked while still alive and are consumed claws and all. In the following recipe the claws are trimmed off, but this is not usual.

Trim off the claws of 1½ pounds crabs and wash the crabs in salted water; then pat them dry. Beat 2 eggs with a pinch of salt. Roll the crabs in the beaten egg, then in flour. Deep-fry in hot oil until they change color, then take them from the pan with a perforated spoon, drain, sprinkle lightly with salt, and serve at once.

Serves 4.

Granseola
Crab Salad in the Shell

US		UK
3	crabs – see method	3
	salt	
	olive oil	
1	lemon	1
	pepper	
3 sprigs	parsley, finely chopped	3 sprigs

Granseola is the name for a large crab found only in the Adriatic and considered a great delicacy in Venice. It turns a bright scarlet color when cooked. Ordinary large crabs may be used instead.

Blanch the crabs in boiling salted water for 10 to 15 minutes. Leave them to cool. Clean them carefully without using undue pressure or squeezing, and shell them. Wash the shells. Chop the crab meat, making sure there are no shell splinters left. Return to the washed shells.

Dress with plenty of olive oil, lemon juice, salt and pepper, and garnish with parsley. Serve well chilled.

Serves 3.

Cape Sante
Scallops

US		UK
18	scallops	18
	fine dry breadcrumbs	
2–3 tablespoons	olive oil	2–3 tablespoons
3 tablespoons	butter	1½ ounces
1 clove	garlic, finely chopped	1 clove
2–3 sprigs	parsley, finely chopped	2–3 sprigs
½ cup	dry white wine	6–8 tablespoons
1	lemon	1

Usually scallops are bought opened, cleaned and neatly resting on the flat side of their shells. However, should it be necessary to prepare scallops yourself, this is how it is done. Put the scallops into a thick dry pan, cover and heat over a high heat until the shells open. Prise them open and lift off the scallops with a palette knife. Remove the beard and sac from each scallop, and clean the shell.

Coat the scallops with breadcrumbs. Heat the oil and butter together, and sauté the garlic and parsley. Add the scallops and fry them gently until browned. Moisten with wine and sprinkle with a little lemon juice. Continue cooking gently until the wine has evaporated. Replace the scallops in their shells (which should be heated) and serve hot.

Serve 2 or 3 scallops per person.

Bovoloni
Snails

US		UK
12 large	snails	12 large
	vine leaves and bread	
	coarse salt, flour and wine vinegar	
¼ cup	olive oil	3 tablespoons
1 clove	garlic, finely chopped	1 clove
2–3 sprigs	parsley, finely chopped	2–3 sprigs
	salt and pepper	

Bovoli are a species of large snail, traditionally eaten on Christmas Eve. *Bovoloni* means they are extra large.

Leave the snails for 2 days in a wicker basket with a few vine leaves and some pieces of bread soaked in water, covered to prevent them escaping but not so tightly as to stop the air circulating.

Put a mixture of coarse salt, flour and vinegar in a bowl (enough to coat the snails), add the snails and stir them round and about until the snails are completely covered with foam. Repeat this procedure several times until there is no more foam. Wash the snails under cold running water until quite free of the flour, salt and vinegar mixture. Put them in a pan with water to cover and leave them for 5 minutes. Drain well.

Fill a pan with cold water, add the snails and cook over a gentle heat until they begin to show their heads. Immediately increase the heat and cook rapidly for 10 minutes. Drain the snails (reserving the liquid) and once more drop them into cold water. Drain.

In another pan, heat the oil and gently sauté the garlic and parsley. Add 1¼ cups (U.K. ½ pint) of the snail liquid to make a sauce. Add the snails, season to taste with salt and pepper, and simmer for 1½ hours. Serve the snails in their shells, accompanied by their sauce.

Serves 2 to 3.

Omelette con i Gamberetti
Shrimp Omelette

US		UK
2 tablespoons	butter	1 ounce
½ pound	shrimps, peeled	½ pound
	salt and pepper	
8	eggs	8
2½ tablespoons	olive oil	2 tablespoons
2 sprigs	parsley, finely chopped	2 sprigs

Melt the butter and gently cook the peeled shrimps over a very low heat for a few minutes, adding a pinch of salt. Beat the eggs lightly with ¼ teaspoon salt and a little pepper.

Heat the oil in a frying pan and pour in the eggs. Draw the mixture from the sides with a fork so that the whole omelette cooks quickly. When the omelette is set on the bottom, add the shrimps and fold the omelette over. Continue cooking a minute or so until the top is just beginning to set but is still slightly runny, unless a dry omelette is preferred, in which case, cook a little longer until the desired dryness is obtained. Serve garnished with parsley.

Serves 4.

Frittata coi Piselli
Green Pea Omelette Veneto Style

US		UK
4 tablespoons	butter	2 ounces
1 small	onion, finely chopped	1 small
½ cup	diced ham	2 ounces
1 small bulb	Florence fennel, shredded – see page 68	1 small bulb
2 cups	shelled green peas	½ pound
	salt and pepper	
6	eggs	6
2–3 sprigs	parsley, finely chopped	2–3 sprigs

Melt half the butter and sauté the onion, ham, fennel and peas for a few minutes. Sprinkle with salt and pepper, add a little boiling water or stock, and simmer until the fennel is tender – by which time all the other ingredients in the pan will also be cooked.

Beat the eggs lightly with a pinch of salt and stir in the parsley. Drain the vegetable mixture and add it to the beaten eggs.

Melt the remaining butter in a large frying pan. Pour in the egg mixture and fry until the underside is set and golden brown. Turn the omelette out on to a large plate and slip it back into the pan to brown the other side. Serve flat, not folded over like a French omelette.

Serves 3 to 4.

Patate alla Triestina
Potato Cake Trieste Style

US		UK
3½ pounds	potatoes	3½ pounds
	salt	
6 tablespoons	pork fat, finely chopped	3 ounces
2 tablespoons	butter	1 ounce
2½ tablespoons	olive oil	2 tablespoons
1	onion, sliced	1
⅔ cup	stock	¼ pint

Scrub the potatoes and boil them in salted water until tender. Drain them, peel and cut into slices.

Sauté the pork fat in butter and oil in a large frying pan. Add the onion slices and sauté until golden. Add the sliced potatoes, season to taste with salt and pepper, and moisten with stock. Crush the potatoes with a fork – they should be somewhat lumpy, not smooth like mashed potatoes – and cook them over a moderate heat until the underside is crisp and brown. Turn the potato cake out on to a plate and slide it into the pan to brown the other side. Serve hot.

Serves 4 to 6.

Carciofi alla Venezia Giulia
Artichokes Venezia Giulia Style

US		UK
6	very young artichokes – see method	6
1	lemon	1
6–8 tablespoons	fresh breadcrumbs	5–7 tablespoons
1 clove	garlic, finely chopped	1 clove
2–3 sprigs	parsley, finely chopped	2–3 sprigs
1 cup	olive oil	scant ½ pint
	salt and pepper	

The artichokes must be so young that they have not yet formed a choke. Prepare the artichokes by cutting the stalk so close that each artichoke will stand easily on its base, and trim off the tougher and lower leaves. Open out the remaining leaves and soak the artichokes in water acidulated with lemon juice for 15 minutes.

Combine the breadcrumbs, garlic, parsley and 2 or 3 tablespoons of the olive oil to make a stuffing. Season to taste.

Drain the artichokes and push the stuffing in between the leaves. Arrange them side by side in a pan, standing upright, pour over the remaining oil and add enough water to come half-way up the sides of the artichokes. Cover the pan, bring to the boil and simmer until tender. Young artichokes will take 30 minutes to cook, older ones up to an hour. A little more hot water may be required while the artichokes are cooking.

Serves 6.

"Papriche Stufate"
Stewed Sweet Peppers

US		UK
2 pounds	sweet green or yellow peppers	2 pounds
1 cup	olive oil	scant ½ pint
1 clove	garlic	1 clove
2 pounds	tomatoes, peeled and chopped	2 pounds
	salt and pepper	
2–3 sprigs	parsley, finely chopped	2–3 sprigs

Wash the peppers, cut them in half and discard cores and seeds. Cut the flesh into even strips. Heat the oil in a pan and sauté the garlic until it browns, then discard it. Add the strips of pepper and cook them gently for 15 minutes. Cover with the tomatoes, season to taste, and continue cooking until the tomatoes are reduced to a thick sauce. Serve hot or cold, garnished with parsley.

Serves 6.

"Fugazza di Pasqua"
Easter Bread

US		UK
3½ cakes	compressed (fresh) yeast	2½ ounces
	lukewarm milk	
9 cups	all-purpose (plain) flour	2¼ pounds
	salt	
6	eggs, well beaten	6
1¼ cups	granulated (caster) sugar	10 ounces
1 cup	melted and cooled butter	½ pound
	butter for baking sheet	
	beaten egg, to glaze	

Dissolve the yeast in a little lukewarm milk. Sift 2 cups (½ pound) of the flour into a large warmed bowl with a pinch of salt. Add the yeast and work into the flour with enough extra milk to make a smooth dough. Cover the bowl and leave to rise for about 1 hour, or until doubled in bulk. Sift the remaining flour into another bowl and let it warm gently.

When the dough has risen, punch it down and work in half the eggs, half the sugar, 2½ cups (10 ounces) of the remaining flour, and finally half the melted butter. Knead vigorously until the dough is smooth and no longer sticky. Cover the bowl and leave to rise again until doubled in bulk. This time it will take at least 2 hours.

Punch down the dough again and work in the remaining flour (4½ cups or 1 pound 2 ounces) and the remaining eggs, sugar and butter. Knead until smooth and leave to rise for at least 5 hours.

Punch the risen dough down, knead lightly and shape it into 2 or 3 large buns. Transfer them to buttered baking sheets, brush the tops with beaten egg and leave to rise for the final time.

Bake in a moderately hot oven (400°F. Mark 5) for 30 to 40 minutes, or until the buns are well risen and golden brown.

The dough may be flavored with vanilla, grated orange or lemon rind, or almond extract.

"Fritole"
Spiced Rum Fritters

US		UK
⅔ cup	seedless white raisins (sultanas)	3 ounces
⅔ cup	rum	¼ pint
1½ cakes	compressed (fresh) yeast	1 ounce
½ cup	lukewarm water	6–8 tablespoons
4 cups	all-purpose (plain) flour	1 pound
¼ cup	vanilla sugar	2 ounces
pinch	salt	pinch
	grated rind of 1 lemon	
5 tablespoons	pine nuts	2 ounces
pinch	ground cinnamon	pinch
⅓ cup	candied peel, finely chopped	2 ounces
	oil for deep-frying	
	confectioners' (icing) sugar	

Soak the white raisins (sultanas) in rum until plump and swollen.

Dissolve the yeast in lukewarm water. Sift the flour into a large warmed bowl and make a well in the middle. Add the dissolved yeast, sugar, salt, grated rind, pine nuts, the raisins with their rum, a pinch of cinnamon and the peel. Mix thoroughly with a wooden spoon, adding a little more lukewarm water if necessary, cover the bowl with a cloth and leave to rise in a warm place for about 4 hours, or until doubled in bulk.

Punch the dough down and knead until smooth, adding a little more water if necessary to make a soft, very pliable dough.

Heat a large pan of oil and fry teaspoonfuls of the dough, a few at a time, until golden. Drain on paper towels and serve immediately, dusted with sifted confectioners' (icing) sugar.

Serves 8 to 10.

"Zaleti" – Gialletti
Yellow Diamonds

US		UK
1½ cups	fine cornmeal	½ pound
2 cups	all-purpose (plain) flour	½ pound
¾ cup	seedless white raisins (sultanas)	¼ pound
⅔ cup	rum	¼ pint
3 large	egg yolks	3 large
¾ cup	granulated (caster) sugar	6 ounces
	salt	
pinch	vanilla powder or vanilla extract to taste	pinch
	grated rind of 1 lemon	
1 cup	butter, melted	½ pound
⅓ cup	pine nuts	2 ounces
	butter for baking sheet	
	confectioners' (icing) sugar	

Sift the cornmeal and flour together into a bowl. Soak the white raisins (sultanas) in rum until swollen. Drain and pat dry. Beat the egg yolks and sugar until smooth and thick. Gradually add the cornmeal and flour, a pinch of salt, the vanilla, grated rind and melted butter. Work to a smooth dough, knead well, then knead in the raisins and pine nuts. Roll out fairly thickly on a lightly floured board and cut into small diamond shapes. Arrange on well-buttered baking sheets and bake in a moderate oven (375°F. Mark 4) for about 20 minutes, or until golden.

Sprinkle with confectioners' (icing) sugar and eat warm or cold.

Strangolapreti
Nut Cake

US		UK
½ pound	sponge cake, crumbled	½ pound
½ cup	seedless white raisins (sultanas), soaked in	3 ounces
½ cup	rum	6 tablespoons
¾ cup	shelled walnuts	3 ounces
½ cup	pine nuts	3 ounces
½ cup	almonds, peeled and finely chopped	3 ounces
⅓ cup	diced mixed candied peel	2 ounces
about ½ cup	sugar syrup	6–8 tablespoons
	butter for cake pan	

Mix all the ingredients together until well blended, adding enough sugar syrup (made with 2 parts sugar to 1 part water) to hold the mixture together. Turn into a well-buttered rectangular pan and bake in a moderate oven (375°F. Mark 4) for 20 to 30 minutes.

Leave to cool, turn out and serve cut in thick slices.

Favette
"Little Beans" or Rum Cookies (U.K. Biscuits)

US		UK
2 cups	all-purpose (plain) flour	8 ounces
½ teaspoon	baking powder	½ teaspoon
4 tablespoons	softened butter	2 ounces
2½ tablespoons	granulated (caster) sugar	2 tablespoons
2	eggs	2
3–4 tablespoons	rum	3 tablespoons
	oil for deep-frying	
	confectioners' (icing) sugar	

Make a dough with the flour, baking powder, butter, sugar, eggs and rum, and knead for at least 15 minutes until the dough is light and pliable. Divide it into two pieces and shape each piece into a roll the thickness of a finger. Cut into 2-inch lengths.

Deep-fry the little rolls in hot oil, a few at a time, drain on paper towels and dust with sifted confectioners' (icing) sugar.

LIGURIA

Trenette col pesto, the great Ligurian dish of noodles with *pesto*, or basil sauce (see page 86), whose preparation, though simple, requires meticulous care and great patience.

The heart of Genoa lies in its waterfront—bars and taverns where you may hear a dozen languages spoken at once, booths at which every kind of currency may be exchanged, inns and boardinghouses of every description, restaurants and eating houses to suit all pockets, and both indoor and outdoor markets, often of doubtful legality. Local color predominates, with sailors from every land bringing to the picture just a touch of their own native country. But there is one element that pervades the whole area, as well as the whole of Greater Genoa from Arenzano to Sestri Levante—a characteristic odor that rises above the sharp, pungent smell of sea brine. This is the aroma of *pesto,* the traditional sauce of Genoa, as penetrating and evocative as Bavarian sauerkraut or the perfume of cognac in a cellar in south-west France.

Pesto is made of fresh sweet basil, garlic, ewe's milk cheese, pine nuts (or walnuts) and olive oil. The ingredients are placed together in a mortar and pounded without mercy until they resolve themselves into a smooth, aromatic sauce in which the fragrance of basil predominates. This operation calls for much patience, careful dosage and rapid but skillfully calculated movements. Basil can be seen everywhere in Genoa. In the working-class districts, on the window-sills of tenement houses that are hundreds of years old and that have been reshaped, modernized, patched up but never pulled down and rebuilt, the herb flourishes in vases, saucepans and empty tins, tended with the same loving care that the inhabitants of the Alto Adige bestow on the geraniums with which they decorate their windows and balconies.

Pizza all'Andrea, decorated with black olives and garlic cloves, and dressed with Ligurian olive oil, which is said to be the finest in all Italy. According to legend, this was the favorite dish of the famous Genoese admiral Andrea Doria.

Seafood displayed in the port of Oneglia in the late afternoon when the fishing boats come in.
Below: Specialties of Dolceaqua in the province of Imperia: eel and trout from the River Nervia, casseroled rabbit, late grapes, sweet cakes known as *michette*, and Rossese wine. In the background, the Roman bridge and the ruins of Doria Castle.

Below: By the Well of Garitta in Albisola, home since the seventeenth century of the potters' kilns: a dish of seafood, and *cima alla genovese*, or stuffed veal (see page 88).

Condiglione, an enormous mixed salad (see page 91) prepared for special occasions.
Below: A fine display of fish and shellfish in the Ristorante "Liscia d'oro" at Porto Venere.

Between the loggias of the ancient monastery of Santa Chiara, overlooking the sea at Porto Maurizio, three mouth-watering Ligurian dishes: *sarde ripiene*, or stuffed sardines, *stoccafisso in umido*, or stewed salt cod, and the world-famous *burrida*, Genoese fish stew (see page 89), accompanied by *Sciacchetrà di Pornassio*, a fine local wine with a distinctive *bouquet*.

A selection of Ligurian cakes and candies, photographed in the historic center of Genoa behind the church of Our Lady of the Vines: a basket of Lenten sweetmeats known as *quaresimali*, candied fruits, sugared almonds, fondants, little meringues, and *pandolce*, the great, golden brown, sweet bread of Genoa (see page 92).

The sea provides many of the raw materials of Genoese cooking. Fish is the main ingredient of two classic soups or stews, *burrida* (see page 89) and *ciuppin* (a puréed fish soup similar to the French *bouillabaisse*), and with the exception of a few but excellent meat dishes, it dominates the menu. Dried salt cod from distant Norway, which we have already met in the Veneto, is popular here too, and vegetables blend with every dish, above all with fish in the classic *cappon magro* (see page 90), the most fanciful fish salad in all Italy.

Genoa is also celebrated for having invented ravioli at a time when it had not yet been discovered that pasta could be made with soft-grain flour by binding the dough with eggs (a problem not posed by hard-grain flour). Ravioli then spread throughout Italy, especially to Emilia, where they appear under different names but with the same subtle and delicate flavors. *Farinate*, or soups made with flour, are also characteristic of Genoese cooking, which has, too, its own version of pizza, made with large quantities of anchovies, garlic and black olives, which distinguish it from the more familiar Neapolitan version.

As in so many other parts of Italy, Ligurian cooking relies heavily on the use of olive oil. The coast of the two Ligurian Rivieras provides ideal conditions for the cultivation of olives. Changes in temperature are gradual and never extreme, and the sun shines from a clear sky all the year round, even when the neighboring plain of the Po is wrapped in a thick blanket of fog. The remarkable lightness and transparency of Ligurian oil is due to its being unrefined. The olives are gathered and sent to the mills without delay, instead of being stored for several months in warehouses, as happens in so many other regions. The center of the oil trade is at Oneglia, situated on the Riviera west of Genoa, where, too, can be seen some of the most enchanting gardens in the world and magnificent plantations of carnations which stretch all along the coast from Bordighera and San Remo to the French border.

Liguria also has its own special sweet dishes: sugar beans filled with cocoa, fruit and almond pastes, candied fruits and the celebrated *pandolce genovese* (see page 92). If your tooth is less sweet, however, there is *focaccia*, a savory bread made with olive oil and sage or cheese (see page 85).

Beyond Genoa, beyond Rapallo, Portofino and Sestri, perched high above the rocky coast, are the Cinque Terre, the five villages of Riomaggiore, Manarola, Corniglia, Vernazza and Monterosso, whose vineyards provide the wines for which the region is famous. Among these are Sciachettrà Bianco, a white wine with a slightly bitter *bouquet*, not to be confused with Sciachettrà Rosso, a red dessert wine. Other light Ligurian wines include Rossese, the best of which comes from Val Nervia, Vermentino, Ligasolio (which delighted Napoleon), and Polcevera, which is made in the valley of the same name in the Genoese hinterland.

Focaccia alla Salvia
Sage Bread

US		UK
8 cups	all-purpose (plain) flour	2 pounds
3 cakes	compressed (fresh) yeast	2 ounces
about 1 cup	lukewarm water	scant ½ pint
	olive oil	
	salt	
6 leaves	sage, finely chopped	6 leaves

Sift the flour into a warmed bowl. Dissolve the yeast in lukewarm water. Make a well in the middle of the flour, add the yeast, gently cover with flour (from the bowl) and leave for 20 minutes in a warm place. Knead well, adding just enough lukewarm water to make a firm dough which comes away from the sides of the bowl. Cover and again leave in a warm place until the dough rises – between 1 and 2 hours, according to the quality of the yeast and flour, and the warmth of the room. When the dough is doubled in bulk, knead it again until smooth, adding ½ cup oil (U.K. 6 to 8 tablespoons), a little salt and the sage. Roll out on a floured board to a thickness of about ½ inch.

Grease the required number of baking sheets with oil, add the rolled-out dough and again cover and leave until it has risen. Prick the surface with a fork, sprinkle lightly with salt and bake in a moderately hot oven (400°F. Mark 5) for about 30 minutes, or until golden brown. Serve hot or warm.

Serves 6 to 8.

Pesto alla Genovese
Genoese Green Sauce or Basil Sauce

This is a famous sauce rarely met outside of Genoa and is considered an invention of the Ligurians, who live in a land which is always green. There is a saying that he who eats *pesto* never leaves Genoa. It is used in all kinds of pasta dishes and is an essential and traditional part of *trenette* (a dish of egg noodles) and Genoese vegetable soup. The housewives of Liguria collect the fresh young leaves of the basil plant (which they insist is the best in Italy) and put them into a mortar with garlic, and pound with great patience and diligence until they have a piquant, delicious paste. Some cooks insist that only a marble mortar can be used, others, more modern, use a blender, which is quick and very effective.

Put 2 cloves garlic, 4 small bunches of fresh basil leaves, a pinch of coarse salt, and a tablespoon of toasted pine nuts, if liked, in a mortar. Pound to a paste. Continue pounding, gradually adding 3 or 4 tablespoons each of grated Parmesan and Pecorino cheese. When the paste is smooth, stir in a cup of olive oil.

This quantity of *pesto* is sufficient for 1 pound noodles and will serve 3.

Agliata
Garlic Sauce

US		UK
	soft pith of 1 large bread roll	
4 teaspoons	wine vinegar	1 tablespoon
3 cloves	garlic, finely chopped	3 cloves
2–3 sprigs	basil, chopped	2–3 sprigs
2–3 sprigs	parsley, chopped	2–3 sprigs
	salt	
1 cup	olive oil	scant ½ pint
	pepper	

This sauce is somewhat reminiscent of the Provençal *aïoli* which consists of garlic, egg yolks and olive oil, but similar recipes run right through the Latin countries and the Balkans. Even this recipe, although claimed as Ligurian, originated in Marseilles. It is frequently served with fried salt cod or fried calf's liver.

Soak the bread in the vinegar and squeeze it dry. Pound the garlic with the basil, parsley, salt and bread to a thick, creamy paste. Add the oil, a drop at a time, stirring constantly. When the oil is completely blended into the sauce, add pepper to taste.

Serves 6.

Salsa di Noci
Walnut Sauce

US'		UK
½ pound	walnut kernels, ground (UK minced)	½ pound
⅓ cup	toasted pine nuts	2 ounces
½ clove	garlic	½ clove
2½ tablespoons	finely chopped marjoram or parsley	2 tablespoons
	salt	
½ cup	Ricotta or good-quality cottage cheese	4 ounces
½ cup	olive oil	6 tablespoons

Put the walnuts, pine nuts, garlic and marjoram or parsley in a mortar, add a pinch of salt and pound to a smooth paste. Add the cheese and about 1 tablespoon water. When blended, gradually add the olive oil and continue stirring until the sauce is creamy.

This sauce is frequently served with pasta and in particular with *pansôti*, a variety of ravioli – see page 87. It is sufficient for 1½ pounds noodles. When serving the walnut sauce with noodles, Ligurians (and other Italians) also mix in butter and grated Parmesan cheese.

Sugo di Carne
Meat Sauce

US		UK
3 tablespoons	beef suet, finely chopped	1½ ounces
4 tablespoons	butter	2 ounces
1 pound	lean beef, chopped	1 pound
¼	onion, sliced	¼
¼ clove	garlic	¼ clove
1 stalk	celery, finely chopped	1 stalk
1	carrot, sliced	1
pinch	rosemary *or*	pinch
1 ounce	dried mushrooms, soaked	1 ounce
1 cup	red wine	scant ½ pint
3 large	ripe tomatoes, peeled and chopped	3 large
	salt and pepper	
1¼ cups	meat stock	½ pint

Gently heat the suet and butter together in a large pan. When completely melted and hot, add the meat and brown it lightly all over. Add the onion, garlic, celery, carrot and rosemary (some recipes used mushrooms instead of rosemary).

Add the wine, stir well and cook over a moderate heat for about 15 minutes to reduce the wine a little. Add the tomatoes. Lower the heat, season to taste with salt and pepper, and cook slowly, covered, for about 4 hours. Add the stock in small quantities from time to time, and let the meat cook to a pulp.

Rub the meat and its sauce through a fine sieve.

This sauce is used with noodles and is sufficient for 1½ pounds noodles, or for 6 people. It is often served with *corzetti* – see page 87.

Torta Pasqualina
Easter Cheese and Spinach Pie

US		UK
Dough		
8 cups	all-purpose (plain) flour	2 pounds
5 tablespoons	olive oil	4 tablespoons
1 teaspoon	salt	1 teaspoon
2 pounds	spinach or spring greens, *or*	2 pounds
10	artichoke hearts	10
	olive oil	
½	onion, finely chopped	½
1 pound	Ricotta or cottage cheese	1 pound
1 cup	milk	scant ½ pint
	salt	
4 tablespoons	butter	2 ounces
6	eggs	6
	pepper	
pinch	marjoram	pinch
¾ cup	grated Parmesan cheese	3 ounces

This recipe is reminiscent of the Balkan cheese pies. It takes some time to make the pastry and roll it out into rounds of the required thinness, but this work can be circumvented by using either *strudel* pastry or Balkan *filo* pastry, both of which are obtainable in Greek and other shops dealing in Balkan foods.

Dough
If making your own pastry and it tears while rolling, do not worry. The sheets with holes can be used for the bottom section. The four top sheets should be near perfect, and the top sheet must be perfect.

Mix the flour, oil and salt, and gradually add enough water to make a stiff dough which leaves the sides of the bowl cleanly – be careful when adding water; the dough will become sticky if too much is used. Knead the dough thoroughly and divide it into 10 equal-sized balls (originally the dough was divided into 33 pieces, one for each year of our Lord's life). Put these on a lightly floured pastry board, cover with a damp cloth and leave for 15 minutes.

If using spinach or spring greens, wash these in two or three waters and cook in as little water as possible until soft. If using artichoke hearts, they will probably be canned, so drain them from their liquid, chop and put aside until required.

Heat 5 tablespoons (U.K. 4 tablespoons) oil and sauté the onion until soft but not brown. Drain the spinach or spring greens and chop finely. Add whatever vegetable is being used to the pan, and mix gently with the onion. Continue cooking for a few moments longer and put aside to cool until required.

Mix the Ricotta with the milk and add a pinch of salt. Put aside. Brush a large, deep pie dish with oil.

Roll one ball of pastry into a wafer-thin sheet, keeping the rest of the pastry balls under the damp cloth. Line the prepared pie dish, brush lightly with oil and trim off excess pastry. Repeat this with five more balls of pastry, brushing each layer with oil, and laying one on top of the other.

Spread the sixth layer of pastry with the cooked onion and vegetables, and on top of this spread the Ricotta cheese. Hollow out 6 wells in the filling and into each well drop a sliver of butter and one egg. Sprinkle with salt, pepper, marjoram and Parmesan.

Roll out the remaining balls of pastry in precisely the same manner and pile them, one by one, on top of the filling, brushing each layer with oil. Prick the top layer with a fork, brush it generously with oil and trim off any overlapping pastry. Bake in a moderately hot oven (400°F. Mark 5) for about 40 minutes, or until the pie is golden brown. Serve hot or cold.

, Serves 6.

Tagliatelle Verdi
Green Ribbon Noodles Liguria Style

US		UK
2½ tablespoons	olive oil	2 tablespoons
1 small	onion, finely chopped	1 small
4 small	Italian pork sausages, skinned and crumbled	4 small
1	calf's sweetbread, cooked and chopped	1
1 cup	shredded cooked borage and spinach	5–6 ounces
	salt	
2½ tablespoons	grated Parmesan cheese	2 tablespoons
5 cups	all-purpose (plain) flour	1¼ pounds
4	eggs	4
Dressing		
	well-flavored mushroom sauce or gravy from roast beef	
	grated Parmesan cheese	

Tagliatelle are the most common type of noodles still made at home. The following recipe is somewhat unusual, but not difficult.

Heat the oil and sauté the onion until golden brown and soft. Add the sausage meat and the sweetbread, and when these are browned add the borage and spinach, and stir well. (If borage is not available, use only spinach.) Season to taste with salt and leave for 5 minutes to develop flavors. Stir in the cheese, then rub everything through a fine sieve to make a paste.

Sift the flour on to a pastry board and make a well in the middle. Add the eggs, start working a little of the flour into them, and then add the meat and spinach paste. Continue to work all the flour into the eggs and paste, adding enough warm water to make a soft but firm, smooth dough. Knead the dough vigorously until elastic, keeping the board and your hands well floured. Roll the dough out into a thin sheet. Leave it to dry, uncovered, for 30 minutes, then cut into strips just under ½ inch wide (the correct width is that of a cotton tape, called *picaggia*, hence these noodles are locally called *picagge*). Leave the strips of dough to dry.

Bring 3 or 4 quarts of salted water to a bubbling boil in a large pan. Cook the noodles for 10 minutes, or until tender. Drain well and turn into a heated serving dish. Mix at once with a good mushroom sauce or gravy, and serve with a large bowl of grated Parmesan cheese.

Serves 6.

Trenette col Pesto
Trenette Noodles with Pesto

US		UK
1½ pounds	trenette noodles – see method	1½ pounds
4 medium-sized	potatoes, peeled	4 medium-sized
	salt	
1¼ cups	Pesto alla Genovese – page 85	½ pint
	grated Pecorino or Parmesan cheese	

Trenette are ribbon-shaped noodles. Many Genoese declare that traditionally *pesto* should be served only with *trenette*. Traditional or not, for many people, not only the Genoese, *trenette* with *pesto* make one of the best noodle dishes in the whole of Italy.

Dice the potatoes and put them into a very large pan with plenty, at least 3 or 4 quarts, of salted water. Bring this to the boil and then add the *trenette*; stir well and continue cooking until tender but *al dente* or slightly resistant to the bite – about 12 minutes for commercially prepared noodles.

Drain and drop the noodles and potatoes into a deep heated serving dish. Dilute the *pesto* with a ladleful of the liquid in which the noodles were cooked and mix it in quickly. Serve very hot, accompanied by a bowl of grated cheese.

Serves 6.

Corzetti
Ligurian Noodles or "Figures of Eight"

US		UK
6 cups	all-purpose (plain) flour	1½ pounds
6–8	eggs, lightly beaten	6–8
	salt	
1 recipe	Meat Sauce – see page 85	1 recipe
¾ cup	grated Parmesan cheese	3 ounces

These noodles are a specialty of Polcevera, and are often available ready-made in Ligurian shops.

Sift the flour on to a large pastry board, make a well in the middle and carefully pour in the eggs. Add salt and gradually work the flour into the eggs to make a smooth, soft dough. Flour the board and knead the dough until smooth and elastic.

Break off small pieces of the dough, roughly the size of a large pea. Roll into small balls and then press each one between the thumb and the first finger to make the noodle look like two joined discs or a figure of eight. Spread out on a clean cloth to dry.

Bring a large pan of salted water to the boil and add the *corzetti*, cooking them in batches so they do not stick together. As they float to the top of the pan, take them out with a perforated spoon and drain them well in a colander. Serve with Meat Sauce and grated Parmesan cheese.

Serves 6.

"Pansôti" di Rapallo
Ravioli Rapallo Style

US		UK
Dough		
5 cups	all-purpose (plain) flour	1¼ pounds
5–6	eggs	5–6
	salt	
Stuffing		
¾ pound	spinach, spinach beet or spring greens	¾ pound
3	hard-boiled eggs, chopped	3
⅓ cup	grated Pecorino or Parmesan cheese	2 ounces
	salt	
Garnish		
1¼ cups	Walnut Sauce – page 85	½ pint
¾ cup	grated Parmesan cheese	3 ounces

The literal translation of *pansôti* is "pot-bellied".

Dough
Prepare the dough as above. Cover with a cloth and leave for 30 minutes.

Stuffing
Thoroughly wash the greens and cook with very little water until tender. Drain well and chop finely. Put into a bowl, add the hard-boiled eggs, cheese and salt to taste, and blend until smooth.

Divide the dough into two equal pieces and roll these out into two thin sheets identical in size and shape. Arrange teaspoonfuls of stuffing in neat rows about 1½ inches apart on one of the sheets. Cover with the second sheet of dough and press down well between the small mounds of stuffing to seal them. Cut between the mounds with a pastry wheel or a very sharp knife to form squares. Spread them on a clean cloth and leave them, uncovered, for 30 minutes.

Bring a large pan of salted water to the boil, add the ravioli, a few at a time, and cook for about 10 minutes, or until tender. Take them out with a perforated spoon and drain in a colander. Serve dressed with Walnut Sauce and grated Parmesan.

Serves 6.

Minestrone alla Genovese
Genoese Vegetable Soup

US		UK
1⅓ cups	fresh or dried white (haricot) beans	½ pound
6–7 pints	water	5–6 pints
	salt	
1	onion, thinly sliced	1
2 stalks	celery, diced	2 stalks
1	carrot, sliced	1
½ cup	olive oil	6 tablespoons
3	zucchini (courgettes), sliced	3
3	potatoes, peeled and diced	3
4 large	tomatoes, peeled and chopped	4 large
small bunch	borage, finely chopped	small bunch
½ pound	maccheroncini rigati, broken into short lengths – see method	½ pound
5 teaspoons	Pesto alla Genovese – page 85	1½ tablespoons
4 tablespoons	Pecorino Sardo cheese, grated	3 tablespoons

Genoese vegetable soup is made when there is a good and varied supply of fresh vegetables in the market. The vegetables can be changed according to taste as well as season. Genoese cooks use leeks, pumpkin, cabbage, squash (marrow), dried or fresh mushrooms, peas and often eggplants (aubergines). It is a good, thick soup like any other similar vegetable soup the world over. What distinguishes the Genoese vegetable soup is the addition of *pesto*. This favorite sauce is always added to a Genoese vegetable soup, whatever the choice of vegetables.

Maccheroncini rigati are a variety of ribbed macaroni, and Pecorino Sardo is a very piquant ewe's milk cheese. If not available, use ordinary Pecorino, or even Parmesan, a more generous portion of the latter.

If using dried white (haricot) beans they must be soaked overnight and partially cooked *without* salt before being added to the soup.

Put the beans into a large pan with the water, salt, the onion, celery, carrot and 5 tablespoons (U.K. 4 tablespoons) oil. Bring to the boil, lower the heat and simmer for 1 hour. Add the zucchini (courgettes), potatoes, tomatoes and borage. Continue cooking for another 30 minutes. Add the *maccheroncini*, and as soon as they are tender, stir in the *pesto*, the remaining oil and the cheese.

Serves 6 to 8.

Trippa con il Sugo di Tocco
Tripe with Meat Sauce

US		UK
2 pounds	dressed tripe – see page 46	2 pounds
1	onion	1
1	carrot	1
2 stalks	celery	2 stalks
1½ ounces	dried mushrooms	1½ ounces
1 recipe	Meat Sauce – see page 85	1 recipe
	salt and pepper	

Wash the tripe, put into a pan with the onion, carrot and celery, and cover with boiling water. Cook until tender, between 2 and 3 hours depending on the type of tripe which is being used.

While the tripe is cooking, soak the mushrooms in warm water for 30 minutes, drain them well and chop.

When the tripe is tender, take it from the pan, drain thoroughly and cut into strips. Return it to the pan, add the Meat Sauce and the mushrooms, and stir well. Add a few tablespoons of the tripe liquid, season to taste with salt and pepper, cover and continue cooking over a low heat for 30 minutes longer, stirring frequently.

Serves 6.

Manzo alla Genovese
Genoese Braised Beef

US		UK
3½ pounds	top ribs of beef, rolled and tied	3½ pounds
1½ ounces	dried mushrooms	1½ ounces
¼ cup	olive oil	3 tablespoons
3 tablespoons	pork fat, finely chopped	1½ ounces
3 tablespoons	bacon fat, finely chopped	1½ ounces
1¼ cups	red wine	½ pint
1 clove	garlic, finely chopped	1 clove
1 small	onion, finely chopped	1 small
2	carrots, finely chopped	2
2 stalks	celery, finely chopped	2 stalks
2–3 sprigs	parsley, finely chopped	2–3 sprigs
1	clove	1
7-ounce can	Italian peeled tomatoes	7-ounce can
	salt	
	stock	

Soak the mushrooms in warm water for 30 minutes. Drain, wipe dry and chop finely. In a large, heavy casserole into which the meat will fit comfortably, heat the oil with the pork and bacon fat. Add the meat and brown it well all over. Pour in the wine, increase the heat slightly and continue cooking until the wine has reduced a little. Add the garlic, onion, carrots, celery, parsley, clove, the tomatoes (without the juice) and a little salt.

Cook slowly with the pan tightly covered for about 3 hours, adding the juice from the can of tomatoes after 1 hour of cooking, and moistening from time to time with a very little boiling stock or water.

Half an hour before the meat is ready, add the mushrooms, check seasoning and continue cooking until the meat is very tender. Take the meat from the pan, cut into medium-thick slices and arrange on a hot serving platter. Keep hot in a warm oven. Rub the sauce through a sieve, return to the pan, re-heat and pour it over the meat for serving. (If there is any sauce left over, this is used by Italians as a dressing for noodles.)
Serves 6 to 8.

Cima alla Genovese
Genoese Cold Stuffed Veal

US		UK
2 pounds	breast or shoulder of veal, boned	2 pounds
¼ pound	calf's brain	¼ pound
1	calf's sweetbread	1
	salt	
¼ cup	veal bone marrow	2 ounces
¼ cup	butter	2 ounces
¼ pound	lean veal, very finely chopped	¼ pound
1 small	onion, finely chopped	1 small
1 clove	garlic, finely chopped	1 clove
1 cup	shelled green peas	4–5 ounces
4	eggs, lightly beaten	4
5 tablespoons	grated Parmesan cheese	4 tablespoons
pinch	marjoram	pinch
5 pints	stock or water	4 pints

This most useful dish, a specialty of Genoa, is considered a dish of the people. Thus it will not be found in the larger elegant restaurants but rather in a small *trattoria*. Although not difficult to prepare at home, it can be bought in shops specializing in cold cuts of meat.

Ask your butcher to make a bag or pouch from the meat (it is much easier using the shoulder). This is done by slicing it horizontally nearly in half, in such a way that three sides remain closed while the fourth side is open, forming a bag.

Soak the brain and sweetbread for several hours in cold water to remove blood, etc. Drain and put into a pan with fresh cold salted water, add the marrow and bring to the boil. Again drain, return to the pan with fresh cold water, bring to the boil, lower the heat and cook until tender. Take from the pan and remove the skin and membranes.

Melt the butter in a frying pan and brown the veal, onion and garlic lightly. Add the brains, sweetbread and marrow, and sauté until golden brown. Put into a bowl and add the peas, eggs, Parmesan cheese, a pinch of marjoram and salt to taste. Mix thoroughly.

Push this stuffing into the prepared breast of veal and sew the opening up carefully. Put the veal into a large pan, add the stock or water, bring to a gentle boil, lower the heat and let it cook for between 1½ and 2 hours, with the water just rippling. For the first hour the pan should be uncovered. Let the veal cool in the liquid. Take it from the pan, put it on a board, cover with a cloth or foil, and put a heavy weight on top.

Before serving, remove the threads and cut the meat into slices. The cooking liquid makes an excellent base for a soup.
Serves 6 to 8.

Tomaxelle
Ligurian Veal Rolls

US		UK
12 slices	veal, cut from the leg	12 slices
1½ ounces	dried mushrooms	1½ ounces
	soft pith of 1 bread roll	
¼ pound	calf's udder – see method	¼ pound
¼ pound	lean veal	¼ pound
4 teaspoons	pine nuts	1 tablespoon
1 clove	garlic	1 clove
2–3 sprigs	parsley	2–3 sprigs
2	eggs, lightly beaten	2
2½ tablespoons	grated Parmesan cheese	2 tablespoons
	salt and pepper	
pinch	marjoram	pinch
4 tablespoons	butter	2 ounces
½ cup	dry white wine	6–8 tablespoons
5 tablespoons	Meat Sauce – page 85	4 tablespoons

This recipe appears throughout Italy in many guises and with many different names. This particular version was originally a way of using up left-overs. Therefore, if there is no left-over calf's udder in the refrigerator, do not feel obliged to go out and buy some – it will be exceedingly difficult to find. *Tomaxelle* are often prepared with left-over brains, sweetbreads or even ham.

Soak the mushrooms in warm water for 30 minutes. Drain and chop finely. Soak the inside of the bread roll in water (or better still stock) until swollen, then squeeze dry.

Lightly pound the veal slices until thin, but try to keep them a neat shape. Cook the udder (if used) with the lean veal in boiling water until tender. Drain, reserve the liquid, and chop the meats finely.

Pound the pine nuts with the garlic and parsley to a paste, then mix with half the mushrooms and all of the soaked bread (this can be done in a blender). Add the eggs, beating well, followed by the Parmesan, salt, pepper and a pinch of marjoram.

Arrange all the slices of meat on a table and in the middle of each piece put a small portion of the stuffing. Roll up each slice and either tie securely with thread or fix with toothpicks.

Brown the veal rolls in butter. Add the wine and the Meat Sauce, the remaining mushrooms and ½ cup (U.K. 6 to 8 tablespoons) of the reserved veal stock. Continue cooking over a low heat for about 20 minutes longer, or until the veal is tender. If Meat Sauce is not available, any well-flavored thick gravy can be used instead, or perhaps a glass of red wine.

Serves 4 to 6.

Anatra con Olive
Duck with Olives

US		UK
1 large	duck, dressed	1 large
2½ tablespoons	olive oil	2 tablespoons
3 tablespoons	butter	1½ ounces
1	onion, finely chopped	1
1	carrot, finely chopped	1
1 stalk	celery, finely chopped	1 stalk
2–3 sprigs	parsley, finely chopped	2–3 sprigs
	salt and pepper	
⅔ cup	boiling stock	¼ pint
16	"white" Ligurian olives – see method	16

The "white" olive is thus called because, although perfectly ripe, it has very little color. Its flesh is rather more tender than that of the usual type of olive and it is also fairly large, with a very small pit. If this type of olive is not available (it is grown in California), use the largest and palest olives you can find.

Heat the oil and butter in a large, heavy casserole and sauté the onion, carrot, celery and parsley. Add the duck and brown it slowly on all sides. Sprinkle with salt and pepper. Cover and cook for 30 minutes, moistening from time to time with hot stock. Pit and chop half the olives, and add them to the pan. Stir gently and continue cooking until the duck is tender.

Take the duck from the pan and put aside. Rub the sauce through a sieve and return it to the pan. Add the duck, turn it round and about to coat it with the sauce, and then add the remaining olives, whole. Continue cooking for 15 minutes longer. Serve the duck in a deep heated platter, covered with the sauce.

Serves 3 to 4.

Coniglio in Umido
Ligurian Rabbit Stew

US		UK
1	rabbit	1
¼ cup	olive oil	3 tablespoons
2 tablespoons	butter	1 ounce
2 cloves	garlic	2 cloves
1 sprig	rosemary	1 sprig
2	bay leaves	2
1 small sprig	thyme	1 small sprig
1	onion, thinly sliced	1
1 stalk	celery, diced	1 stalk
1	carrot, diced	1
1 cup	dry white wine	scant ½ pint
	salt and pepper	
	grated nutmeg – optional	
½ pound	tomatoes, peeled and chopped	½ pound
4 teaspoons	pine nuts	1 tablespoon

Clean and wash the rabbit, and cut into serving pieces. In a large heavy pan heat the oil and butter, and sauté the garlic, rosemary, bay leaves and thyme. Add the pieces of rabbit and brown them all over. When the garlic is brown, take it from the pan together with the herbs, and discard them all.

Add the onion, celery, carrot and the wine, season to taste with salt and plenty of pepper and, if liked, a good pinch of nutmeg. Cook over a moderate heat until the wine has reduced a little. Add the tomatoes and the pine nuts. Cover the pan and cook over a moderate heat until the rabbit is tender, about 1 hour.

Serve the rabbit with its sauce, accompanied by a dish of thick polenta.

Serves 3 to 4.

Burrida
Genoese Fish Stew

US		UK
3–3½ pounds	assorted fish – see method	3–3½ pounds
⅔ cup	olive oil	¼ pint
1 clove	garlic	1 clove
1	onion, finely chopped	1
1–2	anchovy fillets, finely chopped	1–2
2–3 sprigs	parsley, chopped	2–3 sprigs
1 pound	ripe tomatoes, peeled and chopped	1 pound
6	walnuts, shelled and pounded	6
1¼ cups	dry white wine	½ pint
1	bay leaf	1
	salt	
	slices of toasted bread	

Burrida is the famous Genoese fish soup or stew which is cooked and served in the same casserole. The Genoese use a variety of fish, sometimes all of one kind, including salt cod, sometimes an assortment. The *rospo*, also called frog-fish or angler fish, is a favorite fish for this stew. In the Mediterranean it has several names: in France it is the *baudroie* and the *lotte*; on the Tyrrhenian coast of Italy it is called *boldro* and *pescatrice*. *Rospo*, its Adriatic name, means toad and is a reference to its hideous appearance. Only the tail is considered edible but this is well worth eating – in fact, it is a delicious fish. Incidentally, if when traveling in the Adriatic you find a menu announcing with pride "Fried Toad Tail", do not be put off. It is simply the *rospo*.

Other fish used in the preparation of a Genoese *burrida* are conger eel, *palombo* (a kind of mackerel), dog fish, octopus and inkfish. A similar soup can be made using rock salmon, cod fillets and even mackerel. Therefore, in the recipe which follows, the choice of fish is left to the cook.

Clean the fish thoroughly, cut it into pieces and wash it well. Heat the oil in the casserole in which the soup is being made and sauté the garlic clove and onion over a moderate heat. When the garlic turns brown, discard it. Add the anchovy, parsley and tomatoes. Mix the pounded walnuts together with the wine, and add them to the pan. Cook until the wine has reduced a little, then add the fish, bay leaf and salt. Continue cooking slowly for about 20 minutes, and serve the stew in the casserole, accompanied by slices of toasted bread.

Serves 6.

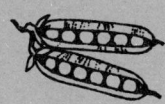

Bianchetti Fritti
Fried Small Fish

US		UK
1½ pounds	small fry: sardines, anchovies, whitebait, etc.	1½ pounds
	flour	
	oil for deep-frying	
2–3 sprigs	parsley, chopped	2–3 sprigs
2	lemons, quartered	2

Wash the fish, drain well and dry carefully in a cloth. Toss lightly in flour and shake gently in a sieve to remove excess flour.

Heat plenty of oil in a deep-frying pan, preferably one with a wire frying basket. Fry the fish a few at a time, otherwise they will stick together. They will be ready in a matter of minutes. Shake the basket gently if using one, or separate the fish with a fork if cooking them directly in the oil. Drain well. If using the basket, return them to the hot oil to crisp and drain a second time before serving. Serve garnished with parsley and lemon.

Serves 3 to 4.

Cappon Magro
Genoese Fish Salad

US		UK
Fish		
1 large	gurnard or sea bass	1 large
1	crawfish (UK crayfish)	1
24	shrimps (UK prawns)	24
10 slices	dried dolphin or tuna fish – see method	10 slices
Vegetables		
1 small	cauliflower	1 small
½ pound	snap (French) beans	½ pound
4	carrots	4
1 stalk	celery	1 stalk
4	artichoke hearts	4
1 bunch	scorzonera – see method	1 bunch
Sauce		
	pith of 1 bread roll soaked in wine vinegar	
1 clove	garlic	1 clove
2–3 sprigs	parsley, finely chopped	2–3 sprigs
3 tablespoons	pine nuts	1 ounce
2 tablespoons	capers	1 ounce
3–4 small	gherkins, chopped	3–4 small
8–10	pickled mushrooms, chopped	8–10
2–3 tablespoons	black olives, pitted and chopped	2–3 tablespoons
2	hard-boiled eggs	2
2	raw egg yolks	2
	salt	
⅔ cup	olive oil	¼ pint
½ cup	wine vinegar	6–8 tablespoons
	lemon juice, salt and olive oil	
	ship's biscuits – see method	
	whole shrimps (UK prawns) and pickles, to decorate	

The following recipe at first glance does appear frightening, and indeed it is not a dish to be lightly undertaken. Much of the success depends on the variety of the fish and vegetables used, as well as a careful hand in the arranging.

If the suggested fish are not available, then with a little thought substitutes can be found. Instead of dried dolphin, tuna fish, a cheap variety of smoked salmon and/or smoked oysters can be used. The vegetables present no problem, except the *scorzonera* (black salsify), but beetroot can take its place, being of a similar color when cooked. Fennel can also be used and this is not at all difficult to find. Instead of the recommended ship's biscuits, thick slices of stale sandwich loaf can be used. These serve as a base or platform to the salad.

Clean and cook the fish and shellfish to be used. Remove all skin and bones, and cut into fairly small pieces. Put all the fish into a bowl and dress with lemon juice, salt and olive oil. Put aside.

Clean the vegetables. The artichoke hearts, if canned, simply require draining and cutting into pieces. Leave the celery raw, thickly sliced. Cook the cauliflower, beans and carrots until just tender – over-cooking will produce a sodden mass. Divide the cauliflower into small flowerettes and snap the beans into pieces. Slice the carrots. Put all the vegetables into a bowl and dress with lemon juice, oil and salt. Put aside and prepare the sauce.

Squeeze the bread dry. Mix together and then pound (or purée in a blender) the garlic, parsley, pine nuts, capers, gherkins, mushrooms, black olives, the bread, and the cooked and raw egg yolks. When all this is reduced to a smooth paste (and without a blender this is quite hard work), rub it through a sieve. Add a pinch of salt, the oil and half the vinegar, beating constantly as if making a mayonnaise.

Moisten the biscuits or bread with the remaining wine vinegar diluted with an equal quantity of water. Arrange these on a round or oval flat dish as a platform to the salad. Cover with a layer of dried dolphin or substitute, such as smoked salmon. Over this pour a tablespoon of the sauce. Make a layer of mixed vegetables and sprinkle them with sauce. Repeat this until all the vegetables are used up, sprinkling each layer with sauce and arranging it all in a pyramid shape.

Finally add the fish, arranging them attractively, and over this pour the rest of the sauce. Garnish with small whole shrimps (U.K. prawns) and pickles.

This is the basic *cappon magro* recipe and its name suggests a fasting dish with a strong flavor of garlic. However, 1 clove of garlic is not too much for most of us. Some recipes rub the biscuit (or stale bread) base with garlic. Some recommend drying the bread in a hot oven and soaking it in oil and wine vinegar overnight. As this is a dish which for most of us would be a party effort, surround the base with cooked lobster, shrimps, prawns, etc.

Serves 6 to 8.

Triglie alla Ligure
Red Mullet Liguria Style

US		UK
2½ pounds	red mullet	2½ pounds
½ cup	olive oil	6–8 tablespoons
1 clove	garlic, finely chopped	1 clove
2 large	anchovy fillets, finely chopped	2 large
2–3 sprigs	parsley, finely chopped	2–3 sprigs
½ cup	dry white wine	6–8 tablespoons
4 large	tomatoes, peeled and chopped	4 large
	salt and pepper	
12	black olives, pitted and halved	12
4 teaspoons	capers	1 tablespoon
2	lemons	2

The following recipe is unusual as red mullet, which is one of the best of the Mediterranean fish, is usually broiled (grilled), fried, baked or cooked *en papillote*. Although this recipe stresses that the fish should be cleaned and scraped, there are cooks who claim that red mullet are best cooked without being cleaned.

Clean the fish very carefully, drawing out the gills, which will at the same time pull out the intestines. Wash and scrape lightly.

Heat the oil in a wide, shallow pan and gently sauté the garlic, anchovies and parsley. Add the wine, simmer for a short time until slightly reduced, then add the tomatoes, stirring gently. Cook slowly for 15 minutes, stirring occasionally. Add the fish, season with salt and pepper, and continue to simmer for 15 minutes longer, or until the fish are tender.

Just before serving, add the olives and capers, and a generous squeeze of lemon. Serve garnished with thick wedges of lemon.

Serves 6.

Baccalà all'Agliata
Dried Salt Cod with Garlic Sauce

US		UK
2 pounds	pre-soaked salt cod – see page 50	2 pounds
	flour	
	oil for frying	
1 recipe	Garlic Sauce – page 85	1 recipe

If pre-soaked salt cod is not available, the dried fish should be soaked for at least 24 hours, changing the water several times.

Cut the salt cod into strips. Dry it thoroughly and coat lightly with flour. Heat plenty of olive oil and fry the pieces of cod until golden. Drain on paper towels and serve with Garlic Sauce.

Serves 6.

Frittelle di Mitili
Mussel Fritters in Batter

US		UK
2–2½ quarts	mussels	2–2½ pounds
½ cup	all-purpose (plain) flour	2 ounces
	olive oil	
	salt and pepper	
1	egg white, lightly beaten	1
1–2	lemons, quartered	1–2

First prepare the batter. Mix the flour with 2½ tablespoons (U.K. 2 tablespoons) olive oil, add salt and pepper to taste, and enough water to make a not too thin batter. Leave for 30 minutes, then fold in the egg white.

Brush and scrape the mussels clean, discarding any which are not tightly closed. Heat a large, deep frying pan, add 2 or 3 tablespoons oil, then the mussels. Cover and cook over a high heat until they open. Put the mussels aside to cool, then shell them, remove the beards and discard any tough ones. Press each mussel well between the palms of the hands.

Heat plenty of oil for deep-frying. Dip the mussels into the batter, drop into the hot oil and fry until crisp and brown. Drain on paper towels and serve hot, garnished with lemon wedges.
Serves 6.

Coccoli di Patate
Ligurian Fried Potato Balls

US		UK
2 pounds	floury potatoes	2 pounds
	salt	
3	eggs, separated	3
½ cup	butter	4 ounces
2–3 tablespoons	pine nuts, very finely chopped	1 ounce
pinch	marjoram	pinch
	fine dry breadcrumbs	
	oil for deep-frying	

Wash the potatoes and cook them in boiling salted water until tender. Drain, cool slightly, peel and mash, making quite sure there are no lumps.

Beat the egg yolks. Add the butter, pine nuts, marjoram, egg yolks and a pinch of salt to the mashed potatoes. Beat well, cover with a cloth and leave for 2 hours in a cool place. Then shape the mashed potatoes into balls or small croquettes.

Stiffly beat the egg whites. Coat the potato balls in egg whites and then roll lightly in breadcrumbs. Deep-fry the potato balls in hot oil until golden brown all over, drain on paper towels and serve immediately.
Serves 4 to 6.

Funghi al Funghetto
Mushrooms with Garlic and Oregano

US		UK
2 pounds	field mushrooms	2 pounds
1 cup	olive oil	scant ½ pint
2 cloves	garlic	2 cloves
pinch	oregano	pinch

Clean the mushrooms, take off the stems (these can be used in another dish) and cut the caps into medium-thin slices. Heat the olive oil, add the garlic, 1 clove chopped and 1 clove whole, then the mushrooms. When the whole clove of garlic is brown, take it from the pan and discard it.

Sprinkle the mushrooms with a generous pinch of oregano, season to taste with salt and continue cooking over a gentle heat for 15 to 20 minutes, or until the mushrooms are tender.
Serves 4.

Melanzane alla Ligure
Eggplants (Aubergines) Liguria Style

US		UK
4 large	eggplants (aubergines)	4 large
	salt and pepper	
1 cup	olive oil	scant ½ pint
1	onion, thinly sliced	1
3 large	ripe tomatoes, peeled and quartered	3 large
3	eggs	3

Wipe the eggplants (aubergines) with a damp cloth and slice them thickly, discarding the stems. Put the slices into a colander, sprinkle with salt, put a weight on top and leave for 1 hour. This will rid them of their bitter juices.

Heat the oil and sauté the onion until golden. Then add the eggplants and simmer for 5 minutes. They will quickly absorb a lot of the oil. Add the tomatoes, salt and pepper, cover the pan and continue cooking for 30 minutes, or until the eggplants are very soft and amalgamated with the tomatoes.

Uncover the pan, beat the eggs lightly with a pinch of salt and pepper and pour into the pan. Continue cooking, uncovered and without stirring, until the eggs are set, and serve immediately.
Serves 6.

Condiglione
Mixed Salad Liguria Style

US		UK
6 large	firm ripe tomatoes, peeled	6 large
1 large	sweet pepper, cored and seeded	1 large
3 cloves	garlic, peeled	3 cloves
1	cucumber, peeled and thinly sliced	1
2	pearl (button) onions, thinly sliced	2
	basil leaves, chopped, to taste	
2 large	anchovy fillets, finely chopped	2 large
pinch	oregano	pinch
12	black olives, pitted	12
2	hard-boiled eggs, quartered	2
	salt and pepper	
1 small can	tuna fish in oil, flaked	¼ pound
	olive oil, to dress salad	

Cut the tomatoes into wedges. Cut the pepper into strips. Rub the salad bowl generously with the garlic cloves. Arrange in the bowl with all the remaining ingredients, rather in the order given, although this is not arbitrary, adding the olive oil last of all, and gently stir it into the salad. Leave for about 1 hour before using. Remove the garlic cloves, stir the salad again gently and serve.
Serves 6.

Zucchine Ripiene
Stuffed Zucchini (Courgettes) Liguria Style

US		UK
12 large	zucchini (courgettes)	12 large
	salt	
	soft pith of 1 bread roll soaked in milk	
2	eggs, beaten	2
	pepper	
1 teaspoon	oregano	1 teaspoon
2½ tablespoons	grated Parmesan cheese	2 tablespoons
½ ounce	dried mushrooms, soaked and chopped	½ ounce
½ cup	olive oil	6–8 tablespoons

Wash the zucchini (courgettes) and cook them for 10 minutes in boiling salted water. Drain and scoop out the flesh through the stem end with an apple corer, taking care not to break the shells.

Squeeze the bread dry and put it in a bowl. Add the zucchini pulp, eggs, salt and pepper to taste, oregano, cheese and mushrooms. Mix thoroughly but do not mash to a paste.

Fill the zucchini with this mixture. Heat the oil in a large, shallow frying or baking pan, add the zucchini and brown quickly over a good heat. Lower the heat and continue cooking for 20 minutes longer, or until the zucchini are tender, moistening with a little hot water or stock if necessary.

If preferred, the zucchini, after first being browned on top of the stove, can be baked in a moderate oven (375°F. Mark 4).

Serves 6.

Latte alla Grotta (Sciumette)

Snow Dumplings with Pistachio Sauce

US		UK
4	eggs, separated	4
4–5 tablespoons	confectioners' (icing) sugar	1 ounce
5 cups	milk	2 pints
$\frac{1}{4}$ cup	granulated sugar	2 ounces
5 teaspoons	all-purpose (plain) flour	4 teaspoons
$2\frac{1}{2}$ tablespoons	pistachio nuts, ground	2 tablespoons
pinch	ground cinnamon	pinch

Beat the egg whites until smooth and gradually add the confectioners' (icing) sugar, beating constantly until the mixture is stiff and smooth. Put aside.

Bring all but $\frac{1}{2}$ cup (U.K. 6 to 8 tablespoons) of milk to the boil in a large, wide, shallow pan. Take the egg white mixture, a tablespoonful at a time, and drop it carefully on top of the boiling milk. As the dumplings set on one side, turn them carefully. Take them from the pan with a perforated spoon as soon as they are firm, and put aside.

Take the milk from the heat and stir in the granulated sugar. Beat the flour smoothly with the egg yolks and half the reserved milk; stir this into the cooled milk. Mix the ground pistachios with the rest of the milk and stir this into the egg and milk mixture. At this point it can be rubbed through a fine sieve if an absolutely smooth sauce is required, otherwise pour the milk mixture as it is into a thick pan and cook over a low heat until it thickens to a sauce. Do not let it boil, or it will curdle.

Arrange the dumplings in a fairly deep glass serving bowl. Pour the sauce carefully over them and sprinkle lightly with cinnamon.

This is a simple, rather everyday Ligurian dish. Instead of pistachios, almonds or walnuts may be used.

Serves 6.

Pizza di Noci e Canditi

Ligurian Walnut and Candied Peel Pie

US		UK
$1\frac{2}{3}$ cups	shelled walnuts	6 ounces
5	eggs, separated	5
$\frac{2}{3}$ cup	granulated (caster) sugar	5 ounces
5 squares	bitter chocolate, grated	5 ounces
	grated rind of $\frac{1}{2}$ lemon	
$\frac{1}{3}$ cup	diced mixed candied peel	2 ounces
	butter and fine dry breadcrumbs for pie pan	

This is not a pie as we in the United States or Britain understand it, but rather more like a cake.

Pound or grind the walnuts to a powder. Beat the egg yolks with the sugar until fluffy. Beat the egg whites until stiff. Mix the egg yolks with the powdered walnuts, chocolate, grated rind and candied peel, and fold in the egg whites.

Pour the walnut mixture into a buttered and breadcrumbed pie pan (tart tin) and bake in a moderate oven (375°F. Mark 4) for about 1 hour.

When cooked, the pie should be about $\frac{1}{2}$ inch thick, rather like a pizza. Turn it out and leave to cool on a cake rack before serving.

Pesche Ripiene

Ligurian Stuffed Peaches

US		UK
13	ripe peaches	13
$\frac{1}{2}$ cup	chopped candied peel	3 ounces
$\frac{1}{2}$ cup	chopped candied pumpkin or other fruit	3 ounces
6 tablespoons	sugar	5 tablespoons
1 cup	white wine	scant $\frac{1}{2}$ pint

Halve all the peaches and remove the stones. Split the stones, take out the kernels and chop them finely. Scoop out the flesh from one peach and put this into a bowl. Add the chopped kernels, the candied peel and pumpkin. Mix well but not to a paste. Fill the halves of the remaining peaches with this mixture. Re-join the halves and secure with cotton or thin skewers.

Dissolve the sugar in the wine. Place the peaches in a shallow baking pan, pour over the wine and sugar mixture, and bake in a moderate oven (375°F. Mark 4) for about 40 minutes, or until soft, basting occasionally with the pan juices.

Serve one or two peaches per person.

Pandolce Genovese

Genoese Sweet Bread

US		UK
8 cups	all-purpose (plain) flour	2 pounds
pinch	salt	pinch
3 cakes	compressed (fresh) yeast	2 ounces
$\frac{1}{2}$ cup	lukewarm milk	6–8 tablespoons
4 tablespoons	orange flower water	3 tablespoons
$1\frac{1}{8}$ cups	granulated (caster) sugar	8 ounces
$\frac{3}{4}$ cup	melted butter	6 ounces
$\frac{1}{4}$ cup	pine nuts	2 ounces
$\frac{1}{8}$ cup	peeled pistachio nuts	1 ounce
scant 1 cup	seedless white raisins (sultanas), soaked in Marsala	4 ounces
4 teaspoons	fennel seeds	1 tablespoon
$\frac{1}{4}$ pound	candied pumpkin or other fruit, finely chopped	4 ounces
	butter and flour for baking sheet	

This is one of the best and certainly the most typical Genoese sweet for Christmas, New Year and Twelfth Night festive occasions.

Sift the flour on to a pastry board or into a bowl. Make a well in the middle and pour in the yeast, dissolved in milk. Leave this for 20 minutes. Add the remaining ingredients in the order given (except the butter and flour for the baking sheet) and mix well. Knead thoroughly for at least 30 minutes (those with an electric mixer can achieve this quickly and with ease), adding a little more milk if the dough is too firm. Shape into a ball, cover with a cloth and leave in a warm place to rise until doubled in bulk – this will take several hours.

Punch the dough down, knead lightly and shape into a round. Transfer it to a well-buttered and floured baking sheet. Make three incisions in the form of a triangle on top, and bake in a moderate oven (375°F. Mark 4) for about 1 hour, or until a skewer inserted in the thickest part comes out clean. Leave to cool before serving.

EMILIA-ROMAGNA

Mortadella sausages and *tortellini*, an Emilian variation on the ravioli theme, photographed in Bologna at the foot of the towering Due Torri.

Emilia offers a rich choice of fine pork products: *culatello* (cured rump of pork) from the Parma district, *zamponi* sausages stuffed into the skin of a pig's trotter, Mortadella from Bologna, savory *ciccioli*, which are the crisp remains of rendered fat pork, and a variety of fine salami.

Zamponi sausages served smoking hot with other boiled meats. In the background, the Ghirlandina of Modena, home of the finest *zamponi* in Italy.

In Emilia, cooking is an art to which creators and consumers are equally devoted. Nowhere is this more striking than in Parma which, after Bologna, is the most interesting and unusual town of the region. Parma owes much of its grace and originality to the fact that in 1815, after the defeat of Napoleon, the victorious allies decided to dispose of his second wife, the daughter of the Austrian Emperor, by granting her this small Italian Duchy. For over two centuries the Farnese family had enriched Parma with elegant buildings and great works of art. Maria Luigia (as the beloved duchess is still called) transformed it into a model town, a perfect court where music and art flourished, and everything bore an indelible seal of good taste. Today, some of the most elegant women in Italy are to be found here, some of the finest critics of lyrical music and connoisseurs of antiques —and, not least, some of the most splendid gourmets.

The Teatro Regio in Parma is still the most difficult testing ground for any opera singer. Not so long ago, the occupants of the boxes at the opera used to dine there between acts. Today, their successors sing *Cortigiani, vil razza dannata!*, *Bella figlia dell'amore* or *La donna è mobile* between courses in the local restaurants. Those same singers will not hesitate to boo some famous tenor at the Regio who does not succeed in giving a perfect rendering of a favorite passage or note. It therefore comes as no surprise to learn that both Verdi and Toscanini were born in this area. Verdi's birthplace is at Busseto, where nearby one of the finest of all Emilian delicacies, *culatelli*, are made. Similar to ham, but more spicy, with a penetrating, aggressive aroma, and easily recognizable on account of its pear shape, the *culatello* is one of the few specialties that industry has not succeeded in mass-producing. It is still made by hand by a small number of families, who pass down the secrets of production from father to son. The finest *culatelli* are made by peasants, who "improve" them by a very old process involving hand massage during the months when the hams are maturing; this makes the meat more tender and allows the spices and salt to penetrate.

The neighborhood of Parma is also the home of Parmesan cheese, which is mentioned by Boccaccio in the *Decameron*. As with all good things, no less than three provinces, Parma, Reggio and Piacenza, claim to have invented it, and to keep everyone happy a compromise has been reached whereby the cheese is sold under the trade name of *parmigiano-reggiano*—a description which enables local producers to control the quality and protect their rights by law. The vast warehouses where the Parmesan is left to mature are themselves well worth a visit. Thousands of glistening whole cheeses giving out a most appetizing aroma are lovingly watched by experts, who occasionally check on the ripening process by removing small fragments with a gimlet.

One might well ask: where does all this grating cheese go? The answer is that it goes to flavor a variety of Emilian pastas—*tagliatelle, lasagne, tortellini, pappardelle,* to name but a few. The noodles are made from *sfoglia*, a dough of flour, eggs and salt, worked with loving care into a golden sheet, and then reduced to the required thinness with a rolling pin.

Above: The specialties of the province of Ferrara include eels and grey mullet from Comacchio, game, excellent sausages called *salama da sugo, panpepato* (spiced bread), and a delicious white bread with a characteristic shape known as *ciupeta*, which once graced the tables of the d'Este family. *Below:* A selection of exquisite dishes of poultry, veal and ham on display at the Ristorante Pappagallo in Bologna.

Fine Emilian wines, the most popular of which is Lambrusco from Modena, the ideal partner for its great compatriot *zampone*—see page 96.
Below: These delicacies of the Ristorante Pappagallo reflect the love of the people of Bologna for good food, well cooked and beautifully presented: Bologna tart surrounded with vanilla and chocolate profiteroles, baked ravioli, capon in aspic, suprême of chicken, chocolate meringues, and finally a selection of classic pork products —Mortadella, hams and fine salami.

The simplest product of *sfoglia* is *tagliatelle*, a typical Bolognese dish devised in 1487 by one Mastro Zafirano, a cook from the village of Bentivoglio, on the occasion of the marriage of Lucrezia Borgia to the Duke of Ferrara. It is said that the cook was inspired by the beautiful fair hair of the bride. To go with *tagliatelle*, the Bolognese invented *ragù*, a rich sauce made with beef, ham, vegetables, butter and cream (see page 105). This sauce is used to flavor many other pasta dishes, especially *tortellini*, those delightful little parcels of pasta dough which can contain either a meat or vegetable filling. To explain the invention of the *tortellino*, Emilians love to quote a legend involving the Greek gods who once roamed the world, feasting and making love. According to this story, Venus, Mars and Bacchus arrive one night at a *trattoria* in Castelfranco. After a splendid meal, the lusty trio retired. When dawn broke Venus remained alone. Seeing her in all her naked glory, the cook was overcome by her beauty, and to immortalize the memory of the moment he created the *tortellino,* shaped like the beautiful navel of Venus. Nowadays, each province boasts its own version of the *tortellino.* These are the *tortellini d'erbetta del Parmigiano,* flavored with only butter and cheese, the *anolini* of Piacenza, the *cappelletti* of Reggio, the *ravioli* of Modena, and the *tortellini* of Bologna, one of whose ingredients is Mortadella.

Already known to have been produced in Bologna in the early Middle Ages, Mortadella is the father of all those seasoned sausages, known collectively as *salumi,* which make their way into almost every dish. Every province of Emilia has its own special *salumi.* In

A selection of gay and enticing sweets from Emilia, including fruit tarts, almond macaroons, *certosino Viscardi*, a rich fruit cake served at Christmas (see page 116), *panpepato di Ferrara*, or spiced bread, the ring-shaped *ciambellone* of Bologna (see page 116), pastries from Parma delle Bizzi, and *torta di riso*, or rice cake (see page 115).

the Piacenza area it is *coppa* and *pancetta*, in Reggio it is called *fiorettino* and *zucco*, and the famous *salama da sugo* of Ferrara once had a local reputation as an aphrodisiac. These sausages are not easy to make. First the meats are prepared, flavored with wine and seasoned with various spices; they are then left to mature for a year in special ashes, and finally they must be boiled for several hours before being brought to the table. In Modena, where they cook the best boiled meats in Emilia, the specialty is *zampone*, which was invented about two hundred years ago, at the same time as the *cappello da prete*, to which it bears a strong resemblance. Both are made of pork—meat and skin—seasoned with pepper, garlic, salt and spices.

In spite of the lavish use of pork in Emilian cooking, of the strong seasonings and "pagan" richness of many of their regional dishes, their diet, so the Emilians claim, is not heavy. Perhaps this is partly due to their wines, some of which are among the finest in Italy. Unfortunately, one of the best, Lambrusco, which has a characteristic aroma of violets and goes admirably with highly spiced food, does not travel well and is therefore not as popular abroad as it deserves to be. Sangiovese from the province of Forli is deep red in color with a strong aroma, and from the same area comes Albana, the ideal partner to the exquisite fish found off the coast of Romagna. Other excellent local wines include Trebbiano, which was popular with the Romans, Malvasia di Maiatico, Fortanella, Scandiano and Sauvignon.

The rich cooking of Emilia reaches its peak in Bologna. It is not for nothing that this town has been called *la grassa* or "the fat one", and the nickname does not compare unfavorably with many others bestowed upon it. Bologna is also known as *la turrita* ("the turreted one") and *la dotta* ("the learned one")—her university is over 1,500 years old. It is a wonderful city which, with its arcades, its churches and its famous palaces, epitomizes the qualities—and perhaps the defects—of the Emilians. Theirs is a humanity which involves all five senses, in which love, food, art and business are joined to perfection.

Crescente
Savory Bread

US		UK
8 cups	all-purpose (plain) flour	2 pounds
4 teaspoons	salt	1 tablespoon
3 cakes	compressed (fresh) yeast	2 ounces
2½ teaspoons	sugar	2 teaspoons
about 2 cups	lukewarm milk	about ¾ pint
½ pound	"flavoring" – see method	½ pound
	oil	

The "flavoring" in this recipe can be small dice of ham, tiny rendered down bits of fat unsmoked bacon, or even diced, rather fatty meat.

Sift the flour and salt into a large warmed bowl and make a well in the center. Melt the yeast with the sugar, add a little of the milk, and pour into the well. Work into the flour, gradually adding more milk, and knead the dough until it is soft and elastic, and leaves the sides of the bowl cleanly. Add the "flavoring" of your choice, and knead until smooth again.

Roll the dough into a sheet about 1 inch thick and place it on a well-oiled baking sheet. Make criss-cross incisions with a knife over the entire surface, cover and leave to rise in a warm place until doubled in bulk. Bake in a moderately hot oven (400°F. Mark 5) for 15 minutes, then lower the heat to 375°F. (Mark 4) and continue to bake for about 30 minutes longer, or until puffed and golden.

Serves 6.

Erbazzone
Spinach Pie

US		UK
5 pounds	fresh spinach	5 pounds
	salt	
2 tablespoons	butter	1 ounce
½ pound	fat salt pork, finely chopped	½ pound
1	clove garlic, finely chopped	1
6	green (spring) onions	6
2 cups	all-purpose (plain) flour	½ pound
2 tablespoons	lard or butter	1 ounce
2	eggs	2
1 cup	grated Parmesan cheese	4 ounces

Wash the spinach carefully, pulling off any discolored leaves and coarse ribs or stalks. Put it into a pan without any water other than that clinging to the leaves, add salt to taste and cook, covered, over moderate heat until soft. Drain the spinach in a sieve or colander and press down firmly to extract all the moisture. Chop finely and reserve.

Heat the butter in a large, deep frying pan, add the salt pork and cook until the fat runs. Add the garlic and the onions, which you have chopped finely, green parts and all. When these are golden, stir in the chopped spinach. Mix well and simmer for 5 minutes longer. Check seasoning and reserve.

Sift the flour into a bowl. Rub in the lard or butter, add a pinch of salt and work in enough warm water to make a firm dough. Knead well, roll the dough into a ball and cut it in half. Roll each piece out thinly into two rounds, making one round larger than the other. Line a shallow pie pan with the larger round, overlapping the sides, and fill it with the spinach mixture. Beat the eggs, add the Parmesan cheese and pour over the spinach. Cover with the remaining round of dough, and seal the two rounds firmly. Trim off untidy edges and prick the top with a fork.

Bake the pie in a hot oven (425°F. Mark 6) for 20 minutes, or until the top is golden brown. Serve hot.

Serves 6.

Torta Fritta
Fritters

US		UK
4 cups	all-purpose (plain) flour	1 pound
1¼ teaspoons	salt	1 teaspoon
3 tablespoons	softened lard	1½ ounces
2 cakes	compressed (fresh) yeast	1⅓ ounces
about 1¼ cups	lukewarm milk or water	about ½ pint
	lard or oil for frying	

Sift the flour and salt into a warmed bowl and rub in the softened lard. Dissolve the yeast in a little of the milk and work it into the flour, together with enough of the remaining milk to make a firm, pliable dough. Knead vigorously until the dough is smooth and leaves the sides of the bowl cleanly. Roll it into a ball, cover the bowl and leave in a warm place to rise.

When the dough has doubled in bulk, punch it down and knead it again lightly. Roll it into a sheet about ⅛ inch thick and cut into diamond shapes with a floured pastry cutter or a sharp knife. Arrange the shapes on a clean cloth sprinkled with flour and leave them to rise again.

Heat the lard or oil – enough for fairly deep frying – and fry the fritters until they are puffed and golden brown on both sides. Drain on absorbent paper and serve hot, accompanied by fresh cheese or sliced salami.

Serves 4 to 6.

Ragù
Bolognese Meat Sauce

US		UK
6 tablespoons	butter	3 ounces
2½ tablespoons	olive oil	2 tablespoons
1	onion, finely chopped	1
1	carrot, finely chopped	1
1 stalk	celery, finely chopped	1 stalk
⅔ cup	bacon, finely chopped	3 ounces
¾ cup	ground (minced) pork	6 ounces
¾ cup	ground (minced) beef	6 ounces
¼ cup	sausage meat	2 ounces
2–3	chicken livers – optional	2–3
⅔ cup	dry white wine	¼ pint
	salt and pepper	
4 teaspoons	tomato paste	1 tablespoon
about 1¼ cups	stock	about ½ pint
4 tablespoons	light (single) cream or milk	3 tablespoons

Heat half the butter and all the oil in a deep frying pan. Add the onion, carrot, celery and bacon, and fry over a low heat until the vegetables soften and begin to change color. Add the pork, beef, sausage meat and chicken livers, if used, and fry these gently until they begin to brown, crumbling with a fork. Moisten with wine and cook until it evaporates, then season to taste with salt and pepper. Dilute the tomato paste with a little stock. Stir this into the sauce, cover and cook slowly, stirring from time to time, and gradually adding the rest of the stock.

After the sauce has been cooking for 1½ hours, stir in the cream and continue cooking until reduced. Finally add the remaining butter and stir until melted and thoroughly mixed into the sauce.

About ¼ pound chopped mushrooms, sautéed in butter and flavored with garlic and finely chopped parsley, may be added to the sauce at the last moment, if liked.

The above quantities will make enough sauce for 1 to 1¼ pounds spaghetti.

Serves 6.

Salsa Besciamella
Béchamel Sauce

US		UK
6 tablespoons	butter	3 ounces
6 tablespoons	flour	1½ ounces
1 teaspoon	salt	scant 1 teaspoon
5 cups	hot milk	2 pints

Melt the butter in a pan, preferably a heavy one with a copper bottom. Stir in the flour and about 1 teaspoon salt to make a *roux*. Cook gently for a few minutes without letting it brown, then gradually add the hot milk, stirring constantly with a wire whisk or a wooden spoon. Continue cooking and stirring until the sauce is thick and smooth, and the raw taste of the flour has completely disappeared.

Pour the sauce into a bowl and beat it lightly. Any additional flavorings may now be stirred in – grated Parmesan cheese, an egg, tomato paste, oysters, shrimps or prawns, parsley, capers.

Salsa per il Pesce
Sauce for Fish

US		UK
2	hard-boiled egg yolks	2
2–4	anchovy fillets	2–4
about ⅔ cup	olive oil	about ¼ pint
a few drops	lemon juice	a few drops

Chop the egg yolks and the anchovy fillets separately, then combine them in a mortar and pound until smooth and well blended. Gradually stir in the oil and lemon juice until the sauce has the consistency of a creamy mayonnaise. Serve with broiled (grilled) fish.

Pasta Gialla
Egg Pasta

US		UK
1 cup	all-purpose (plain) flour, depending on the size of the egg	3½ ounces
1	egg	1

For *pasta asciutta* (lit. "dry pasta", i.e. noodles eaten by themselves or in a sauce, but not in a soup) these quantities will make one portion. For *pasta in brodo*, i.e. noodles to be served in a soup, the above will serve two.

Eggs with dark yolks are preferred by Italian cooks in making pasta in order to give it a strong yellow color – but this is not essential.

Sift the flour on to a pastry board and make a well in the center. Break each egg separately into a cup, then tip it into the well. Mix the eggs into the flour with a fork or with the fingertips, and work the dough energetically. It will be fairly stiff to begin with, but after 15 minutes' kneading, it will become smooth and pliable, and little air bubbles will start forming all over the surface. Roll it into a ball and leave it to rest for 20 minutes on a lightly floured pastry board, covered with a bowl or a cloth.

Roll the dough out into a paper-thin, even sheet, using as little pressure on the rolling pin as possible. Sprinkle lightly with flour to prevent sticking. Do not roll the dough in a draught or in a room which is too warm and dry, as this may make it dry too quickly to be rolled out completely.

The dough can be cut into the required shapes immediately, while it is still fresh, or it can be left for a further 30 minutes to dry.

Recipes for using the pasta dough as soon as it is made:

Stricchetti (Bows or Butterflies)
For these, some people like to add a little grated nutmeg and grated Parmesan cheese to the dough. With a pastry wheel, cut the dough into strips a little under an inch wide and less than 2 inches long. Press the middle of each little rectangle with your fingers to form a butterfly shape. *Stricchetti* are usually cooked and eaten in soup. If they are to be eaten "dry", they should be cut a little larger (1 inch by 2 inches) and served with a well-flavored meat or tomato sauce.

Lasagne
Cut out squares from the sheets of dough just over 3 inches by 3 inches, or cut into rounds. Let the dough dry thoroughly and cook it in plenty of boiling, salted water (2 minutes will be enough if the pasta has been made only a couple of hours beforehand); drain and spread on a napkin to dry.

Tortellini di Bologna (Little Hats of Bologna)
As soon as the dough is rolled out, cut it into circles about 1½ inches in diameter; put a little meat filling on each and shape immediately into "little hats". This is done by folding the circle of dough in half over the filling, taking the semi-circle in your right hand and folding it round your left index finger so that the two ends curl round and overlap slightly. They should be pressed firmly together and turned upwards.

Spread out on a cloth to dry. *Tortellini* can be served either in soup or "dry", with cream, grated Parmesan cheese and truffles, or with a meat sauce (see page 105).

Anolini di Parma (Parma Ravioli)
Cut the dough immediately it has been made into circles about 1½ to 2 inches in diameter. Put a little filling on each and fold in half at once, sealing well. *Anolini* are generally cooked and served in a chicken or meat stock with plenty of grated Parmesan cheese, rarely "dry".

Anolini di Piacenza (Piacenza Ravioli)
Cut the dough into long strips about 1½ inches wide, and arrange little heaps of filling along half of the strips, about 1½ inches apart. Cover with the rest of the strips and, using a round pastry cutter, cut out circles at least 1¼ inches in diameter. Leave to dry on a napkin. These are cooked and served in beef or chicken stock with plenty of grated Parmesan cheese.

Cappelletti di Romagna (Little Hats of Romagna)
Cut the dough immediately it has been made into circles about 3 inches in diameter. Put a little filling (with or without meat) on each one, and form at once into a "hat" (see *tortellini* above), sealing well. These are boiled in water or stock and served "dry" with a meat sauce; they are also excellent served in broth, but are then made somewhat smaller.

Tortelli
Cut out circles about 2 inches in diameter and put a little filling made with a mixture of spinach and cheese on each. Shape as for *tortellini* and seal well. Dry on a cloth. These can be cooked and served either in soup, or "dry" with a dressing of melted butter and grated Parmesan cheese.

Tortelloni (lit.: Big Tortelli)
Cut the dough as soon as it has been made into circles about 3 inches in diameter. Put a little cheese filling on each, fold in half and seal well, pressing the edges firmly with a fork to seal them. Cook the *tortelloni* in stock, drain and serve with plenty of butter and grated Parmesan cheese.

If the dough is left to dry for about ½ hour, the following can be made:

Tagliatelle (Ribbon Noodles)

Roll up the sheet of dough until it is about 2 inches wide. Using a very sharp knife, cut it into rounds about ½ inch wide. Open up the rounds and spread out the strips to dry on a pastry board or a cloth. Cook in boiling water or stock until just tender, drain and serve with a sauce or with melted butter and grated Parmesan.

Tagliolini

Prepare as *tagliatelle* but cut the strips much thinner. These are usually served in broth but can also be eaten "dry".

Quadrucci (Little Squares)

Roll up the sheet of dough and with a sharp knife cut it into rounds about ½ inch wide; unwind the rounds and cut the strips into squares. These are cooked and served in a meat or vegetable stock.

Maltagliati (lit. Badly Cut)

Roll up the sheet of dough and with a sharp knife cut it into rounds about ½ inch wide; unroll them and cut the strips diagonally to form triangles. When cooked in minestrone or in a pea or bean soup these noodles are called *malmaritati* – "unhappily married".

Pasta Verde
Green Pasta

US		UK
1¾ cups	all-purpose (plain) flour	7 ounces
1	egg	1
about ¾ cup	cooked spinach – when squeezed dry it should be the size of an egg	4–5 ounces

For "dry" noodles (see the preceding recipe) the above quantities will serve two. If cooked in a soup, there will be enough for four.

Proceed as for Egg Pasta but include the spinach. Roll the dough out paper-thin.

If it is cut before it dries, i.e. as soon as it is made, it can be made into *maccheroncini*: Cut the dough into strips about ½ inch wide; cut these in turn into pieces about ¾ inch long. These are then wrapped round a special gadget, not unlike a thick knitting needle, which can be used instead. Wrap the strips of dough round a thick knitting needle, pressing them and rotating them until you have little *maccheroni*, i.e. little tube-like shapes. Leave these to dry on a lightly floured pastry board or cloth. Cook in boiling water until tender, 4 minutes or so, drain well and serve with cream, sausage meat and chopped fried mushrooms, or with a tomato and meat sauce.

For *stricchetti*, *lasagne*, *tortellini*, *tagliatelle*, *tagliolini*, and *quadrucci*, proceed in exactly the same way as for Egg Pasta, above.

Tortellini Pasticciati alla Bolognese
Baked Tortellini Noodles Bologna Style

US		UK
4 recipes	Egg Pasta – see opposite	4 recipes
	stock or water	
½ recipe	Bolognese Meat Sauce – page 105	½ recipe
1¼ cups	light (single) cream	½ pint
3 tablespoons	butter	1½ ounces
¾–1 cup	grated Parmesan cheese	3–4 ounces

Prepare the Egg Pasta and make *tortellini* noodles as directed on page 106. Bring a large pan of stock or water to a fast boil and cook the *tortellini* for 5 minutes, or until tender. Drain well and turn them into a baking dish.

Mix the hot Bolognese Sauce with the cream and butter, and pour over the noodles. Sprinkle with grated cheese, mix well and put into a moderately hot oven (400°F. Mark 5) for a few minutes to heat through. Serve hot with plenty of additional grated Parmesan.

Serves 6.

Malfattini
Little Pasta "Grains"

US		UK
3 recipes	Egg Pasta – see opposite	3 recipes
	freshly grated nutmeg – optional	
8 cups	meat or vegetable stock	about 3 pints
	grated Parmesan cheese	

Prepare the Egg Pasta and roll it into a large sausage about 2 inches thick. Cut the sausage into slices ¼ inch thick and spread them out on a floured cloth to dry for about ½ hour – the time this takes will depend on the temperature of the room. Then chop the slices into small pieces no bigger than grains of rice. This can be done most easily with a *mezzaluna* – a crescent-shaped chopper with two handles – but failing this, use a sharp knife. Spread the grains out on the cloth to dry completely. The time will again depend on the surrounding temperature.

When ready to serve, bring a pan of meat or vegetable stock to the boil, add the grains all at once, stirring lightly to ensure that they do not stick together, and cook for only a minute or two. When the grains are tender, drain them in a sieve or colander and serve, accompanied by a bowl of grated Parmesan.

Serves 6.

Cappelletti di Romagna
"Little Hats" of Romagna Stuffed with Cheese

US		UK
5 recipes	Egg Pasta – see opposite	5 recipes
	meat stock	
⅝ cup	melted butter *or*	5 ounces
1 recipe	Bolognese Meat Sauce – page 105	1 recipe
¾ cup	grated Parmesan cheese	3 ounces
Filling		
2 cups	Ricotta or good-quality cottage cheese	1 pound
¾ cup	Stracchino cheese – see method	6 ounces
2	eggs, lightly beaten	2
1 cup	grated Parmesan cheese	4 ounces
	salt	
	freshly grated nutmeg	

If Ricotta cheese is not available, any rather dry cottage cheese may be used instead. Stracchino is a rich, creamy white cheese, rather like a soft Bel Paese. Another alternative would be Taleggio.

Prepare the dough as directed on page 106, using the quantities given above. Roll it out into a thin sheet and cut out circles about 3 inches in diameter.

Blend the filling ingredients together, seasoning the mixture with salt and freshly grated nutmeg, and put a little of this on each circle of dough. Shape into "little hats" similar to *tortellini* (see opposite) and spread them out on a floured cloth to dry.

Bring a large pan of meat stock to the boil, add the "little hats" and cook them rapidly for about 5 minutes, or until tender. Drain immediately and serve dressed with melted butter or hot Bolognese Meat Sauce, and grated Parmesan.

Serves 6.

The same dough and stuffing can also be used to make ravioli, which are then cooked and served in a well-flavored meat stock, garnished with grated Parmesan. This soup is known as *minestra ripiena alla romagnola*.

Cappellacci con la Zucca
"Little Hats" with Pumpkin

US		UK
5 recipes	Egg Pasta – page 106	5 recipes
	salt	

Filling		
3½ pounds	pumpkin	3½ pounds
½ pound	grated Parmesan cheese	½ pound
	freshly grated nutmeg	
	salt and pepper	

Sauce		
⅝ cup	melted butter	5 ounces
1 cup	grated Parmesan cheese	4 ounces

Filling
Wash the pumpkin and slice off the top. Carefully scoop out the seeds, replace the top and place the pumpkin in a shallow baking pan. Bake in a moderate oven (375°F. Mark 4) for 1½ hours, or until tender. Let the pumpkin cool, then peel off the skin and cut the flesh into small pieces. Mash well, mix with the Parmesan and season to taste with nutmeg, salt and pepper.

Dough
Prepare the dough as directed on page 106. Roll it into a paper-thin sheet and cut out circles about 3 inches in diameter. Place a little of the pumpkin mixture on each circle and shape into little "hats" – see *tortellini*, page 106. Spread them out on a floured cloth to dry.

When ready to serve, bring a large pan of salted water to a fast boil and cook the "little hats" until tender – about 5 minutes. Drain and serve immediately with melted butter and grated Parmesan.
Serves 6.

Tortelli di Erbette
Spinach-stuffed Tortelli (Ravioli)

US		UK
6 recipes	Egg Pasta – page 106	6 recipes
	salt	
½–¾ cup	melted butter	4–6 ounces
¾ cup	grated Parmesan cheese	3 ounces

Stuffing		
1 pound	spinach, spinach beet or spring greens	1 pound
	salt	
2¼ cups	Ricotta or fresh cottage cheese	1 pound 2 ounces
10 tablespoons	grated Parmesan cheese	8 tablespoons
2	eggs, lightly beaten	2
½ teaspoon	freshly grated nutmeg	½ teaspoon

Stuffing
Wash the spinach leaves very carefully. Put them in a thick-bottomed pan, sprinkle lightly with salt and cook, covered, until soft. The water remaining on the leaves will be sufficient to cook the spinach. Drain in a sieve or colander, press dry and chop finely. Mix the spinach with Ricotta cheese, Parmesan and eggs, and season to taste with salt and grated nutmeg. Mix thoroughly and put aside until required.

Prepare the Egg Pasta as directed on page 106. Roll it out thinly and cut into circles about 2 inches in diameter. Put a little spinach stuffing on each circle and shape into *tortelli* (page 106). Leave them to dry on a floured cloth.

Bring a large pan of salted water to the boil and cook the *tortelli* until tender. Drain and serve immediately, dressed with melted butter and Parmesan cheese.
Serves 6.

Lasagne Bolognesi

US		UK
3 recipes	Egg Pasta – page 106	3 recipes
	salt	
1 recipe	Bolognese Meat Sauce – page 105	1 recipe
6 tablespoons	butter	3 ounces
1 clove	garlic	1 clove
1½ ounces	dried mushrooms, soaked	1½ ounces
2–3 sprigs	parsley, finely chopped	2–3 sprigs
1¼ cups	milk	½ pint
1 cup	grated Parmesan cheese	4 ounces

Béchamel Sauce		
6 tablespoons	butter	3 ounces
6 tablespoons	all-purpose (plain) flour	5 tablespoons
about 1 teaspoon	salt	about 1 teaspoon
6 cups	hot milk	2½ pints

Prepare the lasagne noodles as directed on page 106. Cook them in boiling salted water and drain thoroughly.

Make a thin Béchamel Sauce, following the directions on page 106. Prepare the Bolognese Meat Sauce.

Heat 2 tablespoons (1 ounce) butter in a pan and gently fry the garlic clove until golden brown. Discard the garlic. Drain and dry the mushrooms, and chop them roughly. Add them to the pan together with the parsley, milk and a pinch of salt, and simmer gently for 15 minutes.

Grease a deep round baking dish about 9 inches in diameter with butter. Cover the bottom with a layer of lasagne, spread it thinly with Béchamel Sauce and Bolognese Meat Sauce, and sprinkle with a tablespoon of grated Parmesan. Continue until all the ingredients are used up, substituting the mushroom mixture for two or three layers of meat sauce. The top layer should be one of lasagne sprinkled with grated cheese and dotted with the remaining butter.

Bake in a moderate oven (375°F. Mark 4) for 1 hour, or until a light golden crust has formed on top. Serve straight from the oven.
Serves 6 to 8.

Timballo di Lasagne alla Modenese
Timbale of Lasagne Modena Style

US		UK
2 recipes	Green Pasta – page 107	2 recipes
6–8 tablespoons	butter	3–4 ounces
1 recipe	Bolognese Meat Sauce – page 105	1 recipe
1 cup	grated Parmesan cheese	¼ pound

Béchamel Sauce		
4 tablespoons	butter	2 ounces
4 tablespoons	all-purpose (plain) flour	3 tablespoons
1 teaspoon	salt	1 teaspoon
4½ cups	hot milk	1¾ pints

Prepare the pasta dough as directed on page 107, roll it out thinly and cut it into 9-inch rounds. Cook in fast-boiling water for 2 or 3 minutes and drain thoroughly.

Grease a round baking dish about 9 inches in diameter generously with butter, and place a round of lasagne in the bottom. Spread with some of the Béchamel Sauce, prepared with the ingredients listed above according to the directions on page 106. Cover with a generous layer of meat sauce, with chicken livers added, and sprinkle with grated Parmesan. Repeat these layers until all the ingredients are used up, leaving aside 2 to 3 tablespoons grated cheese and finishing with a layer of pasta spread with meat sauce. Dot the surface generously with the remaining butter and sprinkle with the remaining Parmesan. Bake in a moderate oven (375°F. Mark 4) for about 1 hour, or until the top is crisp and bubbling. Serve very hot.

Serves 6 to 8.

Paglia e Fieno
"Straw and Grass"

US		UK
2 recipes	Egg Pasta – page 106	2 recipes
2 recipes	Green Pasta – page 107	2 recipes
Garnish		
1 pound	fresh mushrooms	1 pound
4–6 tablespoons	butter	2–3 ounces
1 clove	garlic	1 clove
	salt	
1 cup	pork sausage meat	½ pound
1 cup	light (single) cream	8 fluid ounces
¾ cup	grated Parmesan cheese	3 ounces

Prepare the plain pasta and green pasta doughs as directed. Roll them out thinly, leave them to dry for 30 minutes, then cut them into *tagliatelle* or *tagliolini* (thick or thin ribbon noodles). Leave them to dry on a cloth.

Meanwhile, prepare the remaining ingredients. Clean and slice the mushrooms. Heat half the butter in a deep frying pan, add the garlic clove and sauté gently until browned. Discard the garlic and add the prepared mushrooms; sprinkle lightly with salt and sauté for 10 minutes. In another pan melt the remaining butter and fry the sausage meat until browned, crumbling it with a fork. Heat the cream in a *bain-marie* or in the top of a double boiler. Keep all these ingredients hot.

Bring two large pans of salted water to the boil and cook the two portions of pasta separately until tender. If freshly made, they will be ready almost as soon as the water comes back to the boil. However, if using commercially made, dried pasta, follow the instructions on the package. When the noodles are tender but still firm, drain them, turn them into a deep heated serving dish and toss them together. Dress them with the mushrooms, sausage meat, cream and grated cheese, and serve immediately.

Serves 6.

Instead of mushrooms, cooked peas, gently heated in a mixture of finely chopped sautéed onion and bacon, may be used.

Risotto alla Bolognese
Risotto Bologna Style

US		UK
½ cup	butter	¼ pound
¼ pound	bacon, finely chopped	¼ pound
2 ounces	raw Parma ham, finely chopped	2 ounces
1½ pounds	rice – see page 66	1½ pounds
⅔ cup	dry white wine	¼ pint
6–7½ cups	boiling meat stock	2½–3 pints
4 tablespoons	butter *or*	2 ounces
1¼ cups	Bolognese Meat Sauce – page 105	½ pint
¾ cup	grated Parmesan cheese	3 ounces
1 medium-sized	truffle, sliced paper-thin – optional	1 medium-sized

Melt the butter in a large, heavy pan and sauté the bacon and ham for a few minutes. Add the rice and continue to sauté gently for 5 minutes to allow it to absorb some of the fat and flavor. Pour in the wine, let it reduce, then add the stock, a cupful at a time, stirring gently, until the rice is tender. A few minutes before the rice is ready, stir in the Bolognese sauce, if used. Otherwise, remove the pan from the heat when the rice is tender, stir in the remaining butter and the Parmesan cheese, and leave for 2 minutes before serving.

Serve the risotto on a hot platter with thin slices of truffle scattered over the top.

Serves 6.

Tortellini in Brodo
Consommé with Tortellini (Small Ravioli)

US		UK
3 recipes	Egg Pasta – page 106	3 recipes
10 cups	stock	4 pints
	grated Parmesan cheese	
Stuffing		
3 tablespoons	butter	1½ ounces
¼ pound	loin of pork	¼ pound
2 ounces	chicken, turkey or capon breast	2 ounces
¼ cup	bone marrow	2 ounces
2–3 thin slices	raw Parma ham	1 ounce
4 slices	Mortadella	2 ounces
1 cup	grated Parmesan cheese	¼ pound
2	eggs, beaten	2
	salt, pepper and freshly grated nutmeg	

Heat the butter and gently sauté the pork, chicken breast and bone marrow until golden brown. Put through the coarse blade of a grinder (mincer) together with the ham and Mortadella. Mix with the grated cheese and eggs, and season to taste with salt, pepper and freshly grated nutmeg.

Prepare the Egg Pasta, roll it out thinly and cut into circles about 1½ inches in diameter. Put a little stuffing on each circle and shape into *tortellini* as directed on page 106. Leave to dry on a lightly floured cloth for about 30 minutes.

Bring a pan of stock to the boil. (A very large pan is required, as this recipe allows 20 *tortellini* per person.) Drop the *tortellini* into the boiling stock, a portion at a time, and serve as soon as they are tender (about 5 minutes), accompanied by a bowl of grated Parmesan.

Serves 10.

Minestra del Paradiso
Paradise Soup

US		UK
4	eggs	4
	salt and pepper	
	freshly grated nutmeg	
10 tablespoons	grated Parmesan cheese	8 tablespoons
5 tablespoons	soft breadcrumbs	4 tablespoons
7½–10 cups	meat stock	3–4 pints

Some Italian recipes for this soup recommend sautéeing the breadcrumbs in butter until they are golden brown, before mixing them with the eggs.

Beat the eggs with salt, pepper and a little nutmeg to taste; add the Parmesan cheese and the breadcrumbs, and mix well. Bring the stock to the boil and pour in the beaten egg mixture, stirring vigorously all the time to prevent the eggs from curdling. Bring to a gentle boil again and serve at once, generously sprinkled with additional grated Parmesan cheese.

Serves 6 to 8.

Il Grande Fritto Misto all'Emiliana
The Emilian Great Mixed Fry

This basically consists of a great many different ingredients – the more variety you have, the better. Generally, it includes chicken croquettes, fried sweet custard, baby lamb chops, veal cutlets, Bolognese-style skewers, little beignets, apple fritters, semolina fritters, Ricotta or cottage cheese fritters, squash (marrow) flowers, fried zucchini (courgettes) and eggplants (aubergines), artichokes fried in butter, fried bone marrow and brains, rice croquettes and tagliatelle fritters.

Chicken Croquettes
Coarsely grind (mince) left-over boiled or roast chicken; add an equal amount of fairly stiff Béchamel Sauce, a little diced ham, a few tablespoons of grated Parmesan cheese, egg to bind the mixture, and salt, pepper and grated nutmeg to taste. Mix well and shape into small croquettes. Coat with fine breadcrumbs, dip into beaten egg and coat with breadcrumbs again. Deep-fry in hot oil.

Fried Sweet Custard
Beat together 5 egg yolks, 1 egg white, a scant ½ cup (U.K. 6 tablespoons) granulated (caster) sugar and a pinch of salt. Add a generous ½ cup (U.K. 8 tablespoons) all-purpose (plain) flour and beat until well blended. Stir in 2½ cups (U.K. 1 pint) warm milk and add the rind of 1 small lemon in a strip. Cook in a double boiler, stirring constantly, until the mixture thickens. Discard the lemon rind and pour the custard out in a thick layer into a wet dish. Leave to cool and to become quite firm. Then cut into large diamond shapes, dip in stiffly beaten egg white and coat with fine dry breadcrumbs. Deep-fry in hot oil, drain on absorbent paper and sprinkle with fine sugar. Serves 4 to 6.

Baby Lamb Chops
Lightly flour the chops and fry them quickly in butter until golden brown on both sides, but not cooked through. Take them from the pan and drain on absorbent paper. Dip into seasoned beaten egg and coat with breadcrumbs. Deep-fry in hot oil.

Veal Cutlets (or Pork Cutlets or Chicken Breasts)
Beat them lightly to flatten them and brown them in butter on one side only. Remove them from the pan and put a slice of ham on the cooked side. Spread with a little stiff Béchamel Sauce, sprinkle generously with grated Parmesan and season with a little pepper. Press the top lightly, then carefully dip each cutlet into seasoned beaten egg, coat it with breadcrumbs and fry in plenty of hot oil.

Bolognese-style Skewers
Dice 6 ounces lean veal, 4 ounces brains (blanched) and bone marrow, 3 ounces Mortadella, 4 ounces calf's liver and 3 ounces Gruyère or Emmenthal cheese. Thread the dice on to skewers in suitable sequence. Dip the skewers into a thin Béchamel Sauce, then into seasoned beaten egg and finally in breadcrumbs. Fry in plenty of hot oil and serve immediately. Makes about 12 small skewers.

Apple Fritters
Make a batter with 1 egg yolk, 5 tablespoons (U.K. 4 tablespoons) all-purpose (plain) flour, 1 tablespoon water, 1 cup (U.K. scant ½ pint) milk and a pinch of salt. Let it rest for 30 minutes. Peel and core 4 to 6 apples and slice them into thick rounds. When ready to make the fritters, fold 2 stiffly beaten egg whites into the batter and dip the apple slices into it. Fry in hot oil until puffed and golden, drain thoroughly and dust with confectioners' (icing) sugar.

Savory Beignets
Bring 7 tablespoons (U.K. 3½ fluid ounces) water to the boil with 3 tablespoons (U.K. 1½ ounces) butter and a generous pinch of salt. Remove from the heat and beat in all at once ½ cup (U.K. 2 ounces) all-purpose (plain) flour. Beat vigorously until the mixture forms a ball, then beat in 2 eggs, one at a time. Continue beating until the mixture is smooth. Drop teaspoonfuls of the mixture into hot oil and fry until puffed and golden. Drain on absorbent paper and serve immediately. Makes about 30 fritters.

Semolina Fritters
Bring 3 cups (U.K. 1¼ pints) milk to the boil in a thick-bottomed pan. Sprinkle in 1 scant cup (U.K. 5 ounces) coarse semolina and a pinch of salt, stirring constantly, and simmer, stirring, for about 20 minutes, or until the mixture is very thick. Remove from the heat and beat in 1 egg and 2 tablespoons (U.K. 1 ounce) butter. Turn into a deep dish rinsed in cold water, making a thick layer. Leave to cool, then cut into diamond shapes. Dip into seasoned beaten egg, coat with breadcrumbs and fry in deep hot oil until golden. Drain on absorbent paper and serve, sprinkled with fine sugar. Makes about 40 small fritters.

Ricotta Fritters
Blend together 1 cup (U.K. ½ pound) Ricotta or cottage cheese, ¼ cup (U.K. 3 tablespoons) all-purpose (plain) flour, 1 egg and about 1 tablespoon Marsala or rum to taste. Fry tablespoonfuls of the mixture in hot oil and drain well. Serve dusted with sugar.

Fried Zucchini (Courgettes)
Cut them into short lengths, dredge with flour and deep-fry until soft and golden brown.

Fried Eggplants (Aubergines)
Cut them into slices, sprinkle with salt and leave to drain for 2 hours on a sloping plate or in a colander. This will rid them of their bitter juices. Wipe the slices dry, dip them into seasoned beaten egg and coat them with breadcrumbs. Fry at once in deep hot oil.

Fried Artichokes
Remove the outer leaves from 6 artichokes. (Italian artichokes, which do not seem to form a choke, are obviously the most suitable. Otherwise, use only very young, tender artichokes.) Only the more tender, light-colored leaves may be left. Rinse them in water acidulated with a few drops of lemon juice. Dry them and cut them into thin slices or rounds. Make a batter with 1 egg yolk, ¼ cup (U.K. 3 tablespoons) all-purpose (plain) flour, a pinch of salt and a scant cup (U.K. ⅓ pint) milk. Leave for ½ hour to settle. When ready to fry the slices, fold 2 stiffly beaten egg whites into the batter. Dip the artichoke slices into it and fry in deep hot oil until golden brown. Drain and serve immediately.

Squash (Vegetable Marrow) Flower Fritters
Make a batter as for the artichokes, dip the squash flowers in it and fry in deep hot oil.

Bone Marrow and Brains
Lightly sauté some bone marrow and cleaned and blanched brains in a little hot oil for a minute or two only. Make a coating batter with all-purpose (plain) flour, grated Parmesan cheese, a pinch of salt and water. Stir in about 1 tablespoon olive oil and leave to settle for ½ hour. When ready to cook the ingredients, beat 1 or 2 egg yolks into the batter and fold in the stiffly beaten egg white(s). Cut the marrow and brains into pieces, dip them in batter and fry in deep hot oil until golden.

Rice Croquettes
In a large, thick-bottomed pan gently sauté 2 to 3 tablespoons each finely chopped onion and bacon in mixed butter and oil until soft. Add 1¼ cups (U.K. ½ pound) starchy rice and sauté until transparent. Pour in about 2½ cups (U.K. 1 pint) hot stock and simmer the rice until tender but still slightly resistant to bite. Remove the pan from the heat, drain off any remaining liquid and stir in 2 to 3 tablespoons grated Parmesan cheese, 1 egg and freshly grated nutmeg to taste. Shape the mixture into 12 croquettes, putting a little Bolognese Meat Sauce (page 105) or chopped mushrooms sautéed in butter inside. Dredge with flour and fry in deep hot oil.

Tagliatelle Fritters
These are made with left-over cooked tagliatelle ribbon noodles – or indeed with any cold cooked pasta. Chop the noodles finely and mix with grated Parmesan, salt and pepper to taste. Bind with eggs lightly beaten with a little milk. Drop tablespoonfuls of the mixture into fairly deep hot oil or lard and fry until golden brown all over. Drain well and serve very hot, dusted with sugar if you wish.

Agnello Dorato in Salsa d'Uovo
"Golden" Lamb in Egg Sauce

US		UK
3½ pounds	baby lamb chops	3½ pounds
6 tablespoons	butter	3 ounces
2–3 tablespoons	olive oil	2 tablespoons
¼ pound	raw Parma ham or fat salt pork, diced	¼ pound
½ cup	dry white wine	6–7 tablespoons
3	egg yolks	3
2½ tablespoons	grated Parmesan cheese	2 tablespoons
	juice of ½ lemon	
2–3 sprigs	parsley, finely chopped – optional	2–3 sprigs

Heat the butter and oil together in a heavy flameproof casserole and gently sauté the lamb and ham or fat pork until brown all over. Sprinkle with salt and pepper, and moisten with wine. Cover the casserole, transfer to a moderate oven (375°F. Mark 4) and bake for 30 to 40 minutes, or until the meat is tender.

Beat the egg yolks until smooth and add the grated cheese, lemon juice and parsley if used. Check seasoning, adding a little salt and pepper if necessary. Just before serving, pour the egg mixture into the casserole. Stir and serve immediately before the eggs are set.

Serves 6 to 8.

Costolette di Vitello alla Modenese
Veal Cutlets Modena Style

US		UK
6	veal cutlets, on the bone	6
1	egg	1
	salt	
	fine dry breadcrumbs	
6 tablespoons	butter	3 ounces
2 tablespoons	fat salt pork	1 ounce
4 teaspoons	finely chopped or minced onion – optional	1 tablespoon
1–2 tablespoons	Marsala	1–2 tablespoons
½ tablespoon	tomato paste	½ tablespoon
½ cup	stock	6 tablespoons
	pepper	

Lightly beat the cutlets with a cutlet bat and nick the edges so that they will not curl up while cooking. Dip them into the egg beaten with a pinch of salt, then coat them with breadcrumbs.

Heat the butter with the pork fat in a heavy frying pan and fry the onion gently (if used). Add the cutlets and brown them on both sides. Moisten with Marsala and cook until it evaporates. Dilute the tomato paste in the stock and pour this over the cutlets. Season to taste with salt and pepper, and continue cooking for another 5 to 10 minutes, or until the cutlets are tender.

Serve one or two cutlets per person.

Scaloppine di Vitello alla Bolognese
Veal Scaloppini (Escalopes) Bologna Style

US		UK
2 pounds	fillet of veal, cut into 12 thin slices or scaloppini (escalopes)	2 pounds
	flour	
2½ tablespoons	olive oil	2 tablespoons
3 tablespoons	butter	1½ ounces
	salt and pepper	
2½–4 tablespoons	Marsala or dry white wine	2–3 tablespoons
12 slices	raw Parma ham	12 slices
12 slices	Gruyère or Emmenthal, *or*	12 slices
5 tablespoons	grated Parmesan cheese	12 teaspoons

Lightly flatten the veal slices and dip them in flour. Heat the oil with the butter in a large heavy frying pan and sauté the slices quickly on both sides until tender and golden brown. Transfer them to a baking pan and season with salt and pepper. Add the Marsala to the fat remaining in the pan and cook for a minute or so until slightly reduced, stirring in the crusty bits from the bottom with a wooden spoon. Pour this mixture over the veal. On each slice of veal place a slice of ham and one of cheese (or sprinkle the ham with a generous teaspoon of Parmesan cheese). Put into a hot oven (425°F. Mark 6) just long enough to melt the cheese.

Serves 6.

Noce di Vitello Farcito
Stuffed Veal

US		UK
2 pounds	veal steak (noisette of veal)	2 pounds
	salt and pepper	
	lemon juice	
½ pound	pork or turkey meat	½ pound
2 ounces	cooked ham	2 ounces
2 ounces	Mortadella	2 ounces
2 ounces	calf's liver	2 ounces
2 ounces	tongue pickled in brine	2 ounces
1	carrot, boiled and shredded	1
⅔ cup	cooked green peas	4 ounces
4–5	"ovette" – see method	4–5
	freshly grated nutmeg	
2½–4 tablespoons	Marsala	2–3 tablespoons
5 tablespoons	olive oil	4 tablespoons
	milk – optional	

Ovette are the unlaid eggs sometimes to be found inside a freshly killed chicken. They lack both shells and egg whites. Substitute the yolks of 2 large eggs.

Lightly beat the piece of veal to flatten it out into a thin rectangle. Trim the edges to make a neat shape. Chop the trimmings finely and spread them out over the veal. Sprinkle with salt, pepper and a few drops of lemon juice. Grind (mince) the pork and put it into a bowl. Add the other meats, cut into thin strips, the carrot, peas and *ovette* or egg yolks. Mix together very carefully, season lightly with salt, pepper and a little grated nutmeg, pour over the Marsala and leave to "marinate" for at least an hour.

Drain the stuffing of excess moisture and spread it over the slice of veal. Roll up carefully and tie securely with string. Place the roll in a baking pan, pour the oil over the top and roast in a slow oven (350°F. Mark 3) for about 1½ hours, or until the veal is tender. A little hot milk may be added to the pan during cooking time if necessary, to keep the meat moist. Serve hot or cold, cut into slices.

Serves 6 to 8.

Lombatine alla Parmigiana
Veal Cutlets Parma Style

US		UK
6	veal cutlets, from the loin	6
	salt	
4 tablespoons	butter	2 ounces
¼ pound	raw Parma ham, finely chopped	¼ pound
2–3 sprigs	parsley, finely chopped	2–3 sprigs
¼ cup	grated Parmesan cheese	3 tablespoons
2½ tablespoons	Marsala	2 tablespoons

Beat the cutlets lightly with a cutlet bat to flatten them. Sprinkle them with salt and fry on both sides until golden brown in a heavy frying pan large enough to take them all in one layer. Put a little chopped ham, parsley and grated Parmesan on each cutlet, and sprinkle with Marsala. As soon as the cheese begins to melt, take the cutlets from the heat and serve them immediately, with any remaining sauce poured over them.

Serve one or two cutlets per person.

Trippa Dorata alla Bolognese
"Golden" Tripe Bologna Style

US		UK
2½ pounds	pre-cooked fresh tripe – see method	2½ pounds
	salt	
5 tablespoons	olive oil	4 tablespoons
1 clove	garlic, finely chopped	1 clove
2–3 sprigs	parsley, finely chopped	2–3 sprigs
¼ pound	bacon, finely chopped	¼ pound
1	onion, very thinly sliced	1
	pepper	
1 teaspoon	meat extract	1 teaspoon
4	eggs	4
5 tablespoons	grated Parmesan cheese	4 tablespoons

Usually tripe in Italy comes from veal, which has a more delicate flavor than the beef tripe more commonly available abroad. However, in this dish beef tripe is specified. Buy tripe which has already been cleaned, scalded, soaked and boiled. Take care not to overcook it, or it will turn into a slithery tough mass.

Wash the tripe and cook it for about 1 hour in boiling salted water. Drain and cut it into 1½-inch squares.

Heat half the oil in a small pan and sauté the garlic and parsley over moderate heat until the garlic turns golden. Do not let it brown. Set aside. Heat the remaining oil in another pan, large enough to take the tripe, add the bacon and onion slices, and sauté gently until these change color. Stir in the garlic and parsley mixture, add the tripe and season generously with salt and pepper. Simmer for 2 minutes. Dilute the meat extract in a little hot water and add it to the pan. Cover and cook over very low heat for about 30 minutes.

Beat the eggs, add the grated Parmesan and pour the mixture over the tripe. Stir lightly and leave for only 3 or 4 minutes longer, just long enough to set the eggs to a creamy consistency. Serve immediately.

Serves 6.

Fegatelli alla Petroniana
Baked Skewered Liver

US		UK
¾ pound	pig's caul – see page 133	¾ pound
1½ pounds	pig's liver	1½ pounds
	salt and pepper	
2–3 sprigs	sage, finely chopped	2–3 sprigs
1 sprig	rosemary, finely chopped	1 sprig
	juice of ½ lemon	
	small croûtons	
	bay leaves	
¼ cup	olive oil	3 tablespoons
½ cup	dry white wine	6 tablespoons
	sliced of fried cornmeal mush (polenta)	

Soak the pig's caul (*rete*) in water to soften it. Cut the liver into even-sized cubes. Sprinkle with salt and pepper, the finely chopped herbs and lemon juice, toss well and leave to marinate for 30 minutes.

Cut the softened caul into as many pieces as there are pieces of liver. Wrap each piece of liver in caul. Thread the liver bundles two at a time on to skewers, with a croûton on either side and a bay leaf in the middle, making a sort of five-decker sandwich.

Arrange the skewers in a baking dish, pour over the oil and bake in a moderately hot oven (400°F. Mark 5) for about 30 minutes. When the caul is browned, spoon over the wine and bake for a few minutes longer, or until the liver is cooked but still pink inside.

Serve the liver cubes with Bolognese pan juices poured over them, accompanied by slices of fried cornmeal mush (polenta).

Serves 4 to 6.

The liver is also excellent cooked without first being wrapped in caul.

Zuppa di Anguille di Comacchio
Comacchio Eel Soup or Stew

US		UK
2½ pounds	eels	2½ pounds
2½ tablespoons	tomato paste	2 tablespoons
2	onions, thinly sliced	2
1	carrot, sliced	1
2 stalks	celery, diced	2 stalks
2–3 sprigs	parsley, finely chopped	2–3 sprigs
	grated rind of ½ lemon	
	salt and pepper	
2 tablespoons	wine vinegar	1½ tablespoons
	slices of toasted bread	

Comacchio eels are renowned throughout Italy.

If the eels are large, skin them, otherwise leave them intact and simply cut them into medium-thick rounds. Dilute the tomato paste in a little water.

Put a layer of eels at the bottom of a large heavy pan, cover with a layer of onion slices, carrot, celery, parsley and lemon rind, and continue in the same order until all these ingredients are used up. Add water to cover, season with salt and pepper, cover the pan and cook slowly, stirring from time to time. After the soup has been simmering for about 15 minutes, add the vinegar and the diluted tomato paste. Cover again and continue cooking for another 20 to 25 minutes, or until the eels are tender.

Serve garnished with slices of crisply toasted bread.

Serves 6.

Anguilla in Gratella
Broiled (Grilled) Eel

US		UK
a 2½-pound	eel (or 2–3 smaller ones)	a 2½-pound
	croûtons	
a few	bay leaves or sage leaves	a few
	salt and pepper	
1–2	lemons, cut in wedges	1–2

A large eel should be skinned; smaller ones do not require it.

Cut the eel(s) into chunks about 1 inch long. Thread them on to skewers, alternating them with croûtons. Put a bay leaf (or a sage leaf) in the middle of each skewer.

Heat the broiler (grill). Season the eels with salt and pepper, and cook them under (or over) the heat until done, turning the skewers from time to time to ensure even cooking. Serve immediately, accompanied by large wedges of lemon.

Serves 6.

Anguilla Marinata
Marinated Eel

US		UK
2½ pounds	eels (2–3 eels)	2½ pounds
a few	bay leaves	a few
	salt and pepper	
Marinade		
6 cups	wine vinegar	2½ pints
2–3 sprigs	sage	2–3 sprigs
2 cloves	garlic	2 cloves
	peel of 2 oranges or lemons	
1 tablespoon	seedless white raisins (sultanas)	1 tablespoon
1 tablespoon	pine nuts	1 tablespoon
1 teaspoon	chopped candied peel	1 teaspoon
5–6	black peppercorns	5–6

Cut the (unskinned) eels into 2-inch lengths and thread them on to skewers, with a bay leaf in the middle of each skewer. Sprinkle with salt and pepper, and broil (grill) as directed in the preceding recipe.

Marinade

Pour the vinegar into a non-metallic pan. Add the next five ingredients, bring to the boil and simmer for ½ hour. After 25 minutes add the candied peel and peppercorns.

Remove the pieces of eel from the skewers and put them into another non-metallic pan. Pour over the marinade and bring to the boil again. Transfer to a large earthenware jar, cover and leave in a cool place for at least 2 days before using. Eels prepared in this manner will keep for some time, provided they are completely covered with marinade.

Serves 6.

Brodetto di Rimini
Rimini Fish Soup

US		UK
3½ pounds	assorted fish – see method	3½ pounds
	salt	
1 cup	olive oil	6–8 tablespoons
2	onions, finely chopped	2
1 pound	tomatoes, peeled, seeded and chopped	1 pound
	pepper	
4 teaspoons	wine vinegar	1 tablespoon
2–3 sprigs	parsley, finely chopped	2–3 sprigs
	slices of toasted bread	

Fish stock		
1	onion, finely chopped	1
2½ tablespoons	olive oil	2 tablespoons
2 large	tomatoes, peeled, seeded and chopped	2 large
2–3 sprigs	parsley, chopped	2–3 sprigs
	salt and pepper	
4 teaspoons	wine vinegar	1 tablespoon

Several towns on the Adriatic coast, which abounds in excellent fish, boast a *brodetto* or fish soup as their specialty. The version from Rimini is famous. The following fish would all be used, and it must be left to the imagination of the reader to devise a creditable substitute: sole, flounder, *cannochie* (see below), turbot or brill, red and grey mullet, small bass, dogfish, hake, fresh sardines, cuttlefish, squid, baby clams, etc. The greater the variety of fish, the finer the soup.

Clean and wash the fish in salted water and cut off their heads. Cut the larger fish into thick slices and leave the smaller ones whole. Use the heads to prepare the stock.

Fish stock

Sauté the onion in oil in a large pan. When it turns golden, add the tomatoes and cook briskly for 15 minutes. Then stir in the parsley and the fish heads, season with salt and pepper, and add the vinegar mixed with 5 cups (U.K. 2 pints) water. Bring to the boil, cover the pan and simmer for about 40 minutes. Strain the stock through a sieve, pressing the fish heads firmly with a wooden spoon, and return to the pan.

In a large, deep, heatproof casserole, preferably an earthenware one, in which the fish will all fit in one layer, heat the oil and brown the onions lightly. Add the tomatoes and cook over a moderate heat for 20 minutes.

Meanwhile, pick over the fish and divide it into two categories. The toughest will go into the casserole first, not necessarily the largest. If using cuttlefish or squid, for example, these must be added at the very beginning as they will take at least 30 minutes to cook.

Start adding the fish to the casserole in this manner, ending up with all the fish in a single layer if possible. Season to taste with salt and a generous sprinkling of black pepper. When all the fish are in the casserole, sprinkle with vinegar and let it evaporate. Finish cooking the fish with the casserole covered (about 15 minutes longer). Finally, sprinkle with finely chopped parsley.

This dish can be served in two ways. Formerly, the stock and fish stew were served separately so that each person might choose for himself which kind of fish he preferred. Nowadays it is more common to pour the stock into the fish before serving it with slices of bread toasted in the oven.

Serves 6 to 8.

Canocchie Fritte
Fried "Canocchie"

US		UK
4½ pounds	canocchie – see method	4½ pounds
5 tablespoons	soft breadcrumbs	4 tablespoons
2 cloves	garlic, finely chopped	2 cloves
3–4 sprigs	parsley, finely chopped	3–4 sprigs
8 tablespoons	olive oil	6½ tablespoons
	salt	
	flour	
	oil for deep-frying	

Cannochie or *squilla mantis* are rather like shrimps (U.K. prawns) in appearance. They are considered to have a particularly delicate flavor.

Clean the *cannochie* and make a cut across their backs with a pair of sharp-pointed scissors. Mix the breadcrumbs, garlic, parsley and olive oil to a paste; season with salt. Put a little of this mixture into the incisions in the *cannochie*. Dust them with flour and fry quickly in deep hot oil. Drain on absorbent paper and serve very hot.

Serves 6.

Seppie in Umido con Piselli
Stewed Cuttlefish or Squid with Peas

US		UK
2½ pounds	small cuttlefish or squid, cleaned	2½ pounds

Marinade		
1¼ cups	wine vinegar	½ pint
1 small	onion, sliced	1 small
	salt and pepper	

Sauce		
5 tablespoons	olive oil	4 tablespoons
1 clove	garlic	1 clove
1 small	onion, finely chopped	1 small
2–3 sprigs	parsley, finely chopped	2–3 sprigs
2½ tablespoons	tomato paste	2 tablespoons
3 cups	shelled green peas	¾ pound
	salt and pepper	

Cut the cuttlefish or squid into thin strips. Mix the marinade ingredients in a large earthenware or porcelain bowl, add the cuttlefish and leave to marinate for several hours.

Heat the oil in a large pan and fry the garlic clove until brown. Discard it and fry the onion in the same oil until golden. Add the cuttlefish, thoroughly drained, parsley, a tablespoonful of the marinade and the tomato paste diluted in a cup of water. Cook gently for 15 minutes. Add the peas, check seasoning and simmer until the cuttlefish are tender. The cooking time will depend entirely on their size.

Serves 6.

Pesce in Graticola alla Maniera dell'Adriatico
Broiled (Grilled) Fish Adriatic Style

For this particular recipe the following fish are suggested, but the method can, of course, be applied to other fish which may be more easily available: sole, cuttlefish, grey mullet, shrimps or prawns – these are threaded on to skewers – turbot, John Dory, angler fish – tail only. Marinate the chosen fish for 30 minutes in a mixture of olive oil, salt, pepper, breadcrumbs, garlic and chopped parsley. Slash the skin of the fish in two or three places on both sides and put them on a very hot oiled grid over glowing charcoal. Between 7 and 10 minutes' cooking on both sides is sufficient for most fish. As the fish are cooked, place them on a hot platter, sprinkle lightly with olive oil and a few drops of wine vinegar, and keep hot.

If shrimps or prawns are used, rub their shells with olive oil and salt, and impale them, face to face, on tiny skewers. When they are almost cooked, flatten them lightly with a mallet – this helps them to finish cooking evenly and makes shelling easier.

Large squid and similar fish must be pre-cooked before broiling (grilling), or they will never become tender. Grey mullet should first be cleaned with more than usual care as they can have a muddy flavor which is unpleasant.

All the fish should be served with thick wedges of lemon.

Melanzane alla Parmigiana
Eggplants (Aubergines) Parma Style

US		UK
6 medium-sized	eggplants (aubergines)	6 medium-sized
	coarse salt	
	olive oil	
	butter	
6 ounces	raw Parma ham, thinly sliced – see method	6 ounces
1 cup	tomato sauce – see method – or Bolognese Meat Sauce – page 105	½ pint
	pepper	
¾–1 cup	grated Parmesan cheese	3–4 ounces

By tomato sauce Italians understand a well-flavored sauce made from either fresh or canned tomatoes gently simmered in oil or butter with onion, garlic and herbs. If raw Parma ham (*prosciutto crudo*) is not available, use thinly sliced lean bacon.

Trim the eggplants and cut them into rounds. Sprinkle with salt and leave on a sloping plate or in a colander for at least 1 hour to allow the bitter juices to drain away. This procedure also helps them to absorb less oil when fried. Rinse the slices and pat them dry.

Heat a generous layer of olive oil in a frying pan and fry the eggplant slices on both sides until golden brown. Drain them on absorbent paper. Put a layer of eggplants at the bottom of a well-buttered baking dish, cover with slices of ham, a few tablespoons of tomato or meat sauce, a little pepper and a generous sprinkling of Parmesan cheese. Repeat the layers until the ingredients are all used up. Dot the surface with butter and bake in a slow oven (325°F. Mark 2) for about 1 hour. Serve hot.

Serves 6.

Verdure alla Parmigiana
Vegetables Parma Style

The vegetables vary according to season, but favorites include asparagus, zucchini (courgettes), spinach, fennel and cardoons or Swiss chard. They are first cooked in a little salted water until tender, drained thoroughly, then simmered slowly in butter until thoroughly re-heated, and served generously sprinkled with grated Parmesan cheese.

Sformato di Besciamella
Béchamel Mold (Mould)

US		UK
½ cup	butter	4 ounces
1 cup	all-purpose (plain) flour	4 ounces
3¾ cups	warm milk	1½ pints
1¾ cups	grated Parmesan cheese	7 ounces
	salt	
7	eggs, separated	7
	butter	
	fine dry breadcrumbs	
	Bolognese Meat Sauce – page 105 *or* Vegetables Parma Style – see above	

Make a stiff Béchamel Sauce with the butter, flour and milk, following the directions given on page 106. Pour it into a bowl and beat in the grated Parmesan and salt to taste. Leave to cool, then add the egg yolks, one at a time, beating well after each addition. Beat the egg whites until stiff and fold them into the sauce. Pour immediately into a large, deep, well-buttered mold or soufflé dish coated with fine dry breadcrumbs. Cover with a piece of foil to prevent the top from browning too quickly and place in a *bain-marie* (or a baking pan into which you have poured warm water to come halfway up the sides of the mold). Bake in a moderate oven (375°F. Mark 4) for about ½ hour.

Turn the mold out and serve immediately with meat sauce or vegetables.

Serves 6 to 8.

Tortino di Zucchine
Zucchini (Courgette) Mold (Mould)

US		UK
3½ pounds	zucchini (courgettes)	3½ pounds
4 tablespoons	butter	2 ounces
4 tablespoons	olive oil	3 tablespoons
	salt	
4 tablespoons	grated Parmesan cheese	3 tablespoons
1	egg yolk	1
	pepper	
	freshly grated nutmeg	
Béchamel Sauce		
6 tablespoons	butter	3 ounces
8 tablespoons	all-purpose (plain) flour	2 ounces
1 teaspoon	salt	1 teaspoon
4½ cups	hot milk	1¾ pints

Wash the zucchini and slice them fairly thickly. Sauté gently in a mixture of butter and oil until soft and golden.

Prepare a Béchamel Sauce with the ingredients above, following the directions on page 106. Cook it very gently, in a double boiler if available, so that it becomes really stiff. Remove from the heat and beat in the Parmesan, egg yolk, pepper and nutmeg to taste.

Arrange the zucchini in an ovenproof dish, pour the sauce over them and brown the top in a very hot oven (450°F. Mark 7) for a few minutes.

Serves 6.

Crauti alla Modenese
Sauerkraut with Sausage Modena Style

US		UK
1	Zampone sausage – see method	1
1½ pounds	sauerkraut – see method	1½ pounds

A Zampone is a highly spiced sausage made from pork which is stuffed into the skin of a pig's trotter. It is a specialty of the area.

Instead of using commercially prepared sauerkraut, it can be prepared at home in the Italian manner. Simply take a large Savoy or white cabbage, trim off the stem and discolored leaves, and shred it finely. Pack it into a large earthenware jar, cover with wine vinegar and leave for at least 48 hours.

Loosen the strings which are tied round the Zampone and make two incisions with a sharp knife. Wrap it in a cloth and drop it into a large pan so that it lies flat on the bottom. Cover generously with cold water, bring to the boil and simmer for 3 hours, longer if the weight of the sausage exceeds 4 pounds.

Put the sauerkraut (well drained) into a shallow pan, add a ladleful of the liquid in which the sausage was cooked and if necessary a little water. Cover the pan and cook gently for 30 minutes.

Cut the Zampone into thick slices and serve it very hot with the sauerkraut.

Serves 6.

Castagnole Fritte
Sweet Lemon Fritters

US		UK
4	eggs	4
5 tablespoons	granulated (caster) sugar	4 tablespoons
2½ cups	all-purpose (plain) flour	10 ounces
5 tablespoons	mild olive oil	4 tablespoons
5 teaspoons	brandy	4 teaspoons
pinch	salt	pinch
½ teaspoon	vanilla extract	½ teaspoon
	grated rind of 4 lemons	
	oil for deep-frying	
	confectioners' (icing) sugar	

Beat the eggs lightly, add the sugar and beat until fluffy. Add the flour, oil, brandy, salt, vanilla and grated lemon rind, and mix thoroughly with a wooden spoon until well blended.

Heat a large pan of oil for deep-frying. Drop teaspoonfuls of the fritter batter into the oil, using 2 teaspoons to shape it into neat balls, and fry until puffed and golden. The fritters will swell, so do not attempt to fry too many at a time. Drain on absorbent paper, dust generously with confectioners' (icing) sugar and serve immediately.

Serves 6 to 8.

Sfrappole di Carnevale
Carnival Fritters or Knots

US		UK
4 cups	all-purpose (plain) flour	1 pound
2 tablespoons	butter	1 ounce
3	egg yolks, lightly beaten	3
1	egg white, lightly mixed	1
2½ tablespoons	granulated (caster) sugar	2 tablespoons
1 teaspoon	salt	1 teaspoon
pinch	vanilla powder *or* vanilla extract to taste	pinch
about 1 cup	white wine	about ½ pint
	oil for deep-frying	
	confectioners' (icing) sugar	

Sift the flour and work in the butter. Add the egg yolks, egg white, sugar, salt, vanilla and enough wine to make a smooth, pliable, fairly soft dough. Wrap in wax paper and leave in a cool place for 1 hour.

Roll the dough out very thinly, then cut it into long ribbons about ½ inch wide and 8 inches long. Carefully tie these into knots or bows and fry them quickly in deep boiling oil until golden. Drain the fritters on absorbent paper, dust with confectioners' (icing) sugar and serve, either alone, or with fruit salad, cold mousse or similar types of sweet dishes.

Torta di Riso
Rice Cake

US		UK
6½ cups	milk	generous 2½ pints
1½ cups	rice	10 ounces
pinch	salt	pinch
1 cup	sugar	8 ounces
½ cup	sweet almonds	3 ounces
3–4	bitter almonds	3–4
4	eggs, separated	4
	grated rind of 2 lemons	
½ cup	diced candied citron and orange peel	3 ounces
pinch	vanilla powder *or* vanilla extract to taste	pinch
	butter	
	fine dry breadcrumbs	
5 tablespoons	Maraschino	4 tablespoons
	confectioners' (icing) sugar	

Bring the milk to the boil in a heavy pan, stir in the rice, salt and half the sugar, and simmer gently until the rice is almost tender. Meanwhile, blanch the almonds in boiling water for 1 or 2 minutes, peel them, toast them in a hot oven and chop them finely. When the rice is ready, remove it from the heat and allow to cool.

Beat the egg yolks with the remaining sugar. Stir in the rice mixture, the grated lemon rind, diced candied peel and vanilla. Beat the egg whites until stiff and fold them into the mixture. Pour into a well-buttered 12-inch cake pan coated with breadcrumbs. Bake for at least 1½ hours, longer if necessary. The cake should be firm and light, although not stodgy, with a creamy brown top. Take it from the oven and let it cool. Then prick all over the surface with a skewer or toothpick and pour over the Maraschino. Leave until the following day, then turn it out, dust with confectioners' (icing) sugar and serve.

Ravioli di San Giuseppe
St. Joseph's Sweet Ravioli

US		UK
1 cup plus 2 tablespoons	potato flour – obtainable in health food and specialty stores	6 ounces
1 cup	all-purpose (plain) flour	4 ounces
3 tablespoons	butter	1½ ounces
6 tablespoons	granulated (caster) sugar	3 ounces
pinch	salt	pinch
2	eggs	2
	grated rind of 1 lemon	
pinch	cream of tartar	pinch
¼ teaspoon	baking soda	¼ teaspoon
2½ tablespoons	milk	2 tablespoons
	jam or thick custard cream	
	butter for baking sheet	
	confectioners' (icing) sugar	

Sift the flours into a bowl and cut in the butter. Add the sugar, salt, 1 egg, beaten, lemon rind, cream of tartar and baking soda dissolved in milk. Mix to a firm dough and knead well. Cover the bowl and leave in the refrigerator for 1 hour.

Roll the dough out very thinly and cut into circles about 2 inches in diameter. Put a teaspoon of jam (or custard cream) on each circle and fold in half. Seal the edges well. Arrange the ravioli on a buttered baking sheet, brush with the remaining egg, beaten, and bake in a slow oven (350°F. Mark 3) for about 30 minutes. Cool and serve, dusted with confectioners' (icing) sugar.

Ciambellone Bolognese
Bolognese Fruit and Nut Ring

US		UK
4	eggs	4
¾ cup	granulated (caster) sugar	6 ounces
4 cups	all-purpose (plain) flour	1 pound
5 teaspoons	baking powder	4 teaspoons
6 tablespoons	softened butter	3 ounces
1 cup	milk	8 fluid ounces
pinch	vanilla powder *or* vanilla extract to taste	pinch
pinch	salt	pinch
½ cup	diced mixed candied peel	3 ounces
2 tablespoons	pine nuts	1 ounce
2½ tablespoons	almonds, peeled, toasted and halved	1 ounce
¼ cup	raisins, soaked in Marsala	1½ ounces
	butter for cake pan	
2–3 tablespoons	sugar sprinkles (strands) – optional	1 ounce

Beat 3 eggs with the sugar until thick and fluffy. Sift the flour and baking powder into a bowl. Add the flour to the egg mixture gradually, beating well between each addition with a wooden spoon. Cut the butter into small pieces and add to the batter, beating until well blended. Then, still beating vigorously, add the milk, vanilla, salt, diced peel, pine nuts, almonds, and the raisins, squeezed dry and dusted with flour. Mix thoroughly and turn into a well-buttered tube pan. Brush with the remaining egg, beaten, and sprinkle with sugar sprinkles (strands). Bake in a slow oven (350°F. Mark 3) for about 45 minutes, or until the cake tests done.

Certosino
Christmas Fruit Cake

US		UK
1⅓ cups	honey	1 pound
5 cups	all-purpose (plain) flour	1¼ pounds
½ pound	peeled almonds	½ pound
4–5 tablespoons	pine nuts	2 ounces
½ cup	white seedless raisins (sultanas)	3 ounces
½ pound	mixed candied fruit, diced	½ pound
scant 1 cup	cooked fruit, sieved	½ pound
4 squares	bitter chocolate, chopped	¼ pound
pinch	ground cinnamon	pinch
4 teaspoons	anise seed	1 tablespoon
4 tablespoons	softened butter	2 ounces
2½ teaspoons	baking soda	2 teaspoons
	butter for cake pan	
	candied peel or fruit, to decorate	

This cake is made by the Carthusian monks of Bologna.

Pour the honey into a heavy pan, add 2 or 3 tablespoons water and heat gently, stirring, until liquid. Take the pan from the heat. Sift the flour into a large bowl and slowly pour in the liquid honey, stirring vigorously until thoroughly blended. Mix well with the remaining cake ingredients, adding the soda, dissolved in a little warm water, at the very end. Turn the mixture into a generously buttered tube pan and decorate with candied peel or fruit, cut in half or left whole. Bake in a slow oven (350°F. Mark 3) for about 1 hour, or until the cake tests done.

This cake will keep for some time if stored wrapped in wax paper or foil.

Zuppa a Due Colori
Vanilla and Chocolate Pudding

US		UK
½ pound	sponge cake	½ pound
	rum	
	Alkermes liqueur (page 156) or syrup from a can of fruit tinted with red food coloring	
	grated bitter chocolate and 12 liqueur cherries, pitted, to decorate	

Vanilla custard

5	egg yolks	5
5 tablespoons	sugar	4 tablespoons
pinch	vanilla powder *or* vanilla extract to taste	pinch
1 rounded teaspoon	flour	1 teaspoon
	rind of 1 lemon	
2¼ cups	milk, scalded	generous ¾ pint
1 tablespoon	butter	½ ounce

Chocolate cream

2	eggs	2
5 tablespoons	sugar	4 tablespoons
2½ tablespoons	flour	2 tablespoons
2½ tablespoons	cocoa	2 tablespoons
pinch	vanilla powder *or* vanilla extract to taste	pinch
2 cups	milk, scalded	¾ pint
1 tablespoon	butter	½ ounce

If preferred, the vanilla powder or extract can be omitted in both creams, and a piece of vanilla pod infused in the milk instead.

Vanilla custard
Mix the egg yolks with the sugar, vanilla (see above) and flour in the top of a double boiler. Add the strip of lemon rind and stir in the scalded milk gradually, beating well with a wooden spoon. Cook over water, stirring constantly, until the custard thickens. On no account let it boil or it will curdle. When the custard is smooth and thick, stir in the butter. Remove from the heat, discard the lemon rind, and pour into a jug. Leave to cool, stirring occasionally to prevent a skin from forming on the surface.

Chocolate cream
This should again be cooked carefully in the top of a double boiler, but somewhat longer to ensure that the flour is well cooked. Mix the ingredients together with the milk and cook as above. When thick and smooth, beat in the butter, pour into a jug and leave to cool, with an occasional stir.

Cut the sponge cake into thin slices and line a deep glass dish with a layer of cake. Sprinkle generously with rum and cover with a layer of vanilla custard. Cover with another layer of cake slices and this time soak with Alkermes (a cochineal liqueur) or syrup tinted with red food coloring. Spread with a layer of chocolate cream. Continue in this manner until the ingredients are used up, finishing with a layer of vanilla custard. Grate a little chocolate over the top, decorate with cherries, and chill for several hours before serving.
Serves 6.

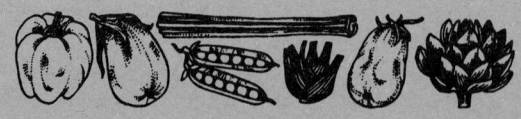

TUSCANY

Against a background of Florence viewed from the Piazzale Michelangelo, the classic flask of Chianti surrounded by Florentine specialties: in the foreground, the inimitable Florentine steak (see page 132), together with beans in olive oil and a dish of peas and ham.

The word Tuscany evokes an image of a world that has been described by poets as often as it has been depicted by artists. It is a world whose clear and tranquil landscape matches the temperament of its people, which in turn is reflected by their speech, the purest in the Italian language, their caustic wit, clarity of mind and realism. In the same way, purity is the keynote of Tuscan cooking. And whereas elsewhere in Italy cooking may be said to be a passion, in Tuscany it is an art, as decorous and as formal as that of the great masters of the Florentine school.

The task of the Tuscan cook is not easy. He cannot fall back on elaborate sauces and gravies to disguise the flavor of the food, nor may he employ the garnishes which are so dear to some schools of cooking. In preparing dishes of classic simplicity he must rely on his skill alone, aided by the excellence of his raw materials. For instance, the *bistecca alla fiorentina* is so simple to prepare, but it is essentially a rite, for the cut of meat must be of just the right size and thickness, from the right sort of animal, the *vitellone*, a young steer that is no longer a calf but has not yet become an ox. And this is only part of the secret. At the last moment, while the meat is still on the heat, and after it has been seasoned with salt and pepper, it is lightly brushed with Tuscan olive oil.

Olive oil is the only luxury permitted in Tuscan cooking. Lucca, the center of the olive oil trade, is famous for the oil which it exports all over the world. But the oil the Tuscans like best is that made for them in their local mills, to which every season they take the olives that they have grown on their own small farms.

An ancient, uniquely Tuscan dish, *fagioli nel fiasco*, or beans cooked in a wine flask (see page 138), is still prepared today, both in the countryside and in fashionable city restaurants. Traditionally, the beans should be cooked on special charcoal-burning braziers.

The art of cooking the celebrated Florentine steak is handed down among restaurateurs from father to son. One of the best-known *trattorie* in which to eat this typical Tuscan dish is "da Sostanza", also known as "Il Troia", in Florence.

Despite the poverty of the Tuscan soil, this oil is the most precious product of their land.

Another example of Tuscan culinary genius is the manner in which they prepare vegetables, especially the classic dish of beans, which gourmets still cook directly over a fire in wine flasks, and artichokes which, although Rome is their acknowledged capital, are prepared here with consummate skill. Indeed, it would be true to say that Tuscan cooking revolves round the old-fashioned hearth, where pride of place is taken by the grill and the roasting spit. The countless restaurants in Tuscany called *Girarrosto* (The Roasting Spit) owe their name to those huge spits, loaded with chickens, pork, suckling kids, guinea fowls and game of all kind, from birds to boar, which rotate perpetually over the fire.

By the coast, an altogether different kind of cooking flourishes. The Tyrrhenian Sea abounds in fish of all kinds and Leghorn is the main center of the fishing industry. Here the *cacciucco* was invented, a fish soup (but woe betide you if Tuscans hear you calling it a soup!) in which every imaginable kind of fish and shellfish is included, according to the whim of the cook. The result is a splendid, spicy dish, poured over slices of toasted bread and garnished with fried tomatoes and red peppers. A *cacciucco* is meant to contain the full flavor of the sea; at Viareggio they believe that the height of perfection is reached by boiling a stone from the sea bed with the fish. Other Tuscan fish dishes include *fritto del mare*, a mixture of small fried fish, red mullet, and the celebrated *cieche*, tiny, blind baby eels caught in large numbers at the mouth of the Arno.

Some local specialties photographed before the Palazzo Pretorio in Arezzo.
Below: The turning spit, a familiar sight in Tuscany, laden with delicious meats—chickens, loin of pork, kid and guinea fowl.

In Albarese, in the heart of the Tuscan Maremma (see page 126), some of the typical products of the region: pork, wild boar and Pecorino cheese.

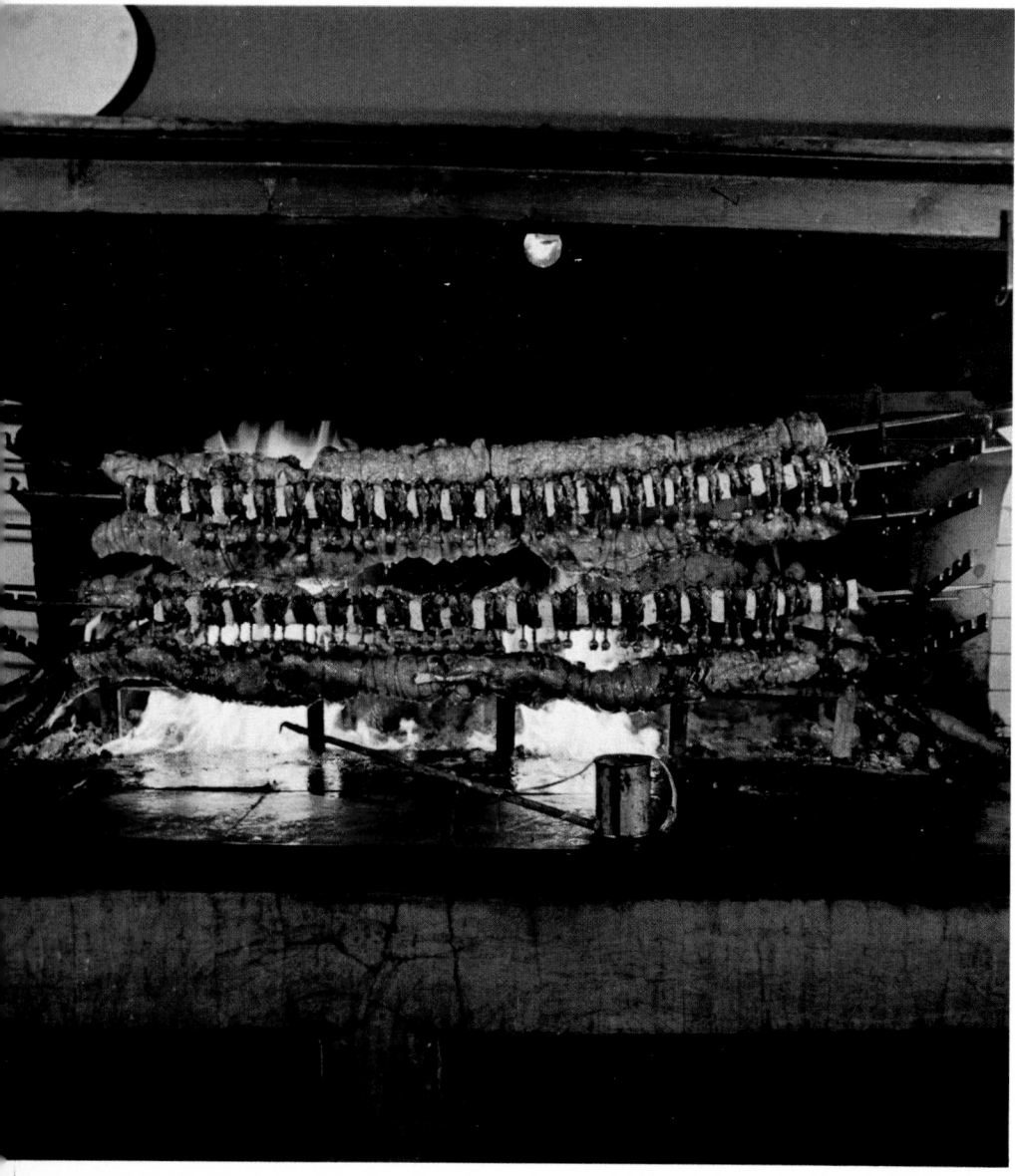

The towers of San Gimignano set the scene for a display of the finest local dishes—risotto, veal, chicken and delicious fresh vegetables—all washed down with Vernaccia wine.

Blind baby eels known as *cieche*, caught at the mouth of the Arno in the early spring, are a favorite dish of Pisan gourmets.
Below, left: Rice is an important ingredient of Tuscan cooking. Pictured here are *riso nero* or "black rice", prepared with the ink of cuttlefish, and risotto with seafood.

Livorno (Leghorn) is justly proud of
its fish dishes. *Cacciucco*, the local
fish stew (see page 135), and red
mullet *alla livornese* (see page 136)
are two fine examples of the
local cuisine.

The masts of fishing boats anchored
in the harbor of Viareggio make a
picturesque setting for a selection of
local dishes of fish and shellfish.

Tuscany is a fascinating blend of town and country. One of the strangest landscapes is the Maremma, like another Far West, over which herds of cattle roam, and where, surprisingly enough, one can still find wild boar. Every town, large or small, interprets cooking in its own individual way, yet a perfect unity is achieved from the cliffs of Volterra to the valley of the Tiber, from Prato, where the wool trade has flourished since the Middle Ages, down to Lucca, whose peddlers travel all over the world selling picturesque plaster statuettes.

Siena, the city of the Palio, is the home of *panforte*, a delicious Christmas cake made of flour, almonds, hazelnuts, cocoa, spices and fruit, which is now as well known as the battle which takes place twice a year between the seventeen quarters of the town in the Piazza del Campo. But Tuscany also offers less extravagant sweet dishes: *brigidini*, small, spiced, wafer-like pastries which are sold from barrows and stalls at markets and country fairs, and *castagnaccio*, a simple chestnut-flour cake covered with pine nuts and raisins, invented by the woodcutters of the Pistoian Apennines.

Both at home and abroad, Tuscan cooking is well supported by its wines. The vine is cultivated throughout the region and every valley boasts its own specialty. Chianti has become a legend. Already famous six centuries ago to the extent that it was known then as far away as England, it was originally produced by a small group of villages in the provinces of Florence and Siena. With time, and because of the ever-increasing demand, the area grew, so that today, although the individual districts of production are protected

Olive oil from the hills around Lucca, delicate and light to taste, is indispensable in many traditional recipes, including the two chestnut-flour cakes pictured here: *tortini di castagnaccio* eaten with fresh Ricotta cheese, and the classic *castagnaccio* itself, sometimes sprinkled with pine nuts and raisins, and flavored with a sprig of rosemary (see page 140).

by trademarks, the name Chianti is synonymous with Tuscan wine. Other famous wines include the Vernaccia of San Gimignano, the Aleatico of Portoferraio, which is made on Elba, and Brunello Montalcino and Moscadello from Siena. There is also *vinsanto*, or "holy wine", which takes a long time to mature, becoming darker, sweeter and more full-bodied the longer it is kept in the barrel.

Finally, eating in Tuscany may also mean a picnic lunch on a hillside, perhaps just ham with great chunks of Tuscan bread, and wine from a farmhouse, drunk straight from the bottle. On such occasions the meal is even more glorious if through the vines and the silvery grey leaves of the olive trees one can catch a glimpse of the outline of Florence, with the dome of Brunelleschi, Giotto's Campanile, the tower of the Signoria and the silver ribbon of the River Arno.

Crostini di Fegatini di Pollo
Chicken Livers on Toast

US		UK
½ pound	chicken livers	½ pound
4 teaspoons	olive oil	1 tablespoon
2 tablespoons	butter	1 ounce
2 tablespoons	ham fat	1 ounce
3–4 slices	onion	3–4 slices
1 sprig	sage	1 sprig
	salt	
6 slices	bread, halved	6 slices
	lemon juice	
4 teaspoons	grated Parmesan cheese	1 tablespoon

Clean the chicken livers and chop them into small pieces. Heat the oil, butter and ham fat, and sauté the onion gently until golden brown. Add the chicken livers and the sage. Season with salt and cook over a low heat for about 10 minutes. Meanwhile, toast the bread. Add a few drops of lemon juice and the cheese to the chicken livers, and discard the sage. Spread the livers on the toast, pour any remaining fat over the top, and put into a hot oven for a minute or so to heat through.

Serves 3 to 4.

Pan di Ramerino
Rosemary Buns

US		UK
1 pound	once-risen bread dough, made with 2½ cups (10 ounces) flour	1 pound
½ cup	olive oil	6 tablespoons
1 sprig	rosemary, chopped	1 sprig
½ cup	seedless white raisins (sultanas), soaked in warm water	3 ounces
	flour	

Heat the oil and gently sauté the rosemary sprig for several minutes, but do not let it turn black. Strain the oil and discard the rosemary. Put the dough on a pastry board, make a hollow in the middle and add the rosemary-flavored oil. Work it in thoroughly. Pat the white raisins (sultanas) dry, add these to the dough, and knead well. Grease your hands with oil and shape the dough into small buns. Arrange them, well spaced apart, on a floured baking sheet. With a knife, make a cross-shaped incision on each bun. Cover and leave in a warm place until doubled in bulk. Then bake for 15 minutes in a hot oven (425°F. Mark 6), lower the heat to moderate (375°F. Mark 4) and continue baking until the little buns are golden.

Makes about a dozen buns.

Spaghetti alla Viareggina
Spaghetti Viareggio Style

US		UK
4 pounds	baby clams	4 pounds
	salt	
2 cloves	garlic	2 cloves
1 cup	olive oil	scant ½ pint
1 small	onion, thinly sliced	1 small
½ cup	dry white wine	6–8 tablespoons
1½ pounds	tomatoes, peeled, seeded and chopped	1½ pounds
small piece	hot chili pepper	small piece
1½ pounds	spaghetti	1½ pounds
2–3 sprigs	parsley, chopped	2–3 sprigs
	pepper	

Soak the baby clams in salted water to draw out all the sand. Rinse them thoroughly and put them in a pan with the garlic and a few tablespoons of the oil. Cook over a moderate heat, tightly covered, until the clams open. Take them out of their shells and reserve the liquor.

Heat the remaining oil and sauté the onion gently until golden. Add the wine and continue cooking until reduced. Add the tomatoes and the clam liquor; season to taste with the chili pepper and a pinch of salt, and cook over a brisk heat for about 20 minutes.

Boil the spaghetti in a large pan of salted water until just tender. Meanwhile, add the clams and parsley to the tomato sauce, season with plenty of pepper and leave for a minute for the clams to absorb the flavors. Drain the spaghetti as soon as it is cooked, dress immediately with the hot sauce and serve at once.

Serves 6.

Pappardelle con la Lepre
Noodles with Hare Sauce

US		UK
Dough		
6 cups	all-purpose (plain) flour	1½ pounds
6–8	eggs	6–8
	salt	
Sauce		
1	hare – back and legs only	1
4 tablespoons	butter	2 ounces
2½ tablespoons	olive oil	2 tablespoons
2 ounces	bacon, finely chopped	2 ounces
1 small	onion, finely chopped	1 small
1 stalk	celery, finely chopped	1 stalk
	salt and pepper	
pinch	thyme	pinch
4 teaspoons	flour	1 tablespoon
1 cup	dry white wine	scant ½ pint
2 cups	boiling meat stock	¾ pint
Garnish		
	grated Parmesan cheese	

Dough
Prepare the dough according to the recipe for Egg Pasta on page 106. Roll it out thinly and cut into long strips about ½ inch wide. Put aside to dry. (Or use commercially prepared wide ribbon noodles.)

Sauce
Remove all the bones and sinews from the hare, and cut the flesh into small pieces. Heat the butter and oil, and gently sauté the bacon, onion and celery. Add the hare, season to taste with salt and pepper, and sprinkle with thyme. Brown the hare all over, dust with the flour and let this brown. Pour in the wine and cook gently until reduced. Then add the boiling stock, cover and cook over a low heat for about 2 hours.

Cook the noodles in plenty of boiling salted water until *al dente* (home-made noodles cook very quickly). Drain them and immediately toss them with the hot sauce. Serve with plenty of Parmesan cheese.

Serves 6.

Strisce e Ceci
Ribbon Noodles with Chick Peas

US		UK
2 cups	chick peas, soaked overnight	¾ pound
½ cup	olive oil	6–8 tablespoons
1	onion, thinly sliced	1
1 clove	garlic, finely chopped	1 clove
2–3 sprigs 1 sprig	parsley, finely chopped, *or* rosemary, finely chopped	2–3 sprigs 1 sprig
1 teaspoon	tomato paste	1 teaspoon
	salt and pepper	
¾ pound	wide ribbon noodles	¾ pound
	grated Parmesan cheese	

Bring a large pan of unsalted water to the boil and simmer the chick peas in it until tender. Heat the oil, and gently sauté the onion and garlic; add the parsley. When the mixture begins to turn golden, add the tomato paste diluted with a little hot water. Drain off half the chick peas and rub them through a fine sieve (or put through a blender). Add to the pan with remaining whole chick peas and their cooking liquid. Season with salt and plenty of pepper, and simmer for 30 minutes to develop flavors. Then bring to the boil, add the noodles, stir and cook them until tender but still firm.

The result should be noodles with a chick pea sauce rather than a soup of chick peas with noodles in it, as the noodles will swell during cooking. Serve with plenty of Parmesan cheese.

Serves 6.

Gnocchi di Polenta
Polenta Pie

US		UK
Polenta		
3 cups	cornmeal	1 pound
9 cups	water	3½ pints
	salt	
Sauce		
1½ ounces	dried mushrooms	1½ ounces
¼ cup	olive oil	3 tablespoons
3 tablespoons	butter	1½ ounces
¼ cup	ham fat	2 ounces
1	carrot, finely chopped	1
1 stalk	celery, finely chopped	1 stalk
1 small	onion, finely chopped	1 small
¾ cup	lean pork sausage meat	6 ounces
½ pound	tomatoes, puréed	½ pound
	salt and pepper	
Garnish		
6 tablespoons	butter	3 ounces
1 cup	grated Parmesan cheese	4 ounces

Polenta

Make the polenta in the usual way (see page 43). Take it from the pan and spread it out on a wetted surface to a thickness of about ½ inch. Leave to cool.

Sauce

Soak the mushrooms in warm water for 30 minutes. Squeeze dry and chop finely. Put aside until required. Heat the oil and butter, and gently fry the ham fat and vegetables until transparent. Add the sausage meat, crumble it with a fork and cook for a few minutes longer. Dilute the tomato purée with a little water, add to the pan, cover and cook slowly. After 15 minutes, add the mushrooms, season to taste with salt and pepper, and continue cooking for a further 15 minutes.

Cut the polenta into rounds. Put a layer of these into a well-buttered baking dish, spread with a few tablespoonfuls of sauce, dot with butter and sprinkle with Parmesan cheese. Continue in this way until all the ingredients are used up. Put into a hot oven (450°F. Mark 7) to heat through and brown the top, and serve very hot with a bowl of additional grated Parmesan.

Serves 6.

Risotto alla Toscana
Tuscan Risotto

US		UK
2¼ cups	rice	1 pound
¼ cup	olive oil	3 tablespoons
5 tablespoons	butter	2½ ounces
1 small	onion, thinly sliced	1 small
1 small	carrot, finely chopped	1 small
1 stalk	celery, finely chopped	1 stalk
1 cup	ground (UK minced) lean beef	½ pound
¼ pound	calf's liver, chopped	¼ pound
¼ pound	calf's kidney, sliced	¼ pound
1–2	chicken livers	1–2
½ cup	red wine	6 tablespoons
1–2 teaspoons	tomato paste	1–2 teaspoons
6¼ cups	boiling stock	2½ pints
	salt and pepper	
	grated nutmeg	
¾ cup	grated Parmesan cheese	3 ounces

See page 66 for general instructions on the technique of making risottos.

Heat the oil and half the butter in a large pan, and gently sauté the onion, carrot and celery until they begin to brown. Add the beef, calf's liver and kidney, and the chicken liver. Brown well, add the wine and cook gently until reduced. Dilute the tomato paste in a little hot stock. Stir this into the pan, season with salt, plenty of pepper and a pinch of grated nutmeg, cover and cook gently for 30 minutes.

Dribble the rice into the pan and stir it well until it has become brown and almost transparent, about 5 minutes' cooking. Add the boiling stock a little at a time, stirring constantly. When all the stock is in the pan, cover and cook over a moderate heat, with the liquid just bubbling, until the rice is tender and has absorbed most of the liquid. Take the pan from the heat, gently stir in the remaining butter and Parmesan cheese, cover and leave for 2 minutes before serving.

Serves 4 to 6.

Minestra di Pasta Grattata
Grated Noodle Soup

US		UK
3 cups	all-purpose (plain) flour	¾ pound
	salt and grated nutmeg	
3 large	eggs	3 large
7½ cups	meat stock	3 pints
	grated Parmesan cheese	

Make a very stiff dough with the flour, a pinch each of salt and grated nutmeg, and the eggs. Knead thoroughly and leave to rest until dry enough to grate. Then grate it on the coarsest side of a cheese grater and spread out on a cloth to dry.

Bring the stock to the boil, add the grated noodles and cook for about 2 minutes, or until the stock stops foaming. Serve with a large bowl of grated Parmesan.

Serves 6.

Minestrone Toscano
Tuscan Vegetable Soup

US		UK
2 cups	dried white (haricot) beans, soaked overnight	¾ pound
½ cup	olive oil	6 tablespoons
2 cloves	garlic, finely chopped	2 cloves
1 small	onion, thinly sliced	1 small
2 stalks	celery, diced	2 stalks
1	carrot, diced	1
2 sprigs	rosemary, finely chopped	2 sprigs
½ cup	finely chopped bacon – optional	2 ounces
5 teaspoons	tomato paste	4 teaspoons
½ head	Savoy cabbage, shredded	½ head
2–3	leeks, chopped	2–3
3	zucchini (courgettes), diced	3
	finely chopped basil, to taste	
2–3 sprigs	parsley, finely chopped	2–3 sprigs
1	clove	1
	salt and pepper	
⅔ cup	rice or noodles, or pieces of toasted bread	5 ounces

Cook the beans in their soaking water for about 2 hours, or until tender. Drain, reserving the liquid, and put about half of them through a fine sieve (or blender). Put aside. Heat the oil in a large pan and gently sauté the garlic, onion, celery, carrot, rosemary and bacon until they begin to brown. Dilute the tomato paste with a little warm water, stir it into the pan, then add the cabbage, leeks, zucchini (courgettes), basil, parsley and clove, as well as the puréed and whole beans, and their cooking water. Add a little extra hot water if necessary. Check seasoning and cook slowly for 30 minutes.

If using rice or noodles, add them to the broth at this point and cook until tender. Otherwise, serve the thick soup poured over slices of toast, adding a little extra olive oil.

Serves 6.

Minestrone alla Fiorentina
Florentine Vegetable Soup

US		UK
¾ cup	olive oil	9 tablespoons
1	onion, thinly sliced	1
2 ounces	raw Parma ham, shredded	2 ounces
½ head	Savoy cabbage, shredded	½ head
2 stalks	celery, diced	2 stalks
¼ pound	fresh pork	¼ pound
2 sprigs	thyme	2 sprigs
2 cups	cooked white (haricot) beans	½ pound
5 pints	stock or water	4 pints
2 cloves	garlic	2 cloves
2 sprigs	rosemary	2 sprigs
	salt	
	grated Parmesan cheese	

Heat ¼ cup (U.K. 3 tablespoons) oil in a large pan and sauté the onion and ham gently. Add the cabbage, celery, pork, thyme and beans. Let them brown, then add a ladleful of stock and cook slowly for 5 minutes. Pour in the rest of the stock and continue to cook gently for an hour.

Heat the remaining oil and add the garlic and rosemary. When the garlic cloves are brown, strain the oil into the soup. Simmer for another 15 minutes, check seasoning and serve, with plenty of grated Parmesan.

Serves 6 to 8.

Zuppa di Verdura
Summer Vegetable Soup

US		UK
	olive oil	
3	carrots, diced	3
3	potatoes, cubed	3
1 small	cauliflower, divided into flowerettes	1 small
2	leeks, chopped	2
2 stalks	celery, diced	2 stalks
1 small	onion, sliced	1 small
4–5 leaves	lettuce, shredded	4–5 leaves
4 tablespoons	shelled green peas	3 tablespoons
½ pound	snap (French) beans, chopped	½ pound
12	asparagus tips	12
	salt	
7½ cups	stock	3 pints
	toasted bread	
	grated Parmesan cheese	

Heat ¼ cup (U.K. 3 tablespoons) olive oil in a large pan and sauté the vegetables gently until they soften and begin to change color. Season with salt, add a ladleful of water and simmer over the lowest possible heat for about 30 minutes. Add the hot stock and simmer for ½ hour longer. Serve very hot with slices of toasted bread, plenty of Parmesan and a trickle of olive oil over each soup bowl.

Serves 6.

"La Ribollita"
Tuscan Bean Soup au Gratin

US		UK
2½ cups	dried white (haricot) beans, soaked overnight	1 pound
2–3 tablespoons	olive oil	2 tablespoons
1 clove	garlic, finely chopped	1 clove
1	onion, finely chopped	1
1	carrot, finely chopped	1
1 stalk	celery, finely chopped	1 stalk
2	leeks, finely chopped	2
1 sprig	rosemary, finely chopped	1 sprig
small piece	hot chili pepper	small piece
1	ham bone	1
	salt and pepper	

Garnish		
¾ cup	olive oil	generous ¼ pint
2 cloves	garlic, crushed	2 cloves
pinch	thyme	pinch
8 slices	bread, toasted	8 slices
¾ cup	grated Parmesan cheese	3 ounces
1	onion, thinly sliced	1

Drain the beans. Heat the olive oil in a large pan and gently sauté the garlic, onion, carrot, celery, leeks, rosemary and the piece of chili until they begin to turn brown. Add the beans and ham bone. Cover with water, season with salt and pepper, and simmer very gently for about 2 hours, or until the beans are tender. Remove the ham bone and rub half the beans through a fine sieve (or purée in a blender). Return the purée to the soup.

Heat ¾ cup olive oil and sauté the crushed garlic cloves and thyme until golden. Strain half the oil into the soup, and discard the garlic. Stir the soup well.

Arrange the slices of toast at the bottom of a fireproof tureen, sprinkle with half the Parmesan cheese and pour the soup over the top. Cover with the onion slices and add the rest of the oil and grated cheese. Cook in a moderate oven (375°F. Mark 4) for about ½ hour.

Serves 6 to 8.

Acquacotta
Tomato and Sweet Pepper Soup

US		UK
½ cup	olive oil	6–8 tablespoons
3	onions, sliced	3
½ pound	sweet red or green peppers	½ pound
1 cup	diced celery	4–6 ounces
1½ pounds	tomatoes, peeled and chopped	1½ pounds
	salt and pepper	
9 cups	boiling water	3½ pints
4	eggs	4
¾ cup	grated Parmesan cheese	3 ounces
12 slices	bread, toasted	12 slices

The literal translation of *acquacotta* is "cooked water". This Tuscan soup is internationally famous.

Heat the oil in a large heavy pan and sauté the onions until soft and transparent. Remove the seeds and cores from the peppers, and cut the flesh into strips. Add them to the pan together with the celery and tomatoes, season to taste with salt and cook over a brisk heat for 30 minutes. Pour in the boiling water, check seasoning and boil for 5 minutes.

Beat the eggs until smooth with a pinch of salt and stir in the grated cheese. Pour the soup into a heated tureen and quickly stir in the egg mixture. Ladle into soup bowls over slices of toast. Serves 6.

Bistecche alla Fiorentina
Florentine Steaks

A Florentine steak is at least 1 inch thick, cut from the rib of a young steer, and well hung.

Allow a 3-pound steak – prime, sirloin or T-bone – for 6, and broil (grill) over charcoal if possible. Otherwise use either gas or electricity. Keep the meat about 3 inches from the heat and cook for about 4 minutes on each side – a Florentine steak should never be overcooked. Sprinkle each side with salt and freshly ground pepper about 1 minute before it is ready. Serve immediately, garnished with lemon wedges.

Stracotto di Manzo
Tuscan Beef Pot Roast

US		UK
2½ pounds	beef, cut from the rump	2½ pounds
2 tablespoons	fat salt pork, diced	1 ounce
½ cup	olive oil	6–8 tablespoons
4	onions, finely chopped	4
1 clove	garlic, finely chopped	1 clove
2	carrots, finely chopped	2
1 stalk	celery, diced	1 stalk
1 cup	red wine	scant ½ pint
	salt and pepper	
1 pound	tomatoes, peeled, seeded and chopped	1 pound
⅔ cup	hot stock	¼ pint

Stud the meat with the fat pork, roll it neatly and tie securely with strong thread. Heat the oil in a large heavy pan or casserole and brown the meat all over. Add the chopped vegetables (not the tomatoes) and continue cooking until they begin to brown. Moisten with wine, let it reduce over a brisk heat, then season to taste with salt and pepper, and add the tomatoes. Cover tightly and cook over a low heat for about 3 hours, or until the meat is very tender. Turn the meat occasionally, basting with a little stock each time.

Take the meat from the pan and cut it into medium-thick slices. Arrange these on a heated serving dish and keep hot in a warm oven. Strain the sauce through a fine sieve, rubbing as much of the vegetables through with it as possible. Pour over the meat and

serve, accompanied by sliced polenta or boiled white (haricot) beans or *fagioli all'uccelletto* (page 137).

Tuscan cooks prefer to leave the meat in its sauce in the pan until the day after it has been cooked, then reheat gently before serving. Serves 6.

Polpettine alla Salvia
Meat Rissoles with Sage

US		UK
1½ cups	ground (UK minced) lean beef	¾ pound
6 leaves	sage, finely chopped	6 leaves
6 tablespoons	butter	3 ounces
¼ teaspoon	salt	¼ teaspoon
2½ tablespoons	grated Parmesan – optional	2 tablespoons
	flour	
¼ cup	Marsala	3 tablespoons

Mix the beef, sage, 2 tablespoons (1 ounce) butter, salt and the Parmesan cheese, if used, to a smooth paste. With floured hands break off pieces and shape them into rissoles. Dredge with flour. Melt the remaining butter and fry the rissoles until brown on both sides, about 5 to 7 minutes. Sprinkle with Marsala and let it reduce. Serve the rissoles immediately with their cooking juices. Serves 3.

Stufato di Muscolo
Tuscan Casseroled Veal

US		UK
1½ pounds	lean veal, cubed	1½ pounds
	flour	
2½ tablespoons	tomato paste	2 tablespoons
2–3 tablespoons	butter	1–1½ ounces
4 tablespoons	olive oil	3 tablespoons
2 cloves	garlic, crushed	2 cloves
½ cup	white wine	6–8 tablespoons
	salt and pepper	
2–3 sprigs	parsley, finely chopped	2–3 sprigs
	boiled peas or sautéed mushrooms – optional	

Dredge the cubed veal with flour. Dilute the tomato paste with a little warm water. Heat the butter and oil in a heavy casserole, and sauté the garlic until brown. Discard the garlic and brown the veal. Moisten with wine and let it reduce over a moderate heat. Add the tomato paste, salt and pepper, lower the heat and continue cooking, covered, until the meat is tender. Garnish with parsley and, if liked, a cupful of boiled peas or sautéed mushrooms, or serve with *fagioli all'uccelletto* (page 137). Serves 4.

Costatine al Finocchio
Pork Chops with Fennel

US		UK
6	pork chops, thinly cut	6
4 teaspoons	tomato paste	1 tablespoon
2 tablespoons	butter	1 ounce
2½ tablespoons	olive oil	2 tablespoons
	salt and pepper	
½ cup	Marsala	6 tablespoons
½ cup	dry red wine	6 tablespoons
1 clove	garlic, finely chopped	1 clove
¼ teaspoon	fennel seeds	¼ teaspoon

Dilute the tomato paste with a little warm water. Heat the butter and oil in a shallow pan, and fry the chops over a moderate heat for about 10 minutes, browning them well on both sides. Season with salt and pepper, arrange on a heated serving dish and keep hot in a warm oven. Add the Marsala, red wine, garlic, fennel seeds and tomato paste to the pan. Check seasoning, reduce the sauce a little over a brisk heat and pour it, boiling hot, over the chops.

Serves 6.

Fegato all'Aceto
Calf's Liver with Vinegar

US		UK
1½ pounds	calf's liver, very thinly sliced	1½ pounds
4 tablespoons	butter	2 ounces
	salt and pepper	
2½ tablespoons	wine vinegar	2 tablespoons
2–3 sprigs	parsley, finely chopped	2–3 sprigs

Melt the butter in a frying pan. Add the slices of liver (Italians cut liver very thinly indeed), and brown on both sides for 3 minutes. Season with salt and pepper, sprinkle with vinegar and cook for just 2 minutes longer. Garnish with parsley and serve immediately.

Serves 4 to 6.

Fegato di Vitello al Pomodoro
Calf's Liver with Tomatoes

US		UK
1½ pounds	calf's liver, thinly sliced – see above	1½ pounds
	flour	
½ cup	olive oil	6–8 tablespoons
2 cloves	garlic, crushed	2 cloves
1 sprig	sage	1 sprig
	salt and pepper	
1¼ cups	freshly made tomato sauce	½ pint

Dredge the liver slices with flour. Heat the oil and sauté the garlic and sage gently. When the garlic cloves are brown, discard them and add the liver. Fry this for about 5 minutes on both sides over a brisk heat, but take care not to overcook it. Season with salt and pepper, and add the warm tomato sauce. Lower the heat and cook for 2 minutes to reheat the tomato sauce and bring out its flavor. Serve the liver at once in the sauce.

Serves 4 to 6.

Fegatelli alla Toscana
Pig's Liver Tuscan Style

US		UK
2½ pounds	pig's liver, cut into 24 pieces	2½ pounds
¾ pound	pig's caul – see method	¾ pound
¼ teaspoon	fennel seeds	¼ teaspoon
	salt and pepper	
	stale white breadcrumbs	
18	bay leaves	18
12 small squares	bread	12 small squares
	olive oil – optional	

Pig's caul or fry (*rete*) is sometimes obtainable from Italian shops and pork butchers. Caul fat is stiff and tears easily when pulled, so before using it, soak it in warm water acidulated with a little vinegar. This will make it soft and pliable, and easy to cut into portions with kitchen scissors. For the following recipe cut the caul into 24 pieces.

Sprinkle the pieces of liver with fennel seeds, salt, pepper and breadcrumbs. Wrap each piece in caul and thread on to 6 skewers, alternating with a bay leaf and a square of bread. Broil (grill) over charcoal, or cook over a high heat in a heavy frying pan with very little oil, for no longer than 8 minutes. Serve immediately.

Serves 6.

Zampa di Vitello alla Toscana
Calf's Foot Tuscan Style

US		UK
6	calf's feet	6
	salt	
2	onions	2
2 stalks	celery	2 stalks
1	carrot	1
2 tablespoons	butter	1 ounce
4 tablespoons	olive oil	3 tablespoons
	salt and pepper	
3 ounces	tomato paste	3 ounces
2 sprigs	parsley, finely chopped	2 sprigs
pinch	ground cinnamon	pinch
¼ cup	grated Parmesan cheese	3 tablespoons

Singe the feet if necessary, wash them well and boil them in plenty of salted water with 1 onion, the celery and carrot for about 3 hours. Take the feet from the pan, pull the meat off the bones and cut it into pieces. Heat the butter and oil, and gently fry the remaining onion, diced, until it begins to brown. Add the meat and a few tablespoons of the stock. Season with salt and pepper, and cook over a brisk heat to let it reduce. Dilute the tomato paste with some of the stock. Add this to the pan and let it cook until you have a good thick sauce. Finally, sprinkle with the parsley, cinnamon and grated Parmesan cheese, and serve very hot.

The stock can be used as a base for a soup. It should be carefully strained and will be so rich that it will become a thick jelly.

Serves 6.

Trippa e Zampa alla Fiorentina
Tripe with Calf's Foot Florentine Style

US		UK
2½ pounds	dressed calf's tripe – see page 46	2½ pounds
1	calf's foot, cleaned – see above	1
	salt	
1½ large	onions	1½ large
3 stalks	celery	3 stalks
3	carrots	3
4 sprigs	parsley	4 sprigs
⅔ cup	olive oil	¼ pint
2 cloves	garlic	2 cloves
1 sprig	rosemary, finely chopped	1 sprig
3–4 leaves	basil, finely chopped	3–4 leaves
¾ pound	tomatoes, peeled and chopped	¾ pound
	salt and pepper	
⅔ cup	stock	¼ pint
3 tablespoons	butter	1½ ounces
⅔ cup	grated Parmesan cheese	2 ounces

Put the calf's foot in a large pan of salted water, adding ½ onion, 1 stalk celery, 1 carrot and a sprig of parsley. Bring to the boil, lower the heat and simmer for about 3 hours, or until the meat comes easily off the bone.

In another pan cover the tripe with salted water and add ½ onion, 1 stalk celery, 1 carrot and 1 sprig parsley. Bring to a slow boil and continue cooking for 1 to 1½ hours, or until the tripe is tender.

Take the tripe and the calf's foot from their pans. Cool slightly. Cut the tripe into slices. Pull the meat from the calf's foot and cut this into small pieces.

Dice the remaining ½ onion, the celery and carrot. Heat the oil, add the garlic, rosemary, parsley, chopped, basil and the vegetables, and brown them lightly. Add the tomatoes, stir well, then add the tripe and the meat from the calf's foot. Season with salt and pepper, and cook slowly for 2 hours, stirring occasionally and moistening with hot stock. Stir in the butter and Parmesan, and serve.

Serves 6.

Pollo Fritto
Tuscan Fried Chicken

US		UK
1	frying chicken – 3½ pounds	1
½ cup	olive oil	6–8 tablespoons
	juice of 1 lemon	
2 sprigs	parsley, finely chopped	2 sprigs
	salt and pepper	
	flour	
2	eggs, beaten	2
	olive oil for deep-frying	

Clean and singe the chicken if necessary, and cut into small pieces: two pieces from each leg and wing, four from the breast and the back. Marinate for 1 hour in olive oil mixed with lemon juice, parsley, salt and pepper.

Drain the chicken pieces, pat them dry and dredge with flour, then dip into beaten egg. Deep-fry in hot oil until golden brown, drain on paper towels and serve immediately.

Serves 4.

Pollo in Salsa Piccante
Chicken in Piquant Sauce

US		UK
1	tender chicken – 3½ pounds	1
½ cup	olive oil	6 tablespoons
1	onion, finely chopped	1
4 teaspoons	flour	1 tablespoon
½ cup	dry white wine	6–8 tablespoons
4 teaspoons	tomato paste	1 tablespoon
	salt and pepper	
½ cup	wine vinegar	6 tablespoons
1 1 large	salted anchovy, filleted and chopped, *or* anchovy fillet, finely chopped	1 1 large
3	gherkins, finely chopped	3
4 teaspoons	capers, finely chopped	1 tablespoon
½ clove	garlic, finely chopped	½ clove
2 sprigs	parsley, finely chopped	2 sprigs

Cut the chicken into serving pieces. Heat the oil, add the onion and the chicken pieces, and sauté gently. When lightly browned, sprinkle with flour, add the wine and cook until it evaporates. Dilute the tomato paste with hot water. Add it to the pan, season to taste with salt and pepper, and continue to cook slowly until tender.

Meanwhile, simmer the vinegar in a small enamelled pan until reduced by half. Add the anchovy, gherkins, capers, garlic and parsley, and stir well. Pour this sauce over the chicken pieces and continue to cook over a low heat for a final 10 minutes.

Serves 4.

Pollo alla Fiorentina
Chicken Florentine Style

US		UK
1	tender chicken – 3½ to 4 pounds	1
1 ounce	dried mushrooms	1 ounce
½ cup	olive oil	6–8 tablespoons
1 clove	garlic, crushed	1 clove
2 slices	fat salt pork or ham, finely chopped	2 slices
1 small	onion, finely chopped	1 small
½ cup	Marsala or dry white wine	6 tablespoons
	salt and pepper	
¾ pound	tomatoes, peeled, seeded and chopped	¾ pound
2 sprigs	parsley, finely chopped	2 sprigs

Soak the mushrooms in warm water for 30 minutes. When soft, squeeze them dry and cut them into thin strips. Cut the chicken into serving pieces. Heat the oil and gently brown the pieces of chicken with the garlic, fat pork and onion. When the garlic clove begins to brown, discard it and add the Marsala. Season with salt and pepper, and add the mushrooms, tomatoes and parsley. Check seasoning and cook gently for about ½ hour longer, or until the chicken is tender. If necessary, moisten with a little hot stock. The sauce should be fairly thick.

Serves 4.

Piccioni alla Diavola
Barbecued Pigeons

US		UK
3	squabs or young pigeons	3
½ cup	olive oil	6–8 tablespoons
	salt and cayenne pepper	
	baked or broiled (grilled) tomatoes	
1	lemon, cut in wedges	1

Clean, singe and wash the pigeons, and dry them with paper towels. Split them in half, chop off their heads and beat the carcasses lightly to flatten them. Marinate them for about an hour in the oil with salt and plenty of cayenne pepper, turning them occasionally. Thoroughly heat a broiler (grill), if possible a charcoal one, and cook the pigeons, basting them from time to time with the oil from the marinade. Serve very hot, garnished with tomatoes and lemon wedges.

Spring chicken can be cooked in the same way.

Serves 3.

Lepre in Agrodolce
Hare in Sweet-sour Sauce

US		UK
1	hare, well hung and cleaned	1
2	onions, sliced	2
2 cloves	garlic, crushed	2 cloves
2 stalks	celery, diced	2 stalks
1	bay leaf	1
3 sprigs	rosemary, finely chopped	3 sprigs
2–3 sprigs	sage	2–3 sprigs
2 sprigs	parsley	2 sprigs
1 bottle	red wine	1 bottle
	salt and pepper	
½ cup	olive oil	6 tablespoons
2 tablespoons	ham fat, chopped	1 ounce
	flour	
2½–3 tablespoons	sugar	2 tablespoons
½ cup	wine vinegar	6 tablespoons
1 square	bitter chocolate, grated	1 ounce
2–3 tablespoons	pine nuts	1 ounce
3–4 tablespoons	seedless white raisins (sultanas)	1½ ounces
2 tablespoons	mixed diced candied peel	1½ tablespoons

Cut the hare into pieces, wash them well and dry them. Marinate the hare overnight with the vegetables, herbs, wine, salt and pepper, tightly covered, in a cool place. Drain and dry the hare, reserving the marinade.

Heat the oil with the ham fat in a large enamelled or earthenware pan and brown the pieces of hare. Dust with flour and as soon as it has browned add the marinade with its vegetables. Cover and cook gently for about 2 hours, turning the hare occasionally.

Meanwhile, slowly dissolve the sugar in the vinegar in a small enamelled pan. Add the chocolate, pine nuts, white raisins (sultanas) and candied peel. Strain off the liquid in which the hare is cooking and mix it with the sweet-sour sauce. Pour this back over the hare.

The hare is reheated and served on the day after it has been cooked so that its meat is thoroughly impregnated with the sauce.

Serves 6 to 8.

Cacciucco alla Livornese
Leghorn Fish Stew

US		UK
4–5 pounds	assorted fish – see method	4–5 pounds
	salt and pepper	
	olive oil	
1	onion, finely chopped	1
1	carrot, finely chopped	1
2 stalks	celery, finely chopped	2 stalks
2 sprigs	parsley, finely chopped	2 sprigs
2 cloves	garlic	2 cloves
2 small	hot chili peppers	2 small
2	bay leaves	2
1 sprig	thyme	1 sprig
1¼ cups	red wine	½ pint
2 pounds	tomatoes, peeled and chopped	2 pounds
	toasted or fried bread	

In this famous fish dish, which is meant to be served as a main course and *not* as a glorified fish soup, all or any of the following fish could be used: eel, squid, a delicate crustacean, *squilla mantis*, for which shrimps or prawns could well be substituted, gurnard, whiting, hake, red mullet, small octopus, John Dory, cuttlefish and crawfish (U.K. crayfish).

Clean the fish, cut off their heads and put them aside. Cut the larger fish, including the squid, eel, cuttlefish and octopus, into pieces. Put them into a shallow dish and leave for 30 minutes, sprinkled with salt, pepper and olive oil.

Meanwhile, heat ½ cup (U.K. 6 to 8 tablespoons) olive oil in a large pan. Add the vegetables, parsley, garlic, chilies, bay leaves, thyme and finally the fish heads. Brown the heads well, moisten with wine and continue cooking until this has reduced. Add the tomatoes and about 6 cups (U.K. 2½ pints) water. Season and continue cooking for 30 minutes. Rub the soup through a fine sieve.

In another large pan, preferably an earthenware one, heat another ½ cup (U.K. 6 to 8 tablespoons) olive oil. Add the squid, cuttlefish and octopus, and cook these for 15 minutes. Add the crawfish (U.K. crayfish) and the *squilla mantis* (or shrimps or prawns), and 5 minutes later, the remaining fish. Add salt if necessary, and plenty of pepper, and cook for another 10 minutes.

Fry in oil or toast in the oven 2 or 3 slices of bread per person. Put these in the bottom of a large soup tureen or into large individual soup bowls. Add the fish and pour the soup over the top.

Serves 6.

Anguilla alla Fiorentina
Eel Florentine Style

US		UK
2 pounds	fresh eel	2 pounds
	salt and pepper	
1 cup	olive oil	scant ½ pint
	fine dry breadcrumbs	
2 cloves	garlic, crushed	2 cloves
1 sprig	sage	1 sprig

Clean and skin the eel, and cut it into pieces about 2½ inches long. Wash and dry them thoroughly, and put them into a shallow bowl. Sprinkle with a little salt and pepper and a trickle of olive oil, and leave for 2 hours. Dry well and coat with breadcrumbs. Heat the remaining oil in a casserole large enough to take the pieces of eel in one layer, and sauté the garlic and sage gently. Discard the garlic as soon as it begins to brown. Add the pieces of eel and bake in a slow oven (350°F. Mark 3) for 30 to 40 minutes.

Serves 4.

Anguilla coi Piselli
Eel with Peas

US		UK
2 pounds	eel	2 pounds
	salt and pepper	
⅔ cup	olive oil	¼ pint
2 cloves	garlic, crushed	2 cloves
1	onion, sliced	1
½ cup	dry white wine	6–8 tablespoons
4 teaspoons	tomato paste	1 tablespoon
4 cups	shelled green peas	1 pound

Clean and skin the eel. Cut it into pieces about 2½ inches long. Wash and dry them, and put them into a shallow bowl. Sprinkle with a little salt, pepper and a trickle of olive oil. Leave for 2 hours.

Heat the remaining oil and very gently sauté the garlic and onion. Discard the garlic as soon as it begins to brown and add the pieces of eel. Brown them gently, add the wine and continue cooking until the wine evaporates. Dilute the tomato paste with ⅔ cup (U.K. ¼ pint) boiling water. Add this to the pan, stir well, then add the peas. Check seasoning and cook slowly for another 30 minutes.

Serves 4 to 6.

Tonno Fresco coi Piselli
Fresh Tuna Fish with Peas

US		UK
2–2½ pounds	tuna fish, thinly sliced	2–2½ pounds
½ cup	olive oil	6 tablespoons
1 clove	garlic, crushed	1 clove
1 small	onion, finely chopped	1 small
½ cup	dry white wine	6–8 tablespoons
4 teaspoons	tomato paste	1 tablespoon
	salt and pepper	
3 cups	cooked green peas	1 pound
2–3 sprigs	parsley, finely chopped	2–3 sprigs

Use slices of fresh tuna, if possible cut from the belly (*ventresca*).

Heat the oil and sauté the garlic and onion gently. When the garlic is brown, discard it and add the fish. Lightly brown the slices on both sides, add the wine and let it reduce over a moderate heat. Dilute the tomato paste with a little hot water. Add this to the pan, season to taste with salt and pepper, and cook very slowly for 30 minutes. Add the peas and parsley, and continue cooking for a few minutes over a simmering heat. Serve very hot.

Serves 6.

Baccalà alla Livornese
Dried Salt Cod Leghorn Style

US		UK
2 pounds	dried salt cod – see page 50	2 pounds
	flour	
1 cup	olive oil	scant ½ pint
2 cloves	garlic, finely chopped	2 cloves
1¼ cups	freshly made tomato sauce	½ pint
1–2 sprigs	parsley, finely chopped	1–2 sprigs

Soak the dried salt cod for 24 hours under cold running water. If this is not possible, change the water at least once every 8 hours.

Skin the cod and cut it into 4-inch squares. Dry well and roll in flour. Heat the oil in a large frying pan and sauté the garlic gently until golden. Then add the pieces of cod and brown them well on both sides. Add the tomato sauce and cook over a low heat, stirring occasionally, for 30 minutes. Check seasoning and serve, garnished with chopped parsley.

Serves 6.

Pesce Marinato
Marinated Fish Tuscan Style

US		UK
2 pounds	grey mullet, fried, *or*	2 pounds
2 pounds	baby cuttlefish and octopus, boiled separately	2 pounds
2–3 tablespoons	olive oil	2 tablespoons
2 cloves	garlic, finely chopped	2 cloves
1 small	onion, thinly sliced	1 small
3–4 sprigs	sage	3–4 sprigs
2	bay leaves	2
2 sprigs	rosemary	2 sprigs
scant 2½ cups	wine vinegar	scant 1 pint

It is important to cook baby cuttlefish and octopus separately, since the former will be ready much more quickly. Use salted water with a tablespoon of vinegar and an onion.

Cut the grey mullet, if used, into large pieces. Arrange the fish in an earthenware dish. Heat the oil and sauté the garlic and onion until golden, then add the herbs and vinegar. Bring to the boil. Pour this mixture over the fish and leave in a cool place for 2 days, covered, before serving.

Serves 6.

Triglie alla Livornese
Red Mullet Leghorn Style

US		UK
12 small	red mullet, cleaned	12 small
	flour	
½ cup	olive oil	6–8 tablespoons
1 clove	garlic, finely chopped	1 clove
1 small	onion, finely chopped	1 small
1	bay leaf, crumbled	1
pinch	thyme	pinch
	salt and pepper	
2 cups	thin tomato sauce	¾ pint
2–3 sprigs	parsley, finely chopped	2–3 sprigs

Wipe the mullet, dry them and roll them in flour. Heat the oil in a frying pan, add the mullet and cook them on each side for 4 minutes, or until browned. Add the garlic, onion, bay leaf and thyme, salt, pepper and finally the tomato sauce. Continue cooking for a further 5 minutes. Serve at once, garnished with parsley.

Serves 6.

Totani al Prezzemolo
Baby Squid with Parsley

US		UK
3½ pounds	baby squid – or cuttlefish	3½ pounds
½ cup	olive oil	6–8 tablespoons
2 cloves	garlic, crushed	2 cloves
	salt and pepper	
3–4 sprigs	parsley, finely chopped	3–4 sprigs
	juice of ½ lemon	
	slices of fried bread	

The squid or cuttlefish must be very tiny or this method of cooking them will not be successful.

Clean, wash and dry them. Heat the oil and sauté the garlic gently until it begins to brown; discard it. Add the squid, season with salt and pepper, and cook over a brisk heat for about 10 minutes. Sprinkle with parsley and lemon juice, and serve very hot, garnished with slices of fried bread.

Serves 6.

Uova alla Fiorentina
Florentine Eggs

US		UK
Pastry		
1 cup	all-purpose (plain) flour	4 ounces
¼ cup	melted butter	2 ounces
pinch	salt	pinch
2–3 tablespoons	water	2 tablespoons
	dried beans or rice	
1½ cups	cooked spinach	¾ pound
2 tablespoons	butter	1 ounce
¼ cup	creamy milk	3 tablespoons
	salt	
4 tablespoons	grated Parmesan cheese	3 tablespoons
12 small	eggs, poached	12 small

Pastry

Sift the flour into a bowl, add the melted butter, salt and water. Mix to a dough and knead well. Roll into a ball and leave, covered, for 30 minutes. Roll out very thinly, cut into small rounds and line 12 individual pie pans (small tartlet tins) about 2 inches in diameter. Fill the cases with dried beans and bake them "blind" in a moderately hot oven (400°F. Mark 5) for about 15 minutes. Take from the oven, remove the beans but leave the pastry cases in the pans (tins).

Squeeze the spinach dry, chop finely and mix with the butter, milk, salt and half the cheese. Heat this mixture through in a pan over a low heat.

Fill the little pastry cases with the spinach mixture and top each one with a poached egg. Trim off any overhanging egg white. Sprinkle with a pinch of salt and the remaining cheese, and bake in a hot oven for a few minutes until heated through.

Serves 6.

Frittata con le Arselle
Omelette with Baby Clams

US		UK
1½ pounds	baby clams	1½ pounds
5 tablespoons	olive oil	4 tablespoons
6	eggs	6
	salt and pepper	
2 sprigs	parsley, finely chopped	2 sprigs

Wash the clams in several changes of fresh water. Shake dry and put into a thick pan with half the olive oil. Cover and cook until the shells open. Take the clams from their shells and put them into a bowl.

Beat the eggs lightly with a pinch of salt and rather more pepper. Add the parsley and mix into the clams.

Heat the remaining oil in a heavy frying pan, add the egg and clam mixture, and cook over a low heat until the underside is set. Holding a dish over the top of the pan, turn it over, then slide the omelette back into the pan to cook and brown the other side. Serve very hot.

Serves 4.

Frittata "in Zoccoli"
Bacon Omelette

Dice a slice of bacon weighing about ¼ pound and sauté gently in 2 or 3 tablespoons oil until cooked but not too crisp. Drain thoroughly. Beat 6 eggs lightly with a pinch of salt and pepper, and add 2 or 3 tablespoons parsley and the bacon.

Heat 2 or 3 tablespoons oil in a heavy frying pan and pour in the egg mixture. Let the omelette cook until set and golden brown on one side, then invert it on to a plate and slip it back into the pan to brown the other side.

Serves 4.

Tortino di Carciofi
Baked Artichokes

US		UK
6	artichokes	6
1	lemon	1
	flour	
1 cup	olive oil	scant ½ pint
	salt and pepper	
6	eggs	6
4 tablespoons	milk	3 tablespoons

Remove the outer leaves of the artichokes, leaving only the more tender ones. Cut into thick slices. (If using other than Italian artichokes, take away all the chokes.) Soak in water acidulated with lemon juice for 15 minutes. Drain, dry and dust with flour.

Heat half the oil in a wide pan, add the slices of artichoke and cook over a low heat until they are golden brown on both sides. This will take between 20 and 30 minutes. Sprinkle lightly with salt and lay them in one layer in a shallow fireproof baking dish. Pour the remaining oil over the top.

Beat the eggs, adding salt, pepper and the milk. Pour this mixture over the artichokes, and bake in a moderately hot oven (400°F. Mark 5) for about 15 to 20 minutes, or until the eggs are set. Serve immediately.

Serves 6.

Sformato di Carciofi
Artichoke Mold (Mould)

US		UK
2 pounds	artichokes	2 pounds
1	lemon	1
2½ tablespoons	olive oil	2 tablespoons
6 tablespoons	butter	3 ounces
	salt and pepper	
¼ pound	calf's sweetbreads	¼ pound
¼ pound	veal bone marrow	¼ pound
2–3 tablespoons	fine dry breadcrumbs	2 tablespoons

Béchamel sauce		
¼ cup	butter	2 ounces
½ cup	all-purpose (plain) flour	2 ounces
	salt	
2½ cups	hot milk	1 pint
2	egg yolks	2
	pepper	
2½ tablespoons	grated Parmesan cheese	2 tablespoons

The most suitable artichokes for this recipe are Italian ones which do not form a choke. Only the outer leaves need be removed and they are then cut into wedges. If these are not available, use the most tender artichokes possible. Remove the outer leaves, cut the artichokes in half and cut out their chokes or fibrous beards. Drop them into water acidulated with the juice of 1 lemon for 15 minutes and drain well.

Heat the oil and 2 tablespoons (1 ounce) butter in a pan, add the artichokes, sprinkle with salt and pepper, and cook gently for ½ hour, or until the artichokes are golden. Put aside.

Béchamel Sauce
Melt the butter in a heavy pan and stir in the flour and a pinch of salt off the heat. Return the pan to the heat and cook the *roux*

for a few minutes, stirring all the while. Gradually add the milk, stirring constantly with a wooden spoon. Continue stirring and cooking over a moderate heat until the sauce is thick and smooth. Take the pan from the heat and beat in the egg yolks, a sprinkling of pepper and the cheese. Put aside.

Drop the sweetbreads into cold water, bring to the boil and cook for 15 minutes. Take them from the pan and drop at once into cold water. When they are cold, trim off all the fat and membrane. Chop finely.

Chop the bone marrow into small pieces and put it into a pan with 3 tablespoons (1½ ounces) butter. Sprinkle lightly with salt and cook over a low heat for a few minutes to bring out flavors.

Mix the cooked artichokes, sweetbreads and bone marrow with the sauce. Grease a deep baking dish with the remaining butter and coat it with breadcrumbs. Fill it with the Béchamel mixture, sprinkle the top lightly with breadcrumbs and place in a baking pan half-full of warm water. Bake in a moderately hot oven (400°F. Mark 5) for about 20 minutes, or until the top is golden. Turn out and serve immediately.

Serves 6.

Fagioli all'Uccelletto
White (Haricot) Beans Cooked Like Small Birds

US		UK
1 pound	fresh white (haricot) beans – see method	1 pound
	salt	
¾ cup	olive oil	generous ¼ pint
2 cloves	garlic, crushed	2 cloves
1 sprig	sage	1 sprig
14-ounce can	Italian peeled tomatoes, chopped	14-ounce can
	pepper	

The "small birds" in the name of this recipe possibly refer to the sage, a popular ingredient in the cooking of small birds.

If fresh haricot beans are not available, dried ones may be used, but they will need soaking overnight and somewhat longer cooking.

Cook the beans in salted water (this will take about 1½ hours if they are fresh). Heat the oil in a large pan and sauté the garlic until brown. Discard the garlic and add the beans, sage and tomatoes. Season to taste with salt and pepper, and cook for about 20 minutes, or until the sauce is thick.

Serves 6.

Fagioli Freschi al Tonno
Fresh White (Haricot) Beans with Tuna Fish

US		UK
1 pound	fresh white (haricot) beans – see above	1 pound
	salt	
½ cup	olive oil	6–8 tablespoons
1 clove	garlic, crushed	1 clove
5–6 large	ripe tomatoes, peeled and chopped	5–6 large
12 ounces	tuna fish in oil, drained and cut in pieces	12 ounces
2–3 sprigs	basil, finely chopped	2–3 sprigs
	pepper	

Cook the beans in salted water until tender, about 1½ hours. Drain. Heat the oil in a large pan and sauté the garlic until brown. Discard the garlic and add the tomatoes. Sprinkle lightly with salt and cook for 10 minutes over a brisk heat. Stir in the beans and the pieces of tuna, and sprinkle with basil and plenty of pepper. Cook for 10 minutes over a low heat and serve very hot.

Serves 6.

Fagioli nel Fiasco
Beans in a Flask

This is an old, very famous Tuscan dish. Use a wine flask – such as Chianti or many other Italian wines are sold in – with a capacity of about 7½ cups (U.K. 3 pints). Remove the straw. Wash 1 pound of shelled fresh white (haricot) beans and pour them into the flask. Do not fill the flask quite full – the beans must have room to swell. Add ½ cup (U.K. 6 tablespoons) oil, a sprig of sage, 2 cups (U.K. ¾ pint) water, 2 cloves garlic, but no salt. Push a little tow or straw loosely into the neck of the flask, leaving an opening for the steam to escape.

Traditionally the beans were then cooked over a smoldering charcoal fire until the water had almost all evaporated. This took about 3 hours, and the same results can be achieved by putting the flask in a slow oven. Turn the cooked beans into a bowl, season them with salt and pepper, and serve hot or cold.

Serves 6.

Dried beans can also be used – in this case they do not have to be pre-soaked.

Fave Stufate
Fava (Broad) Beans with Bacon

US		UK
5 pounds	very fresh young fava (broad) beans	5 pounds
½ cup	olive oil	6–8 tablespoons
1 cup	diced bacon	5 ounces
1 small	onion, sliced	1 small
2 sprigs	parsley, finely chopped	2 sprigs
	salt	
½ cup	dry white wine	6–8 tablespoons
	pepper	

Shell the beans and soak them for several hours in water. Heat the oil in a large pan and sauté the bacon until it begins to change color. Add the onion and parsley. When the onion is golden brown, stir in the beans, salt lightly and cook for about 15 to 20 minutes, or until the beans are tender. Add the wine and continue cooking until reduced. Sprinkle with pepper and serve very hot.

Serves 6.

Cardi alla Fiorentina
Cardoons Florentine Style

US		UK
2 pounds	cardoons	2 pounds
	juice of 2 lemons	
	salt	
6 tablespoons	butter	3 ounces
1 small	onion, thinly sliced	1 small
2–3 tablespoons	grated Parmesan cheese	2 tablespoons

Remove the outer stalks and tough parts from the cardoons, cutting them into pieces about a foot long. Cut off the white, tender stalks, remove the strings with a knife and cut the stalks into pieces about 3 inches long. Wash these in water acidulated with the juice of 1 lemon.

Bring a pan of water flavored with the juice of the remaining lemon to the boil, salt slightly, add the cardoons and cook them slowly for at least 1 hour.

Melt the butter in a pan and sauté the onion until golden brown. Drain the cardoons, reserving their liquid, add them to the pan, season with salt and cook over a low heat for about 20 minutes, moistening with ⅔ cup (U.K. ¼ pint) of the cardoon liquid. Sprinkle with Parmesan cheese and serve the cardoons very hot.

Serves 6.

Fagiolini Rifatti
"Twice-cooked" Beans

US		UK
2 pounds	snap (French) beans	2 pounds
	salt	
½ cup	olive oil	6 tablespoons
2 cloves	garlic, crushed	2 cloves
1 pound	ripe tomatoes, peeled and chopped	1 pound
1–2 sprigs	fresh basil, chopped	1–2 sprigs
	pepper	

Wash and trim the beans, but do not cut them. Cook them in a little boiling salted water until tender and drain well.

Meanwhile, heat the oil in a pan, sauté the garlic until brown and discard it. Add the tomatoes and basil, season to taste with salt and pepper, and cook for 10 minutes over a brisk heat. Add the beans, lower the heat and continue cooking over a low heat until the sauce thickens.

Serves 6.

Funghi Trippati
Mushrooms Cooked Like Tripe

US		UK
1½ pounds	fresh field or cultivated mushrooms	1½ pounds
5 tablespoons	olive oil	4 tablespoons
2 cloves	garlic, crushed	2 cloves
4 teaspoons	tomato paste	1 tablespoon
	salt	
1 teaspoon	oregano	1 teaspoon

The addition of tomato to this dish is typical of the region around Pistoia.

Clean the mushrooms and cut into medium-thick slices. Heat the oil and sauté the garlic gently until it begins to brown; discard it and add the mushrooms. Dilute the tomato paste with a little hot water and add it to the pan. Season to taste with salt, sprinkle with oregano and continue cooking over a low heat for about 15 minutes, or until the mushrooms are tender.

Serves 3 to 4.

Frittata con le Mele
Apple Omelette

US		UK
2½ tablespoons	all-purpose (plain) flour	2 tablespoons
pinch	salt	pinch
½ cup	milk	6 tablespoons
2	eggs, beaten	2
4 teaspoons	sugar	1 tablespoon
	grated rind of 1 lemon	
2	apples, peeled and thinly sliced	2
2–3 tablespoons	butter	1–1½ ounces
	confectioners' (icing) sugar	

Make a thin, smooth batter with the flour, salt and milk. Add the beaten eggs, sugar and lemon rind, and beat well. Stir the apple slices gently into the batter.

Melt the butter in a frying pan about 8 inches in diameter. Pour in the apple mixture, distributing the apple slices evenly over the bottom of the pan. Cook over a medium heat until the omelette is set and golden brown on the underside. Then invert it on to a plate of the same size and very carefully slide it back into the pan to brown the other side, adding a little more butter. Turn the omelette out on to a heated serving dish and sprinkle with sifted confectioners' (icing) sugar. Serve hot.

Serves 2 to 4.

Zuccotto
Pumpkin-shaped Cream Pudding

US		UK
½ cup	peeled almonds	3 ounces
¾ cup	skinned hazelnuts	3 ounces
5 cups	whipping cream	2 pints
⅔ cup	confectioners' (icing) sugar	3 ounces
5 squares	bitter chocolate, grated	5 ounces
4 tablespoons	brandy	3 tablespoons
4 tablespoons	sweet liqueur	3 tablespoons
1 pound	light sponge cake	1 pound
	butter	
	confectioners' (icing) sugar	
	cocoa powder	

Toast the almonds and hazelnuts in the oven, and chop them roughly. Whip the cream with the confectioners' (icing) sugar until very stiff. Fold in the almonds, hazelnuts and chocolate. Cut the sponge cake into slices about ½ inch thick and sprinkle them with the brandy and sweet liqueur, mixed. Line a round bowl with well-buttered wax paper and then with some of the sponge cake slices. Fill with the whipped cream up to the brim, smooth over with a knife blade and cover with the remaining sponge slices. Leave in the refrigerator for at least 2 hours, longer if possible.

Turn out on to a round serving dish and sprinkle either with confectioners' sugar and cocoa powder, mixed, or with first one and then the other in alternate segments – like a brown and white beach ball, which is the traditional way of presenting this rich pudding.

Serves 8.

Crostata alla Crema
Custard Tart

US		UK
Pastry		
2½ cups	all-purpose (plain) flour	10 ounces
½ cup plus 2 tablespoons	butter	5 ounces
½ cup	granulated (caster) sugar	4 ounces
3	egg yolks	3
pinch	salt	pinch
pinch	baking soda	pinch
	grated rind of 1 lemon	
Custard		
4	egg yolks	4
6 tablespoons	sugar	3 ounces
2½ cups	milk	1 pint
½ cup plus 2 tablespoons	all-purpose (plain) flour	2½ ounces
	whole rind of 1 lemon	
	butter and flour for pie pan	
1	egg, beaten	1
	confectioners' (icing) sugar	

Pastry
Sift the flour into a bowl and rub in the butter until the mixture resembles coarse breadcrumbs. Add the sugar and egg yolks, salt, baking soda and lemon rind. Work to a smooth dough but do not handle it more than necessary. Cover and leave in the refrigerator for 1 hour.

Custard
Beat the egg yolks with the sugar until smooth. Mix the milk into the flour, stirring all the time, to make a smooth batter. Pour this into a pan, add the rind, and cook over a low heat until the mixture thickens like a sauce and no longer tastes of raw flour. Take the pan from the heat and pour the sauce into the beaten eggs, stirring all the time. Return it to the pan and continue to cook over a low heat until it thickens again. Pour into a bowl, remove the rind and leave to cool, stirring occasionally to prevent a skin from forming.

Butter and lightly flour a pie pan about 11 inches in diameter. Roll out a little more than half of the pastry and line the pan. Pour in the custard sauce and smooth over the top with a palette knife. Roll out and cut the remaining pastry into strips to make a lattice pattern over the top of the custard. Brush the pastry with the beaten egg and bake in a moderate oven (375°F. Mark 4) for 30 minutes, or until golden brown. Cool and sprinkle with sifted confectioners' (icing) sugar.

Cenci
Lovers' Knots – Tuscan Fried Pastries

US		UK
1¾ cups	all-purpose (plain) flour	7 ounces
2 tablespoons	butter	1 ounce
4 teaspoons	granulated (caster) sugar	1 tablespoon
2	eggs	2
pinch	salt	pinch
	grated rind of ½ lemon	
2½ tablespoons	wine	2 tablespoons
	lard or oil for deep-frying	
	confectioners' (icing) sugar	

The word *cenci* literally means "rags and tatters".

Sift the flour into a bowl and rub in the butter. Add the sugar, eggs, salt, lemon rind and wine, and work to a rather stiff but very pliable dough. If it is too stiff, add a little more wine. Knead well and leave in a cool place for 1 hour, wrapped in a cloth.

Roll out rather thinly, and cut into rectangles about 3 by 4½ inches. Make three lengthwise cuts in each rectangle. The effect should be of 4 thin strips joined at each end – these strips can then be intertwined to look like knots. Fry the strips or knots, two or three at a time, in plenty of hot lard until puffed up and golden. Drain on paper towels and when cold sprinkle with sifted confectioners' (icing) sugar.

Cenci can be served alone or with a fruit salad, cold mousse or a similar type of dessert.

Brigidini
Aniseed Wafers

US		UK
2 cups	all-purpose (plain) flour	8 ounces
1 teaspoon	baking powder	1 teaspoon
7 tablespoons	butter	3½ ounces
3 tablespoons	granulated (caster) sugar	1½ ounces
1 teaspoon	anise seeds	1 teaspoon
2	eggs	2
5 tablespoons	milk	4 tablespoons

Brigidini are often seen in Tuscany, where they are sold on street stalls and at country fairs.

Sift the flour and baking powder into a bowl, and rub in the butter. Add the sugar, anise seeds, eggs and milk, and mix thoroughly with a wooden spoon. Work to a smooth dough. Break off small pieces and roll them into balls no bigger than a walnut. Roll each one out into a thin round wafer.

Traditionally, the wafers are cooked in a special gadget similar to a waffle iron, which is heated in a fire. However, they can also be cooked on both sides on a hot griddle or heavy iron frying pan. They should be crisp and golden.

Ricciarelli di Siena
Siennese Macaroons

US		UK
1⅓ cups	almonds, peeled and toasted	½ pound
¾ cup	granulated (caster) sugar	6 ounces
1⅓ cups	confectioners' (icing) sugar	6 ounces
pinch	vanilla powder or vanilla sugar	pinch
2	egg whites, beaten	2
25 rounds	rice paper	25 rounds

Pound or grind the almonds to a powder; add the granulated (caster) sugar and half the confectioners' (icing) sugar. Add the vanilla and fold in the egg whites, a little at a time, until you have a smooth but not too runny mixture. Put a little of the mixture on each circle of rice paper. Shape into diamonds and sprinkle with the remaining sugar. Leave overnight.

Bake in a slow oven (325°F. Mark 2) for 20 minutes or so, just long enough to dry the little macaroons. Remove them before they brown. Leave to cool and dust with more sifted sugar.

Ciambelline Rustiche
Country Doughnuts

US		UK
2 cups	all-purpose (plain) flour	8 ounces
5 tablespoons	granulated (caster) sugar	2–2½ ounces
pinch	salt	pinch
½ cup	white wine	6 tablespoons
½ teaspoon	anise seeds, or to taste	½ teaspoon
½ cup	olive oil	6 tablespoons
	oil for baking sheet	
1	egg, beaten	1

Sift the flour into a bowl and add the sugar, salt, wine, anise seeds and olive oil. Mix to a dough and knead thoroughly. Cover and leave for 1 hour. Divide the dough into 20 pieces, shape these into cylinders the thickness of a finger, and then into rings.

Arrange them on a greased baking sheet, brush with beaten egg and bake in a hot oven (425°F. Mark 6) for about 20 minutes.

Stiacciata Unta
Tuscan Sweet Bread

US		UK
4 cups	all-purpose (plain) flour	1 pound
1 cake	compressed (fresh) yeast	⅔ ounce
1¼ cups	lukewarm water	½ pint
2	eggs	2
pinch	salt	pinch
½ cup	granulated (caster) sugar	4 ounces
	grated rind of 1 orange	
½ cup plus 2 tablespoons	butter, melted and cooled	5 ounces
	butter or oil for baking sheet	
	confectioners' (icing) sugar	

Sift the flour into a warmed bowl. Make a well in the middle and pour in the yeast, dissolved in lukewarm water. Knead very thoroughly until the dough is elastic and comes away easily from your hand and the sides of the bowl, adding 2 or 3 tablespoons more water if the dough is very hard. Cover the bowl with a cloth and leave the dough in a warm place to rise for about 1 hour, or until doubled in bulk.

Punch the dough down again and work in the eggs, lightly beaten to mix the yolks and whites, salt, sugar and grated orange rind. This will make the dough very soft. Continue to knead it vigorously in the bowl as you would a baba dough for about 10 minutes, or until it regains its elastic texture and comes away easily from the

sides of the bowl. Finally, work in the melted butter, beating and kneading by hand until the butter is completely incorporated.

Grease two rectangular baking pans about 8 by 12 inches (traditionally these breads are baked in pans about 20 inches long and 12 inches wide). Divide the dough in half and press each piece out thinly with the palm of your hand to cover the bottom of the pan. Cover the pans and leave for 1 to 1½ hours for the dough to rise again. Bake in a moderately hot oven (400°F. Mark 5) for 20 to 25 minutes, or until cooked through and golden. Turn out on to wire racks to cool, and when cold dust the side which has acquired the pattern of the rack with sifted confectioners' (icing) sugar.

This cake should be only 1 to 1½ inches thick, as indicated by its name, *stiacciata*, which means "squashed".

Buccellato
Tuscan Sweet Ring-shaped Bun

US		UK
3 cakes	compressed (fresh) yeast	2 ounces
1¾ cups	lukewarm milk	¾ pint
7 cups	all-purpose (plain) flour	1¾ pounds
1¾ cups	granulated (caster) sugar	12 ounces
6 tablespoons	softened butter	3 ounces
2 teaspoons	pork fat, finely chopped	¾ ounce
pinch	baking soda	pinch
¼ cup	Marsala wine	3 tablespoons
4	eggs	4
pinch	salt	pinch
	grated rind of 1 lemon	
	butter for tube pan	

Buccellato is a specialty of the small town of Lucca.

In a large bowl, dissolve the yeast in half the milk and add enough flour to make a sponge batter. Cover and leave to rise until foamy.

Beat down the batter, add the rest of the flour and milk, and the remaining ingredients, reserving a little egg white and beating the eggs lightly. Knead the dough thoroughly until smooth and pliable, and shape into 1 or 2 long rolls. Fit the rolls into 1 or 2 tube pans brushed with melted butter – the dough should come about half-way up the pan. Leave to rise for about 1 hour longer.

Brush with the reserved egg white, lightly beaten, and bake in a moderate oven (375°F. Mark 4) for 1 hour. Cool before turning the bun out of the pan.

Castagnaccio alla Toscana
Tuscan Chestnut Cake

US		UK
3 tablespoons	white seedless raisins (sultanas)	2–3 tablespoons
½ pound	chestnut flour	½ pound
2½ tablespoons	olive oil	2 tablespoons
pinch	salt	pinch
4 teaspoons	sugar	1 tablespoon
2–2½ cups	cold water	¾–1 pint
	oil for cake pan	
3 tablespoons	pine nuts	2–3 tablespoons
1 sprig	rosemary	1 sprig
6–8	walnut halves, chopped – optional	6–8

Soak the white raisins (sultanas) in warm water. Drain and pat dry.

In a bowl, mix the chestnut flour, oil, salt and sugar with enough cold water to make a fairly thin, smooth batter. Beat well and pour into a wide, shallow cake pan about 9 inches in diameter, brushed with oil. The cake should be not more than 2 inches deep. Sprinkle with pine nuts, white raisins, rosemary and walnuts, if used. Bake in a moderately hot oven (400°F. Mark 5) for about 1 hour, or until the top of the cake is crisp and covered with tiny cracks.

UMBRIA-
THE MARCHES

At the foot of the picturesque Falls of Le Marmore in the province of Terni, an irresistible invitation to gastronomes: spit-roasted chickens, shrimps (U.K. prawns), risotto, broiled (grilled) trout, and croûtes spread with truffles.

The Umbrian countryside, immortalized by these sculptures in the Romanesque church of San Pietro, boasts an abundance of delicacies, including *strangozzi*, or ribbon noodles Spoleto style (see page 150), and *pizza di Pasqua* (see page 149).

Nature has endowed Umbria with a soft, typically Italian landscape that has preserved its beauty intact throughout the centuries. At Gubbio one steps straight into the Middle Ages, and at Fonti del Clitunno, a few miles from Spoleto, it is still possible to catch a glimpse of the world of Virgil, Pliny, Byron and Carducci. Also in Umbria is that golden city, Perugia, which crowns a hill like another Acropolis, with its delightful Fontana Maggiore, graced with the works of such famous sculptors as Nicolo, Giovanni Pisano and Arnolfo di Cambio. There, too, is Orvieto, with its majestic cathedral, and Assisi. Beyond Gubbio, on the other side of the Apennines, the landscape gradually changes as we near the Adriatic. This is the region known as Marche—"the Marches"—birthplace of Rossini and Leopardi, and also renowned for the piano accordions made there. This area is cut by a dozen or so rivers and torrents, which all run in parallel lines towards the sea, and the skill of the local fishermen is famous throughout Italy.

The cuisines of Umbria and the Marches have much in common, especially in their use of *porchetta*, which, though now typical of Roman cookery, originated here between Macerata and Ascoli Piceno. Many gourmets contend that the best *porchetta* comes from Umbria, where they fill the pig's belly with herbs, including a special kind of wild fennel, which make it particularly tasty. The main pig-breeding district is around Norcia, the birthplace of St. Benedict. So great is the fame of the district that in Central Italy the word *norcino*, meaning a native of Norcia, is synonymous with butcher.

Broiled (grilled) trout surrounded by a selection of sausages and a dish of noodles garnished with black truffles from Norcia.
Below, left: More fine Umbrian dishes—sausages, chicken *all'arrabbiata* (see page 151) and *spiedini misti*, or mixed kebabs (see page 150)—together with a selection of local fruits and vegetables. In the background, the town of Spoleto and the Ponte delle Torri or "Bridge of Towers".

Below: The hinterland of the Marches is rich in raw materials and offers an excellent traditional cuisine: *pollo in potacchio* (see page 151), fresh beans "country style" (see page 153), fine noodles known as *maccheroncini*, pork chops and deep-fried stuffed olives.

Left: Torta sul testo, a sheet of dough cooked on a heated slab, is typical of the cooking in the district around Lake Trasimeno.

Both regions specialize in oven and spit roasts, and in the preparation of these much use is made of the *pilotto*, a piece of lard wrapped in paper, which is then set alight and held so that the melting fat drips over the meat roasting on the spit. The most famous spit roast is the *arrosto alla ghiotta*. The *ghiotta* (sometimes also known as a *leccarda*) is a dish which is placed under the spit to collect the fat that drips from the meat. White wine, vinegar, slices of lemon, sage leaves and black olives are placed all together in the *ghiotta*, and as the boiling fat drips into this mixture it releases an aromatic vapor which rises and impregnates the meat above.

Black truffles, which are as famous as the white truffles of Alba, are to be found at Norcia and in the neighborhood of Val di Nera and Montagna di Spoleto. Unlike the practice in Piedmont, only the owners of the land where the truffles are hidden are allowed to search for them. This they do with the help of specially trained dogs and even with pigs that have a highly delicate sense of smell. Experts claim to be able to tell from the way the flies are flying exactly where black truffles are to be found buried in the soil.

The Marches supply almost all the fish dishes of the region— almost all because Umbria, which has no coastline, does have trout in its local streams. On the other hand, the Marches boast the principal fishing port of Italy, San Benedetto del Tronto, from which fishermen sail all over the world. The finest fish soup of the area, the *brodetto*, is comparable with the best fish soups of Italy, as well as with the French *bouillabaisse*. The best-known *brodetti* are those of Ancona and Porto Recanati. In the former, shallow

A rich display of shellfish seen against a background of the Riviera del Conero. In the foreground, a local dish of stuffed lasagne, and *stoccafisso* or dried salt cod Ancona style (see page 154). On the right, some of the fine wines produced in Umbria and the Marches.

No visitor to Porto Recanati in the province of Macerata should miss the delicious *brodetto* or local fish soup (see page 153). Other seaside specialties include baby clams, boiled scampi, mussels *au gratin*, *latterini* (sand smelts), and baked fish.

water fish, red mullet and squid are the main ingredients; a touch of vinegar is added, the fish are coated with flour, and the soup is served poured over slices of toasted bread. The Porto Recanati *brodetto* is traditionally made with cuttlefish, dogfish, cod and mullet. It does not need vinegar, nor is the fish dusted with flour; the bread is rubbed with garlic, but not toasted. Wild saffron is used to give the dish an attractive color and aroma. *Brodetto* is the finest dish of the Marches, a masterpiece of imaginative cooking.

The two rival regions, Umbria and the Marches, stoutly defend the merits of their respective white wines, Orvieto and Verdicchio, both of which are considered to be among the best in Italy. Orvieto is produced on the borders of Umbria and Lazio, and has been famous for centuries. It is said than when Pinturicchio was commissioned to paint the interior of the cathedral in Orvieto, he stipulated that he was to be supplied on demand with local wine for the duration of the work. There are two kinds of Orvieto, one slightly sweet, which is ideal as a table and dessert wine, and a dry one, highly recommended for serving with fish and hors d'oeuvre. Verdicchio is the most famous wine of the Marches and, as its name implies, it is of a yellowish-green color, with a high alcoholic content. It is made in the area of the Castelli di Jesi which also includes Cupramontana, Monteroberto, Castelplano and Castelbellino. Other wines of the Marches are Sangiovese, Bianchello, and an oddity called *vino cotto*—see page 151. Besides Orvieto, other good Umbrian wines include the red Montefalco, Sacrantino and Greco di Todi.

Pizza di Pasqua
Easter Pizza

US		UK
½ pound	once-risen bread dough, made with 1¼ cups (5 ounces) flour	½ pound
4	eggs	4
	salt	
¾ cup	grated Parmesan cheese	3 ounces
¾ cup	grated Pecorino cheese	3 ounces
1¼ cups	strong all-purpose (plain) flour	5 ounces
6 tablespoons	olive oil	5 tablespoons
	lard	

Beat the eggs with a pinch of salt, and the grated cheeses. Leave to rest. Meanwhile, punch down the risen dough; make a hole in the center and add the flour and the oil. Mix thoroughly and knead energetically until smooth again. Make another hole in the bread dough and add the cheese mixture. Knead again until the dough is perfectly smooth and comes away cleanly from the pastry board. Put it into a bowl, cover with a cloth and leave to rise in a warm place for about 2 hours, or until doubled in bulk.

Grease a deep fireproof dish – traditionally earthenware – with lard. Knead the dough lightly and spread out in the dish. Cover and leave to rise again for an hour or so in a warm place.

Bake in a moderately hot oven (400°F. Mark 5) for 20 to 30 minutes, or until the pizza is golden brown. Serve hot with chopped black truffles, salami and hard-boiled eggs.

Serves 6.

Pizza al Formaggio
Cheese Pizza

US		UK
1 pound	once-risen bread dough, made with 2½ cups (10 ounces) flour	1 pound
2	eggs	2
¾ cup	grated Parmesan cheese	3 ounces
scant ½ cup	grated Pecorino cheese	1½ ounces
½ cup	grated Gruyère or Provolone	2 ounces
	olive oil	

Beat the eggs and add the cheeses. Punch down the dough and knead it again with 2½ tablespoons (U.K. 2 tablespoons) olive oil until completely absorbed. Make a hole in the center of the dough and add the beaten egg and cheese mixture. Knead again thoroughly until smooth.

Turn into a deep, narrow baking pan, well oiled, and bake in a moderately hot oven (400°F. Mark 5) for 20 to 30 minutes, or until the dough is well risen and a light golden brown color. Serve hot.

Serves 6.

Spaghetti al Tartufo Nero
Spaghetti with Black Truffle

US		UK
1½ pounds	spaghetti	1½ pounds
	salt	
1 cup	Spoleto olive oil – see method	⅓ pint
1–2	anchovy fillets, chopped	1–2
2 cloves	garlic, crushed	2 cloves
1 large	black Norcia truffle, thinly sliced	1 large

Spoleto olive oil is of particularly fine quality with a delicate flavor. Norcia is the center of the black truffle area.

Bring a large pan of salted water to a fast boil and cook the spaghetti briskly until *al dente*, tender but still firm.

Meanwhile, heat the olive oil, preferably in a double boiler. Add the anchovy and cook gently until dissolved. Add the garlic and continue to cook gently until softened, but on no account let it become browned. Finally add the black truffle.

Drain the spaghetti, which by this time should be just tender, and turn it into a hot serving dish. Add the oil and truffle sauce, stir and serve immediately.

Serves 6.

Spaghettini Aromatici
Spaghettini with Anchovy Sauce

US		UK
1½ pounds	spaghettini (very fine spaghetti)	1½ pounds
	salt	
1 cup	olive oil	scant ½ pint
2 cloves	garlic, crushed	2 cloves
3–4 large	anchovy fillets, chopped	3–4 large
4 leaves	mint, finely chopped	4 leaves
3 sprigs	parsley, finely chopped	3 sprigs
4 teaspoons	capers	1 tablespoon
12	black olives, pitted and chopped	12

Bring a large pan of salted water to the boil and throw in the spaghettini. Cover, bring the water back to the boil and give the noodles a good stir with a large fork. Cook briskly until tender but still firm.

Meanwhile, heat the oil in a pan. Add the garlic cloves, sauté until brown and discard them. Then add the anchovies and cook gently, stirring until they are completely dissolved to a paste. Take the pan from the heat and stir in the mint and parsley.

Drain the spaghettini, pour into a heated dish and add the anchovy-flavored oil, the capers and the olives. Mix well and serve, in this case without cheese.

The quantity of olive oil may be increased for those who are particularly fond of it.

Serves 6.

Spaghetti al Guanciale
Spaghetti with Bacon

US		UK
1½ pounds	spaghetti	1½ pounds
	salt	
2½ tablespoons	olive oil	2 tablespoons
½ pound	bacon, diced	½ pound
1	onion, thinly sliced	1
1½ pounds	ripe tomatoes, peeled and chopped	1½ pounds
1 sprig	marjoram, finely chopped	1 sprig
	pepper	
1 cup	grated Pecorino or Parmesan cheese	¼ pound

Bring a large pan of salted water to a rapid boil and add the spaghetti. While this is cooking, prepare the sauce.

Heat the oil in a pan and fry the diced bacon gently over a low heat until all the fat has run out. Add the onion and continue cooking gently until transparent; then add the tomatoes, marjoram, a little salt and a good sprinkling of pepper. Raise the heat and cook briskly for 10 minutes.

By this time the spaghetti will be just tender. Drain thoroughly and turn it into a deep heated serving dish. Dress with the bacon sauce and grated Pecorino cheese, and serve immediately.

Serves 6.

Strangozzi di Spoleto
Ribbon Noodles Spoleto Style

US		UK
4 cups	all-purpose (plain) flour	1 pound
½ cup	olive oil	6 tablespoons
2 cloves	garlic, crushed	2 cloves
2 pounds	ripe tomatoes, peeled and chopped	2 pounds
3–4 sprigs	parsley, finely chopped	3–4 sprigs
2–3 sprigs	basil, finely chopped	2–3 sprigs
	salt and pepper	
	grated Parmesan cheese – optional	

Ribbon noodles, made with only flour and water, are called *strangozzi* in Spoleto.

Sift the flour into a bowl and gradually work in enough cold water to make a pliable dough. Knead until it is light and smooth and little air bubbles begin to form, then roll it out into one very thin sheet and leave for 15 minutes to dry out a little. Roll the sheet up tightly and cut into strips about ¼ inch wide. Unroll the "ribbons" and leave to dry for another 30 minutes.

Meanwhile, heat the oil in a heavy pan and fry the garlic gently. When the cloves begin to turn brown, discard them. Stir in the tomatoes, parsley, basil and a pinch of salt and pepper. Raise the heat and cook briskly for 20 minutes.

Bring a large pan of salted water to the boil, add the ribbon noodles and cook rapidly. If freshly made they will be cooked almost as soon as the water comes back to the boil. Drain and cover with the tomato sauce. Serve at once, with or without grated cheese.

Serves 6.

Minestra di Passatelli d'Urbino
Consommé with Meat Dumplings Urbino Style

US		UK
1 pound	finely ground (minced) beef	1 pound
¾ pound	spinach, cooked	¾ pound
1½ ounces	beef marrow	1½ ounces
1 cup	grated Parmesan cheese	¼ pound
2½ cups	soft breadcrumbs	¼ pound
3 tablespoons	softened butter	1½ ounces
5	eggs	5
	freshly grated nutmeg	
	salt	
4 pints	consommé	3½ pints

Passatelli are dumplings not much larger than peppercorns. They are usually pushed through a gadget called a *ferro per passatelli*.

The meat should be ground (minced) to a smooth paste. Squeeze the cooked spinach dry and chop it very finely. Chop the marrow very finely. Mix the meat, spinach, marrow, Parmesan cheese, breadcrumbs, butter and eggs to a smooth paste, and season to taste with grated nutmeg and salt. Bring the consommé to the boil. Put the meat mixture into a colander and press it through the holes into the consommé. Simmer for 5 minutes and serve with plenty of additional grated Parmesan cheese.

Serves 8.

Bracioline con Cipolle
Pork Chops with Onions

US		UK
6	pork chops, cut from the loin	6
3	large onions	3
	olive oil	
	salt and pepper	

Peel the onions and cut them in half horizontally. Put them into a shallow pan with ¼ cup (U.K. 3 tablespoons) olive oil; sprinkle with salt and cook over a low heat until soft. Keep hot.

Brush the chops lightly with the remaining oil. Place them on the broiler (grill) rack and broil (grill) on both sides, as near as possible to the heat, until well cooked. Sprinkle with salt during cooking. Arrange the chops in a fireproof dish, sprinkle with pepper and put half an onion on top of each chop. Then transfer the dish to a moderate oven (375°F. Mark 4) and bake for 5 minutes, or until thoroughly heated through. Serve immediately.

Serves 6.

Spiedini Misti Spoletini
Mixed Kebabs Spoleto Style

US		UK
6 small slices	loin of pork	6 small slices
6 small pieces	boned chicken	6 small pieces
6 slices	pig's liver	6 slices
6	baby lamb chops	6
24 slices	streaky bacon	24 slices
24 leaves	sage	24 leaves
2 sprigs	rosemary, finely chopped	2 sprigs
	pepper	
½ cup	olive oil	6–8 tablespoons
3–4	juniper berries	3–4
	salt	

Thread a piece of pork, chicken, liver and a lamb chop on to each of 6 skewers, alternating them with a slice of bacon and a leaf of sage; sprinkle each skewer with a little rosemary. Put the skewers in a wide shallow dish, sprinkle them with pepper and pour the olive oil over them. Add the juniper berries and leave for 5 to 6 hours.

Cook the skewers over charcoal if possible, or under a very hot broiler (grill) for 15 minutes, turning frequently. Serve as soon as the meat is cooked, lightly sprinkled with salt. Alternatively, the skewers may be cooked in a hot oven, placed on a rack in a baking pan.

Serves 6.

Trippa alla Marchigiana
Tripe Marche Style

US		UK
3 pounds	dressed calf's, or beef, tripe – see page 46	3 pounds
2–3	pig's trotters	2–3
	salt	
4 tablespoons	butter	2 ounces
¼ pound	bacon, finely chopped	4 ounces
1 clove	garlic, finely chopped	1 clove
1 stalk	celery, finely chopped	1 stalk
1	carrot, finely chopped	1
2–3 sprigs	parsley, finely chopped	2–3 sprigs
1	ham bone	1
1 sprig	marjoram	1 sprig
	rind of ½ lemon	
	pepper	
2–3 tablespoons	tomato paste	2 tablespoons
1 head	Savoy cabbage	1 head
24	pearl (button) onions	24
3 large	potatoes, thickly sliced	3 large
	grated Parmesan cheese	

Wash and scrape the trotters thoroughly, and scald them in boiling water. Cut the tripe into smallish squares; drop them into a pan of cold water, bring to the boil and drain. Put the trotters **and** tripe into a large, heavy pan and cover with plenty of cold, salted water. Bring to a gentle boil, lower the heat and simmer gently for 2 hours.

Take the tripe from the pan and cut it into strips about ¼ inch wide. Reserve. Take the trotters from the pan and gently pull out all the bones. Reserve the boned meat. Strain and reserve the stock.

Wipe the pan clean, heat the butter in it, and gently fry the bacon with the garlic, celery, carrot and parsley. Add the ham bone, marjoram, lemon rind, tripe and the meat from the trotters, and season to taste with a very little salt (the ham bone may already be salty) and pepper. Dilute the tomato paste with a little of the reserved stock and add it to the pan, together with the remaining stock. Bring to the boil again, lower the heat and simmer gently, covered, for 1½ hours.

In the meantime, trim off the outer leaves from the cabbage, cut it into 6 pieces and blanch for 2 minutes in boiling water. Drain well, add this to the pan with the onions and potatoes, and continue cooking for a further 30 minutes. Just before serving, discard the ham bone.

Serve the stew very hot with plenty of grated Parmesan cheese. Serves 6.

Pollo in Potacchio
Chicken in Tomato Sauce

US		UK
1	chicken – about 2½ pounds	1
½ cup	olive oil	6 tablespoons
6 tablespoons	butter	3 ounces
2 cloves	garlic, crushed	2 cloves
1 medium-sized	onion, thinly sliced	1 medium-sized
	salt	
½ cup	dry white wine	6–8 tablespoons
Sauce		
1 pound	ripe tomatoes	1 pound
¼ cup	olive oil	3 tablespoons
1	onion, finely chopped	1
1 sprig	rosemary, finely chopped	1 sprig
	salt	
pinch	chili powder *or* black pepper	pinch

Cut the chicken into small pieces. Heat the oil and 4 tablespoons (2 ounces) butter in a two-handled shallow pan, and gently fry the pieces of chicken with the garlic and onion until golden brown all over. Sprinkle with salt. When the garlic cloves are browned, discard them. Add the wine and continue cooking slowly, covered, until the chicken is tender.

Sauce
Peel and chop the tomatoes, and discard the seeds. Heat the oil in a heavy pan and sauté the onion and rosemary gently until the onion is golden brown; then add the tomatoes and sprinkle lightly with salt and chili or black pepper. Bring to a gentle boil, lower the heat and simmer for 20 minutes.

Pour this sauce over the chicken, dot with the remaining butter and continue cooking in a slow oven (325°F. Mark 2) for about 20 minutes longer.

If a two-handled frying pan is not available, simply transfer the chicken to an oven casserole before adding the sauce.

Serves 4.

In some parts of Italy near Ascoli *vino cotto* (cooked wine) is used instead of the dry white wine, and the tomatoes are left out altogether. The dish is then called *pollo in cip-ciap* – "cheep-chap chicken".

Vino cotto is made as follows: press the juice from several bunches of either black or white grapes, strain it into a flameproof earthenware or glass pan, and simmer very gently until thick, about 4 hours.

Pollo alla Maceratese
Chicken Macerata Style

US		UK
1	tender chicken – about 2½ pounds	1
	salt	
6 tablespoons	olive oil	5 tablespoons
3 tablespoons	butter	1½ ounces
2 cups	meat stock	¾ pint
2	egg yolks	2
	juice of 1 lemon	

Choose a free-range chicken for this recipe, if possible. Wash it well, singe if necessary, and rub generously inside and out with salt. Carefully clean the giblets and chop them finely.

Take a flameproof casserole, preferably an oval one, into which the chicken will fit snugly; heat the oil and butter in it and sauté the giblets for 2 minutes. Then add the chicken and continue to cook until golden brown all over. Pour in the stock – there should be almost enough to cover the bird. Cover the casserole with wax paper and then the lid, and cook over a low heat for about 1 hour. When the chicken is tender, uncover the casserole and cook over a brisk heat to reduce the sauce.

Take the chicken from the pan and cut it into serving pieces. Arrange them on a heated serving dish, re-forming them into the original shape of the chicken. Keep hot while the sauce is being finished.

Beat the egg yolks until well mixed but not frothy; add the lemon juice and stir into the sauce. Season to taste with salt, stir well and cook over a low heat for 1 minute. Pour the sauce over the chicken and serve at once.

Serves 4.

Pollo all'Arrabbiata
Chicken with Chili

US		UK
1	chicken – about 2½ pounds	1
½ cup	olive oil	6 tablespoons
4 tablespoons	butter	2 ounces
	salt	
1 cup	dry white wine	⅓ pint
3 large	ripe tomatoes	3 large
pinch	chili powder	pinch

Cut the chicken into serving pieces. Heat the oil and butter in a deep frying pan or flameproof casserole and fry the pieces of chicken until golden brown all over. Sprinkle with salt, add the wine and continue cooking until reduced by half.

Peel and chop the tomatoes, discarding seeds. Add the tomato pulp to the chicken, lower the heat and sprinkle with a generous pinch of chili powder. Cover the pan and continue cooking until the chicken is tender. Serve the chicken very hot in its sauce.

Serves 3 to 4.

Spezzato di Tacchino
Casseroled Turkey with Olives

US		UK
2½–3 pounds	turkey joints	2½–3 pounds
½ cup	olive oil	6–8 tablespoons
2 cloves	garlic, crushed	2 cloves
	salt	
small piece	hot chili pepper, finely chopped	small piece
½ cup	dry white wine	6–8 tablespoons
1¼ cups	sweet black olives, pitted	8 ounces
⅔ cup	stock	¼ pint

This dish should be made with the sweet black olives of Umbria. Curiously, these are known all over the area as *olive bianche* or "white olives".

Heat the oil in a large casserole and gently fry the garlic cloves until they begin to brown. Discard them and add the pieces of turkey. Brown these all over. Sprinkle with salt to taste and a pinch of finely chopped chili; add the wine, let it reduce a little, then add the olives and a little of the stock. Cover and cook over a very low heat for about 2½ hours, moistening from time to time with the remaining stock. The sauce should be thick and full of flavor.

Serves 6.

Oca Arrosta Ripiena
Stuffed Roast Goose

US		UK
1	young goose, dressed – about 7 pounds	1
	salt	
½ pound	Italian pork sausage meat	½ pound
¾ cup	green olives, pitted and chopped	5 ounces
1	truffle, chopped	1
	pepper	
1 cup	olive oil	⅓ pint
about 2½ cups	boiling stock	about 1 pint

Clean the goose carefully both inside and out. Wash the goose giblets and chop them finely. Mix them with the sausage meat, olives and truffle. Rub the cavity of the goose with salt and pepper, and fill it with the stuffing. Sew up the opening.

Put the goose on the rack of a large roasting pan and pour the olive oil over the top. Roast in a moderate oven (375°F. Mark 4) until the goose is golden brown all over; then lower the heat to 325°F. (Mark 2) and continue cooking, basting occasionally with boiling stock, for about 2 hours – this allows approximately 18 minutes per pound of goose. Test the goose by wriggling its legs; if they move easily it is done.

Serves 4 to 6.

Coniglio in Porchetta
Stuffed Rabbit

US		UK
1	rabbit – 3 to 3½ pounds	1
1 cup	wine vinegar	scant ½ pint
	salt and pepper	
2–3 slices	Parma ham, shredded	2–3 slices
3 cloves	garlic, finely chopped	3 cloves
1 sprig	rosemary, finely chopped	1 sprig
2 sprigs	fennel, finely chopped	2 sprigs
½ cup	olive oil	6–8 tablespoons
¼ cup	fat salt pork, chopped	2 ounces
½ cup	dry white wine	6–8 tablespoons

The literal translation of this recipe is "rabbit cooked like suckling pig", the reference being to the fennel, the herb traditionally used with suckling pig.

Wash the rabbit in a mixture of water and vinegar, wipe it dry with paper towels, and rub the cavity with salt and pepper. Chop the rabbit's heart and liver finely, and mix with half the ham, garlic, rosemary and fennel. Season the mixture with a little salt and stuff it into the rabbit. Sew it up with thread and tie it neatly, to keep its shape while cooking.

Heat the oil and the fat salt pork in a flameproof casserole; add the rabbit and the remaining ham, garlic and herbs, and cook gently until the rabbit is browned all over, turning it from time to time. Add the wine, cover the pan and cook over a moderate heat for 30 to 45 minutes, or until the rabbit is tender.

Serves 4.

Coniglio in Potacchietto
Casseroled Rabbit

US		UK
1	rabbit – 3 to 3½ pounds – disjointed	1
½ cup	wine vinegar	6–8 tablespoons
2 cloves	garlic, lightly crushed	2 cloves
2 sprigs	rosemary	2 sprigs
small piece	hot chili pepper, finely chopped	small piece
½ cup	olive oil	6–8 tablespoons
	salt and pepper	
1 cup	dry white wine	⅓ pint
	stock – optional	

Wash the rabbit joints in a mixture of water and vinegar, wipe them dry with paper towels, and put them in a flameproof casserole with the garlic, rosemary, chili pepper, olive oil and a little salt and pepper. Cover and leave in a cool place to marinate for 12 hours, turning the pieces from time to time.

Put the casserole on a moderate heat and cook the rabbit pieces until they are lightly browned all over. Discard the garlic and add the wine. Cover and cook over a low heat for about 40 minutes, or until the rabbit is tender, adding a little more wine, water or stock if necessary. Arrange the rabbit pieces on a heated serving dish and pour the remaining sauce over them. Serve immediately.

Serves 4.

Palombacci allo Spiedo
Spit-roasted Wood Pigeons

US		UK
3	wood pigeons	3
1 cup	herb vinegar – see method	scant ½ pint
	salt and pepper	
½ cup	olive oil	6–8 tablespoons
1 cup	red wine	scant ½ pint
6 slices	lemon	6 slices
1 sprig	sage	1 sprig
12	black olives, pitted	12

This dish is traditionally prepared with fresh young wood pigeons but it is also delicious made with tame pigeons or squabs. The herb vinegar used in this recipe is not, as might be expected, seasoned with tarragon, and an Italian recipe for it is given below.

Pluck the pigeons, draw them and wash them carefully with all but 2 or 3 tablespoons of herb vinegar. Clean the giblets and put them back inside the birds. Season with salt and pepper both inside and out, brush with oil and thread on to a spit. Spit-roast the pigeons, turning them slowly and brushing occasionally with oil. Season with salt. Catch the drippings in a shallow pan (this is known as a *leccarda* or *ghiotto*) into which you have poured the wine, the remaining herb vinegar, the lemon slices, sage leaves and olives. As this mixture becomes hot, the vapor rising from it will add flavor to the birds.

As soon as the pigeons are cooked (about 40 minutes) remove

them from the spit, cut them in half and chop the giblets finely. Add the latter to the drippings in the pan and cook briskly for a few minutes. Serve the pigeons with the hot sauce poured over them.

Serves 3.

Herb Vinegar

In an enamel pan simmer about 5 cups (U.K. 2 pints) good quality wine vinegar until reduced by half. In the meantime, prepare the following: 2 shallots, finely chopped, 1 clove garlic, crushed, 1 bay leaf, a sprig of thyme, 1 or 2 black peppercorns, crushed, and a pinch of salt. Mix these together in a bowl and pour over the reduced vinegar. Cover and leave for 1 hour. Strain through fine cloth or muslin and store in a tightly corked bottle.

Salsa per la Cacciagione
Sauce to Accompany Game

US		UK
1 cup	red wine	⅓ pint
1 cup	dry white wine	⅓ pint
1 cup	wine vinegar	⅓ pint
½ cup	olive oil	6–8 tablespoons
2 ounces	Parma ham, shredded	2 ounces
½	lemon, peeled and sliced	½
3 cloves	garlic, crushed	3 cloves
2 leaves	sage	2 leaves
1 sprig	rosemary	1 sprig
4	juniper berries	4
	salt and pepper	
2	chicken livers, finely chopped	2

Put all the ingredients, except the chicken livers, into an enamel pan. Bring to the boil, lower the heat and simmer for 30 minutes. Remove the garlic, sage and rosemary, and add the chicken livers. Cover and cook slowly until the sauce is reduced by more than half.

Serve hot as an accompaniment to any kind of roast game.

Fave alla Campagnola
Fresh Fava, Lima or Broad Beans Country Style

US		UK
3 pounds	fresh beans	3 pounds
	salt and pepper	
	olive oil	
1–2	green (spring) onions, finely chopped	1–2

Do not shell the beans until just before cooking. Then cook them in plenty of unsalted, boiling water. They should cook slowly and absorb quite a lot of liquid. As soon as they are tender, drain them, turn them into a salad bowl and dress them while still hot with a little salt, a good sprinkling of pepper, plenty of olive oil, and the finely chopped onion. Mix well and serve.

Serves 6.

Olive al Forno
Baked Green Olives

Remove the pits from 24 large green olives pickled in brine. Failing an olive pitter, use a small sharp knife to cut round the pit in a spiral; if you are careful not to break the olive spiral it can be re-formed into the original shape. Cut 12 slices of bacon in half. Wrap each olive in a half-slice of bacon and secure them, two by two, with toothpicks. Oil an ovenproof dish, arrange the olives in it and bake in a moderate oven (375°F. Mark 4) until the bacon fat runs. Arrange on a heated serving dish and serve immediately.

Serves 6.

Brodetto di Porto Recanati
Porto Recanati Fish Soup or Stew

US		UK
3½ pounds	assorted fish – see method	3½ pounds
1 pound	small cuttlefish or squid	1 pound
	salt	
1 cup	olive oil	⅓ pint
1	onion, thinly sliced	1
pinch	safflower or saffron	pinch
	pepper	
1¼ cups	dry white wine	½ pint
1–2 tablespoons	wine vinegar	1–1½ tablespoons
	slices of fried bread	

Safflower is not to be confused with the true saffron, which comes from Aquila and is made from the stigmas of *crocus sativus*. Safflower is extracted from *carthamus tinctorius*, a locally grown plant, and serves simply to give the soup an orange color. Real saffron can, of course, be used instead. Both should be dissolved in a little water.

The fish used for this soup would include cod, angler fish, dogfish, skate, grey and red mullet, sole and *cicale*, small crustaceans with a delicate flavor found in the Adriatic and Mediterranean.

Clean the fish and cut the larger ones into even-sized pieces. Remove the ink-sac, eyes and cuttle-bone from the cuttlefish, and cut them into strips. Wash all the fish carefully in plenty of salted water.

Heat the oil in a large heavy pan and sauté the onion gently until golden. Add the cuttlefish and the dissolved safflower, and continue to cook gently. When the cuttlefish turn yellow, season with salt and pepper, and cover with water. Bring to the boil and cook over a low heat for 30 minutes.

Now take another large, wide pan, if possible one with two handles (so as to be able to shake the fish from time to time without using a fork or ladle). Cover the bottom of it with a layer of *cicale*; on top of them put the cooked cuttlefish, without their liquid – this comes later. Then add the pieces of firmer-fleshed fish; finally, add the more delicate-fleshed fish and the stock from the cuttlefish. There should be not more than three layers of fish. Mix the wine and wine vinegar with enough hot water almost to cover the fish, pour into the pan, check seasoning and cook over a brisk heat for 15 minutes, or until all the fish are tender, gently shaking the pan from time to time. Serve very hot with slices of fried bread.

Serves 6.

Calamaretti delle Marche
Cuttlefish (or Squid) Marche Style

US		UK
3 pounds	baby cuttlefish – or squid	3 pounds
	salt	
½ cup	olive oil	6–8 tablespoons
2 cloves	garlic, crushed	2 cloves
3–4 sprigs	parsley, finely chopped	3–4 sprigs
small piece	hot chili pepper, finely chopped	small piece
1 cup	dry white wine	⅓ pint
⅔ cup	hot stock	¼ pint

Clean the cuttlefish or squid as directed in the preceding recipe, rinse them thoroughly in salted water and dry them well. Heat the oil and fry the garlic gently until golden brown; discard the garlic and add the cuttlefish, parsley, a little salt and the chili. Cook over a brisk heat for about 10 minutes. Moisten with the wine and let it reduce. Then add a little hot stock (or water), lower the heat, cover and simmer gently for about 15 minutes longer, or until the cuttlefish are tender.

Serves 6.

Zuppa di Baccalà
Salt Cod Soup

US		UK
2 pounds	dried salt cod, pre-soaked (page 50)	2 pounds
$\frac{2}{3}$ cup	olive oil	$\frac{1}{4}$ pint
2	onions, thinly sliced	2
2 cloves	garlic, finely chopped	2 cloves
1	bay leaf	1
1 sprig	thyme	1 sprig
$\frac{3}{4}$ pound	ripe tomatoes	$\frac{3}{4}$ pound
1 stalk	celery, finely chopped	1 stalk
3–4 sprigs	parsley, finely chopped	3–4 sprigs
1 cup	dry white wine	$\frac{1}{3}$ pint
4	potatoes, peeled and quartered	4
	pepper	
	slices of fried bread	

Cut the cod into pieces about $2\frac{1}{2}$ inches wide. Skin and bone them. Heat all but 2 or 3 tablespoons of the oil in a large pan and sauté the onion and garlic gently over a low heat until golden but not brown. Tie the bay leaf and thyme together. Peel and chop the tomatoes, and rub the pulp through a sieve.

Add the celery, the tied herbs and the parsley to the pan, and cook gently. When the celery begins to turn golden, add the tomato purée and cook for 10 minutes longer. Moisten with wine, stirring it well into the juices, then cook until reduced. Add the potatoes and about 5 cups (U.K. 2 pints) boiling water. When the potatoes are almost cooked, discard the tied herbs and add the salt cod, together with the remaining olive oil. Check seasoning and continue cooking over a low heat for about 1 hour. If the soup becomes too thick, dilute it with a little more hot water. Serve garnished with additional finely chopped parsley and slices of crisply fried bread.

Serves 6.

Stoccafisso all'Anconetana
Dried Salt Cod Ancona Style

US		UK
$2\frac{1}{2}$ pounds	dried salt cod, pre-soaked (page 50)	$2\frac{1}{2}$ pounds
	olive oil	
1	onion, thinly sliced	1
1	carrot, finely chopped	1
1 stalk	celery, finely chopped	1 stalk
2–3 sprigs	parsley, finely chopped	2–3 sprigs
$\frac{3}{4}$ pound	ripe tomatoes	$\frac{3}{4}$ pound
pinch	marjoram	pinch
	salt and pepper	
4	potatoes, peeled and sliced	4
$\frac{1}{2}$ cup	milk	6–8 tablespoons

Bone the salt cod but leave it unskinned. Cut into large pieces. Heat 5 tablespoons (U.K. 4 tablespoons) oil and sauté the onion, carrot, celery and parsley gently until the vegetables begin to soften. Peel and chop the tomatoes, discarding seeds. Add the tomato pulp to the pan with the marjoram, salt and pepper. Cook over a brisk heat for about 20 minutes.

Take a large heavy pan and in the bottom put a rack. On this arrange a layer of salt cod. Pour over some of the tomato sauce, add another layer of fish and continue in this manner until all the fish and tomato sauce are used up. Cover with a layer of potatoes, sprinkle lightly with salt (remember the fish is already salty enough), then pour over about 2 cups (U.K. $\frac{3}{4}$ pint) oil and the milk. For those less fond of olive oil, the amount can be halved and the milk increased instead. Cover and cook over a very low heat for $1\frac{1}{2}$ hours, carefully shaking the pan from time to time. Then uncover the pan (do not stir or shake) and continue cooking for a little less than 1 hour longer.

The rack is placed in the pan to prevent the fish from sticking. Traditionally, a layer of reeds or bamboo canes was used, and those with a fish kettle can do the same.

Serves 6.

Muscioli al Forno
Baked Mussels

US		UK
3 pounds	mussels	3 pounds
	salt	
1 pound	ripe tomatoes, peeled	1 pound
$\frac{1}{4}$ cup	soft breadcrumbs	3 tablespoons
3 sprigs	parsley, finely chopped	3 sprigs
	olive oil	

Clean the mussels thoroughly with a stiff brush. Wash them in several changes of salted water and open them with an oyster-knife (or sauté them in a pan with a little olive oil until they open). Remove the mussels and put two or three on each half-shell.

Rub the tomatoes through a fine sieve. Mix together the tomato pulp, breadcrumbs, parsley, a trickle of olive oil and a pinch of salt to taste. Spread a little of the mixture on top of the mussels and arrange them side by side in a large, shallow, fireproof dish. Trickle a little olive oil over them and bake in a slow oven (350°F. Mark 3) for 10 to 15 minutes, or until the breadcrumbs are lightly browned.

Serves 6.

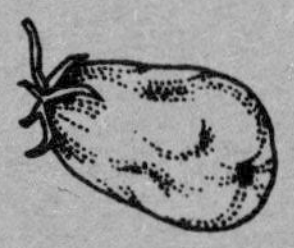

Triglie all'Anconetana
Red Mullet Ancona Style

US		UK
6	red mullet	6
	salt	
	juice of 1 lemon	
2 cloves	garlic, crushed	2 cloves
1 sprig	rosemary, finely chopped	1 sprig
	pepper	
2–3 sprigs	parsley, finely chopped	2–3 sprigs
	fine dry breadcrumbs	
6 large slices	Parma ham	6 large slices
$\frac{1}{2}$ cup	olive oil	6–8 tablespoons

Red mullet are often sold already scaled. However, if this operation is necessary, do it carefully, as the skin of the mullet is very fragile. As for cleaning, this is a matter of taste. Some mullet lovers believe that the intestines of the mullet, like the trail of small game birds, add flavor to the cooked fish.

Wash the fish gently in salted water and drain. Put them in a shallow earthenware dish and sprinkle with lemon juice, garlic, rosemary and a little salt and pepper. Leave for 1 hour in a cool place.

Combine the parsley with enough breadcrumbs to coat the fish. Take the fish from the marinade, drain them, and then roll in the mixed breadcrumbs and parsley. Wrap each fish in a slice of ham. Put the wrapped fish in a shallow ovenproof dish. Strain the remains of the marinade and mix with the olive oil. Pour this over the top of the fish and bake in a slow oven (350°F. Mark 3) for about 20 minutes, or until cooked. Serve the mullet immediately in the same dish to avoid the danger of breaking them.

Serves 6.

Trota del Nera
Trout from the River Nera

US		UK
6	trout	6
10 tablespoons	soft breadcrumbs	8 tablespoons
	salt and pepper	
4–5 sprigs	parsley, finely chopped	4–5 sprigs
	juice of 2 lemons	
1 cup	olive oil	$\frac{1}{3}$ pint

The delicious trout caught in the Nera and Sordo rivers are usually carefully cleaned and washed, brushed with oil, sprinkled with a little finely chopped rosemary and parsley, salt and pepper, and broiled (grilled). Just before serving, a little more olive oil is trickled over them.

However, for a change they are also prepared in the following manner. Clean the trout and wash them well. Combine the breadcrumbs, a little salt, a generous quantity of freshly ground pepper, the chopped parsley and lemon juice. Mix this well to a paste and stuff a little of it into each trout. Spread what is left over the top of the fish.

Heat the oil in a large, heavy pan (one that can be transferred to the oven), arrange the trout in it in one layer and cover the pan – or use two pans. Transfer to a moderate oven (375°F. Mark 4) and bake for about 20 minutes, or until the fish flake easily with a fork.

Serves 6.

Omelette ai Tartufi
Truffle Omelette

US		UK
2 small	black Umbrian truffles	2 small
5 tablespoons	olive oil	4 tablespoons
	salt	
2 sprigs	parsley, finely chopped	2 sprigs
8	eggs	8
2$\frac{1}{2}$ tablespoons	grated Parmesan cheese	2 tablespoons
4 tablespoons	butter	2 ounces

Clean the truffles thoroughly and slice them very thinly.

Heat the oil in a thick-bottomed frying pan and add the truffles, a pinch of salt and the parsley. Leave over a low heat for a couple of minutes to bring out the flavors.

Beat the eggs with a pinch of salt and the Parmesan cheese. Heat the butter in a large frying pan, add the eggs and swirl the pan around to spread them evenly – or just stir them with the back of a fork. When the eggs are set, put the truffles down the center, fold up one side of the omelette, then the other. In Umbria, this dish is served either hot or cold.

Serves 4 to 6.

Pinoccate di Perugia
Pine Nut Fondants

US		UK
$\frac{1}{2}$ pound	pine nuts	$\frac{1}{2}$ pound
1$\frac{1}{2}$ cups	sugar	$\frac{3}{4}$ pound
1 cup	water	$\frac{1}{3}$ pint
$\frac{1}{4}$ pound	candied orange peel cut into strips – optional	$\frac{1}{4}$ pound
	circles of rice paper	

Spread the pine nuts on a baking sheet and dry them out slightly in a very low oven.

Put the water into a pan and add the sugar. Let this dissolve slowly, then bring to the boil at 240°F. Pour the boiled syrup into a bowl and stir it with a wooden spoon until it is thick and white or opaque. Knead it well until it has an even texture all through. Add the nuts and orange peel if used. Put small balls of the mixture on the circles of rice paper and leave to cool, trimming off surplus bits of rice paper from around each fondant later.

Frustenga
Corn (U.K. Maize) Fruit Cake

US		UK
$\frac{1}{4}$ pound	dried figs	$\frac{1}{4}$ pound
scant 1 cup	seedless white raisins (sultanas)	$\frac{1}{4}$ pound
	salt	
1 pound	fine cornmeal	1 pound
7$\frac{1}{2}$ tablespoons	olive oil	6 tablespoons
24	walnut halves, finely chopped	24
	butter	
	fine dry breadcrumbs	
	oil	

Soak the figs and white raisins (sultanas) in warm water overnight. Drain, reserving the liquid. Cut the figs into small pieces.

Measure the soaking liquid and add enough fresh water to make it up to 8$\frac{3}{4}$ cups (U.K. 3$\frac{1}{2}$ pints). Pour it into a large pan, add a little salt and bring to the boil. Add the cornmeal gradually, stirring constantly, then cook, stirring frequently, for 40 minutes. Make sure that the mixture is thick and free of lumps.

Take the pan from the heat, beat the "polenta", then add the figs, raisins, $\frac{1}{4}$ cup (U.K. 3 tablespoons) olive oil and the walnuts.

Grease 2 layer cake pans about 10 inches in diameter with butter and sprinkle lightly with breadcrumbs. Pour the mixture into the pans (the cakes should not be more than 1 inch thick, preferably even a little less). Brush each cake with a little oil, cover with wax paper (or foil) and bake in a slow oven (325°F. Mark 2) for about 30 minutes.

Frustenga may be served hot or cold.

Pestringolo
Rich Fruit Cake with Figs

US		UK
3 cups	dried figs	1 pound
$\frac{1}{2}$ cup	seedless white raisins (sultanas)	2 ounces
$\frac{1}{3}$ cup	almonds, toasted and finely chopped	2 ounces
$\frac{1}{3}$ cup	candied peel, diced	2 ounces
$\frac{1}{2}$ cup	cocoa	2 ounces
2$\frac{1}{2}$ cups	soft breadcrumbs	3$\frac{1}{2}$ ounces
5 tablespoons	olive oil	4 tablespoons
pinch	ground cinnamon	pinch
pinch	grated nutmeg	pinch
4 teaspoons	honey	2 ounces
	oil and dry breadcrumbs for cake pan	
4 teaspoons	pine nuts	1 tablespoon
about $\frac{1}{2}$ cup	walnut kernels	about 2 ounces

Soak the figs overnight in warm water. Next day, bring them to a gentle boil in the same water, lower the heat and simmer gently until tender. While the figs are cooking, soak the white raisins (sultanas) in warm water.

Drain the figs and put them into a bowl. Drain the raisins, squeeze them dry and add them to the figs. Add the almonds, candied peel, cocoa, breadcrumbs, oil, cinnamon and nutmeg to taste, and honey. Stir well to as smooth a consistency as possible.

Rub a layer cake pan with oil and sprinkle lightly with breadcrumbs. Pour in the fruit mixture. Cover the surface with pine nuts and walnuts, and bake in a moderate oven (375°F. Mark 4) for 30 to 45 minutes, or until firm. Serve cold.

Cicerchiata
Umbrian Honey Cake

US		UK
about 1¼ cups	all-purpose (plain) flour	about 5 ounces
¼ cup	granulated (caster) sugar	3 tablespoons
5 tablespoons	olive oil	4 tablespoons
2	eggs, lightly beaten	2
	oil for frying	
½ cup plus 1 tablespoon	honey	7 ounces
2–3 tablespoons	blanched almonds, slivered	2–3 tablespoons
	ground cinnamon	
	hundreds and thousands – see method	

"Hundreds and thousands" are decorative, brightly dyed sweet grains, almost as fine as granulated sugar. They come in colors of pink, blue, green, mauve, etc., and are sold in small glass cylinders.

Sift the flour into a bowl, make a well in the middle and add the sugar, oil and eggs. Work to a firm dough, using a little more flour if necessary, and knead until smooth and pliable.

Break off pieces of the dough and roll into long, thin "sausages". Cut each sausage into slices and roll each slice into a ball the size of a large pea. Heat plenty of olive oil in a deep frying pan. Drop the dough "peas" into the hot oil, a few at a time, and fry until golden. Take from the pan and drain on absorbent paper.

Melt the honey in a pan and cook until it begins to change color. Add the fried dough "peas" and stir carefully with a wooden spoon until well mixed. Turn out on to a plate or marble slab brushed with water. When the mixture is cool enough to handle, wet your hands and form it into a ring-shape, like a large doughnut. Sprinkle with the almonds, cinnamon and hundreds and thousands.

Pizza Dolce
Sweet Pizza

US		UK
1 pound	once-risen bread dough, made with 2½ cups flour	1 pound
	grated rind of 1 lemon	
3 tablespoons	granulated (caster) sugar	1½ ounces
¼ cup	olive oil	3 tablespoons
1	egg yolk	1
⅔ cup	sweet white wine	¼ pint
	lukewarm milk	
	oil or butter and fine dry breadcrumbs for cake pan	
1	egg, beaten – optional	1
	confectioners' (icing) sugar	

Punch down the bread dough and knead it again, adding the lemon rind, sugar, oil, egg yolk, wine and, if necessary, a little milk. The dough should be perfectly smooth, but not too stiff. Work it thoroughly until it is light and springy, and comes away from the pastry board in one piece.

Grease a deep, wide cake pan and sprinkle it with breadcrumbs. Add the pizza dough. Cover with a cloth and leave to rise again in a warm place for 1 hour. Brush the top with beaten egg. Bake in a moderately hot oven (400°F. Mark 5) for about 40 minutes without opening the oven door.

Sprinkle with confectioners' (icing) sugar before serving.

Ciaramicola
Umbrian Cochineal Cake

US		UK
2	eggs	2
3	egg yolks	3
1⅛ cups	granulated (caster) sugar	½ pound
⅝ cup	softened butter	5 ounces
5 teaspoons	baking powder	4 teaspoons
4 cups	all-purpose (plain) flour	1 pound
2–3 tablespoons	Alkermes liqueur – see method	2–2½ tablespoons
½ cup	milk	6–8 tablespoons
pinch	salt	pinch
	grated rind of 1 lemon	
	butter and flour for cake pan	
3	egg whites	3
6 tablespoons	confectioners' (icing) sugar	1½ ounces
	hundreds and thousands – see above	

Alkermes is an Italian liqueur made with alcohol and sugar, colored with cochineal and flavored with spices, cinnamon, nutmeg, cloves, etc.

Beat the whole eggs and the egg yolks with the sugar to a thick, fluffy cream. Add the butter in small pieces and continue to beat until the mixture is smooth and like a thick cream. Sift the baking powder with the flour and gradually work this into the egg and butter cream. Mix the liqueur with the milk and work this thoroughly into the dough, beating or kneading until the color of the liqueur has worked evenly through the dough, and adding a little more milk if necessary. Add the salt and lemon rind. Knead until smooth, then break off a piece of dough, about one-quarter of the whole amount.

Grease a round cake pan lightly with butter and coat with flour. Add the large piece of dough, shaping it in the pan like a doughnut with a hole in the center. Cut off a small piece of the reserved dough and roll this out. Cut into 2 strips and make a cross over the hole with them. Divide the remaining dough into 3 pieces and roll these into 3 small balls. Arrange these on top of one of the strips of the cross. This is the traditional shape for a *ciaramicola*.

Bake the cake in a moderate oven (375°F. Mark 4) for 40 minutes. In the meantime, beat the egg whites until stiff, then gradually add the confectioners' (icing) sugar. When the *ciaramicola* is a golden brown color, spread the meringue over it and sprinkle with hundreds and thousands. Return the cake to the cooling oven to allow the meringue to dry without changing color.

ROME-LAZIO

In former days, the walls of the old, traditional Roman *trattorie* were decorated with large paintings depicting appropriate subjects such as Bacchus astride a cask. Film stars and pinups have long since taken their place, but everywhere one traditional element still survives. This represents a giant cock with a bright red crest, multicolored feathers and large claws, and bears the following inscription in large, block letters:

> *Quando questo gallo canterà*
> *allora credenza si farà.*
> (Credit will be given the day this cock crows.)

This notice is typical of the Romans, who would never dream of writing a solemn warning like "No credit given here," or "Only cash accepted." The people of Rome are "people" in the old sense of the word. They are jealous defenders of their traditions, their coarse but vivid language, their love of pleasure. They loathe respectability and treat strangers with the utmost familiarity, addressing them by nicknames at the first meeting.

Such people cannot help but express their character in their cooking, where their inspiration explodes. No other city in Italy has as many restaurants, *trattorie* or inns as Rome where, in the district of Trastevere, the bastion of Roman cooking, there are literally hundreds. Nor has any city the same past tradition of Gargantuan banquets. Modern ideas about diet have made these a thing of the past, but Roman cooking remains inimitable. Nowhere else have such sayings as "*Acqua e pane, vita da cane*" (Bread and water

A rich display of specialties of the Lazio photographed in "Checco er carrettiere" ("Checco the carter's"), a typical *trattoria* in Trastevere.

Two Roman dishes of humble origin, now considered delicacies: *rigatoni con la pagliata*, large ribbed maccheroni noodles with ox duodenum, and *coda* (oxtail) *alla vaccinara*. To sample them you will have to visit one of the many *trattorie* in the popular quarters of Testaccio and Trastevere in Rome.

Frascati is one of the most famous of Italian wines. It is stored in the natural caves of the *Castelli romani* (see page 166) and comes in three qualities: dry, medium and sweet.

In the cool, delightful atmosphere of
the gardens of the Villa Lante at
Bagnaia, rosé wine from the
Etruscan Hills surrounded by four
exquisite dishes: saddle of veal,
broiled (grilled) veal chops,
fettuccine noodles, and galantine of
chicken in aspic.

Pork, served in a variety of ways, is also an important ingredient of Roman cooking, not only in the form of *strutto*, but also as *guanciale*, a type of bacon, and especially as *porchetta*, which is a pig killed when it is six or seven months old, and weighs about 112 pounds, then boned, flavored with aromatic herbs and roasted. *Porchetta* originated in Ariccia in the Alban Hills, from where it is supplied not only to Rome, but to the whole of Italy. Once it was eaten as a snack and could be bought from street vendors, but today it is considered fit to be served to the most discerning gourmet. The secret of *porchetta* lies in its preparation and stuffing, which is made with cheese, fat salt pork, garlic, rosemary and pepper. This brings out the flavor of the meat and makes it easily digestible. Other meat dishes include oxtail, tripe, and *pagliata*, which is made from part of the intestine of oxen and sheep cut into rings, and used in many recipes, especially with pasta.

The most famous of all pasta dishes is *spaghetti all'amatriciana* or *alla matriciana* (page 170), the origin of which is said to be Amatrice, a little village in the Sabine country, on the border between Lazio and the Abruzzo. The sauce is based on *guanciale*, diced and mixed with tomatoes, peppers, onions and fat salt pork (purists omit tomatoes), and it is also sometimes eaten with very thin tagliatelle ribbon noodles.

Artichokes are used in the most typical Roman dishes, such as *carciofi alla romana*, artichokes stuffed with breadcrumbs, parsley, anchovies, salt and pepper, but the most famous dish of all is fried artichokes *alla giudia*, the name of which indicates its Jewish

Left, top: In the shade of the trees that line the Appian Way: a pot-roast of beef, Roman Ricotta cheese and the world-famous *saltimbocca* (see page 174). In the foreground, three delicious pasta dishes: *ziti* with Parma ham, *stracci* (a kind of *cannelloni*), and *bucatini all'amatriciana*.
Center: Three classics of the cuisine of the Lazio, photographed on Janiculum Hill overlooking Rome: *saltimbocca* garnished with peas, *fettuccine* noodles, and a dish of sweet peppers.
Bottom: The cooking of Ciociaria remains authentic and unspoilt. Its specialties include Pecorino cheese, *involtini con fagiolini*—stuffed rolls of veal served with beans, also popular in the Abruzzo (see page 192)—a variety of noodles, and pot-roasted beef with tomatoes.
Below, right: Before the Temple of Vesta, one of the most noble products of the Roman region, the artichoke, which gourmets have held in high esteem since ancient times. *Carciofi alla giudia* (see page 176) are one of the most magnificent dishes which the fine cuisine of Rome can offer.

Above, left: A selection of fish and shellfish photographed against the background of the rocky coast of San Felice Circeo.
Above, right: Gaeta offers a rich variety of seafood, prepared in many different ways: *risotto alla taverna, spaghetti alla pescatora* (fisherman's style), giant shrimps (U.K. prawns) and skewered squid.
Right: Before the medieval castle of the Contessa Matilde at Tarquinia, a selection of traditional dishes, including red mullet, *langouste* and sea bass from the Tyrrhenian Sea, *cannelloni,* galantine of chicken and veal, fish steaks with mussels, *ferlenghi* mushrooms and *rigatoni* (ribbed noodles) Etruscan style.

origin. In spite of its simplicity, few but the Romans know how to prepare this dish to perfection.

Wine is the worthy accompaniment of great Roman cooking, and the best comes from the area of the Castelli. There are thirteen of these in thirteen villages which line the road leading from Rome to the Alban Hills, a favorite spot for picnics. Leaving Rome by the Via Tuscolana, you come in turn to Frascati (where Cicero used to retire to work over two thousand years ago), Monte Porzio Catone, Monte Compatri, Rocca Priora, Grotta-ferrata, Marino and Rocca di Papa. From here you skirt Lake Albano and Lake Nemi (where Roman galleys have been found), and turning back at Velletri, return to Rome through Genzano, Ariccia, Albano and Castelgandolfo, the Pope's summer residence, along the Appian Way. Each of these villages produces a famous wine, the celebrated *vine dei Castelli* which, though made in large quantities, are almost all drunk by the inhabitants of Rome, leaving little to be exported. Most of the *vine dei Castelli* are white. They can be dry or sweet, and are full of that special aroma that comes from the volcanic nature of the soil. Today, the wine is sent to Rome in trucks, but in the past it arrived in horse-drawn carts, each loaded with eight sixty-litre barrels. The journey to Rome lasted the whole night, and the roads were crowded with carts, their drivers, with a little mongrel dog to keep them company, dozing on top of the barrels, resting their heads on a cushion of tree branches covered with goatskin.

In Rome itself you will also find Falerno, a wine which was

already a great favorite in the days of the Caesars, and the equally famous Est! Est!! Est!!! from Montefiascone and Bolsena. Legend has it that this wine was discovered by a servant of Bishop Fugger of Augsberg, who had come to Italy in search of the best wines. The servant's task was to precede the bishop and write the word "Est" on the doors of inns where they served good wine. When he reached Montefiascone, he found the wine so good that he wrote the word "Est" three times on the tavern door. The bishop seems to have shared his enthusiasm, for he never got any farther, and his tomb is to be found in the local cemetery.

Crostini alla Provatura
Bread and Cheese Skewers

US		UK
1 pound	Provatura or Mozzarella cheese	1 pound
	salt and pepper	
	home-made bread, sliced	
1 tablespoon	melted butter	½ ounce
4 large	anchovy fillets	4 large
½ cup	butter	4 ounces

This recipe is traditionally made with Roman Provatura, a small, fresh, soft cheese the size and shape of an egg.

Cut the cheese into medium-thick slices. Sprinkle with salt and pepper. Cut from the bread as many pieces as there are of cheese, plus 6 extra, all of the same size and thickness as the cheese. Thread the bread and cheese alternately on to 6 skewers, beginning and ending each one with a piece of bread. Ideally these skewers are then placed over the embers of a wood fire, turned from time to time until brown and slightly smoked. Alternatively, use a baking dish deep and wide enough to allow the skewers to rest on the sides without the bread or cheese touching the bottom of the dish. Bake in a moderately hot oven (400°F. Mark 5) for 15 minutes, or until the bread is lightly toasted and the cheese has softened and begun to melt. Baste from time to time with melted butter.

While the *crostini* are cooking, chop the anchovies and mix with the remaining butter. Cook this gently in a small frying pan until the anchovies have dissolved into the butter to make a sauce.

Arrange the *crostini* in a heated serving dish and pour the hot anchovy butter over the top.

Serves 6.

Crostini col "Merollo"
Bone Marrow on Toast

US		UK
12 slices	bread	12 slices
¼ pound	beef bone marrow	¼ pound
	salt	

Toast spread with bone marrow is hardly ever met with today, even in Rome. It used to be served as a light snack, especially to children. The recipe is worth reviving since it is simple, nourishing and tasty.

Lightly toast the bread on both sides. Spread with bone marrow, sprinkle with salt and put into a hot oven (450°F. Mark 7) for a few minutes until the bone marrow begins to melt. Serve very hot.

Serves 6.

Pandorato
"Golden Bread" or Poor Knights of Windsor

US		UK
12 slices	bread, medium-thick	12 slices
⅔ cup	warm milk	¼ pint
2–3	eggs	2–3
	salt	
	oil or lard for shallow frying	

Trim the crusts from the bread and arrange the slices in a flat dish. Sprinkle with the milk. Beat the eggs with a pinch of salt. Pour them over the bread slices, covering them, and leave until the bread has absorbed the eggs.

Heat a good quantity of olive oil, not, however, enough for deep-frying. Lift out the slices of bread, one at a time, using a spatula, and place carefully in the hot oil. Fry on both sides until golden brown. Take from the pan with a perforated spoon. Drain

on paper towels and put into a hot oven until all the slices are fried. Serve hot.

The fried bread can be served plain, sprinkled with vanilla sugar or ground cinnamon, or with stewed fruit.

Serves 6.

Cuscinetti di Pandorato
Fried Bread "Cushions"

US		UK
1 large	sandwich loaf	1 large
1 pound	Provatura or Mozzarella cheese, thinly sliced	1 pound
5 ounces	raw ham, sliced *or*	5 ounces
6 large	anchovy fillets, chopped	6 large
	flour	
	milk	
3	eggs	3
	salt	
	lard or oil for deep-frying	

The traditional *pandorato* (golden bread) is made as described in the recipe above, but there is also this version in which it is stuffed with cheese and ham or anchovies. It then becomes *cuscinetti* or "little cushions".

Slice the loaf thickly, trim off the crusts and with a sharp knife slit each slice through the middle without cutting it completely through, like a cushion cover. Stuff each slice with a mixture of cheese and ham or anchovies. Flour each "cushion" lightly, dip quickly into milk and arrange in a deep dish. Beat the eggs with a little salt and pour them over the top. Leave until the eggs are completely absorbed by the bread.

Heat plenty of lard or oil and deep-fry the "cushions", two at a time, until golden brown on both sides. Drain on paper towels. Keep hot in a warm oven until all the "cushions" are fried. Serve hot.

Serves 6.

Sugo Finto
Tomato Sauce Roman Style

US		UK
2–2½ pounds	ripe or canned tomatoes	2–2½ pounds
4 tablespoons	butter	2 ounces
2½ tablespoons	olive oil	2 tablespoons
4 tablespoons	bacon fat	2 ounces
1 small	onion, finely chopped	1 small
1 stalk	celery, finely chopped	1 stalk
1	carrot, finely chopped	1
½ clove	garlic, finely chopped	½ clove
2–3 sprigs	parsley, finely chopped	2–3 sprigs
	hot meat stock	
	salt and pepper	

Heat the butter and oil together in a large pan. Add the bacon fat, fry for 2 minutes, then add the onion, celery, carrot, garlic and parsley, and sauté for 5 minutes. Moisten with a few tablespoons of hot stock to allow the mixture (*soffritto*) to brown without burning.

Peel and chop the tomatoes, discarding seeds. As soon as the vegetables begin to brown, add the tomatoes, season to taste with salt and pepper, and cook with the lid half on the pan for about 45 minutes, stirring from time to time.

The sauce, which is sufficient to garnish 1½ pounds noodles, can be served as it is, or strained. It is called "mock sauce" in Roman culinary parlance.

Serves 6.

Spaghetti all'Amatriciana
Spaghetti Amatrice Style

US		UK
1½ pounds	spaghetti	1½ pounds
2½ tablespoons	lard or oil	2 tablespoons
1	onion, thinly sliced	1
5 ounces	lean bacon, diced	5 ounces
½ cup	dry white wine – optional	6–8 tablespoons
1 pound	ripe or canned tomatoes	1 pound
	salt and pepper	
¾ cup	grated Pecorino, or mixed Parmesan and Pecorino cheese	3 ounces

In Rome, this way of serving spaghetti, which takes its name from the little town of Amatrice in the Sabine Hills, is frequently known, erroneously, as *spaghetti alla matriciana* – the sound of the phrase when spoken being exactly the same.

Heat the lard and sauté the onion over a very low heat until soft. Add the bacon and fry it slowly for a few minutes. Moisten with white wine and continue cooking until it evaporates a little. Peel, chop and seed the tomatoes, and add them to the pan. Season to taste with salt and pepper, and cook over a brisk heat for not more than 15 minutes.

Bring a large pan of salted water to a fast boil. Lower the spaghetti into the water, stir well and cook until just tender. Drain and dress the spaghetti immediately with the hot sauce, and sprinkle with the grated cheese.

Serves 6.

Spaghetti a "Cacio e Pepe"
Spaghetti with Cheese and Pepper

Bring a large pan of salted water to a fast boil. Slowly add the spaghetti and cook until just tender. Drain in a colander, but not too thoroughly. Serve immediately with freshly ground black pepper and Pecorino cheese.

As the spaghetti would be far too dry with simply the pepper and cheese dressing, the cooking water which adheres to it is allowed to remain to keep it moist. Sometimes a little oil, or lightly fried pork fat or bacon is added but this is not traditional.

Serves 6.

Rigatoni alla Carbonara
Ribbed Noodles Charcoal-burner's Style

US		UK
4 teaspoons	lard or oil	1 tablespoon
5 ounces	streaky bacon, diced	5 ounces
1 clove	garlic, crushed	1 clove
	salt	
1¼ pounds	rigatoni – ribbed noodles	1¼ pounds
5	eggs	5
5 tablespoons	grated Parmesan cheese	4 tablespoons
5 tablespoons	grated Pecorino cheese	4 tablespoons
	pepper	

Heat the lard and sauté the bacon and garlic. As soon as the garlic is browned, discard it. Bring a large pan of salted water to a bubbling boil. Add the *rigatoni* and cook until tender but still firm.

Meanwhile, beat the eggs thoroughly in a large shallow pan with a pinch of salt, the Parmesan and Pecorino cheeses, and plenty of freshly ground black pepper. Do not heat.

As soon as the *rigatoni* are tender, drain them and add them to the pan with the egg mixture. Add the bacon with its cooking fat, then cook over a very low heat, stirring constantly, for a couple of minutes to heat the eggs through. Serve immediately.

This method of cooking can, of course, be used with any noodles – spaghetti is frequently served *alla carbonara*.

Serves 6.

Fettuccine alla Romana
Ribbon Noodles Roman Style

US		UK
Dough		
6 cups	all-purpose (plain) flour	1½ pounds
6–8	eggs	6–8
	salt	
	or	
1½ pounds	ready-made fettuccine ribbon noodles	1½ pounds
Sauce		
4 tablespoons	bacon fat, finely chopped	2 ounces
½ cup	butter	4 ounces
1	onion, finely chopped	1
1 clove	garlic, crushed	1 clove
¾ pound	ripe or canned tomatoes	¾ pound
1 ounce	dried mushrooms, soaked	1 ounce
	salt and pepper	
¾ pound	chicken giblets, chopped	¾ pound
5 tablespoons	dry white wine	4 tablespoons
	stock	
½ cup	Meat Gravy – page 173	6–8 tablespoons
4 tablespoons	melted butter	2 ounces
	grated Parmesan cheese	

Dough

Make a firm dough with the flour and eggs, but do not use water (see page 106). Roll it out very thinly and leave for 30 minutes to dry. Cut into strips about ½ inch wide. Spread these out on a large pastry board or table to dry completely.

Sauce

Heat the bacon fat with 5 tablespoons (2½ ounces) butter, add the onion and garlic, and sauté gently until golden brown. Discard the garlic. Peel and chop the tomatoes, discarding seeds. Squeeze the mushrooms dry. Add both to the pan, season with salt and pepper, and cook over a brisk heat for 20 minutes.

Heat the remaining butter in another pan, add the chicken giblets and sauté for 2 or 3 minutes. Sprinkle with salt, add the wine and continue cooking until it evaporates. Add pepper and a few tablespoonfuls of hot stock and continue cooking until the giblets are tender. Add the giblets and the Meat Gravy to the tomato sauce, stir and continue to simmer while the noodles are being cooked.

Bring a large pan of salted water to a brisk boil. Add the *fettuccine*, stir well and cook until tender but still slightly resistant to bite (*al dente*). Drain them as soon as they are ready, turn into a hot dish and garnish with the sauce, butter and plenty of Parmesan.

Serves 6.

Maccheroni con la Ricotta
Sweet Macaroni with Cheese

US		UK
1¼ pounds	macaroni	1¼ pounds
	salt	
1 cup	fresh Ricotta or cottage cheese	½ pound
½ cup	warm milk	6–8 tablespoons
2½ tablespoons	sugar	2 tablespoons
pinch	ground cinnamon	pinch

This way of serving macaroni is generally liked by children.

Pour the macaroni into a large pan of rapidly boiling salted water, stir and cook for about 10 minutes, or until tender. Beat the Ricotta, milk, sugar and cinnamon together until smooth.

Drain the macaroni and pour into a heated dish. Add the Ricotta dressing, mix well and serve immediately.

Serves 6.

Supplì
Stuffed Rice Croquettes

US		UK
2½ cups	rice	1 pound
	salt and pepper	
1¼ cups	Meat Gravy – see page 173	½ pint
6 tablespoons	butter	3 ounces
¾ cup	grated Parmesan cheese	3 ounces
2	eggs, well beaten	2
5 ounces	Provatura or Mozzarella cheese, diced	5 ounces
	fine dry breadcrumbs	
	oil for deep-frying	

Filling		
3 tablespoons	butter	1½ ounces
4 teaspoons	finely chopped onion	1 tablespoon
2–3 slices	raw Parma ham, shredded	2–3 slices
3	chicken livers, chopped	3
½ cup	ground (UK minced) meat	4 ounces
1	sweetbread, blanched and chopped	1
1 ounce	dried mushrooms, soaked	1 ounce
1 teaspoon	tomato paste	1 teaspoon

Supplì can be prepared correctly only with Provatura or Mozzarella cheese as these cheeses are elastic and when the supplì are cut into they stretch into long threads. For this reason they are known in Rome as "telephone-wire croquettes".

Pour 2 pints (U.K. 2½ pints) water into a large pan, add salt and bring to a quick boil. Add the gravy, stir it well into the water, then dribble in the rice. Continue boiling until the rice is tender but still firm. Drain and put into a bowl. Add salt and pepper, the butter, Parmesan cheese and eggs. Mix thoroughly, stirring until the butter has melted into the rice. Put aside to cool.

Filling
Melt the butter and lightly brown the onion over a low heat. Add the ham, chicken livers, meat and sweetbread, and sauté gently until they begin to change color. Drain the mushrooms and squeeze dry. Dilute the tomato paste with a little warm water. Add both these ingredients to the pan, and continue to cook slowly until the liquid is completely reduced. Take from the pan and put into a bowl.

Take a good heaped tablespoonful of rice and put it into the palm of one hand. Smooth it out with the back of a wooden spoon. Place a portion of the filling and a little of the diced cheese in the middle, and close your hand in such a manner that the rice completely envelopes the filling; then shape it into a large round croquette. Repeat until all the rice and filling are used up. Roll the croquettes in breadcrumbs.

Deep-fry the croquettes until crisp and golden brown all over. Drain on paper towels and serve at once. The above quantity makes between 18 and 20 croquettes, depending on their size.

Serves 6.

Gnocchi di Patate
Potato Gnocchi Roman Style

US		UK
4½ pounds	floury potatoes	4½ pounds
	salt	
about 1¾ cups	all-purpose (plain) flour	7 ounces
2	egg yolks	2
	melted butter	
	grated Parmesan cheese	

Wash but do not peel the potatoes. Cook them in boiling salted water until soft. Take them from the pan, peel and mash them in a large bowl until quite smooth. Add the flour and salt to taste. Beat in the egg yolks and mix to a firm dough or paste.

Break the dough into pieces and shape these into long rolls about the thickness of a finger. Cut the rolls into pieces about 1 inch long. Press each piece against a lightly floured cheese grater to make a sickle-shape, then spread out on a pastry board or table to dry.

Bring a large pan of salted water to the boil, add the gnocchi, a few at a time, and as they rise to the surface, take them out with a perforated spoon, draining them well. Put at once into a hot dish and dress with melted butter and Parmesan cheese. If preferred, the gnocchi can be dressed with either Meat Gravy (page 173) or Tomato Sauce (page 169).

Serves 6.

Gnocchi di Semolino
Semolina Gnocchi

US		UK
5 cups	milk	2 pints
1½ cups	semolina	½ pound
	salt	
8 tablespoons	butter	4 ounces
2	egg yolks, well beaten	2
¾ cup	grated Parmesan cheese	3 ounces

Bring the milk to the boil in a large pan and sprinkle in the semolina slowly, stirring constantly with a wooden spoon to prevent lumps forming. When the semolina is all absorbed, stir energetically, scraping away any from the sides and bottom of the pan, and cook over a low heat for about ½ hour, or until thick.

Pour the semolina into a bowl, add 3 tablespoons (1½ ounces) butter, the egg yolks and a little of the Parmesan cheese. Mix thoroughly and spread out on a wetted marble surface or a large plate. Using a wetted spatula, smooth out to about ½-inch thickness and leave to get cold. Cut into small circles with a liqueur glass.

Generously butter a round fireproof dish. Cover the bottom with a layer of gnocchi and sprinkle with Parmesan cheese. Repeat this until all the gnocchi and cheese are used up, arranging the layers in such a manner as to form a dome-shape, i.e. making each layer smaller than the previous one. Melt the rest of the butter, pour this over the top and bake in a moderate oven (375°F. Mark 4) for about 30 minutes, or until the gnocchi are a light golden brown.

Serve the gnocchi in the dish in which they were cooked, very hot, with plenty of additional grated Parmesan.

Serves 6.

Stracciatella
Egg and Cheese Soup

US		UK
3	eggs	3
	salt	
4 tablespoons	semolina	3 tablespoons
4 tablespoons	grated Parmesan cheese	3 tablespoons
	freshly grated nutmeg – optional	
7½ cups	meat stock	3 pints

Beat the eggs in a bowl with a good pinch of salt, the semolina, Parmesan and grated nutmeg, to taste. Dilute the mixture with a ladleful of cold stock.

Bring the remaining stock to the boil, pour in the egg mixture and stir thoroughly, using a wire whisk. Lower the heat and simmer for 2 minutes, beating constantly. Serve boiling hot, with the beaten eggs just breaking up into strands.

Serves 6.

Brodetto Pasquale
Easter Soup

US		UK
1 pound	lean beef	1 pound
1 large	onion, stuck with a clove	1 large
2	carrots	2
1 stalk	celery	1 stalk
1–2	ripe tomatoes, peeled and chopped	1–2
2 sprigs	parsley	2 sprigs
	salt	
6 pints	cold water	5 pints
1 pound	shoulder or breast of lamb	1 pound
6	egg yolks, well beaten	6
	juice of 1 lemon	
1 sprig	marjoram, finely chopped	1 sprig
¾ cup	grated Parmesan cheese	3 ounces
	pepper	
6 slices	toasted bread	6 slices

This is the dish which traditionally begins the Easter feast.

Put the beef into a large pan with the vegetables, a little salt and the water. Bring to the boil and simmer for a good hour. Add the lamb and continue cooking, tightly covered, for another hour. After it comes to the boil, remove any scum from time to time with a skimmer.

Take out the meat (this can be served separately as a main course if desired), strain the broth and return it to the pan. Re-heat but do not let it boil again.

Pour the egg yolks into a soup tureen. Add the lemon juice, marjoram, Parmesan cheese and a pinch of pepper, and stir well. Add the hot soup rather slowly, stirring constantly (the soup should not be boiling, for this would curdle the egg). Put a slice of toast into each soup bowl and pour the hot soup over it. Serve with plenty of additional grated Parmesan.

Serves 6.

Abbacchio alla Cacciatora
Baby Lamb Hunter's Style

US		UK
3–3½ pounds	milk-fed lamb – see method	3–3½ pounds
3 tablespoons	lard	1½ ounces
	salt and pepper	
2 sprigs	rosemary	2 sprigs
2 cloves	garlic, finely chopped	2 cloves
2 sprigs	sage	2 sprigs
	flour	
½ cup	wine vinegar	6 tablespoons
½ cup	water	6 tablespoons
3–4	anchovy fillets, chopped	3–4

Abbacchio is the Roman word for suckling or milk lamb, which is eaten mainly at Easter time. The best cuts are the leg and lion, as the shoulder gives too much bone in proportion to meat.

Cut the lamb into small, even-sized pieces. Wipe dry with a cloth. Heat the lard in a large pan, add the meat and sauté until brown all over. Season with salt and pepper, and add the rosemary, garlic and sage. Stir with a wooden spoon and dust with flour. Let it brown and add the vinegar and water. Stir well, scraping the bottom of the pan, cover and cook over a low heat for 15 minutes. If the sauce reduces too much while cooking, add a little more vinegar and water.

In another pan, dissolve the anchovies in a tablespoon of the liquid from the lamb. Pour this sauce over the lamb, leave for a few minutes to develop its flavor, then stir and reduce over a brisk heat. The sauce should be fairly thick, dark and not too plentiful, enough to cover the meat like a glaze, making each piece shine. Discard the rosemary and sage, and serve very hot.

Serves 6.

Abbacchio o Capretto Brodettato
Baby Lamb or Kid with Egg Sauce

US		UK
3–3½ pounds	milk-fed lamb – see above – or kid	3–3½ pounds
1½	lemons	1½
4 tablespoons	olive oil	3 tablespoons
2 tablespoons	butter	1 ounce
2 slices	Parma ham, shredded	2 slices
1	onion, finely chopped	1
	salt and pepper	
4 teaspoons	flour	1 tablespoon
1 cup	dry white wine	scant ½ pint
	hot stock or water	
3	egg yolks	3
2 sprigs	parsley, finely chopped	2 sprigs
1 sprig	marjoram, finely chopped	1 sprig

Cut the meat into bite-sized pieces. Wipe it dry with a cloth and rub with half a lemon. Heat the oil and butter in a heavy pan, add the pieces of meat, ham and onion, and brown over a very low heat, stirring from time to time. Season with salt and pepper. When the meat is brown, sprinkle it with flour and turn all the pieces carefully. Add the wine, cover and cook slowly for 30 minutes, or until the meat is tender. If necessary, add a few tablespoonfuls of hot stock, but although the sauce should be fairly plentiful, it must not be too liquid.

Beat the egg yolks. Grate the rind of the half lemon and squeeze the juice from the remaining lemon. Beat this into the eggs and add the parsley, marjoram and a pinch of salt. When the lamb is cooked, lower the heat, pour in the eggs and simmer for 2 minutes, stirring constantly so that the sauce will not set in "strings". Serve immediately.

Serves 6.

Bracioline di Agnello con Carciofi
Baby Lamb Chops (U.K. Cutlets) with Artichokes

US		UK
3–3½ pounds	baby lamb chops (UK cutlets)	3–3½ pounds
6 young	artichokes, without chokes if possible	6 young
1	lemon	1
4 tablespoons	butter	2 ounces
4 tablespoons	olive oil	3 tablespoons
2 tablespoons	ham fat	1 ounce
1 clove	garlic, finely chopped	1 clove
1 small	onion, finely chopped	1 small
2–3 sprigs	marjoram, finely chopped	2–3 sprigs
	salt and pepper	
1 cup	dry white wine	scant ½ pint
4 teaspoons	tomato paste	1 tablespoon

Even though *agnello* is not suckling lamb, it is still killed very young indeed. Italian lamb chops (cutlets) are very small, and sold by weight rather than number. There is hardly more than one good mouthful per chop.

Young Italian artichokes do not have chokes. In this recipe, unless such artichokes are available, canned baby artichokes would be the best choice. However, if using fresh artichokes, it is desirable to prepare them before starting to cook the meat. Remove the hard leaves, cut the artichokes into wedges and wash them in water to which the juice of 1 lemon has been added.

Heat the butter and oil in a large pan, and sauté the lamb with the ham fat, garlic, onion and marjoram. Season with salt and pepper, moisten with wine and cook until it evaporates. Dilute the tomato paste with a cup of water, and add this to the pan, stirring gently. Add the artichokes, check seasoning, cover the pan, and cook over a low heat for 30 minutes.

Serves 6.

Cosciotte di Agnello Arrosto
Pot-roasted Leg of Lamb with Herbs

US		UK
3–3½ pounds	leg of lamb	3–3½ pounds
2–3 sprigs	parsley, finely chopped	2–3 sprigs
2 cloves	garlic, finely chopped	2 cloves
1–2 sprigs	marjoram, finely chopped	1–2 sprigs
2 sprigs	rosemary, finely chopped	2 sprigs
¼ pound	Parma ham, cut in thin strips	¼ pound
	salt and pepper	
4 tablespoons	lard	2 ounces
1 cup	dry white wine	scant ½ pint

Wipe the meat with a damp cloth. Remove some of the harder skin and make a dozen or so deep cuts over the entire surface. Mix together the parsley, garlic, marjoram and rosemary. Coat the strips of ham with the herbs and push them into the slits in the meat. Rub the meat with salt and pepper, and the remainder of the chopped herb and garlic mixture.

In a heavy pan or casserole, brown the meat in lard, turning it occasionally and basting it with some of the wine. When the meat is brown all over, pour in the rest of the wine, cover the pan and cook slowly for 40 minutes longer, or until tender, moistening with a little more wine if necessary.

Serves 6.

Garofolato e Sugo d'Umido
Beef Casserole with Cloves

US		UK
2½ pounds	lean beef rump	2½ pounds
¼ pound	fat salt pork	¼ pound
1 clove	garlic, finely chopped	1 clove
2 sprigs	marjoram, leaves only, finely chopped	2 sprigs
	salt and pepper	
2–3	cloves	2–3

Sauce (Meat Gravy)

¼ cup	ham fat, finely chopped	2 ounces
¼ cup	butter	2 ounces
1 clove	garlic, crushed	1 clove
	salt and pepper	
⅔ cup	red wine	¼ pint
2–3	cloves	2–3
1	onion, finely chopped	1
2	carrots, finely chopped	2
2 stalks	celery, finely chopped	2 stalks
3 sprigs	parsley, finely chopped	3 sprigs
4 teaspoons	tomato paste	1 tablespoon

The Italian name for this dish comes from its use of cloves. *Garofolo* is the Roman name for carnation, hence *garofolato*.

Beat the meat with a cutlet bat to tenderize it. Cut the fat pork into small strips. Mix the chopped garlic and marjoram together, add salt and pepper to taste, and roll the strips of pork in this mixture. Make some small incisions all over the meat and insert 2 or 3 cloves and the strips of fat pork. Roll the meat into a neat shape and tie securely.

Sauce
Heat the ham fat and butter together, add the crushed garlic and sauté until it browns. Discard the garlic and add the meat to the pan. Brown this gently all over, add salt and pepper and the wine. Continue cooking until the wine has evaporated, then take the meat from the pan and put it aside. Add the remaining cloves, the onion, carrots, celery and parsley to the pan. Cook very gently until the vegetables are tender.

Dilute the tomato paste with a little warm water. Return the meat to the pan and cook over a low heat for another 10 minutes. Add the tomato paste, cover the pan and simmer for 2 hours.

Take the meat from the pan, slice it and serve it as a main course.

It is usual in Italian, and in particular Roman, cooking practice for the gravy in this type of dish to be strained and reserved for use in other dishes. This is one of the reasons why so many recipes call for "meat gravy".

Serves 6.

Stufatino
Beef Stew Roman Style

US		UK
1½ pounds	lean stewing beef	1½ pounds
5 tablespoons	lard	2½ ounces
1 small	onion, finely chopped	1 small
4 tablespoons	ham fat, finely chopped	2 ounces
1 stalk	celery, diced	1 stalk
1 clove	garlic, finely chopped	1 clove
pinch	marjoram	pinch
	salt	
1¼ cups	red wine	½ pint
2½ tablespoons	tomato paste	2 tablespoons
	hot stock	
2 pounds	celery or cardoons, boiled	2 pounds

Cut the meat into small chunks. Heat the lard and sauté the onion until transparent. Add the ham fat, diced celery and garlic, cook for a minute or two and add the meat, a pinch of marjoram and a little salt. Brown over a low heat, then add the wine and let it evaporate slowly. Dilute the tomato paste with 2½ cups (U.K. 1 pint) hot stock and add to the pan. Cover and cook slowly for about 2 hours, moistening from time to time with a little more hot stock if necessary.

Cut the cooked celery or cardoons into serving pieces. Add them to the pan and continue cooking for a few minutes longer.

In Rome, when this dish is cooked with cardoons, it is known as *stufatino al gobbo*, "stew with hunchbacks", since cardoons are known as *gobbi* or hunchbacks, due to their habit of drooping over at the top.

Serves 6.

Uccelletti di Campagna
Beef Birds Country Style or "Country Birds"

US		UK
1½ pounds	lean beef, broiling (grilling) quality, cut into thin slices	1½ pounds
6 ounces	Parma ham, thinly sliced	6 ounces
	sage leaves	
	pepper	
5 ounces	fat salt pork, thinly sliced	5 ounces
	slices of French bread	
4 tablespoons	melted lard or oil	2 ounces
	salt	

"Country birds" is the Roman name for thin slices of beef rolled up and broiled (grilled) on skewers over charcoal. In other parts of Italy they are known as "crazy birds" or "birds that go away", probably because the meat is cooked on skewers, as small birds nearly always are.

Cut the slices of meat into strips about 1 inch wide and a little over 2 inches long. Beat them flat and on each piece lay a slice of ham and a leaf of sage. Sprinkle with pepper. Roll up each slice of meat (with the ham and sage) separately and put a thin slice of fat salt pork on either side. Thread these "sandwiches" on to skewers with a piece of bread between each one.

Brush the meat and bread with melted lard or oil, and season with a pinch of salt. Broil (grill) over charcoal, turning the skewers slowly, or bake in the oven at 375°F. (Mark 4) for 30 minutes. If using charcoal, fix a bowl or baking pan underneath the meat to collect the drippings. When the meat is cooked and the bread and pork fat nicely browned, remove the "little birds", pour the drippings over them and serve very hot.

Serves 6.

"Coppiette"

Rissoles Roman Style

US		UK
1½ pounds 1 pound	raw lean beef *or* cooked beef	1½ pounds 1 pound
4 tablespoons	ham or pork fat, finely chopped	2 ounces
½ clove	garlic, finely chopped – optional	½ clove
2–3 sprigs	parsley, finely chopped	2–3 sprigs
2–3 sprigs	marjoram, finely chopped	2–3 sprigs
2½ tablespoons	soft breadcrumbs	2 tablespoons
	salt and pepper	
	grated nutmeg	
¼ cup	milk	3–4 tablespoons
2	eggs, lightly beaten	2
4 tablespoons	grated Parmesan cheese	3 tablespoons
4 teaspoons	seedless white raisins (sultanas)	1 tablespoon
4 teaspoons	pine nuts	1 tablespoon
	fine dry breadcrumbs	
	lard or oil for deep-frying	

Put the meat, fresh or cooked, twice through a meat grinder (U.K. mincer). Put it into a bowl and mix with the remaining ingredients, except the fine breadcrumbs and lard. Knead to a smooth paste. Break off small pieces, shape them into balls and lightly flatten each one top and bottom. Roll in fine breadcrumbs and leave, covered, in the refrigerator for 30 minutes.

Deep-fry the rissoles in lard until crisp and golden brown. Take from the pan with a perforated spoon. Drain on paper towels and serve immediately. Alternatively, arrange the rissoles in a wide, shallow pan, cover with Meat Gravy (page 173) or Tomato Sauce (page 169) and heat through for a few minutes over a very low heat.

Serves 6.

Frittura Piccata

Veal Scallopini (Escalopes) in Lemon Sauce

US		UK
12 small	veal scallopini (escalopes)	12 small
	flour	
¼-pound slice	Parma ham	¼-pound slice
6 tablespoons	butter	3 ounces
	salt	
2 sprigs	parsley, finely chopped	2 sprigs
	juice of 1 lemon	
2½ tablespoons	hot stock	2 tablespoons

Carefully but thoroughly beat the scallopini (escalopes) until thin and flat but not broken, and sprinkle them with flour. Cut the ham into strips. Heat two-thirds of the butter in a wide pan; add the ham and the veal. Turn up the heat and fry the meat quickly – it will take only a few minutes. Salt lightly. As soon as the meat is done, remove it to a heated serving dish and keep hot.

Add the parsley, lemon juice, the remaining butter and the stock to the pan. Stir well and, as soon as the sauce is bubbling, pour it over the veal. Serve immediately.

Serves 6.

I "Saltimbocca"

Veal Scallopini (Escalopes) with Ham and Sage

US		UK
12 small	veal scallopini (escalopes)	12 small
12 slices	Parma ham	12 slices
12 leaves	sage	12 leaves
4 tablespoons	butter	2 ounces
	salt and pepper	
½ cup	dry white wine – optional	6–8 tablespoons

The literal translation of *saltimbocca* is "jump in the mouth". The recipe, it is claimed, originated in Brescia, but it is so popular in Rome that it has become naturalized.

Carefully beat the scallopini (escalopes) with a cutlet bat until very thin. On each slice put a slice of ham and a sage leaf. Secure with a short toothpick. Do *not* roll up.

Melt the butter in a wide pan, add the veal slices and brown them on both sides over a brisk heat for a few minutes. Salt lightly, remembering the ham is already salty, sprinkle with pepper and, if liked, moisten with wine. The cooking time should be no more than 5 minutes in all. Serve very hot, arranged on a serving dish, with the sauce poured over the top.

Serves 6.

Costarelle con la "Panuntella"

Broiled (Grilled) Pork Chops

US		UK
12 small	pork chops	12 small
	lard	
	salt and pepper	
12 slices	bread, home-made if possible	12 slices

Bread fried in drippings is known as *panunta* or *panuntella*, literally "greased bread".

Spread a little lard on both sides of the chops and season lightly with salt and pepper. Lay the pieces of bread flat on the bottom of the broiling (grilling) pan. Arrange the chops on the rack over the bread so that it catches the drippings. Broil (grill) under a moderate heat until one side is brown and crisp. Turn the chops and brown them on the other side. Make sure the meat is thoroughly cooked.

Serve the chops, one on each slice of bread, sprinkled with freshly ground pepper.

Serves 6.

"Lombello" Arrosto

Broiled (Grilled) and Skewered Pork Fillet

US		UK
2–2½ pounds	pork fillet	2–2½ pounds
24 slices	French bread from a long thin loaf	24 slices
24 small slices	Parma ham, cut thick	24 slices
4 tablespoons	lard	2 ounces
	salt and pepper	

Lombello is the Roman name for a fillet of pork, from which they make this delicious dish.

Wipe the fillet and remove all fat and skin. Cut it into 18 slices, each about the thickness of a finger and all of the same size.

Take one large skewer (or 6 small ones) and thread on it a slice of bread, one each of ham and pork, another slice of ham and one of bread. Repeat until all the ingredients are used up.

Melt the lard and pour it over the meat and bread. Season with salt and pepper, and broil (grill) over charcoal embers, in a rotisserie or in the oven (375°F. Mark 4), turning the skewer continually and basting from time to time with melted lard. The cooking time will be about 30 minutes; the bread should be crisp and golden, and the meat cooked through. Serve immediately.

Serves 6.

Frittura di Cervella
Fried Brains

US		UK
1½ pounds	lambs' or calves' brains	1½ pounds
1 small	onion	1 small
	salt	
4 tablespoons	wine vinegar	3 tablespoons
1	lemon	
	olive oil	
2 sprigs	parsley, finely chopped	2 sprigs
	flour	
2	eggs, beaten with salt	2
	oil for deep-frying	

Soak the brains in cold water, changing it frequently, to draw out the blood. Put them into a pan with the onion, a little salt, the vinegar and water to cover, and bring to the boil. Remove the brains, rinse them in cold water and remove the membranes. Cut them into pieces, put into a bowl and sprinkle with a little lemon juice, olive oil and parsley. Leave for 1 hour.

Drain the pieces of brain and pat them dry. Roll them in flour, then dip into beaten egg. Deep-fry until a pale golden color. Drain on paper towels and serve immediately.

Serves 6.

Trippa
Tripe Roman Style

US		UK
3–3½ pounds	dressed veal – or ox – tripe – see page 46	3–3½ pounds
	salt	
1	onion	1
2 stalks	celery	2 stalks
1	carrot	1
1 recipe	Meat Gravy – page 173 – *or*	1 recipe
1 recipe	Tomato Sauce – page 169	1 recipe
4–5 leaves	mint	4–5 leaves
	grated Parmesan or Pecorino cheese	

This famous Roman dish can be cooked with either Meat Gravy or Tomato Sauce, but the basic method is the same in both cases.

Cut the tripe into fairly large pieces and put into a large pan of cold water. Bring to the boil and drain off the water. Add the same quantity of water, salt and the vegetables, and bring to the boil. Cover and cook for about 3 hours.

Drain and cut the tripe into strips about the width of a finger. Put into a large pan with plenty of Meat Gravy or Tomato Sauce, and cook over a very low heat for about ½ hour. Check seasoning and sprinkle with mint and a little Pecorino (or half Pecorino and half Parmesan). Serve with a bowl of grated cheese flavored with mint.

Serves 6.

Rognone di Manzo in Umido
Stewed Ox Kidney

US		UK
1½ pounds	ox kidneys	1½ pounds
2 tablespoons	butter	1 ounce
2½ tablespoons	olive oil	2 tablespoons
2 tablespoons	lard	1 ounce
2	onions, thinly sliced	2
5–6 large	ripe tomatoes, peeled and sliced	5–6 large
	salt and pepper	
½ cup	dry white wine	6–8 tablespoons
2–3 sprigs	parsley, finely chopped	2–3 sprigs

Ox kidneys have a strong flavor and certain precautions are necessary to rid them of this before they are cooked. Skin them and remove all traces of fat. Cut the halves in two again and slice thinly. Plunge them for a second only into boiling water. Drain and pat dry on a cloth.

Heat the butter and oil in a frying pan, and brown the kidney slices over a brisk heat, turning with a wooden spoon. As soon as they are lightly browned, drain them for 15 minutes on a sloping plate to rid them of their strong, unpleasant taste. Discard the fat in which they were cooked.

Heat the lard and sauté the onions until golden brown. Add the tomatoes and the kidneys. Season to taste with salt and pepper, and moisten with wine. Cook over a brisk heat for 5 to 6 minutes. Garnish with parsley and serve very hot.

Serves 6.

Pollo in Padella (alla Romana)
Fried Chicken Roman Style

US		UK
1	frying chicken – about 3½ pounds	1
¼ cup	olive oil	3 tablespoons
¼ cup	butter	2 ounces
	salt and pepper	
1 clove	garlic, finely chopped	1 clove
1 sprig	marjoram, finely chopped	1 sprig
⅔ cup	dry white wine	¼ pint
5–6 large	ripe tomatoes	5–6 large

Cut the chicken into serving pieces. Heat the oil and butter in a large, deep frying pan, and fry the chicken pieces until golden brown all over. Sprinkle with salt, pepper, garlic and marjoram. Pour over the wine and cook until it evaporates.

Peel and chop the tomatoes, discarding seeds. Add the pulp to the pan, check seasoning and continue cooking over a brisk heat for 20 minutes, or until the chicken is tender. The chicken must not be overcooked, and its sauce should be thick and dark, but not too plentiful – a typical feature of any dish styled *alla romana*.

Serves 4.

Filetti di Baccalà Fritti
Fried Fillets of Salt Cod

US		UK
1¾ pounds	dried salt cod, pre-soaked – see page 50	1¾ pounds
	oil for deep-frying	
1	lemon	1
Batter		
1 cup	water	⅓ pint
5 tablespoons	all-purpose (plain) flour	4 tablespoons
2½ tablespoons	olive oil	2 tablespoons
pinch	salt	pinch
2	egg whites	2

Unless using pre-soaked salt cod, it must be soaked for at least 24 hours in several changes of cold water until softened.

Blanch the cod in boiling water for 5 minutes, skin and bone it, then cut into fillets.

Make a batter. Stir the water into the flour until the batter is smooth, then add the oil and, still stirring, the salt. Put aside for 1 hour.

At this point, heat enough oil for deep-frying to smoking point. While it is heating, beat the egg whites until stiff and fold them into the batter. Dip the cod fillets immediately into the batter and fry them, a few at a time, until golden brown. Drain on paper towels and serve very hot, garnished with lemon wedges.

Serves 6.

Carciofi al Tegame
Fried Artichokes

US		UK
12 young	artichokes	12 young
2 cloves	garlic, finely chopped	2 cloves
3–4 sprigs	mint, finely chopped	3–4 sprigs
	salt and pepper	
$\frac{2}{3}$ cup	olive oil	$\frac{1}{4}$ pint

Use only the most tender young artichokes which have not yet had a chance to form a choke.

Remove the tougher outer leaves from the artichokes and cut off the stalks, leaving only the tenderest part. Open out the middle slightly and into each artichoke put a little of the garlic and mint, and a pinch of salt and pepper. Arrange the artichokes side by side in a heavy pan. Trickle the oil over them and add 2 cups (U.K. $\frac{3}{4}$ pint) water. Cover and cook over a low heat for about 1 hour. Uncover the pan and reduce the cooking juices over a brisk heat. Serve the artichokes hot or cold.

Serves 6.

Carciofi Fritti
Artichoke Fritters

US		UK
8	artichokes	8
2	lemons	2
	oil for deep-frying	
Batter		
4 tablespoons	all-purpose (plain) flour	3 tablespoons
	salt and pepper	
4 tablespoons	olive oil	3 tablespoons
3	eggs	3

Remove any tough outer leaves from the artichokes and the tough part of the stalk, leaving only a small piece of the latter which must be scraped clean with a small sharp knife. Cut each artichoke into 8 wedges and soak for 30 minutes in water acidulated with the juice of 1 lemon.

Prepare the batter. Sift the flour, salt and pepper into a bowl, add the oil, blend well, then add the eggs, one at a time, beating well between each addition, until quite smooth.

Heat a large pan of oil for deep-frying until smoking hot. Drain and pat the artichokes dry, dip them into the batter, shaking off any surplus, and drop into the hot oil. Fry until golden brown and drain on paper towels. Sprinkle lightly with salt and serve hot, garnished with lemon wedges.

Serves 6.

Carciofi alla Giudia
Artichokes "alla Giudia"

US		UK
12 young	artichokes	12 young
	juice of 2 lemons	
	salt and pepper	
2 cups	olive oil	$\frac{3}{4}$ pint

This is one of the traditional dishes of Rome, where the artichokes are so tender that the whole vegetable can be eaten. Fairly large artichokes are used. The dish may not be easy to prepare outside Italy, but if visiting Rome around Easter, when artichokes are in season, it should not be missed.

Remove the slightly tougher leaves of the artichokes and shorten the stems slightly, leaving at least 2 inches. Scrape the stems with a knife from the bottom towards the top. Soak in cold water acidulated with lemon juice. Drain well.

Take each artichoke and carefully flatten out the leaves slightly with the hands to the shape of a flower. Season them inside with salt and pepper.

Heat plenty of oil in a large pan (traditionally this should be of earthenware) and arrange the artichokes in it, side by side, stalks uppermost. Cook the artichokes until tender. While they are cooking, keep the oil at an even temperature and turn the artichokes round and round in the pan so that they all cook evenly, eventually returning them to their original place.

When they are tender, gently press them down with a wooden spoon to the bottom of the pan so that their leaves spread out. Leave them for 10 minutes. By this time they should look like bronze chrysanthemums, no longer conical, but squat with flattened-out leaves. At the last moment dip your hand in cold water and, keeping as far away from the stove as possible, shake the cold water over the boiling oil in which the artichokes are cooking. This will complete the crisping of the outer shell which is typical of artichokes cooked in this manner. Leave over the heat for 2 minutes longer, then drain well, arrange on a dish and serve very hot.

Serves 6.

Broccoli "a Crudo"
Broccoli Sautéed with Wine and Garlic

US		UK
2 pounds	broccoli	2 pounds
	salt	
5 tablespoons	olive oil	4 tablespoons
2 cloves	garlic, finely chopped	2 cloves
	pepper	
2 cups	dry white wine	$\frac{3}{4}$ pint

Clean the broccoli, discarding any coarse leaves but retaining tender ones. Divide the heads into small pieces and wash well in cold water, then leave in cold salted water until ready to be cooked. Drain well.

Heat the oil in a large pan and sauté the garlic until golden but not brown. Add the broccoli leaves, season to taste with salt and pepper, and continue to sauté gently until the leaves are tender. Add the heads and more salt and pepper if required. Pour in the wine, bring to the boil slowly and cook gently, stirring occasionally, until tender.

Serve very hot, either as a vegetable by itself, or as an accompaniment to boiled or roast meat.

Serves 4 to 6.

Broccoletti di Rape "Strascinati"
Turnip Tops with Garlic

US		UK
3–3$\frac{1}{2}$ pounds	fresh young turnip tops	3–3$\frac{1}{2}$ pounds
$\frac{2}{3}$ cup	olive oil	$\frac{1}{4}$ pint
2 cloves	garlic, crushed	2 cloves
	salt and pepper	
	stock	
	slices of fried bread	

Turnip tops are one of the most popular of Roman vegetables. Wash them thoroughly and discard all coarse leaves, hard stalks and veins. Drain the rest and chop finely.

Heat the oil in a large pan and sauté the garlic cloves until brown. Discard them and add the turnip tops. Add salt and pepper to taste, cover and cook over a low heat until tender, about 30 minutes. Moisten with a little stock occasionally, mixing it well into the turnip tops. Make sure all the liquid has evaporated. Pile neatly on a hot dish and serve with slices of fried bread.

If in a hurry, the turnip tops can be cooked in boiling water, drained and cooked for a few minutes only in the oil and garlic.

Serves 6.

Indivie Intere "a Crudo"
Belgian Endive Braised with Garlic

US		UK
6 large	Belgian endives – see method	6 large
½ cup	olive oil	6–8 tablespoons
2 cloves	garlic, crushed	2 cloves
1–2 sprigs	mint or basil	1–2 sprigs
	salt and pepper	

Indivie are the firm, white, cigar-shaped Belgian endives.

Trim the endives and remove the outer leaves. Wash thoroughly to remove all traces of earth. Arrange them, still dripping with water, side by side in a heavy pan. Add the oil, garlic, mint and a little salt and pepper. Cover and cook over a low heat until tender.

Discard the garlic and the mint, and serve the endives, either on their own or as an accompaniment to roast meat, especially veal.

Serves 6.

Zucchine Ripiene di Carne
Meat-stuffed Zucchini (Courgettes)

US		UK
12	zucchini (courgettes)	12
2 tablespoons	butter	1 ounce
2½ tablespoons	olive oil	2 tablespoons
2 tablespoons	ham fat, finely chopped	1 ounce
1 small	onion, finely chopped	1 small
4 tablespoons	tomato paste	3 tablespoons
	salt and pepper	
2–3 sprigs	parsley, finely chopped	2–3 sprigs

Stuffing		
1¼ cups	ground (UK minced) lean beef	10 ounces
2	eggs	2
4 tablespoons	grated Parmesan cheese	3 tablespoons
2–3 tablespoons	fresh breadcrumbs	2 tablespoons
2 ounces	ham, finely chopped	2 ounces
	salt and pepper	
	milk – optional	

Choose fairly large zucchini for this recipe as they are much easier to stuff. Wash them, cut off the stem end and then scoop out the pulp through the stem end with an apple corer, taking care not to break the shell.

Mix together the stuffing ingredients; if the mixture seems a little too thick, add enough milk to loosen it. Stuff this mixture into the zucchini, pushing it in firmly.

Heat the butter and oil in a large, wide frying pan, and sauté the ham fat and onion over a low heat until the onion begins to change color. Add the zucchini and sauté gently, turning them over from time to time to brown them evenly but lightly.

Dilute the tomato paste with a cup of warm water and pour over the zucchini. Check seasoning, add the parsley, cover and cook gently until tender, about 30 minutes. Handle the zucchini carefully when taking them from the pan or they will break. Serve hot.

Serves 4 to 6.

Fritto di Fiori di Zucca
Fried Squash (Marrow) Flowers

For this unusual dish the flowers must be very fresh and still closed.

First, make a simple batter with 4 to 5 tablespoons flour and enough cold water to make a thin paste, the consistency of cream. Beat until smooth and leave to rest for 1 hour.

Wash and dry about 1½ pounds flowers. Trim off the stems and remove the threads.

Make a stuffing with 2 to 3 tablespoons fresh breadcrumbs, 4 anchovy fillets, pounded, a tablespoon of olive oil, 2 to 3 sprigs parsley, finely chopped, and black pepper to taste.

Carefully open the petals of the flowers and put a little stuffing into each one. Close them up again. (Sometimes the flowers are simply stuffed with a little anchovy and a few cubes of Provatura or Mozzarella, or they can be fried without stuffing.)

Heat a large pan of olive oil until smoking hot. Dip the flowers into the batter, then quickly deep-fry in hot oil, a few at a time. As soon as they are golden, take them from the pan with a perforated spoon and drain on paper towels. Serve very hot. If the flowers are not stuffed, they should be sprinkled lightly with salt before serving.

Serves 6.

Fagiolini in Padella
Snap (French) Beans with Tomatoes

US		UK
1½ pounds	snap (French) beans	1½ pounds
1¼ pounds	ripe tomatoes	1¼ pounds
2 tablespoons	oil or butter	1½ tablespoons
1 small	onion, finely chopped	1 small
	salt and pepper	
2 sprigs	parsley, finely chopped	2 sprigs

The following method of cooking beans applies not only to small snap (French) beans but also to the larger variety known as *fagiolini a corallo* in Italy. Really small beans can be cooked whole; somewhat larger ones should be broken, not cut, into 2-inch lengths.

Trim the beans and wash them. Leave in cold water until required. Peel the tomatoes, chop them into small pieces and discard seeds.

Melt the oil or butter in a large pan and sauté the onion until golden. Add the tomatoes, stir well and let them come to a gentle boil. Add the beans and season with salt and pepper. Cover the pan and cook slowly for 30 minutes, or until the beans are tender and the sauce reduced. Garnish with parsley and serve hot.

Serves 6.

Fagioli Freschi con Pomodoro
Fresh White (Haricot) Beans in Tomato Sauce

US		UK
2 pounds	fresh white (haricot) beans	2 pounds
	salt	
2 pounds	ripe tomatoes	2 pounds
4 tablespoons	ham fat, finely chopped	2 ounces
2 tablespoons	butter	1 ounce
4 tablespoons	olive oil	3 tablespoons
1 small	onion, finely chopped	1 small
1 stalk	celery, finely chopped	1 stalk
1–2 sprigs	parsley, finely chopped	1–2 sprigs
	pepper	

If fresh beans are not available, use 2½ cups (1 pound) dried beans, first soaking them for several hours in water.

Shell the beans and put them into a pan with cold water and a little salt. Cook over a low heat until tender but not broken, about 1 hour. While the beans are cooking, peel and chop the tomatoes, and rub them through a sieve.

Heat the ham fat, butter and olive oil in a pan, and sauté the onion, celery and parsley until they begin to brown. Add the tomatoes, season with salt and pepper, and cook over a brisk heat for 30 minutes. Drain the beans, add them to the tomato sauce and continue to cook for about 20 minutes over a very low heat to let them absorb the tomato flavor. Serve hot with the sauce.

Serves 6.

Fagioli con le Cotiche
White (Haricot) Beans with Pork Sausages

US		UK
6 ounces	Italian pork sausages – see method	6 ounces
4 cups	dried white (haricot) beans, soaked overnight	1½ pounds
	salt	
4 teaspoons	lard	1 tablespoon
4 tablespoons	ham fat, finely chopped	2 ounces
1 clove	garlic, finely chopped	1 clove
2–3 sprigs	parsley, finely chopped	2–3 sprigs
1 small	onion, finely chopped	1 small
2½ tablespoons	tomato paste	2 tablespoons
	pepper	

The sausages used in this dish, *cotiche*, are made with pork rind and meat, and are rather hard. If not available, use Cotechino.

Scrape the sausages and put them into a large pan of cold water. Bring to the boil and boil for 5 minutes. Throw out the water, rinse the sausages in cold water and return them to the pan. Add the beans, cover generously with water and bring to the boil again. Lower the heat and simmer for 2 hours, or until the beans are tender. Add salt to taste.

Melt the lard with the ham fat in a large pan and sauté the garlic, parsley and onion gently until the onion begins to brown. Dilute the tomato paste with 1 cup (U.K. scant ½ pint) warm water taken from the beans, add this to the onion mixture, season with salt and pepper, and simmer for 30 minutes longer.

Drain the beans and sausages, transfer them to the other pan and stir well. Cook over a moderate heat for another 30 minutes so that they absorb the flavor of the sauce. Serve very hot.

Serves 6.

Fava al Guanciale
Fava (Broad) Beans with Bacon

US		UK
1 pound	shelled fresh fava (broad) beans	1 pound
4 teaspoons	butter or oil	1 tablespoon
2–3 slices	lean bacon, diced	2–3 slices
1 small	onion, finely chopped	1 small
	salt and pepper	
	stock or water	

This dish is considered something of a Roman specialty, as Roman broad beans are particularly tender and well-flavored. They can be served alone as a separated dish, or as an accompaniment to boiled or roast meat.

Melt the butter in a pan and sauté the bacon and onion over a low heat until golden. Add the beans, season with salt and pepper, and moisten with a few tablespoons of stock or water. Increase the heat and cook briskly for 20 minutes. Serve very hot.

Serves 6.

Peperoni al Guanciale
Sweet Peppers with Bacon

US		UK
10 large	ripe tomatoes	10 large
½ pound	lean bacon, thinly sliced	½ pound
9	sweet green peppers	9
4 tablespoons	olive oil	3 tablespoons
1	onion, thinly sliced	1
	salt and pepper	

Peel the tomatoes, chop them finely and discard seeds. Put aside until required. Cut the bacon into pieces, not too small, and discard the rind.

Char the peppers under a hot broiler (grill) or in a hot oven until their skins blacken and blister. As soon as they are cool enough to handle, rub off the thin outer skin. Wash in running water and cut them in half, discarding cores and seeds. Cut the flesh into neat strips.

Heat the oil in a wide pan over a low heat and sauté the onion, adding 2 or 3 tablespoons water so that the onion will not burn but turn translucent. Add the tomatoes and cook for 20 minutes over a brisk heat. Add the peppers, salt and pepper, and cook over a moderate heat for 15 minutes. Finally add the bacon. Continue cooking for another 10 minutes, or until the bacon is almost transparent. Serve very hot.

Serves 6.

Piselli al Prosciutto
Peas with Parma Ham

US		UK
3–3½ pounds	fresh green peas	3–3½ pounds
4 tablespoons	butter	2 ounces
1 small	onion, finely chopped	1 small
	salt and pepper	
⅔ cup	hot stock or water	¼ pint
pinch	sugar – optional	pinch
3–4 ounces	Parma ham, cut in strips	3–4 ounces
	triangles of bread fried in butter – optional	

This dish, which can be a gastronomic experience, is a true Roman creation. Roman peas are deliciously sweet and tender.

Shell the peas. Melt the butter and sauté the onion over a low heat until it begins to change color. Add the peas, season with salt and pepper, and moisten with stock. Cook over a brisk heat for 10 minutes, if cooking fresh young peas, or until tender with older ones. No sugar is required with Roman peas—but some peas may require a little sugar to sweeten them. Two minutes before the peas are ready, add the ham and stir gently.

Correctly arranged, this dish can look very attractive with the fresh green of the peas and the bright red of Parma ham. It can be served with triangles of crisply fried bread, if desired.

Serves 4.

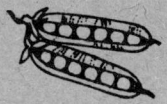

Funghi Porcini al Tegame
Mushrooms with Garlic and Mint

US		UK
2 pounds	fresh field mushrooms – cèpes or boletus edulis	2 pounds
½ cup	olive oil	6–8 tablespoons
3–4	anchovy fillets, finely chopped	3–4
2 cloves	garlic, crushed	2 cloves
6 large	ripe tomatoes, peeled, seeded and chopped	6 large
2–3 sprigs	mint, finely chopped	2–3 sprigs
	salt and pepper	
	slices of French bread fried in butter	

Clean and wash the mushrooms, and cut them into slices. Heat the oil in a shallow pan (preferably earthenware), add the anchovies and cook them until dissolved to a paste. Add the mushrooms, garlic and tomatoes, the mint, a little salt and a good sprinkling of freshly ground pepper. Cover the pan and cook over a brisk heat, stirring from time to time, for about 15 minutes. Discard the garlic and serve the mushrooms very hot, garnished with fried bread.

Serves 6.

Uova in Trippa alla Romana
Eggs Cooked To Look Like Tripe, Roman Style

US		UK
8	eggs	8
10 tablespoons	grated Parmesan cheese	8 tablespoons
	salt and pepper	
	olive oil	
1¼ cups	hot Meat Gravy or Tomato Sauce – page 173 or 169	½ pint
a few leaves	mint, finely chopped	a few leaves

Break the eggs into a bowl, add half the Parmesan cheese and season to taste with salt and pepper. Beat lightly with a fork.

Heat a little oil in a frying pan and pour in about a quarter of the beaten egg mixture. Lower the heat and, as the omelette begins to cook underneath, prick with a fork and run a knife round the edges. When the underside is golden, turn the omelette over and brown it on the other side. Repeat this with the remaining egg mixture, making 4 omelettes.

Cut the omelettes into strips to resemble tripe and arrange a layer at the bottom of a fireproof baking dish. Sprinkle this with grated cheese, hot sauce and a little mint. Repeat this until all the ingredients are used up, ending with a layer of cheese. Heat through in a moderate oven (375°F. Mark 4) and serve immediately.

If the correct type of Italian sauce is not to hand, almost any kind of home-made sauce may be used in this recipe, as long as it has a well-developed flavor.

Serves 6.

Bigne di San Giuseppe
St Joseph's Fritters

US		UK
1 cup	water	8 fluid ounces
7 tablespoons	butter	3½ ounces
pinch	salt	pinch
4 teaspoons	sugar	1 tablespoon
1¼ cups	all-purpose (plain) flour	5 ounces
4	eggs	4
	grated rind of 1 lemon	
	oil for deep-frying	
	confectioners' (icing) sugar	

The Feast Day of St Joseph, patron saint of the hearth and home, is celebrated in Italy with much eating and ceremony. As a result, many dishes are accepted as St Joseph's Day specialties.

Put the water, butter, salt and sugar into a heavy pan. Bring to the boil, and as soon as the butter has melted, take from the heat and add the flour, all at once, stirring quickly and thoroughly with a whisk or a wooden spoon. Return the pan to the heat and cook over a low heat, stirring constantly, until the paste comes away from the sides of the pan, making a light crackling sound. Cool the paste slightly and then add the eggs, one at a time, beating vigorously and making sure each egg is completely incorporated into the mixture before another is added. Add the lemon rind and then knead the paste until bubbles begin to form over the surface. Leave to rest for 1 hour.

Heat plenty of oil in a tall pan (a pressure cooker would be a good choice) until hot but not smoking. Drop the paste into the hot oil in heaped teaspoonfuls (over a moderate heat) and fry the fritters until they puff up. Raise the heat slightly and fry the fritters to a golden brown. Take from the pan with a perforated spoon and drain on paper towels. Continue until the paste is finished, letting the oil cool a little each time before adding a fresh batch.

Heap the fritters on a plate and dust generously with sugar.
Makes about 60 fritters.

"Gnocchi" Teneri al Latte
Soft Milk Gnocchi

US		UK
6	egg yolks	6
4 teaspoons	sugar	1 tablespoon
4 tablespoons	all-purpose (plain) flour	3 tablespoons
4 teaspoons	cornstarch (cornflour)	1 tablespoon
1 teaspoon	potato flour	1 teaspoon
2½ cups	milk	1 pint
pinch	salt	pinch
	freshly grated nutmeg	
7 tablespoons	softened butter	3½ ounces
¾ cup	grated Parmesan cheese	3 ounces
	ground cinnamon	

A traditional dish served at weddings or christenings, feasts and during carnival. These *gnocchi* are very typical of Roman cooking and worthy of a gourmet's appreciation.

In a pan, beat the egg yolks with the sugar until fluffy. Add the flour, cornstarch (cornflour), potato flour, milk, salt and nutmeg to taste. Mix thoroughly. Add half the butter and beat well. Put the pan on the stove and cook over a low heat until the mixture thickens and is creamy and elastic.

Rinse a smooth, flat surface or a flat plate and pour the paste over it. Spread it out with a spatula to an even thickness of about ½ inch. Leave to cool, then cut into diamond shapes.

Butter a baking dish and arrange a layer of the *gnocchi* at the bottom. Sprinkle with Parmesan cheese and a pinch of cinnamon, and continue in this manner until all the *gnocchi* are used up. Melt the remaining butter and sprinkle over the *gnocchi*. Bake in a moderate oven (375°F. Mark 4) for 20 minutes, or until the top is golden brown. Serve hot.

Serves 6.

Budino di Ricotta
Ricotta Cheese Pudding

US		UK
1½ pounds	Ricotta or good-quality cottage cheese	1½ pounds
4 teaspoons	seedless white raisins (sultanas)	1 tablespoon
5 tablespoons	diced mixed candied peel	4 tablespoons
¼ cup	rum	3 tablespoons
4	eggs	4
	butter and fine dry breadcrumbs for baking dish	
4 teaspoons	all-purpose (plain) flour	1 tablespoon
5 tablespoons	confectioners' (icing) sugar	4 tablespoons
pinch	ground cinnamon	pinch
	grated rind of ½ lemon	
	vanilla sugar	

Soak the white raisins (sultanas) and peel in the rum. Separate 3 eggs. Grease a deep round baking dish generously with butter and coat it with fine breadcrumbs. Beat 3 egg yolks and 1 whole egg until smooth. Beat the egg whites until stiff.

Rub the Ricotta through a fine sieve. Put into a bowl, add the eggs, flour, sugar, the beaten egg yolks, the white raisins, rum, candied peel, cinnamon and lemon rind. Add more sugar to taste if preferred. Mix thoroughly, then fold in the egg whites. Pour into the prepared dish, filling it not more than half-full; otherwise, when the pudding rises, it will spill over the sides. Bake in a moderate oven (375°F. Mark 4) for about 1 hour.

When the top is a pale golden color, turn off the heat and let the pudding cool in the oven; this prevents it from sinking in the middle. Turn out and serve cold, sprinkled with vanilla sugar.

Serves 6.

"Fave" Dolci

Sweet Almond and Cinnamon "Beans"

US		UK
$\frac{2}{3}$ cup	sweet almonds	4 ounces
$\frac{3}{4}$ cup	sugar	6 ounces
$\frac{3}{4}$ cup	all-purpose (plain) flour	3 ounces
1 teaspoon	ground cinnamon	1 teaspoon
4 tablespoons	butter	2 ounces
1	egg	1
	grated rind of $\frac{1}{2}$ lemon	
	butter and flour for baking sheet	

A traditional sweet for All Souls' Day, November 2. There are a dozen or more recipes for making sweet beans, also more morbidly named "Dead Man's Beans". Their origin is somewhat obscure but they are eaten all over Italy. Beans were connected with death and with the souls of the departed in many countries in more ancient times.

Spread the almonds, unpeeled, on a baking sheet and dry them in the oven. Pound them in a mortar with the sugar until fine, or use a blender. Shake through a sieve and return any pieces which will not go through the sieve to be pounded or blended again. Take care not to use all the sugar at the beginning, otherwise it is possible to end up with only almonds for either pounding or blending and this will make their oil run.

Put the powdered sugar and almonds into a bowl. Add the flour, cinnamon and butter, mix well, then add the egg and the lemon rind, and work to a smooth paste. More cinnamon may be added if wished. Flour your hands and roll the paste into a long roll. Cut this into bean-sized pieces. Arrange them, well spaced, on a greased and floured baking sheet, and squash them lightly to give them an oval shape, like a fava (broad) bean. Bake in a moderate oven (375°F. Mark 4) for 20 minutes, or until a pale golden color. Cool before serving. The "beans" will keep well in an airtight container.

These quantities will make about 50 "beans".

Ricotta Fritta

Ricotta Cheese Fritters

US		UK
$\frac{1}{2}$ pound	almond macaroons	$\frac{1}{2}$ pound
1 pound	fresh Ricotta or good-quality cottage cheese	1 pound
pinch	ground cinnamon	pinch
2 large	eggs	2 large
	flour	
1	egg, beaten	1
	fine dry breadcrumbs	
	lard or butter for frying	
	confectioners' (icing) sugar	

Crush the macaroons to a powder. Put them in a bowl and add the Ricotta, cinnamon to taste and 2 eggs. Mix thoroughly. Flour your hands, break off pieces of the mixture and roll them into balls. Dip into beaten egg and coat with breadcrumbs.

Fry the little balls in lard or butter, a few at a time, until golden brown. Take from the pan with a perforated spoon, drain on paper towels and sprinkle lightly with confectioners' (icing) sugar. Serve hot or cold.

Alternatively, cut the Ricotta mixture into diamond shapes about $\frac{1}{2}$ inch thick, flour them lightly, dip in beaten egg and fry as above.

Maritozzi Uso Fornaio

Lenten Buns Baker's Style

US		UK
$\frac{3}{4}$ cup	seedless white raisins (sultanas)	4 ounces
1 pound	once-risen bread dough, made with $2\frac{1}{2}$ cups (10 ounces) flour	1 pound
5 tablespoons	olive oil	4 tablespoons
4 tablespoons	granulated (caster) sugar	3 tablespoons
pinch	salt	pinch
$\frac{1}{3}$ cup	pine nuts	2 ounces
$\frac{1}{3}$ cup	diced candied orange peel	2 ounces
	butter for baking sheet	

Soak the white raisins (sultanas) in warm water until soft and swollen, and pat dry before using.

Place the bread dough on a floured board and punch it down. Make a hole in the middle and add the oil, sugar and salt. Fold the dough over the hole, then knead it until these ingredients are completely incorporated and the dough is pliable and smooth again. Add the pine nuts, raisins and orange peel, and knead vigorously.

Butter a baking sheet lightly. Break off pieces of the dough and shape into small buns. Arrange them on the baking sheet, well spaced apart. Cover with a cloth and leave to rise until doubled in bulk.

Bake in a very hot oven (450°F. Mark 7) for 20 minutes, or until the buns are golden brown.

Makes about 12 to 14 buns.

Crostata di Visciola

Cherry Tart Roman Style

US		UK
$1\frac{1}{3}$ cups	sour or black cherry jam	1 pound
1	egg, beaten	1
	confectioners' (icing) sugar	
Pastry		
$2\frac{1}{2}$ cups	all-purpose (plain) or pastry flour	10 ounces
5 tablespoons	butter	$2\frac{1}{2}$ ounces
5 tablespoons	lard	$2\frac{1}{2}$ ounces
$\frac{2}{3}$ cup	granulated (caster) sugar	5 ounces
3	egg yolks	3
	grated rind of 1 lemon	
pinch	salt	pinch

It is a Roman pastry-making tradition that fruit tarts are almost invariably prepared with jam made from *visciole* – sour cherries.

Pastry

Sift the flour into a bowl, rub or cut in the butter and lard until the mixture resembles fine breadcrumbs. Add the remaining ingredients and knead quickly to a dough. Work it as little as possible and roll into a ball. Wrap in a cloth or foil and leave to rest in the refrigerator for at least 1 hour.

Break off three-quarters of the dough, roll it out thinly on a floured board and line a 1-inch-deep cake or pie (tart) pan about 9 inches in diameter with it, overlapping the sides. Trim neatly. Roll out the remaining dough and cut it into even strips, about $\frac{1}{2}$ inch wide and 9 to 10 inches long.

Spread the dough in the pan with jam and cover with the strips arranged in a lattice pattern. Brush with beaten egg and bake in a moderate oven (375°F. Mark 4) for about 40 minutes, or until the pastry is golden. Cool and dust generously with sifted confectioners' (icing) sugar.

ABRUZZO-MOLISE

The landscape of the Abruzzo is solemn, tranquil and very beautiful. The fine local cheeses include Scamorza and Pecorino.

Descriptions of rich and prolonged meals are to be found in innumerable works of literature, ranging from Homer to Rabelais, and from Petronius to Dickens. The ancient Greeks held day-long banquets by the seashore. Trimalchio turned such occasions into ritual spectacles which blended hospitality with music, love-making, fantasy and gluttony, so as to titillate all the five senses of his guests. In Gargantua and Pantagruel Rabelais created two characters of prodigious vigor and voracity, who were best able to express themselves in the manner in which they satisfied their appetites at table.

In one region of Central Italy this historical tradition of gigantic meals has survived, still something of a ritual but, alas, increasingly rare, for the appetite and digestion of twentieth-century man cannot match those of his ancestors. This region is the Abruzzo, a mountainous area which stretches from the Adriatic to the highest peaks of the Apennines. Some of the most skilled fishermen of Italy live along its coast, while the central region contains the National Park of the Abruzzo, a great game reserve where the few bears, wolves and other wild animals that remain in Italy are allowed to live peacefully under the protection of the law.

This wild, mountainous region forms the setting to the *panarda*, a colossal meal the origins of which go back to pagan antiquity, now held only on great occasions. Today, the *panarda* has no deistic significance; it is merely an occasion of celebration. The meal begins at midday and often continues far into the night. With merciless regularity, as it must seem to those of modest appetite, dish follows dish. From time to time there is a short pause for conversation, then

Maccheroni alla chitarra (see page 190), together with the traditional "guitar" on which these noodles are cut, could well be called the symbol of Abruzzese cooking.

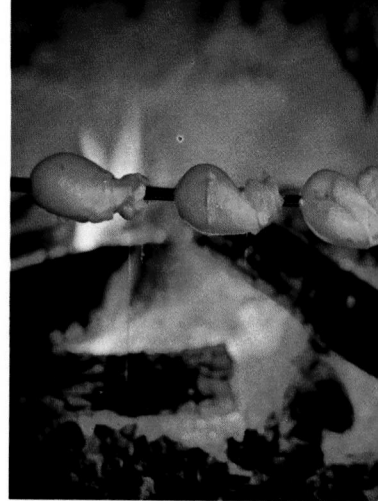

the interminable procession of dishes, which include every kind of local specialty, starts again. A famous Neapolitan journalist of the nineteenth century, Edoardo Scarfoglio, describes how he was once a guest at one of these feasts. After the thirtieth dish he felt that he could eat no more. Consequently, he refused the next dish, but in doing so he ran a serious risk. His host, quite indifferent to the limitations of Scarfoglio's digestive system, snatched up a rifle and threatened to kill him if he refused to finish the meal, as honor demanded.

These are tales of the distant past and in this sober age we must forget gastronomic legends and instead turn our attention to individual local specialties. There are many of these, and the most famous dish of the region is undoubtedly *maccheroni alla chitarra* (see page 190), made with the help of an implement known as a *chitarra* or "guitar", to be found in the kitchen of every self-respecting cook in the region. This characteristic pasta dish is served with a tomato sauce flavored with sweet peppers and smoked fat pork, and crowned with a sprinkling of delicious Pecorino cheese.

As in every other part of the Apennines, the region is the home of shepherds, and lamb is a great specialty, prepared in a variety of ways. It may be roasted, or it may be fried, or cooked *alla cacciatora* with red peppers, or as a fricassée with an egg and lemon sauce. The local shepherds are also masters in the art of making cheese. Besides the world-famous Pecorino there is the less familiar Scamorza—the local peasantry prefer it roasted over a fire—which comes mainly from Rivisondoli and Pescoconstanzo.

Porchetta (roast suckling pig) forms the pretext for numerous popular country fairs; the best-known of these is held at the beginning of October at Campli in the province of Teramo.

Scapece, or fish steaks with vinegar and saffron, and a fish soup or stew known as *brodetto* (both on page 194) are typical specialties of Vasto in the province of Chieti.
Below: The cooking of Molise is related to that of nearby Apulia. The specialty of the region is lamb, prepared in various ways, seen here with a selection of other local dishes, including *fusilli* noodles with broccoli.
Left: In a region renowned for its cheeses these skewered Scamorzine cooked over an open fire are regarded as a particular delicacy.

Centerbe, one of the many liqueurs produced in the Abruzzo, is a potent digestive flavored with herbs. It is often served flambé with fruit.
Below, left: Photographed before the Abbey of San Clemente, some specialties of Casauria in the province of Pescara: Ricotta-stuffed ravioli, broiled (grilled) baby lamb chops, trout and shrimps (U.K. prawns) from the River Tirino, and a sweet pizza.
Below, right: A table spread for a feast with some of the best dishes of Chieti, including a pizza made with cornmeal, stuffed veal, and a selection of local sausages.

The cuisine of Teramo occupies a place of honor in Abruzzese cookery. Here, against a backdrop of the city, are some local dishes: turkey *alla canzanese* (in aspic—see page 193), and roasted *alla neretese, crispelle 'mbusse*, or cheese-stuffed pancakes, which are served in soup, and *spiedini alla ruota* (lit: "skewers on the wheel").

Pigs may often be seen grazing with the sheep on the mountain slopes, whose high altitudes are said to make their flesh lean and very tasty. The local ham, reminiscent of the Spanish *jamon serrano*, is particularly worthy of mention, and so, too, is the *ventricina*, a sausage made with pig's intestine, pork, sweet peppers, fennel and orange peel. As in the neighboring regions, roast *porchetta* is considered to be a great delicacy.

Pescara, the birthplace of Gabriele d'Annunzio, is situated on the Adriatic and well known as a fishing port. Here they make *brodetto alla pescarese*, a fish soup that is particularly good because of the use of a special kind of red pepper known as *diavolillo*. Vasto, another large port, and a rival to Pescara in the matter of fish dishes, is renowned for its *scapece*, an unforgettable dish of fish marinated in vinegar and colored with saffron (see page 194).

Produced almost exclusively in the Abruzzo, and for this reason known, both in Italy and abroad, as "Aquila saffron", this spice has no real substitute. It is obtained by drying the stigmas of the saffron flower, and one hundred and thirty thousand flowers are said to be needed to produce about two pounds. Local cooks make little use of it, however, and large quantities are exported to gild the risotto of Milan and the *bouillabaisse* of Marseilles.

The most famous of local desserts is the *parrozzo*, a soft cake covered with chocolate (see page 196). Its inventor was an Abruzzese pastrycook called Luigi d'Amico, and its praises have been sung in verse by no less a poet than d'Annunzio.

A small amount of saffron is used in the manufacture of some well-known local liqueurs, made from herbs gathered in the woods and mountains. The two best-known liqueurs are Aurum, the ingredients of which include tea, rum and tangerines, and Centerbe, which is the most powerful of all Italian liqueurs. Its color is emerald green, it has an extremely high alcoholic content, and it was first produced (as its name, "one hundred herbs", suggests) by skillful herbalists. Centerbe may well have been devised to help the digestion of those who have to face a gargantuan *panarda*.

The rocky landscape of the Abruzzo means that few wines are produced in the region. There are, however, three types which blend well with the local cooking: Cerasuolo d'Abruzzo, which is cherry-red in color and should be served with soups, vegetables, and roasted Scamorza; Trebbiano, a white wine to be drunk with fish; and Montepulciano d'Aquila, which is ideal with roasts and *porchetta*.

The cooking of the Abruzzo, as varied as it is refined, is intended for strong, healthy digestions. Cooks from this region are to be found in restaurants all over the world. In every country they bring to the table the secrets of their local cookery, and perhaps the hope that one day they may be permitted to serve up a gigantic and interminable *panarda*.

Bruschetta
Garlic Bread

US		UK
12 slices	bread	12 slices
2 cloves	garlic, lightly crushed	2 cloves
	olive oil	
	salt and pepper	

The best bread for this recipe naturally is home-made bread, but if this is not available use fresh-baked bakers' bread or a long French or Italian stick. Pre-sliced or packaged bread will not do.

Toast the bread in the oven until brown and crisp. Rub at once with crushed garlic, brush lightly with olive oil and sprinkle generously with salt and freshly ground pepper. Serve hot.

Serves 6.

Fiadone
Cheese Pie

US		UK
2 cups	all-purpose (plain) flour	½ pound
	salt	
6–7	eggs	6–7
	olive oil	
¾ pound	Scamorza cheese – see method – diced	¾ pound
1½ cups	grated Pecorino or Parmesan	6 ounces
	pepper	

Scamorza is a locally produced soft cheese, similar to Mozzarella, which can be used in this recipe if the former is not available.

Sift the flour and a pinch of salt into a bowl. Add 2 eggs and work with the flour to a dough, adding a third egg if it is still too stiff. Knead the dough until elastic, then roll it out into a thin sheet. Lightly brush a baking sheet with olive oil and line it with the pastry. Trim off untidy edges.

Lightly beat 4 eggs, add the diced and grated cheeses, and season to taste with salt and pepper. Spread this mixture down the middle of the pastry sheet. Fold one side of the pastry over to enclose the filling completely, sealing the edges firmly with a fork. Bake at once in a moderate oven (375°F. Mark 4) for about 30 minutes, or until the pastry is a light golden color.

Serves 6.

Timballo di Scamorza dell'Abruzzo
Potato and Cheese Pie

US		UK
1 pound	waxy potatoes	1 pound
	salt and pepper	
	oil or lard for frying	
	flour	
2	eggs	2
6 tablespoons	butter	3 ounces
¾ pound	Scamorza or Mozzarella cheese, sliced	¾ pound
¼ pound	sliced Parma ham, cut into thin strips	¼ pound
4 tablespoons	grated Parmesan cheese	3 tablespoons

Wash the potatoes and drop them, without peeling, into a pan of boiling, salted water. Cook them steadily until soft. Take from the pan, cool, peel and cut into medium-thick slices.

Bring plenty of olive oil or lard to the boil in a deep frying pan. Coat the potato slices with flour, then dip them into the eggs, lightly beaten with a little salt. Fry in hot oil until crisp and brown, and drain thoroughly on absorbent paper. Sprinkle with salt.

Lightly grease a baking dish with butter and arrange the potatoes in it in layers. Cover with the sliced cheese, sprinkle generously with salt and freshly ground pepper, and dot with thin slivers of butter,

using half the remaining quantity. Bake in a moderate oven (375°F. Mark 4) for 20 minutes, or until the cheese has melted.

Take the dish from the oven, cover with strips of ham and sprinkle with grated Parmesan. Melt the remaining butter and sprinkle it over the top. Serve at once.

Serves 6.

Sugo di Pomodoro Fresco
Fresh Tomato Sauce

US		UK
2–3 thin slices	smoked pancetta – see method	2–3 thin slices
½ cup	olive oil	6 tablespoons
1	onion, sliced	1
2 cloves	garlic, crushed	2 cloves
2 pounds	ripe tomatoes	2 pounds
	salt	
small piece	hot chili pepper	small piece
4–5 leaves	mint, chopped	4–5 leaves

Pancetta is smoked, salted belly of pork. This is often available in Italian shops, but if not, use salted belly of pork instead, or even fat bacon. The recipe will make enough sauce for 1½ pounds pasta.

Cut the *pancetta* into small dice. Heat the oil in a pan and fry the onion, garlic and diced pork. Remove the garlic cloves as soon as they begin to brown and discard them. Peel the tomatoes, chop them finely and rub them through a sieve. Add the tomato purée to the pan, together with salt to taste, the chili and the mint. Cover the pan and simmer for at least 30 minutes. Remove the chili just before serving, and serve the sauce poured over freshly cooked, hot pasta.

Serves 6.

Ragù d'Agnello e Peperoni
Meat Sauce with Peppers

US		UK
½–¾ pound	lean lamb	½–¾ pound
	salt and pepper	
½ cup	olive oil	6 tablespoons
2 cloves	garlic, crushed	2 cloves
3	bay leaves	3
½ cup	dry white wine	6 tablespoons
4 large	ripe tomatoes, peeled	4 large
3	sweet peppers	3
	stock or water	

This is a thick meat sauce suitable for serving with spaghetti, noodles, macaroni, etc. If fresh tomatoes are not available, use a small can of Italian peeled tomatoes.

Wipe the meat and cut it into small cubes. Sprinkle with salt and pepper, and leave for 1 hour.

Heat the oil in a pan and sauté the garlic and bay leaves. As soon as they begin to brown, discard them and brown the meat in the same oil, turning the pieces to color them evenly. Add the wine and continue cooking until reduced.

Chop the tomatoes, discarding seeds. Cut each pepper in half, discard the core and seeds, and cut the pepper into thin strips. Add the tomatoes and peppers to the pan. Season to taste with salt and pepper, cover and cook over a low heat for 1½ hours. Stir from time to time and add a little stock or water if the sauce seems dry. (If using canned tomatoes, no extra liquid will be required as there will be sufficient in the can.) Serve the sauce very hot, poured over cooked pasta.

Serves 6.

Polenta Stufata
Baked Polenta

US		UK
3 cups	coarsely ground cornmeal	1 pound
9–10 cups	water	3½–4 pints
	coarse salt	
2½ tablespoons	olive oil	2 tablespoons
½ pound	Italian pork sausage meat	½ pound
2½ cups	freshly cooked tomato sauce	1 pint
pinch	chili powder	pinch
4 tablespoons	butter	2 ounces
⅔ cup	grated Pecorino cheese	2 ounces
¾ cup	grated Parmesan cheese	3 ounces

This is another particularly regional dish popular with those who like polenta. When cooking with cornmeal it is difficult to assess the exact quantity of liquid which will be required, for flours differ not only from country to country but often from day to day. The traditional Italian utensil for cooking polenta is the *paiolo*, a deep copper pan, and the polenta itself is stirred with a special spoon, slightly different in shape from our wooden spoons.

Bring the water to the boil in a large, heavy pan, add coarse salt to taste (about 2 tablespoons) and sprinkle in the cornmeal, stirring continuously with a wooden spoon to avoid lumps. Continue cooking over a moderate heat, stirring frequently, for about 50 minutes, or until the polenta comes away cleanly from the sides of the pan. Turn it on to a marble slab or a large wooden pastry board. It will shape itself into a dome. Leave until quite cold.

While the polenta is cooling prepare the sauce. Heat the oil in a pan, add the sausage meat and fry it until it begins to brown, crumbling it with a fork. Pour in the tomato sauce and season to taste with a pinch of chili powder and salt. Simmer for 10 minutes.

Cut the cold polenta into slices about ⅛ inch thick, using either strong thread or fine wire. Butter a deep baking dish and fill it with alternate layers of polenta, sauce and the grated cheeses, dotting each layer of cheese with a few slivers of butter. The top layer should be one of polenta sprinkled with cheese and butter. Bake for about 1 hour in a moderate oven (375°F. Mark 4), by which time the polenta will have formed a golden crust. Serve hot.

Serves 6.

Fettuccine in Salsa
Ribbon Noodles with Tomatoes and Cheese

US		UK
1½ pounds	fettuccine (ribbon noodles)	1½ pounds
½ cup	olive oil	6 tablespoons
2 cloves	garlic, finely chopped	2 cloves
6 leaves	basil, finely chopped	6 leaves
3 leaves	mint, finely chopped	3 leaves
2–3 sprigs	parsley	2–3 sprigs
14-ounce can	Italian peeled tomatoes	14-ounce can
	salt and pepper	
small piece	hot chili pepper, finely chopped	small piece
⅔ cup	grated Pecorino or Parmesan	2 ounces
¼ pound	Scamorza cheese (page 189), thinly sliced	¼ pound

Heat the olive oil and gently sauté the garlic, basil, mint and parsley. Drain the tomatoes, chop them coarsely and add them to the pan, together with their liquid. Season to taste with salt, a pinch of pepper and the chili, and cook over a brisk heat for 20 minutes.

Bring a large pan of salted water to the boil and cook the *fettuccine* until just tender, i.e. *al dente*. Drain thoroughly and turn into a deep earthenware baking dish. Pour over the sauce, stirring gently to allow it to penetrate the dish; sprinkle with the grated cheese and cover with slices of Scamorza. Bake in a hot oven (425°F. Mark 6) for a few minutes until the cheese is melted and bubbling.

Serves 6.

Maccheroni alla Chitarra
Matchstick Noodles

This is a typical Abruzzo spaghetti dish, not a recipe which the amateur need attempt, but interesting to know about as a local specialty.

The noodles are made on a special instrument known locally as a "guitar", consisting of a rectangular frame on which are strung a large number of steel wires, like the strings or cords of a guitar. The dough is prepared in the usual manner, rolled into strips and placed on the steel wires, then rolled out with a rolling pin to give matchstick-thin strips. These are cooked in boiling, salted water and served with a meat or tomato sauce and a generous portion of grated Pecorino cheese.

Spaghetti Aglio, Olio e Peperoncino
Spaghetti with Olive Oil, Garlic and Chili

US		UK
1½ pounds	spaghetti	1½ pounds
	salt	
1 cup	olive oil	⅓ pint
3–4 cloves	garlic, crushed	3–4 cloves
1	hot chili pepper pod	1
3–4 sprigs	parsley, finely chopped	3–4 sprigs
	black pepper	

According to this and other recipes, both the garlic and the chili are removed from the oil as soon as they begin to brown. But this, curiously enough, does not happen when the dish is served in a *trattoria* in Italy. On the contrary, there is great willingness to provide both extra garlic and chili. Therefore, if a strong flavor of garlic is liked, chop it very finely and let it remain in the oil dressing, but be sure not to let it burn, as this will make it bitter.

Bring plenty of salted water to the boil in a large pan. Add the spaghetti, lowering it slowly into the pan so that the water remains rapidly boiling all the time. Simmer gently.

Heat the olive oil and add the garlic, chili and parsley. As soon as the garlic cloves begin to brown, discard them (see above), together with the chili.

When the spaghetti is tender but still firm, drain it thoroughly and turn it into a deep heated serving dish. Pour the olive oil over the spaghetti straight from the pan, sprinkle with black pepper, stir well and serve immediately.

Serves 6.

Minestra di Sedani all'Uso di Teramo
Teramo Celery Soup

US		UK
1 large bunch	celery	1 large head
4 tablespoons	olive oil	3 tablespoons
1	onion, sliced	1
1–2 slices	fat salt pork, chopped	1–2 slices
2½ tablespoons	tomato paste	2 tablespoons
10 cups	beef stock	4 pints
1½ cups	rice	10 ounces
¾ cup	grated Parmesan cheese	3 ounces

This makes a very thick, filling soup. The quantity of rice may be cut down, even halved, if preferred.

Wash the celery carefully, discarding coarse leaves or really bruised stalks, and separate the remaining stalks. Cut these into dice.

Heat the oil in the pan in which the soup is to be made, and fry the onion and pork over a low heat until the onion is soft and a light golden color. Add the diced celery and the tomato paste, and continue frying for about 5 minutes longer.

In the meantime, bring the stock to the boil in another pan. Pour it gradually over the celery, stirring all the time. Cover and simmer for 20 minutes.

Bring the soup back to a gentle boil, pour in the rice, stirring, and continue to simmer until the rice is tender but not overcooked, about 15 minutes. Serve very hot, garnished with grated Parmesan cheese.

Serves 6 to 8.

Minestrone Abruzzese

US		UK
generous ½ cup	flageolets (dried haricot beans)	4 ounces
¼ cup	chick peas	2 ounces
¼ cup	brown lentils	2 ounces
½ pound	pork rind	½ pound
1	ham bone *or* pig's trotter	1
1	pig's ear	1
	salt	
¼ cup	olive oil	3 tablespoons
¼ cup	finely chopped fat salt pork	3 tablespoons
1 clove	garlic, finely chopped	1 clove
2–3 sprigs	parsley, finely chopped	2–3 sprigs
2	carrots, diced	2
4 large	ripe tomatoes	4 large
1 bulb	fennel, finely chopped – see page 68	1 bulb
1 cup	fresh lima (broad) beans	6 ounces
2 cups	shelled green peas	12 ounces
4–5 leaves	fresh mint	4–5 leaves
3–4 leaves	marjoram	3–4 leaves
	pepper	
½ pound	fresh spinach, cut in ribbons	½ pound
½ pound	short thick noodles – optional	½ pound
	grated Parmesan or Pecorino	

Soak the dried vegetables in water overnight. The following day, half-cook them in unsalted water. In another pan boil the pork rind, ham bone or trotter and pig's ear in salted water for about 2 hours. When the meat is tender, drain and cut into small pieces.

Heat the oil and fat salt pork in the pan in which the soup is to be made, and sauté the garlic, parsley and carrots until the garlic is golden but not brown and the carrot has softened. Add the tomatoes, the dried vegetables, drained, and all the remaining fresh vegetables and herbs, except the spinach. Season to taste with salt and freshly ground pepper, and cover with about 12 cups (U.K. 5 pints) water. Bring to the boil and simmer gently for 1 hour. Add the spinach and the meat, and cook until the spinach is soft.

Noodles may be added if an even thicker *minestrone* is preferred, but as always, care must be taken not to overcook them.

Serve hot or cold, sprinkled generously with grated Parmesan or Pecorino.

Serves 6 to 8.

Bracioline di Maiale al Vino Bianco
Pork Cutlets in White Wine

US		UK
6	pork cutlets	6
1 clove	garlic, finely chopped	1 clove
1 sprig	rosemary, finely chopped	1 sprig
	salt	
pinch	chili powder	pinch
4 tablespoons	olive oil	3 tablespoons
½ cup	dry white wine	6 tablespoons
⅔ cup	beef stock	¼ pint

Flatten the pork cutlets lightly with a cutlet bat. Trim off all the fat, cut into small pieces and pound to a paste with garlic, rosemary,

a little salt and a pinch of chili powder. Spread this paste on both sides of each cutlet.

Heat the oil in a frying pan large enough to take all the cutlets at once, and fry first on one side until brown, then turn and brown them on the other side. Pour the wine into the pan and cook, uncovered, until reduced.

Heat the stock (if none is available, use hot water), add this to the pan, cover and cook gently until completely absorbed. Serve immediately, allowing one or two cutlets per person. If using pork loin chops, which can also be prepared in this manner, allow one per person.

'ndocca 'ndocca
Boiled Pork

US		UK
3½–4 pounds	mixed salted pork – see method	3½–4 pounds
2–3 tablespoons	wine vinegar	2–3 tablespoons
3	bay leaves	3
1 sprig	rosemary	1 sprig
2 cloves	garlic, crushed	2 cloves
small piece	hot chili pepper	small piece
6	peppercorns	6
	salt	
4 teaspoons	tomato paste	1 tablespoon

This is a characteristic dish of the province of Teramo. It is prepared in the autumn and winter when the pigs are killed and the meat is freshly salted. Trotters, skin, ribs, snout and ears can all be used.

Soak the meat overnight in cold water to which you have added the vinegar. This will rid it of some of the salt. Cut up the skin and the snout, split the trotters and put them all in a casserole, preferably an earthenware one. Add the herbs, garlic, chili, peppercorns and a little salt. Pour in plenty of water, cover the casserole and cook very slowly for 4 hours.

Half an hour before the end of cooking time, stir in the tomato paste. Serve the pork very hot with the sauce, which by now will be considerably reduced.

Serves 6.

Agnello, Cacio e Uova
Lamb Stew with Cheese

US		UK
3½ pounds	leg of lamb, boned	3½ pounds
	salt and pepper	
½ cup	olive oil	6 tablespoons
1	onion, sliced	1
1 cup	dry white wine	⅓ pint
about ½ cup	beef stock	about 6 tablespoons
4	eggs *or*	4
6	egg yolks	6
⅔ cup	grated Pecorino or Parmesan	2 ounces

This typical Italian dish of lamb should be cooked in an earthenware casserole. If this is not available, choose a pan as near to earthenware as possible, one which can be brought to the table.

Wipe the lamb with a damp cloth, cut it into cubes, sprinkle lightly with salt and pepper, and leave for 1 hour.

Heat the oil in the earthenware pan and lightly fry the onion until it is soft but not brown. Add the pieces of lamb and brown them lightly on all sides, turning frequently. Pour in the wine and cook, uncovered, until it has evaporated. Cover the pan and cook slowly for about 1 hour, or until the meat is very tender, adding a little stock from time to time if required.

Beat the eggs, add the grated cheese and a pinch of salt and pepper, and pour this mixture over the meat. Stir and leave over a low heat for 2 minutes. Serve immediately.

Serves 6.

Bracioline d'Agnello
Baby Lamb Chops

US		UK
12	baby lamb chops	12
½ cup	olive oil	6 tablespoons
2–3 sprigs	sage	2–3 sprigs
	salt and pepper	
½ cup	dry white wine	6 tablespoons
	juice of ½ lemon	

Heat the oil in a large frying pan. Add the sage and the lamb chops, fitting them all into the pan at the same time, and brown on both sides. Sprinkle with salt and pepper, pour in the wine and continue cooking until the chops are tender and the wine has evaporated. Serve immediately, sprinkled with lemon juice.

Serves 4 to 6.

Agnello Rustico
Roast Leg of Lamb Abruzzo Style

US		UK
3–3½ pounds	leg of lamb	3–3½ pounds
	salt and pepper	
½ cup	olive oil	6 tablespoons
1 small	onion, sliced	1 small
	juice of ½ lemon	
⅔ cup	grated Pecorino or Parmesan	2 ounces

Wipe the meat with a damp cloth, sprinkle it with salt and pepper, and leave for 1 hour.

Pour the oil into a shallow ovenproof casserole with a lid, and add the onion and the meat. Cover and bake in a moderate oven (375°F. Mark 4) for 1 hour, or until tender, turning the meat from time to time and basting it occasionally with the pan juices.

Just before serving, sprinkle the meat with lemon juice and grated cheese.

Serves 6.

Agnello in Fricassea
Fricassée of Lamb

This dish is prepared in exactly the same manner as the previous recipe, except that garlic is used instead of onion and lemon juice, and finely chopped parsley is substituted for the grated cheese.

Agnello alla Pecorara
Lamb Casserole

US		UK
3–3½ pounds	tender young lamb	3–3½ pounds
	salt	
4 tablespoons	butter	2 ounces
1	onion	1
	slices of toasted bread	

In order to cook this dish a casserole with two handles and a tightly fitting lid is essential.

Wipe the meat with a damp cloth, trim and cut it into even-sized cubes. Sprinkle with salt and leave for 1 hour. Cut the butter into small pieces and put these at the bottom of the casserole. Add the cubed meat and bury the onion in it. Cover the casserole tightly and cook over a very low heat for 1 hour, shaking it from time to time to prevent the meat sticking. The lid should not be raised until the meat has been cooking for 1 hour. Test to see whether it is tender; if not, continue cooking, still firmly covered, for another 30 minutes. Serve the meat with its sauce on slices of toasted bread.

Serves 6.

Involtini con Fagioloni Bianchi
Stuffed Veal with White Beans

US		UK
12 thin slices	veal	12 thin slices
	olive oil	
3 tablespoons	unsmoked ham fat	1½ ounces
2 cloves	garlic	2 cloves
6 sprigs	parsley, finely chopped	6 sprigs
4 large	ripe tomatoes, peeled and chopped	4 large
3 cups	cooked dried white (haricot) beans	1 pound
¼ pound	mushrooms, sliced	¼ pound
2½ tablespoons	stock	2 tablespoons
1 cup	ground (UK minced) lean pork	½ pound
2½ tablespoons	grated Parmesan cheese	2 tablespoons
1	egg	1
	pepper	
4 tablespoons	clarified butter	2 ounces

The veal for this recipe should be cut almost wafer-thin and then gently flattened between two layers of wax paper with a cutlet bat. Trim the veal slices if necessary to give them a neat shape.

Heat ½ cup (6 tablespoons) oil in a heavy pan, add the ham fat and 1 clove garlic, finely chopped, and fry gently until golden, taking care not to let the garlic brown, as this will make it bitter. Add half the parsley, the chopped tomatoes and the cooked beans, mix well and season to taste with salt. Simmer gently for 30 minutes.

In another pan heat 2 to 3 tablespoons oil and fry the remaining garlic clove, lightly crushed, until brown. Discard the garlic and add the mushrooms. Moisten with stock and cook over a moderate heat for 20 minutes. Drain the mushrooms and chop them finely.

Mix the pork to a paste with the Parmesan cheese, the egg, the remaining parsley and the mushrooms, and season to taste with salt and pepper. Spread a little of this mixture on each slice of veal, roll the slices up firmly and secure with thread or toothpicks.

Heat the butter in a large pan and sauté the veal rolls until golden brown all over, turning them once or twice and keeping the heat constant. Cook for 10 minutes, then add the beans together with their sauce, and simmer gently for a further 15 minutes.

Serves 6.

Rollè di Filetto
Pot-roasted Fillet of Beef

US		UK
3 pounds	beef fillet, in one piece	3 pounds
	salt and pepper	
5 tablespoons	olive oil	4 tablespoons
1 sprig	rosemary	1 sprig
3	bay leaves	3
½	lemon	½
1 rounded teaspoon	flour	1 teaspoon
3 tablespoons	butter	1½ ounces
½ cup	dry white wine	6 tablespoons

Cut the sinews along the fillet and tie it up – this helps the meat to keep its shape while cooking. Rub it with salt and pepper.

Heat the oil in a casserole and add the rosemary, bay leaves and lemon. Place the fillet on top, cover the casserole and cook over a moderately high heat for between 30 and 40 minutes. Turn the meat over once or twice during this time to ensure that it browns evenly. Discard the lemon and herbs.

Knead the flour and butter together. Add this to the casserole in small pieces, stirring it thoroughly into the juices until smooth; then add the wine and continue cooking for 5 minutes longer, turning the fillet round several times. Check seasoning. Serve the meat cut into medium-thick slices.

Serves 6.

Pollo all'Abruzzese
Chicken with Tomatoes and Sweet Peppers

US		UK
1	tender chicken – 3 to 3½ pounds	1
½ cup	olive oil	6 tablespoons
1 small	onion, chopped	1 small
	salt and pepper	
1 pound	ripe tomatoes, peeled, seeded and chopped	1 pound
2 large	sweet peppers	2 large

Chop the chicken into serving pieces. Heat the oil in a heatproof casserole and sauté the onion until golden. Add the pieces of chicken and continue to sauté gently, turning them to brown them all over. Season to taste with salt and pepper, and add the tomatoes. (A can of Italian peeled tomatoes may be used instead of fresh ones.) Cover the casserole and simmer gently for ½ hour.

In the meantime, char the peppers over a high flame or put them under the broiler (grill) as near to the source of heat as possible, until their skins blacken and blister all over. Peel off their thin outer skins and cut the peppers into strips, discarding cores and seeds. Add the pepper strips to the casserole with the chicken and continue to simmer gently for about 15 minutes longer, or until the chicken and peppers are soft.

Serves 4.

Tacchino alla Canzanese
Boned Turkey in Aspic

US		UK
1	turkey – 8 to 10 pounds	1
	salt and pepper	
1	carrot	1
1	onion	1
1 stalk	celery	1 stalk
4	peppercorns	4
	oil	

Usually the butcher will bone a customer's turkey if asked. However, this is how it is done. Cut the neck off as close to the body as possible. Cut through the skin with the point of a sharp knife until the sockets of the wings and thighs are reached. Bone these joints before proceeding further, for once these are detached nearly the whole of the carcass may be separated from the flesh and taken out complete. Only the neck bones and the forked bone between the neck and the breast (the merrythought) remain to be removed and the empty body will be ready to be rolled.

Place the boned body of the turkey flat on a table, skin side down. Sprinkle it with salt and pepper, and roll it up tightly so that it looks like a large, thick, firm sausage. Sew up along the side with a needle and thread.

Pour about 2½ cups (U.K. 1 pint) water for each pound of turkey meat into a large pan. Add the carrot, onion, celery, peppercorns and a little salt. Bring to the boil and add the turkey. Cover the pan tightly, lower the heat and continue cooking until the turkey is quite tender – about 3 hours, depending on the size of the bird.

Take the turkey from the pan, but leave the stock simmering over a low heat until considerably reduced. Brush the turkey with oil and roast it in a hot oven (425°F. Mark 6) for about 30 minutes. Then take it from the oven, cool it and remove the threads. Cut into neat, medium-thin slices and arrange these in a large, fairly deep, oval platter.

Strain the stock and chill in the refrigerator until it just begins to jell, then pour it over the slices of turkey, smoothing it down evenly with a warm palette knife. Leave the turkey in the refrigerator until the aspic is quite firm.

Serves 6 to 8.

Coniglio alla Molisana
Skewered Rabbit with Sausages

US		UK
1	large rabbit – about 3½ pounds	1
	salt and pepper	
1 sprig	parsley, finely chopped	1 sprig
1 sprig	rosemary, finely chopped	1 sprig
¼ pound	Parma ham, thinly sliced – 12 slices	¼ pound
12 leaves	sage	12 leaves
6 small	Italian sausages	6 small
½ cup	olive oil	6 tablespoons

Bone the rabbit carefully, keeping the pieces of meat as large as possible. Wipe the rabbit meat with a damp cloth. Cut it into 12 even-sized pieces, flatten them out lightly, and season with salt, pepper and a little finely chopped parsley and rosemary. Put a slice of ham on each slice of rabbit and roll up tightly.

Take 6 skewers. Thread a roll of rabbit, 1 sage leaf, 1 sausage, another rabbit roll and another sage leaf on to each skewer. Brush the skewers with oil and broil (grill), over charcoal if possible, or on a rack placed as close as possible to the source of heat. Alternatively, the skewers can also be baked in a slow oven (350°F. Mark 3) for about 1 hour. Turn the skewers occasionally, each time brushing with oil.

Serves 6.

Trote del Sangro al Pomodoro
Sangro River Trout in Tomato Sauce

US		UK
6	trout	6
2 pounds	ripe tomatoes	2 pounds
⅔ cup	olive oil	¼ pint
1 clove	garlic	1 clove
3–4 sprigs	parsley	3–4 sprigs
	salt and pepper	

Traditionally, trout from the Sangro river should be used in this recipe. However, it can be prepared with other trout, and in particular with deep-frozen fish.

Peel and chop the tomatoes, discarding seeds. Sauté gently in the oil in a large, wide, heatproof casserole, together with the garlic, 2 to 3 sprigs parsley, finely chopped, and salt and pepper to taste. Then cook over a brisk heat for 20 minutes.

In the meantime, clean and wash the trout, and rub the cavities lightly with salt and pepper. Place them carefully in the tomato sauce, cover the casserole and cook very gently for about 10 minutes longer, or until the fish flake easily with a fork. Serve in the casserole, garnished with the remaining parsley, finely chopped.

Serves 6.

Trote sulla Brace
Broiled (Grilled) Trout

US		UK
6 small	trout	6 small
	salt and pepper	
4–6 sprigs	parsley, finely chopped	4–6 sprigs
2 cloves	garlic, finely chopped	2 cloves
	best-quality olive oil	
1	lemon, cut in wedges	1

Wash and clean the trout. Sprinkle the cavities lightly with salt and pepper, and fill with the finely chopped parsley and garlic. Brush the fish lightly with olive oil and broil (grill) them over charcoal if possible. Turn after 5 minutes, brush lightly with oil again, and cook the other side. Serve immediately, sprinkled with a little more olive oil and garnished with lemon wedges.

Serves 6.

Triglie sul Focone
Broiled (Grilled) Red Mullet

US		UK
12 small	red mullet	12 small
	salt	
4 tablespoons	olive oil	3 tablespoons
2	bay leaves	2
2–3 sprigs	parsley	2–3 sprigs
pinch	thyme	pinch
a few	chives	a few
3–4	black peppercorns	3–4

Clean and wash the mullet in salted water. Put the oil, bay leaves, parsley, thyme, chives and peppercorns into a large shallow dish and add the fish. Turn them round so that they are all thoroughly coated with oil and leave to marinate for about 1 hour.

In the Abruzzo mullet are broiled (grilled) over charcoal in the following manner. A dozen or so reeds are whittled down into thin strips, then one reed is threaded into each fish from head to tail. The tails are tied to the reeds with thread to prevent them slipping off. The fish are then cooked over charcoal, the reeds being gently turned from time to time, and the fish basted with the oil from the marinade.

However, failing the reeds, the mullet can be put into a wire fish frame specially designed for outdoor charcoal cooking and broiled (grilled) slowly and carefully, basting occasionally with the marinating oil.

Serves 6.

Tranci di Palombo con Seppie alla Scapece
Fried Soused Fish

US		UK
2 pounds	dogfish steaks – see method	2 pounds
1 pound	small cuttlefish, or squid, cleaned	1 pound
	flour	
	olive oil for deep-frying	
	salt	
5 cups	wine vinegar	2 pints
1	onion, sliced	1
4–5 sprigs	parsley	4–5 sprigs
2	bay leaves	2
1 sprig each	rosemary and sage	1 sprig each
pinch	marjoram	pinch
2–3	black peppercorns	2–3
3 cloves	garlic, sliced	3 cloves
2–3 sprigs	basil, finely chopped	2–3 sprigs

Large fish steaks other than dogfish may be used in this recipe.

Lightly coat the fish steaks and cuttlefish with flour. Fry the fish steaks in plenty of oil until golden brown. Take them out with a perforated spoon and drain on absorbent paper. Sprinkle lightly with salt. Fry the cuttlefish for a few minutes only, drain and dry on absorbent paper.

Pour the vinegar into a non-metallic pan and add a teaspoon of salt. Add the onion, 2 sprigs parsley, the bay leaves, rosemary, sage, a little marjoram and the peppercorns. Bring to the boil and boil for 20 minutes. Strain.

Arrange a layer of fish and cuttlefish at the bottom of a shallow earthenware or porcelain dish. Chop the remaining parsley and sprinkle a little of it over the fish, together with some of the garlic and basil. Spoon over some of the vinegar marinade. Repeat until all the ingredients are used up, finishing with a sprinkling of garlic and herbs, and pour over the remaining marinade. Cover the dish and leave it in a cool place for 2 days before serving.

Serves 6.

Scapece alla Vastese
Fish Steaks with Vinegar and Saffron Vasto Style

US		UK
2½ pounds	thick white fish steaks – see method	2½ pounds
	flour	
	olive oil for deep-frying	
	salt	
generous pinch	saffron	generous pinch
5 cups	white wine vinegar	2 pints

In Italy, skate and dogfish are preferred for this dish.

Lightly coat the fish steaks with flour and deep-fry in hot oil until golden brown. Take from the pan with a perforated spoon, drain on absorbent paper and sprinkle with salt.

Dissolve the saffron in a little of the vinegar and stir it into the rest of the vinegar. Pour into a non-metallic pan, bring just to boiling point, then immediately remove the pan from the heat.

Cover the bottom of a shallow earthenware or porcelain dish with a layer of fish steaks and sprinkle with some of the hot vinegar. Add the remaining fish and pour over the rest of the vinegar. Cover the dish and leave to marinate in a cool place for 24 hours. Serve the fish thoroughly drained of vinegar.

Serves 6.

Teglia di Pesce al Forno
Swordfish Casserole

US		UK
1½ pounds	swordfish	1½ pounds
	salt and pepper	
⅔ cup	olive oil	¼ pint
2 pounds	potatoes, thinly sliced	2 pounds
1 large	onion, sliced	1 large
1 clove	garlic, finely chopped	1 clove
4 sprigs	parsley, finely chopped	4 sprigs
½	hot chili pepper, finely chopped	½

Swordfish is plentiful in the Mediterranean and is particularly appreciated. However, if this is not available, use fresh tuna, dogfish, or even the humble rock salmon for this dish.

Cut the fish into medium-thick steaks and sprinkle them with salt and pepper on both sides.

Brush a moderately deep baking dish with oil and cover the bottom with half of the potato and onion slices. Sprinkle with salt and pepper, and add all the fish steaks in a single layer. Sprinkle them with some of the oil, all the garlic and parsley, and scatter a few pieces of chili pepper over the top. Cover with the remaining potato and onion slices, sprinkle with a little more salt and pepper, and pour in the rest of the oil. Bake in a moderate oven (375°F. Mark 4) for at least 1 hour, or until the potatoes are soft.

Serves 6.

Brodetto alla Vastese
Fish Soup or Stew Vasto Style

US		UK
3–3½ pounds	mixed fish – see method	3–3½ pounds
6–8 tablespoons	olive oil	6–8 tablespoons
10	dried sweet peppers	10
3 cloves	garlic, finely chopped	3 cloves
1 cup	red wine vinegar	⅓ pint
3–4 sprigs	parsley, finely chopped	3–4 sprigs
	salt and pepper	
	slices of home-made bread	

Clean the fish (whiting, red mullet, sole, goby, dogfish, squid or cuttlefish, baby clams, lobster, mussels, etc.). Cut the larger ones into thick steaks or simply into large chunks.

Heat the oil in a large heavy pan or casserole and add the sweet peppers and garlic. Fry these over a high heat for 15 minutes. Remove the peppers and pound them in a mortar, gradually adding the vinegar. Stir this mixture back into the casserole.

Add the larger pieces of fish and cook these for a few minutes until they begin to soften. Add the rest of the fish, the chopped parsley, and salt and pepper to taste. Cover the casserole and continue to cook gently for about 20 minutes, shaking the pan from time to time to prevent the fish from sticking. Serve the soup very hot poured over slices of home-made bread, taking great care not to break the fish when taking them out of the pan.

Serves 6.

Timballo di Melanzane

Eggplant (Aubergine), Ham and Cheese Pie

US		UK
4 large	eggplants (aubergines)	4 large
	salt	
	flour	
	olive oil for deep-frying	
	butter	
¼ pound	raw Parma ham, thinly sliced	¼ pound
½ pound	Scamorza – see page 189 – or Mozzarella cheese, sliced	½ pound
4	eggs	4

Slice the eggplants, sprinkle the slices with salt and leave them to drain for about 1 hour on a tilted plate or in a colander. This will rid them of their bitter juices. Wipe the slices dry and dust them with flour. Deep-fry in hot oil. When golden brown, take them out with a perforated spoon, drain well and dry on absorbent paper.

Butter a baking dish. Cover the bottom with a layer of fried eggplant slices, a layer of ham and one of cheese. Cover with another layer of eggplant slices, and continue in this manner until all the ingredients are used up, finishing with a layer of eggplants.

Melt 4 tablespoons (2 ounces) butter and pour it over the top of the dish. Bake in a moderate oven (375°F. Mark 4) for 15 minutes. Beat the eggs with a pinch of salt and pour them over the dish. Return it to the oven for another 15 to 20 minutes, or until the cheese has melted and the eggs are set.

Serves 6.

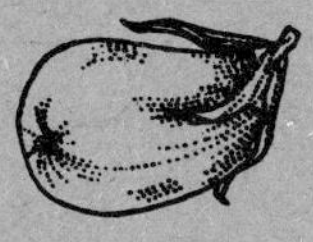

Frittata con le Patate

Potato Omelette

US		UK
1 pound	potatoes	1 pound
3 cups	milk	1¼ pints
	salt	
3 tablespoons	butter	1½ ounces
pinch	chili powder	pinch
6	eggs	6
2–3 tablespoons	grated Pecorino or Parmesan	2 tablespoons
2–3 tablespoons	olive oil	2–3 tablespoons

A *frittata* is a type of omelette. Italians prefer to serve their omelettes round and not folded over in the French manner, and this particular recipe produces almost a potato pancake. If dubious about taking the *frittata* out of the pan, brown the top under a hot broiler (grill), or make two or even three omelettes instead of one large one.

Wash the potatoes, peel them and cut them into quarters. Pour the milk into a heavy pan, add the potatoes and a little salt, and cook over a moderate heat until soft. Then mash them to a smooth purée together with the butter, and salt and chili to taste. Beat the eggs, add a pinch of salt and the grated cheese, and blend thoroughly with the potato purée.

Brush a large, heavy frying pan generously with oil. When it is very hot, add the egg and potato mixture, lower the heat and fry gently until the underside is crisp and brown. Carefully turn the *frittata* out on to a large, flat plate, then slide it back into the pan to brown the other side, adding a little more oil to the pan. Serve very hot.

Serves 6.

Pasticcio di Patate con le Salsicce

Sausage and Potato Pie

US		UK
3–3½ pounds	floury white potatoes	3–3½ pounds
	salt	
	butter	
about 2½ cups	lukewarm milk	about 1 pint
5 tablespoons	grated Parmesan cheese	4 tablespoons
	freshly grated nutmeg	
	pepper	
6	Italian sausages	6

Wash the potatoes and cook them in their jackets in boiling, salted water until soft. Drain and peel them, and rub them through a potato ricer or sieve. Add 3 tablespoons (1½ ounces) butter, the milk, cheese, and salt, freshly grated nutmeg and a little freshly ground pepper to taste. Mix well and beat until fluffy. Skin the sausages, crumble the meat and cook in a small pan over low heat without any additional fat for 15 minutes. Mix into the potato.

Generously butter a deep baking dish and fill it with the potato and sausage mixture. Bake in a moderate oven (375°F. Mark 4) for about 20 minutes, or until a golden brown crust has formed on top.

Serves 6.

Cuscinetti di Teramo

Fried "Jam Cushions" Teramo Style

US		UK
1 cup	all-purpose (plain) flour	4 ounces
pinch	salt	pinch
2½ tablespoons	granulated (caster) sugar	2 tablespoons
4 teaspoons	olive oil	1 tablespoon
2–3 tablespoons	white wine	2–3 tablespoons
5 tablespoons	jam	4 tablespoons
2 squares	bitter chocolate, grated	2 ounces
⅓ cup	almonds, toasted and chopped	2 ounces
	oil for deep-frying	
	honey	

Sift the flour on to a pastry board or into a bowl and make a well in the center. Add the salt, sugar and oil, and enough wine to make a firm but pliable dough. Knead vigorously. Roll the dough out into a very thin sheet and cut into circles about 3 inches in diameter.

Mix the jam, chocolate and almonds together. Place a little of this mixture on each circle, fold the pastry over it and press the edges firmly to seal them.

Heat plenty of oil or lard until hot but not boiling (about 350°F.) and deep-fry the little "cushions", a few at a time, until a deep golden color. Take them from the pan with a perforated spoon and drain on absorbent paper. Serve warm or cold, lightly coated with honey.

Calciuni del Molise
Sweet "Ravioli" Stuffed with Chestnuts

US		UK
Pastry		
1¾ cups	all-purpose (plain) flour	7 ounces
2	egg yolks	2
1 tablespoon	water	1 tablespoon
1½ tablespoons	white wine	1 tablespoon
4 teaspoons	mild olive oil	1 tablespoon
Filling		
½ pound	cooked chestnuts or canned puréed chestnuts	½ pound
4 teaspoons	honey	1 tablespoon
2½ tablespoons	grated bitter chocolate	2 tablespoons
1–2 tablespoons	rum	1–2 tablespoons
3 tablespoons	chopped toasted almonds	1 ounce
¼ cup	chopped candied peel	1 ounce
	ground cinnamon	
	vanilla powder or extract	
	oil for deep-frying	
	confectioners' (icing) sugar	

Calciuni are prepared at Christmas and are a variety of fried ravioli.

Pastry

Sift the flour on to a pastry board, make a well in the center, and add the egg yolks, water, wine and olive oil. Work the flour from the sides into the center, mixing well to a firm dough. Knead vigorously until smooth, cover and set aside while you prepare the filling.

Filling

Rub the chestnuts through a sieve. Add the honey, chocolate, rum, almonds and candied peel, a pinch of cinnamon and vanilla, to taste. Blend thoroughly.

Roll the pastry out into a thin sheet. Cut out circles about 3 inches in diameter. Put a little of the filling on each circle, fold it over and press the edges firmly to seal them. Deep-fry the *calciuni* until a deep golden color. Take from the pan with a perforated spoon and drain on absorbent paper. Serve sprinkled with confectioners' (icing) sugar sifted with ground cinnamon.

Torrone di Cioccolata
Chocolate Nougat

US		UK
⅔ cup	honey	½ pound
1½ pounds	shelled hazelnuts	1½ pounds
1⅛ cups	granulated (caster) sugar	½ pound
8 squares	bitter chocolate	½ pound
2	egg whites	2
	rice paper	

In Italy, the name *torrone* is applied to all kinds of nougat, some soft, some hard. Soft *torrone* require hardly any cooking at all, simply dissolving the sugar, and very little attention. A harder *torrone* needs more cooking and some care. The following recipe belongs to the latter type. After the *torrone* has been cooked it is spread either on a thin sheet-like wafer, called *ostia* (but ordinary wafers can be used instead, placed close together) or on rice paper.

Pour the honey into the top of a double boiler and cook until liquid over boiling water, stirring all the time with a wooden spoon. Let it cook over simmering water, stirring frequently, for 1 hour or until a little dropped into cold water forms a hard ball.

While the honey is cooking, prepare the remaining ingredients. Toast the hazelnuts in a moderate oven (375°F. Mark 4) and rub off their thin outer skins. Dissolve ¼ cup (U.K. 3 tablespoons) sugar in the same quantity of water and let it cook slowly until it thickens. Add the chocolate, broken into small pieces, and continue cooking, stirring all the time, until the chocolate is completely melted and blended into the sugar. Put aside but keep warm.

Dissolve the remaining sugar with 1 or 2 tablespoons water and cook slowly until it caramelizes, stirring with a wooden spoon from time to time.

Beat the egg whites until very stiff. By this time the honey should be ready; add the egg whites to the honey slowly, beating constantly. The mixture will become white and fluffy. Stir the caramelized sugar into the honey and egg white mixture, and when thoroughly blended add the warm chocolate. Mix well, then add the nuts. All this should be done with the pan on the heat.

Remove the pan from the heat and spread the mixture over wafers or rice paper. Quickly smooth it down with a wet palette knife into an even layer about 1½ to 2 inches thick. Some recipes also cover the top with a layer of wafers, which is rather nice. Cool for 20 minutes, then with a sharp, wetted knife, cut the *torrone* into two long strips, and each of the strips into equal-sized pieces – the size is a matter of preference. Let the *torrone* become quite cold; then, if keeping for later use, wrap each piece in foil or wax paper and store in a cool dry place.

Parrozzo
Almond and Chocolate Cake

US		UK
scant 1 cup	sweet almonds	5 ounces
2–3	bitter almonds – optional	2–3
¾ cup	granulated (caster) sugar	6 ounces
	butter and flour for the cake pan	
½ cup	all-purpose (plain) flour	2 ounces
6 tablespoons	potato flour	2 ounces
pinch	ground cinnamon	pinch
pinch	vanilla powder or vanilla extract to taste	pinch
5 tablespoons	butter	2½ ounces
5	eggs	5
Topping		
5 squares	bitter chocolate	5 ounces
4 teaspoons	butter	⅔ ounce
	chocolate strands or vermicelli	

Blanch the almonds, both sweet and bitter, for 1 or 2 minutes. Drain them and peel off their skins as soon as they are cool enough to handle. Pound the almonds in a mortar with 2 to 3 tablespoons of the sugar until reduced to a powder (or use an electric blender).

Grease a 9-inch layer cake pan with butter and coat lightly with flour, shaking out the excess. Sift together the flour, potato flour, cinnamon and vanilla powder. Melt the butter and let it cool.

Separate the egg whites from the yolks. Beat the yolks one at a time, gradually adding the remaining sugar and the almond-sugar mixture, until the whole is white and fluffy. Add the flour mixture little by little, beating vigorously between each addition. Beat in the cooled melted butter, and lastly, fold in the egg whites, stiffly beaten. Pour the mixture into the prepared cake pan and bake in a slow oven (350°F. Mark 3) for about 40 minutes, or until the cake has risen and the top is firm and golden. Leave the cake to cool before turning it out.

Break the chocolate into small pieces and melt it in the top of a double boiler together with the butter and a tablespoon of water. Beat to a smooth paste, then pour it quickly over the top of the cake, smoothing it down over the top and sides with a palette knife dipped in boiling water. Let the chocolate dry, then decorate the cake with chocolate strands.

NAPLES-
CAMPAGNA

Pizza is the pride of Naples, but today there are many other cities all over the world where the cheerful, convivial sign of the *pizzeria* brightens the downtown streets.

Wandering through the streets of old Naples, you may suddenly find yourself face to face with the local busker, the *pazzariello*, a strange creature whose fantastic costume seems to belong to a bygone age before the fall of the Bourbons. He entertains the delighted crowds with songs and jokes, and by playing the tarantella on his one-man band. The *pazzariello* is often hired by restaurants to attract customers, and when he wanders through the alleys of Spaccanapoli, in the heart of the old city, he is besieged by children. Here the Neapolitans live in what one writer has called a "mutual help society". From dawn to dusk they engage in countless activities in the bustling streets, working, resting, arguing, eating and doing business. Here, too, you will find another Neapolitan character, the *ramariello*, whose task it is to find the necessary funds for engaged couples to get married.

In those narrow alleyways festooned with washing and echoing with the colorful language of the seething crowds, where candles flicker before innumerable shrines and the air is redolent of the oil from the fried fish shops and oregano from the ubiquitous *pizzerie*, you can eat at any time of the night or day. Until a few years ago, you could buy two sorts of spaghetti, floating in the milky water in which they had been boiled—plain spaghetti without sauce, and spaghetti flavored with *pommarola*, the famous Neapolitan tomato sauce—all for a few pennies. Today you will buy *pizze* folded in two like a pocketbook and called *libretti*, which you eat as you stroll along the street.

Speed is the keynote of Neapolitan cooking. Food goes straight from the pan into the mouth with the minimum of fuss. What are known as *passatempi* (pastimes)—tiny dishes of seafood, miniature *pizze* and small helpings of vegetables—are eaten standing up at any time of the day, and oyster-sellers' pushcarts are to be found on every street corner.

Pizza and spaghetti are the main attractions of Neapolitan cooking. Pasta in a variety of shapes and sizes besides spaghetti and macaroni, such as *bucatini, vermicelli* and countless others, are always popular. Contrary to popular belief, spaghetti was not invented in Naples. Pasta is said to have come from Sicily, but it was in the little town of Gragnano, a few miles from Naples, that it was discovered how to dry it and keep it. Pasta is made from durum wheat flour, which is difficult to knead, and for this reason Neapolitans usually prefer to buy it ready-made. Their skill comes out in the cooking—spaghetti must be cooked *al dente* (to the tooth), which means that it must remain slightly resistant to the tooth, neither too soft nor too sticky—and in the sauce. The simplest sauce, which many Neapolitans prefer, is made with oil and garlic, but the classical accompaniment is the rich tomato *pommarola* that has made Neapolitan cooking famous the world over. Indeed, it is difficult to imagine what Neapolitan cooking could have been like before the earliest European travelers brought the first tomato seeds back from Peru, for neither pasta nor pizza can do without tomatoes.

In Italy, pizza and spaghetti are synonymous with Naples, and throughout the world they have become a synonym of Italy

Bucatini alla Principe di Napoli as served at the Ristorante Transatlantico in Naples. These delicious noodles are garnished with tongue, veal in aspic, Parma ham and black truffles, all thinly sliced. *Far right: Cannelloni alla napoletana* (see page 213) provide another delicious first course for an important dinner.

Ziti al ragù, or maccheroni in Neapolitan meat sauce (see page 211) which, though different, is just as good as the famous meat sauce of Bologna. It is traditionally prepared on Sundays in Neapolitan homes.

Squid *alla napoletana* with mussels and baby clams, photographed on the coast of Amalfi.
Below, left: Three dishes of eels accompanied by a selection of wines from Campagna, before the House of the Faun at Pompeii.
Below, right: Two delicious Neapolitan dishes of sweet peppers —stuffed peppers and *peperonata*— together with a *parmigiana di melanzane* or casserole of eggplants (aubergines) and Parmesan cheese (see page 218).

Three specialties of the Ristorante Giuseppone on the seafront at Posillipo: baby octopus, *dentice* (a large white fish), and sautéed mussels and baby clams.
Below: With the picturesque houses of Positano in the background, a superb seafood risotto which marries happily with a bottle of rosé wine from Ravello.

Every evening, thousands of lights twinkle around the curve of the Bay of Naples, among them those of the gaily decorated oyster-sellers' stands. Apart from oysters, the one below, photographed at Mergellina, sells sea dates, sea truffles, razor-shells, baby clams and mussels.

itself. Simple though this cliché may be, it delights the Neapolitans, who revel in the image of a pleasure-loving people enjoying good food and popular songs, strumming guitars and mandolins, and indulging in ancient superstitions which they cling to obstinately even today.

Over all this generous, lively world presides Vesuvius. Since the eruption of 1944, the tuft of smoke has vanished from the volcano, but the sulfurous fumes at Pozzuoli and the earth tremors at Baia—a popular resort since Roman times—are a constant reminder to the people of the volcanic nature of the region they inhabit. Pompeii and Herculaneum are the museum towns of Naples' ancient greatness. Capri, Ischia and the glorious coastline round Sant'Agata, Positano, Amalfi and Ravello, make this one of the most beautiful tourist areas in the world.

The Neapolitans, who love cooking, have the advantage of splendid vegetable gardens. Tomatoes grow everywhere, even on the slopes of Vesuvius, up to the lava and heather in sight of the crater, and local fruit and vegetables are excellent.

According to historians, the origins of the pizza go back to the Neolithic Age. With the arrival of tomatoes in the sixteenth century, and other ingredients in the eighteenth century, the pizza became a dish fit for a king. It was offered by the Bourbons at their receptions in the Palace of Caserta, and Ferdinand IV had them cooked in the ovens of the famous porcelain factory of Capodimonte. There are an infinite number of pizza recipes, from *pizza Margherita,* created in honor of the first Queen of All

Some of the finest Neapolitan fish dishes are made with octopus, which are caught in large numbers in the deep waters of the Bay of Naples.

In the charming Art Nouveau interior of the Gay-Odin, the oldest pastry-shop in Naples: *struffoli alla napoletana*, little balls of pastry covered with honey and sprinkled with multi-colored sugar strands or "hundreds and thousands" (see page 220), and sugared almonds. These are invariably prepared at Christmas time.

Italy, and combining the colors of the Italian flag by the use of red tomatoes, white Mozzarella cheese and green basil, to pizza with various kinds of fish and shellfish.

Mozzarella is one of the chief constituents of pizza. There is also a celebrated dish called *mozzarella in carrozza*, which is made by sandwiching slices of cheese between two slices of bread, coating the sandwiches in egg and breadcrumbs, and frying them in hot olive oil.

Fish has an important place in Neapolitan cooking, either on its own, or with pasta and rice. In Posillipo, octopus is cooked with garlic, olives, capers, parsley and oil, in hermetically sealed earthenware pots. In the tiny harbor of Santa Lucia they serve the celebrated *polpi alla luciana*, cooked in earthenware pans with peppers and tomatoes. Mussels, baby clams and squid provide the raw materials for many splendid dishes.

The wines of Naples deserve a chapter on their own. Tourists are rarely aware that the wines they are being offered are the same as those served in ancient Rome. The best come from Capri and Ischia. White Capri should be drunk with fish, and is considered by experts to be one of the best in Italy. It improves with age up to five years. Ischia has white Piedimonte, red and white Epomeo and Forio d'Ischia. White, red and rosé Ravello are found along the coast of Amalfi, and red Gragnano on the Sorrento peninsula. The famous Falerno, used by the ancient Romans to accompany banquets which lasted for days, is still produced in Campi Flegrei. Amber-colored Lacrima Christi comes from vineyards on the slopes of Vesuvius stretching from Resina to Torre del Greco, and Asprinto, which should be drunk as soon as it is made, is produced in the hinterland of Caserta.

Mozzarella in Carrozza
Fried Mozzarella Sandwiches

US		UK
	olive oil for deep-frying	
3	eggs	3
2–3 tablespoons	milk	2 tablespoons
	salt	
1	sandwich loaf, about 1 pound	1
about 1½ pounds	Mozzarella cheese	about 1½ pounds
	flour	

Heat a large pan of olive oil for deep-frying. Beat the eggs with the milk and a pinch of salt. Cut the bread into 24 slices, removing all crusts. Trim each slice into a triangle and round off the corners. Cut the Mozzarella into 12 slices, matching the shape and size of the bread slices as nearly as possible. Sandwich a slice of Mozzarella between two slices of bread. Dust lightly with flour and drop each sandwich into the beaten eggs. Deep-fry, two or three at a time, until golden brown on both sides. Take from the pan with a perforated spoon and drain on paper towels. Serve immediately.
Serves 6.

Fritto di Mozzarella
Fried Mozzarella Cheese

US		UK
	olive oil for deep-frying	
3	eggs	3
	salt	
12 slices	Mozzarella or Scamorza cheese, ½ inch thick – about 1½ pounds	12 slices
	flour	
	fine dry breadcrumbs	

Heat plenty of olive oil in a deep pan. Beat the eggs with a pinch of salt. Coat the slices of cheese with flour, dip them in the beaten eggs, roll in breadcrumbs and then dip once again in beaten eggs. Drop a few at a time into the hot oil. As soon as the cheese is golden brown, take it from the pan with a perforated spoon and drain on paper towels. Serve immediately.
Serves 6.

Taralli
Baked Pastry Rings with Fennel

US		UK
1½ cakes	compressed (fresh) yeast	1 ounce
1 cup	lukewarm water	scant ½ pint
3 cups	all-purpose (plain) flour	12 ounces
½ teaspoon	salt	½ teaspoon
2½ teaspoons	fennel seeds	2 teaspoons

Prepare a dough with the yeast, water, flour and salt, following the directions given for Neapolitan Pizza below. It should be rather soft.
Divide the dough into 24 pieces. Roll into small "sausages" about ½ inch thick. Shape each sausage into a ring, closing the ends firmly together. Arrange them on a floured baking sheet and leave to rise in a warm place for about 2 hours.
Sprinkle the rings with fennel seeds and bake in a moderate oven (375°F. Mark 4) for about 1 hour. They must be crisp.
Makes 24 rings.

Panzarotti
Neapolitan Fried Turnovers

US		UK
Pastry		
4 cups	all-purpose (plain) flour	1 pound
1 teaspoon	salt	1 teaspoon
4 tablespoons	lard	2 ounces
2	egg yolks – optional	2
Filling		
½ pound	Mozzarella cheese, diced	½ pound
¼ pound	smoked Provola cheese *or*	¼ pound
½ pound	Ricotta cheese	½ pound
1 cup	grated Parmesan cheese	¼ pound
2	eggs	2
2–3 sprigs	parsley, finely chopped	2–3 sprigs
	salt and pepper	
2	egg whites	2
	oil or lard for deep-frying	

Pastry
Sift the flour and salt into a bowl, cut in the lard and rub it in finely. Add the egg yolks, mix well, then add enough water to make a firm, pliable dough. Knead vigorously for 30 minutes, shape into a ball and leave to rest for 30 minutes, covered with a cloth. Roll out slightly, re-form into a ball and knead again for 10 minutes. Put aside.

Put the filling ingredients into a bowl and mix thoroughly, adding salt and pepper to taste.
Roll the pastry out into a very thin sheet and cut into rounds about 3 inches in diameter. Put a little of the filling on each round and fold over to form half-moons. Beat the egg whites very slightly and brush each half-moon of pastry; seal tightly.
Heat plenty of oil and deep-fry the pastries, a few at a time, until golden brown. Take them out with a perforated spoon, drain on paper towels and serve very hot.
Serves 6.

Pizza alla Napoletana
Neapolitan Pizza

The following ingredients – dough and filling – will make one large pizza 12 by 14 inches, or two or four smaller ones.

US		UK
Dough		
1½ cakes	compressed (fresh) yeast	1 ounce
about 1 cup	lukewarm water	scant ½ pint
4 cups	all-purpose (plain) flour	1 pound
1 teaspoon	salt	1 teaspoon
Filling		
½ pound	peeled ripe or canned tomatoes	½ pound
½ pound	Mozzarella cheese, diced	½ pound
6	anchovy fillets, chopped	6
4 teaspoons	finely chopped oregano or marjoram, or to taste	3 teaspoons
	pepper – optional	
	olive oil	

Dough
Dissolve the yeast in the water. Add enough of the flour to make a soft, smooth dough, cover the bowl and leave in a warm place to rise, about 30 minutes. Sift the remaining flour and salt together and make a well in the middle. Fill it with the risen dough and mix well. Knead vigorously, adding a little more water if necessary, until the dough is smooth and elastic. Roll into a ball, place in a large

bowl and leave covered with a damp cloth in a warm place for about 2 hours, or until the dough has doubled its bulk. If desired, it may be divided into two or four pieces before being left to rise.

In Italy, pizzas are baked in a brick oven heated by faggots. When this is not possible, pre-heat a gas or electric oven until very hot (475°F. Mark 8) before baking the pizza.

When the dough has risen, flatten it down lightly with a rolling pin and then place it on a well-oiled rectangular baking pan, about 12 by 14 inches. Push the dough evenly with the fingers until it is stretched to cover the bottom of the pan. (If making more than one pizza, use smaller pans but otherwise proceed in the same manner.) The edges of the pizza should be slightly thicker than the middle, and none of it should be thicker than ¼ inch.

Either canned or fresh tomatoes may be used in a pizza, finely chopped and drained of excess liquid.

Make tiny depressions on the surface of the dough with the fingers. Spread with the tomatoes, Mozzarella cheese and anchovy fillets, and sprinkle with oregano and pepper (no salt) to taste, and a little olive oil.

Place in the hottest part of the oven. Bake a whole pizza for about 30 minutes, and smaller ones for 15 to 20 minutes. Serve at once, otherwise the pizza will toughen as it cools.

Fillings for Pizzas — sufficient for 1 large pizza or 2 or 4 smaller ones

Pizza alla Romana — Roman-style Pizza

US		UK
½ pound	Mozzarella cheese, diced	½ pound
5 tablespoons	grated Parmesan cheese	4 tablespoons
⅓ cup plus 2 tablespoons	olive oil	8 tablespoons
8 leaves	basil, finely chopped	8 leaves
	pepper — optional	

Pizza alla Siciliana — Sicilian-style Pizza

US		UK
14-ounce can	Italian peeled tomatoes, drained and chopped	14-ounce can
2 tablespoons	capers	1½ tablespoons
4 large	anchovy fillets, chopped	4 large
12–18	black olives, pitted	12–18
5 tablespoons	olive oil	4 tablespoons
	pepper — optional	

Pizza Aglio e Olio — Pizza with Garlic and Olive Oil

US		UK
2–4 cloves	garlic, finely chopped	2–4 cloves
2 sprigs	parsley or oregano, finely chopped	2 sprigs
	salt	
⅓ cup plus 2 tablespoons	olive oil	8 tablespoons
	pepper — optional	

Pizza Aglio, Olio e Pomodoro — Pizza with Garlic, Olive Oil and Tomatoes

US		UK
14-ounce can	Italian peeled tomatoes, drained and chopped	14-ounce can
2 sprigs	parsley or oregano, finely chopped	2 sprigs
2–4 cloves	garlic, finely chopped	2–4 cloves
⅓ cup plus 2 tablespoons	olive oil	8 tablespoons
	salt and pepper	

Pizza Margherita — Tomato and Mozzarella Pizza

US		UK
½ pound	tomatoes, peeled, drained and chopped	½ pound
1 cup	diced Mozzarella cheese	6 ounces
6 leaves	basil, finely chopped, or to taste	6 leaves
	salt and pepper	
10 tablespoons	olive oil	8 tablespoons
5 tablespoons	grated Parmesan cheese	4 tablespoons

Pizza Quattro Stagioni — Pizza of the Four Seasons

Lay two strips of pastry over the pizza dough in the form of a cross in order to divide it into four even compartments.

In the first compartment (*Posillipo*) scatter a tablespoonful each of cooked shrimps or prawns and boiled baby squid, coarsely chopped.

In the second compartment (*Cassuola*) spread a small tomato, peeled and chopped, and top with 3 finely chopped anchovy fillets.

In the third compartment (*Margherita*) scatter a tablespoonful of diced Mozzarella cheese and a teaspoon of grated Parmesan, a small tomato, peeled, drained and chopped, and a pinch of oregano.

In the fourth compartment (*alla Romana*) put a small tomato, peeled, drained and chopped, 2 or 3 finely chopped anchovy fillets, a pinch of oregano and a small pinch of pepper.

Sprinkle the pizza with 2 or 3 tablespoons olive oil and break an egg in the middle. Season lightly with salt and bake as above.

Pizza alle Vongole o Cozze — Pizza with Baby Clams or Mussels

US		UK
14-ounce can	Italian peeled tomatoes, drained and chopped	14-ounce can
	salt	
3–4 teaspoons	finely chopped fresh oregano, or to taste	2–3 teaspoons
6–8 tablespoons	olive oil	5–6 tablespoons
2 quarts	baby clams or mussels	2 pounds
2–4 cloves	garlic, finely chopped	2–4 cloves
2–3 sprigs	parsley, finely chopped	2–3 sprigs
	pepper	

Spread the tomatoes evenly over the pizza dough, sprinkle lightly with salt and oregano, and half the olive oil. Bake in a very hot oven (475°F. Mark 8) as directed above.

Meanwhile, clean the clams or mussels thoroughly and arrange them in a pan with the remaining olive oil, and the garlic and parsley. Cook over a moderate heat until they open, shaking the pan occasionally. Then discard the shells and keep the clams or mussels warm in their liquor.

As soon as the pizza comes out of the oven, spread it evenly with the shellfish and sprinkle generously with pepper.

Pizza ai Funghi — Mushroom Pizza

US		UK
1 pound	fresh mushrooms	1 pound
2–4 cloves	garlic	2–4 cloves
10 tablespoons	olive oil	8 tablespoons
2–3 sprigs	parsley, finely chopped	2–3 sprigs
	salt	
	pepper — optional	

Wash and peel the mushrooms thinly. Slice the caps thinly, discarding stems. Crush the garlic cloves with a knife blade and sauté in the oil until brown. Discard the garlic cloves and add the mushrooms, parsley and a pinch of salt to taste. Sauté gently for about 10 minutes. Spread this mixture over the pizza dough, sprinkle with a little pepper if liked, and proceed as above.

Pizza co' Cecinielle – Fish Pizza

US		UK
1 pound	cleaned cecinielli – see method	1 pound
1–2 cloves	garlic, finely chopped	1–2 cloves
	olive oil	
	finely chopped oregano, to taste	
	salt and pepper	

Cecinielli are the small fry of fish which are so small that they do not require pre-cooking.

Clean the fish in the usual manner, removing heads, tails, etc., and wash them. Pat dry with paper towels and spread over the unbaked pizza dough. Sprinkle lightly with garlic, olive oil, oregano, salt and pepper, and bake in the hottest part of a thoroughly preheated hot oven (475°F. Mark 8) until done. Serve at once.

Pizza Rustica
Country Cheese Pie

US		UK
Short pastry		
3 cups	all-purpose (plain) flour	12 ounces
$\frac{3}{4}$ cup	softened butter	6 ounces
	salt	
2 small	eggs, lightly beaten	2 small
Filling		
$1\frac{1}{4}$ cups	Ricotta or good-quality cottage cheese	10 ounces
$\frac{1}{3}$ pound	smoked Provola cheese, diced	5 ounces
scant $\frac{1}{2}$ pound	Mozzarella cheese, diced	6–7 ounces
$1\frac{2}{3}$ cups	grated Parmesan cheese	5 ounces
4	eggs, lightly beaten	4
$\frac{1}{4}$ pound	Parma ham or salami, diced	$\frac{1}{4}$ pound
2–3 sprigs	parsley, finely chopped	2–3 sprigs
	salt and pepper	
1	egg, beaten, to brush pastry	1

Pizza has a much wider meaning in Italy than it does in the United States or Britain. In its wider sense it means pie, and to call the following recipe a pizza would be misleading for other than Italians.

Short pastry
Sift the flour on to a pastry board or into a bowl and rub in the butter. Add a pinch of salt and the eggs. Work quickly, just enough to mix the ingredients to a dough. Put aside in a floured bowl and leave, covered, for 30 minutes.

Filling
Mix the four cheeses in a bowl, add the eggs, Parma ham or salami, parsley and a pinch of salt and pepper. Put aside.

Divide the dough into two pieces, one slightly larger than the other. Roll both pieces into round sheets – sufficient to cover a 12-inch pie pan. Line the pan with the larger sheet of pastry. Spread with the filling and cover with the remaining sheet of pastry. Press the edges down firmly. Gather together the remaining ends of the pastry and roll them into a strip, like a thin cord. Press this lightly round the edges. Prick all over with a fork and brush with beaten egg. Bake in a moderate oven (375°F. Mark 4) for about 1 hour, or until the top is golden brown. Serve warm or cold.

In winter, two Italian pork sausages are added to the pie. They are first fried until brown, then skinned, and the meat crumbled and spread over the bottom of the pastry before the rest of the filling is added.

Serves 6.

Tortano
Neapolitan Savory Cake

US		UK
3 pounds	pork fat to make about $\frac{1}{2}$ pound ciccioli – see method	3 pounds
4 cups	all-purpose (plain) flour	1 pound
pinch	salt	pinch
$1\frac{1}{2}$ cakes	compressed (fresh) yeast	1 ounce
$1\frac{1}{4}$ cups	lukewarm water	$\frac{1}{2}$ pint
10 tablespoons	softened lard	5 ounces
	pepper	

Ciccioli are the crisp solid bits left over after rendering down a piece of fat pork. Chop the pork into small pieces and fry over a moderate heat until the fat is completely rendered. The small solid remains are *ciccioli* or *grattons* in France, cracklings in the United States.

Sift the flour and salt into a mound on a pastry board. Dissolve the yeast in water. Make a well in the flour and pour in the yeast. Add about 6 tablespoons (3 ounces) of the lard and work to a fairly stiff but smooth dough, adding a little more lukewarm water if necessary. Roll the dough into a ball, put it into a floured bowl and leave in a warm place to rise for 2 hours.

When doubled in bulk, punch the dough down again and knead in 2 tablespoons (1 ounce) of the remaining lard, the *ciccioli*, and plenty of freshly ground pepper. When the dough is smooth again roll it into a long, twisted sausage.

Grease a 12-inch tube (or savarin) pan with lard and arrange the dough in it. The pan should be not more than half full. Cover with a cloth and leave to rise again, this time for 3 hours. Brush lightly with melted lard and bake in a moderate oven (375°F. Mark 4) for about 1 hour. Cool before serving.

Sometimes the *tortano* is stuffed with sliced hard-boiled eggs and diced Parma ham (3 or 4 hard-boiled eggs and about $\frac{1}{4}$ pound Parma ham). Press the dough down lightly after it has risen the second time and shape it into a rectangle. Cover it with the eggs and ham, and fold it over. Bake as above.

Serves 6.

Ragù alla Napoletana
Neapolitan Meat Sauce

US		UK
2 pounds	lean pork or beef rump	2 pounds
4 tablespoons	fat salt pork, diced	2 ounces
4 tablespoons	lard	2 ounces
	salt	
$\frac{1}{2}$ clove	garlic, finely chopped	$\frac{1}{2}$ clove
3	onions, finely chopped	3
2	carrots, finely chopped	2
1 stalk	celery, finely chopped	1 stalk
$\frac{2}{3}$ cup	red wine	$\frac{1}{4}$ pint
4 teaspoons	tomato paste	1 tablespoon
$1\frac{1}{4}$ cups	Tomato Sauce – see overleaf	$\frac{1}{2}$ pint

Wipe the meat with a damp cloth and make a few incisions in it with the point of a sharp knife. Into each incision push a small piece of fat pork. Melt the lard in a large pan, add the meat and brown it all over. Sprinkle with a little salt and add the garlic, onions, carrots and celery. Cook slowly until the vegetables are lightly browned. Add the wine, bring it to the boil and let it evaporate.

Dilute the tomato paste in $\frac{2}{3}$ cup (U.K. $\frac{1}{4}$ pint) tepid water. Add to the pan and simmer for 30 minutes. Then add about $\frac{2}{3}$ cup (U.K. $\frac{1}{4}$ pint) hot water, or better still stock, and the tomato sauce. Continue cooking slowly for a further 2 hours.

Almost all Italian meals start with a dish of pasta. When this recipe is prepared, the meat is served separately and the sauce used for whatever pasta is chosen.

Serves 6.

Salsa di Pomodoro alla Napoletana
Tomato Sauce Neapolitan Style

US		UK
2½ pounds	ripe or canned tomatoes	2½ pounds
3 cloves	garlic	3 cloves
1 cup	olive oil	⅓ pint
2–3 sprigs	basil	2–3 sprigs
2–3 sprigs	parsley – optional	2–3 sprigs
	salt and pepper	
1 teaspoon	finely chopped oregano – optional	1 teaspoon

Wash, peel and chop the tomatoes, discarding seeds. Crush the garlic cloves with the blade of a knife. Heat the oil in a moderately deep pan and sauté the garlic cloves until brown. Discard them and add the herbs, tomatoes, and salt and pepper to taste. Cook for 30 minutes over a moderate heat. If using oregano, which should be fresh, add this at the last moment.

The quantity of basil used in this recipe is very much to taste. It is a popular herb in Italy.

This quantity of sauce will dress 1½ pounds pasta and serve 6.

Cannolicchi e Fagioli Freschi
White (Haricot) Beans and Noodles in Tomato Sauce

US		UK
1 pound	shelled fresh white (haricot) beans	1 pound
	salt	
3½ pounds	ripe tomatoes	3½ pounds
2 cloves	garlic, crushed	2 cloves
½ cup	olive oil	6–8 tablespoons
1 teaspoon	finely chopped fresh oregano	1 teaspoon
2–3 sprigs	parsley, finely chopped	2–3 sprigs
small piece	hot chili pepper	small piece
¾ pound	cannolicchi noodles – see method	¾ pound
2–3 sprigs	fresh basil, finely chopped	2–3 sprigs

Cannolicchi are small, curved noodles with a hole in the middle. If preferred, use a large can (about 18-ounce) of Italian peeled tomatoes plus one or two teaspoons of tomato paste, instead of the fresh tomatoes.

Cook the beans in a large pan of salted water until tender, about 1 hour. Peel and chop the tomatoes, and rub them through a sieve. If using canned tomatoes, chop them finely; dilute the tomato paste with a little water, and mix the two together.

Sauté the garlic cloves in oil in a large pan, and when brown discard them. Add the tomatoes, oregano, parsley and chili, and cook over a high heat until the sauce is thick. Drain the beans and stir them into the tomato sauce. Simmer for 10 minutes.

In another large pan of salted water boil the noodles until tender but still firm – *al dente*. Drain and add to the beans. Stir gently and simmer for 5 minutes longer. Remove the piece of chili, sprinkle with basil and leave for 2 minutes (off the heat) before serving.

Serves 6.

Linguine Aglio e Olio
Linguine Noodles with Oil, Garlic and Parsley

US		UK
1½ pounds	linguine or vermicelli noodles	1½ pounds
	salt	
3–4 cloves	garlic, finely chopped	3–4 cloves
1¼ cups	olive oil	½ pint
3–4 sprigs	parsley, finely chopped	3–4 sprigs
	pepper	

Bring a large pan of salted water to the boil. In the meantime, sauté the garlic cloves in oil until brown and discard them. Add the parsley to the same oil and simmer gently. Drop the noodles into the boiling water and cook until tender but still firm. Drain and arrange them on a heated serving dish. Dress with the oil and parsley; sprinkle generously with pepper. Serve without cheese.

Serves 6.

Spaghetti alla Caprese
Spaghetti Capri Style

US		UK
1 pound	ripe tomatoes	1 pound
½ cup	olive oil	6–8 tablespoons
	salt	
1 ounce	salted boned anchovies	1 ounce
about 4 ounces	canned tuna fish	4 ounces
6–8 large	black olives, pitted	6–8 large
1¼ pounds	spaghetti	1¼ pounds
¾ cup	diced Mozzarella cheese	5 ounces
	pepper	

Peel and chop the tomatoes, discarding seeds. Heat 4 tablespoons (U.K. 3 tablespoons) olive oil in a frying pan, and add the tomatoes and a little salt. Cook briskly for 15 minutes.

Wash the anchovies, remove their heads and tails, and wipe them dry. Pound them in a mortar together with the tuna fish and olives. Rub this mixture through a sieve and dilute it with enough olive oil to produce a medium-thick paste. Heat gently but do not let the sauce become really hot.

Bring a large pan of salted water to the boil, add the spaghetti and cook until tender but still firm. Drain and dress immediately with the hot tomato sauce, the diced Mozzarella, the anchovy sauce, and a generous sprinkling of freshly ground pepper. Stir well and serve at once.

Serves 6.

Spaghetti "alla Puttanesca"
Spaghetti with Chili

US		UK
½ cup	olive oil	6–8 tablespoons
3 cloves	garlic	3 cloves
1 pound	tomatoes, peeled and chopped	1 pound
1–2 tablespoons	capers, or to taste	1–2 tablespoons
12–16 large	black olives, pitted	12–16 large
1	hot chili pepper	1
1 teaspoon	finely chopped fresh oregano	1 teaspoon
	pepper	
3 ounces	salted boned anchovies	3 ounces
2–3 sprigs	parsley, finely chopped	2–3 sprigs
1¼ pounds	spaghetti	1¼ pounds
	salt	

The literal translation of this recipe is "as a prostitute would prepare spaghetti", *puttanesca* being a vulgar word for prostitute.

Heat the oil in a deep frying pan and sauté 2 cloves garlic, crushed, until browned. Discard them and add the remaining garlic clove, finely chopped, the tomatoes, capers, olives, chili, oregano and a little freshly ground pepper. Cook over a brisk heat for 20 minutes.

Wash the anchovies and remove their heads and tails. Cut the anchovies into small pieces and add them to the sauce, together with the parsley. Lower the heat and cook gently for 2 minutes. Discard the chili and add a little salt if required. If a very hot sauce is preferred, chop the chili finely and return it to the sauce.

Bring a large pan of salted water to the boil, and cook the spaghetti until tender. Drain and dress with the sauce. Serve hot.

Serves 6.

Maccheroni alle Alici Freschi
Noodles and Fresh Anchovies

US		UK
1 pound	fresh anchovies	1 pound
	salt	
4 large	ripe tomatoes	4 large
⅔ cup	olive oil	¼ pint
2 cloves	garlic, crushed	2 cloves
	pepper	
2–3 sprigs	parsley, finely chopped	2–3 sprigs
1¼ pounds	maccheroni noodles — see method	1¼ pounds

Maccheroni are spaghetti-like noodles but much thicker, with a hole through the middle like macaroni.

Other small fish such as smelts can be used instead of anchovies when these are not available.

Clean the anchovies, cut off their heads and remove their backbones. Cut them in half, wash them in salted water and wipe them on paper towels.

Peel and chop the tomatoes, discarding seeds. Heat the olive oil, sauté the garlic cloves until brown and discard them. Add the tomatoes and anchovies, and cook for 5 minutes. Add 3 or 4 tablespoons water, a pinch of salt and pepper, and the parsley. Raise the heat and cook for 5 minutes.

Bring a large pan of salted water to the boil. Break the noodles into 3-inch lengths. Cook briskly until just tender and drain well. Cover the bottom of a casserole with half the noodles, add half the anchovy and tomato sauce, cover with the remaining noodles and spread with the remaining sauce. Cover the pan and cook over a low heat for 2 minutes. Serve immediately.

Serves 6.

Vermicelli con le Vongole (o le Cozze) in Bianco
Noodles with Baby Clams or Mussels

US		UK
3½–4 quarts	baby clams or mussels	3½–4 pounds
	salt	
	olive oil	
3 cloves	garlic	3 cloves
2–3 sprigs	parsley, finely chopped	2–3 sprigs
	pepper	
1¼ pounds	vermicelli or spaghetti	1¼ pounds
	Neapolitan Meat Sauce — optional	

Thoroughly scrub the clams (or mussels) and leave them for 1 hour in a bowl with plenty of heavily salted water. Wash them several times under running water and wipe them until they are clean and shining.

Put 2 or 3 tablespoons olive oil in a large pan, and sauté 2 cloves garlic, crushed, until brown. Discard the garlic, add the clams and cook covered for 5 minutes, shaking the pan occasionally. Those clams which do not open should be thrown away. Take the pan from the heat and remove the clams from their shells. Put them all into a bowl with their liquor. Wait until all the liquor has fallen to the bottom of the bowl, then strain it.

Heat ½ cup (U.K. 6 to 8 tablespoons) oil, add the remaining garlic, chopped, and as soon as this is golden add the clams with their liquor, the parsley and a good sprinkling of freshly ground pepper. Cook over a low heat for 2 minutes – no longer, as the clams will become tough.

Bring plenty of salted water to the boil, add the vermicelli and cook until just tender. Drain well and dress with the sauce. Serve without cheese. If liked, however, a cup of hot Neapolitan Meat Sauce (page 211) may be added just before serving.

Serves 6.

Fusilli alla Vesuviana
Noodles with Tomato and Cheese, Vesuvius Style

US		UK
1¼ pounds	fusilli noodles — see method	1¼ pounds
1 pound	ripe tomatoes	1 pound
½ cup	olive oil	6–8 tablespoons
	finely chopped basil, to taste	
1 teaspoon	finely chopped oregano	1 teaspoon
	salt	
1 cup	diced Mozzarella cheese	6 ounces
¾ cup	grated Pecorino or Parmesan cheese	3 ounces
	pepper	

Fusilli are noodles which look like pulled-out watch springs or coils. Any similar noodles may, of course, be used as a substitute.

Chop the tomatoes (without peeling them), squeeze out the seeds and discard them. Heat the olive oil in a frying pan, add the tomatoes, herbs and a little salt, and cook briskly for 15 minutes.

Bring a large pan of salted water to the boil. Add the noodles, stir and cook until just tender. Drain thoroughly and put into a casserole. Stir in the tomato sauce, the Mozzarella and Pecorino or Parmesan cheese. Mix well and cook over a low heat until the two cheeses have melted. Sprinkle with freshly ground pepper and serve immediately.

Serves 6.

Cannelloni alla Napoletana
Neapolitan Cannelloni

US		UK
Dough		
3 cups	all-purpose (plain) flour	12 ounces
3	eggs	3
	salt	
4½ pounds	ripe tomatoes	4½ pounds
½ cup	olive oil	6–8 tablespoons
	salt	
	finely chopped basil, to taste	
¾ pound	Mozzarella cheese, diced	¾ pound
4–6	anchovy fillets, chopped	4–6
¾ cup	grated Parmesan cheese	3 ounces

Dough

Prepare the dough with the ingredients above, following the directions for Egg Pasta on page 106. Roll it out and leave it to dry for 20 to 30 minutes. The dough must not become too dry or it will be too brittle to cut. Cut into 2½-inch squares.

Bring a large pan of salted water to the boil and cook the squares, a batch at a time, until tender but still firm. Drain and cool on a well-wrung-out cloth, each square separate from the other.

Peel and chop the tomatoes, discarding seeds. Heat the olive oil in a heavy pan, add the tomatoes, season lightly with salt and cook over a high heat for 20 minutes. Rub half the tomatoes through a sieve and flavor with basil. Put aside for later use.

Put a little of the unsieved tomato on to each square of pasta. Add a little Mozzarella, anchovy and a sprinkling of Parmesan cheese. Roll each square of pasta like a small pancake to enclose the filling, and arrange the rolls in one layer in a shallow baking dish. Cover with the sieved tomatoes and the rest of the Parmesan cheese, and bake in a moderate oven (375°F. Mark 4) for about 20 minutes. Serve the *cannelloni* as soon as they are taken from the oven.

Serves 6.

Peperoni Imbottiti alla Napoletana
Stuffed Sweet Peppers Neapolitan Style

US		UK
6 large	yellow sweet peppers	6 large
	olive oil	
1 clove	garlic, finely chopped	1 clove
3 large	ripe tomatoes, peeled, seeded and chopped	3 large
1½–2½ tablespoons	capers	1–2 tablespoons
6–8 large	black olives, pitted and chopped	6–8 large
3–4 large	anchovy fillets	3–4 large
1 teaspoon	finely chopped oregano	1 teaspoon
	pepper and salt	
½ pound	maccheroncini noodles – see method	½ pound

Maccheroncini are short, thick, hollow noodles like macaroni.

Wipe the peppers with a damp cloth and slice off the tops to use later as "lids". Discard cores and seeds.

Heat 5 tablespoons (U.K. 4 tablespoons) olive oil and sauté the garlic until golden. Add the tomatoes and cook over a brisk heat for 10 minutes. Take the pan from the heat and stir in the capers, olives, anchovies, oregano and a good sprinkling of freshly ground pepper.

Bring plenty of salted water to the boil and cook the noodles until just tender. Drain and mix with the tomato sauce.

Fill the peppers with the noodle mixture, cover with their tops and arrange them upright in a shallow casserole. Sprinkle with about ½ cup (U.K. 6 to 8 tablespoons) olive oil and bake in a moderate oven (375°F. Mark 4) for about 45 minutes, or until the peppers are soft but still retain their shape.

Serves 6.

Lasagne di Carnevale
Noodle and Cheese Pie, or Carnival Lasagne

US		UK
1 pound	lasagne noodles	1 pound
	salt	
½ pound	Italian pork sausages	½ pound
3½–4 cups	Neapolitan Meat Sauce – page 211	1½ pints
	butter	
2 cups	Ricotta or good-quality cottage cheese	1 pound
1⅔ cups	grated Parmesan cheese	5 ounces
2	eggs	2
	salt and pepper	
½ pound	Mozzarella cheese, sliced	½ pound

Cook the lasagne noodles in a large pan of salted water, a few pieces at a time, and when tender but still firm, drain them and spread them out to dry on a damp cloth.

Prick the sausages and fry them without any additional fat until brown. Add 2 or 3 tablespoons water and continue cooking for 15 minutes. Take the sausages from the pan, skin them and crumble the meat.

Heat the sauce with 2 tablespoons (1 ounce) butter.

Beat the Ricotta in a bowl with half the Parmesan cheese, 2 eggs, a pinch of salt and a little pepper. Spread a little of this mixture over all but 4 or 5 pieces of lasagne.

Grease a baking dish, approximately 12 by 14 inches in diameter, with butter and line the bottom with the Ricotta-spread lasagne. Cover with a thin layer of sausage, a few slices of Mozzarella, a few tablespoonfuls of the sauce and a generous sprinkling of Parmesan cheese. Continue until all these ingredients are used up, reserving a few tablespoons of sauce, the last layer being of plain lasagne. Spread with the remaining sauce and dot with slivers of butter. Bake in a moderate oven (375°F. Mark 4) for 45 minutes. Serve the lasagne very hot in the same dish.

Serves 6.

Sartù di Riso alla Napoletana
Neapolitan Rice Timbale

US		UK
Meat balls		
½ pound	ground (UK minced) lean beef	½ pound
1⅓ cups	soft breadcrumbs	2 ounces
2½ tablespoons	grated Parmesan cheese	2 tablespoons
2–3 sprigs	parsley, finely chopped	2–3 sprigs
	salt and pepper	
1–2	eggs	1–2
	flour	
	oil for deep-frying	
1¼ cups	Neapolitan Meat Sauce – page 211	½ pint
Filling		
2½ tablespoons	olive oil	2 tablespoons
2–3 slices	streaky bacon, diced	2–3 slices
2 cups	shelled green peas	½ pound
	salt	
5 small	Italian pork sausages	5 small
2	chicken livers, chopped	2
2½ tablespoons	dry white wine	2 tablespoons
Rice mixture		
6 cups	beef stock	2½ pints
8 tablespoons	Neapolitan Meat Sauce–page 211	6 tablespoons
2½ cups	risotto rice–see page 66	1 pound
¾ cup	grated Parmesan cheese	3 ounces
2	eggs, well beaten	2
	pepper	
	oil and fine dry breadcrumbs	
½ pound	Mozzarella cheese, diced	½ pound
¼ pound	Parma ham, sliced	¼ pound
2	hard-boiled eggs, sliced	2
1 ounce	dried mushrooms, soaked and chopped	1 ounce
	butter and breadcrumbs, to garnish	

Recipes for this famous rice dish, sometimes called *timballo di riso*, are many and varied. As the recipe is a little complicated, the ingredients have been kept distinctly separate for easier preparation and cooking in stages.

Brush a 5-pint (U.K. 4-pint) mold (mould) 8 to 10 inches in diameter with oil and sprinkle lightly with breadcrumbs. Put aside.

Meat balls

Put the beef, breadcrumbs, Parmesan, parsley, salt and pepper in a bowl, and knead well by hand until thoroughly mixed. Add 1 egg, mix well, and add the second egg only if the mixture is still not completely blended and of a medium-soft consistency. Break off small pieces the size of large cherries, roll them into balls and coat them lightly with flour. Deep-fry in oil until golden brown, but take care not to let them become too dark. Drop the meat balls into a pan with the meat sauce, and leave simmering until required.

Filling

Heat the oil in a pan and add the bacon, peas, a pinch of salt and a few tablespoons of water. Bring to the boil and cook gently for 15 minutes. Skin and crumble the sausages. Add the sausage meat to the pan and simmer, stirring occasionally, for about 10 minutes, or until it has changed color. Stir in the chicken livers and moisten with wine. Simmer for 5 minutes. Taste for salt and put aside.

Rice mixture

Bring the beef stock to the boil in a heavy oven casserole together with the meat sauce. Stir in the rice, cover and put into a moderate oven (375°F. Mark 4) for 10 minutes. When it comes out of the oven the rice will still be slightly underdone and very moist. Stir in the Parmesan, eggs and a little freshly ground pepper. Mix thoroughly.

Spoon at least three-quarters of the rice into the prepared mold, pressing it well against the sides and bottom with a wooden spoon to make a hollow in the middle for the filling. Fill the hollow as follows: cover the bottom with half the Mozzarella and Parma ham and 1 sliced hard-boiled egg. Then add the prepared filling, then the meat balls with their sauce, the mushrooms, and finally the remaining Mozzarella, ham and sliced hard-boiled egg. Cover with the remaining rice, sprinkle the top with breadcrumbs and dot with slivers of butter.

Bake in a moderate oven (375°F. Mark 4) for 1 hour, or until a golden crust has formed on top. Remove from the oven and leave for 10 minutes to settle before turning out. Serve immediately.

Serves 6.

Migliaccio Napoletana
Neapolitan Polenta

US		UK
3 cups	cornmeal	1 pound
1 teaspoon	salt	1 teaspoon
5 pints	water	4 pints
1 pound	Italian pork sausages	1 pound
⅔ cup	grated Parmesan cheese	2 ounces
	pepper	
½ pound	pork ciccioli – see page 211 – optional	½ pound
4 tablespoons	butter	2 ounces
1 pound	Mozzarella cheese, thinly sliced	1 pound
4 tablespoons	grated Pecorino cheese	3 tablespoons

Traditionally, polenta is made in a large copper pan, but any kind of heavy pan may be used instead.

Bring the salted water to the boil and as soon as it is bubbling add the cornmeal, pouring it from a height. Stir continuously with a wooden spoon for 50 minutes, or until the polenta is thick and comes away from the sides of the pan.

Prick the sausages and put them in a frying pan with a little water. Cook them slowly until the water has evaporated, then fry them in their own fat until brown. Take from the pan, cool, skin and slice. Take the fat in which they were cooked and mix it with the Parmesan, a little freshly ground pepper and the *ciccioli*, if used. Mix with the polenta.

Rinse a large bowl and pour in the polenta. Leave until cold, then turn it out on to a board. Cut into slices approximately ¼ inch thick.

Grease a deep baking dish about 12 inches in diameter with butter. Cover the bottom with a layer of polenta slices. Add a layer of Mozzarella, spread lightly with sausage meat, and sprinkle with Pecorino. Continue in this manner until all the ingredients are used up. The top layer should be of polenta, dotted with slivers of butter. Bake in a moderate oven (375°F. Mark 4) for about 30 minutes, or until a golden crust has formed on top. Serve hot.

Serves 6.

Minestra di Erbe Maritata
Neapolitan Pork and Vegetable Soup

US		UK
¼ pound	Italian pork sausage	¼ pound
¼ pound	bacon	¼ pound
1	ham bone	1
¼ pound	pork skin	¼ pound
	salt	
1	onion	1
1 stalk	celery	1 stalk
1	carrot	1
1 small	cabbage	1 small
1 pound	Belgian endives – see page 177	1 pound
½ pound	escarole (curly endive)	½ pound
2½ tablespoons	olive oil	2 tablespoons
4 tablespoons	fat salt pork, finely chopped	2 ounces
1 clove	garlic, finely chopped	1 clove
8½ cups	chicken stock	3½ pints
	grated Parmesan cheese	

This Neapolitan soup is traditionally served on Easter Sunday.

Bring the sausage, bacon, ham bone and pork skin to the boil in plenty of lightly salted water. Add the onion, celery and carrot, cover the pan and simmer gently. As soon as the various meats are cooked, take them from the pan and keep them hot in a little of the cooking liquid.

Wash the cabbage, discard any coarse leaves and cut the remaining leaves in half. Wash the endives and escarole (curly endive) and quarter them lengthwise. Scald the cabbage, endive and escarole in boiling salted water. Drain and squeeze dry.

In a small frying pan, heat the oil and sauté the salt pork and garlic. Do not let the garlic brown. Pour the oil mixture into the green vegetables.

Heat the chicken stock. Cut the meat and green vegetables into small pieces, and add them to the stock. Simmer very slowly for 2 hours. By this time the soup will be thick, and most of the stock will have been cooked away. Serve hot, accompanied by a bowl of grated Parmesan.

Serves 6.

Fettine di Manzo alla Pizzaiola
Beef Slices with Tomatoes and Oregano

US		UK
6 slices	frying beef – about 2½ pounds	6 slices
2 pounds	ripe tomatoes	2 pounds
½ cup	olive oil	6–8 tablespoons
2 cloves	garlic, crushed	2 cloves
	salt and pepper	
2–3 sprigs	fresh oregano, or to taste	2–3 sprigs
½ cup	dry white wine – optional	6–8 tablespoons

Do not attempt to make this dish unless you have the oregano which gives it its distinctive flavor.

Beat the slices of beef with a cutlet bat until very thin, taking care not to break them. Discard any skin and sinews. Peel and chop the tomatoes, discarding seeds.

Heat the oil in a large frying pan, brown the garlic cloves and discard them. Brown the meat slices very quickly on both sides in the same oil. Sprinkle them lightly with salt and keep them warm between two plates. Add the tomatoes to the oil in the pan, season with salt, freshly ground pepper and plenty of oregano, finely chopped. Add the wine, if used, and cook over a moderate heat until the tomatoes are soft but not reduced to a pulp.

Arrange the beef slices in a wide, shallow pan, smother them with the tomatoes, cover and simmer for a few minutes only to re-heat the meat.

Serves 6.

Polpette di Carne
Meat Balls in Tomato Sauce Neapolitan Style

US		UK
4–5 cups	soft breadcrumbs	8 ounces
2–3 tablespoons	milk	2 tablespoons
1½ pounds	ground (UK minced) lean beef	1½ pounds
2–3 sprigs	parsley, finely chopped	2–3 sprigs
2	eggs, lightly beaten	2
1⅔ cups	grated Parmesan cheese	5 ounces
	salt and pepper	
1 clove	garlic, very finely chopped	1 clove
4 tablespoons	lard	2 ounces
⅓ cup	seedless white raisins (sultanas)	2 ounces
⅓ cup	pine nuts	2 ounces
	flour	
	oil for deep-frying	
5 tablespoons	olive oil	4 tablespoons
1 small	onion, sliced	1 small
1½ pounds	tomatoes	1½ pounds
1 teaspoon	tomato paste	1 teaspoon

Moisten the breadcrumbs with the milk. Put the meat, breadcrumbs, parsley, eggs, Parmesan cheese, salt, pepper, garlic, lard, white raisins (sultanas) and pine nuts into a bowl, and knead until thoroughly blended. Break off small pieces of the mixture and shape them into round balls. Roll them in flour. Deep-fry the meat balls in hot oil, a few at a time, until golden brown. Take from the pan with a perforated spoon and drain on paper towels. Put the meat balls aside but keep them warm.

In another pan, heat the fresh olive oil and sauté the onion until it changes color. Peel and chop the tomatoes, discarding seeds. Stir the tomatoes into the onion, and cook over a brisk heat for 5 minutes. Dilute the tomato paste with a little hot water, adding a pinch of salt and pepper. Stir this into the tomatoes, cover the pan tightly, and simmer for 40 minutes.

Drop the meat balls into the tomato sauce and cook them gently for 10 minutes to let them absorb the flavor of the sauce.

Serves 6.

Saltimbocca alla Sorrentina
Veal Slices Sorrento Style

US		UK
12 slices	milk-fed veal – generous 1½ pounds	12 slices
scant ½ cup	olive oil	6 tablespoons
4 tablespoons	butter	2 ounces
	salt and pepper	
¾ pound	tomatoes, peeled and chopped	¾ pound
2–3 sprigs	parsley, finely chopped	2–3 sprigs
1 teaspoon	finely chopped fresh oregano	1 teaspoon
12 slices	Parma ham, paper-thin	12 slices
12 thin slices	Mozzarella cheese	12 thin slices
¼ cup	grated Parmesan cheese	3 tablespoons

This recipe should not be attempted without genuine milk-fed veal.

Flatten out the slices of veal as thinly as possible, removing any skin or sinews. Heat 5 tablespoons (U.K. 4 tablespoons) oil and all the butter together, and lightly fry the slices on both sides. Sprinkle with salt and pepper, and keep hot.

Heat the remaining oil in another pan, add the tomatoes, salt, freshly ground pepper, parsley and oregano, and cook quickly for 10 minutes, or until the tomatoes are reduced to a pulp.

Take the veal slices and on each one lay a slice of ham and one of Mozzarella. Spread with a tablespoonful of tomato sauce and a generous sprinkling of Parmesan cheese. Arrange the veal slices in one layer in a shallow baking dish and bake in a hot oven (425°F. Mark 6) until the cheese has melted.

Serves 4 to 6.

Lombatine di Maiale alla Napoletana
Loin of Pork Neapolitan Style

US		UK
½ cup	olive oil	6 tablespoons
1 clove	garlic, crushed	1 clove
6 slices	pork, cut from the loin	6 slices
	salt and pepper	
2 large	sweet peppers	2
2 large	ripe tomatoes, peeled and roughly chopped	2 large
½ pound	fresh mushrooms, sliced	½ pound

Heat the oil in a frying pan and sauté the garlic clove until brown. Discard the garlic and add the pork slices. Brown them on both sides, sprinkle lightly with salt and pepper, and simmer gently.

Char the peppers and rub off their thin outer skins. Cut the peppers in half, discard cores and seeds, and cut the flesh into thin strips.

Take the meat from the pan and keep hot. Add the peppers and tomatoes to the remaining fat, sprinkle with salt and pepper, and cook over a moderate heat for 20 minutes. Stir in the mushrooms, cover the pan and simmer for 10 minutes longer. Return the pork slices to the pan, coat them with the sauce, and simmer for a few minutes longer to blend flavors.

Serve one or two slices of pork per person.

Petto di Tacchino alla Napoletana
Turkey Breast with Mozzarella and Tomatoes

US		UK
6 slices	raw turkey breast – about 2 pounds	6 slices
6 tablespoons	butter	3 ounces
	salt and pepper	
6 slices	Mozzarella cheese	6 slices
3 large	tomatoes, peeled and chopped	3 large
	finely chopped parsley or basil, to garnish	

Melt 4 tablespoons (2 ounces) butter in a wide frying pan. Add the slices of turkey breast and fry them until golden brown on both sides. Sprinkle lightly with salt and pepper. Place the turkey slices in one layer in a wide, shallow baking dish. Cover each slice of turkey with a slice of Mozzarella and some of the tomatoes. Dot with slivers of butter and bake in a moderate oven (375°F. Mark 4) for about 20 minutes, or until the tomatoes are cooked and the cheese has melted. Just before serving, sprinkle with parsley or basil.

This recipe can be prepared with sliced, cooked turkey, in which case the turkey should be put straight into the baking dish (previously greased with butter) without first frying it.

Serves 3 to 6.

Zuppa di Pesce di Pozzuoli
Pozzuoli Fish Soup

US		UK
4½–5 pounds	assorted fish - see method	4½–5 pounds
	salt	
1¼ cups	olive oil	½ pint
2 cloves	garlic, finely chopped	2 cloves
small piece	hot chili pepper	small piece
1 pound	ripe or canned tomatoes, peeled and chopped	1 pound
3 sprigs	parsley, finely chopped	3 sprigs
6 slices	toasted bread	6 slices

In this dish any or all of the following fish would be included: sea scorpion, gurnard, skate, dogfish, swordfish, cuttlefish, baby squid, shrimps or prawns, baby clams, mussels, etc.

Thoroughly clean the fish. Leave the small ones whole; cut up the larger fish, discarding heads and tails. Clean and chop the cuttlefish and squids. Wash and scrub the mussels and clams, and soak them in a bowl of cold salted water for 1 hour to allow the sand to fall to the bottom of the bowl.

If possible, use an earthenware pan or casserole for the soup. Add all but 2 or 3 tablespoons of the oil and sauté the garlic and chili. Add the tomatoes and 2½ cups (U.K. 1 pint) warm water, stir well, then add the larger fish. Season with salt and cook for 20 minutes, adding the smaller fish after about 10 minutes.

In the meantime, put the mussels and clams into a large pan with the remaining olive oil, cover and cook over a high heat for 10 minutes, shaking the pan from time to time to help the shells open. Add them to the soup with their shells at the last minute. Sprinkle generously with parsley and serve at once in soup bowls, garnished with slices of toasted bread.

It is vitally important that the mussels and clams be perfectly clean and scrubbed before they are cooked, otherwise any sand remaining on them will go into the soup.

Serves 6.

Zuppa di Vongole
Baby Clam Soup

US		UK
4½–5 pounds	baby clams	4½–5 pounds
	salt	
⅔ cup	olive oil	¼ pint
2 cloves	garlic	2 cloves
2–3 sprigs	parsley, finely chopped	2–3 sprigs
1 pound	ripe tomatoes, peeled and coarsely chopped	1 pound
	pepper	
	slices of toasted bread	

Like so many Italian soups, this one is very thick, and we would be inclined to call the dish "clams in tomato sauce".

Wash and scrub the clams and soak them in cold, salted water for 30 minutes to allow any remaining sand to fall to the bottom of the bowl. Rinse thoroughly in a colander under running water.

Heat the oil in a large, heavy pan and sauté 1 clove garlic, crushed, until it browns. Discard it, add the remaining clove of garlic, chopped, and the parsley, and fry over a very low heat for 2 to 3 minutes, then add the tomatoes. Season with salt, raise the heat to moderate and cook for 15 minutes. Add the clams, cover the pan, lower the heat again and cook for about 10 minutes, or until the shells have opened and the clams are ready. Sprinkle with freshly ground pepper. Serve immediately, poured over slices of toast in individual soup bowls.

Serves 6.

Insalata di Frutti di Mare
Seafood Salad

US		UK
3–3½ pounds	mussels	3–3½ pounds
1½ pounds	baby clams	1½ pounds
	salt	
	olive oil	
1½ pounds	octopus	1½ pounds
1½ pounds	shrimps or prawns	1½ pounds
1 teaspoon	French mustard	1 teaspoon
	juice of 2 lemons	
2–3 sprigs	parsley, finely chopped	2–3 sprigs
	pepper	

Wash the mussels and clams in plenty of salted water and scrape them thoroughly with a stiff brush.

Pour 2 or 3 tablespoons olive oil into a large pan, add the mussels and clams, and cook, covered, over a high heat for 10 minutes, shaking the pan from time to time. When the shells open, take the mussels and clams out, catching the liquor in a bowl. Strain the liquor and put aside.

Turn out the inside bag of the octopus and empty it. Remove and discard the eye and "beak", which is at the bottom of the bag. Wash the octopus well and beat it vigorously with a cutlet bat to tenderize it. Put the octopus into a large pan, add the strained liquor from the shellfish and cook gently for about 2 hours. Add the shrimps or prawns and continue cooking for 10 minutes longer.

Take the octopus and shrimps from the pan. Shell the shrimps and cut the octopus into small pieces. Arrange all the fish together attractively in a salad bowl. Mix plenty of oil (here the quantity is to taste but use at least twice as much as there is of lemon juice) with the mustard, lemon juice, parsley, a little salt and a good sprinkling of freshly ground pepper. Pour over the fish, mix lightly and leave for about 2 hours before serving.

Serves 6.

Polpo alla Luciana
Boiled Octopus

Clean and "tenderize" an octopus (3 to 3½ pounds) as directed in the preceding recipe. Put it into a large pan – it should fill about two-thirds of the pan – and cover with water. If living near the sea, this should be three parts sea water to one part fresh water. Bring to the boil slowly and simmer for 2 hours, or until tender. If using small octopus, they will require less "tenderizing" and be cooked in a much shorter time.

In the meantime, prepare a dressing of 6 to 8 tablespoons olive oil, 2 to 3 tablespoons lemon juice, 2 cloves garlic, finely chopped, 2 or 3 sprigs parsley, finely chopped, salt and pepper. More or less oil and lemon juice may be used according to individual taste.

Drain the cooked octopus and cut it into thin strips. Pour the dressing over it while it is still hot, and serve warm or cold.

Serves 6.

Baccalà alla Napoletana
Neapolitan Salt Cod

US		UK
2½ pounds	salt cod, pre-soaked – see page 50	2½ pounds
	flour	
	oil for deep-frying	
5 tablespoons	olive oil	4 tablespoons
2 cloves	garlic, crushed	2 cloves
1 pound	ripe tomatoes, peeled and chopped	1 pound
4 teaspoons	capers, chopped	1 tablespoon
20 large	black olives, pitted and chopped	20 large
	salt and pepper	

If using dried salt cod, soak it for at least 24 hours under cold running water, or changing the water every 8 hours, until softened.

Skin and bone the soaked cod, and cut it into 2-inch squares. Wipe them dry and coat lightly with flour. Deep-fry in hot oil until golden brown, drain on paper towels and keep hot in a baking dish in a low oven.

In a deep frying pan heat the fresh olive oil and sauté the garlic cloves until brown. Discard them and add the tomatoes, capers and olives. Season very lightly with salt and generously with pepper, stir well and cook over a brisk heat for 15 minutes. Pour over the cod slices, cover the dish and bake in a slow oven (300°F. Mark 1) for 15 minutes, or until thoroughly hot.

Serves 6.

Capitone Marinato
Conger Eel in Vinegar

US		UK
1	conger eel – 3 to 3½ pounds	1
2 cloves	garlic, sliced	2 cloves
	salt and pepper	
3–4	bay leaves	3–4
1¼ cups	olive oil	½ pint
2 cups	wine vinegar	¾ pint

Clean the eel but do not remove the head. Rinse it several times in running water and wipe dry.

Starting from the head, roll the eel round and round like the springs of a clock and place it in a non-metallic casserole just large enough to hold it. Add the garlic, a little salt, plenty of freshly ground pepper, bay leaves, olive oil and vinegar. The eel must be completely covered with the liquid. Cover the casserole and bring to the boil slowly, then lower the heat and simmer for 1 hour. By this time the eel should be tender and the vinegar will have evaporated.

Transfer the eel, still in its coiled position, to a round dish, cover with the oil and leave in a cool place, preferably for several days, when its flavor will be at its best.

Serves 6.

Melanzane a Fungetielli
Eggplants (Aubergines) Cooked Like Mushrooms

US		UK
3–3½ pounds	eggplants (aubergines)	3–3½ pounds
	salt	
6 tablespoons	olive oil	5 tablespoons
4 large	ripe tomatoes, peeled and chopped	4 large
6–8 large	black olives, pitted and chopped	6–8 large
4 teaspoons	capers	1 tablespoon
2–3 sprigs	basil or parsley, finely chopped	2–3 sprigs
1 teaspoon	fresh oregano, finely chopped	1 teaspoon
1 clove	garlic, finely chopped	1 clove

Trim and peel the eggplants (aubergines) thinly and cut them into 1-inch cubes. Sprinkle lightly with salt and leave in a colander for 1 hour to drain off their bitter liquid. Wipe dry.

Heat the oil in a deep pan, add the eggplants and sauté over a high heat for 15 minutes. Add the tomatoes, olives and capers. Lower the heat and continue cooking for about 15 minutes, or until the eggplants are soft. Add the herbs and garlic, taste for salt and stir gently. Serve either hot or cold.

Serves 6.

Parmigiana di Melanzane
Eggplant (Aubergine) and Parmesan Casserole

US		UK
3–3½ pounds	eggplants (aubergines)	3–3½ pounds
	salt	
	olive oil	
2½ pounds	ripe tomatoes, peeled and chopped	2½ pounds
2–3 sprigs	basil, chopped	2–3 sprigs
	pepper	
1–1¼ cups	grated Parmesan cheese	4–5 ounces
½ pound	Mozzarella cheese, sliced	½ pound
1	egg, beaten, *or*	1
2	hard-boiled eggs, sliced – optional	2

Trim and peel the eggplants (aubergines) thinly, and cut them lengthwise into thin slices. Sprinkle with salt and leave to drain for

1 hour on a plate set at an angle or in a colander. This will rid them of their bitter juices. Wipe the slices dry. Fry them in plenty of hot olive oil until golden brown and drain on paper towels.

Take 4 tablespoons (U.K. 3 tablespoons) of the frying oil and heat in a deep pan. Add the tomatoes and basil, and cook over a brisk heat until the tomatoes are soft and thick, like a sauce. Season with salt and pepper.

Arrange a layer of eggplant slices in a shallow, wide baking dish, sprinkle with Parmesan cheese and cover with a few slices of Mozzarella cheese; spread with tomato sauce and, if liked, either beaten egg or slices of hard-boiled eggs. Continue in this manner until all the ingredients are used up, the top layer being one of eggplant, lightly sprinkled with Parmesan cheese. Bake in a moderate oven (375°F. Mark 4) for about 40 minutes. Serve hot or cold.

Serves 6.

Timballo di Zucchine alla Pizzaiola
Baked Zucchini (Courgettes) with Mozzarella

US		UK
3–3½ pounds	zucchini (courgettes)	3–3½ pounds
	salt	
	olive oil	
4 teaspoons	tomato paste	1 tablespoon
1 small	onion, finely chopped	1 small
¾ pound	ripe tomatoes, peeled and coarsely chopped	¾ pound
2–3 sprigs	basil, finely chopped, or to taste	2–3 sprigs
½ pound	Mozzarella cheese, sliced	½ pound
3–4	anchovy fillets, halved lengthwise	3–4
	pepper	

Trim the zucchini (courgettes), wash them and cut them into slices about ⅛ inch thick. Sprinkle with salt and leave them to drain for 1 hour, then wipe dry. Fry the slices in hot oil until golden and drain on paper towels.

Dilute the tomato paste with a little warm water. Take 2½ tablespoons (U.K. 2 tablespoons) oil from the frying pan and heat it in a smaller pan. Add the onion, and when it softens, add the tomatoes, tomato paste and basil, and cook briskly for 10 minutes.

Brush a baking dish with oil and cover the bottom with zucchini slices. Spread with the tomato sauce, then cover with the sliced cheese. Arrange the anchovies in a pattern on top and sprinkle with pepper. Bake in a moderate oven (375°F. Mark 4) for about 30 minutes, or until the cheese has melted and begun to brown.

Serves 6.

Cipolle di Napoli
Neapolitan Onions

Onions cooked in this way may be served as a dish on their own.

Remove the outer skins of 12 large mild onions – all of which should, if possible, be of the same size. Insert 2 cloves into each onion and arrange them in a baking dish into which they will all fit in one layer. Sprinkle with salt and pepper, pour over ½ cup (U.K. 6 tablespoons) olive oil, and bury a sprig of thyme among them. Cover and bake in a moderate oven (375°F. Mark 4) for about 1 hour, or until the onions are soft but still retain their shape, shaking the dish occasionally. Then sprinkle the onions with 3 or 4 tablespoons Marsala and return to the oven, uncovered, to allow it to evaporate – if Marsala is not available, use a medium or sweet sherry, not wine.

Arrange the onions on a heated serving dish and discard the cloves. Sprinkle with 3 or 4 teaspoons capers and serve immediately.

Serves 6.

Peperoni Ripieni
Cheese-stuffed Peppers

US		UK
6 large	sweet peppers	6 large
	olive oil	
2 tablespoons	butter	1 ounce
½	onion, finely chopped	½
⅔ cup	rice	5 ounces
⅔ cup	hot stock or water	¼ pint
½ pound	Provola cheese, diced – see method	½ pound
4 tablespoons	grated Parmesan cheese	3 tablespoons
1 teaspoon	finely chopped fresh oregano	1 teaspoon
2	hard-boiled eggs, chopped	2
1 clove	garlic, crushed	1 clove
4 large	ripe tomatoes, peeled, seeded and chopped	4 large
	salt and pepper	

If Provola, a fresh soft cheese, is not available, use Mozzarella.

Slice off the tops of the peppers and reserve them to use later as "lids". Scoop out cores and seeds.

Heat 2½ tablespoons (U.K. 2 tablespoons) oil with the butter in a medium-sized pan, and sauté the onion until golden. Stir in the rice and when it is transparent, add the stock. Stir well and simmer, tightly covered, until the rice is tender, about 15 minutes. Take the rice from the heat and stir in the cheeses, oregano and the hard-boiled eggs. Stuff the peppers with this mixture, cover with their "lids", and arrange them upright in one layer in a shallow baking dish. Pour in a few tablespoons of hot water and bake in a moderate oven (375°F. Mark 4) for 40 minutes.

Sauté the garlic clove in ¼ cup (U.K. 3 tablespoons) oil until brown and discard it. Add the tomatoes, season to taste with salt and pepper, and cook over a brisk heat for 10 minutes. Pour over the peppers and bake for about 20 minutes longer, or until the peppers are soft but have not collapsed.

Serves 6.

Pomodori Ripieni di Riso
Tomatoes Stuffed with Rice

US		UK
6 large	firm tomatoes – see method	6 large
	salt	
¾ cup	rice	4 ounces
	olive oil	
4 tablespoons	grated Parmesan cheese	3 tablespoons
½ clove	garlic, finely chopped	½ clove
3–4	anchovy fillets, finely chopped	3–4
4 teaspoons	capers	1 tablespoon
2–3 sprigs	parsley, finely chopped	2–3 sprigs
2–3 sprigs	basil, finely chopped, or to taste	2–3 sprigs
	pepper	

Large Neapolitan tomatoes weigh about ½ pound each and are very juicy. If only smaller ones are available, increase the number accordingly.

Wipe the tomatoes, slice off their tops and reserve them to use as "lids". Pour out their juice and reserve it; squeeze or scoop out the seeds and discard them. Sprinkle the empty shells with salt.

Mix the tomato juice with the remaining ingredients, adding salt and pepper to taste. Stuff into the tomato shells – they should not be more than half-full as the rice will swell during cooking. Cover with the tops and arrange the tomatoes upright in a shallow baking dish. Sprinkle with several tablespoons of olive oil and pour in 1 cup (U.K. scant ½ pint) water. Bake in a slow oven (350°F. Mark 3) for about 1 hour, or until the tomatoes are soft but still firm.

Serves 6.

Carciofi Ripieni
Stuffed Artichokes Neapolitan Style

US		UK
6	artichokes	6
	salt	
1	egg	1
	pepper	
4 teaspoons	grated Parmesan cheese	1 tablespoon
⅔ cup	diced Mozzarella cheese	¼ pound
2–3 sprigs	parsley, finely chopped	2–3 sprigs
4 teaspoons	soft breadcrumbs	1 tablespoon
1	salted anchovy, filleted, *or*	1
2	anchovy fillets, slivered	2
5 tablespoons	olive oil	4 tablespoons

Use tender young artichokes without chokes if possible. Discard their outer leaves and cut off the stalks at the base. Scoop out chokes if necessary. Push the leaves apart to separate them and sprinkle with salt.

Beat the egg, add a pinch of salt and freshly ground pepper, and the Parmesan and Mozzarella cheeses and parsley. Mix well and stuff this mixture in between the leaves of the artichokes. Sprinkle with breadcrumbs. Press the filling well into the artichokes and put a sliver of anchovy on top of each one.

Arrange the artichokes upright in a large wide baking dish or oven casserole, well spaced apart. Sprinkle with olive oil and add a few tablespoons of warm water. Cover and bake in a moderate oven (375°F. Mark 4) for about 25 minutes, then uncover and continue to bake for 15 minutes longer, or until the artichokes are browned.

Serves 6.

Frittata con la Ricotta
Ricotta Cheese Omelette

US		UK
1 cup	olive oil	scant ½ pint
½ small	onion, finely chopped	½ small
	salt	
2 leaves	basil, finely chopped	2 leaves
¾ pound	tomatoes, peeled and sliced	¾ pound
¾ pound	Ricotta or good-quality cottage cheese	¾ pound
5 tablespoons	grated Parmesan cheese	4 tablespoons
2–3 sprigs	parsley, finely chopped	2–3 sprigs
8	eggs	8
	pepper	
3 tablespoons	butter	1½ ounces

In a small pan heat the oil, add the onion, a pinch of salt, the basil and tomatoes, and cook briskly for 20 minutes. Beat the Ricotta in a bowl with half the Parmesan, a pinch of salt and the parsley, until smooth and creamy. Beat the eggs with the remaining Parmesan, adding a pinch of salt and pepper to taste.

Heat half the butter in an omelette pan, pour in half the egg mixture and fry this until the underside is golden brown and the omelette is set and fairly dry. Place half the Ricotta filling down the middle and fold the omelette over. Slide from the pan on to a hot platter and keep hot. Quickly make a second omelette in the same manner and slide on to the same platter. Serve hot, garnished with the tomato sauce.

Serves 4 to 6.

Struffoli alla Napoletana
Neapolitan Honey Sweets

US		UK
4 cups	all-purpose (plain) or pastry flour	1 pound
8	eggs	8
2	egg yolks	2
pinch	salt	pinch
4 tablespoons	softened butter	2 ounces
	grated rind of ½ lemon	
	grated rind of ½ orange	
	oil for frying	
⅔ cup	honey	½ pound
4 tablespoons	sugar	2 ounces
¾ cup	diced candied orange peel	4 ounces
¾ cup	diced candied citron	4 ounces
6 pieces	candied pumpkin, diced – optional	6 pieces
	"hundreds and thousands" – see page 156	

This is a traditional and delicious Neapolitan Christmas sweet.

Sift the flour into a bowl. Make a well in the middle and add the whole eggs and yolks, salt, butter and the grated rinds. Mix to a smooth dough, knead thoroughly and leave to rest for 1 hour, covered with a damp cloth.

Heat plenty of oil in a deep pan. Break off pieces of the dough, roll into "sausages" roughly ½ inch thick and break off pieces ¼ inch long – in other words make small pieces of dough ½ inch thick by ¼ inch long. When the oil is very hot, add the pieces of dough a few at a time and fry them until golden. Drain on paper towels.

Put the honey, sugar and a few tablespoons of water into a pan, bring to the boil and simmer until the foam disappears and the mixture is yellow and clear. Lower the heat and immerse the *struffoli* and approximately half the diced fruit. Stir quickly and pour on to a round plate. Wet your hands with cold water and quickly shape the *struffoli* into a ring or, if easier, a round dome. Sprinkle evenly with "hundreds and thousands" and the rest of the candied fruit. Serve after several hours or, better still, the next day.

Struffoli will keep for a week or more if carefully wrapped in wax paper or foil.

Zeppole
Neapolitan Sweet Pastry Rings

US		UK
3 cups	water	1¼ pints
pinch	salt	pinch
3 tablespoons	sugar	1½ ounces
2½ tablespoons	brandy – optional	2 tablespoons
3 cups	all-purpose (plain) flour	1¼ pints
	oil for deep-frying	
	confectioners' (icing) sugar	
	ground cinnamon	

Put the water, salt, sugar and brandy (no more than stipulated or the *zeppole* will immediately darken when fried) into a pan, and bring to the boil. As soon as the water bubbles, but is not quite boiling, add the flour (the same *volume* as that of water) all at once, stirring vigorously with a wooden spoon. Continue cooking and stirring until the paste comes away from the sides of the pan. Beat it with the spoon until light and elastic, then turn it out on to an oiled marble slab or pastry board. It must be in one piece, like a ball. Beat the ball with a wooden pestle, keeping it in one piece, and continue beating for 10 minutes. As it becomes flat, re-shape it back to its ball shape.

Break off small pieces of the dough and roll them into ½-inch-thick sticks about 10 inches long. Shape these into rings, pressing the ends together firmly, and prick with a fork.

Heat plenty of oil for deep-frying. Add the rings, a few at a time, and fry until crisp and golden. Take from the pan with a perforated spoon and drain on paper towels. Serve hot, sprinkled lightly with confectioners' (icing) sugar sifted with cinnamon.

If the *zeppole* have been prepared correctly, they will be very light and "empty" inside when they are fried.

Sfogliatelle Frolle
Sweet Ricotta Turnovers

US		UK
Short pastry		
1¾ cups	all-purpose (plain) flour	7 ounces
6–7 tablespoons	granulated (caster) sugar	3 ounces
	salt	
6 tablespoons	softened lard	3 ounces
Filling		
2 cups	water	¾ pint
¾ cup	semolina	5 ounces
	salt	
⅝ cup	Ricotta cheese	5 ounces
¾ cup	granulated (caster) sugar	5½ ounces
1	egg, beaten	1
¾ cup	diced candied fruit	¼ pound
	vanilla extract, to taste	
pinch	ground cinnamon	pinch
1–2	egg yolks, beaten	1–2
	confectioners' (icing) sugar	

Short pastry

Sift the flour on to a pastry board or into a bowl, add the sugar, a pinch of salt and then work in enough cold water to make a very firm dough – the actual quantity of water depends on the kind of flour being used. Cut the lard into small pieces and knead into the dough. Continue kneading until the dough is smooth and pliable, roll into a ball and put aside until required.

Filling

Bring the water to the boil in a small pan and pour in the semolina slowly, stirring. Add a pinch of salt and cook briskly for 5 minutes, stirring vigorously with a wooden spoon. Turn into a large bowl and let it cool.

Mix the Ricotta cheese, sugar, beaten egg, candied fruit, vanilla and cinnamon together, then stir into the semolina and beat the mixture until smooth.

Break the pastry dough into 12 pieces and roll them into ovals ⅛ inch thick. Put a little of the filling on each oval of pastry, fold over and seal the edges firmly. Now, using a glass, cut the turnovers into perfect rounds, trimming off the excess dough neatly, and again make sure that the edges are firmly sealed.

Butter a baking sheet and arrange the turnovers on it. Brush with beaten egg yolk(s) and bake in a moderate oven (375°F. Mark 4) at its hottest point. The turnovers should be cooked and golden brown in 15 minutes; if not, bake them for a little longer. Sprinkle with confectioners' (icing) sugar and serve warm or cold, not hot.

Serves 4 to 6.

CALABRIA-
LUCANIA

This is one of the few regions in the world where time seems to have stood still. At almost any point along the coast, with its bare, sun-bleached rocks and incredibly blue sea, it seems possible to imagine that a Greek galley will appear over the horizon and drop anchor. The scenery of Calabria and Lucania encourages this imaginary journey backwards in time for the region bears few traces of modern life. Dozens of different races have landed on this coast: Phoenicians, Greeks, Arabs, Albanians, Normans, and Spaniards, as well as Turkish pirates, a gallimaufry of races that have all left their mark on the customs of the area. Yet the countryside itself has preserved its wild, primitive appearance which, if anything, has been emphasized by time.

The men of Lucania built their towns on high ground, far from the sea and sheltered from malaria and the raids of Turkish pirates. Until comparatively recently, the people of Matera lived in caves hewn in the rocks. Poverty, ancestral beliefs and customs, and what are virtually tribal attitudes, have prevented the population of Lucania from evolving like the rest of Italian society. Calabria has similar, though slightly different characteristics. The Apennines not only dominate the whole region geographically, they also determine the conditions of life. The Sila, a forest of oaks and pine trees, is governed by tradition, an area where austere customs and primitive craftmanship still prevail. The soil is difficult to cultivate, and consequently the tourist trade is as yet in its infancy. However, those parts of the land that can be cultivated yield splendid crops. The plains of Santa Eufemia, Sibari, Rosarna, and the arable land

Above: Morseddu, a delicious savory with bread (see page 229), is a speciality of Catanzaro. Here it is shown together with roast chicken, Ricotta, and a basket of limes.
Above, right: The regions of Calabria and Lucania take pride in their excellent cheeses and pork products. Here we see the famous *luganega* or *lucaniche* pork sausages surrounded by local country delicacies.
Below: On the green Sila plateau can be had excellent hams, roast kid, trout, mushrooms and a type of Ricotta cheese known as *abbespata*, accompanied by Cirò, a fine wine of ancient origin, and Amaro Silano, a local aperitif which is medicinal as well as pleasant.

With the Punta di Scilla (the legendary "rock of Scylla") in the background, a selection of fish dishes from Calabria and Lucania, including swordfish steaks, baked maccheroni with tomatoes, *risotto agli angeli*, spaghetti with cuttlefish ink, and tuna fish *alla marinara*.

Above, left: A sumptuous fish banquet laid out on the wide, sunny beach of the Lido di Catanzaro. *Below:* The fish from the Straits of Messina naturally play an important role in the cooking of Calabria. Some of the typical dishes of the region include fresh anchovy pie (see page 233), stuffed mussels and seafood salad.

Maratea is the home of some of the best fish dishes of the region, such as the salad of *unnatelle*—minute small fry of sardines and sprats, so tiny that they form one gelatinous mass—mussels and shrimps (U.K. prawns) *alla mariposa*.

around Reggio Calabria, are exceedingly fertile, and vegetables of the highest quality, especially sweet peppers and eggplants (aubergines), are grown here, as well as excellent citrus fruits. Almost half the world's production of bergamot comes from this region. There are also vast olive groves and fine plantations of jasmine, roses, mimosa and lavender, which supply the most important flower-essence industry in Italy. Apart from these small oases of cultivation, Lucania and Calabria are poor regions, populated largely by shepherds and, until a few years ago, brigands. And for centuries it was believed in these areas that trees were "soil robbers". They were therefore cut down ruthlessly and huge areas were despoiled and desolated in this way.

In many parts of the region, the most important event of the year is the killing of the pig, on whose products half the dishes of the region are based. The ancient Romans knew and appreciated the local sausage, which both Cicero and Martial called *lucanica*, and which is still known in many parts of Italy, such as Lombardy and the Veneto, as *luganega*. It is made with a mixture of pork spiced with black and sweet peppers and chili, and may be eaten fresh—roasted or fried—or smoked and dried.

The region offers a wide choice of sausages. The *soppressata,* so called because in order to mix the contents it is pressed with heavy weights after it has been packed, is made of lean meat and lard seasoned with salt, black pepper and sweet peppers, and packed into a pig's intestine. After this has been done, the *soppressata* is hung over the hearth to allow the hot air and smoke from the chimney to bring

it to perfect maturity. *Capocollo,* another type of sausage, is made of meat from the pig's neck and shoulder packed into a bladder and then smoked. Many people preserve their *capocolli* by soaking them in oil. Of recent years another sausage has become popular in this region. It is called *pezzente* and, as its name suggests (*pezzente* means "beggar"), it was originally eaten only by the very poor because it is made with bits and pieces from the butcher's shop, such as sinews, liver and lungs. These are all finely ground and packed together with large quantities of pepper and garlic. The local ham is excellent, and among other delicacies of the region are *cotiche,* which is pig's skin preserved in lard, and *ciccioli* (see page 229), which are given to children as a treat at the annual killing of the pigs.

Fish, though less in evidence than pork, is another ingredient of local dishes and there is no limit to the inventiveness which is displayed in its preparation. All fish dishes contain dried and ground red chili pepper, as well as black pepper, and are exceedingly tasty.

Another feature of the local cooking is the bread. Here in Calabria they still make huge round loaves, some weighing more than 20 pounds, which will last a whole family for a week. The Calabrians also specialize in a whole series of bread-like products known as *pitte,* a word derived from the Latin *pictae,* which means painted. These are "colored" with ingredients that range from tomatoes to sardines, and from sweet peppers to mixed herbs. The origin of Calabrian *pitta* can be traced back to antiquity, once the ritual food of one of the many civilizations that invaded the shores of Calabria.

Desserts in this part of Italy, like certain wines, are associated

Below, left: Some delicious varieties of dried fruit, with in the background the picturesque houses of Guardia Piemontese, a historic little village which, in 1240, offered shelter to a group of Waldensian refugees from Piedmont.
Below, right: Pigs reared according to traditional methods provide the delicious cured pork products of Calabria and Lucania pictured below.

with ancient traditions and contain a variety of delicious ingredients, such as honey, figs, almonds and dried fruits, which are exported from Calabria all over the world. *Mostaccioli*, for instance, which are of Arabic origin, are made with flour, honey and white wine (see page 236). The dough is shaped into images of saints and knights, or to look like fish, animals or baskets. These are colored and stuck on foil, to the delight of the local children.

There are many shepherds in this part of the world and there are therefore many cheeses to choose from, for the shepherds while away their time during the long periods of isolation that they spend in the vast mountain pastures by making cheese from the milk of their ewes. Among them are Caciocavallo and Pecorino, as well as small cheeses stuffed with butter, called *caciotte*.

To counterbalance the spicy flavors that are characteristic of the local cooking, Lucania and Calabria produce heavy wines with a high alcoholic content and vivid colors. In Lucania, at Barile, Melfi and Rionero, round the extinct volcano of Vulture, they make Agliatico, a red wine which, when mature, is ideal with spiced foods and roasts. From Calabria comes a wine called Cirò, which, according to legend, was favored for the festivities that took place in ancient days in honor of Bacchus along the coast near Catanzaro. This splendid wine, which has a very pleasant *bouquet*, should be drunk with the local cheese. Heavy wines, such as Greco di Gerace and Montonico, which can be kept for as long as twenty years, are to be found along the Ionic coast of Calabria. And from the western coast come two exquisite wines, Nicastro and Squillace.

Morseddu
Savory Morsels on Toast

Morseddu literally means "big bite", describing the way in which the dish is eaten, i.e. without using a knife or fork.

Peel, chop and seed about 1 pound ripe tomatoes. Slice ¾ pound liver (all the meat can be either pork or veal), and finely chop ½ pound each of heart and lung.

In a heavy pan, heat a cup of olive oil or lard and fry the meats gently until brown. Then add 2 cloves garlic, finely chopped, the tomatoes, salt, pepper and a small piece of hot chili pepper to taste. Cover the pan and cook over a moderate heat for 30 minutes.

Serve hot, spread on small squares of toasted bread. The mixture can also be used to stuff a *pitta* (see below).

Serves 6.

Cullurelli
Sweet Christmas Pastries

US		UK
1 cake	compressed (fresh) yeast	⅔ ounce
4 cups	all-purpose (plain) flour	1 pound
	salt	
2	potatoes, boiled and mashed	2
	oil for deep-frying	
	sugar	

These small sweet pastries are traditionally eaten on Christmas Eve.

Dissolve the yeast in lukewarm water and mix to a very soft dough with about ½ cup (2 ounces) of the flour. Put aside in a warm place to rise. It should become frothy within about 20 minutes.

Sift the remaining flour on to a pastry board with a pinch of salt. Make a well and pour in the risen yeast mixture. Work to a dough, adding the mashed potatoes and a little more lukewarm water if necessary. Knead until smooth and shape into small rounds. Put these aside to rise again, then deep-fry, a few at a time, in hot oil until golden brown. Drain on paper towels, sprinkle with sugar and serve hot.

Makes about 40 small pastries.

Cuzzupe di Pasqua
Easter Egg Rolls

US		UK
1½–1¾ pounds	once-risen bread dough, made with about 4 cups (1 pound) flour	1½–1¾ pounds
2½–3 tablespoons	softened lard	1¼–1½ ounces
	salt	
pinch	chili powder	pinch
6	eggs in their shells, hard-boiled	6

Cuzzupe are typical small Easter breads made in the shape of a ring, either plain or plaited, and garnished with an egg. They are usually given to children at Easter time.

Put the dough on a pastry board, punch it down and open it up to incorporate the lard, and a pinch of salt and chili. Knead until elastic, roll into a ball and leave in a warm place, covered with a cloth, for about 1 hour, or until it has risen again. Divide the dough into 6 pieces. Shape these into rings or, if preferred, pull the dough out, cut each piece into three and plait them. Make a dent in the middle, large enough to rest the egg in its shell, and push in an egg. Leave to rise again for a short time until the bread looks puffy, then bake in a moderately hot oven (400°F. Mark 5) until golden brown, about 20 minutes.

Serves 6.

Pagnottine Brusche
Calabrian Savory Rolls

US		UK
1¼ cups	water	½ pint
½ teaspoon	salt	½ teaspoon
5 tablespoons	lard	2½ ounces
1½ cups	all-purpose (plain) flour	6 ounces
4	eggs	4
1 cup	diced salami	4 ounces
1 cup	diced Caciocavallo cheese	4 ounces
	lard for baking sheet	

Put the water, salt and lard in a pan, and bring to the boil. Take from the heat and add the flour all at once, beating vigorously with a wooden spoon. When it is completely blended, return the pan to the heat and continue cooking until the paste comes away from the sides of the pan. Stir for 2 or 3 minutes longer, then take from the heat and let the paste cool. Beat the eggs in, one at a time. The paste will form air bubbles and also break apart. Add the salami and cheese, still beating hard.

Rub a baking sheet with lard and drop teaspoonfuls of the mixture on to it, rounding them off with a second teaspoon. Make sure each mound of dough is well and evenly spaced apart. Bake in a hot oven (450°F. Mark 7) for 15 minutes. The rolls should be light, hollow and golden brown.

Makes 40 rolls.

Pitta Inchiusa
Stuffed Pizza

US		UK
2 pounds	once-risen bread dough, made with 5 cups (1¼ pounds) flour	2 pounds
½ cup	softened lard	4 ounces
2 large	eggs, beaten	2 large
	salt and pepper	
	lard for pan	
¾ pound	frittoli — see method	12 ounces

Frittoli is another name for *ciccioli* (see page 211) – they are made from rendered down pork fat. As they take 2 hours to cook and become crisp, it is better to make these first unless using canned *ciccioli*.

Put the dough on a pastry board, pull it open in the middle, punch it down lightly to deflate it and then add the lard and about three-quarters of the beaten eggs (save a little for brushing the pizza later). Add a pinch of salt and a generous pinch of pepper. Knead the dough until it is elastic and smooth again, and comes away from the board. Cover and leave to rise for 1 hour, or until it is doubled in bulk.

Divide the dough into two pieces, one slightly larger than the other. Grease a 12-inch-diameter baking pan with lard. Line this with the larger portion of dough, stretching it out evenly with your thumbs and overlapping the sides of the pan. Cover with the *frittoli* and then with the rest of the dough, stretching it out in the same way. Press the edges firmly to seal them, and brush the top with the remaining egg. Put the *pitta* aside to recover and puff up, then bake in a hot oven (450°F. Mark 7) for about 20 to 30 minutes, or until an even golden brown. Serve hot.

Instead of *frittoli*, a filling of cooked spinach or other greens may be used, or fresh sardines cooked in tomato sauce, or cooked red peppers.

Serves 6.

Pizza Calabrese
Calabrian Fish Pie

US		UK
1½ pounds	once-risen bread dough, made with about 4 cups (1 pound) flour	1½ pounds
7 tablespoons	softened lard	3½ ounces
	salt and pepper	
2½ pounds	ripe tomatoes	2½ pounds
4 tablespoons	olive oil	3 tablespoons
8 ounces	canned tuna fish	8 ounces
3–4	anchovy fillets	3–4
scant 1 cup	black olives, pitted	6 ounces
2–3 tablespoons	capers	2–2½ tablespoons
	melted lard	

Put the dough on a pastry board, open it up in the middle, add the lard and a little salt and pepper, and knead vigorously until smooth and elastic. Cover and put aside in a warm place to rise.

In the meantime, peel and chop the tomatoes, discarding seeds. Heat the olive oil in a large pan, add the tomatoes, sprinkle with salt and cook over a brisk heat for 15 minutes. Drain the canned fish, and chop the anchovies and olives. Mix these ingredients into the tomato sauce, together with the capers.

Break the dough into two pieces, one larger than the other. Grease a deep baking pan 12 inches in diameter with melted lard and line it with the larger piece of dough (see previous recipe). Fill with the fish mixture, cover with the remaining dough and press the edges firmly to seal them. Brush the surface with a little melted lard. Leave to rise again until the dough looks puffy, then bake in a moderate oven (375°F. Mark 4) for a little over 1 hour, until the pastry is risen and golden brown. Serve hot or cold.

Serves 6.

Maccheroni alla Pastora
Shepherd's Noodles

US		UK
2 cups	Ricotta or good-quality cottage cheese	1 pound
	salt and pepper	
1 cup	pure pork sausage meat – optional	½ pound
5 cups	macaroni	1¼ pounds
¾ cup	grated Pecorino cheese	3 ounces

Bring plenty of salted water to a bubbling boil in a large pan. While it is heating, mix the Ricotta with a little salt and pepper, and beat until smooth. (If using the sausage meat, it should be crumbled and lightly fried until brown.) Add the macaroni to the boiling water and cook until tender but still firm.

Take a little of the water in which the macaroni is cooking and mix this into the Ricotta – just enough to make a thick sauce. Drain the macaroni, turn into a heated serving dish and dress with the Ricotta sauce, Pecorino and a little freshly ground pepper. Mix well and serve immediately.

Serves 6.

Pasta e Finocchiella
Noodles with Fennel

US		UK
1 pound	bulb fennel – see page 68	1 pound
	salt	
1¼ pounds	spaghetti or macaroni	1¼ pounds
	olive oil – optional	
	grated Pecorino or Parmesan cheese	

Wash the fennel thoroughly, cut the bulbs in two and cook them in salted water until tender. Drain, reserving the liquid, gently squeeze dry and then cut into thin strips. Keep hot.

Bring the fennel water back to a bubbling boil, add the noodles and cook until tender but still firm. Drain quickly and mix with the fennel. No other dressing is necessary, except perhaps a little olive oil. Serve with plenty of grated Pecorino cheese.

Serves 6.

Timballo di Maccheroni
Timbale of Macaroni and Eggplants (Aubergines)

US		UK
6–8	eggplants (aubergines)	6–8
	olive oil	
2 pounds	ripe tomatoes	2 pounds
2 cloves	garlic, crushed	2 cloves
	salt and pepper	
4 cups	macaroni	1 pound
¾ cup	grated Pecorino cheese	3 ounces
3–4 sprigs	basil, finely chopped	3–4 sprigs

Peel the eggplants (aubergines) and slice them lengthwise into fairly thin slices. Fry them, a few at a time, in plenty of hot oil until well-browned and drain on paper towels. Keep hot. (The eggplants should not be washed, nor salted, nor floured.)

Peel the tomatoes, slice them and put the juice and seeds into a separate bowl. Pour off most of the oil in the pan, leaving only about a cupful, and sauté the garlic cloves until brown. Discard them, add the tomatoes and stir well. Strain the juice and pour it over the tomatoes. (Discard the seeds.) Sprinkle with salt and pepper, and cook quickly for 10 minutes. Meanwhile, bring a large pan of salted water to a bubbling boil and cook the macaroni until tender but firm. Drain and mix with half the tomato sauce.

Brush a deep earthenware baking dish with oil. Cover the bottom with a layer of macaroni, followed by one of eggplants, and sprinkle generously with grated Pecorino and a little basil. Continue in this manner until all the ingredients are used up, finishing with a layer of eggplants, which should completely cover the top. Spread with the rest of the tomato sauce and sprinkle with cheese and a little olive oil. Bake in a hot oven (450°F. Mark 7) for 15 minutes to allow the ingredients to absorb the mixed flavors and to become very hot. Serve immediately.

Serves 6.

Maccheroni alla Calabrese
Noodles Calabria Style

US		UK
2½ pounds	ripe tomatoes	2½ pounds
½ cup	olive oil	6 tablespoons
1 clove	garlic, crushed	1 clove
small piece	hot chili pepper, finely chopped	small piece
1	onion, finely chopped	1
¼ pound	Parma ham, finely chopped	¼ pound
	salt and pepper	
5 cups	broken macaroni	1¼ pounds
1 cup	grated Caciocavallo cheese	4 ounces

Peel and chop the tomatoes, discarding seeds. Heat the oil in a large pan and sauté the garlic and chili pepper. Discard the garlic as soon as it browns, add the onion and cook until it becomes translucent. Add the ham, continue cooking for 2 or 3 minutes longer, then add the tomatoes. Season to taste with salt and pepper, raise the heat and cook briskly for 30 minutes.

Bring a large pan of salted water to a bubbling boil and cook the macaroni until tender but still firm. Drain and dress with a little of the sauce. Put a layer of macaroni in a hot serving dish, sprinkle with plenty of grated cheese and add about 2 tablespoons of the sauce. Continue in this manner until all the ingredients are used up, and serve immediately while still very hot.

Serves 6.

Pasta Ammuddicata
Noodles with Anchovy Sauce

US		UK
7	salted anchovies, boned	7
1¼ cups	olive oil	½ pint
3–3½ cups	coarsely grated fresh breadcrumbs	5 ounces
pinch	chili powder	pinch
	salt	
1¼ pounds	bucatini noodles – thick spaghetti	1¼ pounds

If substituting canned anchovies for the salted ones, use about half the number of large fillets, i.e. 7 or 8 fillets, and drain them well. If salted anchovies are used, wash them thoroughly to rid them of some of their salt.

Cut the anchovies into small pieces. Heat half the olive oil, add the anchovies and cook them until dissolved to a paste. Put aside but keep hot. Heat the remaining oil in another pan and sauté the breadcrumbs until golden. Sprinkle with plenty of chili and keep hot.

Bring a large pan of salted water to a bubbling boil. Add the noodles and cook them rapidly until tender but still firm. Drain and dress them with the anchovy sauce. Serve immediately, accompanied by the breadcrumbs in a separate bowl. No cheese is served with this dish.
Serves 6.

"Sagne Chine"
Calabrian Lasagne

US		UK
3 young	artichokes, without chokes if possible	3 young
1	lemon	1
4 tablespoons	olive oil	3 tablespoons
	salt	
1¼ pounds	lasagne noodles	1¼ pounds
1¼ cups	Meat Sauce – page 211 – or home-made tomato sauce	½ pint
4	hard-boiled eggs, quartered	4
½ pound	fresh Provola or Mozzarella cheese, diced	½ pound
¾ cup	grated Pecorino cheese	3 ounces

Meat balls

1 cup	finely ground (UK minced) pork	½ pound
	olive oil	
4 tablespoons	grated Pecorino cheese	3 tablespoons
1	egg	1
	salt and pepper	

Vegetable mixture

½ cup	olive oil	6 tablespoons
1 small	onion, finely chopped	1 small
1	carrot, finely chopped	1
1 stalk	celery, finely chopped	1 stalk
1 ounce	dried mushrooms, softened	1 ounce
	salt	

Meat balls
Sauté the pork gently in 2½ tablespoons (U.K. 2 tablespoons) olive oil until browned, crumbling it with a fork. Take the pan from the heat and mix the pork with the grated cheese, egg, a pinch of salt and a generous sprinkling of pepper. Shape into tiny balls the size of large peas, and fry in plenty of hot oil until well browned. Drain on paper towels and keep warm.

Vegetable mixture
Heat the oil in a pan and sauté the onion, carrot and celery until softened. Add the soaked mushrooms, squeezed dry and chopped, season with a little salt, and simmer for 10 minutes. Keep warm.

Trim the artichokes, cut them into quarters (and remove chokes if necessary). Drop them into cold water acidulated with lemon juice until they are all prepared. Drain, pat dry and sauté in olive oil for about 20 minutes. Add a pinch of salt and moisten occasionally with a few tablespoons of boiling water (or stock).

Boil the lasagne noodles, a few at a time, in a large pan of salted water. As soon as they are tender, drain them and leave them to dry on a damp cloth, well spaced apart.

Moisten the bottom of a deep earthenware baking dish about 12 inches in diameter with hot meat or tomato sauce. Cover with a layer of lasagne and spread with a tablespoon of the sauce. Scatter a few meat balls over the surface, followed by some of the mushroom mixture, a few pieces of artichoke and hard-boiled egg, diced cheese and a generous sprinkling of grated cheese. Continue in this manner until all the ingredients are used up, ending with a layer of lasagne noodles spread with sauce and sprinkled generously with grated cheese. Bake in a slow oven (350°F. Mark 3) for 30 minutes, or until the top is bubbling and golden, and serve very hot.
Serves 6 to 8.

Pancotto
"Bread" Soup

US		UK
1 pound	ripe tomatoes	1 pound
1 cup	olive oil	scant ½ pint
3 sprigs	parsley	3 sprigs
2	bay leaves	2
1 clove	garlic, crushed	1 clove
2 stalks	celery	2 stalks
	salt	
small piece	hot chili pepper	small piece
12 slices	bread, preferably home-made	12 slices
	grated Pecorino cheese	

Peel and chop the tomatoes, discarding seeds. Heat the olive oil in a large pan, add the tomatoes, parsley, bay leaves, garlic, celery, a little salt and the chili. Stir well and sauté for a minute or two, then gradually pour in about 5 pints (U.K. 4 pints) hot water. Bring to the boil, cover the pan, lower the heat and cook gently for about 30 minutes. Strain the stock and return it to the pan.

Toast the bread lightly and drop it into the hot stock. Leave for 2 minutes, then serve at once, with a bowl of grated cheese.
Serves 6.

Zuppa di Cipolle
Onion Soup

US		UK
2½ pounds	large mild onions	2½ pounds
6 tablespoons	butter	3 ounces
	salt	
4 teaspoons	sugar	1 tablespoon
7½ cups	boiling stock	3 pints
5 tablespoons	grappa, marc or cheap brandy	4 tablespoons
	slices of toasted bread, preferably home-made	
	grated Parmesan or Pecorino cheese	

Peel the onions and slice them thinly. Heat the butter in a casserole, add the onions and cook them until they are translucent and beginning to change color. Sprinkle with a little salt and the sugar, and gradually pour in the boiling stock. Cover, lower the heat and simmer for 30 minutes. Stir in the brandy and continue cooking for 5 minutes longer. Then drop in the toast and serve immediately, with plenty of grated cheese. If the slices of toast are small, allow two per person.
Serves 6.

Crocchette di Carne Arrostite
Meat Croquettes on Skewers

US		UK
1 pound	finely ground (UK minced) meat – veal, pork or beef	1 pound
	soft pith of a small bread roll	
	milk	
2	eggs	2
2½ tablespoons	grated Pecorino cheese	2 tablespoons
4 teaspoons	softened lard	1 tablespoon
¼ pound	finely chopped salami	¼ pound
2 sprigs	parsley, finely chopped	2 sprigs
¼ pound	fat salt pork, thinly sliced	¼ pound
6 large slices	toasted bread, cut into squares	6 large slices
1 tablespoon	melted lard	½ ounce

Put the meat in a bowl. Soak the bread in a little milk until quite soft and squeeze dry. Beat the eggs. Mix the eggs and cheese into the meat, kneading until completely incorporated, then add the bread. Continue kneading, then add the softened lard, salami and parsley. Knead to a firm and well-blended paste.

Break off small pieces of the meat mixture and roll into balls or croquettes. Thread the meat balls on to 6 skewers, alternating them with a thin slice of fat pork and a square of toast. Arrange the skewers in a baking pan, resting the ends on the sides of the dish to prevent the meat from touching the bottom of the pan. Trickle melted lard (or olive oil) over the top and bake in a moderate oven (375°F. Mark 4) for 20 to 30 minutes, turning the skewers occasionally. Serve very hot.

Serves 6.

Salsicce Arroste
Roasted Sausages

The sausage traditionally used for this dish is the *salsiccia lucana*, which is very long and thin, and made of pure pork.

Cut the sausages into 6-inch lengths and roll each length into a coil. Secure the coils with toothpicks. Wrap each coil separately in dampened wax paper or foil, and roast in the ashes of a hearth for about 20 minutes – a barbecue fire would be the closest alternative. Serve on slices of toasted, home-made bread.

Capretto alla Paesana
Roast Kid Country Style

US		UK
2½ pounds	kid	2½ pounds
12	pearl (button) onions, peeled	12
1½ pounds	new potatoes	1½ pounds
1½ pounds	ripe tomatoes	1½ pounds
	salt and pepper	
	finely chopped oregano, to taste	
1 cup	olive oil	⅓ pint
1 cup	water	⅓ pint
¾ cup	grated Pecorino cheese	3 ounces

This dish is usually cooked in a wood-burning oven.

Wipe the meat with a damp cloth and cut it into even-sized chunks. Put them in an earthenware casserole, and add the onions and potatoes (if the potatoes are large, they may be halved or quartered). Peel and slice the tomatoes, discarding seeds, and add them to the casserole. Sprinkle with salt, pepper and a generous pinch of oregano. Add the olive oil and water, cover the casserole and cook in a slow oven (350°F. Mark 3) for about 1 hour, or a little longer if necessary. Just before serving, sprinkle the meat with grated cheese.

Serves 6.

Capretto e Carciofi
Kid with Artichokes

US		UK
3–3½ pounds	saddle of kid	3–3½ pounds
1 cup	olive oil	scant ½ pint
2 ounces	Parma ham, finely chopped	2 ounces
1 medium-sized	onion, finely chopped	1 medium-sized
2–3 sprigs	parsley, finely chopped	2–3 sprigs
5 teaspoons	flour	4 teaspoons
1¼ cups	dry white wine	½ pint
	salt and pepper	
6 young	artichokes	6 young
	juice of 3 lemons	
4	egg yolks	4
pinch	marjoram	pinch

Wipe the meat with a damp cloth and cut into fairly even, medium-sized chunks. Heat the oil in a flameproof casserole, add the meat, ham and onion, and the parsley (reserving a little for later use). Sauté gently until the pieces of meat are golden brown. Sprinkle lightly with flour and continue cooking for a further 10 minutes, stirring carefully to distribute the flour, then add the wine. Raise the heat and cook briskly until evaporated. Sprinkle with salt and pepper, cover the pan, lower the heat and cook for 30 to 45 minutes.

Meanwhile, clean the artichokes. In Italy at the time of year when kid is available, artichokes are very young and tender, without chokes. They are simply washed, the outer leaves removed and each artichoke cut into four. They are then washed in water acidulated with half the lemon juice and added to the meat. (If such tender artichokes are not available, Italian canned artichokes would be the best substitute.) Check seasoning, and continue cooking until the meat is tender. If the sauce seems too thick, thin it slightly with stock or water, but not too much. When the meat is served the sauce should be thick and sparse.

Beat the egg yolks in a bowl with a pinch of salt and pepper and the remaining lemon juice. Add the reserved parsley and the marjoram. Pour this mixture into the simmering meat, stirring constantly. Take from the heat, cover and leave for a few minutes to allow the eggs to thicken without curdling. Serve immediately.

Serves 6.

Pollo Ripieno alla Lucana
Stuffed Chicken Lucania Style

US		UK
1	chicken – 2½ pounds	1
4 tablespoons	lard – or butter	2 ounces
4–5	chicken livers	4–5
	salt and pepper	
2	eggs	2
4 tablespoons	grated Pecorino cheese	3 tablespoons
1–2 sprigs	sage – optional	1–2 sprigs
1 sprig	rosemary – optional	1 sprig

Clean the chicken and wipe it with a damp cloth. Heat 1 tablespoon (½ ounce) lard in a small pan, add the livers and a pinch of salt and pepper, and sauté gently for 5 minutes. Chop finely.

Beat the eggs, add the cheese, salt and pepper, and the chopped livers. Sprinkle salt inside the chicken and then fill it with the egg, liver and cheese mixture. Sew up the opening and truss the chicken, or simply tie with string to keep it in shape. Sage and rosemary can be inserted underneath the string if liked. Rub the chicken with lard and sprinkle with salt and freshly ground pepper.

Put the chicken in a roasting pan into which it will fit neatly and roast in a moderate oven (375°F. Mark 4) for about 1 hour. Turn the chicken occasionally and baste with pan juices. Cut into portions and serve with pan juices.

Serves 3 to 4.

Coniglio alla Cacciatora
Rabbit in Wine Vinegar

US		UK
1	rabbit – 3 to 3½ pounds	1
½ cup	olive oil	6 tablespoons
2 cloves	garlic	2 cloves
2–3 sprigs	sage	2–3 sprigs
	salt and pepper	
2 cups	wine vinegar	¾ pint
3	anchovy fillets, finely chopped	3
2–3 tablespoons	capers	2–2½ tablespoons
2 teaspoons	potato flour	½ tablespoon

Clean the rabbit and cut it into serving pieces. Wash it carefully and wipe dry.

Heat the olive oil in a shallow casserole and sauté the rabbit pieces with the garlic and sage until brown all over. Sprinkle with salt and pepper to taste. Dilute the vinegar with an equal amount of water and pour half of it into the casserole. Cover, lower the heat and simmer for 45 minutes, adding most of the remaining vinegar, a little at a time, as the rabbit dries out.

When the rabbit is tender, transfer the pieces to a deep heated serving dish. Keep hot. Discard the garlic cloves. Stir the anchovies and capers into the sauce, and continue cooking and stirring until the anchovies are reduced to a paste. Mix the potato flour to a smooth paste with the remaining vinegar and stir this into the sauce. Bring to the boil and stir over a moderate heat until the sauce has thickened. Pour over the rabbit and serve immediately.

Serves 6.

Aringhe alla Calabrese
Herrings Calabria Style

US		UK
2–2½ pounds	fresh herrings	2–2½ pounds
	salt	
½ cup	olive oil	6–8 tablespoons
1 clove	garlic, finely chopped	1 clove
½	hot chili pepper, very finely chopped	½
12 thin slices	bread, trimmed of crusts	12 thin slices

Clean the herrings, slit them open carefully and remove their backbones. Cut each herring in two and remove all the smaller bones. Wash in plenty of salted water and wipe dry.

Heat the olive oil in a fish pan, add the garlic and chili, and finally the herrings. Sprinkle *very* lightly with salt and simmer, mashing lightly with a fork, until the herrings are reduced to a paste. Spread the herring paste on slices of bread and serve immediately. The bread may be toasted if preferred.

Serves 6.

Sarde all'Olio e Origano
Fresh Sardines with Olive Oil and Oregano

US		UK
2½ pounds	fresh sardines	2½ pounds
	salt	
1 cup	olive oil	scant ½ pint
½ small	hot chili pepper, finely chopped	½ small
	finely chopped oregano, to taste	
	juice of 1 lemon	

Clean the sardines and chop off their heads. Slit each fish open, just enough to pull out the backbone without separating the two halves of the fish. Wash in salted water and wipe dry.

Brush a baking dish liberally with olive oil. Cover the bottom with a layer of sardines, sprinkle with salt, a little chili pepper, plenty of oregano and a little olive oil. Repeat these layers until all the sardines are used up. Sprinkle the top with a little more oil and bake in a slow oven (350°F. Mark 3) for about 15 minutes, or until the sardines are tender.

Take the sardines from the oven, sprinkle with lemon juice and serve immediately in the same dish.

Serves 6.

Alici al Limone
Baked Fresh Anchovies

US		UK
2–2½ pounds	large fresh anchovies	2–2½ pounds
	salt	
1⅓ cups	soft breadcrumbs	2½ ounces
	pepper	
2 sprigs	oregano, finely chopped	2 sprigs
pinch	chili powder	pinch
½ cup	olive oil	6–8 tablespoons
	juice of 1 lemon	

Cut off the heads of the anchovies, slit the bodies open carefully and remove the backbones. Wash in cold salted water and wipe dry.

Close the fish again firmly and arrange them in a shallow baking dish. Sprinkle lightly with salt, the breadcrumbs, plenty of freshly ground pepper and oregano, a pinch of chili powder and finally the olive oil and lemon juice. Bake in a slow oven (350°F. Mark 3) for about 30 minutes, or until the fish are cooked through and a golden crust has formed on top. Serve hot or warm.

Serves 6.

Tortiera di Alici
Anchovy Pie

US		UK
2½ pounds	fresh anchovies	2½ pounds
1¼ cups	olive oil	½ pint
5 cups	soft breadcrumbs	½ pound
¾ cup	grated Pecorino cheese – optional	3 ounces
2–3 sprigs	parsley, finely chopped	2–3 sprigs
1 clove	garlic, finely chopped	1 clove
12	green olives, pitted and chopped	12
4 teaspoons	capers, chopped	1 tablespoon

For this recipe, neither anchovy fillets nor salted anchovies can be substituted. However, fresh sprats or smelts or similar small fish could be prepared in the same manner.

Clean the anchovies, slit them open to pull out the backbone but do not separate the two halves. Brush a wide baking dish with oil and coat it with breadcrumbs. Cover the bottom with a layer of fish.

Mix the remaining breadcrumbs to a paste with the cheese, ½ cup (U.K. 6 tablespoons) olive oil, the parsley, garlic, olives and capers. Spread some of this over the layer of fish, cover with a second layer of anchovies and continue in this manner until all the ingredients are used up. Pour over the remaining olive oil and bake in a slow oven (350°F. Mark 3) for about 40 minutes, or until the fish are cooked and the breadcrumbs lightly browned. Serve hot or warm.

Many cooks cover the top of the pie with thinly sliced peeled tomatoes before baking.

Serves 6.

Triglie alla Calabrese
Red Mullet Calabria Style

US		UK
12	red mullet	12
	salt	
1 cup	olive oil	scant ½ pint
	finely chopped oregano, to taste	
	juice of 1 lemon	

Clean the fish with extreme care and wash them in salted water. If they have not been scaled, do this lightly as the skin is brittle. Many people leave in the liver and entrails, but this is a matter of taste.

Pour about ½ cup (U.K. 6 tablespoons) olive oil into a shallow baking dish and lay the mullet on top in one layer. Season with salt, sprinkle generously with oregano, and pour over the remaining olive oil and the lemon juice. Bake in a moderate oven (375°F. Mark 4) for about 15 minutes, or until the fish are cooked through but still firm, and serve immediately in the same dish.

Serves 6.

Anguille Stufate
Baked Eels

US		UK
2–2½ pounds	small eels	2–2½ pounds
5 tablespoons	olive oil	4 tablespoons
1	onion, finely chopped	1
	flour	
1¼ cups	dry white wine	½ pint
1 pound	ripe tomatoes	1 pound
	salt and pepper	
2–3 sprigs	parsley, finely chopped	2–3 sprigs
1 clove	garlic, crushed	1 clove
1	bay leaf	1

Clean the eels, chop off their heads but do not skin them. Wash carefully under running water and chop each eel into pieces about 4 inches long.

Heat the olive oil in a casserole (preferably of earthenware) and sauté the onion until golden brown. Coat the pieces of eel lightly with flour and add them to the pan. Fry the eels gently, turning them from time to time with a wooden spoon. Moisten with the wine and let this evaporate slowly.

Peel and chop the tomatoes, discarding seeds. Add the tomatoes to the casserole, season with salt and freshly ground pepper, and add the parsley, garlic and bay leaf. Cover the casserole and cook over a gentle heat for 30 minutes longer, or until the eels are tender. Serve very hot in the same casserole.

Serves 6.

Melanzane sott'Olio
Pickled Eggplants (Aubergines)

US		UK
2 pounds	eggplants (aubergines)	2 pounds
	salt	
2½ cups	wine vinegar	1 pint
1–2 sprigs	basil, finely chopped	1–2 sprigs
3–4 cloves	garlic, finely chopped	3–4 cloves
½	hot chili pepper, finely chopped	½
	olive oil	

For this recipe the eggplants (aubergines) should not be too large. They must be fresh and young with good, smooth, unbroken skins. Wash them and cut off the stem ends, then cut the egg-plants lengthwise into thin slices. Sprinkle them lightly with salt, place on a rack, cover with a plate and press down with a heavy weight. Leave for 24 hours.

Wipe the eggplants dry, squeeze well and arrange them in layers in a bowl. Cover with the vinegar. Leave to marinate for 24 hours.

Arrange the slices neatly in layers in preserving jars, sprinkling a little basil, garlic and chili between the layers. Press down firmly to avoid empty spaces or air pockets. Pour olive oil into the jars right to the top and cover tightly. The jars must be airtight.

After a few days look at the jars – it might be necessary to add some more oil, as the eggplants absorb quite a lot.

They are now ready for storing.

Crocchettine di Patate
Potato Croquettes with Salami and Cheese

US		UK
2½ pounds	potatoes	2½ pounds
	salt	
3	eggs, beaten	3
4 tablespoons	grated Parmesan cheese	3 tablespoons
¼ pound	salami, diced	¼ pound
¼ pound	Mozzarella cheese, diced	¼ pound
	pepper	
2 sprigs	parsley, finely chopped	2 sprigs
1	egg, beaten – for coating	1
	fine dry breadcrumbs	
	oil for deep-frying	
1–2	lemons, quartered	1–2

Wash the potatoes without peeling them and cook them in boiling salted water until tender. Cool, peel and mash them. Beat in 3 eggs and mix thoroughly with the Parmesan and salami, Mozzarella, a generous amount of pepper and the parsley. Break off pieces of the potato mixture and shape into croquettes. Dip into beaten egg and coat with breadcrumbs. Deep-fry the croquettes in hot oil, a few at a time, until golden brown. Take from the pan with a perforated spoon and drain on paper towels. Work quickly and serve the croquettes as hot as possible, garnished with lemon wedges.

Serves 6.

Zucchine e Peperoni
Zucchini (Courgettes) and Peppers

US		UK
6 medium-sized	zucchini (courgettes)	6 medium-sized
	salt	
	olive oil	
2	yellow sweet peppers	2
5 large	ripe tomatoes	5 large
1 clove	garlic, crushed	1 clove
2–3 sprigs	basil	2–3 sprigs
6	anchovy fillets	6
12 slices	Caciocavallo cheese	12 slices

Trim the ends of each zucchini (courgette), cut them in half lengthwise and scoop out some of the pulp. Blanch the halves for 2 minutes in boiling salted water. Drain them at once or they will become soft. Brush a shallow baking dish with olive oil and arrange the zucchini halves in it in one layer.

Roast or broil (grill) the sweet peppers until they blacken and blister, then peel off their thin outer skins. Cut the flesh into long, thin strips.

Peel and chop the tomatoes, discarding seeds. Heat a table-spoon of oil in a small pan, add the garlic, a few leaves of basil and the tomatoes, sprinkle with salt and cook briskly for 20 minutes. Cut each anchovy fillet in half lengthwise.

Put a tablespoonful of the cooked tomato on each zucchini half. Add a few strips of pepper, a slice of cheese, and a piece of anchovy. Sprinkle with olive oil and bake in a slow oven (350°F. Mark 3) for about 15 minutes, or until the cheese has melted and the zucchini are slightly browned. Serve hot or cold.

Serves 6.

Zucchine Gratinate
Zucchini (Courgettes) with Cheese

US		UK
3 pounds	medium-sized zucchini (courgettes)	3 pounds
	flour	
	oil	
	salt	
2 pounds	ripe tomatoes	2 pounds
	pepper	
½ pound	Mozzarella cheese, thinly sliced	½ pound

Wash the zucchini (courgettes), trim the ends and cut the zucchini into medium-thick rounds. Dredge with flour. Heat plenty of olive oil and fry the zucchini, a few at a time, until golden brown. Take from the pan with a perforated spoon, drain on paper towels and sprinkle lightly with salt. Keep hot.

Peel, chop and rub the tomatoes through a sieve. Drain off all but 2½ tablespoons (U.K. 2 tablespoons) of the oil, add the tomatoes, season to taste with salt and pepper, and cook over a brisk heat for 20 minutes.

Heat 2½ tablespoons (U.K. 2 tablespoons) oil in an earthenware baking dish, add the fried zucchini and cover with the tomato sauce. Heat gently, stirring carefully with a wooden spoon. Take the dish from the stove and cover the zucchini with the sliced cheese. Sprinkle with olive oil and bake in a hot oven (450°F. Mark 7) for 5 to 10 minutes, or long enough to let the cheese melt and begin to change color. Serve at once in the same dish.

Serves 6.

Cannariculi
Fried Honey Cookies (U.K. Biscuits)

US		UK
4 cups	all-purpose (plain) flour	1 pound
1 cup	dry white wine	scant ½ pint
pinch	salt	pinch
4 teaspoons	granulated (caster) sugar	1 tablespoon
	oil for deep-frying	
	honey	

Sift the flour on to a pastry board, make a well in the middle and pour in the wine. Add a pinch of salt and the sugar, and work to a dough, adding a little more wine if necessary. Knead vigorously until the dough, which should be rather stiff, is smooth. Roll into a ball, wrap in a cloth and leave in a cool place for 2 hours.

Roll the dough out on a floured pastry board to a thickness of about ¼ inch. Cut into 4-inch squares. Wrap these round metal tubes or, if the tubes are not available, make little sticks of pastry about the thickness of a pencil and 2½ to 3 inches long.

Heat plenty of olive oil for deep-frying and fry the pastries until golden. Take them from the pan with a perforated spoon and drain on paper towels. If using the metal tubes, take them out as soon as they are cool enough to handle. Spread the pastries with plenty of warm honey and serve at once.

In Italy special metal tubes can be bought for making this kind of sweet.

Fichi al Cioccolato
Stuffed Figs in Chocolate

US		UK
1 pound	large dried figs	1 pound
1 cup	toasted almonds	5 ounces
¾ cup	diced candied peel	4 ounces
2	cloves, pounded, or powdered cloves, to taste	2
¾ cup	cocoa	3 ounces
¾ cup	confectioners' (icing) sugar	3½ ounces

For this recipe only the best-quality figs should be used. Trim off any stalks, and with a sharp knife cut the figs open down one side. Stuff each fig with an almond, a few pieces of diced peel and a pinch of clove. Gently press them shut again. Arrange them on a baking sheet and bake in a slow oven (350°F. Mark 3) for 15 minutes, or until they darken slightly.

While the figs are baking, sift the cocoa and sugar together into a shallow dish. Take the figs from the oven and immediately roll them in the cocoa mixture. Serve cold. The figs will also keep well in an airtight container.

Instead of rolling the figs in sifted cocoa and sugar, the same quantity (3 squares or 3 ounces) of bitter chocolate may be melted with the sugar and a tablespoon or two of water or wine. As the figs come out of the oven, coat them in this syrup and leave them to dry completely.

Fichi in Sciroppo
Fresh Figs in Rum Syrup

US		UK
2 pounds	slightly under-ripe figs	2 pounds
1⅛ cups	sugar	½ pound
5 tablespoons	rum	4 tablespoons

Wash the figs in running water and drain well in a colander. Dissolve the sugar in a casserole with about 1¼ cups (U.K. ½ pint) water. Add the figs, lower the heat and simmer, covered, for 2 hours. Turn into a bowl and let the figs cool.

Arrange the cooled figs carefully in a glass preserving jar, add the syrup and fill the jar to the top with rum. Cover the jar with a disc of wax paper dipped in alcohol and the lid, and leave for several days before eating.

Prugne Farcite
Stuffed Prunes

US		UK
1 pound	large dried prunes	1 pound
1 cup	shelled walnuts	3 ounces
5 squares	bitter chocolate, grated	5 ounces

Choose good-quality prunes for this recipe. Soak them in boiling water for 5 minutes, and rinse well. Wipe the prunes dry and make a slit in each one, just large enough to extract the pit. Push the sides of the slit apart slightly to make room for the filling.

Chop the walnuts roughly and mix with the chocolate. Fill the prunes with this mixture, close the openings and re-form them into their natural shape.

They may be served in small paper cases or, if preferred, simply piled in a pyramid on a dish.

Mostaccioli
Chocolate Cookies (U.K. Biscuits)

US		UK
$1\frac{2}{3}$ cups	almonds	10 ounces
$\frac{1}{2}$ cup	honey	5 ounces
pinch	ground cinnamon	pinch
1	clove, pounded, or a pinch of powdered cloves	1
$1\frac{1}{2}$ cups	cocoa	6 ounces
5 tablespoons	weak coffee	4 tablespoons
1 cup	all-purpose (plain) flour	4 ounces
	butter or rice paper	
$1\frac{1}{2}$ cups	confectioners' (icing) sugar	7 ounces
1	egg white, lightly beaten	1
	lemon juice	

Blanch the almonds for 1 minute and peel them as soon as they are cool enough to handle. Toast them in a slow oven (350°F. Mark 3) for a few minutes, then chop or crush them until reduced to a powder.

Put the powdered almonds in a bowl, add the honey, cinnamon and clove. Blend the cocoa with the coffee and mix this into the almond-honey mixture. Sift in the flour and knead the mixture to a smooth dough, adding a little more coffee if necessary.

Roll the dough out on a floured pastry board to a thickness of about $\frac{3}{4}$ inch, and cut out small fancy shapes – crowns, puppets, animals, stars etc.

Lightly butter a baking sheet or line it with rice paper and arrange the pastry shapes on it evenly spaced apart. Bake in a moderate oven (375°F. Mark 4) for about 15 minutes, or until just golden. Cool.

In the meantime, prepare the icing. Sift the sugar into a bowl and blend with the egg white and a few drops of lemon juice (if preferred, a few drops of liqueur may be used instead). As soon as the icing is smooth, spread a little over each cookie, smoothing it down with the blade of a wet knife.

These cookies are usually kept for some time before being eaten as they are very hard when straight from the oven. They are of Arab origin.

Torta di Noci
Walnut Cake

US		UK
$\frac{3}{4}$ pound	walnut kernels	$\frac{3}{4}$ pound
	butter and flour for cake pan	
4	eggs, separated	4
$1\frac{1}{8}$ cups	granulated (caster) sugar	$\frac{1}{2}$ pound
	grated rind of 1 lemon	
	confectioners' (icing) sugar	

Chop or pound the walnuts until almost reduced to a powder. Put them in a bowl. Grease a deep cake pan about 9 inches in diameter with butter and coat lightly with flour.

Beat the egg yolks, add the sugar and beat again until light and fluffy. Stir in the grated lemon rind. Beat the egg whites until stiff and fold a few tablespoons of them into the egg yolk mixture to "loosen" it. Beat the walnuts into the egg yolks and when thoroughly blended fold in the egg whites.

Pour the batter into the prepared pan and bake in a moderate oven (375°F. Mark 4) for about 1 hour, or until the top is firm and golden brown. Allow the cake to cool before turning it out, and serve generously dusted with sifted confectioners' (icing) sugar.

This cake is also delicious if split and sandwiched with a light lemon butter icing. It will remain moist for several days.

Torta con le Prugne
Sponge Cake with Prunes

US		UK
$\frac{1}{2}$ cup	dried prunes	3 ounces
4 teaspoons	sugar	1 tablespoon
	grated rind of $\frac{1}{2}$ lemon	
1 cup	red wine	8 fluid ounces
6 tablespoons	butter	3 ounces
$\frac{1}{3}$ cup	granulated (caster) sugar	3 ounces
2	eggs, separated	2
1 cup plus 2 tablespoons	all-purpose (plain) flour	$4\frac{1}{2}$ ounces
$3\frac{3}{4}$ teaspoons	baking powder	3 teaspoons
	butter and fine dry breadcrumbs for cake pan	
	confectioners' (icing) sugar	

Soak the prunes in hot water for about 1 hour to soften them. Slit them carefully all round the middle and remove the pits. Dissolve the first quantity of sugar with the lemon rind and red wine, and drop in the prunes. Cover the pan and simmer over very low heat until all the liquid has been absorbed. Allow to cool.

Cream the butter with the sugar and beat in the egg yolks, one at a time. Sift the flour and baking powder together twice, and beat gently but thoroughly into the butter. Beat the egg whites and fold them gently into the batter. Pour immediately into a deep cake pan (about 10 inches in diameter), buttered and coated with breadcrumbs. Arrange the prunes on top and bake in a moderate oven (375°F. Mark 4) for 45 minutes to 1 hour, until the sponge is firm and a pale golden color. The cake will rise and the prunes will sink. Turn the cake out on to a rack, dust with confectioners' (icing) sugar and leave to cool before serving.

Torta di Frutta Secca
Fruit Cake

US		UK
1 cup	hazelnuts	$4\frac{1}{2}$ ounces
$\frac{1}{3}$ cup	almonds	2 ounces
$\frac{3}{4}$ cup	dried figs	4 ounces
3 squares	bitter chocolate	3 ounces
$1\frac{1}{4}$ cups	all-purpose (plain) flour	5 ounces
4 teaspoons	baking powder	1 tablespoon
	butter and flour for cake pan	
3	eggs	3
$\frac{2}{3}$ cup	granulated (caster) sugar	$4\frac{1}{2}$ ounces
$\frac{3}{4}$ cup	diced candied peel	4 ounces

Toast the hazelnuts in a slow oven (350°F. Mark 3) for 10 minutes. Rub off their thin outer skins and chop them roughly. Blanch the almonds in boiling water and peel them. Dry them out in the oven for a few minutes, then shred finely. Chop the figs, discarding any stems, and crush the chocolate. Sift the flour with the baking powder. Grease a 2-pound cake pan with butter and coat it with flour.

Beat the eggs in a large bowl, add the sugar and beat again until white and fluffy. Mix in the nuts, figs, chocolate and peel, and finally beat in the flour lightly but thoroughly. Pour the mixture into the prepared pan and bake in a slow oven (350°F. Mark 3) for 45 minutes, or until the cake is golden brown and tests done. Do not open the oven door for the first 30 minutes so that the cake will rise properly. Leave to cool slightly, then turn out on to a rack and allow to become quite cold before serving.

APULIA

A rich selection of vegetables
photographed at a typical *masseria*,
or farmstead, in the Tavoliere.
These products are justly renowned
for their fine flavor and freshness.

A typical dinner in Bari starts with a magnificent variety of hors d'oeuvre: tomatoes, eggplants (aubergines), beans, locally grown onions with a slightly bitter flavor, known as *lampasciuni*, mushrooms, lupin seeds, pickled fruits, and sausages, octopus and mussels.

The landscape of Apulia contrasts vividly with that of the Po Valley. Here we are unmistakably in the south. The sun blazes down on sparse vegetation, caused not only by the climate but even more through the fault of man, who for centuries has waged a war against plants, cutting them down senselessly as if he loathed their shade.

A hundred years ago, shepherds ruled the countryside of Apulia. Then wheat was sown, and the region now resembles a huge tablecloth of green and gold. Within this greenery the vegetables of Apulia are to be found, especially fine in the area around Tavoliere—turnip tops, cauliflowers, green, red and Savoy cabbages, broccoli, onions, eggplants (aubergines), beans, sweet peppers and tomatoes—the raw materials of a cuisine which consists essentially of a mixture of pasta and vegetables.

The Apulians are the champion pasta eaters of Italy. In addition to the usual noodles and lasagne, they have a number of their own: *orecchiette*, made with semolina worked into a thick stick and cut into small pieces, which are then squashed with the thumb to look like small shells; *minuicchi*, small gnocchi made with flour dough; and *laganelle*, small stuffed lasagne. Macaroni is, of course, very popular, and cooked in several ways. The pasta dough is also used to make several kinds of *pizze* and small pies. One of these is *panzarotti* (see page 245), a wrapping of dough filled with Ricotta, Mozzarella or onions according to taste.

Fish and shellfish are both abundant and varied in Apulia. Some are caught by fleets of trawlers or by offshore fishermen, others are "cultivated" in inland catchments and between piers in structures resembling glasshouses. In Taranto, for example, oysters and other mollusks spawn in the very heart of the city in the Mar Piccolo and Mar Grande, where they remain for eighteen months until they have fully matured. These, incidentally, are the oysters served in many an expensive Italian restaurant, but here they are eaten raw with only a squeeze of lemon. Another favorite dish, a specialty of Bari, is *polpi arricciati* (curled octopus). *Triglie coi baffi* (red mullet) is enjoyed in Polignano, and fish soups, stuffed mussels and squid stew are other delicacies of this culinary-conscious region.

Apulian cooking is of a simple nature, giving the housewife a fair amount of work, but also much satisfaction because of the excellence of her raw materials. Meals often revolve around one main dish, perhaps some pasta and vegetables, a tasty dish of fish, a *coratella* or lamb's fry roasted on skewers, or even just a *stuzzica appetito*, an hors d'oeuvre of vegetables pickled in vinegar or olive oil. Like Tuscany, Apulia owes much to the quality of its olive oil. This being a region where almonds grow as well as olives, the oil has a distinct aroma of bitter almonds. The finest comes from the district of Bitonto, Andria Barletta and Molfetta, and is a bright golden color with streaks of green.

Cheese plays a leading role in the cooking of the region. Provole di bufala, Mozzarella, Scamorza, Bocconcini di latte di vacca, fresh Ricotta and Caciocavallo are used to flavor many of its splendid dishes, as well as being delicious to eat on their own.

Tempting yet simple fare displayed before the early thirteenth-century castle of Frederick of Swabia: Ricotta cheese, a dish of chicken *alla Federico*, braised turnip tops, sausages, and spaghetti with olive oil and garlic.

Right: The impressive panorama of Polignano, with its culinary specialties: shellfish hors d'oeuvre, baked *saragno* (a kind of porgy or sheepshead), red mullet and shrimps (U.K. prawns) on the spit, and octopus fisherman's style.
Below: The cooking of Barletta is robust and full of flavor, in keeping with its generous wines: skewered meats, ragoût of kid and hare, Canosa mushrooms, and baked noodles, photographed in the Cantina al Fieramosca.

Traditional dishes in the fairy-tale country of the *trulli* (beehive dwellings) at Alberobello: baked lamb with potatoes and tomatoes (see page 247), little pasta shells called *orecchiette* with green Apulian cauliflower, beans, turnip tops and the classic *capuzzedde*, or lambs' heads.
Below, left: By the Well of the Seminary at Lecce: Pecorino cheese with raw beans and radishes, *orecchiette* with tomato sauce (see page 247), *pizza rustica* and meat kebabs.

Typical Apulian sweetmeats,
in the lovely setting of the
caves at Castellana.
Below: A collection of dishes from
the Daunia area—pasta, lamb,
mushrooms in breadcrumbs,
potato pie and sweet
pastries—photographed before
the Romanesque church of San
Leonardo, near Manfredonia.

Apulia is one of the richest wine-growing regions of Italy. The heavy wines of Cerignola, Squinzano, Canosa, Andria and Barletta are widely used for blending and improving many other Italian wines on account of their body and high alcoholic content. Sansavere del Tavoliere (a dry, straw-colored white wine) is a local specialty, as is Santo Stefano, a bright red wine from the same district. Torre Quarto comes from the area round Cerignola, Primitivo, a red wine, is produced in Gioia del Colle, and a variety of wines, red, white and rosé, come from Castel del Monte. Malmsley, Aleatico and Muscatel conclude this list, which is by no means a complete one, for every village prides itself on producing a wine of distinction.

Calzoni Pugliesi
Apulian Pasties

US		UK
1 pound	once-risen bread dough, made with 2½ cups (10 ounces) flour	1 pound
	olive oil	
1 pound	mild onions	1 pound
about 12	anchovy fillets	about 12
2–3 tablespoons	capers	2–3 tablespoons
6–8 large	black olives, pitted and chopped	6–8 large

A *calzone* is a version of the pizza which varies from district to district. Sometimes it is like a large envelope of dough stuffed with cheese and deep-fried in olive oil. Sometimes a large piece of yeast dough is spread out on a baking sheet, roughly indented to take the filling, and then baked. It is all a matter of local tradition, and there are no set rules.

Put the bread dough on a pastry board and make a deep dent in the center. Add ¼ cup (U.K. 3 tablespoons) olive oil and work this into the dough until it is completely absorbed. Knead the dough until it is smooth and elastic again, then roll out into a sheet about ½ inch thick. Cut this into 3-inch squares. Put them aside, covered with a clean damp cloth, until doubled in bulk.

Slice the onions, not too thinly. Heat 5 tablespoons (U.K. 4 tablespoons) olive oil, and sauté the onions over a low heat until soft, without letting them brown. Cool.

Oil a large flat baking sheet and arrange the *calzoni* on it, evenly spaced. Spread each *calzone* with a little of the onion mixture, add an anchovy fillet, some capers, a few slivers of olive and a trickle of olive oil. Fold each square in half to make a rectangle and press the edges firmly with a fork to seal them tightly. Brush the rectangles lightly with olive oil and bake in a very hot oven (450°F. Mark 7) for 15 to 20 minutes, or until golden brown. Serve hot.

Serves 6.

The filling may be varied by using slices of tomato, grated cheese, onion slices softened in oil, and a few pieces of anchovy, instead of the ingredients listed above.

Panzarotti
Fried Cheese-stuffed Ravioli

US		UK
Dough		
2½ cups	all-purpose (plain) flour	10 ounces
½ cup	olive oil	6 tablespoons
2	egg yolks	2
	salt	
Stuffing		
1 cup	diced fresh Mozzarella cheese	½ pound
2	eggs	2
5 tablespoons	grated Parmesan cheese	4 tablespoons
	salt	
¼ pound	salami or Parma ham, diced – optional	¼ pound
	oil for frying	

Panzarotti, or fried ravioli, are always made smaller than the boiled variety and are often served as hot canapés with drinks.

Dough
Sift the flour into a mound on a pastry board or into a bowl. Make a well in the center. Add the oil, a pinch of salt, the egg yolks and about 1 tablespoon lukewarm water. Work the flour into the liquid and knead to a firm dough. If it seems too thick, add a little more water, if too thin, more flour. Knead the dough until smooth and elastic; gather it into a ball, put into a lightly floured bowl, cover and leave for about 30 minutes to rest. Roll out into one thin sheet and cut into circles about 2½ inches in diameter.

Stuffing
Put the Mozzarella into a bowl with the eggs, Parmesan cheese, salt to taste, and salami or ham, if used. Mix thoroughly and put a teaspoon of the mixture on each circle of dough. Fold the dough over to cover the filling and seal tightly with a fork.

Deep-fry the *panzarotti* a few at a time until crisp and golden brown. Drain on absorbent paper and serve very hot.

Serves 6.

Pizza con Uova e Cipolle
Egg and Onion Pie

US		UK
5 cups	all-purpose (plain) flour	1¼ pounds
	salt	
1½ cakes	compressed (fresh) yeast	1 ounce
	olive oil	
2 pounds	mild onions, sliced	2 pounds
	salt and pepper	
3 sprigs	parsley, finely chopped	3 sprigs
4	eggs, hard-boiled	4

Sift the flour into a warmed bowl with a pinch of salt. Melt the yeast in a few tablespoons of lukewarm water. Make a well in the center of the flour, add the dissolved yeast, ¼ cup (U.K. 3 tablespoons) oil and enough warm water to make a firm dough (about ½ pint in all). Work the flour into the liquid and knead until smooth and pliable. Cut in two and roll each piece into a ball. Leave to rise in a warm place, in two covered bowls, until each piece has doubled its bulk.

Heat about ¼ cup (U.K. 3 to 4 tablespoons) olive oil in a deep frying pan, and sauté the onions gently until soft without letting them change color. Add salt and pepper to taste, and the parsley. Mix well and cool slightly.

Grease a deep baking or pie pan with oil. Knead each ball of dough lightly and roll out into a sheet about ¼ inch thick. Use one sheet of dough to line the pan, stretching it as much as possible. Spread with the onion and parsley mixture, then distribute the quartered eggs evenly over the surface. Cover with the remaining sheet of dough, brush lightly with olive oil and prick all over with a fork. Bake in a moderately hot oven (400°F. Mark 5) for about 40 minutes, or until well risen and a golden brown color.

Serves 6 to 8.

Torta Tarantina di Patate
Potato "Pizza" with Cheese

US		UK
3 pounds	floury potatoes	3 pounds
	olive oil	
	salt	
	flour	
½ pound	Mozzarella or other fresh soft cheese, diced	½ pound
4 large	ripe tomatoes, sliced	4 large
	pepper	
⅔ cup	grated Parmesan cheese	2 ounces
1 teaspoon	finely chopped oregano	1 teaspoon
12	black olives, pitted and sliced	12

Scrub the potatoes clean and boil them until soft. Drain and cool slightly, and as soon as they can be handled, peel and mash them with ¼ cup (U.K. 3 tablespoons) olive oil and a little salt to taste.

Brush the bottom of a wide, shallow baking dish with oil, sprinkle with flour, spread with the mashed potato, and cover with the cheese and slices of tomato. Sprinkle lightly with salt and pepper, the Parmesan cheese, oregano and olives. Trickle ¼ cup (U.K. 3 tablespoons) olive oil over the top and bake in a hot oven (425°F. Mark 6) for 15 minutes, or until the potato crust is brown and beginning to crisp. Serve immediately.

Serves 6.

Pizza Rustica Leccese
Onion Pie as made in Lecce

US		UK
1–1¼ pounds	once-risen bread dough, made with 2½–3 cups (10–12 ounces) flour	1–1¼ pounds
	olive oil	
1 pound	mild onions, sliced	1 pound
1 pound	ripe or canned tomatoes	1 pound
	salt	
12	anchovy fillets, chopped	12
½ cup	black olives, pitted and slivered	3–4 ounces

Put the risen dough on a pastry board, make a dent in the center and add 2½ tablespoons (U.K. 2 tablespoons) olive oil. Work it into the dough and then knead until the dough is again smooth and elastic. Cut it into two pieces, cover and leave each piece to rise separately until doubled in bulk.

Heat 4 tablespoons (U.K. 5 tablespoons) oil and sauté the onions over a low heat until soft without letting them change color. Peel and chop the tomatoes, discarding seeds. Add the tomatoes to the onions with salt to taste, and cook over a brisk heat for 20 minutes.

Brush a shallow, round baking dish lightly with oil. Roll out both pieces of dough into two sheets about ¼ inch thick. Line the baking dish with one sheet of dough, stretching it out as thinly as possible and overlapping the sides of the dish. Spread with the onion and tomato mixture, arrange the anchovy fillets on top, and sprinkle with olive slivers. Cover with the second sheet of dough and press down firmly all round to seal; trim off surplus dough. Brush lightly with oil and prick all over with a fork. Bake in a moderately hot oven (400°F. Mark 5) for 45 minutes, or until the pie is puffed and golden brown.

Serves 6.

Pizza Lievitata di Verdure
Vegetable Pie made with Yeast Dough

US		UK
Dough		
3 cups	all-purpose (plain) flour	12 ounces
	salt and white pepper	
1½ cakes	compressed (fresh) yeast	1 ounce
2½ pounds	mixed green leaf vegetables	2½ pounds
5 tablespoons	olive oil	4 tablespoons
1 clove	garlic, lightly crushed	1 clove
	salt and pepper	
2½ tablespoons	salted capers, well rinsed	2 tablespoons
about 12	black olives, pitted and roughly chopped	about 12
	olive oil	

Dough
Sift the flour with a little salt and white pepper on to a pastry board or into a warmed bowl and make a well in the center. Dissolve the yeast in a little lukewarm water and add to the flour, with enough additional water to make a firm, pliable dough. Knead until smooth and elastic. Put into a lightly floured bowl, cover and leave to rise in a warm place for about 2 hours, or until doubled in bulk.

In the meantime, clean the vegetables – they can be all of one kind or mixed. Wash them well under running water and drain. Chop coarsely. Put the oil and garlic in a pan, add the chopped vegetables, and salt and pepper to taste, cover and cook over a moderate heat until soft. Drain well and leave to cool. Discard the garlic.

Brush a deep, 10-inch baking pan with oil. Knead the risen dough lightly and cut it into two pieces; roll out each piece thinly. Line the pan with one sheet of dough, stretching it out as thinly as possible, and overlapping the sides of the pan. Spread it with the

cooked vegetables and cover the surface with capers and olives. Cover with the remaining sheet of dough, seal the edges firmly and trim off surplus dough.

Prick the surface with a fork, brush with olive oil and bake in a moderately hot oven (400°F. Mark 5) for 45 minutes, or until puffed and golden. Serve hot or cold.

Serves 6.

Bucatini al Cavolfiore
Bucatini Noodles with Cauliflower

US		UK
1 medium-sized	cauliflower	1 medium-sized
2½ pounds	ripe tomatoes	2½ pounds
½ cup	olive oil	6 tablespoons
1 clove	garlic, crushed	1 clove
	salt and pepper	
3–4 sprigs	parsley, finely chopped	3–4 sprigs
1½ pounds	bucatini noodles – see method	1½ pounds
	grated Parmesan or Pecorino	

Bucatini is a variety of pasta which looks like fat spaghetti. If this is not available, spaghetti may be used instead.

Trim the cauliflower, discard the leaves and stalks, and divide the head into flowerettes. Peel the tomatoes, chop them finely and rub them through a sieve. Heat the oil in a pan, add the garlic clove and fry until it begins to brown. Discard the garlic and add the puréed tomatoes. Bring to a gentle boil, then add the pieces of cauliflower. Add ⅔ cup (U.K. ¼ pint) hot water, season with salt, cover the pan and cook over a moderate heat for about 40 minutes, or until the sauce is thick and the cauliflower has disintegrated. Sprinkle generously with freshly ground pepper and the parsley. Keep hot.

Bring a large pan of salted water to a rapid boil, add the *bucatini* and cook over a high heat until *al dente* – just tender. Drain, turn into a large heated serving dish, stir in the sauce and serve with plenty of grated Parmesan or a smaller amount of Pecorino cheese.

Serves 6.

Lasagne con la Ricotta
Lasagne with Ricotta Cheese

US		UK
1¼ pounds	lasagne noodles	1¼ pounds
	salt	
1 cup	Ricotta cheese	½ pound
	olive oil	
⅔ cup	grated Pecorino cheese	2 ounces
⅔ cup	grated Parmesan cheese	2 ounces
Sauce		
¼ cup	olive oil	3 tablespoons
1 clove	garlic, crushed	1 clove
1 cup	pork sausage meat, crumbled	½ pound
½ cup	ground (UK minced) loin of pork	¼ pound
½ cup	red wine	6 tablespoons
2½ tablespoons	tomato paste	2 tablespoons
	salt and pepper	
3–4 sprigs	basil, finely chopped	3–4 sprigs

Sauce
Heat the oil, add the garlic clove, and when it turns brown discard it; then add the sausage meat. When the fat from the sausage meat begins to run, add the pork and sauté gently until browned. Add the wine and continue cooking until this is reduced. Dilute the tomato paste with ½ cup (U.K. 6 to 8 tablespoons) warm water and add to the pan; season to taste with salt and pepper. Cover the pan and cook the sauce over a low heat until thick. A few minutes before the sauce is ready, stir in the basil.

In the meantime, bring a large pan of salted water to the boil. Add the lasagne, a few pieces at a time, and cook until tender – the cooking time will vary according to whether the lasagne are home-made or bought. Drain the lasagne and spread them out on a damp cloth.

Beat the Ricotta with 2 or 3 tablespoons of hot water until creamy and smooth. Brush a deep fireproof baking dish lightly with oil. Put a layer of lasagne at the bottom, spread it with a layer of Ricotta, sprinkle with some of both the grated cheeses, and spread with a few tablespoons of the meat sauce. Continue in this manner until all the ingredients are used up, finishing with a layer of lasagne lightly spread with meat sauce. Bake in a slow oven (325°F. Mark 2) for about 40 minutes.

Serves 4 to 6.

Orecchiette al Pomodoro
"Little Ears" or "Priests' Hats" with Tomato Sauce

US		UK
Pasta dough		
2 cups	Graham (durum wholewheat) flour	½ pound
4 cups	all-purpose (plain) flour	1 pound
1 teaspoon	salt	¾ teaspoon
	warm water	
Sauce		
½ cup	olive oil	6 tablespoons
1 clove	garlic, crushed	1 clove
1 cup	ground (UK minced) lamb or pork	½ pound
1	onion, thinly sliced	1
1 pound	ripe tomatoes	1 pound
	salt and pepper	
2 sprigs	parsley, finely chopped	2 sprigs
1–2 sprigs	basil, finely chopped	1–2 sprigs
¼ pound	hard Ricotta cheese, grated	¼ pound

Pasta dough

Mix the flours together in a bowl. Make a well in the center. Dissolve the salt in about 1 cup (U.K. scant ½ pint) warm water. Pour this into the well, then work the flour into the liquid to make a dough similar in consistency to bread dough, but just a little firmer. If necessary, add a little more warm water, but on no account let the dough become too soft. Knead until smooth and elastic.

Break off pieces of the dough and roll them into cylinders about 1 inch thick and 12 inches long. Cover the cylinders with a damp cloth as soon as they are formed to prevent them from drying out. When all the dough is used up, cut the cylinders into rounds and shape each round into an "ear" by pressing the center with the thumb or the rounded end of a knife. Press each "ear" well down over the thumb so that it looks like a little round priest's hat without a brim. Spread out on a lightly floured cloth to dry.

Sauce

Heat the oil, fry the garlic clove until it browns, then discard it. Add the meat and simmer for a few minutes, crumbling it with a fork. Add the onion and continue to cook gently. Peel and chop the tomatoes, discarding seeds, and add to the pan. Season to taste with salt and pepper, stir well, cover and cook over a moderate heat for about 1 hour. Finally, add the parsley and basil.

Bring a large pan of salted water to the boil, add the "priests' hats" and cook them rapidly until tender or *al dente*, about 5 minutes. Drain well, turn into a deep, heated serving dish, stir in the sauce and sprinkle with grated cheese.

Serves 6.

Crema di Ceci
Chick Peas with Noodles

US		UK
2 cups	chick peas	¾ pound
1 sprig	rosemary	1 sprig
2 stalks	celery	2 stalks
1 large	onion, halved	1 large
4	bay leaves	4
	salt	
½ cup	olive oil	6–8 tablespoons
1 clove	garlic, crushed	1 clove
2–3 tablespoons	tomato paste	2–2½ tablespoons
½ pound	"bavette" ribbon noodles	½ pound

It is difficult to say exactly how long chick peas will take to soften as they vary considerably according to their age and their place of origin. If the chick peas are not soft after 1 hour, continue cooking until they are. Chick peas will always retain their shape however long they have been cooked.

Soak the chick peas overnight. Drain and cook in 10 to 11 cups (U.K. 4½ pints) boiling water with the rosemary, celery, onion and bay leaves. Do not add salt at this stage as it will prevent the chick peas from softening. Cook them steadily, covered, for 1 to 1½ hours, or until tender.

Discard the rosemary, celery, onion and bay leaves, add salt to taste and rub the chick peas, with their liquid, through a sieve. Return to the pan.

Heat the oil in a small pan, add the garlic and fry until brown; discard it. Dilute the tomato paste with a little water, stir it into the oil and cook briskly for 15 minutes. Stir this into the chick pea purée. Bring to the boil again, check seasoning, add the noodles, broken into small pieces, and cook until tender, about 10 minutes. Turn off the heat and leave the pan for a few minutes on the cooling stove to settle before serving.

Serves 6.

Agnello al Forno con Patate e Pomodori
Baked Lamb with Potatoes and Tomatoes

US		UK
3–3½ pounds	lamb, leg or loin	3–3½ pounds
½ cup	olive oil	6–8 tablespoons
¼ cup	butter	2 ounces
1 large	onion, sliced	1 large
2 sprigs	rosemary, finely chopped	2 sprigs
1 cup	dry white wine	⅓ pint
	salt	
1 pound	ripe tomatoes	1 pound
1½ pounds	new potatoes	1½ pounds
	pepper	

This is a very typical Italian recipe and one which hardly varies throughout the country, and indeed the whole of the Mediterranean.

Cut the lamb into even-sized pieces. Heat the oil and butter in a heavy casserole, and fry the onion gently until transparent; then add the pieces of lamb and the rosemary. Brown the meat evenly all over, add the wine and simmer gently on top of the stove until it evaporates. Sprinkle with salt. Peel and chop the tomatoes, discarding the seeds. Add to the casserole and continue cooking, uncovered, for 30 minutes.

Heat the oven to 375°F. (Mark 4).

Scrape or peel the potatoes and add them to the casserole. Sprinkle them with salt and a generous amount of pepper. Transfer the casserole to the oven and bake for about 40 minutes, stirring from time to time with a wooden spoon. Serve as soon as the potatoes are brown and soft and the meat well cooked.

Serves 6.

Costolette di Agnello ai Peperoni
Baby Lamb Chops with Sweet Peppers

US		UK
12	baby lamb chops	12
3	sweet peppers	3
⅝ cup	olive oil	8 tablespoons
	salt and pepper	
3–4 large	anchovy fillets	3–4 large
½ clove	garlic, finely chopped	½ clove
3 sprigs	parsley, finely chopped	3 sprigs

Wash the sweet peppers and char them under a hot broiler (grill) or in a very hot oven until their skins begin to blacken and blister. Rub off the thin outer skin and cut each pepper into 4 pieces, discarding the hot white seeds and the core. Arrange the peppers lying flat in a shallow baking dish, add half the oil and a pinch of salt, and bake them in a slow oven (325°F. Mark 2) for about 10 minutes, just long enough to soften them.

Heat the remaining oil in a frying pan and fry the chops briskly on both sides until brown. Sprinkle with salt and pepper. Arrange a chop on each piece of pepper and return them to the oven to keep hot. Add 2 to 3 tablespoons water to the frying pan, stir well, then add the anchovy fillets, garlic and parsley. Simmer over a low heat, stirring gently, until the sauce is hot and the anchovy fillets reduced to a paste. Spoon over the chops and serve immediately.

Serves 6.

Spiedini di Capretto
Baked Kid on Skewers

US		UK
2–2½ pounds	kid, leg or loin	2–2½ pounds
	salt and pepper	
20 thin slices	lean bacon	20 thin slices
½ cup	olive oil	6 tablespoons

Wash the meat, wipe it dry and cut it into 20 even-sized cubes. Season with salt and pepper, and wrap each cube in a slice of bacon. Thread these on to 4 or 5 skewers. Choose a suitable baking dish so that the skewers can rest on its sides without the meat touching the bottom. Brush the skewers with oil and bake in a moderately hot oven (400°F. Mark 5) for about 20 minutes, turning them from time to time until they are evenly browned all over. Slip the pieces of meat off the skewers on to a heated serving dish and pour the cooking juices over the top.

Serves 4 to 5.

Manzo con Cipolle
Beef with Onions

US		UK
2 pounds	beef fillet in one piece	2 pounds
¼ pound	fat salt pork – optional	¼ pound
	juice of 2 lemons	
	salt and pepper	
6 large	sweet onions	6 large
¼ cup	olive oil	3 tablespoons
¼ cup	butter	2 ounces
	stock	

If you wish, you may lard the fillet with strips of fat salt pork. Then put the fillet in an earthenware dish, add the lemon juice and sprinkle with salt and pepper. Leave to marinate for 2 hours.

Peel the onions and make a deep cross-shaped cut in each one without cutting right through. Heat the oil and butter in a pan, add the onions and cook over a low heat. As soon as they begin to

soften, add ⅔ cup (U.K. ¼ pint) stock and let the onions cook slowly, uncovered, for 20 minutes, gently disintegrating. By the end the stock will have almost completely evaporated.

Tie the meat with thread to keep it in shape. Add it to the onions and brown gently on all sides. Continue to cook gently for about 30 minutes for slightly underdone or rare steak, longer if medium-rare is preferred.

Take the meat from the pan and cut it into thick slices, discarding the threads. Keep it hot in a warm oven. Add a little water or more stock to the pan and cook over a high heat for 2 minutes. Rub the onions and stock through a sieve, reheat to boiling point and pour over the meat. Serve immediately.

Serves 4 to 6.

Polpettine ai Capperi
Meat Balls with Capers

US		UK
1 pound	lean beef	1 pound
¼ cup	pith of a stale bread roll *or* soft breadcrumbs	3 tablespoons
	milk	
2 tablespoons	softened butter	1 ounce
	salt	
pinch	marjoram	pinch
1–2 tablespoons	capers	1–2 tablespoons
	flour	
5 tablespoons	olive oil	4 tablespoons
½ cup	dry white wine	6–8 tablespoons

Put the meat twice through a grinder (mincer). Soak the bread or crumbs in a little milk until soft, then squeeze dry. Combine the bread and the meat in a bowl, and add the butter, salt and a pinch of marjoram, to taste. Knead until the mixture is smooth, then break off small pieces and roll them into balls. Push 2 or 3 capers into each meat ball. Smooth over the holes and roll the meat balls in flour.

Heat the oil in a large, shallow pan and arrange the meat balls in this in one layer. Brown them quickly and evenly over a brisk heat, turning carefully. Add the wine, cover the pan and continue cooking for 10 to 15 minutes, adding a little more hot water or stock if necessary. Serve the meat balls very hot in their sauce.

Serves 4.

Coniglio ai Capperi
Rabbit with Capers

US		UK
3½ pounds	rabbit pieces	3½ pounds
3 tablespoons	lard or oil	1½ ounces
1	onion, sliced	1
2½ tablespoons	olive oil	2 tablespoons
4–6 large	anchovy fillets	4–6 large
2½ tablespoons	capers in brine, well drained	2 tablespoons
2–3 sprigs	parsley, finely chopped	2–3 sprigs
1½ teaspoons	flour	1 teaspoon
Marinade		
¾ cup	wine vinegar	6 fluid ounces
1 cup	red wine	8 fluid ounces
1	onion, sliced	1
1 stalk	celery, chopped	1 stalk
1	carrot, chopped	1
	salt and pepper	

Wash the pieces of rabbit and wipe them dry. Put them in an earthenware dish. Make a marinade with the wine vinegar, wine, onion, celery and carrot, and pour it over the rabbit. Sprinkle lightly with salt and pepper. Leave overnight in a cool place, but not in the refrigerator.

Take the rabbit pieces from the marinade and wipe them dry. Heat the lard in a heavy pan and fry the onion and rabbit. Cook over a low heat, turning the pieces from time to time until evenly browned all over. Strain the marinade and pour half of it over the rabbit. Cover and cook over a low heat for another 30 minutes.

In another pan heat the olive oil, add the anchovies and cook them, stirring, to a paste. Stir in the capers and the parsley, and add the rest of the strained marinade. Mix the flour to a smooth thin paste with warm water, stir this into the sauce, bring to a gentle boil and stir well until the sauce thickens; lower the heat again and simmer for 15 minutes. Then pour the hot sauce over the rabbit pieces and leave for 10 minutes over a low heat to bring out the flavors.

Serves 6.

Sarde in Tortiera
Baked Sardines

US		UK
2 pounds	fresh sardines	2 pounds
10 tablespoons	soft breadcrumbs	8 tablespoons
1 large clove	garlic, finely chopped	1 large clove
3 sprigs	parsley, finely chopped	3 sprigs
	salt and pepper	
	olive oil	
1–2	lemons	1–2

If fresh sardines are not available, other fish such as small herring could be used instead.

Clean the sardines and remove the heads. Open them just enough to enable you to remove their insides and backbones. Re-form the sardines as neatly as possible into their original shape.

Mix together the breadcrumbs, garlic, parsley, a little salt and plenty of pepper, adding just enough olive oil to make a thickish paste.

Brush a baking dish with oil and cover the bottom with a layer of sardines. Spread this lightly with some of the breadcrumb mixture and cover with another layer of sardines and another layer of breadcrumbs. Repeat until all the ingredients are used up, finishing with a layer of breadcrumbs. Put the dish into a slow oven (350°F. Mark 3) and bake for at least 30 minutes, or until the breadcrumb mixture is golden brown. Take the sardines from the oven, sprinkle generously with lemon juice and serve immediately.

Serves 6.

Frittura di Pescespada
Fried Swordfish Steaks

US		UK
2 pounds	swordfish steaks	2 pounds
¼ cup	olive oil	3 tablespoons
2–3 sprigs	parsley, finely chopped	2–3 sprigs
	juice of 1 lemon	
	salt and pepper	
	flour	
2	eggs	2
	fine dry breadcrumbs	
	oil for frying	
1–2	lemons	1–2

Skin the steaks and put them in a shallow bowl with the oil, parsley, lemon juice and a little salt and pepper. Leave to marinate for 1 hour. Then drain the steaks, wipe them dry and roll them in flour.

Heat plenty of oil in a deep frying pan. Beat the eggs lightly with a pinch of salt. Dip the swordfish steaks into the eggs, dust them with breadcrumbs, shaking off any excess, and fry at once in very hot oil. Lower the heat as soon as the fish is placed in the oil and fry over a moderate heat to ensure that it cooks right through. When golden brown on both sides remove the fish steaks and drain on absorbent paper. Serve very hot, garnished with lemon wedges.

Serves 4 to 6.

Baccalà con le Olive Verdi
Salt Cod with Green Olives

US		UK
2½ pounds	pre-soaked salt cod (page 50)	2½ pounds
	flour	
1 cup	olive oil	6–8 tablespoons
1 small	onion, finely chopped	1 small
12-ounce can	Italian peeled tomatoes	12-ounce can
	salt and pepper	
3	gherkins, sliced	3
1–1½ tablespoons	capers	1 tablespoon
generous ½ cup	green olives, pitted	4 ounces
2–3 sprigs	parsley, coarsely chopped	2–3 sprigs

Thoroughly rinse the salt cod, skin it and remove the bones. Cut it into neat pieces, as even-sized as possible and about 2½ inches square. Wash the pieces, wipe them dry and roll them in flour. Arrange them in one layer in a shallow pan into which you have poured all but 2 or 3 tablespoons of the olive oil. Brown the pieces of fish gently on both sides. Keep hot.

Heat 2 to 3 tablespoons oil in a pan and fry the onion until soft and a pale golden brown. Chop the tomatoes, and stir them in with their liquid. Season to taste with salt and pepper, and cook over a moderate heat for 15 minutes, or until the sauce thickens slightly.

Drain the cod and arrange the pieces in another ovenproof dish. Cover with the tomato sauce, mixed with gherkins, capers and olives. Bake in a slow oven (325°F. Mark 2) for about 15 minutes. Serve hot, garnished with parsley.

Serves 6.

Pesce al Forno
Baked Fish with Olives

US		UK
3	large red mullet (¾–1 pound each) *or*	3
6	smaller ones	6
	salt	
⅔ cup	olive oil	¼ pint
½ cup	wine vinegar	6 tablespoons
1¼ cups	green olives, pitted	½ pound

Red mullet are usually sold already scaled, but if this has not been done, the operation must be carried out with extreme care as the skin is delicate. Mullet may be cleaned or left uncleaned. Some mullet lovers think the intestines of the mullet, like the trail of small game birds, add to their flavor.

Sprinkle the mullet lightly inside and out with salt, and arrange them in a baking dish, preferably an earthenware one. Trickle the olive oil over the fish, sprinkle lightly with vinegar and salt, and bake in a slow oven (350°F. Mark 3) for about 20 minutes, turning them once carefully with a fish slice or a wooden spatula. Add the olives and continue baking for a few minutes longer until they are heated enough.

Take the fish from the pan. If 3 large fish have been used, divide each one in two lengthwise and remove the backbone. Serve the fish garnished with the olives and a little of the pan juices.

Serves 6.

Zuppa di Cozze alla Tarantina
Taranto Mussel Soup (Stew)

US		UK
3–3½ quarts	mussels	3–3½ pounds
¼ cup	olive oil	3 tablespoons
2 cloves	garlic	2 cloves
¼	hot chili pepper	¼
1 pound	ripe tomatoes *or*	1 pound
¼ cup	tomato paste	3 tablespoons
1 cup	dry white wine – optional	⅓ pint
	salt and pepper	
	slices of toasted bread	

Scrape the mussels with a stiff brush and remove their "beards". Wash them particularly carefully until no trace of sand remains.

Heat the oil in a large pan and sauté 1 clove garlic, lightly crushed, and the piece of chili until browned. Discard both and add the tomatoes, peeled, seeded and chopped, or the tomato paste diluted in water. Cook over a brisk heat for 10 minutes, then drop in the mussels. Cover and cook until the mussels open, shaking the pan occasionally. Stir well, add the wine, if used, and cook briskly until reduced. Sprinkle with the remaining garlic, finely chopped.

The "soup" may be served as it is, with slices of toasted bread, alternatively the mussels may first be scooped out of their shells and returned to the pan.

Serves 6.

Cozze Fritte
Fried Mussels

US		UK
3–3½ quarts	mussels	3–3½ pounds
	flour	
2	eggs	2
	salt	
	fine dry breadcrumbs	
	oil for deep-frying	
1–2	lemons	1–2

Thoroughly wash the mussels, scrubbing them with a brush if necessary. Open them with a strong short-bladed knife and take the mussels from their shells. Drain well and roll in flour.

Beat the eggs lightly with a pinch of salt. Dip the floured mussels into the beaten eggs and then into the breadcrumbs.

Heat plenty of oil – it would be wise to have the oil heating gently while preparing the mussels as they should be fried immediately they are egg-and-breadcrumbed – and fry the mussels until golden brown. Drain on absorbent paper. Serve very hot, garnished with lemon wedges.

Serves 6.

Cozze al Riso
Mussels with Rice

US		UK
4–6 dozen	mussels	2½ pounds
	salt	
1 pound	ripe tomatoes	1 pound
2½ tablespoons	olive oil	2 tablespoons
1 clove	garlic, crushed	1 clove
	pepper	
2½ cups	rice	1 pound

Wash the mussels and scrape them with a stiff brush. Wash again in salted water, drain well and put into a large, deep pan. Cover and place over a moderate heat. Shake the pan from time to time and continue heating for 10 minutes, by which time the mussels should all have opened. Discard any that are still closed. Take the mussels from their shells and strain their liquor into a bowl.

Peel the tomatoes, chop them finely and rub them through a sieve. Heat the oil in a large, heavy pan, and fry the garlic clove gently. When it turns brown, discard it and add the sieved tomatoes, the mussel liquor, and salt and pepper to taste, and cook over a brisk heat for 10 minutes.

Bring a large pan of salted water to the boil. Add the rice and cook it for about 7 minutes, or until it is half-cooked. Drain well. Add the rice to the pan with the tomatoes and continue cooking until soft, about another 10 minutes, not longer. Two or three minutes before the rice is ready to be served add the mussels, stir and leave just long enough to reheat them and develop their flavor – longer cooking will make them tough.

Serves 6.

Ostriche alla Tarantina
Baked Oysters Taranto Style

US		UK
3 dozen	fresh oysters	3 dozen
3–4 sprigs	parsley, finely chopped	3–4 sprigs
¼ cup	soft breadcrumbs	3–3½ tablespoons
	pepper	
	olive oil	
1–2	lemons	1–2

Open the oysters with an oyster knife. Arrange them on their half-shells in a fireproof dish. Sprinkle generously with parsley, lightly with breadcrumbs, and finish with plenty of freshly ground pepper. Trickle a little olive oil over each oyster and bake in a slow oven (325°F. Mark 2) for 10 to 15 minutes. Serve immediately, garnished with lemon wedges.

Serve 6 to 12 oysters per person.

Melanzane alla Foggiana
Eggplants (Aubergines) Foggia Style

US		UK
6 medium-sized	round eggplants (aubergines)	6 medium-sized
	salt	
½ pound	ripe tomatoes, sliced	½ pound
½ cup	olive oil	6–8 tablespoons
Stuffing		
5 tablespoons	olive oil	4 tablespoons
1 clove	garlic, crushed	1 clove
1 pound	ripe tomatoes	1 pound
	salt and pepper	
	sugar	
2 sprigs	basil, finely chopped	2 sprigs
3 sprigs	parsley, finely chopped	3 sprigs
¼ cup	breadcrumbs	3 tablespoons

Wipe the eggplants with a damp cloth. Slice off the stem ends, reserving them to use later as "lids". Scoop out as much pulp as possible, but leave sufficient to make a firm shell. Reserve the pulp. Sprinkle the shells lightly with salt and turn them upside down to drain on a sloping plate or in a colander for 1 or 2 hours.

Stuffing

Heat the oil in a frying pan, and fry the garlic clove until brown. Discard it. Peel and chop the tomatoes, discarding seeds. Add them to the pan, stir well, then add the eggplant pulp. Season to taste with salt, pepper and a pinch of sugar, and stir in the basil and parsley. Cook over a brisk heat for 20 minutes, then remove the pan from the heat and add the breadcrumbs. Mix well.

Rinse the eggplant shells, dry them carefully and fill them with the stuffing. Close the openings with their "lids" and pack them tightly together, lids uppermost, in a shallow pan. Cover with tomato slices, trickle with olive oil and sprinkle with salt. Add about ½ cup

(U.K. 6 tablespoons) water, cover the pan and cook over a low heat, shaking the pan occasionally, for about 1 hour, or until the eggplants are soft. Add a little more water if the liquid in the pan evaporates too quickly. Serve hot or cold.

Serves 6.

Fritto di Melanzane Filanti
Eggplant (Aubergine) and Cheese "Sandwiches"

US		UK
6	eggplants (aubergines)	6
	salt	
	flour	
	olive oil	
3	egg yolks	3
¼ cup	grated Parmesan cheese	3 tablespoons
½ pound	Mozzarella or fresh cheese, diced	½ pound
2	eggs, beaten	2
	fine dry breadcrumbs	

Wash the eggplants and cut them lengthwise into slices about ¼ inch thick. Sprinkle with salt and leave to drain on a sloping plate or in a colander for about 1 hour to rid them of their bitter juices. Pat dry, dust with flour and fry in hot oil until golden. Drain well.

Beat the egg yolks with the grated Parmesan and a pinch of salt. Spread a slice of eggplant with a spoonful of this mixture and top with a little diced cheese; cover with another slice of eggplant and press lightly, making a firm sandwich. Continue until all the ingredients are used up. Roll the "sandwiches" in flour, dip them in beaten eggs and coat with breadcrumbs. Deep-fry in hot oil until golden, drain on absorbent paper and serve very hot.

Serves 6.

Involtini di Peperoni
Stuffed Sweet Peppers

US		UK
6	sweet yellow peppers	6
½ cup	soft breadcrumbs	6–8 tablespoons
6–8	anchovy fillets, chopped	6–8
1–2 tablespoons	chopped capers	1½ tablespoons
2–3 tablespoons	pine nuts	2 tablespoons
2–3 tablespoons	seedless white raisins (sultanas)	2 tablespoons
	salt and pepper	
3 sprigs	parsley, finely chopped	3 sprigs
	olive oil	

Wash the peppers and char them under a hot broiler (grill) until their skins blacken and blister. Rub off the thin outer skin and cut each pepper in half lengthwise, discarding seeds and cores.

Mix together the breadcrumbs, anchovies, capers, pine nuts, seedless raisins (sultanas), salt and pepper to taste, and parsley. Add just enough oil to make a paste. Stuff a little of this mixture into each half-pepper and arrange in a baking dish. Sprinkle with olive oil and bake in a moderate oven (375°F. Mark 4) for 30 minutes.

Serves 6.

Peperoni e Cipolle
Sweet Peppers and Onions

US		UK
6 large	sweet peppers	6 large
3 large	sweet onions	3 large
6 tablespoons	olive oil	5 tablespoons
1 pound	ripe tomatoes	1 pound
	salt	
2–3 sprigs	basil, finely chopped	2–3 sprigs

Green, yellow or red sweet peppers can all be used in this dish. Slice the onions very thinly. Heat the oil in a pan and soften the onions over a very low heat. Peel and chop the tomatoes, discarding seeds. Stir them into the onions, season to taste with salt and cook over a brisk heat for 15 minutes.

Wash the peppers, cut each one in half and scoop out the core and seeds. Cut them into strips about 1 inch wide and add them to the tomato sauce. Check seasoning, add the basil, stir well and cover. Cook over a low heat for 30 minutes, or until the peppers are soft.

Serves 6.

Pomodori Ripieni
Stuffed Tomatoes

US		UK
12 medium-sized	ripe tomatoes	12 medium-sized
5 tablespoons	soft breadcrumbs	4 tablespoons
¼ cup	milk	3 tablespoons
2–3 sprigs	parsley, finely chopped	2–3 sprigs
1 clove	garlic, finely chopped	1 clove
2	egg yolks, lightly beaten	2
¼ cup	grated Parmesan cheese	3 tablespoons
	salt and pepper	
½ cup	olive oil	6 tablespoons

Wash the tomatoes and cut them in half horizontally. Gently squeeze or scoop out their seeds, and discard them; then scoop out some of the flesh, leaving a firm shell. Mash the tomato flesh to a pulp.

Soak the breadcrumbs in the milk. Mix with the tomato pulp, parsley and garlic. Add the egg yolks and Parmesan cheese, and season to taste with salt and pepper.

Brush the bottom of a large, shallow baking dish with olive oil. Stuff the tomato halves with the breadcrumb mixture and place them in the oiled baking dish in one layer. Trickle the remaining olive oil over the top – a little on each tomato half – and bake in a moderate oven (375°F. Mark 4) for about 30 minutes, depending on the size of the tomatoes. They must be soft, but still retain their shape. Serve hot or cold.

Serves 6.

Frittata di Pasta e Uova
Fried Noodles and Eggs

US		UK
1½–2 cups	cooked noodles	½ pound
6	eggs	6
6 tablespoons	grated Parmesan cheese	4–5 tablespoons
	olive oil	
1 cup	pork sausage meat	½ pound
6 ounces	fresh soft cheese, sliced	6 ounces

Any type of left-over cooked noodles can be used in this recipe, spaghetti, macaroni, etc., which have been previously served with a sauce. Cut the cold, cooked noodles into small pieces. Beat the eggs with the Parmesan cheese. Stir this into the noodles and mix well.

Heat 2 to 3 tablespoons olive oil in a frying pan. Add the sausage meat and sauté over moderate heat, crumbling it with a fork, until well browned. In another, larger frying pan heat a scant ¼ cup (U.K. 3 tablespoons) oil; pour in half the noodle mixture, place pieces of soft cheese on top and spread with the cooked sausage meat. Cover with the remaining noodles.

Fry over a moderate heat until brown and crisp on one side. Then turn out of the pan on to a plate and slide back into the pan to brown the other side. Turn out on to a hot serving dish and serve at once.

Serves 4 to 6.

Frittelle di Ricotta
Ricotta Fritters

US		UK
1½ cups	Ricotta cheese	¾ pound
2 cups	soft breadcrumbs	3½ ounces
	milk	
	granulated (caster) sugar	
2	egg yolks, beaten	2
	grated rind of 1 orange	
	oil for frying	
	flour	
2	eggs, well beaten	2

Rub the Ricotta through a sieve. Soak the breadcrumbs in milk and squeeze dry. Mix the breadcrumbs with the Ricotta, ⅓ cup (3 ounces) sugar, the egg yolks and grated orange rind. Blend thoroughly.

Heat plenty of olive oil for deep-frying. Take a little of the Ricotta mixture at a time, roll it first in flour and then in beaten egg. Deep-fry in hot oil until a pale golden color; drain on absorbent paper and serve, sprinkled with sugar.

Makes about 40 fritters.

Carteddate
Honey-coated Pastries

US		UK
1¾ cups	all-purpose (plain) flour	7 ounces
2½ tablespoons	mild olive oil	2 tablespoons
½ cup	sweet white wine	6 tablespoons
pinch	salt	pinch
	oil or lard for frying	
	honey	

Sift the flour into a bowl, make a well in the center and add the oil, wine and a pinch of salt. Mix to a firm dough and knead until smooth and elastic. Cover and leave to rest for about 1 hour.

Roll out the pastry a scant ¼ inch thick and then with a pastry wheel cut it into strips about 1 inch wide. Tie these into bows or shape into triangles or circles, making carnival fritters.

The pastries can either be fried in deep oil or fat until golden – not too fast so that they have a chance to cook right through – or spread out on an oiled baking sheet and baked in a hot oven (425°F. Mark 6) for 20 minutes.

Leave the pastries to cool and serve them coated with honey.

The dough can also be rolled out very thinly, in which case the pastries will become even more puffed and delicate. Drain on paper towels, cool and dust with confectioners' (icing) sugar.

Zeppole di San Giuseppe
St Joseph's Doughnuts

US		UK
8 cups	all-purpose (plain) flour	2 pounds
2 cakes	compressed (fresh) yeast	1⅓ ounces
about 2½ cups	lukewarm milk	about 1 pint
3	eggs	3
¾ cup	granulated (caster) sugar	5 ounces
	grated rind of 1 lemon	
pinch	salt	pinch
6 tablespoons	butter	3 ounces
	oil or lard for frying	
	confectioners' (icing) sugar	

Sift the flour into a large, warmed bowl and make a well in the center. Dissolve the yeast in ½ cup (U.K. 6 to 8 tablespoons) of the lukewarm milk and pour it into the well. Work it with the flour, gradually adding more of the milk, until the dough is workable but fairly stiff. Knead until smooth and elastic, then cover the bowl and leave the dough in a warm place to rise for about 2 hours, or until doubled in bulk.

Punch down the risen dough and work in the eggs, beaten with the sugar, lemon rind and salt. Knead until thoroughly blended and smooth again. Then melt the butter over a low heat in about 7 tablespoons (3½ fluid ounces) milk, cool to lukewarm, and gradually add to the dough, kneading vigorously all the time. The dough will now be fairly soft and sticky. Continue to knead it until it comes away cleanly from the fingers.

Sprinkle a pastry board lightly with flour and roll the dough out about ¼ inch thick (not thinner) with a floured rolling pin. Cut it into circles about 2½ inches in diameter. Spread the circles out on a lightly floured cloth and leave them to rise again until doubled in bulk.

When ready to fry the doughnuts, heat plenty of oil (or lard) in a deep pan. Test the temperature to make sure that it is not too high (350°–360°F.): a cube of bread should brown in 1 minute. Fry the doughnuts, two or three at a time, until puffed and golden brown on both sides. Drain on absorbent paper and dust generously with sifted confectioners' (icing) sugar.

Bocconotti
Apulian Baked Sweet Ravioli

US		UK
Custard		
5	egg yolks	5
⅔ cup	granulated (caster) sugar	5 ounces
¼ cup	all-purpose (plain) flour	1 ounce
pinch	vanilla powder *or* vanilla extract to taste	pinch
2 cups	milk	¾ pint
	rind of ½ lemon	
Ravioli pastry		
4 cups	all-purpose (plain) flour	1 pound
3 tablespoons	granulated (caster) sugar	1½ ounces
pinch	salt	pinch
¼ cup	mild olive oil	3 tablespoons
1 cup	sweet white wine	⅓ pint
	black cherry jam	
1	egg, lightly beaten	1
	oil	

Custard

Beat the egg yolks and sugar until well mixed and blend in the flour. Mix the milk with vanilla to taste (or vanilla sugar), and gradually add it to the egg mixture. Pour the mixture into the top of a double boiler, add the strip of lemon rind and cook over hot water, stirring constantly, until the custard is very thick. Pour into a bowl and leave to become quite cold.

Ravioli pastry

Sift the flour, sugar and salt on to a pastry board or into a large bowl. Make a well in the center, add the oil and enough wine to make a firm, pliable dough. Knead well and roll out very thinly into a square or rectangular sheet.

Arrange a neat row of teaspoonfuls of custard cream about 4 inches apart and 2½ inches from the edge of the dough. Top each mound with a teaspoonful of cherry jam. Fold the nearest edge of the dough over the row of filling and press down firmly between each little mound to seal it completely. Cut out squares with a pastry wheel or a sharp knife. Continue in this manner until all the pastry and filling are used up. Brush each square with beaten egg.

Grease a baking sheet with oil and arrange the squares on it in neat rows. Bake in a moderate oven (375°F. Mark 4) for 15 to 20 minutes, or until golden brown. Serve warm or cold.

SICILY

It seems strange that the seas surrounding this peaceful land of orange blossom and citrus fruit, where early in February the temples of Agrigento are submerged by flowering almond trees, should be the scene of a brutal ritual that takes place every spring. It is then that on the high seas off Trapani the *tonnare* are organized, fierce and bloody tuna-fishing expeditions that provide the Sicilians with some of their most delicious dishes. The *tonnare* begin when the fish surface in large numbers in search of a mate. They are channeled through several enclosed areas which lead to a central "hall of death", a kind of enclave in the middle of the sea, the walls of which are formed by fishing boats and the bottom by a strong net. The chase is led by the *rais*, or leader, who shouts the orders. Slowly, the ends of the net are drawn on board, and as the fish rise to the surface in the gradually diminishing area of water, they are clubbed and hoisted on board. The chanting of the fishermen, the yells of the *rais*, and the thrashing of the great fish make this a violent and dramatic spectacle.

In the Straits of Messina, which separate Sicily from the mainland, the traditional hunt for swordfish is just as cruel. The fish are stopped in the Straits in the spawning season on their way from the Atlantic to the African coast of the Mediterranean. As soon as a fish is sighted, it is followed in rowing boats and harpooned. The harpoon is attached to the boat by a long cable, which gives the fish the illusion that it can escape, but in the end, exhausted by the effort, it weakens and submits.

Tuna and swordfish have inspired many famous Sicilian

Delicacies from Messina, besides swordfish, include salt cod and *pasta 'ncaciata* (see page 266). *Below: Arancini di riso*, or rice croquettes (see page 268), sardines *a beccafico* (see page 271), fresh vegetable salad, *pasta con le sarde*, or macaroni with sardines (see page 266), *involtini*, and *caponata* in sweet-sour sauce (see page 273), with Palermo in the background.

At the foot of Elephant Fountain, emblem of Catania, a dish of red mullet with onions and spaghetti with eggplants (see page 265). *Below:* Two dishes from the country around Mount Etna: pasta with cuttlefish ink, and *farsumagru,* a delicious Sicilian meat loaf (see page 268).

dishes: *tonno alla cipollata,* which consists of tuna fried with large quantities of sliced onions, and swordfish *alla messinese,* swordfish cooked in oil with tomatoes, onions, celery, olives, capers and potatoes. Sardines, too, have an important place in Sicilian cooking, served fried, or *a beccafico,* stuffed with breadcrumbs, grated cheese, pine nuts and raisins (see page 271), or as *pasta con le sarde* (macaroni and sardine pie), Palermo's famous entrée (see page 266). There is also an excellent Sicilian fish soup of Arabic origin, cooked mainly in Trapani, called *cùscusu* (see page 267).

Sicilian fishermen are noted for their bold incursions beyond the Mediterranean. The most highly skilled, who come from Mazara del Valle near Trapani, catch almost half of all the Italian tuna fish, and every year they dispute the fishing primacy of the country with the men of San Benedetto del Tronto (see page 146).

Although there is plenty of fish in Sicily, there is not much meat, and most of the recipes are for rabbit and pork. However, fruit and cereals of every kind abound. Wheat, for instance, has always been an important product, and although Naples is now the main pasta-making center, it is here in Sicily that it was first made. There are references to *maccaruni,* the name given to the original pasta, in records dating from as far back as 1250. A legend concerning William the Hermit tells how he was invited to a meal by a Sicilian nobleman, who served him *maccaruni.* But instead of being stuffed with Ricotta cheese, the noodles were filled with pure earth. Undaunted, William blessed the food and by a miracle the earth became Ricotta, as prescribed in the recipe. This dish still exists, the *cannelloni* of Catania, filled as they were then with Ricotta and meat, and served garnished with a rich and plentiful sauce and grated cheese.

Sicilians serve pasta in many different ways. It is frequently eaten with fish, and invariably flavored with olive oil and tomatoes. Besides *pasta con le sarde*, there is *pasta con le melanzane*, a specialty of Catania (see page 265). This dish is also sometimes known as *pasta alla Norma*, in honor of the composer of *Norma*, Vincenzo Bellini, who was born in Catania in 1801. There is also a strange-looking dish made by cooking spaghetti with squid in their own inky secretion.

Rice, which plays such an important role in Italian regional cooking, is practically unknown here, although it was introduced into Italy through Sicily by the Arabs. Indeed, until a few years ago rice was looked upon exclusively as invalid food, and sold in chemists' shops. *Arancini di riso*, a traditional Sicilian snack (see page 267), is one of the few rice dishes to have been created here.

Butter is not used for cooking in Sicily. There are few cows and any milk that is not drunk is used for making cheese, which is essential for flavoring pasta. Cheeses used for grating are invariably tasty: the salty Incanestrato, Piacentino, made with pepper, and Caciocavallo.

Sicily's huge citrus plantations, the luxuriant vegetation, the fragrance of asphodel and orange blossom, could exist only in a land of sunshine. Sun means grapes and grapes mean wine, and the wines of Sicily are famous all over the world. Oddly enough,

In a symphony of sea and greenery, the specialties of the Ristorante "Il Pescatore" in Mazzarò (Taormina): grey rock mullet, *cannelloni*, rice with seafood, mussels and octopus.

One of Trapani's most traditional dishes is *cùscusu* (couscous), of ancient Arab origin. It is generally served with a rich fish soup (see page 267).

Some Syracusan fish dishes photographed in the Grotto of the Cordari: *sarago* (a kind of porgy) cooked *en papillote*, fish stew, mussels *au gratin*, and *dentice (dentex) alla siracusana*, accompanied by the famous Moscato, or Muscatel, said to have been brought over from Thrace more than 2,600 years ago.

Marsala, one of the best known, was first produced by an Englishman, John Woodhouse, who landed at the small port of Marsala toward the end of the eighteenth century. He soon realized that the local grapes would yield a highly alcoholic and aromatic wine similar to those made in Spain and Portugal. One of Woodhouse's first distinguished customers was Lord Nelson, who was followed by some of the best London families.

The best wines of the province of Palermo are Corvo, a white wine which is ideal with fish, Partinico and Monreale. In the province of Syracuse they make Eloro, a white wine, Pachino, Albanello, and a Muscatel which came over from Thrace at the time of the foundation of Rome. At Messina, Capo Bianco is produced, specially recommended with broiled (grilled) swordfish, and Milazzo and Barcellona. The Etna wines come from the neighborhood of Catania, where the proximity of the volcano is said to make the local vineyards particularly fertile. One of the best Etna wines is Val di Lupo, excellent with fish. One of these "volcanic" wines particularly worthy of consideration is the Malmsley which is produced on the islands of Lipari, Salina and Stromboli, and has a sweet, velvety taste. A Muscatel made with a very sweet grape called *zibibbo* comes from the distant island of Pantelleria, off the African coast.

The quality of the local fruit, almonds, honey and aromatic roots which are the basic raw materials of confectionery have helped to give the Sicilians their great reputation as pastry cooks. They are also well known for *frutti di marturana*, made with almond

Sicilian ice creams are famous the world over. Here is a delicious assortment, with a traditional *cassata* (see page 274) in the foreground. *Below:* Sicilian pastrycooks have brought their art, inherited from the Arabs, to a high degree of perfection. Seen below, some delicious sweetmeats, including a *cassata*, arranged around a Paschal lamb made of sugar. On the facing page, a ring-shaped cake called *buccellato* with *mustazzoli* (see page 276) on the left and a plate of delicious fried stuffed pastries known as *cannoli* (see page 275) on the right.

paste which is shaped and painted in bright colors to look like fruit. And Sicilian ice cream is famous all over the world. One of the most delicious is *cassata granita* with cream. The first and greatest purveyor of ice cream was Procopio Coltelli, who introduced it into France in about 1630. The Café Procope, which he founded in Paris, is said to have counted Voltaire, Balzac and Baudelaire among its distinguished clients.

Caciocavallo al Fumo
Steamed Caciocavallo Cheese

Cut about 2 pounds Caciocavallo cheese into strips about ¼ inch thick and put them into a deep serving dish. Dress with 3 or 4 tablespoons olive oil and a generous teaspoon of chopped oregano.

Fill a medium-sized pan with water, bring it to the boil and rest the dish of cheese over the pan. Continue boiling until the cheese has melted, about 15 minutes, and serve immediately.

Serves 6 to 8.

Formaggio all'Argintera
Fried Cheese

For this dish Caciocavallo or Incanestrato cheese should be used. Incanestrato, literally "basketed", is a popular Italian cheese rather like Pecorino. It is pressed into wicker baskets and the markings show on the surface of the cheese – hence the name.

Cut about 2 pounds cheese into ¼-inch-thick strips. Sauté ½ clove garlic in 3 or 4 tablespoons oil in a frying pan. As soon as the garlic browns, discard it and add the cheese. Fry over a low heat on both sides and sprinkle with 3 or 4 teaspoons wine vinegar. Add a pinch of sugar and a teaspoon of finely chopped fresh oregano, and continue cooking for 5 minutes longer, taking care that the cheese does not overcook, as this will cause it to harden. Serve hot.

Serves 6.

Salmoriglio
Sicilian Sauce

US		UK
1 cup	olive oil	scant ½ pint
	juice of 2 lemons	
4 teaspoons	finely chopped parsley	1 tablespoon
2½ teaspoons	finely chopped fresh oregano	2 teaspoons
	salt	

This sauce is served with both roast meat and baked fish.

Beat the olive oil in a warm bowl, gradually adding ¼ cup (U.K. 3 tablespoons) hot water, the lemon juice, parsley and oregano. Add salt to taste and warm the sauce in the top of a double boiler. Pour it hot over meat or fish, and serve immediately.

Scacciata
Sicilian Bread Pie

US		UK
2 pounds	once-risen bread dough, made with 5 cups (1¼ pounds) flour	2 pounds
	olive oil	
¼ pound	unripened Caciocavallo cheese	¼ pound
6–8	salted anchovies	6–8
¼ pound	cooked ham	¼ pound
1	onion	1
3 large	ripe tomatoes	3 large
12–16	black olives, pitted	12–16
	salt and pepper	

Knead the risen dough, adding 2½ tablespoons (U.K. 2 tablespoons) oil. Divide the dough into two equal parts and roll it out into two rounds of equal size about ½ inch thick. Brush a round baking pan with oil and cover with one round of dough. Put aside.

Cut the cheese into thin slices. Thoroughly wash the anchovies to remove all the salt, drain and cut into small pieces, discarding heads, tails and bones. Cut the ham into long strips. Slice the onion; peel and chop the tomatoes, discarding seeds, and chop the olives.

Cover the dough in the baking pan with slices of cheese, then add the anchovies, ham, onion, tomatoes and olives. Sprinkle lightly with salt and generously with freshly ground black pepper. Cover with the remaining round of dough and press the edges together firmly. Prick the top with a fork and brush lightly with olive oil. Bake the pie in a hot oven (425°F. Mark 6) for about 40 minutes. Serve hot or cold.

Serves 6.

Sfincione di San Vito
San Vito Pizza

US		UK
1 pound	once-risen bread dough, made with 2½ cups (10 ounces) flour	1 pound
	olive oil	
1¼ pounds	ripe tomatoes	1¼ pounds
1	onion, finely chopped	1
	salt and pepper	
¾ pound	salted sardines	¾ pound
¼ pound	Caciocavallo cheese, diced	¼ pound

This particular pizza is popular in the area around Palermo.

Knead the risen dough, adding as you knead 5 tablespoons (U.K. 4 tablespoons) olive oil. When the dough is smooth and elastic, shape it into a ball and leave it to rise again, about 2 hours.

In the meantime, prepare the filling. Peel and chop the tomatoes, discarding seeds. Heat ½ cup (U.K. 6 to 8 tablespoons) olive oil in a pan and sauté the onion; as soon as it changes color add the tomatoes, a little salt and pepper, and cook over a low heat for 30 minutes.

Wash the sardines, cut off heads and tails, open them and remove their backbones. Add half of the sardines to the tomato sauce and continue cooking for another 10 minutes.

Brush a 12-inch shallow baking pan with oil. Roll the dough out lightly and fit it into the pan. Spread it with half the tomato and sardine sauce and all of the cheese. Bake in a moderate oven (375°F. Mark 4) for about 20 minutes. Cover with the rest of the sauce and the sardines, sprinkle with a little oil and bake for 10 minutes longer. Serve very hot.

Serves 6 to 8.

Spaghetti con le Melanzane
Spaghetti with Eggplants (Aubergines)

US		UK
6	eggplants (aubergines)	6
	salt and pepper	
	olive oil	
2 cloves	garlic, crushed	2 cloves
2 pounds	ripe tomatoes	2 pounds
2–3 sprigs	basil, finely chopped	2–3 sprigs
1½ pounds	spaghetti	1½ pounds
¾ cup	grated Pecorino or Parmesan cheese	3 ounces

Wipe the eggplants (aubergines), peel them and cut them into thin slices. Sprinkle with salt and leave in a colander or on a tilted plate for 1 hour to drain off their bitter juices. Wipe the slices dry and fry in hot oil, a few at a time, until brown on both sides. Drain on paper towels.

Pour about ½ cup (U.K. 6 tablespoons) oil into a small pan, sauté the garlic cloves until brown and discard them. Peel and chop the tomatoes, discarding seeds. Stir the tomatoes into the oil and cook for 20 minutes. Add salt, plenty of pepper and basil to taste.

Bring a large pan of salted water to a bubbling boil. Add the spaghetti and cook until tender but still firm. Drain and dress immediately with the fried eggplants, the tomato sauce and the cheese. Serve at once with plenty of additional grated cheese.

Serves 6.

Pasta 'ncaciata

Sicilian Macaroni with Cheese and Eggplants (Aubergines)

US		UK
8	eggplants (aubergines)	8
	salt	
	olive oil	
2 pounds	ripe tomatoes	2 pounds
1 clove	garlic, crushed	1 clove
	pepper	
2–3 sprigs	basil, finely chopped	2–3 sprigs
$1\frac{1}{2}$ pounds	macaroni	$1\frac{1}{2}$ pounds
$\frac{1}{4}$ pound	salami, sliced	$\frac{1}{4}$ pound
$\frac{1}{4}$ pound	Mozzarella cheese, diced	$\frac{1}{4}$ pound
$\frac{2}{3}$ cup	grated Pecorino or Parmesan cheese	2 ounces
2	hard-boiled eggs, sliced	2

The number of eggplants (aubergines) required depends on their size. There must be sufficient to line a deep 12-inch-diameter baking dish. Wipe the eggplants, peel and cut them into $\frac{1}{2}$-inch-thick slices. Sprinkle the slices with salt and leave on a rack or a tilted plate to drain off excess liquid. Dry well.

Heat plenty of olive oil and fry the eggplant slices until brown on both sides. Drain on paper towels. Line the bottom and sides of the dish with the eggplants, overlapping the slices (the dish is turned out to serve). Left-over slices should be finely chopped.

Peel and chop the tomatoes, discarding seeds. Pour off all but about 1 cup (U.K. scant $\frac{1}{2}$ pint) oil from the pan. Sauté the garlic until brown and discard it. Add the tomatoes, season with salt and pepper, and cook over a brisk heat for 20 minutes. Stir in basil to taste.

Bring a large pan of salted water to the boil and cook the macaroni until tender but still firm. Drain well. Turn into a bowl and mix with the salami, Mozzarella and Parmesan cheeses, tomato sauce and if any is left over, chopped eggplant. Cover the bottom of the lined dish with the sliced eggs. Add the macaroni mixture and bake in a moderately hot oven (400°F. Mark 5) for about 20 minutes. Take the dish from the pan, leave to settle for a couple of minutes and turn out. Serve very hot with plenty of additional grated cheese.

Serves 6.

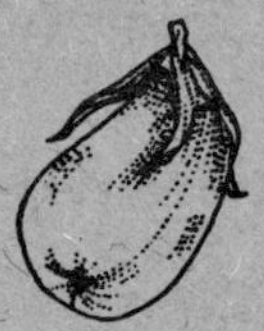

Pasta con le Sarde

Macaroni and Sardine Pie

US		UK
$\frac{3}{4}$ pound	bulb fennel – see page 68	$\frac{3}{4}$ pound
	salt	
1 pound	fresh sardines	1 pound
5	salted anchovies	5
2 cups	olive oil	$\frac{3}{4}$ pint
2	onions, sliced	2
	pepper	
$\frac{1}{2}$ cup	pine nuts	3 ounces
$\frac{1}{2}$ cup	seedless white raisins (sultanas)	3 ounces
$1\frac{3}{4}$ pounds	short thick macaroni	$1\frac{3}{4}$ pounds

Wash and trim the fennel, and put into a pan with about 8 cups (U.K. $3\frac{1}{4}$ pints) cold salted water. Bring to the boil and cook for 10 to 15 minutes, or until tender. Drain thoroughly, gently squeeze dry and chop coarsely. Reserve the cooking liquid for later use.

Wash the sardines carefully, open them and remove backbones and heads. Wash carefully in plenty of salted water, drain and wipe dry on a cloth. Wash and bone the anchovies, discarding heads and tails.

Heat half the oil in a pan and sauté the onions until golden. Add half the sardines and crush them with a wooden spoon until reduced to a paste. Add the anchovies and continue to cook until these have dissolved into the sardine paste. Sprinkle lightly with salt and generously with freshly ground pepper. Add the pine nuts and white raisins (sultanas), cover the pan and cook for a few minutes. If the sauce seems too thick, dilute with a little of the fennel cooking liquid. Keep hot.

Heat a little more oil in another pan and fry the rest of the sardines until brown, turning them once without breaking them. Season with salt and pepper, and continue to cook gently for 10 minutes.

Bring the fennel liquid to the boil, add the macaroni and cook until tender but still firm. Drain, turn into a bowl and mix thoroughly with half the sardine sauce. Put a layer of the dressed macaroni at the bottom of an ovenproof dish. Cover with a few of the cooked whole sardines and a few tablespoons of sauce. Continue in this manner until all the ingredients are used up – the top layer should be of macaroni, spread with sauce. Cover the dish and bake in a moderate oven (375°F. Mark 4) for 20 minutes. Serve hot or cold.

Serves 6.

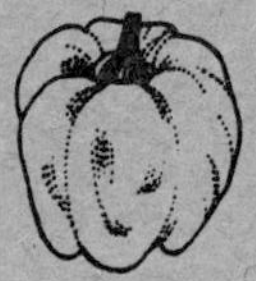

Vermicelli alla Siciliana

Vermicelli Sicilian Style

US		UK
1 large	eggplant (aubergine)	1 large
	salt	
$\frac{1}{2}$ cup	olive oil	6–8 tablespoons
2 cloves	garlic, crushed	2 cloves
6 large	ripe tomatoes	6 large
2	sweet peppers	2
	pepper	
3 3–4 large	salted anchovies, boned, *or* anchovy fillets	3 3–4 large
$\frac{1}{2}$ cup	black olives, pitted and halved	3 ounces
4 teaspoons	capers	1 tablespoon
2–3 sprigs	basil, finely chopped	2–3 sprigs
$1\frac{1}{2}$ pounds	vermicelli	$1\frac{1}{2}$ pounds

Wash the eggplant (aubergine) and cut it into small cubes. Sprinkle with salt and leave on a tilted plate or in a colander to drain off bitter juices.

Heat the oil in a small pan and sauté the garlic cloves until brown, then discard them. Peel and chop the tomatoes, discarding seeds. Add to the pan together with the chopped eggplant. Sprinkle lightly with salt and cook gently for about 20 minutes.

Char the peppers under the broiler (grill) or over heat until their skins are burnt and blistered. Cool, then pull off the thin burnt skin. Cut the peppers in half and discard cores and seeds. Cut the flesh into thin strips and add them to the tomato sauce. Sprinkle generously with freshly ground pepper, and simmer gently until softened. Wash the anchovies and chop them into small pieces. Add to the pan. Stir in the olives, capers and basil. Cover the pan and cook gently for 10 to 15 minutes.

Boil the vermicelli in salted water until tender but still firm. Drain, dress with the hot sauce and serve immediately.

Serves 6.

Cùscusu Trapanese

Couscous Trapani Style

US		UK
1 pound	coarse semolina *or*	1 pound
½ pound each	coarse and fine semolina	½ pound each
pinch	saffron – optional	pinch
⅔ cup	olive oil	¼ pint
	salt and pepper	
1 clove	garlic, finely chopped	1 clove
1	onion, finely chopped	1

Fish stew

3 pounds	assorted fish – see method	3 pounds
	salt	
1 cup	olive oil	scant ½ pint
2 cloves	garlic, finely chopped	2 cloves
1 medium-sized	onion, finely chopped	1 medium-sized
2–3 sprigs	parsley, finely chopped	2–3 sprigs
1–2	tomatoes – optional	1–2
10 cups	hot water	4 pints
	pepper	

This dish, which is of Berber origin, calls for special utensils and takes some time to prepare, but the results are well worth the effort and the utensils can be improvized without much difficulty.

The *pignata di cùscusu* in which the couscous is steamed over boiling water, is a glazed earthenware pan with a rounded and perforated bottom, which can be rested on a pan of the same size. A double steamer, or a metal sieve which fits exactly over a large pan, can be used instead with excellent results.

Contrary to the North Africans, who serve this dish with meat, fish, vegetables, yoghourt, and even sweet, with milk, sugar and raisins, Sicilians eat couscous only with fish: mixed shallow water fish, eel or even large shellfish such as crawfish (U.K. crayfish) or lobster. However, the manner of preparing the grain is identical.

Put two handfuls of the grain into a large bowl and sprinkle with a little water in which you have dissolved the saffron, if used. Work the grains with your fingers to separate them and moisten them evenly. Rake them with one hand and with the other rub into small grains resembling lead shot. If the mixture becomes too wet, add a little dry semolina and start again. Continue in this manner, adding more semolina and water, until all the grains are moistened. Once or twice during the process put the grains into a sieve and shake the dry semolina out gently over the bowl. Spread the grains remaining in the sieve out on a cloth to dry.

Fill the bottom part of the utensil to be used with water – not too much, the couscous should cook in steam and the water must *never* touch it. Put the prepared grains in the top part and dress them with olive oil, a little salt and pepper, the garlic and onion. Mix thoroughly but lightly. Put a damp cloth round the two utensils where they join to prevent steam from escaping, cover and steam over a very low heat for about 1½ hours.

Fish stew – "Ghiotta"

Clean and wash the fish in salted water. In a large casserole sauté the garlic and onion until golden. Add the parsley and the fish, all in one layer. Cover with tomatoes, peeled and chopped, if used. Pour in the water, sprinkle with salt and pepper, and simmer for 20 minutes, or until the fish are cooked. Keep hot.

When the couscous is ready, turn it into a large, heated bowl, stir it with a fork to break up any lumps and pour in enough of the fish stock to make a very thick soup. Cover the bowl, wrap it in a thick woolen cloth and leave for ½ hour in a warm place. The grains will absorb the stock and swell up. Add more stock to moisten the couscous thoroughly, ladle into individual bowls and garnish with some fish. Serve with additional stock and a sprinkling of pepper.

Serves 6.

Arancini di Riso

Sicilian Rice Croquettes

US		UK
5 cups	meat stock	2 pints
1½ cups	risotto rice – see page 66	10 ounces
pinch	saffron – optional	pinch
3 tablespoons	butter	1½ ounces
⅔ cup	grated Parmesan cheese	2 ounces
2	eggs	2
½ cup	diced Provola cheese	3 ounces
	fine dry breadcrumbs	
	oil or lard for frying	

Sauce (Filling)

¼ cup	olive oil	3 tablespoons
2 tablespoons	butter	1 ounce
1 small	onion, finely chopped	1 small
¼ pound	ground (UK minced) lean veal	¼ pound
¼ pound	chicken giblets, finely chopped	¼ pound
4 teaspoons	tomato paste	1 tablespoon
1 cup	shelled green peas	4–5 ounces
	salt and pepper	

Heat half the stock until boiling, stir in the rice and cook over a brisk heat until the stock has evaporated. In the meantime, dissolve the saffron in the remaining stock. Gradually pour this on to the rice and continue cooking for another 15 minutes, or until the rice is tender and dry. Add the butter, Parmesan cheese and 1 egg.

Sauce (Filling)

Heat the olive oil, add the butter and when this is blended into the oil add the onion and cook over low heat until it begins to change color. Stir in the meat, cook for a minute or two, then add the giblets. Fry until the meat and giblets are brown. Dilute the tomato paste with a little water and stir into the pan. Add the peas and salt and pepper to taste, and continue cooking for about 20 minutes. Put aside.

Take small portions of the rice and shape them into ball-shaped croquettes. Make a hole in the middle of each croquette and fill it with some of the sauce and a little diced cheese. Smooth over the opening to enclose the filling. Dip into the remaining egg, beaten, and roll in breadcrumbs. Deep-fry in hot oil or lard until golden all over. Drain quickly and serve at once. (They can be kept hot for a short while in a hot oven.)

Serves 6.

Pallottoline in Brodo

Sicilian Meat Ball Soup

US		UK
½ pound	ground (UK minced) lean beef	½ pound
1	egg	1
8 teaspoons	grated Parmesan cheese	2 tablespoons
4 teaspoons	soft breadcrumbs	1 tablespoon
	salt and pepper	
2–3 sprigs	parsley, finely chopped	2–3 sprigs
½ clove	garlic, finely chopped	½ clove
7½ cups	meat stock	3 pints
½ pound	tagliatelle ribbon noodles	½ pound

Mix the meat, egg, Parmesan cheese, breadcrumbs, salt and pepper, parsley and garlic in a bowl. Knead until smooth, then break off small pieces of the mixture and roll them into balls about the size of a hazelnut.

Bring the stock to the boil, add the meat balls and simmer for 5 minutes. Add the noodles and cook these until tender but still firm. Serve immediately with plenty of additional grated Parmesan.

Serves 6.

Minestra di Piselli Freschi e Carciofi
Fresh Pea and Artichoke Soup

US		UK
3 young	artichokes	3 young
1	lemon	1
4 tablespoons	olive oil	3 tablespoons
1 clove	garlic, crushed	1 clove
1 pound	green peas, shelled	1 pound
2 sprigs	parsley, finely chopped	2 sprigs
7½ cups	water	3 pints
pinch	baking soda	pinch
	salt	
	grated Parmesan or Pecorino cheese	
	slices of toasted bread	

Italian artichokes should be used in this recipe as they are without chokes. Remove the outer leaves and cut the artichokes into quarters. Wash them in water acidulated with a little lemon juice. Heat the olive oil in a large pan and sauté the garlic until brown. Discard it, then add the peas, artichokes and parsley. Fry for 1 minute. Dissolve the soda in a little of the water and add it to the pan, together with the remaining water. Sprinkle lightly with salt, cover the pan and cook over a low heat for 30 minutes.

Serve very hot, garnished with plenty of grated cheese and slices of toasted bread.

Serves 6.

"Farsumagru" – Falso Magro
Sicilian Meat Loaf

US		UK
1 pound	ground (UK minced) lean beef	1 pound
2	eggs	2
2	egg yolks	2
4 tablespoons	grated Caciocavallo cheese	3 tablespoons
2–3 sprigs	parsley, finely chopped	2–3 sprigs
pinch	finely chopped marjoram – optional	pinch
pinch	finely chopped thyme – optional	pinch
	salt and pepper	
	freshly grated nutmeg	
1 thin slice	lean beef – about ¾ pound	1 thin slice
2	hard-boiled eggs	2
¼ pound	Caciocavallo cheese	¼ pound
1 slice	fat salt pork – about 5 ounces	1 slice
1 thick slice	Parma ham – about ¼ pound	1 thick slice
4 tablespoons	lard	2 ounces
2	onions, finely chopped	2
⅔ cup	red wine	¼ pint
2 cups	tomato sauce – optional	¾ pint

Put the first seven ingredients into a large bowl and mix thoroughly until smooth and well blended, adding salt, pepper and nutmeg to taste.

Beat the slice of beef until it is rectangular and make small cuts along the edges to prevent it from curling up when cooking. Slice the hard-boiled eggs and cut the remaining cheese, the salt pork and ham into strips.

Spread the beef slice with the ground (U.K. minced) meat mixture, leaving the edges free. Cover with the sliced hard-boiled eggs, cheese, ham and salt pork. Roll up the meat and tie it securely.

Melt the lard in a heavy casserole, sauté the chopped onions until golden, then the meat roll, turning it until it is brown all over. Add the wine and cook over a moderate heat until it evaporates. Sprinkle with salt and pepper, cover and cook over a moderately low heat for 1½ hours. The meat roll can be served either hot or cold. If hot, serve it smothered with a hot tomato sauce.

Serves 6 to 8.

Agnellino al Forno
Sicilian Roast Lamb

US		UK
3–3½ pounds	leg of lamb	3–3½ pounds
1 slice	Parma ham, about ¼ pound, diced	1 slice
1 sprig	rosemary	1 sprig
5 tablespoons	melted lard	2½ ounces
	salt and pepper	
4 tablespoons	fresh breadcrumbs	3 tablespoons
4 tablespoons	grated Pecorino or Parmesan cheese	3 tablespoons

Lamb in Sicily, as in other parts of Italy, is killed very young. Although a piece of young lamb will be cooked sufficiently for Sicilian taste in 30 minutes, for most people, especially when cooking older lamb, longer cooking is advised.

Wipe the meat with a damp cloth and with the point of a sharp knife make small incisions all over the surface. Into each incision push a piece of ham and a few spikes of rosemary.

Put the meat into a baking pan just large enough to hold it. Spread with lard, season lightly with salt and generously with freshly ground pepper. Mix the breadcrumbs with the cheese and sprinkle over the meat. Roast in a moderate oven (375°F. Mark 4) until tender, turning and basting occasionally with pan juices.

Serves 6.

Bistecche alla Siciliana
Sicilian Beefsteak

US		UK
6 small	beef steaks	6 small
6 large	ripe tomatoes	6 large
½ cup	olive oil	6 tablespoons
2 cloves	garlic, crushed	2 cloves
½ cup	black olives, pitted	3–4 ounces
½ cup	sliced small pickled sweet peppers	3–4 ounces
½ stalk	celery, diced	½ stalk
2–3 tablespoons	capers	2–2½ tablespoons
	salt and pepper	
1 teaspoon	finely chopped fresh oregano	1 teaspoon

Peel and chop the tomatoes, discarding seeds. Heat the olive oil in a heavy frying pan and sauté the garlic cloves until brown. Discard them and sear the steaks in the same oil for 2 minutes on each side. Add the olives, peppers, celery, capers and tomatoes. Season with salt and pepper, and sprinkle with oregano. Cook for a few minutes longer. Serve at once, covered with the sauce.

Serves 6.

Vitello con Melanzane
Veal with Eggplants (Aubergines)

US		UK
6 thin slices	veal fillet	6 thin slices
2 large	eggplants (aubergines)	2 large
	salt	
	olive oil	
5 large	ripe tomatoes	5 large
½ cup	green or black olives, pitted	3–4 ounces
3–4 leaves	basil, finely chopped	3–4 leaves
3 tablespoons	butter	1½ ounces
	flour	

Wipe the eggplants (aubergines) with a damp cloth. Peel and slice them thinly. Sprinkle with salt and leave in a colander or on a tilted plate to drain away their bitter juices. Wipe dry. Heat plenty of oil in a deep frying pan and fry the eggplants, a few slices at a time, until brown on both sides. Take from the pan with a perforated spoon and drain on paper towels. Put aside.

Drain off all but 4 tablespoons (U.K. 3 tablespoons) oil from the pan. Peel and chop the tomatoes, discarding seeds, and cook them in the olive oil for 10 minutes over a high heat. Add salt to taste, the olives, basil and eggplants. Lower heat and simmer for 5 minutes.

Melt the butter in a frying pan. Dust the veal slices with flour and fry quickly for 5 minutes on each side until browned (add more butter if required). Take the veal slices from the pan and place them in one layer in a shallow earthenware baking dish. Cover with the sauce and bake in a moderate oven (375°F. Mark 4) for a few minutes to heat through. Serve hot.

Serves 6.

Polpette di Maiale con Pitaggio
Pork Rissoles with Vegetables

US		UK
1 pound	ground (UK minced) lean pork	1 pound
	soft pith of 1 small bread roll	
	milk	
2 cloves	garlic, finely chopped	2 cloves
2–3 sprigs	parsley, finely chopped	2–3 sprigs
¾ cup	grated Parmesan or Pecorino cheese	3 ounces
2	eggs	2
	salt and pepper	
	flour	
⅔ cup	olive oil	¼ pint
Vegetables		
2 young	artichokes – without chokes	2 young
½	lemon	½
2 cups	shelled green peas	½ pound
	salt	
2 cups	shelled fava (broad) beans	½ pound

Moisten the bread with a little milk and squeeze dry. Mix with the meat, garlic, parsley, grated cheese and eggs, and season with salt and freshly ground pepper. Knead the mixture well, break off small pieces and shape them into rissoles. Coat with flour and reserve.

Wash the artichokes in water acidulated with lemon juice. Discard the coarser leaves and cut the artichokes into quarters. Drop them into boiling water and cook for 5 minutes. Drain and keep hot. Cook the peas and beans until tender. Drain and keep hot.

Heat the oil and fry the rissoles until brown all over, cooking them for at least 5 minutes on each side. Take from the pan and arrange on a heated serving dish. Sauté the artichokes, peas and beans in the same oil for a few minutes, and arrange them round the rissoles as a garnish. Serve hot.

Serves 6.

Scaloppe di Maiale al Marsala
Pork with Marsala

US		UK
2 pounds	pork fillet	2 pounds
4 tablespoons	lard	2 ounces
	salt and pepper	
⅔ cup	Marsala wine	¼ pint
1 teaspoon	flour	1 teaspoon
4 tablespoons	butter, slivered	2 ounces

Trim the pork of any fat and slice it about half-way through. Lay it open flat like a book and flatten it with a cutlet bat rinsed in water. Cut the meat into pieces about 4 inches long and 2 inches wide. Beat these again until very thin, taking care not to break the slices.

Melt the lard in a frying pan and brown the meat slices for 2 minutes on each side over a high heat. Sprinkle lightly with salt and generously with freshly ground pepper. Take the meat from the pan and arrange in a heated oval serving dish, the slices overlapping. Keep hot in a warm oven.

Pour the Marsala into the pan, add the flour and stir this into the pan juices quickly with a wooden spoon. Continue stirring until the sauce is thick and smooth; add the butter and when this has melted, pour the hot sauce over the meat. Serve immediately.

Serves 6.

Pollo Spezzato e Melanzane
Chicken with Eggplants (Aubergines)

US		UK
1	chicken – 3 pounds	1
5	eggplants (aubergines)	5
	salt	
1 cup	olive oil	scant ½ pint
1 clove	garlic, crushed	1 clove
	pepper	
1 cup	dry white wine	scant ½ pint
1 pound	ripe tomatoes	1 pound
¼ pound	ham fat or streaky bacon, finely chopped	¼ pound
	stock or water	
2–3 sprigs	parsley, finely chopped	2–3 sprigs

Wipe the chicken with a damp cloth and cut it into four pieces. Wash the eggplants (aubergines) and cut them into small pieces; sprinkle with salt and leave in a colander or on a tilted plate for 1 hour to drain off their bitter juices.

Heat about a third of the olive oil in a casserole and sauté the garlic until brown. Discard it and add the pieces of chicken. Fry them evenly all over until golden brown. Sprinkle with salt and pepper, add the wine and cook, uncovered, over a moderate heat until it has evaporated.

Peel and chop the tomatoes, discarding seeds, and add them to the chicken as soon as the wine has evaporated. Add the ham fat. Taste for salt, cover and continue cooking for 30 minutes. Moisten with a little hot stock or water if necessary.

Heat the remaining oil in another pan. Wipe the eggplant pieces dry and fry them over a high heat for 15 minutes, sprinkled generously with pepper and parsley. Stir them gently into the casserole a few minutes before the chicken is ready. Serve very hot.

Serves 4.

Pernici alle Olive
Partridges with Olives

US		UK
6	partridges, dressed	6
	salt and pepper	
	sage leaves	
12 small slices	ham	12 small slices
½ cup	olive oil	6 tablespoons
2 cups	dry white wine	¾ pint
½ pound	green or black olives, pitted	½ pound
⅔ cup	hot stock or water	¼ pint

Wipe the partridges gently with a damp cloth, putting aside their livers. Sprinkle the insides with salt and pepper and add a leaf or two of sage – not too much as this is a powerful herb. Lightly sprinkle the outsides with salt and wrap each bird in 2 slices of ham, securing them with strong thread.

Heat the oil in a casserole and fry the partridges until brown all over. Add the wine and cook, uncovered, until it evaporates. Chop the livers and add them to the casserole, together with the olives. Moisten with a little hot stock or water, cover the pan and simmer for 30 minutes.

To serve, discard the threads and arrange the partridges on a heated serving dish. Cover with their sauce and garnish with the ham slices.

Serves 6.

Coniglio in Agrodolce
Rabbit in Sweet-sour Sauce

US		UK
1	rabbit, about 3–3½ pounds, disjointed	1
2½ tablespoons	olive oil	2 tablespoons
4 tablespoons	butter	2 ounces
small piece	fat salt pork, diced	small piece
1	onion, finely chopped	1
	flour	
	salt and pepper	
⅔ cup	stock	¼ pint
2½ tablespoons	sugar	2 tablespoons
½ cup	wine vinegar	6–8 tablespoons
4 tablespoons	seedless white raisins (sultanas)	3 tablespoons
4 tablespoons	pine nuts	3 tablespoons

Marinade		
2 cups	red wine	¾ pint
1 small	onion, sliced	1 small
2	cloves	2
1 sprig	parsley	1 sprig
1	bay leaf	1
1 sprig	thyme	1 sprig
4–5	black peppercorns	4–5
	salt	

Wipe the rabbit clean. Put all the marinade ingredients into a small pan and slowly bring to boiling point. Take from the heat immediately and leave it until just warm. Put the rabbit pieces into a bowl, pour over the marinade and leave for 2 hours.

Heat the oil, butter and salt pork together in a large casserole, and sauté the onion until golden brown. Take the pieces of rabbit from the marinade, dry well, coat with flour and fry with the onion.

Strain the marinade over the rabbit and cook, uncovered, for 20 minutes over a moderate heat. When the wine has almost evaporated and the rabbit has darkened, season with salt and freshly ground pepper. Add enough hot stock or water to cover the rabbit pieces, cover the pan, lower the heat and simmer for another 20 minutes. If the sauce seems rather thin and the rabbit is already tender, cook quickly, uncovered, to reduce it.

Dissolve the sugar in a small (preferably copper) pan with 4 teaspoons (U.K. 1 tablespoon) water. When it begins to change color and becomes almost golden, add the vinegar, stirring constantly with a wooden spoon. Add the white raisins (sultanas) and cook them for a moment to let them swell. Add the sauce to the casserole, pouring it over the rabbit pieces and scraping the bottom of the casserole. Stir in the pine nuts and serve immediately.

Serves 4.

Ragù di Tonno
Fresh Tuna Fish Stew

US		UK
2½ pounds	fresh tuna fish	2½ pounds
2–3 sprigs	mint	2–3 sprigs
2 cloves	garlic	2 cloves
	salt and pepper	
	flour	
1½ pounds	ripe tomatoes	1½ pounds
1¼ cups	olive oil	½ pint
⅔ cup	dry white wine	¼ pint
2	onions, sliced	2

The fish must be in one piece and cut from the tail, a cut which in Sicily is called *tarantello*.

Make a few incisions along the sides of the fish with the point of a knife. Finely chop 1 clove garlic. Into each incision in the fish put

a leaf of mint, a little chopped garlic, salt and pepper. Sprinkle the outside of the fish with salt and pepper, and dredge with flour. Peel and chop the tomatoes, and rub them through a sieve.

Heat the oil in a large pan or oval casserole, add the fish and fry until brown all over, turning it carefully with a spatula. Sprinkle with the wine and continue cooking until this evaporates. Take the fish from the pan, put it aside but keep hot. Add the remaining garlic clove, crushed, and the onions to the pan, and sauté until golden. Return the fish to the pan and cook it for 5 minutes, turning it once or twice. Add the tomatoes and cook for a few minutes, then add 1 cup (U.K. scant ½ pint) hot water. Taste for salt and simmer for 20 minutes.

When the fish is tender, take it from the pan and cut into fairly thick slices. Arrange the slices on a hot oval platter and spoon over a few tablespoons of the sauce. Serve at once.

The rest of the sauce can be served with noodles or rice.

Serves 6.

Zuppa di Pesce Siracusana
Fish Soup Syracuse Style

US		UK
2½–3 pounds	assorted fish – see method	2½–3 pounds
	salt	
1	onion, sliced	1
2 cloves	garlic, crushed	2 cloves
2 stalks	celery, diced	2 stalks
2–3 sprigs	parsley, chopped	2–3 sprigs
2	bay leaves	2
½ cup	olive oil	6–8 tablespoons
1½ pounds	tomatoes, peeled, seeded and chopped	1½ pounds
1 cup	dry white wine	scant ½ pint
	pepper	
	slices of toasted bread	

Any or all of the following fish could be used: dogfish, gurnard, hake, sea bream, cuttlefish, octopus, sea scorpion and mussels.

Clean the fish and cut the larger fish into 2 or 3 pieces – the pieces should not be too small. Wash in cold salted water.

Take a large, deep, ovenproof casserole. Arrange the onion, garlic, celery, parsley, bay leaves, olive oil and tomatoes in the bottom, and put the fish on top. Moisten with the wine and add almost enough warm water to cover. Season with salt and freshly ground pepper. Cover tightly and bake in a moderate oven (375°F. Mark 4) for about 40 minutes, or until the fish are tender but not breaking up. Take the casserole from the oven, remove the bay leaves and garlic (if possible), and serve the soup hot, garnished with slices of toasted bread. (If a strong flavor of garlic is liked, the 2 cloves may be chopped and left in the soup.)

Serves 6.

Triglie alla Siciliana
Broiled (Grilled) Red Mullet Sicilian Style

US		UK
6	red mullet	6
	salt and pepper	
2½ tablespoons	olive oil	2 tablespoons
	peel of 2 oranges	
4 tablespoons	meat gravy	3 tablespoons
4 tablespoons	white wine	3 tablespoons
10 tablespoons	butter	5 ounces
	juice of 2 oranges and 1 lemon	

Scale the fish very carefully – the skin is fragile – wash them, but leave in the entrails, liver, etc., which are considered a delicacy. Put the fish in a bowl, sprinkle them with salt, pepper and the olive oil, and leave them for 10 minutes, turning them once or twice.

Remove every scrap of pith from the orange peel and cut into thin strips. Drop into boiling water for 1 minute. Drain and put in a casserole with the gravy and wine. Bring slowly to the boil and boil for 1 minute. Take from the heat and add the butter, cut into small pieces, and the orange and lemon juice. Keep hot.

Take the mullet from the marinade and broil (grill), over charcoal if possible, for 5 minutes on each side. Serve hot, covered with the sauce.

If meat gravy is not available, meat extract diluted with warm water may be used instead.

Serves 6.

Braciole di Pescespada
Stuffed Swordfish Sicilian Style

US		UK
½ pound	small pieces of swordfish	½ pound
1 small	onion, finely chopped	1 small
1¼ cups	olive oil	½ pint
2½ tablespoons	brandy	2 tablespoons
	salt	
2½ tablespoons	soft breadcrumbs	2 tablespoons
6 thin slices	swordfish	6 thin slices
6 slices	Mozzarella cheese	6 slices
2–3 sprigs	basil, finely chopped	2–3 sprigs
pinch	finely chopped thyme	pinch
	pepper	
1–2	lemons	1–2

Wash and dry the small pieces of swordfish and mix with the onion. Heat the olive oil in a pan and sauté the fish and onion. As soon as the onion begins to brown, add the brandy and sprinkle lightly with salt. When the brandy has evaporated, take the pan from the heat and add the breadcrumbs.

Wash and wipe the sliced swordfish. Spread each slice with the cooked swordfish, onion and breadcrumb mixture. Cover with a slice of Mozzarella and sprinkle with herbs and freshly ground pepper. Roll up the slices to enclose the filling and tie with thread.

Broil (grill) the swordfish rolls, over charcoal if possible, for about 15 minutes – the heat should not be too fierce. Serve immediately, either garnished with lemon quarters, or with Salmoriglio Sauce (page 265).

Serves 6.

Pescestocco alla Messinese
Salt Cod Messina Style

US		UK
2½ pounds	pre-soaked salt cod – see method	2½ pounds
1¼ cups	olive oil	½ pint
2	onions, sliced	2
2 stalks	celery, diced	2 stalks
1 pound	ripe tomatoes	1 pound
1 pound	potatoes, peeled	1 pound
8–10 large	pale green olives, pitted	8–10 large
2½ tablespoons	capers	2 tablespoons
2½ tablespoons	pine nuts	2 tablespoons
4 tablespoons	seedless white raisins (sultanas)	3 tablespoons
	salt and chili powder	

This dish is also called *pescestocco alla ghiotta* — "glutton's salt cod".

If the salt cod is not bought pre-soaked, it must first be soaked under cold running water, or in water which is changed every 8 hours, for at least 24 hours.

Heat the oil in a deep frying pan and sauté the onions and celery. Peel and chop the tomatoes, discarding seeds. As soon as the onions change color, add the tomatoes and about ½ cup (U.K. 6 to 8 tablespoons) warm water, and bring to a gentle boil.

Cut the cod into large pieces of fairly equal size, removing skin and bones, and cut the potatoes into quarters. Add them both to the pan, together with the olives, capers, pine nuts and white raisins (sultanas). Add very little salt and plenty of chili powder (remember it is hot). Cook gently for 30 minutes, stirring occasionally with a wooden spoon. If the sauce seems too thick, add just a little more warm water. Serve very hot.

Serves 6.

Sarde a Beccafico
Stuffed Sardines Sicilian Style

US		UK
2½ pounds	fresh sardines	2½ pounds
	salt	
	olive oil	
6–6½ tablespoons	soft breadcrumbs	5 tablespoons
½ cup	seedless white raisins (sultanas)	3 ounces
½ cup	pine nuts	3 ounces
1 teaspoon	sugar, or to taste	1 teaspoon
6	salted anchovies, boned	6
	pepper	
2–3 sprigs	parsley, finely chopped	2–3 sprigs
1 small	onion, finely chopped	1 small
2–3	bay leaves	2–3
	juice of 1–2 lemons or oranges	

Cut off the heads of the sardines, clean the fish well, slit them open down the belly to pull out the backbones but do not divide them completely. Wash them in salted water and wipe dry.

Heat 1¼ cups (U.K. ½ pint) oil in a small pan, add 5 tablespoons (U.K. 4 tablespoons) breadcrumbs, stir well and sauté until brown. Take them from the pan and put them into a bowl. Add the white raisins (sultanas), pine nuts and sugar. Wash the anchovies until quite clear of salt and pound or chop them into small pieces. Add these to the bowl with plenty of freshly ground pepper, the parsley and onion. Knead until the mixture is well blended and stuff a little into each sardine. Close the sardines firmly.

Rub a baking pan with olive oil and arrange the sardines in one layer on the bottom. Tear the bay leaves into strips and sprinkle them over the sardines. Cover with the remaining breadcrumbs, sprinkle with olive oil and bake in a moderate oven (375°F. Mark 4) for 30 minutes, or until the breadcrumbs are brown and the sardines baked through. Serve immediately, sprinkled generously with lemon or orange juice.

Serves 6.

Sarde al Vino Bianco
Sardines in White Wine

US		UK
2½ pounds	fresh sardines	2½ pounds
	salt	
3	salted anchovies, boned	3
10 tablespoons	butter	5 ounces
	pepper	
1¼ cups	dry white wine	½ pint

Cut off and discard the heads of the sardines. Slit the fish open and lay them flat. Take out the backbones and wash the sardines in cold salted water. Wipe them dry.

Wash the anchovies to remove excess salt and pound to a paste with half the butter. Spread a little of this mixture over each sardine; take two sardines and sandwich them together. Repeat the procedure with the remaining sardines and anchovy butter. Butter an ovenproof dish and arrange the sardines in one layer at the bottom. Cut the rest of the butter into slivers and dot over the top. Add a little salt and freshly ground pepper, and pour in the wine. Cover the dish with wax paper and bake in a moderate oven (375°F. Mark 4) for between 20 and 30 minutes, or until the sardines are cooked through. Serve very hot in the same dish.

Serves 6.

Insalata Siciliana
Sicilian Tomato Salad

US		UK
6 large	firm ripe tomatoes	6 large
	salt	
¼ pound	mushrooms in oil	¼ pound
¼ pound	Italian-style pickles	¼ pound
25	olives, pitted	25
4 teaspoons	capers	1 tablespoon
2½ tablespoons	cooked peas	2 tablespoons
scant 1 cup	cooked white (haricot) beans	¼ pound
1 cup	mayonnaise	scant ½ pint
	pepper	

Wash the tomatoes and cut off their tops. Scoop out the seeds and sprinkle the insides with salt. Leave turned upside down to drain.

Coarsely chop the mushrooms, pickles and olives. Put them in a bowl with the capers, peas and beans. Dress with mayonnaise, sprinkle lightly with salt and pepper, and mix gently with a wooden spoon.

Sprinkle the insides of the tomatoes with pepper and fill them with the vegetable mixture. If any of the filling is left over, place it in a mound on a serving dish and surround with the tomatoes.

Serves 6.

Pomodori alla Siciliana
Baked Tomatoes Sicilian Style

US		UK
12	ripe tomatoes	12
	salt	
4	salted anchovies, boned	4
1	onion, very finely chopped	1
3 sprigs	parsley, finely chopped	3 sprigs
	pepper	
	grated nutmeg	
4 teaspoons	capers	1 tablespoon
1 cup	fine dry breadcrumbs	3–3½ ounces
1 cup	olive oil	scant ½ pint

Wash the tomatoes and cut off their tops, reserving them for later use. Empty the tomatoes, sprinkle the shells with salt and turn them upside down to drain.

Wash and chop the anchovies, and put them in a small bowl with the onion, parsley, salt and pepper to taste, and a sprinkling of freshly grated nutmeg. Mix well. Add the capers and 2½ tablespoons (U.K. 2 tablespoons) each breadcrumbs and olive oil. Mix well and put a little of the mixture into each tomato shell. Replace the tops and arrange the tomatoes in a shallow baking pan. Spoon over the remaining olive oil and breadcrumbs. Bake in a moderate oven (375°F. Mark 4) for about 30 minutes, or until the tomatoes are soft but not reduced to a pulp. Serve hot or cold.

Serves 6.

Peperoni Imbottiti
Stuffed Sweet Peppers

US		UK
6 large	sweet peppers	6 large
6	eggplants (aubergines), diced	6
	salt	
	olive oil	
5 tablespoons	thick tomato sauce	4 tablespoons
25–30	green olives, pitted and chopped	25–30
2½ tablespoons	capers	2 tablespoons

Char the peppers under the broiler (grill) or in a very hot oven until their skins blacken and blister. Peel off the thin skins and slice off the top of each pepper (retain these tops to use later). Scoop out seeds and cores, and discard them.

Sprinkle the eggplants (aubergines) with salt and leave for 1 hour in a colander or on a tilted plate to drain off their bitter juices.

Wipe the eggplants dry and deep-fry in hot oil until golden brown. Drain on paper towels and put in a bowl. Mix well with the tomato sauce, olives and capers.

Sprinkle the peppers lightly with salt and fill each one with some of the eggplant mixture. Replace their tops and arrange the peppers in a baking pan. Sprinkle with oil (some from the pan will do), and bake in a moderate oven (375°F. Mark 4) for about 1 hour, basting occasionally with the pan juices. The peppers should cook slowly until they are golden. Serve hot or cold.

Serves 6.

Piatto Freddo di Ortaggi
A Cold Dish of Mixed Vegetables

US		UK
5 medium-sized	eggplants (aubergines)	5 medium-sized
	salt	
3	sweet yellow peppers	3
3	sweet red peppers	3
1¼ cups	olive oil	½ pint
1¼ cups	water	½ pint
2 medium-sized	mild onions, thickly sliced	2 medium-sized
1 clove	garlic, crushed	1 clove
pinch	thyme	pinch
1	bay leaf	1
½ cup	wine vinegar	6 tablespoons
	pepper	

Cut the eggplants (aubergines) into cubes, salt them and leave to drain as directed in the preceding recipe. Skin the peppers as directed in the same recipe, halve them, discard cores and seeds, and cut the flesh into wide strips.

Mix the oil and water in a large casserole, and bring to a fast boil. Add all the remaining ingredients except the vinegar and pepper, mix lightly and bring to the boil again. Cover the casserole with wax paper or foil and transfer to a moderate oven (375°F. Mark 4). Bake for 1½ hours.

Turn out into a deep dish, sprinkle with vinegar, season generously with freshly ground pepper and serve cold.

Serves 6.

Melanzane alla Trapanese
Eggplants (Aubergines) Trapani Style

US		UK
6 large	eggplants (aubergines)	6 large
	salt	
	olive oil	
	flour	
2 cloves	garlic, crushed	2 cloves
1 sprig	rosemary	1 sprig
2½ tablespoons	tomato paste	2 tablespoons
	pepper	
4 tablespoons	wine vinegar	3 tablespoons

Peel the eggplants (aubergines) and slice them lengthwise, not too thinly. Sprinkle with salt and leave for 1 hour in a colander or on a tilted plate to drain off their bitter juices.

In the meantime, heat a generous layer of oil until very hot. Wipe the eggplant slices dry, dredge lightly with flour, and deep-fry in the oil, a few at a time, until golden brown on both sides. Drain on paper towels and keep hot.

Pour a few tablespoons of the oil into a small pan and sauté the garlic cloves until brown. Discard them and add the rosemary.

Dilute the tomato paste with a little water and stir this into the pan. Season with salt and pepper, and simmer for 5 minutes. Mix 1 tablespoon (U.K. ⅔ tablespoon) flour to a paste with vinegar and stir into the sauce. Season generously with pepper and simmer for 5 minutes longer.

Arrange the eggplant slices in one layer on a heated serving dish, only slightly overlapping. Pour the hot sauce over them and leave for a minute or so to allow them to absorb the flavor of the sauce before serving.

Serves 6.

Caponata
Eggplants (Aubergines) in Sweet-sour Sauce

US		UK
2½ pounds	eggplants (aubergines)	2½ pounds
	salt	
	olive oil	
1 bunch	white celery	1 head
1	onion, sliced	1
1 small can	tomato paste (3-ounce)	1 small can
4 teaspoons	sugar	1 tablespoon
1¼ cups	red wine vinegar	½ pint
1–2 tablespoons	capers	1–1½ tablespoons
½ cup	green olives	3–4 ounces
	pepper	

Wash the eggplants (aubergines) and dice them without peeling. Sprinkle with salt and leave in a colander or on a tilted plate for about 1 hour to drain off the bitter juices. Wipe dry. Deep-fry in hot oil until brown and drain on paper towels.

Clean the celery, discarding any coarse stalks. Cut the remaining stalks into short lengths and wash them under running water. Wipe dry and deep-fry in the same oil until golden brown.

Take 1 cup (U.K. scant ½ pint) of the oil, pour it into another, medium-sized pan and sauté the onion until it changes color. Dilute the tomato paste with a little warm water. Stir this into the onion, season with salt and cook for 15 minutes over a moderate heat. Stir in the sugar, vinegar, capers, olives, eggplants and celery. Sprinkle with plenty of freshly ground pepper, add salt if necessary, and simmer for 10 minutes. Serve cold.

It is essential for this dish that a really good-quality vinegar is used, otherwise the flavor will be ruined.

Serves 6.

Zucchine in Agrodolce
Zucchini (Courgettes) in Sweet-sour Sauce

US		UK
6 large	zucchini (courgettes)	6 large
2½ tablespoons	olive oil	2 tablespoons
1 clove	garlic, crushed	1 clove
2½ tablespoons	wine vinegar	2 tablespoons
2–3 tablespoons	pine nuts	1 ounce
2–3 tablespoons	seedless white raisins (sultanas)	1 ounce
2	salted anchovies	2
	salt	

Wash the zucchini (courgettes), trim off the stem ends and cut each one in four lengthwise. If they are large enough, they can be cut yet again into strips.

Heat the olive oil and sauté the garlic until brown. Discard it and add the zucchini, cover the pan and cook for a few minutes. Add the vinegar and an equal quantity of water. Cook for 10 minutes over a moderate heat, then add the pine nuts and white raisins (sultanas).

Wash and finely chop the anchovies, and add them to the pan. Stir gently, add a little salt if necessary, and cook for 2 or 3 minutes longer.

Serves 3 to 6.

Frittedda
Stewed Artichokes Sicilian Style

US		UK
6 young	artichokes	6 young
1	lemon	1
½ cup	olive oil	6 tablespoons
1 small	onion, finely chopped	1 small
1 pound	peas, shelled	1 pound
2 pounds	fava (broad) beans, shelled	2 pounds
	salt and pepper	
	grated nutmeg	
3–4 leaves	mint, chopped–optional	3–4 leaves
1 teaspoon	wine vinegar – optional	1 teaspoon
4 teaspoons	sugar – optional	1 tablespoon

As with so many recipes in this collection, very tender artichokes are called for, young enough not to have developed chokes. If older ones are used, scoop out the chokes and cook for rather longer.

Trim the artichokes and cut each one into eighths, dropping them into water acidulated with lemon juice until they are all prepared.

Heat the oil in a large pan and sauté the onion until soft but not brown. Add the artichokes and cook for a few minutes longer, then moisten with ⅔ cup (U.K. ¼ pint) hot water. Bring to the boil, simmer for 5 minutes, then add the shelled peas and beans. Season to taste with salt, pepper and nutmeg, cover and simmer for 20 minutes longer, or until all the vegetables are tender, moistening with a little more water if necessary. Serve hot or cold. If to be served cold, stir in the mint, vinegar and sugar before cooling the dish.

Serves 6.

Broccoli alla Siciliana
Cauliflower Sicilian Style

US		UK
2–2½ pounds	cauliflower	2–2½ pounds
3	salted anchovies, boned	3
1 cup	olive oil	scant ½ pint
1 large	onion, finely chopped	1 large
12	olives, pitted and sliced	12
2 ounces	strong Caciocavallo cheese, thinly sliced	2 ounces
	salt	
1 cup	red wine	scant ½ pint
	croûtons	

In several regions of Italy cauliflower is referred to as "broccoli".

Cut off the outer leaves of the cauliflower and separate the head into flowerettes. Wash under running water and drain well. Wash and chop the anchovies.

Pour 2 to 3 tablespoons of the olive oil into a heavy casserole, add a little of the onion and olives, and a few slivers of anchovy. Cover with a layer of flowerettes, some slices of cheese, a very little salt, a sprinkling of oil, then again onion and anchovies. Repeat this until all the ingredients are used up, with a good sprinkling of oil over the last layer of cauliflower. Pour in the wine, cover the pan and cook gently until the cauliflower is tender. By this time all the liquid should have evaporated; if not, increase the heat for a few minutes. Do not stir the cauliflower at all. Turn out on to a round heated serving dish, garnish generously with croûtons (fried snippets of bread), and serve.

Serves 6.

Cassata alla Siciliana

Sicilian Cheese Cake

US		UK
1¾ pounds	Ricotta or good-quality cottage cheese	1¾ pounds
scant 2 cups	granulated (caster) sugar	14 ounces
	ground cinnamon	
5 squares	bitter chocolate, crushed	5 ounces
1 pound	candied fruit	1 pound
4 tablespoons	pistachio or pine nuts, chopped	3 tablespoons
1 pound	sponge cake, made without fat	1 pound
	confectioners' (icing) sugar	
5 tablespoons	Maraschino liqueur	4 tablespoons

For many people the famous Sicilian *cassata* brings to mind a kind of ice cream. Indeed, there is an iced *cassata*, but the traditional *cassata* is a variety of cheese cake.

Beat the Ricotta in a large bowl until smooth. Dissolve the sugar with 2 or 3 tablespoons water over a low heat, and cook gently until it just begins to change color. Take it from the heat immediately and beat into the Ricotta. Add a generous pinch of cinnamon and the crushed chocolate, and mix well. Take half the candied fruits, reserving the best pieces to decorate the cake, and chop them into very small pieces. Add to the Ricotta mixture, together with the nuts, and stir well.

Cut the sponge into ½-inch-thick slices and moisten them with Maraschino. Line a deep round bowl about 10 inches in diameter with some of the slices and fill with the Ricotta mixture, smoothing it down neatly with the blade of a knife. Cover with the remaining slices of sponge and chill in the refrigerator for several hours, or overnight.

Cut out a cardboard base of the same size as the top of the bowl. Cover this with wax paper. Place it on top of the bowl with the waxed side towards the cake and, holding it firmly, turn the cake upside down on to the base. Carefully lift off the bowl. Decorate the cake with the reserved pieces of fruit, either whole or thickly sliced, and sprinkle with sifted confectioners' (icing) sugar. Serve immediately.

As with all recipes, there are variations on this cake. Some use a sugar syrup as a covering instead of the confectioners' sugar; others make a layer cake of the *cassata*.

Cassata Gelata

Cassata Ice Cream

US		UK
5	egg yolks	5
⅔ cup	granulated (caster) sugar	5 ounces
	rind of ½ lemon *or* vanilla to taste	
2 cups	warm milk	generous ¾ pint
1¼ cups	sweetened whipped cream	½ pint
2–3 tablespoons	candied fruit, very finely chopped	2–2½ tablespoons
2–3 tablespoons	sugared almonds, chopped	2–2½ tablespoons

This *cassata* requires both care and a special container called a *stampo da spumone*, which is dome-shaped with a lid. The *cassata* itself is in two separate parts. The outside is made with a custard ice cream and the inside is of cream, very frothy and soft, mixed with candied fruit and sugared almonds. Failing the special container, a metal pudding bowl could be used.

Put the egg yolks into a pan, preferably a copper one with a rounded bottom, and beat them vigorously. Add the sugar and continue beating until the mixture is smooth and creamy. Add the lemon peel or vanilla extract (or both if preferred), then gradually stir in the milk. Cook the custard either over a low heat or, better still, in a double boiler, stirring constantly with a wooden spoon until the custard has thickened and coats the back of the spoon. It must not on any account be allowed to boil. Pour it into a bowl and let it cool, stirring from time to time. Transfer the custard to an ice cube tray, cover with wax paper and leave in the freezing compartment for about 2 hours. Stir every 30 minutes with a wooden spatula.

Take the *stampo da spumone*, which holds about 5 cups (U.K. 2 pints), and put it empty into the freezing compartment. When the ice cream is set, line the *stampo* with it, leaving the middle empty. Fill the empty space with the whipped cream lightly mixed with the candied fruits and sugared almonds. Tap the *stampo* to spread the cream evenly and to get rid of any empty spaces, and smooth off the top. Cover with wax paper and the lid, and return to the freezing compartment of the refrigerator for another 3 or 4 hours.

Turn out to serve. To do this, dip the *stampo* into hot water for a few seconds and quickly invert. Serve at once.

Serves 6.

Spuma Gelata di Crema

Iced Mousse

US		UK
4	egg yolks	4
5 tablespoons	sugar	4 tablespoons
	peel of 1 lemon	
	vanilla extract, to taste	
4 teaspoons	all-purpose (plain) flour	1 tablespoon
2½ cups	warm milk	1 pint
2½ tablespoons	diced candied citron	2 tablespoons
2½ tablespoons	diced glacé cherries	2 tablespoons
2	egg whites	2
4 teaspoons	confectioners' (icing) sugar	1 tablespoon

Beat the yolks in a pan, preferably a copper one with a rounded bottom. Add the sugar and continue beating until smooth. Add the lemon peel and vanilla, and continue beating until the mixture is very stiff, then gradually add the flour, beating all the time. Pour in the milk, still beating. Put the pan over a low heat or better still, cook over water, stirring constantly with a wooden spoon until the mixture begins to thicken. On no account let it come to the boil.

Take the pan from the heat, pour the custard into a bowl and continue beating until it is cool. Take out the lemon peel and stir in the candied citron and cherries.

Beat the egg whites until stiff, add the confectioners' (icing) sugar and continue beating until the egg whites stand in peaks. Fold this into the custard. Cover and put into the coldest part of the refrigerator, but not in the freezing section. As the mousse sets, stir vigorously now and again to make it soft and frothy. Finally, let it set completely.

Serves 4 to 6.

Dolce di Castagne e Riso

Chestnut and Rice Pudding

US		UK
1 cup	dried chestnuts	5 ounces
5 cups	milk or water	2 pints
	salt	
1½ cups	pudding rice	10 ounces
scant ½ cup	sugar	3½ ounces
½ cup	seedless white raisins (sultanas)	2½ ounces
4 tablespoons	butter	2 ounces

Soak the chestnuts overnight in warm water to soften them. Drain, put them in a pan, cover with the milk or water, add a pinch of salt and bring slowly to the boil. Lower the heat and cook gently for

½ hour. Add the rice and continue cooking for another 25 minutes, or until the rice is well cooked but each grain is still separate. It might be necessary to add a little milk or water to the rice – much depends on its quality or type. Just before the rice is ready, add the sugar and the white raisins (sultanas). Melt the butter and stir this gently into the rice.

Turn the rice into a pudding bowl and let it cool before serving. (Or the bowl can be rubbed with butter and sprinkled with sugar, the rice turned into it, chilled for several hours in the refrigerator and turned out for serving.)

Serves 6.

Cannoli alla Siciliana
Sicilian Fried Stuffed Pastries

US		UK
Pastry		
1¼ cups	all-purpose (plain) flour	5 ounces
1¼ teaspoons	cocoa	1 teaspoon
1 teaspoon	instant coffee	scant 1 teaspoon
pinch	salt	pinch
4 teaspoons	granulated (caster) sugar	1 tablespoon
2 tablespoons	lard or butter	1 ounce
1 cup	red or white wine or Marsala	8 fluid ounces
Filling		
½ pound	Ricotta or good-quality cottage cheese	½ pound
1½ cups	confectioners' (icing) sugar	6 ounces
4 teaspoons	orange flower water	1 tablespoon
⅓ cup	diced candied orange, citron or pumpkin	2 ounces
1 square	bitter chocolate, crushed	1 ounce
	oil for deep-frying	
12	glacé cherries	12
	confectioners' (icing) sugar	

Although Sicilians called these fried pastries *cannoli*, they are rather like our cream horns, but fried. To make them it is necessary to have some metal tubes about ½ inch in diameter and about 5 inches long. The casing is made with a pastry, *scorza*, while the filling is a wine, is generally used in making the pastry.
delicious mixture of Ricotta cheese. Marsala, the famous Sicilian wine, is generally used in making the pastry.

Pastry
Sift the flour, cocoa, instant coffee, salt and sugar into a bowl. Cut in the lard or butter and rub it into the flour. Then gradually add sufficient wine to make a firm dough – the quantity of wine does vary slightly according to the type of flour used. Knead the dough until smooth and elastic. Roll it out very thinly into a flat sheet and cut into 12 equal-sized squares, each approximately 3 inches square. Put a metal tube diagonally on each square and bring the two corners over to meet in the middle. Press gently to seal.

Heat plenty of olive oil in a deep pan and deep-fry the pastry-covered tubes, one or two at a time, until dark golden and crisp. Take out with a perforated spoon and drain on paper towels, or better still, on a rack over absorbent paper. As soon as the tubes are cool enough to handle, take them gently out of the pastry, and then let the pastry become quite cold.

In the meantime, prepare the filling. Put all the filling ingredients into a bowl and blend thoroughly.

As soon as the pastry cases are ready, fill them neatly with the mixture, either with a spoon or a piping bag. Cut each of the cherries into two and put a piece at each end of the *cannoli*. Arrange them on a dish, sprinkle with confectioners' (icing) sugar and serve immediately.

Serves 6.

Cannoli alla Crema di Caffè
Sicilian Fried Pastries with Coffee Filling

US		UK
12	cannoli pastry shells – see above	12
1	egg yolk	1
2½ tablespoons	sugar	2 tablespoons
4 teaspoons	all-purpose (plain) flour	1 tablespoon
1¼ cups	warm milk	½ pint
	lemon peel or vanilla, to taste	
½ pound	Ricotta or good-quality cottage cheese	½ pound
	confectioners' (icing) sugar	
2½ teaspoons	instant coffee, dissolved in a few drops of boiling water	2 teaspoons

Prepare the *cannoli* as directed in the preceding recipe, deep-fry them and let them cool.

Beat the egg yolk in a small pan, add the sugar and continue beating until the mixture thickens. Add the flour and again beat until the mixture is smooth and creamy. Put the pan on the heat and gradually add the milk, stirring vigorously all the time. Add the lemon rind or vanilla, and continue stirring until the sauce is thick and smooth. Beat for a moment or two, then leave to become quite cold. Discard the lemon peel if used.

In another bowl mix together the Ricotta, 1 cup (3½ ounces) confectioners' (icing) sugar and the instant coffee, then beat in the custard. Fill the *cannoli* with this mixture, arrange them on a serving dish and dust generously with sifted confectioners' sugar. Serve immediately.

Serves 6.

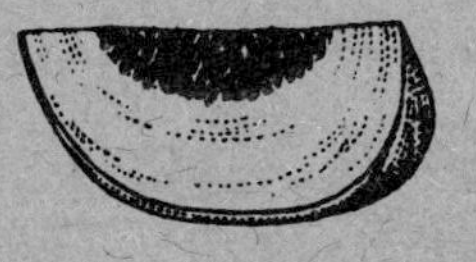

Frittedde di Frutta
Sicilian Fruit Fritters

US		UK
2	egg yolks	2
2½ tablespoons	olive oil	2 tablespoons
	grated rind of ½ lemon	
	vanilla extract, to taste	
pinch	salt	pinch
½ cup	white wine	6 tablespoons
2½ tablespoons	all-purpose (plain) flour	2 tablespoons
2 pounds	ripe firm fresh fruit	2 pounds
	oil for deep-frying	
2	egg whites	2
	confectioners' (icing) sugar	

Beat the egg yolks with the oil, add the lemon rind, vanilla, salt and wine, and mix well. Sift the flour into another bowl and gradually add the egg mixture, beating constantly with a wooden spoon. Leave for 2 hours in a warm place.

Clean, peel and generally prepare whatever fruit is being used. Cut it into small pieces. Dry it (if necessary) in a cloth. Heat plenty of olive oil for deep-frying.

Beat the egg whites until stiff and fold them into the batter. Fold in the prepared fruit. Drop this mixture in tablespoonfuls into the hot oil. As the fritters turn golden, take them out with a perforated spoon and drain on paper towels. Sprinkle generously with sifted confectioners' (icing) sugar and serve hot.

Serves 6.

Cassatine di Ricotta
Ricotta Tarts

US		UK
1 cake	compressed (fresh) yeast	⅔ ounce
4 cups	all-purpose (plain) flour	1 pound
1⅛ cups	granulated (caster) sugar	½ pound
pinch	salt	pinch
	juice of 1 lemon	
1 pound	Ricotta or good-quality cottage cheese	1 pound
2	eggs	2
	ground cinnamon	
	butter for baking sheet	

Dissolve the yeast in ½ cup (U.K. 6 to 8 tablespoons) lukewarm water. Sift the flour into a bowl with 4 teaspoons (U.K. 1 tablespoon) of the sugar and the salt. Add the lemon juice and the yeast. Mix to a dough, adding more warm water if necessary. The dough should be rather stiff. Knead vigorously until smooth. Return it to the bowl and leave to rise for at least 1 hour.

Beat the Ricotta in a bowl until smooth, add the eggs and beat until blended. Beat in the remaining sugar and cinnamon to taste.

Roll out the dough, not too thinly, and cut into 3-inch rounds. Turn up the edges all round to make little cases with a border, and line with a narrow strip of dough to strengthen them. Fill each case with some of the Ricotta mixture and place on a buttered baking sheet. Bake in a hot oven (450°F. Mark 7) for about 20 minutes, or until the pastry is golden brown. Serve hot or cold.

Sfincioni di Riso
Fried Rice Cakes

US		UK
2½ cups	pudding rice	1 pound
	salt	
2½ cups	milk	1 pint
1¼ teaspoons	baking powder	1 teaspoon
1¾ cups	pastry (fine) flour	7 ounces
scant ½ cup	granulated (caster) sugar	3 ounces
	oil for frying	
	confectioners' (icing) sugar	
	ground cinnamon	

Bring a large pan of salted water to the boil, add the rice, stirring, and cook for 8 to 10 minutes, or until it is half-cooked. Drain. Return the rice to the pan, add the milk and cook slowly, stirring from time to time, until the rice has absorbed all the milk. Turn it into a bowl, beat in the baking powder, cover and leave overnight.

The next day, mix in the flour and the sugar. With slightly greased hands break off portions of the rice mixture and shape into "cakes" about 3 inches long and 1 inch thick. Deep-fry in plenty of oil, a few at a time, until lightly browned. Take from the pan with a perforated spoon and drain on paper towels.

Dust the rice cakes with confectioners' (icing) sugar sifted with a little ground cinnamon. Serve hot or cold.

Spumette di Nocciole
Hazelnut Meringues

US		UK
½ pound	hazelnuts	½ pound
4	egg whites	4
2¼ cups	confectioners' (icing) sugar	10 ounces
	grated rind of 1 lemon	
	butter and flour for baking sheet	

Chop the hazelnuts finely without peeling them. Beat the egg whites until stiff and gradually add the confectioners' (icing) sugar.

Continue beating until the whites stand in peaks. Fold in the hazelnuts and lemon rind.

Grease a sheet of wax paper or foil with butter and sprinkle lightly with flour. Drop the meringue mixture on to the baking sheet in teaspoonfuls. Bake in a slow oven (350°F. Mark 3) for about 30 minutes, or until the meringues are firm but still white. Take them from the oven, cool, then peel them off the paper.

These meringues will keep for some time in an airtight container.

Mustazzoli di Erice
Sicilian Almond Cookies (U.K. Biscuits)

US		UK
½ cup	sweet almonds	3 ounces
8 cups	all-purpose (plain) flour	2 pounds
generous 1⅔ cups	granulated (caster) sugar	¾ pound
2½ teaspoons	ground cinnamon	2 teaspoons
5 teaspoons	baking powder	4 teaspoons
pinch	powdered cloves	pinch
	butter and flour for baking sheet	

Toast the almonds, without peeling them, in a slow oven (350°F. Mark 3) for about 15 minutes, shaking the pan occasionally. Take from the oven, rub off the peels and chop the almonds finely.

Sift the flour into a mound on a pastry board, make a well in the middle and add the almonds, sugar, cinnamon, baking powder and cloves. Mix together, then gradually add enough warm water to make a firm dough. Knead until smooth and elastic. Roll out about ½ inch thick. Cut the rolled-out dough into strips 4 inches long. Make a criss-cross pattern on the dough by pulling the tines of a fork down the length of the strips and then across them.

Grease a baking sheet with butter and sprinkle lightly with flour. Place the cookies on the sheet and bake in a moderately hot oven (400°F. Mark 5) for about 10 to 15 minutes, or until a pale golden color. Cool before serving.

Instead of making individual cookies, the dough can be shaped into one cake, patterned as above and baked in a very moderate oven (350°F. Mark 3) for 1 hour.

Crispelle
Sicilian Doughnuts

US		UK
1½ cakes	compressed (fresh) yeast	1 ounce
3 cups	lukewarm water	1¼ pints
8 cups	pastry (fine) flour	2 pounds
pinch	salt	pinch
	olive oil for deep-frying	
	granulated (caster) sugar *or* honey	
	ground cinnamon – optional	

Crispelle are usually made at Christmas or earlier, on November 11 for the Feast of St Martin. However, in many households they are prepared throughout the year.

Dissolve the yeast in ½ cup (U.K. 6 tablespoons) warm water. Heat the remaining water in a large pan and just before it comes to the boil add the flour all at once, beating vigorously all the time. Cool slightly. Beat in a little salt and the yeast, and quickly turn the dough out on to a marble slab or pastry board. Knead with greased hands until smooth. Put the dough into a bowl, cover with a cloth and leave to rise in a warm place until doubled in bulk.

Heat plenty of olive oil and when hot but not smoking fry walnut-sized pieces of the dough until golden brown. Take from the pan and drain on paper towels. Sprinkle with sugar or coat with melted honey. A little ground cinnamon may be sprinkled over the doughnuts as well.

SARDINIA

A traditional dish of the shepherds of Sardinia: wild suckling pigs roasting before a fire of aromatic woods which impart a unique flavor to the meat.

The *nuraghi* of Sardinia are an unforgettable and impressive sight. In the foreground, some of the excellent game of the island, local cheeses, and a crisp, paper-thin bread known as *carasau* or "sheet music", which the shepherds take with them when they leave their homes for the mountains.

Except for its coastal plain and a few small towns in the interior, Sardinia is a barren, windswept land with nothing but rocks and meadows on which little will grow except grass. Dominating the landscape stand the *nuraghi*, which are gigantic rocks held together without visible bond to form massive structures. About their origins historians can only hazard wild guesses. It is thought that they were built about 3,000 years ago, but whether they were fortresses, temples, gigantic tombs, or merely the dwellings of frightened people who felt the need to shelter behind these walls, no one can tell.

The shepherds who roam the mountains, hills and plains with their flocks looking for grass lead an unenviably harsh and lonely life. Away from their homes and families for months on end, they live principally on the game they manage to capture, occasionally lamb, milk and cheese from their ewes, and the bread which they bring with them from their homes. They sleep in crevices in the rocks beside the ancient *nuraghi*, or in primitive circular huts covered with brushwood. When it is cold, they light a fire in the center and sleep on the ground, with their feet to the flame, while one of their numbers keeps watch over the sheep with his dog, or his even more faithful gun.

Sardinia is still a primitive country of shepherds and violence. Game abounds and hunters can always be sure of filling their bags. This is reflected in the cooking of the area. There are two kinds, that of the shepherds and that of their womenfolk, condemned to wait for months at a time for the return of their husbands and

The cooking of Alghero is rich in fish dishes—langoustes, sea bass, tuna fish and baby octopus.
Below, left: Culingiones, or Sicilian ravioli stuffed with spinach and cheese (see page 285), little cheese pastries, and *porceddu*, or roast suckling pig (see page 288), are specialties of the region around Oliena, seen here with the wine of the same name.

With the rocky coastline of Sa Caletta di Siniscola in the background, some typical seaside dishes: skewered eels, baked mussels, langoustes from Santa Lucia, and stuffed squid.
Below: At Santa Margherita di Pula, near Cagliari, many fine dishes are prepared with the seafood from the Bay.
Below, right: Specialties from Monte Ortobene: *pane frattau* (thin sheets of unleavened bread), *cordula*, or plaited lambs' entrails on skewers (see page 286), trout in Vernaccia (see page 290), *zurrette*, or blood puddings, and mountain ham.

sons. Isolated in the mountains, the shepherds have learned to improvise their own methods, of which the roasting spit is the chief implement. Their usual dish is wild suckling pig, skewered and roasted beside an open fire of juniper, mastic and olive wood, whose aromatic properties impart a unique flavor to the meat. An alternative method of roasting, known as *a carraxiu*, begins with the digging of a hole in the ground. A fire is lit in it, and when this has burned itself out, the meat, wrapped in aromatic herbs, is put into the hole, which is then filled with earth, and a slow-burning fire lit on top. Patience is needed, but the results are excellent. Another of the shepherds' dishes is smoked ham made from boars' or wild pigs' legs, and cheese, one of the great specialties of the region. Pecorino, a ewe's milk cheese, is one of the best of its kind, and as such adopted by other cuisines besides that of Italy.

Bread is the masterpiece of the Sardinian women: large, soft loaves called *chivarzu*, which are baked slowly in the large ovens that are to be seen in every house; and *carasau* or "sheet music", so called because it is made in crisp, hard, paper-thin sheets. These have to be stored in damp cloths and softened in boiling water before they can be eaten. To the Sardinian, bread is the symbol of family unity which, because it is interrupted by long periods of absence, seems to be stronger here than anywhere else.

Life on the coast contrasts sharply with the bleakness of the mountains; beaches with fine, dazzlingly white sand and strange, beautiful rocks which shelter the last surviving seals of the Mediterranean. The coast has drawn to it people from all over

Love of tradition, inspiration, and an infinite capacity for taking pains constitute the secret of Sardinian pastry-making. The selection below includes little wedding cakes called *dolci degli sposi*, meringues, orange peel candies, a *gattò*—from the French *gâteau*—and *torrone* (nougat) *di Oliena*.
Below, left: Sausages rolled into a spiral and broiled (grilled) over charcoal are one of the traditional dishes of Campidano di Cagliari.

Europe; there is one village that speaks only Catalan, and in others Genoese is the mother tongue. In recent years, the pleasures of Sardinia's coast have also been discovered by the tourist trade. Not least of these pleasures are the fish, in which the sea around Sardinia abounds, and the magnificent lobsters, which find their way to many of the great European restaurants. In Cagliari, the capital, there is a famous fish soup of Spanish origin known as *sa cassòla*, and in the north of the island another called *sa buridda*, of which dogfish is the chief ingredient (both on page 289).

Whatever effects the tourist trade may have on the economic prospects of the coastal region, the cooking of Sardinia, based largely on the traditional needs of a hardy and self-sufficient island population, is unlikely to show much change.

Like the mainland provinces of Italy, Sardinia, too, has its share of great wines. The finest of all is the amber-colored Vernaccia which, when left to mature for thirty years, acquires a high alcoholic content and gives out a wonderful aroma of orange blossom. It is unsurpassed when served with fish, and especially lobster. Other famous wines include Cannonau, Oliena, a red wine, Muscatel, Nasco, Torbato, Anghelu Ruju and Malvasia, better known as Malmsley, which was brought to Sardinia from Greece in the early Middle Ages.

Culingiones
Sardinian Ravioli with Spinach and Cheese Stuffing

US		UK
4 cups	all-purpose (plain) flour	1 pound
pinch	salt	pinch
5	eggs	5
Stuffing		
¾ pound	spinach	¾ pound
	salt	
2 tablespoons	butter	1 ounce
¾ pound	fresh Pecorino cheese	¾ pound
3	eggs	3
¾ cup	grated Parmesan cheese	3 ounces
pinch	saffron	pinch
	pepper and freshly grated nutmeg	
To serve		
	Meat or Tomato Sauce – pages 211, 212	
	grated Pecorino or Parmesan cheese	

Dough

Sift the flour and salt on to a pastry board or into a large bowl. Make a well in the center and break in 5 eggs. Knead thoroughly, adding a little water if necessary, to make a smooth, pliable dough. Roll it into a ball, wrap it in a clean cloth, paper or foil, and leave it in the refrigerator to rest for 30 minutes.

Stuffing

Clean and wash the spinach carefully, but do not shake all the water off the leaves. Put it in a pan with a little salt, and cook over a moderate heat, covered, until tender. Take from the pan, and as soon as it is cool enough to handle squeeze dry and chop finely. Heat the butter in a frying pan, add the spinach and cook gently for a few minutes.

In a bowl work the fresh Pecorino with a wooden spoon until soft and smooth. Add the eggs, Parmesan cheese, chopped spinach, saffron, and a good sprinkling of pepper and grated nutmeg, to taste. Add more salt only if necessary. Mix thoroughly until well blended.

Take the dough from the refrigerator. Divide it into two equal-sized pieces and roll them both out into sheets, as thinly as possible. On one of the sheets place little heaps of the prepared stuffing, equally spaced apart. Cover with the remaining sheet of dough and press together very firmly between the mounds. Cut between the rows with a pastry wheel or a sharp knife to make ravioli about 1½ inches square.

Have ready a large pan of rapidly boiling salted water. Drop in the ravioli a batch at a time (this type is not meant to dry first). They will be ready almost as soon as they rise to the surface. Drain well and serve hot, with generous portions of meat or tomato sauce, and grated Pecorino cheese.

Serves 6.

"Malloreddus"
Sardinian Gnocchi

US		UK
6 cups	all-purpose (plain) flour	1½ pounds
1 rounded teaspoon	salt	1 teaspoon
generous pinch	saffron, dissolved in a little water	generous pinch
2½ cups	Tomato Sauce – page 212	1 pint
	grated Pecorino or Parmesan	

Sift the flour into a large bowl; add the salt and the saffron with its water. Gradually add enough water to make a smooth, pliable dough, kneading vigorously until the color of the saffron is well disbursed and no longer leaves streaks of yellow in the dough.

Break off pieces of the dough and roll them into small "sausages" about ½ inch in diameter. Cut these again into short lengths and press them lightly against a fine sieve to make a criss-cross pattern. Spread them out on a large tray sprinkled with flour, and leave them in a dry warm place for 2 days.

Bring a large pan of salted water to the boil and add these *gnocchi* a few at a time. Almost as soon as they rise to the top of the pan they are ready. Drain them thoroughly and transfer them to a deep heated serving dish. Dress generously with tomato sauce and grated Pecorino cheese, and serve immediately.

For this dish it is important that the tomato sauce be well flavored and home-made.

Serves 6.

Pillas
Semolina Gnocchi

US		UK
5 cups	milk	2 pints
1½ cups	semolina	10 ounces
	salt	
2	egg yolks	2
	butter	
1 cup	grated Parmesan or Pecorino cheese	4 ounces
6 ounces	ground (UK minced) lean beef or pork	6 ounces
½ cup	dry white wine	6 tablespoons
	pepper	
1–1½ cups	freshly cooked Tomato Sauce – page 212	½ pint
¼ pound	Parma ham, thinly sliced	¼ pound

Bring the milk to the boil in a heavy pan and sprinkle in the semolina, stirring all the time to prevent lumps from forming. Season to taste with salt, and continue cooking, stirring constantly, for about 20 minutes, or until the mixture is very thick. Take the pan from the heat; beat in the egg yolks, 4 tablespoons (2 ounces) butter, and half the cheese. Mix until well blended, then turn the mixture out on to a wet plate – or better still a marble slab – and smooth out with a wet knife to a thickness of about ½ inch. Leave to cool completely – the longer it is left (within reason, naturally) the better.

Put the meat into a small heavy pan with 4 tablespoons (2 ounces) butter and fry it slowly over a low heat, crumbling it with a fork. When well browned, add the wine and continue cooking until reduced. Season to taste with salt and pepper, moisten with a little water, cover the pan and continue cooking slowly for about 30 minutes.

Cut the cold semolina into rounds about 2 inches in diameter – this is most easily done with a lightly floured cutter or glass. Grease a round ovenproof dish with butter and cover the bottom with a layer of semolina rounds. Spread with a layer of warm meat sauce, then cover with 2 or 3 slices of ham, and sprinkle with tomato sauce and grated cheese. Continue in this manner until all the ingredients are used up, leaving aside 2 or 3 tablespoons of grated cheese, and finishing with a layer of semolina rounds. Dot with butter and sprinkle with the remaining cheese. Bake in a slow oven (325°F. Mark 2) for 30 minutes, or until the top is a golden brown color, and serve with plenty of additional grated Parmesan or Pecorino.

Serves 6.

Spaghetti al Formaggio
Spaghetti with Cheese

US		UK
1½ pounds	spaghetti	1½ pounds
⅓ cup	olive oil	4–5 tablespoons
1–2 cloves	garlic, finely chopped	1–2 cloves
2½ tablespoons	finely chopped parsley	2 tablespoons
4 teaspoons	finely chopped basil	1 tablespoon
1 pound	ripe tomatoes, fresh or canned	1 pound
	salt and pepper	
¼ pound	Fiore Sardo cheese, sliced	¼ pound

Fiore Sardo is a hard ewe's milk cheese which is eaten either fresh or mature. If not available use fresh Pecorino, or some other hard, grated, strong cheese.

Heat the oil in a deep frying pan and gently sauté the garlic, parsley and basil. Peel and chop the tomatoes, discarding seeds. Add the tomatoes to the pan, stir well and season to taste with salt and pepper. Cook over a brisk heat for 15 minutes.

Bring a large pan of salted water to the boil. Lower in the spaghetti slowly, making sure that the water does not cease to boil for even one minute, and cook until *al dente* – tender but still firm. Drain thoroughly. Turn into a deep, heated baking dish, preferably of earthenware, and immediately cover with the tomato sauce, mixing it in thoroughly. Cover with slices of cheese and bake in a moderately hot oven (400°F. Mark 5) for a few minutes to allow the cheese to melt. Serve at once.

Serves 6.

Spaghetti alla Rustica
Spaghetti Country Style – with Anchovy and Oregano Sauce

US		UK
1½ pounds	spaghetti	1½ pounds
½ cup	olive oil	6 tablespoons
2 cloves	garlic, crushed	2 cloves
5 large	anchovy fillets	5 large
1 teaspoon	finely chopped oregano	1 teaspoon
	salt	
2–3 tablespoons	finely chopped parsley	2 tablespoons
	grated Pecorino or Parmesan	

Heat the oil in a frying pan and sauté the garlic cloves gently until they turn brown. Discard them, add the anchovies and continue to cook over the lowest possible heat until they have dissolved into a paste. Sprinkle with oregano and stir gently.

Bring plenty of salted water to the boil in a large pan and cook the spaghetti until just tender – *al dente* – and drain well. Turn it into a heated serving dish; add the anchovy paste and the parsley, and stir thoroughly but lightly. Serve at once with plenty of grated Pecorino cheese.

Serves 6.

Zuppa Sarda
Sardinian Soup

US		UK
8 cups	clear stock – see method	3–3½ pints
2	eggs	2
5 tablespoons	grated Parmesan cheese	4 tablespoons
	pepper	
½ pound	Mozzarella cheese, diced	½ pound
4 teaspoons	finely chopped parsley	1 tablespoon
12 slices	fried bread	12 slices

The stock for this soup is made from mixed meats, i.e., lamb, chicken, beef and veal.

Bring the stock to the boil. Beat the eggs with the Parmesan and a sprinkling of freshly ground pepper. As soon as the stock comes to the boil, pour in the egg mixture and let it cook for a minute or so until set. Add the Mozzarella and parsley.

Put 2 slices of hot fried bread into each soup bowl and ladle the hot soup over the top.

Serves 6.

Cavolata
Sardinian Pork and Cauliflower Soup

US		UK
1	pig's trotter	1
½ pound	pork rind	½ pound
1	onion	1
2 stalks	celery	2 stalks
2	carrots	2
2–3 sprigs	parsley	2–3 sprigs
	salt	
1	cauliflower	1
2	potatoes, peeled and diced	2
	grated Pecorino or Parmesan	

Clean the trotter and rind thoroughly, and scrape them if necessary. Put them into a large pan with the vegetables, parsley sprigs and a little salt. Cover with at least 7½ pints (U.K. 6 pints) water, cover the pan, bring slowly to the boil, and simmer over a low heat for about 2 hours.

In the meantime, pull off the outer stalks of the cauliflower and divide the head into flowerettes.

When the trotter and rind are very soft, take them from the pan and put them aside to cool. Strain the stock and return it to the pan, together with the cauliflower and the diced potatoes. Check for seasoning, bring to the boil again and cook, covered, over a low heat for about 20 to 30 minutes.

Bone the trotter and cut the meat into small pieces. Cut the rind into pieces of the same size. Return both to the pan and cook until heated through. Serve the soup very hot, garnished with plenty of grated cheese.

Serves 6.

Vitello al Vino Rosso
Veal with Red Wine Sauce

US		UK
2 pounds	stewing veal, boned and cut into pieces	2 pounds
½ cup	butter	4 ounces
1	onion, finely chopped	1
	salt and pepper	
2 cups	red wine	¾ pint
1 cup	hot stock	scant ½ pint
2–3 sprigs	parsley	2–3 sprigs
1 large clove	garlic, crushed	1 large clove
1	bay leaf	1
1 sprig	thyme	1 sprig
4 teaspoons	flour	1 tablespoon

Heat 6 tablespoons (3 ounces) of the butter in a large pan or casserole and sauté the onion gently until it begins to soften. Add the veal and continue cooking until lightly colored all over; season to taste with salt and pepper, and moisten with the wine and hot stock. Tie the parsley, garlic, bay leaf and thyme together in a small muslin bag, and add it to the pan. Cover, lower the heat, and continue to cook slowly for 1½ hours, or until the veal is tender – the actual time will depend on the quality of the meat.

Knead the remaining butter with the flour. Take the meat from the pan, place it on a hot platter, and keep hot in a low oven. Discard the herbs and add the kneaded butter to the simmering sauce bit by bit, stirring all the time until it thickens. Pour the sauce over the meat and serve at once.

Serves 6.

"Cordula" o "Corda"
Barbecued Skewers of Lambs' Entrails

This is one of the oldest and most traditional of all Sardinian dishes, clearly of shepherd origin. Homer describes the preparation of a very similar dish in Book XII of the *Odyssey*.

Clean and wash the intestines of 4 or 5 baby lambs and plait them together; then cut into 6 portions and thread on to 6 skewers. Mix together a little marjoram and thyme, a crumbled bay leaf and 3 or 4 sprigs sage, and chop them finely.

Heat a thick slice of pork fat until the fat runs and sprinkle lightly with salt and pepper. Brush the skewered intestines with the fat and sprinkle them with the chopped herbs. Broil (grill) over charcoal until brown all over and serve very hot, straight from the fire.

Serves 6.

According to a less traditional version, the intestines are cooked in a frying pan in a tomato sauce with peas.

Favata
Sardinian Bean and Pork Stew

US		UK
1½ pounds	dried fava, Windsor, lima or butter beans	1½ pounds
½ cup	olive oil	6–8 tablespoons
¾ pound	spare ribs, in one piece	¾ pound
1 pound	small Italian pork sausages	1 pound
½ pound	lean bacon, in one piece	½ pound
½ head	Savoy cabbage, shredded	½ head
2–3 bulbs	fennel with leaves, chopped – see page 68	2–3 bulbs
2	onions, thinly sliced	2
2 large	ripe tomatoes, peeled and chopped	2 large
	salt and pepper	
	slices of fried bread	
	grated Parmesan cheese	

Soak the beans overnight if possible, or for at least 12 hours.

Heat the oil in a large pan or heatproof casserole, and fry the pork and sausages. When the pork is well browned, add the drained beans and enough hot water to cover generously. Add the bacon and the prepared vegetables. Check seasoning, adding salt and pepper to taste, and continue cooking slowly for about 2 hours. Add a little more water from time to time if necessary, but never too much as the sauce should be thick.

When the meat is tender, almost to the point of being overcooked by usual standards, first take out the pork and divide it into ribs. Then lift out the bacon and cut it into small pieces. Return both to the pan and reheat.

Serve the stew very hot, accompanied by slices of crisply fried bread and plenty of grated Parmesan cheese.

Serves 6.

Involtini di Maiale al Forno
Stuffed Baked Rolls of Pork

US		UK
12 thin slices	boned loin of pork – 1½ to 2 pounds	12 thin slices
¼ pound	pig's liver, finely chopped	¼ pound
¼ pound	fat salt pork, finely chopped	¼ pound
1 clove	garlic, finely chopped	1 clove
2–3 sprigs	parsley, finely chopped	2–3 sprigs
	soft pith of ½ bread roll, soaked in water	
	salt	
2	egg yolks *or*	2
1	whole egg	1
6	slices bread	6
⅔ cup	olive oil	¼ pint
	pepper	

Flatten the slices of pork with a meat hammer. Combine the liver, salt pork, garlic and parsley. Squeeze the bread dry and mix it into the liver mixture. Add salt to taste and bind with the egg yolks. Spread a little of this mixture on each slice of pork. Roll the slices neatly and secure them with thread.

Impale two of the stuffed rolls on a skewer with a slice of bread in between. Repeat this with the remaining meat rolls and bread, and arrange the skewers in a baking pan. Brush with oil, sprinkle with salt and pepper, and bake in a moderate oven (375°F. Mark 4) for about 30 minutes, or until the meat rolls are brown and cooked through and the bread is crisp. Serve straight from the oven.

Serves 6.

Bistecchine di Cinghiale
Wild Boar Steaks in a Sweet-sour Sauce

US		UK
2 pounds	boar steaks, cut from the rib	2 pounds
5 tablespoons	olive oil	4 tablespoons
¼ pound	fat salt pork, finely chopped	¼ pound
	salt	
4 tablespoons	sugar	3 tablespoons
4	bay leaves	4
1¼ cups	wine vinegar	½ pint
¾ cup	seedless white raisins (sultanas)	3 ounces
scant ½ cup	pitted prunes	3 ounces
3 squares	bitter chocolate, grated	3 ounces
pinch	ground cinnamon or grated nutmeg	pinch
4 teaspoons	flour	1 tablespoon

Wild boar is frequently eaten both in Italy and in France, where it is hunted. The original recipe instructs that the seedless raisins (sultanas) and prunes should first be plumped up in warm water. This depends entirely on the quality of the fruit; however, the pitted prunes should be chopped. Other strong game, for example young venison steaks, is also delicious prepared in this manner.

In a large heavy frying pan heat the oil with the pork over low heat. Add the boar steaks and brown them on both sides. Sprinkle with salt and leave them to cook gently for 15 minutes.

In the meantime, make the sauce. Put the sugar in a small pan with the bay leaves and about two-thirds of the vinegar, and cook gently, stirring, until it has dissolved. Add the white raisins and the chopped prunes, the chocolate, and a pinch of cinnamon or nutmeg. Stir well and cook gently until the sauce has thickened, about 10 minutes.

Mix the flour to a paste with the remaining vinegar and pour over the boar steaks. Stir well and cook for a further 10 minutes. Add the sweet-sour sauce and continue cooking for 10 minutes longer, or until the steaks are tender. Serve the steaks with the sauce poured over them.

Serves 6.

"Porceddu" Arrostito
Roast Suckling Pig

Suckling pig spit-roasted in the open air is one of the traditional dishes of Sardinia. The animal should not weigh more than 10 or 11 pounds.

Clean the pig, scrape it and singe off any bristles if necessary; much depends on where the animal is bought. Remove the entrails, wash and dry the cavity, and rub it well with myrtle leaves.

Impale the pig on a large skewer and spit-roast it about 20 inches from the fire. Thread a thick slice of salt pork (about ½ pound) on to another spit and heat this on the fire, with a pan underneath to catch the drippings, which are then used to baste the pig. Start roasting the pig with its flank nearest the fire; then, when the skin is browned, turn it continuously until it is a good rich brown color all over. Sprinkle the pig with salt and freshly ground pepper, and baste it occasionally with the drippings from the fat salt pork. It will take between 3 and 4 hours.

In Sardinia the spit is supported in a rough and ready fashion, on three sticks at either end arranged like a tripod. The fire is built with aromatic wood, mainly juniper and mastic wood, and it should blaze away merrily.

The meat can be served hot, cut into thick chunks, or cold, in which case it is left to cool covered with myrtle leaves.

Serves 8.

Pernici in Salsa d'Aceto
Partridges in Caper Sauce

US		UK
3	partridges, cleaned and plucked	3
1	onion	1
2 stalks	celery	2 stalks
2	carrots	2
	salt	
Sauce		
scant 1 cup	olive oil	⅓ pint
2½ tablespoons	wine vinegar	2 tablespoons
	salt	
4 teaspoons	finely chopped parsley	1 tablespoon
4 teaspoons	finely chopped capers	1 tablespoon

Put the partridges in a pan with the onion, celery, carrots, a little salt, and enough water to cover. Cover the pan and cook gently for about 45 minutes, or until tender.

Make the sauce by mixing the oil and vinegar with a little salt, to taste, the parsley and capers.

Take the partridges from the pan, cut them into halves and arrange them on a serving dish. Pour the sauce over them and allow to cool before serving. Serve 1 or 2 halves per person.

Other small game birds may also be prepared in this manner.

Piccioni in Salmì
Stewed Pigeons

US		UK
6	pigeons, dressed	6
2–3 sprigs	sage	2–3 sprigs
2–3 sprigs	parsley	2–3 sprigs
6 large	anchovy fillets	6 large
2 cloves	garlic	2 cloves
1–2 tablespoons	capers	1–1½ tablespoons
2 cups	olive oil	¾ pint
	grated rind of 1 lemon	
1 cup	wine vinegar	scant ½ pint
	salt and pepper	

For this recipe it is essential to use fat young pigeons. Cut all the flesh from the bones, keeping the breast meat as intact as possible.

Cut the rest of the flesh into small, even-sized pieces. Mix the giblets with the sage, parsley, anchovies, garlic and capers, and chop together finely.

In a pan, heat the oil, add the pieces of pigeon breast and the grated lemon rind, and cook over moderate heat until the meat is just browned. Sprinkle with vinegar and let it evaporate; then add the rest of the meat together with the chopped flavorings and giblets. Season to taste with salt and pepper, cover the pan tightly, placing a piece of greaseproof paper or foil under the lid, and continue to cook for 1 hour without uncovering the pan. Serve hot.

Pigeons prepared in this manner are considered to improve if cooked a day before they are required, then reheated. Instead of wine vinegar a dry red wine may be used.

Serves 6.

Salmì di Coniglio
Marinated and Stewed Rabbit

US		UK
1	rabbit – 4 to 5 pounds	1
½ cup	wine vinegar	6 tablespoons
1 cup	olive oil	⅓ pint
1	onion, finely chopped	1
1	lemon, sliced	1
1	clove	1
2	bay leaves, crumbled	2
1 cup	hot meat stock	⅓ pint
	salt and pepper	
2–3	anchovy fillets	2–3
3 tablespoons	softened butter	1½ ounces

Wipe the rabbit with a damp cloth and cut it into serving pieces. Put the vinegar, half the oil, the onion, lemon slices, clove and crumbled bay leaves in a large bowl. Add the pieces of rabbit, making sure they are well coated with the marinade, cover the bowl and leave for 24 hours in a cool place. The following day, discard the lemon slices and stir the remaining oil into the marinade.

Transfer the pieces of rabbit to a pan together with the marinade, and cook over a low heat until they are browned. Add the stock, sprinkle lightly with salt and pepper, cover the pan and cook over a low heat for about 1 hour. Stir from time to time and if necessary add a little more stock or water. The gravy should not be too thin.

In the meantime, chop the anchovy fillets finely and pound them with the butter. Just before serving the rabbit, add the anchovy butter to the pan and stir well. Serve hot.

Serves 4.

Monzettas
Snails

Monzette, or snails, are a specialty of Sassari and its province. They can be cooked with a tomato sauce or baked in the oven.

First the snails must be purged. Allow 30 small snails per person. Put them in a wicker basket lined with vine leaves and leave for 2 or 3 days. Take them from the basket and drop them into a bowl of water mixed with salt and vinegar, and leave them for 10 minutes. Drain well and drop them again into a fresh portion of salted acidulated water, stirring vigorously. Drain again and leave the snails in a colander under cold running water until they are thoroughly clean.

Put the snails in a pan, cover them with cold water and bring slowly to the boil. As soon as the snails poke their heads out of their shells, turn up the heat and continue to cook for 10 minutes. Drain, cool slightly, then take the snails out of their shells.

Sauté a little finely chopped garlic and parsley in oil over low heat. Peel 2 large ripe tomatoes per person, chop them finely and discard their seeds. Stir the tomato pulp into the pan, season to taste with salt and pepper, and cook for 15 minutes. Then rub the mixture through a sieve and return the purée to the pan. Add the snails and cook over a low heat for 10 minutes. Serve at once, generously seasoned with freshly milled pepper.

For baking, only large snails are suitable. Allow 15 per person and proceed as above as far as, but not including, shelling the snails. For each portion mix together 2 to 3 tablespoons freshly grated *formaggio sardo* (Sardinian cheese), a pinch of finely chopped garlic, 1 sprig parsley, finely chopped, a pinch of salt, 2 eggs, beaten, and 2 to 3 tablespoons Vernaccia wine (or medium sherry). Stuff each snail with a little of this mixture, arrange them in a baking pan, openings uppermost, trickle a little olive oil over them and bake in a moderate oven (375°F. Mark 4) for 6 minutes.

Burrida
Fish Stew with Dogfish and Skate

US		UK
2½ pounds	dogfish (about 3 fish)	2½ pounds
1 pound	skate	1 pound
	salt	
	wine vinegar	
2–3 slices	lemon	2–3 slices
2 cloves	garlic, finely chopped	2 cloves
1 cup	olive oil	⅓ pint
5 tablespoons	pine nuts	4 tablespoons
5 tablespoons	walnut kernels	4 tablespoons
1 cup	soft white breadcrumbs	1½ ounces
	pepper	
	grated nutmeg	

Unless bought from a seaport fish market, dogfish and skate are usually sold cleaned, skinned and prepared for cooking.

Cut the fish into serving portions and put them in a large fish kettle with a little salted water, about 1 cup (U.K. ⅓ pint) vinegar and 2 or 3 slices of lemon. Bring to a gentle boil, then lower the heat and simmer gently until the fish are tender. Remove them from the pan and leave to cool. Let the fish stock continue simmering.

In another large pan, fry the garlic cloves gently in the oil until they turn a golden color; then add the nuts, ground to a powder, the breadcrumbs, a sprinkling of vinegar, salt, pepper and nutmeg to taste. Stir and cook for a minute or so longer. Add the fish, moisten with a little of the hot fish stock and turn them to coat them with the sauce. Leave over a low heat for 10 minutes, or until the fish are heated through. Serve hot.
Serves 6.

La "Cassòla"
Sardinian Fish Soup or Stew

US		UK
5–6 pounds	assorted fish – see method	5–6 pounds
	salt	
⅔ cup	olive oil	¼ pint
1 clove	garlic, finely chopped	1 clove
1 large	onion, finely chopped	1 large
2–3 sprigs	parsley, finely chopped	2–3 sprigs
1 pound	ripe tomatoes, peeled, seeded and chopped	1 pound
½ cup	dry white wine	6–8 tablespoons
small piece	dried hot chili pepper *or*	small piece
pinch	chili powder	pinch
	slices of fried bread	

In the original recipe the following fish are used: dogfish, eel, grey mullet, skate, sea bass, gurnard, sea scorpion, sea bream, baby squid, or cuttlefish, octopus, crab, and crayfish (crawfish).

Clean the fish, wash them in plenty of salted water and pat dry. Cut off their heads. Cut the larger fish into pieces, and the crayfish tail into small pieces; split the body of the crayfish in half. Put the fish heads in a pan with a little salt and water to cover; bring to the boil and simmer gently for 30 minutes.

In the meantime, heat the olive oil in a very large pan and fry the garlic, onion and parsley. When they begin to change color add the tomatoes and stir well; then pour in the wine and cook until reduced. Stir in a good ½ cup (U.K. ¼ pint) of the hot fish stock, the baby squid or cuttlefish (roughly chopped) and the octopus (cut into strips). Season to taste with salt and chili. Let these cook for 20 minutes, then add the rest of the firmer fish, followed by the crayfish 5 minutes later. Simmer very gently for 15 minutes, then gradually add the remaining fish. Add another cupful of the fish stock, cover the pan and simmer very gently for a further 15 minutes, or until all the fish are tender. Check seasoning.

Put a slice of crisply fried bread in the bottom of each soup bowl (traditionally, ships' biscuits were used). Pour over the fish and stock, and serve at once.
Serves 6.

Zuppa di Arselle
Baby Clam Soup or Stew

US		UK
6 dozen	baby clams	3–3½ pounds
¼ cup	olive oil	3 tablespoons
2 cloves	garlic	2 cloves
1 cup	dry white wine	⅓ pint
	salt and pepper	
1–2 tablespoons	finely chopped parsley	1–2 tablespoons
	slices of bread fried in oil	

Scrub the clams thoroughly with a brush and wash them, changing the water several times; then leave them for an hour in salted water to rid them entirely of their sand. Rinse the clams again under running water and place them close together at the bottom of a large pan. Add about ½ cup (U.K. 6 to 8 tablespoons) water, cover the pan and cook over a low heat until they open, about 8 minutes. Take the clams from the shells and reserve the liquor.

Heat the oil and gently sauté 1 clove garlic, crushed, until it browns. Discard the garlic clove and pour in the wine. Add the shelled clams, salt and pepper to taste, and a cup (U.K. scant ½ pint) of their liquor. Cook over a low heat for 5 minutes, and add the parsley just before serving.

Rub the slices of fried bread with the remaining clove of garlic, lightly crushed or halved, and put a slice in each soup bowl. Pour over the clams with their liquid, and serve steaming hot.
Serves 6.

Calamaretti Ripieni
Stuffed Baby Squid

US		UK
12 small	squid	12 small
1 clove	garlic	1 clove
2–4	anchovy fillets	2–4
2–3	sprigs parsley	2–3
2	eggs, lightly beaten	2
2–3 tablespoons	breadcrumbs	2 tablespoons
	salt and pepper	
	olive oil	
	lemon wedges	

Skin the squid, remove the ink sac and discard it. Rinse the squid thoroughly in cold water. Cut off the tentacles and chop them as finely as possible with the garlic, anchovies and parsley. Mix together the eggs, breadcrumbs, a little salt, a generous amount of pepper and a trickle of olive oil. Add the chopped ingredients and work to a paste.

Stuff the paste into the squid and sew up the openings with strong thread. Sprinkle them with salt and pepper, and brush with oil. Broil (grill) over – or under – moderate heat for 15 minutes, turning and basting with oil. Serve very hot with lemon wedges.
Serves 6.

Trote alla Vernaccia

Trout in Vernaccia Wine

US		UK
6	trout	6
¼ cup	olive oil	3 tablespoons
1 clove	garlic, finely chopped	1 clove
2–3 sprigs	parsley, finely chopped	2–3 sprigs
1 sprig	rosemary, finely chopped	1 sprig
1 teaspoon	finely chopped oregano	1 teaspoon
1 small	carrot, finely chopped	1 small
	salt and pepper	
about 4 cups	Vernaccia wine – see method	about 1½ pints

Vernaccia is the best known of the Sardinian wines and something of a curiosity. It is a dry, pleasantly bitter aperitif made from the Vernaccia grape, with something of the style of sherry. Sardinians drink it both before and after meals. It is difficult to suggest a substitute, since the wine is the whole point of the recipe, but one could perhaps try equal parts of good sherry and dry white wine.

Clean the trout, wash them well and pat them dry. Heat the oil in a pan large enough to take all the trout in one layer, add the garlic, herbs and carrot, and simmer over a low heat until the carrot is soft. Lay the trout on top and season to taste with salt and pepper. Cover completely with Vernaccia wine and cook over a moderate heat until almost all the wine has evaporated. Serve the trout very hot, straight from the pan, with what little sauce remains.

Serves 6.

Acciughe Ripiene

Stuffed Anchovies

US		UK
2 pounds	large fresh anchovies	2 pounds
	salt	
about ¼ pound	anchovy fillets	about ¼ pound
about ½ pound	fresh soft cheese, cut into thin strips	about ½ pound
	flour	
3	eggs, beaten	3
	fine dry breadcrumbs	
	oil for deep-frying	
1–2	lemons, quartered	1–2

This delicious recipe could well be adapted for other small fish.

Clean the anchovies and wash them in plenty of cold salted water. Slit them down the belly and carefully remove the heads and backbones without separating the fillets. Stuff each fresh anchovy with an anchovy fillet and a strip of cheese. Close the anchovies and reshape them. Dust with flour, dip carefully into the beaten eggs and roll in breadcrumbs. Put aside until required.

When ready to serve, heat plenty of oil for deep-frying, and fry the anchovies, a few at a time, until golden brown. Drain on paper towels and serve very hot, garnished with lemon wedges.

Serves 6.

Sardine al Finocchio

Fresh Sardines with Fennel

US		UK
2 pounds	fresh sardines or small herrings	2 pounds
	olive oil	
1 large	onion, thinly sliced	1 large
½ cup	dry white wine	6–8 tablespoons
1 pound	ripe tomatoes, peeled, seeded and chopped	1 pound
	salt and pepper	
	fine dry breadcrumbs	
4 teaspoons	fennel seeds, pounded	1 tablespoon

Heat ⅓ cup (U.K. 4 tablespoons) oil in a pan; add the onion and cook slowly until soft and transparent. Pour in the wine and cook until it is reduced by half. Then add the tomatoes, season to taste with salt and pepper, and cook over a brisk heat until the sauce thickens and the tomatoes are reduced to a purée.

In the meantime, clean the sardines; cut off their heads, wash them in plenty of salted water and drain well. Pat the fish dry, sprinkle them lightly with salt and pepper, and roll them in breadcrumbs. Pour the tomato sauce into a wide shallow baking dish and arrange the sardines neatly on top, in two rows if possible. Trickle a little olive oil over them and sprinkle with pounded fennel seeds.

Bake the sardines in a moderate oven (375°F. Mark 4) for about 30 minutes, or until the breadcrumbs are golden and the sardines tender. Serve in the same dish.

Serves 6.

Uova alla Sarda

Hard-boiled Eggs Sardinian Style

US		UK
6	eggs	6
¼ cup	olive oil	3 tablespoons
4 teaspoons	wine vinegar	1 tablespoon
	salt	
1 clove	garlic, finely chopped	1 clove
2–3 sprigs	parsley, finely chopped	2–3 sprigs
2½ tablespoons	soft breadcrumbs	2 tablespoons

Cook the eggs in boiling water for 7 minutes. Cool them under cold running water, then shell them carefully and slice them in half lengthwise.

Put the oil, vinegar and salt to taste in a frying pan; add the eggs and cook over a low heat until the vinegar has evaporated, turning them carefully from time to time. Transfer them to a heated shallow serving dish, cut sides uppermost, and keep warm in a low oven.

Add the garlic and parsley to the oil remaining in the pan, and cook over a low heat for a few minutes, stirring. Then stir in the breadcrumbs, and when they are a golden color, spread the mixture over the eggs. Serve either at once, warm, or leave until cold.

Serves 6.

Melanzane alla Sarda

Sardinian Baked Eggplants (Aubergines)

US		UK
6 medium-sized	eggplants (aubergines)	6 medium-sized
	salt	
2–3 tablespoons	soft breadcrumbs	2 tablespoons
	pepper	
1 clove	garlic, finely chopped – optional	1 clove
2–3 sprigs	basil, finely chopped	2–3 sprigs
3–4 sprigs	parsley, finely chopped	3–4 sprigs
3 large	ripe tomatoes, peeled and thinly sliced	3 large
about ½ cup	olive oil	6–8 tablespoons

Wash the eggplants and cut them in half lengthwise. Sprinkle with salt and leave to drain for 1 or 2 hours in a colander, or on a plate set at an angle. This will rid them of their somewhat bitter flavor. When ready to cook, wipe them completely dry and make short but fairly deep incisions in the cut surface of each half with the point of a sharp knife.

Mix the breadcrumbs with a pinch of salt and pepper, the garlic if used, and herbs. Spread a little of this mixture on each eggplant half, pressing it well into the cuts. Arrange the eggplants cut side up in a baking dish and cover with tomato slices. Pour the oil over the top and bake in a moderate oven (375°F. Mark 4) for 45 minutes, or until the eggplants are tender – they vary somewhat in size and texture – basting them frequently with their own liquid.

Serve either hot or cold. If intending to serve cold it is imperative that you use only olive oil as this does not congeal when cold.

The quantity of herbs may be increased if preferred, in particular the basil, a great favorite with Italians.

Serves 6.

Zucchine e Peperoni al Forno
Baked Zucchini (Courgettes) and Peppers

US		UK
6	zucchini (courgettes)	6
	salt	
2	sweet yellow peppers	2
	olive oil	
1 clove	garlic, lightly crushed	1 clove
6 large	ripe tomatoes, peeled, seeded and chopped	6 large
4–5 leaves	basil	4–5 leaves
12 slices	fresh soft cheese, e.g. Mozzarella	12 slices
6	anchovy fillets	6

Wash the zucchini and slice off both ends. Drop them into boiling salted water, and parboil them for 5 minutes. Drain and cut into halves lengthwise.

Broil (grill) the peppers until their skins are blackened and blistered. Let them cool, then scrape off their thin outer skins or rub them off under running cold water. Slice the peppers into halves, discarding cores and seeds, and cut them into strips, 6 strips to each pepper.

Heat about 1 tablespoon oil in a pan; add the garlic clove, fry it until it begins to brown, and discard it. Add the tomatoes, sprinkle with salt to taste, and cook over a brisk heat for 15 minutes. After 10 minutes' cooking add the basil.

Arrange the zucchini, cut side up, in one layer in a shallow baking dish. On each half put about 1 tablespoon of the tomato sauce, a strip of pepper, a slice of cheese and half an anchovy fillet. Pour a scant ½ cup (U.K. 4 to 6 tablespoons) olive oil over the whole dish and bake in a moderate oven (360°F. Mark 3–4) for several minutes, or until the cheese has melted. Serve hot or cold.

Serves 6.

Piselli all'Uso Sardo
Sardinian Peas

US		UK
6 cups	shelled green peas	2 pounds
about ¼ cup	olive oil	3 tablespoons
1	onion, thinly sliced	1
	salt	
5	eggs	5
5 tablespoons	grated Pecorino or Parmesan	4 tablespoons
2½ tablespoons	breadcrumbs, soaked in milk	2 tablespoons

Put the peas in a pan with 2 or 3 tablespoons (U.K. 2 tablespoons) oil, the onion, a little salt to taste, and just enough water to cover

the bottom of the pan. Cook over a brisk heat for 15 minutes, or until the peas are tender and the liquid has evaporated.

Beat the eggs with a pinch of salt and the cheese. Squeeze the breadcrumbs dry and mix them into the beaten egg mixture. Drain the peas thoroughly and stir them into the mixture.

Brush a round baking dish about 8 inches in diameter with the remaining oil, pour in the eggs and peas, and bake in a slow oven (325°F. Mark 2) until set, at least 30 minutes. Turn out on to a heated serving dish and serve hot.

Serves 6.

Carciofi Ripieni di Ricotta
Artichokes Stuffed with Ricotta

US		UK
6	tender young artichokes	6
	juice of 1 lemon	
	salt	
5 tablespoons	butter	2½ ounces
½ pound	Ricotta cheese	½ pound
1	egg, lightly beaten	1
¼ cup	grated Pecorino or Parmesan	3 tablespoons
¼ pound	Italian salami, diced	¼ pound
1–2 tablespoons	soft breadcrumbs	1–2 tablespoons

Only really tender young artichokes, without a choke, should be used for this recipe.

Remove the hard outer leaves from the artichokes and scrape their stalks; cut each one in half lengthwise and soak in a bowl of water acidulated with the juice of 1 lemon until they are all prepared. Wash them carefully in the same water, then cook in a pan of boiling salted water for 10 minutes. Drain and arrange in a well-buttered baking dish, cut sides uppermost.

Work the Ricotta with a wooden spoon until soft, then mix thoroughly with the egg, grated cheese, salami and a pinch of salt to taste. When completely blended, put some of the mixture on each of the artichoke halves, piling it in a slightly rounded or domed shape. Sprinkle lightly with breadcrumbs, dot with the remaining butter and bake in a slow oven (325°F. Mark 2) for about 20 minutes. Serve either hot or cold.

Serves 6.

Frittura di Ricotta
Macaroon and Ricotta Fritters

US		UK
½ pound	almond macaroons	½ pound
1 pound	Ricotta cheese	1 pound
	ground cinnamon	
2–3 tablespoons	granulated (caster) sugar	2–3 tablespoons
3	eggs	3
	flour	
	fine dry breadcrumbs	
	butter for frying	

Crush the macaroons to a powder and mix with the Ricotta, a pinch of ground cinnamon, the sugar, and 2 eggs, beaten. Beat until the mixture is smooth and well blended. With floured hands, take small pieces of the dough and shape into balls. Dip the balls in the remaining egg, beaten, and roll them in breadcrumbs.

Heat about ½ cup (4 ounces) butter in a frying pan and fry the Ricotta balls, a few at a time, until golden brown. Add more butter to the pan as necessary, and continue frying the rest of the Ricotta balls in the same manner. Serve hot.

Some people prefer these fritters to be rather sweeter; more sugar may be added to taste, to a maximum of about ½ cup (4 ounces).

Amaretti d'Oristano
Oristano Macaroons

US		UK
1 cup	sweet almonds	6 ounces
⅓ cup	bitter almonds	2 ounces
2	egg whites	2
1 cup	granulated (caster) sugar	8 ounces
	rice paper	
	confectioners' (icing) sugar	

Blanch the almonds in boiling water for about 1 minute and pull off their peels. Dry them in a warm oven, taking care not to color them, then chop or grind (mince) them finely until reduced to a powder – a blender does this job excellently.

Beat the egg whites until stiff but not dry, and fold in the almonds and sugar. Pipe the mixture out on to circles or ovals of rice paper, each piece about 1 inch in diameter. Spread them out on a baking sheet and dust with confectioners' (icing) sugar. Leave for 4 hours.

Bake the macaroons in a moderately slow oven (350°F. Mark 3) for 15 minutes, or until delicately browned. Remove from the oven and allow to cool before trimming off excess rice paper. The macaroons may be served at once, or they will keep for some time in an airtight container.

Makes 14 to 16 macaroons.

Germinus
Sardinian Macaroons

US		UK
¾ pound	almonds	¾ pound
¾ pound	confectioners' (icing) sugar	¾ pound
4	egg whites, stiffly beaten	4
	juice of 1 lemon	

Blanch the almonds in boiling water for 1 minute. Drain, cool and peel them. Spread them on a baking sheet and dry them out in a cool oven for 15 minutes, turning them from time to time, and taking care that they do not color. Cut the almonds into slivers.

Fold the sugar into the beaten egg whites together with the almonds and lemon juice. Cover a baking sheet with greaseproof paper and place teaspoonfuls of the mixture on it, spaced well apart. Bake in a slow oven (325°F. Mark 2) for about 25 minutes, or until the macaroons are lightly colored. Allow them to cool before detaching them from the paper.

Candelaus o "Scandelaus"
Almond Candies

US		UK
1¼ pounds	almonds	1¼ pounds
2¼ cups	sugar	1 pound
	grated rind of 2 lemons	
⅓ cup	orange flower water	2½ fluid ounces
about 2 cups	confectioners' (icing) sugar	about ½ pound

Blanch the almonds in boiling water for 1 minute. Drain, cool and peel them. Chop or grind (mince) finely. Dissolve the sugar in a pan with about ½ cup water. As soon as it is completely dissolved, add the almonds, stirring well with a wooden spoon; then add the lemon rind, stirring all the while, and half of the orange flower water. Cook gently until the mixture comes away from the sides of the pan. Cool slightly.

As soon as the mixture is cool enough to handle, turn it out on to a wooden board. Wet your fingers with the remaining orange flower water, break off pieces of the mixture and shape them into animals, flowers, figures, etc. Spread them out to dry or put them into a slow oven (325°F. Mark 2) for a few minutes.

When the candies are quite dry, mix the confectioners' (icing) sugar with enough boiling water to make a smooth paste of spreading consistency. Dip the candies into it, drain well and leave in a warm place until dry.

Suspirus
Almond "Sighs"

US		UK
½ pound	sweet almonds	½ pound
1⅔ cups	sugar	¾ pound
	rind of ½ lemon	
5 tablespoons	Maraschino or Goccia d'Oro liqueur	4 tablespoons

Blanch the almonds in boiling water for 1 minute; drain, cool and peel them. Dry them in a cool oven for about 5 minutes, taking care that they do not brown. Chop them finely or grind (mince) to a powder.

Dissolve 1 cup plus 2 tablespoons (½ pound) sugar in about 4 tablespoons water with the lemon rind. Bring to the boil and cook gently for 10 minutes, or until quite clear. Discard the lemon rind, add the almonds and cook for a further 2 minutes, stirring well with a wooden spoon. Remove the pan from the heat and add half of the liqueur, mixing it thoroughly into the syrup. Leave to cool.

Mix the remaining liqueur with an equal quantity of water. Moisten your fingers with this, break off pieces of the almond-sugar mixture and shape them into tiny balls. Roll them in the remaining sugar and leave to dry for 5 hours.

Cut out little squares of white or colored paper, snip the ends into fringes and wrap up the little balls like candies or sweets. They will keep for some time if stored in an airtight container.

Biscottini con il Miele
Honey Cookies (U.K. Biscuits)

US		UK
2 cups	all-purpose (plain) flour	½ pound
¼ cup	honey	3 ounces
2 tablespoons	butter	1 ounce
1	egg	1
	salt	
2 teaspoons	baking powder	scant 2 teaspoons
	milk	
	butter and flour for baking sheet	

Sift the flour into a bowl and make a well in the center. Heat the honey and butter together in a double boiler or in a copper pan, stirring until well blended. Beat the egg with a pinch of salt. Dissolve the baking powder in 2 or 3 tablespoons milk.

Pour the honey mixture into the center of the flour, add the egg and the dissolved baking powder, cover with flour from the sides of the bowl, and mix the whole to a smooth dough. Roll out on a floured pastry board to a thickness of about ⅛ inch and cut into shapes – diamonds, squares, ovals or rounds.

Rub a baking sheet with butter and sprinkle with flour, shaking the sheet to distribute it evenly. Arrange the pastry shapes on this, evenly spaced and well apart. Brush them with milk and bake in a moderate oven (375°F. Mark 4) for about 10 minutes, or until they are a light brown color. Cool on wire racks.

The cookies will keep for some time in an airtight container.

Sources for Italian Specialities

Most supermarkets carry a good selection of Italian specialties from tomato paste and imported Italian tomatoes in cans to a wide variety of pastas (spaghetti, spaghettini, lasagna and the like) to such cheeses as Fontina, Parmesan, Mozzarella, Ricotta, Bel Paese. Some Italian fish specialties are available in cans from specialty shops which mail (see below); other fish recipes will have to be adapted to the resources of the local fish market. Certain fresh vegetables, herbs and unusual meat cuts are available only from Italian markets and butchers; a sampling of such shops in Manhattan, and the ingredients they handle, is given below. Readers from other localities will probably know of similar shops in their own areas.

There are also a group of shops featuring specialties which will mail all over the U.S. These shops are starred in the list which follows.

Alleva Dairy
188 Grand Street
New York, N.Y. 10013

Cheese.

*Aphrodisia Products, Inc.
28 Carmine Street
New York, N.Y. 10014

Dried herbs and spices. Catalog.

Balducci Produce Company
1 Greenwich Avenue
New York, N.Y. 10014

Fresh vegetables and fresh herbs in season (including the hard-to-find baby artichokes, fennel, cardoons).

Mario Bosco
263 Bleecker Street
New York, N.Y. 10014

Italian groceries including risotto rice, sausages, flours, lentils, pastas, canned goods including truffles.

Comollo's Market
357 Sixth Avenue
New York, N.Y. 10014

Rabbit, squab, pheasant as well as prosciutto and other hard-to-find meat cuts.

*Il Conte di Savoia
555 West Roosevelt Road
Chicago, Illinois 60607

Cheeses, spices, sausages, beans, cooking implements.

Fretta Brothers
116 Mott Street
New York, N.Y. 10013

Tripe, pancetta, calf's head, sausage meat, mixed salted pork, sausages.

Gennaro's Grocery
133 Mott Street
New York, N.Y. 10013

Homemade pasta; Italian bread.

Italian Food Center
186 Grand Street
New York, N.Y. 10013

Cheese, pasta, Italian sausage.

A. R. Kurtz
125 Mott Street
New York, N.Y. 10013

Cheeses, flours, spices, beans.

*Manganaro Foods
488 Ninth Avenue
New York, N.Y. 10018

Pasta, cheese, sausages, dried herbs, beans, prosciutto, pancetta, risotto rice, cooking implements, canned goods including truffles. Carries fresh pasta but this cannot be mailed. Catalog.

*Maryland Market
412 Amsterdam Avenue
New York, N.Y. 10024

Partridge, pheasant, quail, rabbit, hare, wild boar, suckling pig, squab, wild duck. Catalog.

*H. Roth & Son
1577 First Avenue
New York, N.Y. 10028

Dried herbs and spices, cooking implements, specialized canned goods, flours. Catalog.

*George H. Shaffer Market
1097 Madison Avenue
New York, N.Y. 10021

Partridge, quail, pheasant.

INDEX